W9-ABP-915

$33.90

2-8-94

The Movie List Book

The Movie List Book

A Reference Guide to Film Themes, Settings, and Series

by Richard B. Armstrong *and*
Mary Willems Armstrong

McFarland & Company, Inc., Publishers
Jefferson, North Carolina, and London

210 42521
5 1156

British Library Cataloguing-in-Publication data are available

Library of Congress Cataloguing-in-Publication Data

Armstrong, Richard B., 1956–
    The movie list book : a reference guide to film themes, settings,
and series / Richard B. Armstrong, Mary Willems Armstrong.
      p. cm.
    ISBN 0-89950-240-7 (50# alk. paper) ∞
    1. Motion pictures—Plots, themes, etc. I. Armstrong, Mary
Willems, 1957– . II. Title
PN1997.8.A76   1990
791.43'75—dc20   89-43692
ARM   CIP

Manufactured in the United States of America

McFarland & Company, Inc., Publishers
  Box 611, Jefferson, North Carolina 28640

For our parents
Oran and Jean Armstrong
and
Edward and Jean Willems

Thanks for your love —
and for letting us stay up
to see all those movies

Table of Contents*

*Throughout the work are "see" references not reflected in this table of con-
tents, for instance, "Dionne Quintuplets see Christian, Dr."

TABLE OF CONTENTS

TABLE OF CONTENTS

TABLE OF CONTENTS

Introduction

The Movie List Book strives to fill a void which has hampered both serious film researchers and casual buffs for several years.

Imagine that you're writing a film paper on George A. Romero's *Night of the Living Dead* and you want to contrast it with similar movies about flesh-eating ghouls. You could diligently pore through a variety of books and articles on Romero and the horror genre, hoping to find references to other features. *Or* you could begin your search by turning to the GHOULS entry in *The Movie List Book*.

Here you will find an encyclopedic entry which defines the category (just what is a ghoul?) and presents a representative list of ghoul films. In the book as a whole, you will find over 450 entries, ranging from unusual occupations in movies to themes, settings, and film series.

You will not find filmographies for performers and technical personnel. Many well established reference works have long provided that kind of data.

However, this is not to say *The Movie List Book* does not cover some familiar ground. We have tried to compile an exhaustive list of film series and, in the process, have included information on well-documented characters like Sherlock Holmes and Tarzan. We have done this for two reasons. First, new movies are continually being made about these popular characters (including the 1989 television movie *Tarzan in Manhattan*, just for example), and secondly, we felt the book should be a one-stop reference on all film series, for at least some users. A film buff trying to find out the name of Christopher Lee's Holmes film (it was *Sherlock Holmes and the Deadly Necklace*) will find this a handy volume. A Holmesian scholar seeking more details would be advised to find more specialized reference works.

We formed some general groundrules to limit the scope of the book to a manageable size:

1. Most of the films listed are English-language pictures released during the sound era. Occasionally, we have included silent or foreign films to give the reader an historical or international perspective of the category. For example, no write-up of ROBIN HOOD would be complete without mentioning the 1922 Douglas Fairbanks, Sr., version.

2. The notable exception to the above rule is the inclusion of foreign film series shown on television. The Mexican wrestler Santo appeared in a long-running film series and many of these pictures have eventually shown up on American television. We have listed foreign series films under their most common English-language titles, although the original foreign titles are shown as well.

3. We defined a film series as three or more movies linked by a recurring theme or characters. Thus, we did not include the films of Abbott and Costello, the Marx Brothers, or Laurel and Hardy. For the same reason, we left out Roy Rogers and Gene Autry—although they do play the same character (themselves) in most of their movies. "B" Western fans can rest assured, however, that their favorite genre is well-represented by the Durango Kid, the Range Busters, Red Ryder, and others.

4. We have included many lengthy lists, but the sheer size of others mandated their exclusion. For example, a written overview and a representative sampling of Civil War or World War II movies would require a write-up far beyond the scope of this book. On the other hand, there are relatively few films about the Korean War and Vietnam. Hence, we have included entries on them. We expect that our decisions on what to include and what to exclude will not suit everyone. Constructive criticism is most welcome.

5. Our cut-off point was movies released or broadcast through December 1989.

For each category/entry, we have provided a narrative description followed by a *representative sample* of films in chronological order. The size of the lists varies from three to seventy titles depending on the scope of the entry (i.e. many films have taken place on TRAINS; few movies have featured GORGONS).

Typically, the narratives present an historic overview of the entry or subcategorize films within the entry. For example, the TELEVISION entry traces its treatment in film from the early 1930s to the present. The GANGSTERS (REAL-LIFE) entry discusses how various individuals have been treated in film.

At the conclusion of the narrative portion of some entries are "see also" references to other entries. For example, the ABOMINABLE SNOWMAN entry also refers readers to the BIGFOOT entry.

The films within each entry are listed chronologically, their dates indicating when the films were released or broadcasted in their country of origin. Made-for-television movies are denoted with the abbreviation "TVM." The first title listed is the film's most widely-known U.S. title. Alternative titles, including the original foreign title if part of a series, are shown in parentheses.

We have refrained from listing credits and plot summaries for each

INTRODUCTION

title. Most of the listed films can be found readily in mainstream reference works.

It would be difficult to acknowledge everyone who added a film here and there. But there are some who made significant contributions. The late British film historian and critic Leslie Halliwell was a source of inspiration—both for his handy *Filmgoer's Companion* and for being gracious enough to invite two American strangers to have tea and biscuits with him and his wife Ruth. The Wisconsin Center for Film Research in Madison allowed us to view some of the rarer features in its collection and also gave us access to its fine film reference library. Its excellent staff was always prompt, courteous, and helpful. Tom Hawkins of Elizabethtown, Kentucky, gave us enthusiastic support throughout our endeavor and also chipped in some titles. Finally, we'd like to offer thanks to our families, who gave us encouragement to complete the massive research (even though they may have thought we were slightly looney).

We heartily encourage reader correspondence—whether it be corrections, recommended additions, or comments over exclusions of favorite movies. Please address your letters to us in care of the publisher. We will try to respond to all mail.

> Richard B. Armstrong
> Mary Willems Armstrong
> *December 1989*

Abominable Snowman

Also known as the Yeti, the Abominable Snowman is a hairy, manlike creature reportedly inhabiting the Himalayas. His movie appearances have been almost as scarce as Yeti photographs. His film debut was probably 1954's *Snow Creature,* a *King Kong*–inspired cheapie in which a Yeti is captured and brought back to Los Angeles (where he escapes, of course). *Man Beast* (1955) kept the action in the Himalayas, but didn't live up to its outrageous ad campaign: "See women stalked and captured for breeding by Yeti monsters!" The only semi-intelligent film on the subject was *The Abominable Snowman of the Himalayas,* scripted by sci-fi/fantasy writer Nigel Kneale. See also **Bigfoot.**

Snow Creature (1954)
Half-Human (1955)
Man Beast (1955)
The Abominable Snowman of
   the Himilayas (1957)
The Seven Faces of Dr. Lao

(1964)
The Werewolf and the Yeti
   (aka *Night of the Howling
   Beast*) (1976)
Snowbeast (1977 TVM)
Yeti (1977)

Acronyms in Title

The nondescriptive nature of acronyms have made them unpopular title choices, especially among theater owners. They have been the ones forced to field complaints from irritated patrons, such as the ones distraught to discover that Sylvester Stallone's *F.I.S.T.* was *not* a boxing film (but the story of a truckers' union). Still, that has not deterred the occasional use of acronym titles. Studios concerned about pronounceable titles have shown a preference toward acronyms that also spelled words, as the case of *D.A.R.Y.L.* and *M*A*S*H.* In addition to film titles, acronyms have been used extensively in screenplays. For example, in *Our Man Flint* and *In Like Flint,* secret agent Derek Flint (James Coburn) worked for Z.O.W.I.E.—Zonal Organization on World Intelligence Espionage. On TV and in the movies, Robert Vaughn and David McCallum worked for U.N.C.L.E. (q.v.), which stood for United Network Command for Law and Enforcement.

The Bride Came C.O.D. (1941) CASH ON DELIVERY
D.O.A. (1950) DEAD ON ARRIVAL
The D.I. (1957) DRILL INSTRUCTOR
A Matter of Who (1961) WORLD HEALTH ORGANIZATION
The V.I.P.s (1963) VERY IMPORTANT PERSONS

The T.A.M.I. Show (1964) TEENAGE AWARDS MUSIC INTERNA-
TIONAL
Agent for H.A.R.M. (1966) HUMAN AETIOLOGICAL RELATIONS
MACHINE
U.M.C. (aka *Operation Heartbeat*) (1969 TVM) UNIVERSITY MED-
ICAL CENTER
M*A*S*H (1970) MOBILE ARMY SURGICAL HOSPITAL
R.P.M. (1970) REVOLUTIONS PER MINUTE
F.T.A. (1972) FREE (OR F--K) THE ARMY
Z.P.G. (1972) ZERO POPULATION GROWTH
F.I.S.T. (1978) FEDERATION OF INTERSTATE TRUCKERS
C.H.O.M.P.S. (1979) CANINE HOME PROTECTION SYSTEM
H.E.A.L.T.H. (1979) HAPPINESS, ENERGY AND LONGEVITY
THROUGH HEALTH
H.O.T.S. (1979) HELP OUT THE SEALS
S*H*E (1980 TVM) SECURITY HAZARDS EXPERT
S.O.B. (1981) SON OF A BITCH
T.A.G.: The Assassination Game (1982)
C.H.U.D. (1984) CANNIBALISTIC HUMANOID UNDERGROUND
DWELLERS
R.S.V.P. (1984) RÉPONDEZ S'IL VOUS PLAÎT
D.A.R.Y.L. (1985) DATA ANALYZING ROBOT YOUTH LIFEFORM
C.A.T. Squad (1986 TVM) COUNTER ASSAULT TACTICAL SQUAD
B.O.R.N. (1989) BODY ORGAN REPLACEMENT NETWORK

Ad Lines (Selected)

As a general rule, bad movies have the best ad lines—which makes a lot
of sense when you think about it. After all, if the movie stinks, then there
must be something else—like a catchy advertising phrase—to lure unsuspecting patrons into the theater. That's why some of the most
memorable (and tasteless) ad lines come from bottom-of-the-barrel horror
flicks like *The Driller Killer* ("Several pints of blood will spill when
teenage girls confront his drill"). Of course, a clever phrase can still ac-
company a big-budgeted science fiction film (*Alien:* "In space, no one can
hear you scream") or a cult classic (*I Walked with a Zombie:* "She's
alive...yet dead! She's dead...yet alive!"). Some of the cinema's more
memorable ad lines:

"Out of the dark fantastic madness of his science...He created
them! Pig-Men...Wolf-Women...Thoughtful Human Apes
—and His Masterpiece...The Panther Woman...Throbbing
to the hot flush of new found love!" *Island of Lost Souls*
(1933)
"Jungle love tease! Bob Preston tears the heart out of Preston
Foster by making jungle love to exciting Dorothy Lamour
under that burning Burma moon!" *Moon Over Burma* (1940)

"Bing Bong! Bing Bong! With song and sarong they hit the gong!" *The Road to Singapore* (1940)

"Kiss me and I'll claw you to death." *The Cat People* (1942)

"How'd you like to tussle with Russell?" *The Outlaw* (1943)

"Body of a boy! Mind of a monster! Soul of an unearthy thing!" *I Was a Teenage Frankenstein* (1957)

"It crawls! It creeps!" *The Blob* (1958)

"You'll be sick, sick, sick—from laughing!" *A Bucket of Blood* (1959)

"Beware the beat of cloth wrapped feet!" *The Mummy* (1959)

"Just ring for doom service!" *Horror Hotel* (aka *City of the Dead*) (1960)

"Beware the eyes that paralyze." *Children of the Damned* (1964)

"They're young...they're in love...and they kill people." *Bonnie and Clyde* (1967)

"The story of a homosexual who married a nymphomaniac." *The Music Lovers* (1971)

"You have nothing to lose but your mind." *Asylum* (1972)

"To avoid fainting, keep repeating: It's only a movie...it's only a movie..." *The Last House on the Left* (1972)

"They'll love the very lives out of your body!" *Invasion of the Bee Girls* (1973)

"The only thing more terrifying than the last twelve minutes of this film are the first 80." *Suspiria* (1976)

"Roses are red. Violets are blue. *My Bloody Valentine* is absolute grue." *My Bloody Valentine* (1981)

Addresses in Title

Street addresses have been used infrequently for movie titles, probably since they don't provide much in the way of description. Still, Gary Cooper played a nagging husband who found solace with younger woman Suzy Parker at *Ten North Frederick* (1958). A murder occurred at *10 Rillington Place* (1971), a fact-based account of the Christie-Evans case which ended capital punishment in Britain. On the lighter side, Anthony Hopkins and Anne Bancroft formed a lasting friendship through exchanging letters mailed to *84 Charing Cross Road* (the address of Hopkins' bookstore). Other movies with address titles, to include street names without numbers:

Forty-Second Street (1933)	*99 River Street* (1953)
15 Malden Lane (1936)	*13 West Street* (1962)
52nd Street (1937)	*Madison Avenue* (1962)
13 Rue Madeleine (1946)	*11 Harrowhouse* (aka *Anything*
Green Dolphin Street (1947)	*for Love*) (1974)
Dulcimer Street (aka *London*	*Hester Street* (1975)
Belongs to Me) (1948)	*Hanover Street* (1979)
711 Ocean Drive (1950)	*Cannery Row* (1982)
Sunset Boulevard (1950)	*Half Moon Street* (1986)

3

Airplanes

Airplanes have provided the setting or functioned as the focal point for dozens of movies. Early efforts typically revolved around the adventure of WWI dogfight pilots or pioneer air mail carriers. William Wellman's *Wings* (1927), the first film to win a Best Picture Oscar, established the standard for combat flying sequences and sealed Gary Cooper's stardom. Howard Hughes' *Hell's Angels* (1930) also featured magnificent dogfight footage, but is best remembered for launching Jean Harlow's career (her famous line: "Do you mind if I slip into something more comfortable?"). Despite their now-dated techniques, these WWI aerial actioners, along with both versions of *The Dawn Patrol*, still surpass similar films made in the 1960s and 1970s (e.g. *The Blue Max, Aces High, Von Richthofen and Brown*). The plight of air mail flyers proved an equally popular subject in the 1930s, with such memorable efforts as *Air Mail, Ceiling Zero*, and *Only Angels Have Wings* (the latter two directed by Howard Hawks). Airplanes played a strictly supporting role in most WWII pictures, although Hawks' *Air Force* and (much later) *Battle of Britain* gave them proper recognition. Interest in aviation had hit a low ceiling when, in 1954, Wellman's *The High and the Mighty* transplanted *Grand Hotel* drama into the clouds and added a generous dose of in-flight disaster. This successful formula was not fully exploited until 16 years later, when Ross Hunter mounted an expensive adaptation of Arthur Hailey's best-seller *Airport* (q.v.). This time, a mass of second-class imitators flooded the screens, including three *Airport* sequels and eventually the highly-successful spoof *Airplane!* (1980). Undoubtedly, the most bizarre airplane disaster film was the 1972 TV-movie *The Horror at 37,000 Feet*, in which a sacrificial druid stone unleashed evil spirits on screeching passengers. Films about real-life aviators have been scarce, consisting primarily of *The Spirit of St. Louis* (Charles Lindbergh), *The Winds of Kitty Hawk* (the Wright Brothers), *Amelia Earhart, Flight for Freedom* (Earhart again), *The Right Stuff* (Chuck Yeager), and *The Wings of Eagles* (Frank "Spig" Wead). Jet pilots can also lay claim to being ignored in favor of fictional dogfight specialists. Howard Hughes' *Jet Pilot* sat on the shelf for seven years before its 1957 release. Clint Eastwood's high-tech *Firefox* fared better, but it took 1986's *Top Gun* to give the jet pilot his proper recognition. However, Tom Cruise's cocky hero ("I feel the need— the need for speed!") was a far cry from the serious aviators portrayed in the films of Hawks, Hughes, and Wellman. While the jets in these latter films looked impressive, none of them compared favorably with the Batplane from 1989's *Batman* in terms of sheer aesthetic design. But, alas, the Batplane proved to be just a pretty package when the Joker shot it down with his long-barreled hand gun. Plane crashes have provided the premise for several memorable yarns, most notably *Lost Horizon, Back from Eternity, Fate Is the Hunter*, and *The Flight of the Phoenix*. In the latter film, James Stewart and his fellow crash survivors escaped from the desert by building a mini-plane from the wreckage. On a lighter note, *Flying Down to Rio* deserves an honorable mention for its delirious dance number featuring chorines high-stepping on top of an airplane's wings. See also **Airport**.

Wings (1927)
Hell's Angels (1930)
The Dawn Patrol (aka *Flight Commander*) (1930)
Air Mail (1932)
Christopher Strong (1933)
Flying Down to Rio (1933)
Ceiling Zero (1935)
Wings in the Dark (1935)
China Clipper (1936)
Non-Stop New York (1937)
Lost Horizon (1937)
The Dawn Patrol (1938)
Men with Wings (1938)
Only Angels Have Wings (1939)
Dive Bomber (1941)
Flight for Freedom (1943)
Air Force (1943)
Gallant Journey (1946)
Broken Journey (1948)
Chain Lightning (1950)
Breaking the Sound Barrier (aka *The Sound Barrier*) (1952)
The High and the Mighty (1954)
Escapade (1955)
Back from Eternity (1956)
Zero Hour (1957)
Bombers B-52 (1957)
The Spirit of St. Louis (1957)
The Wings of Eagles (1957)
Jet Pilot (1957)
Wings of Chance (1961)
Fate Is the Hunter (1964)
Those Magnificent Men in Their Flying Machines (1965)
The Doomsday Flight (1966 TVM)
The Flight of the Phoenix (1966)
The Blue Max (1966)
Battle of Britain (1969)
Airport (1970)
Von Richthofen and Brown (aka *The Red Baron*) (1970)
Terror in the Sky (1971 TVM)
Wild in the Sky (aka *Black Jack*) (1971)
Only One More Day Left Before Tomorrow (aka *How to Steal an Airplane*) (1971 TVM)
Skyjacked (aka *Sky Terror*) (1972)
The Horror at 37,000 Feet (1972 TVM)
Ace Eli and Rodger of the Skies (1973)
The Great Waldo Pepper (1975)
Amelia Earhart (1976 TVM)
Aces High (1977)
Crash (1978 TVM)
The Winds of Kitty Hawk (1978 TVM)
Airplane! (1980)
Firefox (1982)
Airplane 2: The Sequel (1982)
The Right Stuff (1983)
The Aviator (1985)
International Airport (1985 TVM)
Top Gun (1986)
Iron Eagle (1986)
Iron Eagle II (1988)
Batman (1989)

Airport

Ross Hunter's glossy adaptation of Arthur Hailey's bestseller has a lot to answer for, although it was little more than a slight variation of William Wellman's *The High and the Mighty* (1954). In addition to begetting three progressively inane sequels, *Airport* refined the all-stars-in-peril formula that kicked off the disaster movie craze (q.v.) of the 1970s. On its own terms, *Airport* was a slick entertainment package that afforded Helen Hayes another opportunity to win an Oscar. Burt Lancaster, as the dependable chief of airport operations, headed a cast that also included Dean Martin as a pilot, Jacqueline Bisset as a stewardess (and Dean's mistress), Van Heflin as a bomber, and sturdy George Kennedy as Burt's righthand man. Kennedy was the only one who returned for *Airport 1975,* a silly sequel requiring stewardess Karen Black to take over the jet's controls after a midair collision. Charlton Heston gave her support from the sidelines (in a Burt Lancaster-type role), while the all-star passenger list included Helen Reddy as a singing nun and Linda Blair as a sick kid. *Airport '77* sent a jet crashing into the ocean, while *The Concorde: Airport '79* featured typically-nice Robert Wagner as a ruthless tycoon out to destroy the jet. George Kennedy stood around in these films as well, just to lend some consistency to the proceedings and remind audiences that it was an *Airport* picture. Oddly, the films never spawned a TV series, perhaps because the ill-fated 1970–71 "San Francisco International Airport" had already beaten the producers to the punch. See also **Airplanes; Disaster Movies**.

Airport (1970)
Airport 1975 (1974)
Airport '77 (1977)

The Concorde: Airport '79 (aka *Airport '79*) (1979)

Alcoholism

The plight of the problem drinker has been glossed over by most major Hollywood pictures. Even Billy Wilder's landmark portrait of an alcoholic, 1945's *The Lost Weekend,* ended on an upbeat note with Ray Milland's "hero" indicating that he's on the road to recovery. Still, Wilder's film broke new ground with its straightforward treatment — Milland begging for drinks, stealing a woman's purse, experiencing D.T.'s, etc. The female side of alcoholism followed three years later, with Susan Hayward giving a mannered performance in *Smash-up, the Story of a Woman.* Bing Crosby, playing against type, gave the best performance of his career as a singer battling the bottle in the film version of Clifford Odets' *The Country Girl* (1954). Once again, though, an optimistic ending blunted the film's impact, with Grace Kelly passing up caring William Holden to stay with unreliable husband Crosby. Blake Edwards' *The Days of Wine and Roses* (1962) injected a jolt of realism into its depressing story of married alcoholics. After introducing wife Lee Remick to the "pleasures" of drinking, Jack Lemmon becomes a reformed drinker by joining Alcoholics Anonymous. His wife lacks his strength, however, and her alcoholism keeps them apart. The drawing power of the stars made the film a hit, but few producers were interested in duplicating its downbeat ending. Subsequently, movies about alcoholism moved to television where they flourished during the 1970s and 1980s. Veteran TV nice guys Dick Van Dyke, David Janssen, and Andy Griffith played self-destructive drunks in *The Morning After* (1974), *A Sensitive, Passionate Man* (1977), and *Under the Influence* (1986), respectively. Linda Blair, who battled a demon in *The Exorcist,* fought her own alcoholic demons in 1975's then-topical *Sarah T. —Portrait of a Teenage Alcoholic.* James Woods played the co-founder of Alcoholics Anonymous in the fact-based TV biography *My Name Is Bill W.* (1989). Dozens of movies, not principally about alcoholism, have featured main characters inflicted with the disease. Some of the most memorable performances have come from Albert Finney in *Under the Volcano* (1984), Dudley Moore in *Arthur* (1981), and Errol Flynn as John Barrymore in *Too Much, Too Soon* (1958).

The Lost Weekend (1945)
Smash-up, the Story of a Woman (aka *A Woman Destroyed*) (1948)
Come Fill the Cup (1951)
Something to Live For (1952)
The Country Girl (1954)
I'll Cry Tomorrow (1955)
The Bottom of the Bottle (1956)
The Voice in the Mirror (1958)
The Days of Wine and Roses (1962)
The Fire Within (1963)
The Late Liz (1971)
The Morning After (1974 TVM)
Sarah T. —Portrait of a Teenage

Alcoholic (1975 TVM)
A Sensitive, Passionate Man (1977 TVM)
A Cry for Love (1980 TVM)
The Boy Who Drank Too Much (1980 TVM)
Special Treatment (1980)
Life of the Party: The Story of Beatrice (1982 TVM)
Under the Influence (1986 TVM)
Shattered Spirits (1987 TVM)
The Betty Ford Story (1987 TVM)
My Name Is Bill W. (1989 TVM)

Aldrich, Henry

"Wimmen—they bore me!" proclaimed the ad to *Henry Aldrich Gets Glamour,* thus separating Henry from rival film teen, and renowned girl chaser, Andy Hardy (q.v.). Yet, for the most part, the Henry Aldrich series was Paramount's B-movie answer to MGM's more successful Andy Hardy films. Ezra Stone originated the character in Clifford Goldsmith's 1937 Broadway play *What a Life.* It spawned a popular radio program (also with Stone) and a big screen version, adapted by Billy Wilder and Charles Brackett and starring veteran child actor Jackie Cooper as Henry. Two years later, Cooper and co-star Eddie Bracken (as pal Dizzy) returned to their roles in *Life with Henry* ("You'll get a bang out of Henry and his gang!"). But Paramount sought a fresh face for its third installment and introduced Jimmy Lydon as Henry in 1942's *Henry Aldrich for President.* Lydon, who had made an impact two years earlier in *Tom Brown's Schooldays,* was the ideal choice for the bumbling, likeable Henry. He made nine films, supported by Charles Smith as Dizzy, John Litel as his stern father, and Olive Blakeney as his mother. Like the Hardy films, the series ended shortly after World War II. However, in 1949, original author Goldsmith revived his characters in the half-hour TV series "The Aldrich Family." It ran for four years and starred five different actors as Henry.

What a Life (1939)
Life With Henry (1941)
Henry Aldrich for President (1941)
Henry and Dizzy (1942)
Henry Aldrich, Editor (1943)
Henry Aldrich Gets Glamour (1943)
Henry Aldrich Haunts a House

(1943)
Henry Aldrich Swings It (1943)
Henry Aldrich, Boy Scout (1944)
Henry Aldrich's Little Secret (1944)
Henry Aldrich Plays Cupid (1944)

The Alilenas [The Peanuts Sisters]

These twin six-inch princesses hailed from Infant Island, home of the giant caterpillar Mothra (q.v.). They had the power to summon Mothra, which unfortunately required them to talk (which they did in unison — a very irritating habit). Stars Emi and Yumi Ito recorded songs in Japan as The Peanuts Sisters.

Mothra (1962)
Godzilla vs. the Thing (aka *Godzilla vs. Mothra*) (1964)
Ghidrah, the Three-Headed

Monster (1965)
Godzilla vs. the Sea Monster (aka *Ebriah, Terror of the Deep*) (1966)

Alligators and Crocodiles

These much-maligned reptiles made their mark in horror films, but are more fondly remembered for their dancing and comedic talents. Dancing gators performed a ballet parody in the "Dance of the Hours" sequence from Disney's *Fantasia*. A pet alligator played cupid for a young British couple in the 1955 romantic comedy *An Alligator Named Daisy*. Daisy proved to be a gifted comic, especially in the scene where she was discovered in an upright piano. Prior to writing and directing intellectual fare like *Matewan* and *Eight Men Out*, John Sayles penned 1980's *Alligator*, a campy horror picture about a giant alligator running amok in Chicago's sewers. Between *The Texas Chainsaw Massacre* and *Poltergeist*, director Tobe Hooper made *Eaten Alive*, a barely-released film about a Louisiana hotel owner who feeds unwelcome guests to his pet crocodile. Stephen McNally really kept alligators in the moat of *The Black Castle*, while Whit Bissell was dead serious when he threatened to throw victims to the alligators in *I Was a Teenage Frankenstein*. Richard Crane slowly turned into an alligator in 1959's *The Alligator People*, a sobering little horror picture with a most sympathetic monster. *Crocodile Dundee* is the most famous "croc" hunter of recent years, while Tarzan (q.v.) surely holds the record for most crocodile wrestling matches. James Bond (Roger Moore) disguised himself as a crocodile to infiltrate a secret hideout in 1983's *Octopussy.*

Fantasia (1940)	*Eaten Alive* (aka *Starlight*
The Black Castle (1952)	*Slaughter; Death Trap, Hor-*
Peter Pan (1953)	*ror Hotel Massacre; Legend of*
An Alligator Named Daisy	*the Bayou*) (1976)
(1955)	*The Rescuers* (1977)
I Was a Teenage Frankenstein	*Crocodile* (1979)
(1957)	*Alligator* (1980)
Naked Earth (1958)	*The Great Alligator* (1980)
The Alligator People (1959)	*Octopussy* (1983)
The Three Worlds of Gulliver	*Romancing the Stone* (1984)
(1960)	*Crocodile Dundee* (1986)
The Happiest Millionaire (1967)	*Lady in White* (1988)
Live and Let Die (1973)	*All Dogs Go to Heaven* (1989)

American Ninja Series

Title tells all in this Cannon Films' action series about a U.S. soldier schooled in ninja-style martial arts. Michael Dudikoff played quiet-but-lethal Joe Armstrong in the first two films. Karate expert David Bradley, portraying a different character, took over in 1989's *American Ninja 3: Blood Hunt.* Steve James appeared in all three movies as the hero's two-fisted sidekick.

American Ninja (1985)	*American Ninja 3: Blood Hunt*
American Ninja 2: The Con-	(1989)
frontation (1987)	

Amityville

In 1979, American International Pictures turned Jay Anson's allegedly nonfiction best-seller about a haunted house, *The Amityville Horror,* into its biggest hit. It was a sorry excuse for a horror picture, despite the presence of the once-reliable Rod Steiger as a troubled priest. The 1982 se-quel, *Amityville: The Possession,* turned out to be a prequel—but no one really cared either way. The third installment, *Amityville 3-D* (1983), made no attempt to connect itself with the first two films. Its boxoffice failure (despite the added allure of 3-D) apparently signalled the end of the series. However, a 1989 TV-movie, *Amityville: The Evil Escapes,* moved Patty Duke and Jane Wyatt into the house for a night of unpleasantries.

The Amityville Horror (1979)	*The Demon*) (1983)
Amityville: The Possession	*Amityville: The Evil Escapes*
(1982)	(1989 TVM)
Amityville 3-D (aka *Amityville:*	

Amnesia

A plot device staple, despite its unlikely real-life occurrence, amnesia has shown no favoritism toward any particular genre nor sex. Screen legend Greta Garbo made it fashionable for women to forget their identities in 1932's *As You Desire Me,* thus inspiring other actresses to ponder "Who am I?" A sample roster spans five decades and includes Jennifer Jones *(Love Letters),* Ava Gardner *(Singapore),* Karen Valentine *(Jane Doe),* and Lindsay Wagner *(Stranger in My Bed).* Males have proven to be equally forgetful, especially William Powell and Gregory Peck, both of whom suffered two bouts of amnesia (Powell in *I Love You Again* and *Crossroads,* Peck in *Spellbound* and *Mirage*). Greer Garson, who dealt with Ronald Colman's loss of memory in *Random Harvest* (1942), experienced it herself earlier in *Remember?* (1939). In an unusual plot twist, she and Robert Taylor played a bickering couple who take a potion that causes amnesia and then wind up falling in love again. Amnesia has also separated lovers in high-class soap operas like *Random Harvest, Love Letters,* and *Singapore.* It's hard to remember many amnesiac comedies, although *Desperately Seeking Susan* and *The Road to Hong Kong* spring to mind with little difficulty. The most interesting amnesiac plots have appeared in mysteries and espionage thrillers. Gregory Peck played the new head of an asylum who turns out to be an impostor with amnesia in Hitchcock's *Spellbound* (1945). Warner Baxter's *The Crime Doctor* (q.v.) was a sleuthing psychologist, who had been a master criminal before being reformed by amnesia. Unethical psychiatrist Tony Perkins tried to manipulate amnesiac killer Charles Bronson into murdering his wife's lover in the 1971 thriller *Someone Behind the Door.* James Garner, unable to remember his name, saw a Budweiser truck and an airplane and decided to call himself *Mr. Buddwing* (1966). It was certainly one of the more commercial films of its time.

As You Desire Me (1932)
Remember? (1939)
Missing Ten Days (aka *Spy in the Pantry; Ten Days in Paris*) (1939)
I Love You Again (1940)
Crossroads (1942)
Dr. Gillespie's New Assistant (1942)
Street of Chance (1942)
Random Harvest (1942)
The Crime Doctor (1943)
Identity Unknown (1945)
Love Letters (1945)
Spellbound (1945)
The Unknown (1946)

Somewhere in the Night (1946)
While I Live (aka *The Dream of Olwen*) (1947)
Singapore (1947)
High Wall (1947)
Lost Honeymoon (1947)
Girl in the Painting (aka *Portrait from Life*) (1948)
Shadow on the Wall (1950)
The Woman with No Name (1950)
A Tale of Five Women (aka *A Tale of Five Cities*) (1951)
Home at Seven (aka *Murder on Monday*) (1952)
The Unholy Four (aka *A*

Stranger Came Home) (1953)
Man in the Dark (1953)
The Long Wait (1954)
The Constant Husband (1955)
Istanbul (1957)
Forger of London (1961)
Sundays and Cybele (1962)
The Road to Hong Kong (1962)
The Double (1963)
Hysteria (1964)
Mirage (1965)
The Third Day (1965)
Mister Buddwing (1966)
Project X (1968)
Jigsaw (1968)
Run a Crooked Mile (1969)
Someone Behind the Door

(1971)
Richie Brockelman: The Missing
   24 Hours (1976 TVM)
Beyond the Door 2 (aka Shock)
   (1979)
The Return of the Soldier
   (1981)
Jane Doe (1983 TVM)
Blackout (1985 TVM)
Desperately Seeking Susan
   (1985)
Stranger in My Bed (1986 TVM)
Lilac Dream (1987)
The Stranger (1987)
Overboard (1987)
Murder by Night (1989 TVM)
The Lady Forgets (1989 TVM)

Amusement Parks *see* Fairs and Carnivals

Androids and Cyborgs

Much to the dismay of science fiction purists, the cinema has often confused androids and cyborgs. The term "android" refers either to an artificial man made of organic substance or, in a looser sense, to a human-like robot. The most famous artificial man, Mary Shelley's Frankenstein Monster (q.v.), is seldom described as an android, though he certainly fits the first definition. On a larger scale, Vincent Price tried to create a race of "synthetic men" and move them into government positions in 1970's *Scream and Scream Again*. However, artificial humans such as these remain rare, with most movie androids hailing from the human-like robot school. In Fritz Lang's highly influential *Metropolis* (1925), a mad scientist kidnapped a peace-minded tunnel worker and replaced her with a trouble-making robot lookalike. Androids ran amok in a fantasy resort in Michael Crichton's *Westworld* (1973) and its semi-sequel *Futureworld* (1976). Men replaced their female companions with more easily controlled androids in *The Stepford Wives* (1975) and *Cherry 2000* (1988), although the hero of the latter film ultimately chose Melanie Griffith over his robot lover. Some androids, such as the "replicants" in *Blade Runner* (1982), gradually became so human-like as to question their own identities. Androids far outnumber their relatives, the cyborgs. The term "cyborg," a contraction of "cybernetic organism," describes a hybrid between man and machine. Television's "The Six Million Dollar Man" and "The Bionic Woman" brought fame to cyborgs. Indeed, the pilot movie for *The Six Million Dollar Man* (q.v.) (1973) was originally called *Cyborg*. Technically, former Jedi knight Darth Vader had become a cyborg by the time Luke Skywalker

11

encountered him for the first time in *Star Wars* (1977). Likewise, the Tin Man was one when he and Dorothy met in *The Wizard of Oz* (1939). In futuristic Detroit, a cop left for dead was transformed into the cyborgic crimefighter *Robocop,* one of the most popular movie heroes of 1987. See also **Computers; Robots; Six Million Dollar Man.**

Metropolis (1925)
The Wizard of Oz (1939)
The Perfect Woman (1949)
Creation of the Humanoids (1962)
Dr. Goldfoot and the Bikini Machine (1965)
The Human Duplicators (1965)
Cyborg 2087 (1966)
Scream and Scream Again (1970)
The Six Million Dollar Man (1973 TVM)
Westworld (1973)
The Questor Tapes (1974 TVM)
The Stepford Wives (1975)
Futureworld (1976)
Future Cop (1976 TVM)
The Cops and Robin (1978 TVM)

Alien (1979)
Galaxina (1980)
Android (1982)
Blade Runner (1982)
Prototype (1983 TVM)
The Terminator (1984)
D.A.R.Y.L. (1985)
J.O.E. and the Colonel (1985 TVM)
Condor (1986)
The Vindicator (aka *Frankenstein '88*) (1986)
Deadly Friend (1986)
Eliminators (1986)
Robocop (1987)
Making Mr. Right (1987)
Not Quite Human (1987 TVM)
Cherry 2000 (1988)
Cyborg (1989)

Angels

One rather expects to find angels in heavenly fantasies like *Green Pastures* (1936), *Stairway to Heaven* (1946), and *Made in Heaven* (1987). However, earthbound angels outnumber their celestial counterparts on film. They have also made a more lasting impression, perhaps because they appear in smaller numbers, one or two to a film, allowing them to become more personable (and in some cases, more mortal-like). Guardian angels are the most common variety and have been sent to Earth to rescue misguided mortals from suicide, ambition, and lousy baseball playing. Henry Travers played Clarence, an angel trying to earn his wings, in Frank Capra's annual Christmas favorite *It's a Wonderful Life* (1946). He dissuades a distraught family man (James Stewart) from ending his life by showing him how he has affected the lives of others. Cloris Leachman replaced Travers as the angel in the sticky-sweet 1977 TV-movie remake *It Happened One Christmas.* Another holiday feature, 1985's *One Magic Christmas,* cast Harry Dean Stanton as an unlikely-looking angel who comes to the aid of a confused woman (Mary Steenburgen) who has lost the Christmas spirit. Cary Grant made a charming angel in *The Bishop's Wife* (1947), helping clergyman David Niven realize that his desire to build a cathedral had begun to cut him off from his family and his own love of God. Grant's angel also found himself in the precarious position of falling in love with Niven's wife (Loretta Young). Other angel-mortal love affairs occurred in the Jeanette MacDonald—Nelson Eddy musical *I Married an Angel* (1942) and the ridiculous comedy *Date with an Angel* (1987). Baseball collided with heavenly forces in *Angels in the Outfield* (1952), in which an angel guides the woebegone Pittsburgh Pirates (not the yet-unformed California Angels) to a winning season. The spirit of baseball great Shoeless Joe Jackson returned to earth to play on farmer Kevin Costner's baseball diamond in 1989's *Field of Dreams*. The role call of performers who have played angels is an impressive one: Edmund Gwenn in *Between Two Worlds* and *For Heaven's Sake*, James Mason in *Forever Darling* and *Heaven Can Wait*, Claude Rains in *Here Comes Mr. Jordan*, Sidney Poitier in *The Angel Levine*, and Clifton Webb in *For Heaven's Sake*.

Green Pastures (1936)
Here Comes Mr. Jordan (1941)
I Married an Angel (1942)
Cabin in the Sky (1943)
Between Two Worlds (1944)
The Horn Blows at Midnight (1945)
That's the Spirit (1945)
It's a Wonderful Life (1946)
Stairway to Heaven (aka *A Matter of Life and Death*) (1946)
The Bishop's Wife (1947)
Heaven Only Knows (aka *Montana Mike*) (1947)
For Heaven's Sake (1950)
Angels in the Outfield (aka *Angels and the Pirates*) (1952)
The Angel Who Pawned Her Harp (1954)

Forever Darling (1956)
Barbarella (1967)
The Angel Levine (1970)
It Happened One Christmas (1977 TVM)
Heaven Can Wait (1978)
Human Feelings (1978 TVM)
Fear No Evil (1981)
The Kid with the Broken Halo (1982 TVM)
Two of a Kind (1983)
It Came Upon a Midnight Clear (1984 TVM)
The Heavenly Kid (1985)
One Magic Christmas (1985)
Date with an Angel (1987)
Made in Heaven (1987)
Wings of Desire (1988)
Field of Dreams (1989)
Always (1989)

Animated Movies (Feature-Length)

Not only was Walt Disney the father of feature-length animated films, but his studio completely dominated the field for nearly three decades. The Disney artists produced 13 movies during that span, beginning with 1937's landmark motion picture *Snow White and the Seven Dwarfs*. For the most part, Disney had little competition, chiefly due to the high costs associated with animation. Nevertheless, Max Fleischer, creator of Betty Boop and Popeye, mounted some rival productions in the early 1940s. His *Gulliver's Travels* and *Hoppity Goes to Town* earned good reviews for their artwork, but critics complained about weak storytelling. Husband-and-wife team John Halas and Joy Batchelor produced an ambitious adaptation of George Orwell's *Animal Farm* in 1954. It was oriented toward a more sophisticated adult audience — but did not find one. The UPA studio, home of Mr. Magoo, tried unsuccessfully to duplicate the Disney magic with 1959's *1001 Arabian Nights* and 1963's *Gay Purr-ee*, a musical tale about Parisian cats. The latter film signalled the end of an era, as even the Disney product began to exhibit a lowering of standards. Rising costs and Walt Disney's death (in 1966) undoubtedly contributed to the decline. However, in 1972, a 32-year-old animator named Ralph Bakshi revived the feature-length cartoon in grand fashion, with his stylish, controversial X-rated film *Fritz the Cat*. Although Bakshi's subsequent movies made little money, they acquired a strong cult following, principally among college-age viewers raised on Disney cartoons. Sadly, soaring costs prevented Bakshi from completing his *Lord of the Rings* films. His 1976 adaptation ended abruptly, promising a sequel that was never made. Meanwhile, internal problems at the Disney studio resulted in scarce output during the 1970s. Several Disney animators, led by Don Bluth, quit and formed their own studio. Bluth's first independent feature *The Secret of NIMH* (1982) was a colorful, heartwarming return to the Disney formula. It led to a revival of quality feature-length cartoons in the 1980s, culminating with the simultaneous 1988 releases of Disney's *Oliver and Company* and Bluth's *The Land That Time Forgot*. Concurrently, however, the genre became glutted with lower quality cartoon features based on best-selling toys such as the Care Bears (q.v.), the Pound Puppies, Rainbow Brite, and My Little Pony. These films, like their Saturday morning counterparts, strove to sell as much as entertain. The most novel animated feature of the 1980s remains *Starchaser: The Legend of Orin* (1985), which holds the distinction of being the only feature-length 3-D (q.v.) cartoon. See also **The Care Bears; Cartoon/Live Action Features; Peanuts.**

Snow White and the Seven Dwarfs (1937)	*Sleeping Beauty* (1959)
Gulliver's Travels (1939)	*1001 Arabian Nights* (1959)
Pinocchio (1939)	*One Hundred and One Dalmations* (1961)
Fantasia (1940)	*Alakazam the Great* (1961)
Dumbo (1941)	*The Sword in the Stone* (1963)
Hoppity Goes to Town (aka *Mr. Bugs Goes to Town*) (1941)	*Gay Purr-ee* (1963)
Bambi (1943)	*Pinocchio in Outer Space* (1964)
Cinderella (1950)	*Hey There, It's Yogi Bear* (1964)
Alice in Wonderland (1952)	*A Man Called Flintstone* (1966)
Peter Pan (1952)	*Gulliver's Travels Beyond the Moon* (1966)
Animal Farm (1954)	*The Jungle Book* (1967)
Lady and the Tramp (1956)	

A Boy Named Charlie Brown (1969)
The Phantom Tollbooth (1969)
The Aristocats (1970)
shinebone alley (1971)
The Point (1971 TVM)
Fritz the Cat (1972)
Snoopy, Come Home (1972)
Robin Hood (1973)
Fantastic Planet (1973)
Journey Back to Oz (1974)
The Nine Lives of Fritz the Cat (1975)
Hugo, the Hippo (1975)
The Rescuers (1976)
Wizards (1977)
The Hobbit (1977 TVM)
Race for Your Life, Charlie Brown (1977)
Watership Down (1978)
The Lord of the Rings (1978)
Animalympics (1979)
American Pop (1981)
The Fox and the Hound (1981)
Heavy Metal (1981)
Grendel, Grendel, Grendel (1982)
Hey, Good Lookin' (1982)
Heidi's Song (1982)
The Secret of NIMH (1982)
The Plague Dogs (1982)
The Last Unicorn (1982)
Fire and Ice (1983)
Twice Upon a Time (1983)

Rock & Rule (1983)
The Smurfs and the Magic Flute (1984)
The Black Cauldron (1985)
The Cosmic Eye (1985)
The Care Bears Movie (1985)
Here Comes the Littles (1985)
Starchaser: The Legend of Orin (1985)
Rainbow Brite and the Star Stealers (1985)
The Great Mouse Detective (1986)
Heathcliff: The Movie (1986)
My Little Pony (1986)
GoBots: Battle of the Rock Lords (1986)
The Care Bears Movie 2: A New Generation (1986)
An American Tail (1986)
The Chipmunk Adventure (1987)
The Brave Little Toaster (1987)
Pinocchio and the Emperor of the Night (1987)
The Care Bears Adventure in Wonderland (1987)
Pound Puppies and the Legend of Big Paw (1988)
Oliver and Company (1988)
The Land Before Time (1988)
All Dogs Go to Heaven (1989)
The Little Mermaid (1989)

Anthologies

Also called "episode films," anthology movies contain two or more separate stories, typically linked by a framing device. The format descended from D.W. Griffith's *Intolerance* (1918), which interwove four stories set in different time periods. One of the first American films to separate its "internal plots" was 1932's *If I Had a Million*. Richard Bennett played a millionaire who gave fortunes to people (e.g. Charles Laughton, Gary Cooper, W.C. Fields) randomly selected from the phone book. In the early 1940s, French immigrant Julien Duvivier directed two highly-acclaimed anthology films, *Tales of Manhattan* and *Flesh and Fantasy*. The former film used a dress tailcoat to link five stories, while Robert Benchley tied the stories together in the latter film. Curiously, the three-part *Flesh and Fantasy* originally included a fourth tale, which was expanded by Reginald LeBorg into 1944's *Destiny.* Britain's initial foray in anthology films resulted in the classic 1945 chiller *Dead of Night.* Ironically, this film is best remembered for its frame, as opposed to the stories. It opens with an architect who visits a country manor and engages in a conversation about dreams with its inhabitants. After the last dream is told, the architect wakes up — for he has been dreaming all along. That morning, he drives to a client's estate in the country and arrives at the same manor. The recurring, and endless, nightmare has begun again. In the wake of *Dead of Night,* British studios produced three highly successful adaptations of Somerset Maugham short stories: *Quartet, Trio,* and *Encore.* These inspired a 1952 U.S. author anthology, *O. Henry's Full House,* featuring John Steinbeck as narrator. Budget-conscious director Roger Corman reacquainted the anthology format with horror tales in his 1962 Edgar Allan Poe collection *Tales of Terror.* Amicus, a small British studio, followed Corman's example with 1964's *Dr. Terror's House of Horrors* and subsequently specialized in producing anthology horror films. It made seven additional anthology movies between 1968's *Torture Garden* and 1974's *From Beyond the Grave.* Throughout the 1960s, episodic films enjoyed great popularity in France and Italy, with distinguished filmmakers such as François Truffaut and Federico Fellini contributing segments to international efforts like *Love at Twenty* and *Spirits of the Dead.* In the 1970s, attempts to adapt the anthology format to U.S. made-for-TV movies met with modest success. Television viewers seemed to prefer the interlocking-story format made popular by the "Love Boat" and "Fantasy Island" TV series.

If I Had a Million (1932)
Tales of Manhattan (1942)
Flesh and Fantasy (1943)
Dead of Night (1945)
On Our Merry Way (1948)
Bond Street (1948)
Quartet (1948)
Trio (1950)
Actors and Sin (1952)
Encore (1952)
O. Henry's Full House (1952)
Tonight at 8:30 (aka *Meet Me Tonight*) (1952)
It's a Big Country (1952)
The Story of Three Loves (1953)
Love in the City (1953)
Daughters of Destiny (aka *Love, Soldiers and Women*) (1953)
Letters from My Windmill (1954)
Three Cases of Murder (1954)

Invitation to the Dance (1957)
Of Life and Love (1957)
Rising of the Moon (1957)
Love and the Frenchwoman (1961)
The Devil and the Ten Commandments (1962)
Tales of Terror (1962)
Seven Capital Sins (1962)
Yesterday, Today, and Tomorrow (1963)
Twice Told Tales (1963)
Dr. Terror's House of Horrors (aka *The Bloodsuckers*) (1964)
Black Sabbath (1964)
Kwaidan (1964)
Bambole! (1965)
Let's Talk About Women (1965)
Woman Times Seven (1967)
The Oldest Profession (1967)
The Torture Garden (1968)

Spirits of the Dead (1968)
The Illustrated Man (1969)
Night Gallery (1969 TVM)
The House That Dripped Blood
  (1970)
The Decameron (1970)
Triple Play (1971 TVM)
Asylum (aka House of Crazies)
  (1972)
Tales from the Crypt (1972)
Tales That Witness Madness
  (1973)
Vault of Horror (aka Tales from
  the Crypt 2) (1973)
From Beyond the Grave (aka
  Creatures from Beyond the
  Grave) (1974)

Immoral Tales (1974)
Trilogy of Terror (1975 TVM)
How Funny Can Sex Be? (1976)
The Uncanny (1977)
Roseland (1977)
Movie Movie (1978)
Tigers in Lipstick (aka Wild
  Beds) (1979)
Sunday Lovers (1980)
Creepshow (1982)
Nightmares (1983)
Twilight Zone: The Movie
  (1983)
Jealousy (1984 TVM)
Cat's Eye (1985)
Creepshow 2 (1987)
New York Stories (1989)

Apartments

The narrow confines of apartment living have created stress-inducing problems for many tenants, while implicating others romantically. In Roman
Polanski's *Repulsion* (1965), a sexually-repressed girl (Catherine Deneuve)
spent a weekend alone in her sister's London flat and wound up murdering the lecherous landlord with a dinner knife. Polanski himself played an
apartment dweller who became obsessed with his pad's former occupant in
1976's *The Tenant.* The Kowalski's claustrophobic apartment served to
feed the sexual tensions in Elia Kazan's 1951 adaptation of *A Streetcar
Named Desire.* Supernatural creatures have displayed a special fondness
for apartment living in films like *The Sentinel* (1977), *Poltergeist III,* and
Demons 2 (both 1988). Even the Devil showed up, amid a building full
of satanic tenants, in *Rosemary's Baby* (1968). A temporary housing shortage forced Jean Arthur to share her small Washington, D.C. apartment
with Joel McCrea and Charles Coburn in the 1943 comedy *The More the
Merrier.* Naturally, she and Joel discovered true love. The same plot, with
a different setting (Tokyo), surfaced in 1966 as *Walk, Don't Run.* Apart-
ments have also been the site for illicit love affairs. Fred MacMurray paid
Shirley MacLaine's rent for *The Apartment* (1960), while Jason Robards
visited Jane Fonda on *Any Wednesday* (1966) at his company-paid flat.
The close proximity to his neighbors inspired James Stewart to engage in
some hazardous window-peeping in Hitchcock's *Rear Window* (1954).
Other nosy apartment neighbors proved meddlesome in *Terraces* (1977)
and *Through Naked Eyes* (1983). In the 1943 comedy *Johnny Doesn't Live
Here Anymore* (1943), Simone Simon discovered that keys to her apartment were distributed freely during the war. *The Key* (1958) was an

emotional drama about a woman (Sophia Loren) who passes the key to her apartment to a series of fighting Naval officers.

Bachelor Apartment (1931)
The More the Merrier (1943)
There Is a Family (1944)
Johnny Doesn't Live Here Anymore (aka *And So They Were Married*) (1944)
Apartment for Peggy (1948)
A Kiss in the Dark (1949)
A Streetcar Named Desire (1951)
Love Nest (1951)
Rear Window (1954)
The Apartment (1960)
Why Bother to Knock? (aka *Don't Bother to Knock*) (1961)
The Notorious Landlady (1962)
Boys' Night Out (1962)
Repulsion (1965)

Any Wednesday (1966)
Barefoot in the Park (1967)
The Penthouse (1967)
Rosemary's Baby (1968)
The Odd Couple (1968)
The Landlord (1970)
Strangers in 7A (1972 TVM)
Nightmare (1974 TVM)
They Came from Within (aka *Shivers; The Parasite Murders; Frissons*) (1975)
The Tenant (1976)
Terraces (1977 TVM)
The Sentinel (1977)
Through Naked Eyes (1983 TVM)
The Family (1986)
Demons 2 (1988)
Poltergeist III (1988)

Apes and Monkeys

Ape and monkey performers have earned a notorious reputation for stealing scenes from their human costars. The chimpanzee Bonzo had little trouble upstaging future president Ronald Reagan in *Bedtime for Bonzo*. Clyde, a mugging orangutan, showed far more facial expression than iron-jawed Clint Eastwood in *Every Which Way But Loose*. King Kong towered over Fay Wray and Robert Armstrong in terms of on-screen impact as well as sheer size in his 1933 film debut. Although Kong reigns as the cinema's biggest ape in terms of popularity, his physical dimensions have been equalled by *Mighty Joe Young* (1949), *Konga* (1961), *Goliathon* (1977), and, to a lesser extent, *Son of Kong* (1933). There have been no oversized monkeys, although an equally unusual winged species abducted Dorothy and took her to the Wicked Witch's castle in *The Wizard of Oz* (1939). Ordinary apes have proven to be meddlesome as well, especially in horror/mystery fare such as *Murders in the Rue Morgue* (1932), *The Ape* (1940), and *Gorilla at Large* (1954). Typically, though, a villainous human lurks behind the ape's ghastly deeds—and in some cases, the true murderer turns out to be a man in an ape suit. David Warner longed to be a gorilla—and carry off his estranged wife—in the 1968 satire *Morgan!* Mad scientist Dr. Moreau (Charles Laughton) transformed apes into men with dubious results ("Are we not men?") in 1933's *The Island of Lost Souls*. John Carradine turned a female ape into pretty Acquanetta in the *Captive Wild Woman* series, while Bela Lugosi injected himself with an

ape-transforming serum in 1943's *The Ape Man*. Apes and humans
became intellectual and sociological equals in *The Planet of the Apes* films
(q.v.). For most of that series, the Simian society was the dominant one,
although it experienced internal conflicts between its chimpanzee scientists, orangutan politicians, and gorilla military leaders. The right to teach
the theory that man evolved from apes was hotly debated in *Inherit the
Wind* (1960), based on the famous Scopes Monkey Trial. A mysterious
monolith brought intelligence to Earthly apes in the dramatic opening of
Stanley Kubrick's *2001: A Space Odyssey* (1968). Finally, Marlene
Dietrich, in one of her most memorable scenes, sang "Hot Voodoo" while
wearing a gorilla suit in 1932's *Blonde Venus*. See also **Dupree, Paula (The
Ape Woman); King Kong; Planet of the Apes.**

Murders in the Rue Morgue
  (1932)
The Monster Walks (1932)
Island of Lost Souls (1933)
King Kong (1933)
The Wizard of Oz (1939)
The Ape (1940)
The Ape Man (aka *Lock Your
  Doors*) (1943)
Captive Wild Woman (1943)
Nabonga (aka *Gorilla*) (1944)
Mighty Joe Young (1949)
Bedtime for Bonzo (1951)
Road to Bali (1952)
Bonzo Goes to College (1952)
Monkey Business (1952)
Phantom of the Rue Morgue
  (1954)
Gorilla at Large (1954)
The Bride and the Beast (aka
  Queen of the Gorillas) (1958)
Alakazam the Great (1960)
Konga (1961)
The Monkey's Uncle (1965)
Morgan! (aka *Morgan—A Suit-
  able Case for Treatment*)
  (1966)
Monkey, Go Home (1967)

2001: A Space Odyssey (1968)
Planet of the Apes (1968)
The Barefoot Executive (1970)
A Cold Night's Death (1973
  TVM)
A.P.E. (1976)
Goliathon (1977)
Every Which Way But Loose
  (1978)
The Mafu Cage (aka *My Sister,
  My Love*) (1978)
Bye Bye Monkey (1978)
The Wild and the Free (1980)
The Ivory Ape (1980 TVM)
Any Which Way You Can
  (1980)
*The Incredible Shrinking
  Woman* (1981)
Going Ape! (1981)
*Greystoke: The Legend of Tar-
  zan, Lord of the Apes* (1984)
In the Shadow of Kilimanjaro
  (1986)
Link (1986)
Project X (1987)
Gorillas in the Mist (1988)
*Monkey Shines: An Experiment
  in Terror* (1988)

Apu Trilogy

Satyajit Ray's simple, powerful films about the son of a Brahmin priest
brought international attention to Indian cinema in the 1950s. Ray
adapted the first film, 1956's *Pather Panchali*, from Bibhuti Bannerji's acclaimed novel. He bought the book's rights for a modest $1300, but

encountered financial problems early in the production. He pawned his wife's jewelry (a last resort in Indian families) before eventually securing backing from the West Bengal government. The film's story dealt with life in a small village as seen through the eyes of Apu, a young boy. He watches his sister die, his father leave to find work, and finally his family forced to move from their home. This visually stunning, emotional drama soon attracted the attention of international critics. It was voted a special award at the 1956 Cannes Film Festival and was subsequently honored by festivals in Berlin, Tokyo, and Denmark. Ray returned to Apu as both a young boy and an adolescent in 1957's *Aparjito*. In 1959's *Apur Sansar*, Apu marries and becomes isolated from village life by his own education.

> *Pather Panchali* (aka *Father Pan-* *vanquished*) (1957)
> *chali; Song of the Road*) (1956)   *Apur Sansar* (aka *The World of*
> *Aparajito* (aka *The Un-*   *Apu*) (1959)

Arthur, King, and the Knights of the Round Table

The legendary 6th century British king, oddly ignored during Hollywood's swashbuckling days, has gradually evolved into one of the cinema's most durable mythic heroes. He was strictly a supporting character in both sound versions of Mark Twain's *A Connecticut Yankee in King Arthur's Court*. British comedian Arthur Askey dreamed he was a knight of the Round Table in 1942's *King Arthur Was a Gentleman*. Then in 1953, MGM followed its blockbuster *Ivanhoe* with the gloss-dripping Arthurian spectacle *Knights of the Round Table*. Mel Ferrer made a noble Arthur, with Ava Gardner (beautiful, but not quite right) as Guinevere and dashing Robert Taylor (a bit old, actually) as Lancelot. Despite its dramatic shortcomings, it remained the standard Arthurian epic for almost three decades. The next version of the legend came from an unlikely source, action star Cornel Wilde. He produced, directed, and starred in *The Sword of Lancelot,* a straightforward well-done drama focusing on the romance between Lancelot (Wilde) and Guinevere (Jean Wallace). Brian Aherne made a low-key Arthur. Novelist T.H. White's *The Once and Future King* provided the basis for Disney's animated feature *The Sword and the Stone* (1963) and the Broadway musical/film *Camelot* (1967). The former was a bland tale of Arthur's youth, while the latter benefitted from star turns by Richard Harris and Vanessa Redgrave as Arthur and Guinevere. In the 1970s, French directors Robert Bresson and Eric Rohmer contributed the atmospheric, sometimes esoteric, knightly tales *Lancelot of the Lake* and *Perceval,* respectively. The Monty Python troupe spoofed Arthurian films hilariously in their finest feature, 1975's *Monty Python and the Holy Grail.* Disney added an unnecessary remake of *A Connecticut Yankee* in 1979, dubiously titled *Unidentified Flying Oddball.* Two years later, director John Boorman brought atmosphere, mystery, and sexuality to his epic *Excalibur.* Based on Malory's *Le Morte d'Arthur,* Boorman's

picture gave equal time to Merlin (played by Nicol Williamson) while telling Arthur's (Nigel Terry) tale in depth. Malcolm McDowell made a
passable Arthur in the otherwise dreadful 1985 TV-movie *Arthur the
King,* which co-starred Dyan Cannon as a contemporary lass who falls
through a hole in Stonehenge and winds up in Camelot. George Romero's
1981 parable *Knightriders* told the Camelot story in a contemporary setting with Ed Harris as the leader of a troupe of jousting motorcycle riders.

A Connecticut Yankee (1931)
King Arthur Was a Gentleman
  (1942)
*A Connecticut Yankee in King
  Arthur's Court* (1949)
Knights of the Round Table
  (1953)
The Black Knight (1954)
The Sword of Lancelot (aka
  Lancelot and Guinevere)
  (1963)
The Sword in the Stone (1963)
Seige of the Saxons (1964)
Camelot (1967)
Gawain and the Green Knight

(1973)
Lancelot of the Lake (aka *Lance-
  lot du Lac; Le Graal; The
  Grail*) (1974)
*Monty Python and the Holy
  Grail* (1975)
Perceval (aka *Perceval le
  Gallois*) (1978)
Unidentified Flying Oddball
  (aka *A Spaceman in King Ar-
  thur's Court*) (1979)
Excalibur (1981)
Knightriders (1981)
The Sword of the Valiant (1982)
Arthur the King (1985 TVM)

Artists *see* Painters

Assumed Identity

The plot device where one person assumes another's identity has evolved
into one of the cinema's most reliable conventions. Frequently, it is paired
with related plotlines, such as amnesia, disguises, and lookalikes (all q.v.).
For example, amnesiac Gregory Peck assumed the identity of asylum director Dr. Edwardes in Hitchcock's *Spellbound.* In *The Great Impostor*
(1961), Tony Curtis played real-life master of disguises Ferdinand Demara
who assumed the identities of a prison warden, a naval doctor, a school
teacher, and others. Ronald Colman played a dashing gent who
substitutes for his lookalike, the king of Ruritania, in an effort to thwart a
usurper in 1937's *The Prisoner of Zenda.* Despite the utilities of these
plotline pairings, some of the more intriguing films about assumed identities involve neither amnesia, disguises, nor lookalikes. In 1975's *The
Passenger,* Jack Nicholson played a man so unhappy with his own life that
he assumed the identity of a dead man he knew nothing about. In *The
Inspector General* (1949), Danny Kaye was *mistaken* for the title character,
but he readily *assumed* the role once he realized the power it possessed.
Gerard Depardieu was executed for assuming another man's identity in
The Return of Martin Guerre (1982), even though everyone seemed to
prefer him to the real Martin Guerre. Poor Janet Leigh woke up from her
wedding night with a stranger in her bed claiming to be her husband in

the appropriately-titled *Honeymoon with a Stranger* (1969). Still, that's not as bad as Gloria Talbott, who actually married an alien who had assumed her fiancé's identity in *I Married a Monster from Outer Space* (1958). See also **Amnesia; Disguises; Lookalikes.**

The Masquerader (1933)	*I Married a Monster from Outer*
Maniac (1934)	*Space* (1958)
The Great Impersonation (1935)	*Libel* (1959)
The Great Impersonation (1942)	*The Great Impostor* (1961)
The Impostor (aka *Strange Con-*	*Honeymoon with a Stranger*
fession) (1944)	(1969 TVM)
Spellbound (1945)	*The Passenger* (1975)
Detour (1945)	*Kagemusha* (aka *Kagemusha,*
Hollow Triumph (aka *The Scar*)	*the Shadow Warrior*) (1980)
(1948)	*The Return of Martin Guerre*
The Inspector General (1949)	(1982)
No Man of Her Own (1949)	*I Married a Shadow* (1982)
The House on Telegraph Hill	*The Impostor* (1984 TVM)
(1951)	*Critical Condition* (1987)

Asylums

The line between sanity and madness has frequently been portrayed as a thin one in films with an asylum setting. A common plot device has a sane person feigning insanity in order to be committed to an asylum. Journalist Peter Breck pulled the trick to win a Pulitzer Prize in Samuel Fuller's *Shock Corridor* (1963). He lost his mind as a result. The following year's *Shock Treatment* found Stuart Whitman as an actor who entered an asylum to discover where Roddy McDowell hid a fortune. However, the most famous picture along these lines was the 1975 multiple Oscar winner *One Flew Over the Cuckoo's Nest.* Jack Nicholson's Randle Patrick Mc-Murphy faked temporary insanity because he preferred a mental institution over hard labor at a prison. He discovered that the patients were saner—in their own way—than the medical staff. Alan Bates made a similar observation in 1966's *King of Hearts,* in which a group of inmates escaped into an evacuated town during WWI. Bates learned that these charming lunatics may be "touched," but at least they were not fighting a war to destroy each other. Another oft-filmed plot—sane people who are revealed to be mad—has been featured prominently in *The Cabinet of Dr. Caligari* and *The Ninth Configuration.* A highly influential expressionistic film, *Caligari* (1919) is ultimately the vision of a lunatic, for in its famous closing scene, the narrator is revealed to be a patient recounting the story to the head of an asylum. William Peter Blatty's *The Ninth Configuration* (1980) takes a similar theme one step further—the asylum director (Stacy Keach) turns out to be a mad impostor. Other movies which take place principally within the confines of an asylum include *Bedlam, The Snake Pit,* and *Marat/Sade.* Escaped inmates are played for laughs in

Road Show and horror in *Alone in the Dark*. *Frances,* the true story of actress Frances Farmer, and the James Stewart comedy *Harvey* have
memorable closing scenes in mental institutions.

The Cabinet of Dr. Caligari (1919)	*Asylum* (aka *House of Crazies*) (1972)
Road Show (1941)	*Don't Look in the Basement* (1973)
Spellbound (1945)	
Bedlam (1946)	*Frankenstein and the Monster from Hell* (1973)
The Snake Pit (1948)	
Behind Locked Doors (1948)	*One Flew Over the Cuckoo's Nest* (1975)
Harvey (1950)	
Blood of the Vampire (1958)	*High Anxiety* (1977)
The Hideout (1961)	*Down the Ancient Stairs* (1977)
The Cabinet of Dr. Caligari (1962)	*The Other Side of Hell* (1978 TVM)
Shock Corridor (1963)	*Dracula* (1979)
Shock Treatment (1964)	*The Ninth Configuration* (aka
Signpost to Murder (1965)	*Twinkle, Twinkle Killer*
King of Hearts (1966)	*Kane*) (1980)
Marat/Sade (1967)	*Alone in the Dark* (1982)
The Big Cube (1969)	*Frances* (1982)
The Night Visitor (1970)	*Hellhole* (1985)

Atomic Bombs

The atomic bomb has been the subject of earnest fact-based dramas,
escapist science fiction, chilling thrillers, and one wild satire. The fact-
based films began with 1947's *The Beginning or the End,* a stilted but
historically interesting, government-approved story of the Manhattan Project. The personal drama behind the bombing of Hiroshima was better explored in 1952's *Above and Beyond* and in the 1980 TV-movie *Enola Gay:
The Men, the Mission, the Atomic Bomb.* PBS's American Playhouse produced 1986's *Desert Bloom,* a perceptive family drama set in Nevada during the 1950's atomic bomb tests. Another American Playhouse production, 1983's *Testament* (1983), featured a powerful performance by Jane
Alexander as a mother coping with her family's survival in the aftermath
of an atomic explosion. It easily eclipsed the similar, heavily-hyped 1983
TV-film *The Day After.* Both films owe a minor debt to Ray Milland's
1962 "B"-movie *Panic in the Year Zero,* a taut tale of a family's struggle
to survive in a post-atomic world, and a major debt to Peter Watkin's
bleak *The War Game* (1967). Using a pseudo-documentary approach,
Watkins showed what an atomic bomb would do to London. It's a brutal,
frightening picture—so scary that its sponsor, the British Broadcasting
Company, refused to air it on television. Today, it's shown frequently in
conjunction with anti-nuclear protests. On a more positive note, scientists
have used atomic devices for worthy purposes, such as destroying city-

crunching monsters like 1953's *The Best from 20,000 Fathoms.* Ironically, as in *The Beast,* many of these creatures were also created by atomic bomb testing. Mutant humans worshipped an atomic bomb in *Beneath the Planet of the Apes* (see **Planet of the Apes**) (1970). It was detonated in the film's climax and destroyed the world. At the conclusion of 1964's *Fail Safe,* President Henry Fonda ordered the atomic destruction of New York City (where his family lives) to avoid a nuclear confrontation with the Soviet Union. Other thrillers pale in comparison, although *The Bedford Incident* (1965) served as a potent reminder of just how easily an atomic war can be initiated. Industrious teenagers almost caused nuclear war in *WarGames* (1983) and *The Manhattan Project* (1986). In the latter film, a high school student built an atomic bomb to prove a point—a sobering premise despite an insufficient amount of credibility. The only film to effectively poke fun at atomic bombs and the threat of nuclear war remains Stanley Kubrick's *Dr. Strangelove, or How I Learned to Stop Worrying and Love the Bomb* (1964). Kubrick's black comedy closed with a classic image: Slim Pickens riding a falling bomb bronco-style to the closing strains of "We'll Meet Again." See also **End of the World/Post-Apocalypse.**

The Beginning or the End (1947)	*The Day the Fish Came Out* (1967)
Children of Hiroshima (1952)	*Finders Keepers* (1966)
Above and Beyond (1952)	*Beneath the Planet of the Apes* (1970)
The 49th Man (1953)	*Enola Gay: The Men, the Mission, the Atomic Bomb* (1980 TVM)
Port of Hell (1954)	
Hiroshima, Mon Amour (1960)	*The Atomic Cafe* (1982)
The Flight That Disappeared (1961)	*Testament* (1983)
Panic in the Year Zero (1962)	*The Day After* (1983)
Dr. Strangelove, or How I Learned to Stop Worrying and Love the Bomb (1964)	*WarGames* (1983)
	Desert Bloom (1986)
Fail Safe (1964)	*The Manhattan Project* (1986)
The Bedford Incident (1965)	*Day One* (1989 TVM)
The War Game (1967)	*Fat Man and Little Boy* (1989)

Ator

Shortly after achieving (very) minor celebrity status playing *Tarzan, the Ape Man* (1981) opposite Bo Derek, hunky Miles O'Keeffe landed in this brief Italian sword-and-sorcery (q.v.) series. Aside from poor dubbing and O'Keeffe's inept thesping, these films are notable for their atrocious special effects (e.g. the hilarious giant spider slain by Ator in the original). Incredibly, Sean Connery played O'Keeffe's father in the non–Atorian *Sword of the Valiant* (1982). See also **Sword and Sorcery.**

Ator, the Fighting Eagle (1983)	*Invincible*) (1984)
Blademaster (aka *Ator, the*	*Iron Warrior* (1987)

Auto Racing

The high-velocity thrills of auto racing date back to Howard Hawks' 1932 speedway drama *The Crowd Roars* with James Cagney as a cocky driver. Yet, despite other vintage efforts like *Indianapolis Speedway* (a 1939 remake of *The Crowd Roars*) and *The Big Wheel* (1949), auto racing was virtually ignored by filmmakers until the late 1950s. The sport's grassroots popularity grew rapidly in the early 1960s and so did the number of big screen racing dramas. Some pictures catered to Southern stock car fans (e.g. 1960's *Thunder in Carolina*), while others offered European locales and sleek formula cars (e.g. 1963's *The Young Racers*). The common denominator in all these films was an inexpensive look supplemented by plenty of stock footage. Then, in 1966, director John Frankenheimer shifted racing films into high gear with his visually spectacular (but emotionally shallow) epic *Grand Prix*. With its trendy split-screen effects and international cast, *Grand Prix* made it fashionable for big stars to get behind the wheel. Paul Newman and Robert Wagner played pit stop rivals in 1969's *Winning* and Steve McQueen took to the track in 1971's *Le Mans*. Other movies substituted real-life stories for big-name stars. Stock car legend Richard Petty played himself in 1972's *Smash-Up Alley*. Jeff Bridges portrayed Junior Jackson in *The Last American Hero* (1973), while his brother Beau played another race car driver in *Heart Like a Wheel* (1983), the biography of drag racing champion Shirley "Cha Cha" Muldowney (Bonnie Bedelia). Beau was also in *Greased Lightning* (1977), the story of Wendell Scott (Richard Pryor), professional racing's first black driver. Of course, not all auto racing films have taken place at racetracks. Cross-country races have made popular film subjects ever since two genteel couples raced their antique roadsters across the English countryside in 1953's *Genevieve*. Blake Edwards' 1965 comedy *The Great Race* added a bevy of stars to the cross-country racing plot—a formula that's been duplicated in numerous films such as *Those Darling Young Men in Their Jaunty Jalopies* (1969), *Cannonball Run* (1981), and *Speed Zone* (1989). College campus cult movie *Death Race 2000* (1975) featured a cross-country race in which drivers earned points for running down pedestrians. See also **Automobiles** (for nonracing films); **Herbie, the Love Bug**.

The Crowd Roars (1932)	*Checkpoint* (1956)
Racing Youth (1932)	*The Killing* (1956)
Indianapolis Speedway (1939)	*The Devil's Hairpin* (1957)
The Big Wheel (1949)	*Speed Crazy* (1959)
To Please a Lady (1950)	*Thunder in Carolina* (1960)
Genevieve (1953)	*The Green Helmet* (1961)
Race for Life (1954)	*The Young Racers* (1963)
Johnny Dark (1954)	*The Killers* (1964)
The Racers (aka *Such Men Are*	*The Lively Set* (1964)
Dangerous) (1955)	*Viva Las Vegas* (aka *Love in Las*

Vegas) (1964)
The Great Race (1965)
Red Line 7000 (1965)
Fireball 500 (1966)
Grand Prix (1966)
Spinout (aka *California Holiday*) (1966)
A Man and a Woman (1966)
Thunder Alley (1967)
Fireball Jungle (1968)
Track of Thunder (1968)
Speed Lovers (1968)
Speedway (1968)
The Wild Racers (1968)
Those Daring Young Men in Their Jaunty Jalopies (aka *Monte Carlo or Bust*) (1969)
Drive Hard, Drive Fast (1969 TVM)
The Love Bug (1969)
Pit Stop (1969)
Winning (1969)
The Challengers (1969 TVM)
Le Mans (1971)
Corky (aka *Lookin' Good*) (1971)

Smash-Up Alley (aka *43: The Petty Story*) (1972)
Baffled (1972 TVM)
The Last American Hero (aka *Hard Driver*) (1973)
Death Race 2000 (1975)
Win, Place or Steal (1975)
Cannonball (aka *Carquake*) (1976)
The Gumball Rally (1976)
Bobby Deerfield (1977)
Checkered Flag or Crash (1977)
Bob Johnson and His Fantastic Speed Circus (1978 TVM)
Greased Lightning (1977)
The Betsy (aka *Harold Robbins' The Betsy*) (1978)
Cannonball Run (1981)
Safari 3000 (1982)
Six Pack (1982)
Heart Like a Wheel (1983)
Stroker Ace (1983)
Cannonball Run II (1984)
Born to Race (1988)
Speed Zone (1989)

Autobiographical Films

Many people have played themselves on film, but few have played themselves in film biographies. The reasons are obvious: The scarcity of motion picture biographies of *living* persons; the fact that "real" people do not necessarily make believable actors; and the image problem—that of having a big ego—created by portraying oneself in a favorable light. Sports players dominated early film autobiographies, tracing the careers of baseball legend Jackie Robinson *(The Jackie Robinson Story)*, track star Bob Mathias *(The Bob Mathias Story)*, and football players Tom Harmon *(Harmon of Michigan)* and Elroy "Crazylegs" Hirsch *(Crazylegs)*. None of these one-time actors went on to pursue an acting career (though Harmon's son Mark eventually did). Boxing great Muhammad Ali once said: "When you're as great as I am, it's hard to be humble." So naturally, he played himself in the modestly-titled biopic *The Greatest* (1977). Actresses Ann Jillian, Sophia Loren, and Shirley MacLaine all played themselves in made-for-TV biographies. Ms. MacLaine's film was adapted from her best-selling autobiography *Out on a Limb*. Ray Charles also appeared as himself in 1964's *Ballad in Blue*. To date, the best autobiographical film remains 1955's *To Hell and Back*, in which Audie Murphy traced his own rise from farm boy to the nation's most decorated soldier in World War II to movie star. Although not autobiographical, Will Rogers, Jr., played his father in *The Will Rogers Story* (1952) and Marie Osmond played her mother in *Side by Side: The True Story of the Osmond Family* (1982). See also **Film Star Biographies.**

Harmon of Michigan (1941)
The Fabulous Dorseys (1947)
The Jackie Robinson Story (1950)
Crazylegs (1953)
The Bob Mathias Story (1954)
To Hell and Back (1955)
Rock Around the World (aka *The Tommy Steele Story*)
(1957)
Ballad in Blue (aka *Blues for Lovers*) (1964)
The Greatest (1977)
Sophia Loren: Her Own Story (1980 TVM)
Out on a Limb (1987 TVM)
The Ann Jillian Story (1988 TVM)

Automobiles

While a number of auto-oriented movies revolve around auto racing (q.v.), they represent but one model in an eclectic line of car pictures. More imaginative auto movies have featured flying vehicles, gimmicky cars, living vehicles, and high-speed car chases. Airborne autos appeared in the children's fantasies *The Absent Minded Professor* (1961) and *Chitty Chitty Bang Bang* (1968). The latter film was adapted from a book by Ian Fleming, whose secret agent James Bond encountered an AMC Matador-turned-airplane in *The Man with the Golden Gun* (1974). Bond movies are well-known for Q's gimmick-laden cars, the most memorable being the Aston-Martin in *Goldfinger* (1964). It boasted radar, machine guns, a smokescreen device, and an ejector seat that shot unwanted passengers out the roof. Its nearest competitor, gimmick-wise, was the Batmobile from 1989's *Batman*. In addition to an impressive battery of Bat-weapons, the Batmobile could be maneuvered at high speed by remote control and cover itself with protective armor in a matter of seconds. The next step up from remote-controlled vehicles are living ones. Alas, most self-functioning vehicles have exhibited a bad streak. *Christine,* a bright-red '58 Plymouth, mowed down quite a few teens after deciding she had been insulted. *The Car* (1977) proved to be equally troublesome, as did other independent-minded vehicles in *Killdozer* (1974), *The Hearse* (1980), *Nightmares* (1983), *Maximum Overdrive* (1986), and *The Wraith* (1986). There have been friendly autos, though, such as Herbie the Love Bug (q.v.), a romance-minded Volkswagen Beetle which starred in four Disney movies. On television, Ann Sothern was reincarnated as a 1928 Porter in the 1965–66 sitcom "My Mother the Car." In Steven Spielberg's 1971 TV-movie *Duel,* the director showed only fleeting shots of the driver of the truck dead-set on running Dennis Weaver off the road. Another 1971 picture, *Vanishing Point,* starred Barry Newman as an obsessed driver who turns a wager (Denver to San Francisco in 15 hours) into a high speed death drive. Consisting mostly of highway car chase footage, *Vanishing Point* attracted an enthusiastic youth audience and set the pattern for similar low-budget outings like *Dirty Mary, Crazy Larry* (1974), *Eat My Dust!* (1976), and *Grand Theft Auto* (1977). However, the most spectacular car chases of the 1970s and 1980s consisted of single extended sequences in cop thrillers, a practice perfected in the classic high-speed pursuit through San Francisco in 1967's *Bullitt*. Some films integrated the chase into the plot (e.g. *The French Connection*), while others hyped the chase scene as the main selling point (e.g. *The Seven-Ups*). Elaborate chase scenes faded in the 1980s, though William Friedkin staged a nail-grinding drive down a wrong-way street in 1985's *To Live and Die in L.A.* The 1988 Dirty Harry picture *The Dead Pool* spoofed the *Bullitt* chase with a scene of Harry being pursued through San Francisco by a remote-controlled toy roadster carrying a bomb. Of related interest, *Free for All* and *The Formula* dealt with the invention of more cost-efficient gasoline. The cars in 1975's *Idaho Transfer* used people for fuel. See also **Auto Racing.**

Jalopy (1953)
Inside Detroit (1955)
Young and Wild (1958)
The Absent Minded Professor (1961)
The Yellow Rolls Royce (1964)
Goldfinger (1964)
Chitty Chitty Bang Bang (1968)
Duel (1971)
Vanishing Point (1971)
Two-Lane Blacktop (1971)
Killdozer (1974)
Dirty Mary, Crazy Larry (1974)
Cars That Eat People (aka *The Cars That Ate Paris*) (1974)
Gone in 60 Seconds (1974)
The Man with the Golden Gun (1974)
Idaho Transfer (1975)
Eat My Dust! (1976)
Car Wash (1976)
The Car (1977)

Double Nickels (1977)
Grand Theft Auto (1977)
Corvette Summer (1978)
Zero to Sixty (1978)
The Charge of the Model Ts (1979)
The Hearse (1980)
Used Cars (1980)
The Last Chase (1981)
Christine (1983)
Nightmares (1983)
Repo Man (1984)
Car Trouble (1985)
Maximum Overdrive (1986)
Black Moon Rising (1986)
Gung Ho (1986)
The Wraith (1986)
Ford: The Man and the Machine (1987 TVM)
Tucker: The Man and the Dream (1988)
Batman (1989)

Babies

Infants have often exhibited a total disregard for adults, dropping in on unlikely fathers and unwed mothers at the most inconvenient times. *The Three Godfathers*, the story of three tough bandits who "adopt" an orphaned baby, has been filmed at least seven times as: *Bronco Billy and the Baby* (1909), *Three Godfathers* (1916), *Marked Men* (1920), *Hell's Heroes* (1929), *Three Godfathers* (1936), *Three Godfathers* (1948), and *The Godchild* (1975 TVM). John Ford's 1948 version remains the most popular, with John Wayne, Pedro Armendariz, and Harry Carey, Jr., as the improbable parents. *The Baby and the Battleship* (1956) updated the premise and increased the number of dads, but still derived its humor out of showing macho males struggling helplessly to care for a little one. The same sturdy plot surfaced again in the 1985 French comedy *Three Men and a Cradle* and its 1987 American remake *Three Men and a Baby*. However, the most unlikely fathers were the dads-to-be in *Night of the Blood Beast* (1958) and *Rabbit Test* (1978) — two bizarre films about pregnant men. Unexpected infants provided the source of obvious misunderstandings for bachelorettes Ginger Rogers and Debbie Reynolds in the comedy *Bachelor Mother* (1939) and its remake *Bundle of Joy* (1956). Betty Hutton forgot who got her pregnant in Preston Sturges's *Miracle of Morgan's Creek* (1944), but her troubles ended when she gave birth to sextuplets. Tragically, no one believed the young mothers-to-be who claimed to have been blessed with immaculate conceptions in *Agnes of God* and *Hail Mary* (both 1985). A psychotic woman conceived (sans husband) "children of rage" in David Cronenberg's complex chiller *The Brood* (1979). Undesirable babies surprised their mothers in *Rosemary's Baby* (1968), *It's Alive* (1974), *The Stranger Within* (1974), *The Devil Within Her* (1975), and, most disturbingly, David Lynch's *Eraserhead* (1977). *Bobbikins* (1960), a baby who could talk like an adult, was surely a shock to his parents, too. Finally, some movies have dealt with societies which outlawed the birth of babies, as in 1971's *Zero Population Growth* and its TV-movie equivalent *The Last Child* (1981). See also **Babysitters; Having Babies Series; It's Alive; Governesses and Nannies.**

Bronco Billy and the Baby (1909)
Three Godfathers (1916)
Marked Men (1920)
The Kid (1921)
Hell's Heroes (1929)
A Bedtime Story (1933)
Three Godfathers (aka *Miracle in the Sand*) (1936)
Bachelor Mother (1939)
East Side of Heaven (1939)
Little Accident (1939)
Miracle on Main Street (1939)
Miracle of Morgan's Creek (1944)
Three Godfathers (1948)
Father's Little Dividend (1951)
The Little Kidnappers (aka *The Kidnappers*) (1953)
The Baby and the Battleship (1956)
Bundle of Joy (1956)
Night of the Blood Beast (aka *Creature from Galaxy 27*) (1958)
Rock-a-Bye Baby (1958)
Unwed Mother (1958)
Bobbikins (1960)
A Global Affair (1964)
Rosemary's Baby (1968)
ZPG (aka *Zero Population Growth*) (1971)

The Last Child (1971 TVM)
A Brand New Life (1973 TVM)
The Godchild (1974)
It's Alive (1974)
The Stranger Within (1974 TVM)
Unwed Father (1974)
The Devil Within Her (aka *I Don't Want to Be Born*) (1975)
Having Babies (1976 TVM)

Eraserhead (1977)
Rabbit Test (1978)
The Brood (1979)
He's Not Your Son (1984 TVM)
Agnes of God (1985)
Hail Mary (1985)
Three Men and a Cradle (1985)
Raising Arizona (1987)
Baby Boom (1987)
Three Men and a Baby (1987)
Look Who's Talking (1989)

Babysitters

Stalked by psychos and harassed by bratty children, it was inevitable that a babysitter or two would turn out bad. It finally happened in the 1980 TV-movie *The Babysitter,* with practically-perfect sitter Stephanie Zimbalist first seducing her employer (much to the chagrin of his wife), then taking over the family and plotting murder. Diane Franklin was equally menacing in 1983's *Summer Girl.* However, nasty babysitters have been the exception, of course. More typically, they have been portrayed as helpless victims in low-grade horror fare like *Fright, Trick or Treats,* and *Halloween* (though Jamie Lee Curtis managed to defend herself reasonably well). The favorite plot of babysitter comedies has been entrusting the child care to hapless males. Actually, Clifton Webb's Mr. Belvedere (q.v.) turned out to be a very capable babysitter in 1948's *Sitting Pretty.* However, Jerry Lewis played a stereotypically inept male babysitter in *Rock-a-bye Baby,* but then triplets could tax even a veteran sitter. Overall, though, the perils of babysitting were best explored in the hectic 1987 comedy *Adventures in Babysitting.* Teen sitter Elisabeth Shue and her charges somehow transformed a dull night of TV watching into a wild series of connected adventures through the streets of Chicago. Fortunately, they still made it back home before the parents' return, but only by a matter of seconds. Marilyn Monroe made the least likely of all babysitters, portraying a mentally disturbed one contemplating suicide in 1952's *Don't Bother to Knock.* See also **Babies** (for similar films like *Three Men and a Baby*); **Belvedere, Mr.; Governesses and Nannies.**

Sitting Pretty (1948)
Rock-a-bye Baby (1958)
The Babysitter (1969)
Fright (1971)
The Babysitter (aka *Wanted: Babysitter*) (1975)
Halloween (1978)
When a Stranger Calls (1979)

The Babysitter (1980 TVM)
Trick or Treats (1982)
Summer Girl (1983 TVM)
First Affair (1983 TVM)
Rita, Sue and Bob, Too (1986)
Adventures in Babysitting (1987)
Uncle Buck (1989)

The Bad News Bears

The combination of Walter Matthau as a beer-guzzling coach and Tatum O'Neal as a foul-mouthed, female pitcher turned this little league baseball comedy into a surprise 1976 hit. Neither star appeared in the 1977 follow-up *The Bad News Bears in Breaking Training,* which weighed down the comedy with a large dose of sentiment. William Devane played the team's new coach. But he too was nowhere to be found in 1978's *The Bad News Bears Go to Japan,* a weak outing that ended the series. Young Jackie Earle Haley was the only Bear to star in all three films. A half-hour CBS TV series aired briefly during 1979. See also **Baseball.**

The Bad News Bears (1976)	*The Bad News Bears Go to*
The Bad News Bears in Break-	*Japan* (1978)
ing Training (1977)	

Baines, Scattergood

Guy Kibbee starred as Clarence Budington Kelland's genial country philosopher in this RKO series. Actually, the films were produced by little Pyramid Pictures Corporation, which convinced RKO that a six-film series based on the popular radio program was bound to be profitable. It wasn't—the public never warmed up to Scattergood, not even when RKO tried to hide the fact that a movie was part of the series (the studio changed the title of *Scattergood Swings It* to *Cinderella Swings It*). Nevertheless, the storekeeper of Coldriver stayed busy for three years, helping horse-loving orphans *(Scattergood Rides High)* and would-be recording stars *(Cinderella Swings It).*

Scattergood Baines (1941)	*Scattergood Rides High* (1942)
Scattergood Meets Broadway	*Scattergood Survives a Murder*
(1941)	(1942)
Scattergood Pulls the Strings	*Cinderella Swings It* (aka *Scat-*
(1941)	*tergood Swings It*) (1943)

Ballet / Ballerinas

The challenge of integrating a dynamic theatrical art form into the confines of cinema has proven to be a difficult task. Consequently, it has been undertaken almost exclusively by filmmakers/ballet lovers, whose artistic successes have been mixed equally with unmitigated failures. British filmmakers Michael Powell and Emeric Pressburger produced two outstanding ballet films, with Powell also contributing a third, less memorable solo effort. The first Powell-Pressburger ballet film was 1948's *The Red Shoes,* which starred real-life ballerina Moira Shearer as a young dancer driven to her death by her inability to choose between ballet and a "normal" life. The highlight of this dazzling, colorful film is a 14-minute ballet of Hans Christian Andersen's fairy tale "The Red Shoes," brilliantly danced and photographed against stylized sets. The elaborate sets returned in 1951's *Tales of Hoffman,* a fusion of drama, singing, and ballet based on Offenbach's opera and featuring ballerina Shearer again. Powell turned to ballet once more, sans Pressburger, in 1959's all-but-forgotten *Honeymoon,* which featured excerpts from the Spanish ballets "Los Amantes de Teruel" and "El Amor Brujo." The most interesting pre–*Red Shoes* ballet picture was *The Specter of the Rose* (1946), an offbeat drama about a young dancer who is slowly losing his mind. It featured a rare screen appearance by drama teacher Michael Chekhov and the potent presence of Dame Judith Anderson. Gene Kelly, after choreographing a modern ballet for a set-piece in *An American in Paris* (1951), incorporated ballet into his all-dance 1956 picture *Invitation to the Dance.* Shot in 1952, this three-part anthology boasted energetic dancing and clever direction (including a combination of live action and cartoon), but it crashed at the boxoffice and almost ended Kelly's career. In contrast, Herbert Ross' *The Turning Point* (1977) was a solid popular and critical favorite. Shirley MacLaine and Anne Bancroft had the starring roles as a pair of former ballerinas, but Mikhail Baryshnikov stole the film every time he took to the dance floor. Ballets filmed in their entirety have been rare, but have nevertheless been captured in *Peter Rabbit and the Tales of Beatrix Potter* (1971), *Nutcracker* (1982), and *Nutcracker: The Motion Picture* (1986). There have been numerous films, not expressly about ballet, which have featured ballerinas as principal characters. The role call of actresses who have played ballerinas is a varied one: Greta Garbo *(Grand Hotel);* Maureen O'Hara *(Dance, Girl, Dance);* Vivien Leigh *(Waterloo Bridge);* Loretta Young *(The Men in Her Life);* Margaret O'Brien *(The Unfinished Dance);* Janet Leigh *(The Red Danube);* Gene Tierney *(Never Let Me Go);* and Leslie Caron *(Gaby).* Ballet segments have highlighted many mainstream musicals, though the sequences in *An American in Paris* and *On Your Toes* stand out.

Grand Hotel (1932)
On Your Toes (1939)
Dance, Girl, Dance (1940)
Waterloo Bridge (1940)
The Men in Her Life (1941)
The Dancing Masters (1943)
Specter of the Rose (1946)
Carnival (1946)
The Unfinished Dance (1947)
The Imperfect Lady (1947)
The Red Shoes (1949)
The Red Danube (1949)
Illicit Interlude (aka *Summer Play; Summer Interlude*) (1950)
An American in Paris (1951)
Tales of Hoffman (1951)
Limelight (1952)
Never Let Me Go (1953)

Dance Little Lady (1955)
Gaby (1956)
Meet Me in Las Vegas (aka *Viva Las Vegas*) (1956)
Invitation to the Dance (1956)
Honeymoon (1959)
Vampire and the Ballerina (1962)
Peter Rabbit and the Tales of Beatrix Potter (aka *The Tales of Beatrix Potter*) (1971)
The Turning Point (1977)
Slow Dancing in the Big City (1978)
Nutcracker (1982)
The Cowboy and the Ballerina (1984 TVM)
Nutcracker, the Motion Picture (1986)
Dancers (1987)

Balloons, Hot Air

Phileas Fogg may be the world's most famous balloonist, but *Around the World in Eighty Days* is but one of several balloon movies (indeed, Phileas' balloon flight is relatively short). Red Buttons and Barbara Eden spent *Five Weeks in a Balloon* in Irwin Allen's 1962 adaptation of Jules Verne's adventure tale. Civil War prisoners escaped via a hot air balloon and blew off course onto a *Mysterious Island* (1961) in another Verne-inspired epic. Toto's mad dash from the Wizard's hot air balloon kept Dorothy from returning home in a conventional fashion in *The Wizard of Oz* (1939). Good thing she kept those ruby slippers. Katharine Hepburn helped two children launch a balloon—and nearly land on an orchestra conductor—in *Olly, Olly, Oxen Free* (1978), while a boy and his grandfather made a trans-continental flight in the 1981 TV-movie *Charlie and the Great Balloon Chase*. Baron von Munchausen can be credited for creating the most inventive hot air balloon—one made of ladies' bloomers—in 1989's *The Adventures of Baron Munchausen*. See also **Dirigibles.**

Queen of the Jungle (1935)
Penrod's Double Trouble (1938)
The Wizard of Oz (1939)
Around the World in Eighty Days (1956)
Flight of the Lost Balloon (1961)
Mysterious Island (1961)
Five Weeks in a Balloon (1962)
Those Magnificent Men in Their Flying Machines (1965)
The Great Race (1965)
Chitty Chitty Bang Bang (1968)
Charlie Bubbles (1968)
Olly, Olly, Oxen Free (aka *The Great Balloon Adventure*) (1978)
Charlie and the Great Balloon Chase (1981 TVM)
Night Crossing (1981)
The Flight of the Eagle (1982)
The Adventures of Baron Munchausen (1989)

Bancroft, Brass

A promising young star named Ronald Reagan played secret service agent Brass Bancroft in a series of four Warner Bros. programmers, beginning with 1939's *Secret Service of the Air*. The films were inspired by the memoirs of William H. Moran, a former secret service chief. Reagan's heroics, though, were strictly Saturday afternoon kid's stuff. Brass fought smugglers, counterfeiters, and experimental death rays in his brief career. In real life, Reagan fought Warner Bros. to shelve his second Bancroft film, *Code of the Secret Service,* because he felt it was unfit for release. Director Bryan Foy backed Reagan and Warner Bros. compromised (slightly) by not releasing the film in Los Angeles. Eddie Foy, Jr., the director's brother, played Brass's sidekick Gabby Watters.

Secret Service of the Air (1939)
Code of the Secret Service (1939)
Smashing the Money Ring (1939)
Murder in the Air (1940)

Barbers/Hairdressers

On those rare occasions when hairdressers are featured characters in a film, their profession rarely receives much exposure. Murder witness Kim Basinger could have easily been mistaken for a model instead of a hairdresser in *Nadine* (1987). Likewise, the fact that Frances McDormand's character was a beautician in *Mississippi Burning* (1988) had little bearing on the plot. Still, hairdressers have made a major impact in a handful of films. Warren Beatty played an amorous one in his 1975 hit *Shampoo* and Julie Walters received an Oscar nomination for portraying an uneducated hairdresser seeking to better herself intellectually in 1983's *Educating Rita*. *Sweeney Todd, the Demon Barber of Fleet Street* (1936) was about a barber who killed his customers and turned them into "meat pies." Composer Stephen Sondheim transformed the same story into the Broadway musical smash *Sweeney Todd*.

Smart Money (1931)
Diplomaniacs (1933)
Sweeney Todd, the Demon Barber of Fleet Street (1936)
Keep Fit (1937)
The Great Dictator (1940)
Abbott and Costello in Hollywood (aka *Bud Abbott and Lou Costello in Hollywood*) (1945)
Monsieur Beaucaire (1946)
Wait 'Til the Sun Shines, Nellie (1952)
Staircase (1969)
Five on the Back Hand Side (1973)
Shampoo (1975)
Outrageous! (1977)
Educating Rita (1983)
Old Enough (1984)
Nadine (1987)
Conspiracy of Love (1987 TVM)
Mississippi Burning (1988)
Getting It Right (1989)
Steel Magnolias (1989)
Earth Girls Are Easy (1989)

Barton, Dick

Barton, a British Dick Tracy, evolved from a popular 1948 radio series. Don Stannard played him in three low-budget movies. The series concluded following the actor's death in 1949.

Dick Barton, Detective (aka *Dick Barton, Special Agent*) (1949)
Dick Barton Strikes Back (1949)
Dick Barton at Bay (1950)

Baseball

Football may have been played in more movies, but no sport surpasses baseball in providing subjects for inspirational film biographies. Lou Gehrig, Babe Ruth, Dizzy Dean, Grover Cleveland Alexander, Jackie Robinson, Jimmy Piersall, Ron LeFlore, Roy Campanella, and Monty Stratton have all had their stories brought to the screen—often with conviction, almost always with sentiment. Baseball fantasies have proven to be popular, too. In *It Happens Every Spring* (1949), college professor Ray

Milland became a star pitcher for St. Louis when he accidentally invented a chemical that repelled wood (i.e. baseball bats). The Devil and an angel turned last-place teams into winners in, respectively, *Damn Yankees* (1958) and *Angels in the Outfield* (1951). In 1989's *Field of Dreams*, Kevin Costner built a baseball diamond in lieu of planting crops, so the legendary Shoeless Joe Jackson and other heavenly ball players would have a place to play their beloved game. Most filmmakers have preferred to gloss over the game's darker days, although John Sayles' *Eight Men Out* (1988) presented a factual account of the 1919 "Black Sox" scandal. Corruption was also an issue in 1984's *The Natural,* an unusual morality tale of a highly-gifted player (Robert Redford) confronted by temptation and evil. Baseball comedies have ranged from the hilarious to the ridiculous, with some of the more successful ones incorporating unusual angles. 1951's *Rhubarb* was about a baseball team owned by a cat. *The Bad News Bears* (1976) were a team of foul-mouthed little leaguers transformed into winners by beer-guzzling coach Walter Matthau. Finally, who can forget Abbott and Costello's famous vaudeville baseball routine "Who's on First?" recreated in their comedy *The Naughty Nineties*? See also **The Bad News Bears.**

Elmer the Great (1933)
Death on the Diamond (1934)
Alibi Ike (1935)
The Pride of the Yankees (1942)
The Naughty Nineties (1945)
The Babe Ruth Story (1948)
It Happens Every Spring (1949)
The Kid from Cleveland (1949)
The Stratton Story (1949)
Take Me Out to the Ball Game (1949)
Kill the Umpire (1950)
The Jackie Robinson Story (1950)
Angels in the Outfield (1951)
Rhubarb (1951)
The Winning Team (1952)
The Pride of St. Louis (1952)
The Kid from Left Field (1953)
The Big Leaguer (1953)
Roogie's Bump! (1954)
The Great American Pastime (1956)
Fear Strikes Out (1957)
Damn Yankees (1958)
Moochie of the Little League (1959)
Safe at Home! (1962)
Bang the Drum Slowly (1973)
It's Good to Be Alive (1974 TVM)
The Bad News Bears (1976)
The Bingo Long Travelling All-Star and Motor Kings (1976)
Murder at the World Series (1978 TVM)
One in a Million: The Ron LeFlore Story (1978 TVM)
Here Come the Tigers (aka *Manny's Orphans*) (1978)
A Love Affair: The Eleanor and Lou Gehrig Story (1978 TVM)
Aunt Mary (1979 TVM)
The Kid from Left Field (1979 TVM)
The Comeback Kid (1980 TVM)
Don't Look Back: The Story of Leroy "Satchel" Paige (1981 TVM)
Tiger Town (1983 TVM)
Blue Skies Again (1983)
The Natural (1984)
Brewster's Millions (1985)

The Slugger's Wife (1985)
A Winner Never Quits (1986 TVM)
Long Gone (1987 TVM)
Bull Durham (1988)

Eight Men Out (1988)
Stealing Home (1988)
Major League (1989)
Field of Dreams (1989)

Basketball

While other sports films, particularly those involving baseball and football, have devoted extensive footage to real-life personalities, basketball movies have emphasized fiction over fact. Naturally, there have been a few exceptions. *The Harlem Globetrotters* (1951) and *Go, Man, Go* (1954) employed realistic settings, even though they took dramatic license with their plots. *Hoosiers* (1986) was a fact-based story about a small-town Indiana high school team which staged an amazing series of upsets route to a state title. However, most basketball movies have opted for make-believe tales which climax in dramatic last-minute "buzzer shots," as in 1977's *One on One*. For a change of pace, *The Absent Minded Professor* and *Teen Wolf* featured some rather bizarre basketball games. In the former film, professor Fred MacMurray ironed "flubber" onto the shoes of his college's team, allowing the players to bounce higher than the backboard. In *Teen Wolf,* mediocre player Michael J. Fox suddenly transformed into a basketball phenomenon after becoming a werewolf. Anthony Perkins *(The Tall Story)* and Robby Benson *(One on One)* played more conventional star players. Inspirational coaches have been played by Robert Mitchum *(That Championship Season),* Bruce Dern *(Drive, He Said),* Gabe Kaplan *(Fast Break),* and Cathy Lee Crosby *(Coach).* And real-life players have appeared in *Cornbread, Earl and Me* (Jamaal Wilkes), *The Fish That Saved Pittsburgh* (Kareem Abdul Jabbar, Meadowlark Lemon, Julius Erving), and *Amazing Grace and Chuck* (Alex English).

Here Come the Coeds (1945)
The Harlem Globetrotters (1951)
Go, Man, Go (1954)
Tall Story (1960)
The Absent Minded Professor (1961)
Drive, He Said (1971)
Shirts/Skins (1973 TVM)
Maurie (aka Big Mo) (1973 TVM)
Mixed Company (1974)
Cornbread, Earl and Me (1975)
One on One (1977)
The Greatest Thing That Almost Happened (1977 TVM)

Coach (1978)
Fast Break (1979)
The Fish That Saved Pittsburgh (1979)
Inside Moves (1980)
The Harlem Globetrotters on Gilligan's Island (1981 TVM)
That Championship Season (1982)
Teen Wolf (1985)
Porky's Revenge (1985)
Hoosiers (1986)
Amazing Grace and Chuck (1987)

Beach Party Series

1959's *Gidget* (q.v.) and 1960's *Where the Boys Are* may have been the first mainstream pictures to put teens on the beach, but AIP's *Beach Party* (1963) was the one that spawned six sequels, accounted for countless clones, and made teen stars of Frankie Avalon and Annette Funicello. The formula was simple: Start with swimsuit-clad teens, add a way-out motorcycle gang, some cameos by ageing stars (e.g. Buster Keaton, Boris Karloff), and plenty of surf music (provided by the likes of Dick Dale and the Del-Tones, the Hondells, and Little Stevie Wonder). In addition to Frankie and Annette, the regulars included Harvey *(Stalag 17)* Lembeck as bike gang leader Eric Von Zipper and Jody McCrea (Joel's son) as Deadhead. Tommy Kirk and one-time *Gidget* Deborah Walley took over for Frankie and Annette in the final series entry, 1966's *The Ghost in the Invisible Bikini*. Annette played the female lead in the first six films, while Frankie headlined four films and made cameo appearances in two others. The Frankie substitutes were Tommy Kirk (a Martian teen in 1964's *Pajama Party*) and Dwayne Hickman (1965's *How to Stuff a Wild Bikini*). *Beach Blanket Bingo* is considered the best of the Beach Party pictures and still shows up on TV regularly. In 1987, Frankie and Annette tried to spoof their old images in *Back to the Beach*, a nostalgic, but generally overdone, effort. See also **Gidget**.

Beach Party (1963)	*How to Stuff a Wild Bikini*
Muscle Beach Party (1964)	(1965)
Bikini Beach (1964)	*The Ghost in the Invisible*
Pajama Party (1964)	*Bikini* (1966)
Beach Blanket Bingo (1965)	*Back to the Beach* (1987)

The AIP *Beach Party* series also fostered rival mid-1960s sand-and-surf pictures, such as:

Ride the Wild Surf (1964)	*Surf Party* (1964)
For Those Who Think Young (1964)	*The Girls on the Beach* (1965)
The Horror of Party Beach (aka *Invasion of the Zombies*) (1964)	*Beach Ball* (1965)
	Seaside Swingers (1965)
	It's a Bikini World (1967)

Bears

Someone at Walt Disney Productions must have had a soft spot for bears, for the company produced four pictures about the furry forest denizens between 1947 and 1974. The first two were animated bears, Brer Bear in *The Song of the South* (1947) and Baloo in *The Jungle Book* (1967). As voiced by Phil Harris, Baloo has the distinction of being the only bear to sing an Oscar-nominated song—"Bare Necessities." The real-life Disney bears proved to be considerably less talented and, as a consequence, *King of the Grizzlies* (1970) and *The Bears and I* (1974) were also less entertaining. *Gentle Giant* (1967) a juvenile tale about a boy with a pet 650-pound black bear, could have passed for a Disney production. Its modest box-office success led to a 1967–69 TV series starring Clint Howard (Ron's brother) and Dennis Weaver. Clint Walker encountered a less sociable bear in the climax of *Night of the Grizzly* (1966), while another wild bear mauled Richard Harris and left him for dead in *Man in the Wilderness* (1971). Christopher George had the worst luck with bears, battling an 18-foot, 2000-pounder in the 1976 *Jaws* rip-off *Grizzly* and then running into another one in the following year's *Day of the Animals* (actually, this latter bear was nice enough to dispose of troublemaker Leslie Nielsen). The mutant, pollution-made monster in John Frankenheimer's *Prophecy* (1979) looked like a conglomeration of several animals, but it was probably more bear than anything else. In the offbeat 1961 fantasy *The Two Little Bears,* Eddie Albert discovered that his two little children could turn into bear cubs at night. Director-actor Jean Renoir dressed as a bear to attend the climactic country manor costume party in his classic social satire *The Rules of the Game* (1939). Natassja Kinski sported a bear costume as well in John Irving's *The Hotel New Hampshire* (1984). In the 1978 TV-movie *B.J. and the Bear,* the "Bear" turned out to be a chimpanzee. Apparently, that was supposed to be funny.

Song of the South (1947)	*The Bears and I* (1974)
The Two Little Bears (1961)	*Grizzly* (aka *Killer Grizzly*)
Hey There, It's Yogi Bear	(1976)
(1964)	*The Life and Times of Grizzly*
Night of the Grizzly (1966)	*Adams* (1976)
The Jungle Book (1967)	*Day of the Animals* (1977)
Gentle Giant (1967)	*Prophecy* (1979)
King of the Grizzlies (1970)	*The Bear* (1989)
Man in the Wilderness (1971)	

Beauty Contests

Behind-the-scene exposés of the beauty pageant business, complete with bickering contestants and deceitful judges, have been the subject of *Contest Girl* (1964), *The Great American Beauty Contest* (1973), *Smile* (1975), and *Miss All-American Beauty* (1982). Ironically, while these films sought to criticize beauty contests, they are best-remembered for the exposure they provided attractive young actresses such as Diane Lane, Farrah Fawcett, Melanie Griffith, and Annette O'Toole. The lighthearted side of beauty contests was on display in 1950's *Peggy,* the story of a Rose Bowl queen, and 1951's *Lady Godiva Rides Again,* which introduced Joan Collins as a young contestant. A nonexistent woman won a beauty contest when Dick Powell submitted a composite photograph in the 1935 comedy *Page Miss Glory. The Queen* was a well-received 1968 documentary about a beauty pageant for transvestites.

Page Miss Glory (1935)	*The Queen* (1968)
Waikiki Wedding (1937)	*The Great American Beauty*
The Crystal Ball (1943)	*Contest* (1973 TVM)
The Duchess of Idaho (1950)	*Smile* (1975)
Peggy (1950)	*The Night They Took Miss*
Lady Godiva Rides Again (1951)	*Beautiful* (1977 TVM)
Hear Me Good (1957)	*Miss All-American Beauty* (1982
Contest Girl (aka *The Beauty*	TVM)
Jungle) (1964)	*Miss Firecracker* (1989)

Belvedere, Mr. (Lynn)

Clifton Webb created pompous, but likable, genius Lynn Belvedere in 1948's *Sitting Pretty,* in which Robert Young and Maureen O'Hara hired the 59-year-old as a babysitter (q.v.). The film inspired two sequels, sending Belvedere back to college and then to stir things up at a home for the elderly. Webb played a similar character in 1953's *Mister Scoutmaster.*

Sitting Pretty (1948)	*Mr. Belvedere Rings the Bell*
Mr. Belvedere Goes to College	(1951)
(1949)	

Bermuda Triangle

In the mid–1970s, Charles Berlitz published two books about this site of several inexplicable disappearances in the Atlantic Ocean. A brief flurry of movie activity followed, beginning with 1974's made-for-TV feature *Satan's Triangle* and the pseudo-documentary *The Devil's Triangle.* Similar sub-par films came in quick succession. Berlitz went on to write about Atlantis, Noah's Ark, and how to speak Italian, French, and German.

The Devil's Triangle (1974)	*Bermuda Triangle* (1977)
Satan's Triangle (1974 TVM)	*The Bermuda Triangle* (1978)
Beyond the Bermuda Triangle	*The Bermuda Depths* (1978
(1975 TVM)	TVM)
Mysteries from Beyond the	

Bicycles

Vittorio De Sica's touching 1949 Italian classic *The Bicycle Thief* chronicled a poor man's desperate search for the stolen bicycle on which his family's livelihood depended. *Breaking Away* (1979) and *American Flyers* (1985), both written by cycling enthusiast Steve Tesich, dealt with amateur riders and their infatuation with bike racing. Stockbroker Kevin Bacon dropped out of the rat race and became a bicycle messenger in *Quicksilver* (1986). Many movies have featured bicycles in memorable scenes, including *E.T., Butch Cassidy and the Sundance Kid,* and *The Wizard of Oz* (Toto jumping off the back of Miss Gulch's two-wheeler).

Six Day Bike Rider (1934)
A Boy, a Girl, and a Bike
  (1947)
The Bicycle Thief (1949)
Isn't Life Wonderful? (1952)
Smiley (1957)
And Soon the Darkness (1970)
The Gang That Couldn't Shoot

Straight (1971)
Breaking Away (1979)
BMX Bandits (1983)
American Flyers (1985)
Pee Wee's Big Adventure (1985)
Quicksilver (1986)
Rad (1986)

Big Town Series

A CBS radio program provided the inspiration for this short-lived Paramount film series about crusading newspaper editor Steve Wilson (Philip Reed). Hillary Brooke played police reporter Lorelei Kilbourne, Wilson's spunky sidekick.

Big Town (aka Guilty Assignment) (1947)
Big Town After Dark (aka Underworld After Dark) (1947)

I Cover Big Town (aka I Cover
  the Underworld) (1947)
Big Town Scandal (1948)

Bigamy

It is amazing that so few filmmakers have explored the dramatic possibilities inherent in a serious film about bigamy. It's as if a discouraging cloud of "uncomfortableness" hung over the subject matter. Interestingly, a woman (Ida Lupino) directed one of the first serious films about a bigamous husband, 1953's appropriately-titled *The Bigamist*. Although it failed to probe deeply into its protagonist's motivations, it was infinitely superior to 1988's *Double Standard*, a pointless TV-movie "inspired by a true-life case." The cinema's inability to deal seriously with bigamy has resulted in a plethora of multiple marriage comedies. William Bendix, an unlikely candidate for bigamy, traveled up and down New York state visiting his two wives in *Don Juan Quilligan* (1945). Alec Guinness played a ferry-boat captain with a wife in every port (well, two ports to be exact) in 1953's hilarious *Captain's Paradise*. Other male bigamists have included Rex Harrison *(The Constant Husband)*, Clifton Webb *(The Remarkable Mr. Pennypacker)*, and Dudley Moore *(Micki and Maude)*. Female bigamists have been rare in the movies, perhaps reflecting a male chauvinistic attitude among filmmakers. Karen Valentine played a stewardess with multiple families in *Coffee, Tea or Me* (1972). Dyan Cannon's fashion design business allowed her to keep a husband on each coast in *Having It All* (1982). Sally Field lived with two husbands in *Kiss Me Goodbye* (1982), but one of them was a ghost (thus, according to the law, she was not a bigamist). Jean Seberg had two husbands in the gold rush musical *Paint Your Wagon* (1969), but that's only because Lee Marvin and Clint Eastwood bought her wifely services jointly at an auction. The movie bigamist with the most spouses was the one found dead on the floor of a hotel room in the beginning of *15 Wives* (1934). Needless to say, there was no shortage of murder suspects.

15 Wives (1934)
Don Juan Quilligan (1945)
Monsieur Verdoux (1947)
Captain's Paradise (1953)
The Bigamist (1953)
The Constant Husband (1955)
Autumn Leaves (1956)
The Remarkable Mr. Penny-packer (1959)
Two Wives at One Wedding (1960)
Decline and Fall of a Bird

Watcher (aka *Decline and Fall*) (1968)
Paint Your Wagon (1969)
Coffee, Tea or Me (1972 TVM)
Handle With Care (aka *Citizen's Band*) (1977)
Child Bride of Short Creek (1981 TVM)
Having It All (1982 TVM)
Micki and Maude (1984)
Double Standard (1988 TVM)

Bigfoot

The Abominable Snowman's North American cousin has been the subject of several bottom-of-the-barrel features, such as *Bigfoot* (1969), *Curse of Bigfoot* (1972), and *Sasquatch* (1978). He was portrayed as a lovable big guy in 1987's *Harry and the Hendersons* and in the same year's made-for-TV feature *Bigfoot*. The pseudo-documentary *The Legend of Boggy Creek* (1973) traced the exploits of a Bigfoot-like creature who roamed around Foulke, Arkansas. John Frankenheimer's *Prophecy* (1979) was about a Bigfoot relative, a gangling mutant monster created by chemical pollution. See also **Abominable Snowman; Boggy Creek.**

Bigfoot (1969)
Curse of Bigfoot (1972)
Shriek of the Mutilated (1974)
Bigfoot, the Mysterious Monsters (1975)
Creature from Black Lake (1976)

Sasquatch (1978)
Harry and the Hendersons (aka *Bigfoot and the Hendersons*) (1987)
Bigfoot (1987 TVM)

Billy Jack

Tom Laughlin's peace-loving, half-breed, former Green Beret first appeared in the 1967 biker film *Born Losers,* in which he protected the innocent, defied ineffective small-town police, and beat up bad guys. He did basically the same things in Laughlin's 1971 follow-up *Billy Jack,* but this time movie-goers identified with his loner hero and made the picture a low-budget smash. The movie's simplistic politics and thematic inconsistencies (Billy Jack preaches peace, but doesn't hesitate to use violence when necessary) dated it almost immediately. Laughlin's overblown 1974 sequel *The Trial of Billy Jack* focused on government corruption, as did *Billy Jack Goes to Washington* (1977). Allegedly, the latter was a remake of Frank Capra's classic *Mr. Smith Goes to Washington.* Neither of the last two films came close to duplicating *Billy Jack's* success, so the series mercifully died. Laughlin and wife/co-star Delores Taylor produced, directed, and wrote most of the series (often using the pseudonym T.C. Frank).

Born Losers (1967)
Billy Jack (1971)
The Trial of Billy Jack (1974)

Billy Jack Goes to Washington (1977)

Billy the Kid/Billy Carson

This low-budget PRC series had little to do with the real Billy the Kid (see **Outlaws, Real-Life**). Its initial entry, 1940's *Billy the Kid Outlawed* presented Billy as a wronged hero, a victim of small-town corruption. He even went on to become a lawman in the next film, *Billy the Kid in Texas.* But when his brother turned up as the brains behind a local outlaw gang.... Veteran screen cowboy Bob Steele, one of the Three Mesquiteers (q.v.) in the 1930s, played Billy in the first six films. Steele left after 1941's *Billy the Kid in Santa Fe,* though he continued to appear in Westerns and eventually wound up as Trooper Duffy on TV's "F Troop" (1965–67). Serial star Buster ("Flash Gordon") Crabbe replaced Steele in 1941's *Billy the Kid Wanted* and remained for the rest of the series. Al St. John played Billy's grizzly sidekick Fuzzy Q. Jones, who was at least as popular as Billy (one film was even titled *Fuzzy Settles Down*). Sam Newfield directed all the films using various pseudonyms (e.g. Sherman Scott, Peter Stewart). Newfield's real name was Neufeld and his brother, Sigmund, was the head of PRC. Newfield shot the *Billy the Kid* films in two or three days, using the same footage for chases and gunfights repeatedly. In the late 1940s, after the series ended, Eagle Lion re-edited (and drastically cut) some of the films and released them with different titles. Thus, the 65-minute *Western Cyclone* became the 39-minute *Frontier Fighters.* See also **Outlaws (Real-Life Western).**

Billy the Kid Outlawed (1940)
Billy the Kid in Texas (1940)
Billy the Kid's Gun Justice (1940)
Billy the Kid's Range War (1941)
Billy the Kid's Fighting Pals (1941)
Billy the Kid in Santa Fe (1941)
Billy the Kid Wanted (1941)
Billy the Kid's Roundup (1941)
Billy the Kid Trapped (1942)
Billy the Kid's Smoking Guns (1942)
Law and Order (aka Billy the Kid's Law and Order) (1942)
Sheriff of Sage Valley (aka Billy the Kid, Sheriff of Sage Valley) (1942)
The Mysterious Rider (aka Panhandle Trail) (1942)
The Kid Rides Again (1943)
Fugitive of the Plains (aka Raiders of Red Rock) (1943)
Western Cyclone (aka Frontier Fighters) (1943)
Cattle Stampede (1943)
The Renegade (1943)
Devil Riders (1943)
Frontier Outlaws (1944)
Thundering Gunslingers (1944)
Valley of Vengeance (1944)

The Drifter (1944)	*Stagecoach Outlaws* (1945)
Fuzzy Settles Down (1944)	*Border Badmen* (1945)
Blazing Frontier (1944)	*Fighting Bill Carson* (1945)
Rustler's Hideout (1944)	*Prairie Rustlers* (1945)
Wild Horse Phantom (1944)	*Gentlemen with Guns* (1946)
Oath of Vengeance (1944)	*Terrors on Horseback* (1946)
Lightning Raiders (1945)	*Ghost of Hidden Valley* (1946)
His Brother's Ghost (1945)	*Prairie Badmen* (1946)
Shadows of Death (1945)	*Overland Riders* (1946)
Gangster's Den (1945)	*Outlaw of the Plains* (1946)

Birds

The mere word has a Hitchcockian ring to it now. But long before Hitch turned them into formidable little killers in 1963, birds were making their cinematic presence known. In Britain, a pair of rare birds disrupted a quiet hamlet in the quaint comedy *Tawny Pipit* (1944). Scottish islanders created some rare birds with a little paint in 1957's *Mad Little Island,* reasoning that such a discovery would block the construction of a government missile base. The establishment of bird sanctuaries provided the background for another British picture *Conflict of Wings* (1953) and an American romantic comedy *Something for the Birds* (1952). Shirley Temple went looking for the blue bird of happiness in the colorful 1940 fantasy *The Blue Bird,* her consolation prize for not being loaned to MGM for *The Wizard of Oz.* A toucan spread a "happiness virus" throughout New York City in George *(Miracle on 34th Street)* Seaton's *What's So Bad About Feeling Good?* (1968). In contrast, giant birds of the horrific variety flew across the screen in the Japanese import *Rodan* and the inept U.S.-lensed *The Giant Claw* (both 1957). A contemporary witch brought a threatening stone eagle to life and sent it on a murderous mission in the 1962 supernatural gem *Burn, Witch, Burn.* Norman Bates (Anthony Perkins) stuffed birds for a hobby in Hitchcock's *Psycho* (1960), a film overloaded with bird symbolism. Its first murder victim, Marion *Crane,* was first glimpsed in *Phoenix,* Arizona. Hitch's next picture was, naturally, *The Birds* (1963), a vague, but exciting, thriller adapted from Daphne du Maurier's short story. There was nothing horrorific or fantastic about 1962's *Birdman of Alcatraz,* an engrossing biography of convict-turned-bird-expert Robert Stroud (Burt Lancaster). However, cruel sorcerer Boris Karloff turned Peter Lorre into a black bird in 1963's amusing *The Raven.* Akim Tamiroff transformed himself into a ridiculous-looking bird/man in *The Vulture* (1967), while fetching Michelle Pfeiffer spent half her days as a hawk in the 1985 sword-and-sorcery fantasy *Ladyhawke.* Roddy McDowell believed himself to be an extinct bird in human form in the oddball satire *Lord Love a Duck* (1966). Army hospital schizophrenic Matthew Modine wanted to become a bird in *Birdy* (1984), while comic book writer Michael Crawford took flight—albeit briefly—as his own crea-tion *Condorman* (1981). Audrey Hepburn played Rima the Bird Girl in the 1959 adaptation of W.H. Hudson's *Green Mansions*. Hunky warrior Marc Singer communicated with birds (and other animals) in 1982's *The Beastmaster*, yet another sword-and-sorcery picture. A frigid woman could make love only to a man in a bird suit in Roger Vadim's bizarre 1980 film *Night Games*. Finally, Larry Cohen's *Q—The Winged Serpent* (1982) flew and lived in a nest, but technically it turned out to be an Aztec god and not a bird at all.

The Blue Bird (1940)	*The Raven* (1963)
Tawny Pipit (1944)	*Those Calloways* (1965)
Champagne for Caesar (1950)	*Lord Love a Duck* (1966)
Something for the Birds (1952)	*The Vulture* (1967)
Conflict of Wings (aka *Fuss Over Feathers*) (1953)	*What's So Bad About Feeling Good?* (1968)
Mad Little Island (aka *Rockets Galore!*) (1957)	*Harpy* (1970 TVM)
The Giant Claw (1957)	*Jonathan Livingston Seagull* (1973)
Rodan (1957)	*The Blue Bird* (1976)
Green Mansions (1959)	*Condorman* (1981)
Psycho (1960)	*Clash of the Titans* (1981)
Burn, Witch, Burn (aka *Night of the Eagle*) (1962)	*The Beastmaster* (1982)
Birdman of Alcatraz (1962)	*Birdy* (1984)
The Birds (1963)	*Ladyhawke* (1985)
	Beaks: The Movie (1987)

Blackie, Boston

Jack Boyle's thief-turned-detective enjoyed a steady screen career, begin-ning with 1919's *Boston Blackie's Little Pal*. Bert Lytell, Lionel Barrymore, and William Russell played Blackie in silent films. However, Chester Mor-ris kicked off the "official" series with 1941's *Meet Boston Blackie*. Morris made an agreeable hero, always willing to bend the law to crack a case, and the series concluded a profitable run in 1949. Just two years later, Blackie turned up on TV, with Kent Taylor replacing Morris. The "Boston Blackie" TV series ran for 58 episodes from 1951–53. Morris starred in all of the following film entries:

Meet Boston Blackie (1941)	*One Mysterious Night* (1944)
Confessions of Boston Blackie (1941)	*Boston Blackie Booked on Sus-picion* (1945)
Alias Boston Blackie (1942)	*Boston Blackie's Rendezvous* (1945)
Boston Blackie Goes to Holly-wood (1942)	*A Close Call for Boston Blackie* (1946)
After Midnight with Boston Blackie (1943)	*The Phantom Thief* (1946)
The Chance of a Lifetime (1943)	*Boston Blackie and the Law* (1947)

Trapped by Boston Blackie (1948)	*Boston Blackie's Chinese Venture* (1949)

Blackouts

Films revolving around power blackouts include *The Night the City Screamed* (1980), *Where Were You When the Lights Went Out?* (1968), and *Blackout* (1978). The latter two films were inspired by real-life power failures in New York City. The Doris Day vehicle *Where Were You* played the massive 1965 blackout for forced laughs, while *Blackout* went for thrills in its tale of apartment tenants victimized by a gang during the 1977 power failure. In other films: A blackout allowed inmates to escape from an asylum in *Alone in the Dark;* Gregory Peck lost his memory during a blackout in *Mirage;* and the entire world suffered a temporary blackout so Michael Rennie could make a point in *The Day the Earth Stood Still.*

The Day the Earth Stood Still (1951)	*Blackout* (1978)
Mirage (1964)	*The Night the City Screamed* (1980 TVM)
Where Were You When the Lights Went Out? (1968)	*Alone in the Dark* (1982)

Blane, Torchy

Short story writer Frederick Nebel's ace reporter Torchy Blane had a knack for getting involved with murder cases, which she did in nine "B" movies churned out by Warner Bros. during 1937–39. Glenda Farrell played Torchy in all but two films, getting support from Barton MacLane as her charmless boyfriend, police detective Steve McBride (Steve to Torchy: "You're going to settle down and marry me before I throw you in jail"). The two non–Farrell films starred Lola Lane *(Torchy Blane in Panama)* and 25-year-old Jane Wyman *(Torchy Plays with Dynamite).* The series dates badly and Steve's thoughtless attitude toward Torchy's career, especially in the Farrell films, is almost offensive. Still, the Torchy series contained a few offbeat touches — such as the appropriately-titled Jerome Kern tune "Why Do I Have to Sing a Torch Song?" in *Smart Blonde* and the absence of a Chinatown setting in *Torchy Blane in Chinatown.*

Smart Blonde (1937)	*Torchy Blane in Chinatown* (1939)
Fly-Away Baby (1937)	
The Adventurous Blonde (1937)	*Torchy Runs for Mayor* (1939)
Blondes at Work (1938)	*Torchy Plays with Dynamite* (1939)
Torchy Blane in Panama (1938)	
Torchy Gets Her Man (1938)	

Blaxploitation Films

The term "blaxploitation" was coined in the early 1970s to describe a rash of low-budget, action pictures that featured mostly black performers and typically played in black neighborhood theaters. Many critics considered these movies offensive, charging that they portrayed blacks as stereotyped private eyes, drug kingpins, and prostitutes. While that may be true, these films nevertheless kept some talented performers employed (e.g. Richard Pryor in *The Mack,* Godfrey Cambridge in *Cotton Comes to Harlem*). A handful of action stars emerged, such as Tamara Dobson (as Cleopatra Jones), karate champion Jim Kelly, and Richard Roundtree (Shaft). However, their fame was fleeting and, by 1975, they were relegated to supporting roles in more mainstream films. A few blaxploitation films, such as *Shaft* and *Blacula,* broke the typical mold, gained wider distribution, and evolved into sizable hits. 1974's *One Down, Two to Go* attempted to revive the genre. Yet, despite a formidable (and now nostalgic) cast headed by Jim Brown, it flopped miserably. Nevertheless, a parody called *I'm Gonna Git You Sucka,* starring the likes of Eve Plumb ("The Brady Bunch") and Clarence Williams III ("The Mod Squad"), surfaced in 1989.

Cotton Comes to Harlem (1970)
Shaft (1971)
Come Black, Charleston Blue (1972)
Cool Breeze (1972)
Melinda (1972)
Hammer (1972)
Hit Man (1972)
Slaughter (1972)
Shaft's Big Score (1972)
Superfly (1972)
Black Caesar (1973)
Cleopatra Jones (1973)
Coffy (ad line: "Coffy...she'll cream you!") (1973)
Detroit 9000 (1973)
Ganja and Hess (1973)
Hell Up in Harlem (1973)
The Mack (1973)
Scream, Blacula, Scream (1973)
Shaft in Africa (1973)
Slaughter's Big Rip-Off (1973)

Superfly TNT (1973)
Abby (1974)
Black Eye (1974)
Black Gunn (1974)
Blacula (1974)
Foxy Brown (1974)
Hangup (aka *Superdude*) (1974)
Three the Hard Way (1974)
Truck Turner (1974)
Blackenstein (1975)
Bucktown (1975)
Cleopatra Jones and the Casino of Gold (1975)
Dr. Black and Mr. Hyde (aka *The Watts Monster; Dr. Black and Mr. White*) (1975)
Friday Foster (1975)
Black Belt Jones (1976)
Black Fist (aka *The Black Streetfighter*) (1976)
Hot Potato (1976)
The Big Score (1983)

The Blind Dead Series

A gory Spanish import, the Blind Dead series based its premise on legendary 13th–century Templarios Knights who were blinded and then executed for their ritualistic killings of young women. In 1974's *The Blind Dead,* they were resurrected (as rotting, hooded ghouls) and promptly set about in search of more nubile females. The film proved immensely popular in Europe and earned a small cult following in the U.S., chiefly due to its Bava-style atmosphere. Director Armando De Ossorio directed three additional, similarly-plotted installments.

The Blind Dead (aka *Tomb of the Blind Dead; La Noche del Terror Ciego*) (1972)
Return of the Blind Dead (aka *El Ataque de los Muertos sin Ojos*) (1973)
Horror of the Zombies (aka *El Buque Maldito*) (1974)
Night of the Seagulls (aka *La Noche de las Gaviotas*) (1975)

Blindness

Although films dealing exclusively with blindness can be narrowed to a select few, there have been a disproportionate number of films featuring blind characters in critical roles. Edward Arnold played a blind detective in *Eyes in the Night* (1942) and *The Hidden Eye* (1945), while sleuths-by-chance have included writer Van Johnson in *23 Paces to Baker Street* (1956), reporter Karl Malden in *The Cat O'Nine Tails* (1971), and insurance investigator James Franciscus in *Longstreet* (1970). Blind people have been portrayed as musicians of startling talent in *The Enchanted Cottage* (1945), *Night Song* (1947), *Goha* (1957), *Blues for Lovers* (1964), and *If You Could See What I Hear* (1982). The latter two films were partially biographical, with Ray Charles playing himself in *Blues* and Marc Singer as composer Tom Sullivan in *If You Could See What I Hear*. 1969's *Seven in Darkness* was a tense tale about a plane which crashed en route to a convention for the blind, thus stranding its seven sightless passengers in the wilderness. An alien-directed "meteorite shower" blinded most of the Earth's population in the opening frames of John Wyndham's *Day of the Triffids* (1963). As for serious films about persons adjusting to the sudden loss of their sight, few movies can match the emotional impact of *Bright Victory* (1951). Arthur Kennedy earned an Oscar nomination for his wrenching portrait of a blind ex-soldier who no longer knows his place in society. A laborador retriever seeing-eye dog provided Elizabeth Montgomery with needed support in the superior TV-movie *Second Sight: A Love Story* (1984). A blind couple desperately fought to adopt a child in the fact-based 1987 TV-movie *Eye on the Sparrow*. Along more traditional lines, a playboy responsible for a woman's blindness became a surgeon so he could cure her in both versions of Lloyd C. Douglas' tear-jerker *Magnificent Obsession*.

Orphans of the Storm (1922)
Thunder Below (1932)
Wings in the Dark (1935)
Magnificent Obsession (1935)
Bride of Frankenstein (1935)
The Human Monster (aka *Dark Eyes of London*) (1939)
The Light That Failed (1939)
Mr. Skeffington (1944)
The Enchanted Cottage (1945)
Pride of the Marines (aka *Forever in Love*) (1945)
The Hidden Eye (1945)
Night Song (1947)
Bright Victory (aka *Lights Out*) (1951)

Journey Into Light (1951)
On Dangerous Ground (1951)
The Green Scarf (1954)
Magnificent Obsession (1954)
23 Paces to Baker Street (1956)
Goha (1957)
Witness in the Dark (1959)
Faces in the Dark (1959)
The Miracle Worker (1962)
Day of the Triffids (1963)
Blues for Lovers (aka Ballad in
Blue) (1964)
A Patch of Blue (1965)
Cauldron of Blood (aka Blind
Man's Bluff) (1967)
Wait Until Dark (1967)
Seven in Darkness (1969 TVM)
How Awful About Allan (1970
TVM)
Longstreet (1970 TVM)

The Cat O'Nine Tails (1971)
See No Evil (aka Blind Terror)
(1971)
In Broad Daylight (1971 TVM)
Butterflies Are Free (1972)
Journey from Darkness (1975
TVM)
Love's Dark Side (1978 TVM)
Ice Castles (1979)
The Miracle Worker (1979
TVM)
To Race the Wind (1980 TVM)
If You Could See What I Hear
(1982)
Second Sight: A Love Story
(1984 TVM)
Eye on the Sparrow (1987 TVM)
See No Evil, Hear No Evil
(1989)
Blind Witness (1989 TVM)

Blondie

Probably more so than any other film series, *Blondie* established the format and style of the television "sitcom" — 13 years before "I Love Lucy." Penny Singleton and Arthur Lake starred as Chic Young's comic strip couple Blondie and Dagwood Bumstead in an amazing 28 films spanning 12 years. Their supporting cast remained intact for most of the series, too, with Larry Simms as Baby Dumpling, Jonathan Hale as Mr. Dithers, and Marjorie Kent as Cookie. In 1950, long after most film series had expired, *Blondie* came to an end. Arthur Lake continued as Dagwood (with Pamela Britton as Blondie) in a short-lived 1957 television series. Meanwhile, Penny Singleton provided the voice for Jane during the original 1962–63 run of the TV cartoon series "The Jetsons." She later became a union activist and then returned to Broadway in the 1970s in *No, No, Nanette.* In 1968, Patricia Harty and Will Hutchins revived the Blondie and Dagwood characters for another TV series. It lasted but a half-season. Ironically, the film series that inspired the sitcom never made it as a successful one. See also **Comic Strip Characters.**

Blondie (1938)
Blondie Brings Up Baby (1939)
Blondie Meets the Boss (1939)
Blondie Takes a Vacation (1939)
Blondie Has Servant Trouble
(1940)
Blondie on a Budget (1940)
Blondie Plays Cupid (1940)

Blondie Goes Latin (1941)
Blondie in Society (1941)
Blondie's Blessed Event (1942)
Blondie for Victory (1942)
Blondie Goes to College (1942)
Footlight Glamour (1943)
It's a Great Life (1943)
Leave It to Blondie (1945)

48

Blondie Knows Best (1946)
Blondie's Lucky Day (1946)
Life with Blondie (1946)
Blondie's Anniversary (1947)
Blondie's Big Moment (1947)
Blondie's Holiday (1947)
Blondie in the Dough (1947)

Blondie's Reward (1948)
Blondie's Big Deal (1949)
Blondie Hits the Jackpot (1949)
Blondie's Secret (1949)
Beware of Blondie (1950)
Blondie's Hero (1950)

The Blue Demon

This masked Mexican wrestler, known in his homeland as El Demonio Azul, briefly challenged fellow-wrestler Santo (q.v.) for the mid-1960s monster-destroyer crown. Santo proved to be the people's favorite, however, and the Blue Demon eventually joined forces with him to create a potent tag team to battle vampires, werewolves, witches, and other evil creatures in a series of lively, but ludicrous, films. See also **Santo; Neutron** (yet another Mexican monster wrestler); **Wrestling.**

The Blue Demon (aka *El Demonio Azul*) (1964)
Blue Demon Against the Satanical Power (aka *Blue Demon contra el Poder Satanicon*) (1964)
The Shadow of the Bat (aka *La Sombra del Murcielago*) (1966)
Blue Demon vs. the Infernal Brains (1968)
Santo Against Blue Demon in Atlantis (aka *Santo contra Blue Demon en la Atlantida*) (1968)
The World of the Dead (aka *El Mundo de los Muertos*) (1969) (also with Santo)
Blue Demon and the Seductresses (1969)
Santo and Blue Demon vs. the Monsters (aka *Santo y Blue Demon contra los Monstrous*) (1971)
Santo and Blue Demon vs. Dracula and the Wolfman (aka *Santo y Blue Demon contra Dracula y el Hombre Lobo*) (1972)

Boarding Schools

Boarding schools have provided atmospheric settings for a wide variety of films—sentimental tales of dedicated teachers, satanic thrillers, mischievous comedies, and student revolutions. Jean Vigo's 1933 surrealistic classic *Zero for Conduct* blended revolution with comedy in the story of mistreated students who rebel against a regimented boarding school run by a midget principal. British director Lindsay Anderson expanded on the same premise in his 1968 film *If...*, in which defiant Malcolm McDowell and fellow students gun down the school's faculty on Speech Day (or is this massacre merely imagined by McDowell's character?). The girls known as *The Belles of St. Trinian's* (q.v.) (1951) were rebellious too, but never mounted a revolt since they pretty much ran the school anyway. Convent and church-run schools have been especially prone to attracting mischief-making students, as evidenced by

The Trouble with Angels (1966), *Heaven Help Us* (1985), and *Goodbye, Children* (1988). Dedicated teachers molded mischievous youths into mature students of life in *Goodbye, Mr. Chips* (1939 and 1969) and *Dead Poets Society* (1989). In contrast, schoolmaster David Hemming's students threatened to murder him—like they did his predecessor—in *Unman, Wittering and Zigo* (1981). Clint Eastwood found himself in a worse situation as a virile male hiding out in a girls' school populated by lonely, jealous females in 1971's *The Beguiled.* Pamela Franklin entered a girl's boarding school to investigate her sister's suicide in the 1973 TV-movie *Satan's School for Girls.* Despite its title, it turned out to be a nicer place than the demonic school run by a witches coven in Dario Argento's stylish *Suspiria* (1976). Many films such as *Jane Eyre* (1944) have been partially set in boarding schools. See also **Military Academies; St. Trinian's.**

Zero for Conduct (aka *Zero de Conduite*) (1933)
Girls' Dormitory (1936)
Housemaster (1938)
Goodbye, Mr. Chips (1939)
Tom Brown's School Days (aka *Adventures at Rugby*) (1940)
The Happy Years (1950)
The Browning Version (1951)
Tom Brown's Schooldays (1951)
Her Twelve Men (1954)
The Belles of St. Trinians (1955)
Les Diaboliques (aka *Diabolique; The Fiends*) (1955)
Tea and Sympathy (1956)
The Ladies' Man (1961)
13 Frightened Girls (1963)
The Trouble with Angels (1966)
If. . . (1968)
Goodbye, Mr. Chips (1969)
The House That Screamed (aka *The Boarding School*) (1969)
Walk a Crooked Path (1969)
The Beguiled (1971)
Child's Play (1972)
Satan's School for Girls (1972 TVM)
Suspiria (1976)
Our Time (aka *Death of Her Innocence*) (1974)
Boarding School (aka *The Passion Flower Hotel*) (1977)
Unman, Wittering and Zigo (1981)
Deadly Lessons (1983 TVM)
Heaven Help Us (1985)
Goodbye, Children (aka *Au Revoir, Les Enfants*) (1988)
The Chocolate War (1988)
Dead Poets Society (1989)

Body Switching

The most overworked premise of 1988 was this one: A young person's soul magically changes places with an older person's, so that the youngster acts like an adult and the adult behaves like a kid. Actually, the plotline dates back to Peter Ustinov's then-original 1947 fantasy *Vice Versa*, in which a magic stone caused stockbroker Roger Livesey and school-aged son Anthony Newley to temporarily switch bodies. Disney updated the plot and changed the gender for 1977's *Freaky Friday*. It starred Barbara Harris and Jodie Foster as the mother and daughter making the switch for a day. A trio of mediocre 1988 releases revived the plotline (although in *18 Again,* George Burns played a body-switching grandfather). The best of the three was *Vice Versa,* a semi-amusing, one-joke affair benefitting from funny performances by Judge Reinhold and Fred Savage. Unfortunately, it was released late in the cycle and faded quickly at the boxoffice. Even fewer people saw the 1989 body switching comedy *Dream a Little Dream,* despite a potentially interesting cast headed by Jason Robards. Of course, not all films have involved a transfer between parent and child. Actually, the first body-switching comedy, 1940's *Turnabout,* had a more risque premise, with husband and wife Adolphe Menjou and Carole Landis switching bodies (courtesy of a magic Buddha). The film, based on a story by *Topper* author Thorne Smith, served as the basis for a very short-lived 1979 sitcom. The 1986 Disney TV-movie *Hero in the Family* altered the body switching premise slightly, with an astronaut finding himself in a chimpanzee's body. Dr. Frankenstein (Peter Cushing) transferred a dying man's soul into the body of his lover in 1967's *Frankenstein Created Woman.* Technically, that's not body switching since both souls resided in one body—but it's certainly close. See also **Brain Transplants.**

Turnabout (1940)	*18 Again* (1988)
Vice Versa (1947)	*Vice Versa* (1988)
Freaky Friday (1977)	*Like Father, Like Son* (1988)
Hero in the Family (1986 TVM)	*Dream a Little Dream* (1989)

Boggy Creek

A "docudrama" about a Bigfoot-type beast glimpsed roaming around Fouke, Arkansas, 1972's *The Legend of Boggy Creek* peaked enough interest to earn a tidy profit for exploitation producer Charles B. Pierce. Sadly, Pierce's extensive use of "reenactments" has become increasingly popular in television news programs. 1977's *Return to Boggy Creek* was not a sequel, but rather a children's film about a friendly monster helping out some lost kids. It co-starred Dawn Wells, better known as Mary Ann on "Gilligan's Island." In 1985, Pierce returned to Boggy Creek by casting himself as an anthropology professor in *The Barbaric Beast of Boggy Creek, Part II.* See also **Bigfoot.**

The Legend of Boggy Creek (1972)	*The Barbaric Beast of Boggy Creek, Part II* (aka *Boggy*
Return to Boggy Creek (1977)	*Creek II*) (1985)

Bomba, the Jungle Boy

After playing "Boy" for eight years, Johnny Sheffield must have expected to find meatier parts following his farewell Tarzan (q.v.) picture, 1947's *Tarzan and the Huntress.* But no one seemed interested in a 16-year-old star so strongly identified with one role. Then, Monogram producer Walter Mirisch came up with a fool-proof series for Sheffield and signed the teen to play Bomba, a junior Tarzan created by Roy Rockwood in the 1920s. *Bomba, the Jungle Boy*, 1949, was a low-budget, blacklot adventure that relied heavily on stock footage (from a 1930 documentary called *Africa Speaks*). The subsequent Bomba films were pretty routine, though journeyman director Ford Beebe managed to make them tolerable. The series ended in 1955, the 24-year-old Sheffield having outgrown the "jungle boy" look.

Bomba, the Jungle Boy (1949)
Bomba on Panther Island (1949)
The Lost Volcano (1950)
Bomba and the Hidden City (1950)
Bomba and the Elephant Stampede (aka *Elephant Stampede*) (1951)
The Lion Hunters (1951)
African Treasure (1952)
Bomba and the Jungle Girl (1952)
Safari Drums (1953)
The Golden Idol (1954)
Killer Leopard (1954)
Lord of the Jungle (1955)

Bond, James

Ian Fleming's super secret agent celebrated 25 years of silver screen success in 1987. Sean Connery debuted as Bond in 1962's *Dr. No* and now — three Bonds and over a dozen movies later — 007 is still going in the person of Timothy Dalton. Interestingly, Connery was not Fleming's first choice for Bond. The author envisioned an actor closer to Cary Grant. And technically, the first Bond was played by American Barry Nelson in an adaptation of *Casino Royale* that appeared on the TV anthology series "Climax" in the late 1950s. The Bond movies, with the lead actor in parentheses, are listed below in chronological order. 1967's *Casino Royale*, a spoof starring David Niven as an elder Bond, is not included since it was not part of the Cubby Broccoli-produced series. *Never Say Never Again*, 1983, which was also not part of the "official" series is included because it starred Connery. As Bond trivia buffs know, *Never* is actually a remake of *Thunderball* and was made only after a long legal dispute.

Dr. No (1962) (Sean Connery)
From Russia with Love (1963) (Connery)
Goldfinger (1964) (Connery)
Thunderball (1965) (Connery)
You Only Live Twice (1967) (Connery)
On Her Majesty's Secret Service (1969) (George Lazenby)
Diamonds Are Forever (1971) (Connery)
Live and Let Die (1973) (Roger Moore)
The Man with the Golden Gun (1974) (Moore)
The Spy Who Loved Me (1977) (Moore)
Moonraker (1979) (Moore)
For Your Eyes Only (1981) (Moore)
Octopussy (1983) (Moore)
Never Say Never Again (1983) (Connery)
A View to a Kill (1985) (Moore)
The Living Daylights (1987) (Timothy Dalton)
Licence to Kill (1989) (Dalton)

Bond Heroines

The ladies who play opposite 007 are famous not only for their beauty, but also their outrageous names. Who can forget such memorable monikers as Pussy Galore, Tiffany Case, and Holly Goodhead? Even more interesting, though, is the fascinating trivia surrounding the actresses. For instance, prior to portraying Ms. Galore in 1964's *Goldfinger,* Honor Blackman played Patrick MacNee's sleuthing partner on "The Avengers." Her popular "Avengers" replacement was Diana Riggs, who went on to play Tracy (aka Mrs. Bond) in 1968's *On Her Majesty's Secret Service.* Maud Adams is the only actress to play in two Bond flicks—she was a supporting villain-turned-good in *The Man with the Golden Gun,* then graduated to the title role in *Octopussy.* Claudine Auger and Kim Basinger played the same character; Claudia played Domino in *Thunderball* and Kim in *Never Say Never Again.* The Bond movies, the leading ladies, and the *characters* are as follows:

Dr. No—Ursula Andress—*Honeychile Rider*
From Russia with Love—Tatiana Romanova—*Daniela Bianchi*
Goldfinger—Honor Blackman—*Pussy Galore*
Thunderball—Claudine Auger—*Domino Vitali*
You Only Live Twice—Mia Hama—*Kissy Suzuki*
On Her Majesty's Secret Service—Diana Rigg—*Teresa (Tracy), the Countess di Vicenzo*
Diamonds Are Forever—Jill St. John—*Tiffany Case*
Live and Let Die—Jane Seymour—*Solitaire*
The Man with the Golden Gun—Britt Ekland—*Mary Goodnight*
The Spy Who Loved Me—Barbara Bach—*Major Anya Amasova*
Moonraker—Lois Chiles—*Holly Goodhead*
For Your Eyes Only—Carole Bouquet—*Melina Havelock*
Octopussy—Maud Adams—*Octopussy*
Never Say Never Again—Kim Basinger—*Domino*
A View to a Kill—Tanya Roberts—*Stacey Sutton*
The Living Daylights—Maryam D'Abo—*Kara Milovy*
Licence to Kill—Carey Lowell—*Pam Bouvier*

Bounty Hunters

What do disenchanted lawmen do when the system won't let them get their man? They become bounty hunters, of course. Thus, Rutger Hauer played an ex-government agent turned modern-day, high-tech bounty hunter in 1987's *Wanted: Dead or Alive.* Interestingly, Rutger's character was supposed to be the grandson of Josh Randall, the Western bounty hunter made famous by Steve McQueen in the 1958–61 TV series "Wanted: Dead or Alive." McQueen played real-life bounty man Pappy Thorson on the big screen in 1980's *The Hunter.* It was his last film. Robert DeNiro and Clint Eastwood played skip tracers, contemporary bounty hunters specializing in bail jumpers, in the light-hearted adventures *Midnight Run* (1988) and *Pink Cadillac* (1989). Westerns typically feature bounty hunters in a negative light. *The Reward* (1965), for example, concerned a group of greedy bounty men who kill each other for a larger share of the reward money.

The Naked Spur (1953)
The Bounty Hunter (1954)
The Bounty Killer (1965)
The Reward (1965)
The Shooting (1966)
Any Gun Can Play (aka *For a Few Bullets More*) (1967)
The Bounty Man (1972 TVM)
Joe Kidd (1972)
Santee (1972)

Manhunter (1974 TVM)
Truck Turner (1974)
The Hunter (1980)
Rivkin: Bounty Hunter (1981 TVM)
Wanted: Dead or Alive (1987)
The Blue Iguana (1988)
Midnight Run (1988)
Pink Cadillac (1989)
The Bounty Hunter (1989)

The Bowery Boys

The chronology of this popular, low-budget juvenile series spans three decades, from the Dead End Kids in the 1930s to the Little Tough Guys and the East Side Kids in the 1940s to (finally) the Bowery Boys in the 1950s. It all began with 1937's *The Dead End,* an adaptation of the sober 1935 Broadway play about New York slum life. That film introduced teen performers Leo Gorcey and Huntz Hall, an odd couple who would eventually form the comedy core of all these movies. At Warner Bros., the Dead End Kids appeared with major stars like James Cagney (1938's *Angels with Dirty Faces*) and John Garfield (1939's *They Made Me a Criminal*). These efforts, though, did not constitute a series since they featured the Kids in changing roles. Some of the Kids (e.g. Billy Halop, Huntz Hall) defected to Universal in 1939 and made *Little Tough Guy,* a *Dead End* imitation with a downbeat ending (Halop goes to reform school). Additional Little Tough Guy movies followed, although the cast and characters again changed on a regular basis. Jackie Cooper even cropped up as the lead Little Tough Guy in 1938's *Newsboy's Home.* In the early 1940s, enterprising producer Sam Katzman brought some of the boys, including Gorcey and Halop, to Monogram Pictures and redubbed them the East Side Kids. Under Katzman's guidance, the series gradually shifted from juvenile drama to broad comedy. Gorcey and Hall also emerged as the principal stars. With their agent Jan Grippo, they revamped the series in 1946 and launched the Bowery Boys pictures for Monogram. As Terence Alyosius Mahoney (Slip) and Horace Debussey Jones (or Sach), Gorcey and Hall mugged their way through 48 Bowery Boy comedies. The humor frequently centered around hapless Sach acquiring some strange power. A throat operation turned him into a great singer in *Blues Busters.* A punch in the nose gave him telepathic powers in *Private Eyes.* He also became clairvoyant *(Master Minds),* acquired great physical strength *(No Holds Barred)*, and learned how to smell diamonds *(Jungle Gents)*. In the end, though, he always returned to normal, inspiring Slip to slap him with his hat. Other Bowery Boys who appeared with some regularity were: Whitey (Billy Benedict), Chuck (Gorcey's brother David), Gabe (Gabriel Dell), and Bobby (Bobby Jordan). The Boys hung out at Louie's Sweet Shop, which was run by Louie Dumbrowsky (Gorcey's father Bernard), who was always sorry for listening to Slip and company. Bernard Gorcey died in 1955, after completing *Dig That Uranium*. His father's death and his own alcoholism caused Leo Gorcey to leave the series after 1957's *Crashing Las Vegas*. Stanley Clements (Gloria Grahame's ex-husband) took over as Duke, the gang's new leader, in the series' final seven films. Huntz Hall continued to appear in movies in supporting roles. He and Gorcey had a cameo together in the dismal 1970 satire *The Phynx*.

The East Side Kids

East Side Kids (1941)	*Kid Dynamite* (1943)
Boys of the City (1941)	*Clancy Street Boys* (1943)
That Gang of Mine (1941)	*Ghosts on the Loose* (1943)
Pride of the Bowery (1941)	*Mr. Muggs Steps Out* (1943)
Flying Wild (1941)	*Million Dollar Kid* (1944)
Bowery Blitzkreig (1941)	*Follow the Leader* (1944)
Spooks Run Wild (1941)	*Block Busters* (1944)
Mr. Wise Guy (1942)	*Bowery Champs* (1944)
Let's Get Tough (1942)	*Docks of New York* (1945)
Smart Alecks (1942)	*Mr. Muggs Rides Again* (1945)
'Neath Brooklyn Bridge (1942)	*Come Out Fighting* (1945)

The Bowery Boys

In Fast Company (1946)	*Ghost Chasers* (1951)
Mr. Hex (1946)	*Crazy Over Horses* (1951)
Spook Busters (1946)	*Let's Go Navy* (1951)
Bowery Bombshell (1946)	*Bowery Battalion* (1951)
Live Wires (1946)	*Hold That Line* (1952)
Hard-Boiled Mahoney (1947)	*Feudin' Fools* (1952)
News Hounds (1947)	*Here Come the Marines* (1952)
Bowery Buckeroos (1947)	*No Holds Barred* (1952)
Angels' Alley (1947)	*Clipped Wings* (1953)
Trouble Makers (1948)	*Jalopy* (1953)
Smuggler's Cove (1948)	*Loose in London* (1953)
Jinx Money (1948)	*Private Eyes* (1953)
Angels in Disguise (1949)	*Paris Playboys* (1954)
Hold That Baby! (1949)	*Jungle Gents* (1954)
Fighting Fools (1949)	*The Bowery Boys Meet the*
Master Minds (1949)	*Monsters* (1954)
Blonde Dynamite (1950)	*Bowery to Bagdad* (1955)
Blues Busters (1950)	*High Society* (1955)
Lucky Losers (1950)	*Spy Chasers* (1955)
Triple Trouble (1950)	*Jail Busters* (1955)

Dig That Uranium (1956)
Crashing Las Vegas (1956)
Fighting Trouble (1956) (first
  with Clements)
Hot Shots (1956)

Hold That Hypnotist (1957)
Spook Chasers (1957)
Looking for Danger (1957)
Up in Smoke (1958)
In the Money (1958)

Boxing

Filmmakers have long been fascinated by the sweaty, brutal world of boxing, making it by far the most popular sport in movies. Film biographies have chronicled the careers of John L. Sullivan *(The Great John L.)*, Jim Corbett *(Gentleman Jim)*, Jack Johnson *(The Great White Hope)*, Joe Louis *(The Joe Louis Story)*, Rocky Graziano *(Somebody Up There Likes Me)*, Jake La Motta *(Raging Bull)*, Muhammad Ali *(The Greatest)*, Jack Dempsey *(Dempsey)*, Rocky Marciano *(Marciano)*, and Boom Boom Mancini *(Heart of a Champion: The Ray Mancini Story)*. Ficticious prizefighters have fared even better, with Rocky Balboa (q.v.), Joe Palooka and Too Sweet (see **Penitentiary**) earning their own film series. Some movie boxers have hailed from other, more unusual professions. John Derek was a young minister who entered the ring to earn money for his congregation in *The Leather Saint* (1956). William Holden played a young man forced to choose between prizefighting and a promising career as a violinist in *Golden Boy* (1939). Almost every male comedy star has included a boxing routine in one of his movies. Danny Kaye made an unlikely boxer in *The Kid from Brooklyn* (1946), but he looked pretty good compared to Donald O'Connor in *Francis in the Navy* (1955), a hypnotised Jimmie Walker in *Let's Do It Again* (1975), Don Knotts in *The Prize Fighter* (1979), and Lou Costello in *Abbott and Costello Meet the Invisible Man* (1951). In the latter film, Costello's boxing prowess was aided considerably—and hilariously—by the presence of an invisible boxing chum. Serious fight films have tended to focus on the corruption within the sport. These include some of the genre's finest films—*The Champ* (1931), *Battling Bellhop* (aka *Kid Galahad*) (1937), *Body and Soul* (1941), *Champion* (1949), *The Set-Up* (1949), and Rod Serling's *Requiem for a Heavyweight* (1962). *The Set-Up* has the added distinction of taking place in real time, as indicated by the clocks shown at the beginning and end of the film. Bare-fisted fighters have been limited to backroom brawls, though Charles Bronson brought one to life memorably in *Hard Times* (1975) and Clint Eastwood had his biggest boxoffice success as slugger Philo Beddoe in *Every Which Way But Loose* (1978). The most bizarre boxer has to be the spunky kangaroo in *Matilda* (1978), though Elvis Presley rates a close second for his pugilist performance in *Kid Galahad* (1962). See also **Rocky; Penitentiary Series; Wrestling.**

Battling Butler (1926)
Iron Man (1931)

The Champ (1931)
Winner Take All (1932)

The Prizefighter and the Lady
(aka *Every Woman's Man*)
(1933) (with real-life boxers
Jack Dempsey and Max Baer)
King for a Night (1933)
The Life of Jimmy Dolan (aka
The Kid's Last Fight) (1933)
Cain and Mabel (1936)
Battling Bellhop (aka *Kid
Galahad*) (1937)
When's Your Birthday? (1937)
Ex-Champ (1939)
Golden Boy (1939)
Invitation to Happiness (1939)
They Made Me a Criminal (1939)
City for Conquest (1940)
Body and Soul (1941)
Here Comes Mr. Jordan (1941)
Knockout (1941)
Ringside Maisie (1941)
Gentleman Jim (1942)
The Great John L. (aka *A Man
Called Sullivan*) (1945)
Leather Gloves (1948)
Whiplash (1948)
The Big Punch (1948)
Champion (1949)
The Set-Up (1949)
The Golden Gloves Story (1950)
Right Cross (1950)
*Abbott and Costello Meet the
Invisible Man* (1951)
The Fighter (1951)
Iron Man (1951)
Flesh and Fury (1952)
The Ring (1952)
The Joe Louis Story (1953)
Champ for a Day (1953)
Tennessee Champ (1954)
The Leather Saint (1956)
The Harder They Fall (1956)
Somebody Up There Likes Me
(1956)
World in My Corner (1956)

Kid Galahad (1962)
Requiem for a Heavyweight
(1962)
Confessions of Tom Harris (aka
Childish Things) (1967)
The Legendary Champions
(1968)
AKA Cassius Clay (1970)
The Great White Hope (1970)
Ripped Off (aka *The Boxer*)
(1971)
Jack Johnson (1971)
Fat City (1972)
The All-American Boy (1973)
Hard Times (1975)
Let's Do It Again (1975)
Rocky (1976)
The Greatest (1977)
Every Which Way But Loose
(1978)
Penitentiary (1978)
Ring of Passion (1978 TVM)
Matilda (1978)
*Movie Movie (the "Dynamite
Hands" segment)* (1978)
The Main Event (1979)
Marciano (1979 TVM)
The Champ (1979)
The Prize Fighter (1979)
Any Which Way You Can
(1980)
Raging Bull (1980)
Body and Soul (1981)
Honeyboy (1982 TVM)
Edith and Marcel (1983)
The Fighter (1983 TVM)
The Last Fight (1983)
Dempsey (1983 TVM)
*Heart of a Champion: The Ray
Mancini Story* (1985 TVM)
Streets of Gold (1986)
Heart (1987)
Spike of Bensonhurst (1988)
Split Decisions (1988)

Boy Scouts

Comedy and sentimentality have dominated movies about Boy Scouts.
Clifton Webb played a grouchy kid-hater who wound up leading a scout

troop—and liking it—in the 1953 comedy *Mister Scoutmaster*. In 1949's *The Great Lover*, scout leader Bob Hope had his hands full aboard a ship filled with his rowdy troupe, a murderer, and luscious Rhonda Fleming. On the sentimental side, Fred MacMurray portrayed a man who devoted his life to his boys in the sticky-sweet Disney picture *Follow Me, Boys!* (1966). *The Wrong Guys* was a 1988 comedy about a Cub Scout reunion, while the 1989 Shelley Long vehicle *Troop Beverly Hills* gave equal time to some *girl* scouts. In the prologue to *Indiana Jones and the Last Crusade* (1989), young Indiana Jones (River Phoenix) showed up in a scout's uniform.

Henry Aldrich, Boy Scout (1944)
The Great Lover (1949)
Mister Scoutmaster (1953)
Follow Me, Boys! (1966)

Scout's Honor (1980 TVM)
The Wrong Guys (1988)
Indiana Jones and the Last Crusade (1989)

Brain Transplants

Mad scientists have been obsessed with transplanting brains since the days of silent films. Almost all Frankenstein films (q.v.), beginning with Edison's 1910 version, have dealt with brain transplanting of some fashion. In James Whales' 1931 *Frankenstein,* the doctor's assistant Fritz stole a criminal's brain from a medical lab, thus explaining the Monster's homicidal tendencies. Yet, the basic Frankenstein operation—the implant of a spare brain into a nonliving body—is but one kind of brain transplant. More interesting films have involved the transplant of a brain from one living creature to another. *On Time* (1924) was a strange little adventure film with a subplot about some thugs trying to replace the hero's brain with a gorilla's. The reversal of that plot describes 1941's *The Monster and the Girl,* in which the implanted brain of a killer transformed an ape into the "Mangle Murderer." Similarly, John Carradine's brain wound up in the skull of a missing link in 1944's *Return of the Ape Man.* In contrast to such silliness, the 1986 TV-movie *Who Is Julia?* was a serious affair about a brain-dead mother (Mare Winningham) who receives new gray cells courtesy of a recently-deceased model. Surprisingly, Terence Fisher's *Frankenstein Must Be Destroyed* (1969) dispensed with the required gruesome monster and opted for a straightforward brain transplant plot. In this ironic tale, Frankenstein (Peter Cushing) "cures" a brain-damaged fellow scientist by transplanting the man's brain into a new body. However, the scientist's gratefulness turns to bitter hate when his wife spurns his new appearance—the face of a stranger. In 1969's *Change of Mind,* a dying white district attorney awoke one day to find his brain in the body of a black man—but, after the initial shocks, it all ended happily. The funny side of brain switching has been explored by Abbott and

Costello *(A&C Meet Frankenstein)*, the Bowery Boys *(Spook Busters)*, and Steve Martin *(The Man with Two Brains)*. Martin's delightful 1983 film cast him as a brain surgeon in love with a body-less brain (although he eventually finds a happy home for it). Although it did not involve brain transplanting, *Hauser's Memory* (1970) deserves special mention for its plot about a man who injected himself with another's brain fluid to learn a valuable secret. See also **Body Switching.**

On Time (1924)	*Frankenstein* (1948)
Frankenstein (1931)	*The Head* (1959)
The Man Who Lived Again	*Monstrosity* (aka *The Atomic*
(aka *The Man Who Changed*	*Brain*) (1964)
His Mind) (1936)	*Frankenstein Must Be Destroyed*
The Ghost of Frankenstein	(1969)
(1940)	*Change of Mind* (1969)
Black Friday (1940)	*Hauser's Memory* (1970 TVM)
The Monster and the Girl	*Brainwaves* (1982)
(1941)	*The Man with Two Brains*
Return of the Ape Man (1944)	(1983)
Spook Busters (1946)	*Who Is Julia?* (1986 TVM)
Abbott and Costello Meet	

Brainwashing

By strict definition, brainwashing is the process by which a person is forcibly induced to forsake political, religious, or social beliefs in favor of contrasting views. *Ticket to Heaven* (1981) and *Split Image* (1982) both explored how susceptible youths were brainwashed by religious cults and then rescued and "deprogrammed." A loathsome punk named Alex (Malcolm McDowell) was brainwashed by Liberals with the "Ludovico technique" in Stanley Kubrick's cult fantasy *A Clockwork Orange* (1971). 1988's fact-based *Patty Hearst* detailed how the famous heiress was kidnapped and subsequently brainwashed into joining her terrorist captors. The Australian horror picture *Thirst* (1979) offered an intriguing twist, whereby a secret society tried to brainwash a young woman into becoming a vampire. Other movies have altered the definition of "brainwashing" to include plots in which a person is controlled subconsciously (usually by hypnosis) and forced to perform uncharacteristic acts. A Robert Frost poem, delivered over the telephone, triggered nice folks into becoming autonomous saboteurs in the thriller *Telefon*. The spy hero of *The Ipcress File* (Michael Caine) used self-induced pain as a defense against hi-tech brainwashing techniques. However, the most famous film of this type remains John Frankenheimer's controversial classic *The Manchurian Candidate* (1962). Frank Sinatra starred as a patriotic soldier turned into a time-delayed assassin — controlled by his own mother (Angela Lansbury). The only brainwashing comedy of note is *Simon,* a decidedly offbeat tale in which a psychology professor (Alan Arkin) was brainwashed into thinking he's an alien from another world. See also **Hypnosis.**

1984 (1956)
Brainwashed (1961)
The Manchurian Candidate (1962)
Thirty-Six Hours (1964)
The Ipcress File (1965)
A Clockwork Orange (1971)
Hunter (1972 TVM)
Telefon (1977)

Thirst (1979)
Simon (1980)
Ticket to Heaven (1981)
Split Image (1982)
Circle of Power (aka *Mystique; Brainwash; The Naked Weekend*) (1983)
1984 (1984)
Patty Hearst (1988)

Bullfights *see* Matadors

Buried Alive

A plot staple in most film adaptations of Edgar Allan Poe, the "buried alive" premise has been best used as a subplot. Nevertheless, it has been the focus of a few movies. In 1958's *Macabre* a doctor frantically searched for his little girl, whom some fiend had buried alive. Producer/director William Castle hyped it by offering viewers fright insurance. In 1972's *The Screaming Woman,* no one believed recently-released asylum resident Olivia de Havilland when she told them she heard a voice in the ground—but there was someone down there, all right. Kidnappers buried their victim in a tiny underground compartment in *The Longest Night* (1972), a film which should have conveyed a more claustrophobic feeling.

Isle of the Dead (1945)
Macabre (1958)
The House of Usher (aka *The Fall of the House of Usher*) (1960)

The Premature Burial (1962)
The Oblong Box (1969)
The Screaming Woman (1972 TVM)
The Longest Night (1972 TVM)

Buses

The Big Bus (1976) may be the only film which takes place almost exclusively on a bus. A disaster movie spoof, it starred Joseph Bologna, Lynn Redgrave, and Ruth Gordon as some of the passengers aboard the world's first nuclear-powered bus during its maiden journey from New York to Denver. In 1980's *Detour to Terror,* O.J. Simpson played a driver whose tour bus is hijacked en route to Las Vegas by a group of terrorists. Carl Betz and family set out aboard a restored bus to rediscover the U.S. in the 1971 TV-movie *In Search of America.* Despite their blue-collar reputation, buses have boasted their share of pulchritudinous passengers. Joan Collins and Jayne Mansfield took a ride on *The Wayward Bus,* adapted from a John Steinbeck story, while *Bus Stop* featured Marilyn Monroe as a rodeo champ's reluctant girlfriend. Alfred Hitchcock considered the bus explosion in *Sabotage* one of his greatest mistakes, since it cruelly killed the heroine's innocent younger brother. The issue of forced busing to schools was examined in the 1980 TV-movie *All God's Children*. On the lighter side, John Candy led fellow bus passengers in singing TV songs (much to Steve Martin's dismay) in 1987's *Planes, Trains, and Automobiles.*

Friday the Thirteenth (1933)	*The Magic Carpet* (1971 TVM)
Sabotage (aka *A Woman Alone*) (1936)	*On the Buses* (1971)
	The Laughing Policeman (1974)
Pardon My Sarong (1942)	*The Big Bus* (1976)
Dead of Night (1945)	*The Gauntlet* (1977)
The Runaway Bus (1954)	*Lady on the Bus* (1978)
Bus Stop (1956)	*Detour to Terror* (1980 TVM)
The Wayward Bus (1957)	*All God's Children* (1980 TVM)
In Search of America (1971 TVM)	*Planes, Trains and Automobiles* (1987)

Butlers

Stereotypically stuffy and very British, butlers have been cast as supporting characters for the most part. Even then, they have managed to upstage the principal stars, as exemplified by John Gielgud's scene-stealing performance in *Arthur* (1981). Arthur Treacher practically made a career of playing butlers, his most famous portrayal being that of P.G. Wodehouse's perfect butler Jeeves in 1936's *Thank You, Jeeves* and its 1937 follow-up *Step Lively, Jeeves.* Irrepressible Eric Blore made a very funny, very cynical valet to Fred Astaire in *Top Hat* (1935) and subsequently specialized in butler roles, too. Although butler leads have been rare, Charles Laughton and William Powell played them in two comedy classics. In 1935's *Ruggles of Red Gap,* Western millionaire Charlie Ruggles won British butler Laughton in a poker game. The cultured butler's clash with American customs provided much of the comedy. But his eventual understanding of American freedom gave the film a surprisingly patriotic ending. Bob Hope reprised the role in the loose 1950 remake *Fancy Pants.* William Powell played a millionaire mistaken by Carole Lombard for a bum in *My Man Godfrey* (1936). She undertakes it as a personal project to transform him into a proper butler. It was also remade in 1957 with David Niven and June Allyson. Niven, who had played opposite Treacher in the first Jeeves film, played a butler again in Disney's *Candleshoe* (1977). Other memorable butlers have been played by Dan Duryea, Ralph Richardson, and Dirk Bogarde. Duryea's butler pretended to be the master of the house while his employer was on vacation in the 1946 comedy *White Tie and Tails.* In *The Fallen Idol* (1948), a young boy idolized the family butler (Richardson) until murderous suspicions took their toll on the friendship. Bogarde played the screen's creepiest valet in Joseph Losey's *The Servant,* a character study in which a butler becomes master of his employer. On television, the future stars of "Dallas" and "Knots Landing," Larry Hagman and Donna Mills, played an average American couple masquerading as a butler and cook for millionaire David Wayne in the 1971–72 sitcom "The Good Life."

Get Off My Foot (1935)
She Married Her Boss (1935)
If You Could Only Cook (1935)
Ruggles of Red Gap (1935)
My Man Godfrey (1936)
Thank You, Jeeves (1936)
Step Lively, Jeeves (1937)
The Baroness and the Butler (1938)
Her Man Gilbey (aka *English Without Tears*) (1944)
Nothing But Trouble (1944)
White Tie and Tails (1946)
The Fallen Idol (1948)

Fancy Pants (1950)
My Man Godfrey (1957)
Light Fingers (1957)
The Admirable Crichton (aka *Paradise Lagoon*) (1957)
The Servant (1963)
The Adventures of Bullwhip Griffin (1967)
Fitzwilly (aka *Fitzwilly Strikes Back*) (1967)
Blue Blood (1973)
Candleshoe (1977)
Arthur (1981)
Clue (1985)

La Cage aux Folles

The 1979 film version of Jean Poiret's French stage farce racked up an impressive $8 million in North America, making it the continent's top all-time grossing foreign-language film. Ugo Tognozzi and Michel Serrault played the gay couple who try to "clean up their act" when Tognozzi's son brings his fiancée and her family over to dinner. Tognazzi and Serrault teamed up again for two mild sequels, neither of which approached the original's raging success. However, *La Cage aux Folles* was adapted into a smash Broadway musical headlining Gene Barry.

La Cage aux Folles (1978)
La Cage aux Folles II (1980)

La Cage aux Folles III: The Wedding (1985)

Camels

Although steadily employed in desert epics, camels have failed to land many starring roles. Indeed, the looney Western comedy *Hawmps* (1976) and its offbeat inspiration, 1954's *Southwest Passage,* may be the only pictures expressly about camels. *Passage* was a 3-D Western which had Rod Cameron experimenting with using camels to transport settlers across the desert. Interestingly, the Indians refrain from attacking the wagon train because they fear the strange-looking camels. Unfortunately, a camel dies and the Indians get wise. The less-serious *Hawmps* headlined James Hampton (Dobbs on TV's "F Troop") as a cavalry officer trying to convince the army to use camels instead of horses. In yet another Western, Disney's *One Little Indian* (1973), James Garner played a cavalryman trudging through the desert with an Indian boy and a trusty camel. Despite its promising title, 1967's *Follow That Camel* was nothing more than a *Carry*

On (q.v.) spoof of *Beau Geste*. Two scene-stealing talking camels added some dry commentary to Hope and Crosby's wacky *Road to Morocco* (1942). Another talking camel had a cameo in Yvonne de Carlo's *Slave Girl*, while a blind camel had the best scene in the Dustin Hoffman–Warren Beatty flop *Ishtar* (1987). There was nary a camel in the 1931 Charlie Chan mystery *The Black Camel*, the title being derived from Charlie's line: "Death is the black camel that kneels unbidden at every gate."

Road to Morocco (1942)
Slave Girl (1947)
Southwest Passage (aka *Camels West*) (1954)
Follow That Camel (aka *Carry On Follow That Camel*) (1967)
One Little Indian (1973)
Hawmps! (1976)
Ishtar (1987)

Cannibalism

Cannibalism, prior to the gore-explicit 1970s, was restricted mostly to jungle adventure films such as *Cannibal Attack* (1954). A pleasantly gruesome exception was the 1936 film version of the old school melodrama *Sweeney Todd, the Demon Barber of Fleet Street*. Tod Slaughter, a noted British ham, portrayed the title character, who not only cut hair, but also cut up his customers and sold them in "meat" pies. The story also served as the basis for 1970's *Bloodthirsty Butchers* and Stephen Sondheim's hit Broadway musical *Sweeney Todd*. By the mid–1960s, cannibalism had crept its way into exploitative, drive-in horror films. Often, the cannibalism was somewhat muted by the inclusion of fantastic elements. A man was barbecued and eaten in *Two Thousand Maniacs* (1964), but the "cannibals" turned out to be ghosts. The flesh-eaters in George Romero's cult classic *Night of the Living Dead* (1968) were ghouls (q.v.), not normal humans. However, the demented family in 1964's *Spider Baby* was physically normal. Its cannibalistic tendencies were a result of inbreeding. Three cannibal films were released in 1972. Both *The Folks at Red Wolf Inn* and *Cannibal Girls* played their grisly subject matter for laughs with jokes about spare ribs and lady fingers. The latter film starred SCTV alumni Eugene Levy and Andrea Martin and was directed by Ivan *(Ghostbusters)* Reitman. *Raw Meat* was an offbeat chiller about descendants of people trapped in a London subway tunnel who devour unsuspecting passers-by. Three other cannibal movies of the 1970s and early 1980s blossomed into cult hits. The most notorious was Tobe Hooper's *The Texas Chainsaw Massacre* (1974), a ghastly tale about a family of flesh-eaters. It was condemned by critics for its violence, which was more implied than explicit. Former cowboy star Rory Calhoun played Farmer Vincent, whose popular sausages were made from human meat, in 1980's *Motel Hell* (the "o" in Motel Hello having burned out). Cannibalism played a small but very significant role in Paul Bartel's *Eating Raoul* (1982), a black comedy about a couple who hit upon a way to finance their dream restaurant when they accidentally commit murder. *Survive!* (1976) was a nonhorror, Mexican import about plane crash survivors who resorted to eating dead fellow passengers to stay alive. The tragic, real-life story of the Donner party, who turned to cannibalism to avoid starvation in the harsh West, was whitewashed in the 1978 TV-movie *Donner Pass: The Road to Survival.* See also **Ghouls.** The following list excludes films featuring cannibal natives:

Sweeney Todd, the Demon Barber of Fleet Street (aka *The Demon Barber of Fleet Street*) (1936)
Spider Baby (aka *The Liver Eaters; Cannibal Orgy or the Maddest Story Ever Told*) (1964)
Mondo Cane (aka *It's a Dog's Life*) (1963)
Do You Like Women? (1964)
The Undertaker and His Pals (1967)
Bloodthirsty Butchers (1970)
The Folks at Red Wolf Inn (aka *Terror at Red Wolf Inn; Terror House*) (1972)
Cannibal Girls (1972)
Raw Meat (aka *Deathline*) (1972)
The Texas Chainsaw Massacre (1974)
Survive! (1976)
Donner Pass: The Road to Survival (1978 TVM)
Motel Hell (1980)
Eating Raoul (1982)
Cannibals in the Street (aka *Invasion of the Flesh Hunters*) (1982)
Raw Force (1982)
C.H.U.D. (1984)
The Texas Chainsaw Massacre 2 (1986)
Eat the Rich (1987)
Parents (1989)
Cannibal Women in the Avocado Jungle of Death (1989)
Chud II: Bud the Chud (1989)

The Care Bears

Media-product tie-ins were the rage of the early 1980s, with toy companies eagerly licensing their bestselling items to TV cartoon producers and vice versa. Few products were more popular than the Care Bears, nice little pastel-colored bears with sentimental names like Wish Bear, Bedtime Bear, and Tenderheart Bear. Just for a touch of realism, there was also Grumpy Bear. The Care Bears, along with My Little Pony and He-Man, were big enough to attract the attention of movie producers, too. Indeed, the first Care Bears film, a feature-length animated musical, did surprisingly well at the boxoffice. However, the law of diminishing returns and short-lived nature of toy trends limited those nice, little bears to two sequels. See also **Animated Movies (Feature-Length).**

The Care Bears Movie (1985)
The Care Bears Movie II: A New Generation (1986)
The Care Bears Adventure in Wonderland (1987)

Carry On Series

This lowbrow British comedy series made an inauspicious debut in 1958 with *Carry On Sergeant,* a silly army farce littered with bad jokes ("Your rank, soldier!" "That's a matter of opinion"). But while the critics scorched it, the public ate it up. Subsequent *Carry On* films were not sequels in a narrative sense, but they featured the same cast members (Kenneth Connor, Charles Hawtrey, Sid James) and the same vaudeville sense of humor. The series highlight was 1960's *Carry On Nurse,* which even earned respectable reviews, although it is chiefly remembered for a scene in which distinguished Wilfred Hyde-White gets a daffodil stuck up his rear end. The series got progressively racier during the 1960s (Cleopatra to Caesar: "I have seen your bust." Caesar: "I wish I could say the same.") and finally featured nudity for the first time in 1969's *Carry On Camping.* The films also suffered a sharp decline in quality (what quality there was), although no one seemed to notice since the *Carry On* movies had become a British institution by then. To its credit, the *Carry On* gang considered nothing sacred and spoofed *Cleopatra (Carry On Cleo), The Third Man (Carry On Spying), The Scarlet Pimpernel (Don't Lose Your Head), Beau Geste (Follow That Camel),* and *Anne of the Thousand Days* (aka *Carry On Henry,* which was memorably subtitled *Anne of a Thousand Lays*). The series finally died in the late 1970s after producing 29 films.

Carry On Sergeant (1958)
Carry On Nurse (1959)
Carry On Teacher (1959)
Carry On Constable (1960)
Carry On Regardless (1961)
Carry On Cruising (1962)
Carry On Cabby (1963)
Carry On Jack (aka *Carry On Venus*) (1963)
Carry On Cleo (1964)
Carry On Spying (1964)
Carry On Cowboy (1965)
Carry On Screaming (1966)
Carry On Doctor (1967)
Don't Lose Your Head (aka *Carry On Don't Lose Your Head*) (1967)
Follow That Camel (aka *Carry On Follow That Camel*) (1968)
Carry On Up the Khyber (1968)

Carry On Again Doctor (1969)
Carry On Camping (1969)
Carry On Henry (1970)
Carry On Loving (aka *One Thing on Top of Another*) (1970)
Carry On Up the Jungle (1970)
Carry On at Your Convenience (aka *Carry On Round the Bend*) (1971)
Carry On Abroad (1972)
Carry On Matron (1972)
Carry On Girls (1973)
Carry On Dick (1974) (as in Dick Turpin, famed British outlaw)
Carry On England (1976)
Carry On Behind (1978)
Carry on Emmanuelle (1978)

(Note: 1957's *Carry On Admiral* was not a part of the series.)

Carson, Billy *see* Billy the Kid

Carter, Nick

Ormond C. Smith and John Russell Coryell created this turn-of-the-century detective for *New York Weekly.* Yet, while Nick Carter seemed a sure bet for a long-running "B"-movie series, his screen career has been modest at best. Andre Liabel made four French serials in 1909–12, while both Edmund Lowe (a future Philo Vance) and Thomas Corrigan appeared in Nick Carter short features in the 1920s. MGM launched an updated three-film series in 1939 with Walter Pidgeon in the lead. The series was dropped when Pidgeon went on to bigger roles in bigger movies (e.g. 1941's *How Green Was My Valley*). Eddie Constantine, best known as tough detective Lemmy Caution (q.v.), played Carter in France while Robert Conrad revived the character for American audiences in the 1972 TV-movie *The Adventures of Nick Carter*. The latter film was the pilot for a television series that never materialized. The detective unexpectedly reappeared in 1978's *Nick Carter in Prague* (aka *Dinner for Adele*), a tongue-in-cheek Czech film that's attracted a minor cult following in the U.S.

Nick Carter, Master Detective (1939) (Pidgeon)
Phantom Raiders (1940) (Pidgeon)
Sky Murder (1940) (Pidgeon)
License to Kill (aka *Nick Carter and the Red Club*) (1964) (Eddie Constantine)

The Adventures of Nick Carter (1972 TVM) (Conrad)
Nick Carter in Prague (aka *Dinner for Adele; Adele Hasn't Had Her Supper Yet*) (1978) (Michael Docolomansky)

Cartoon / Live Action Features

These films fall into two categories: Those which simply intercut "live" footage and animated sequences (e.g. *Allegro Non Troppo*) and those which show live and animated characters *in the same frame*, interacting together. The latter films are the more interesting, typically relying on an expensive optical trick called a travelling matte. The use of mattes can be traced back to 1925's *The Lost World*, in which special effects wizard Willis *(King Kong)* O'Brien masked out the shape of a dinosaur in a crowd scene and then inserted footage of an animated model into that "optical hole." As one might expect, Walt Disney Productions has produced the most cartoon/live action movies, featuring such memorable sequences as the carousel horse race in *Mary Poppins* and Roger Rabbit's initial transition from cartoon-world to real-world in *Who Framed Roger Rabbit?* MGM, however, rates a close second with *Anchors Aweigh* (Tom and Jerry dancing with Gene Kelly), *Dangerous When Wet* (T&J swimming with Esther Williams) and *Invitation to the Dance*. At Warner Brothers, Bugs Bunny showed up in a dream sequence in Doris Day's *My Dream Is Yours* (1949). One of the most unique uses of animation was in 1968's *Charge of the Light Brigade*, in which animated line drawings were used to convey Britain's political atmosphere. See also **Animated Features (Feature-Length)**.

Hollywood Party (1934)
Victory Through Air Power (1943)
The Three Caballeros (1945)
Anchors Aweigh (1945)
Song of the South (1946)
So Dear to My Heart (1948)
Two Guys from Texas (1948)
My Dream Is Yours (1949)
The Four-Poster (1952)
Dangerous When Wet (1953)
The Girl Next Door (1953)
Invitation to the Dance (1957)
The Snow Queen (1959)
The Incredible Mr. Limpet (1964)
Mary Poppins (1964)
The Daydreamer (1966)
The Charge of the Light Brigade (1968)
The Phantom Tollbooth (1969)

The Picasso Summer (1969)
Bedknobs and Broomsticks (1971)
Funnyman (1971)
Two Hundred Motels (1971)
Heavy Traffic (1973)
Monty Python and the Holy Grail (1974)
Coonskin (aka *Streetfight*) (1975)
Allegro Non Troppo (1976)
Pete's Dragon (1977)
Gulliver's Travels (1977)
The Water Babies (1978)
9 to 5 (1980)
Xanadu (1980)
Pink Floyd — The Wall (1982)
Who Framed Roger Rabbit? (1988)
Fletch Lives (1989)

Cartoonists

Dean Martin as a cartoonist? Only in a movie in which he steals the ideas for his comic strips from Jerry Lewis' telepathic dreams — which was precisely the plot of 1955's *Artists and Models.* In the Bob Hope comedy *That Certain Feeling,* a "ghost artist" drew a comic strip for a cartoonist who had lost his touch. James Thurbers' drawings and writings inspired 1972's *The War Between Men and Women,* which starred Jack Lemmon as a half-blind cartoonist hassled by his wife's ex-husband. Two years earlier, the same material had provided the basis for the William Windom TV sitcom "My World and Welcome to It." Michael Crawford played a cartoonist who turned into his own comic book hero in the 1981 Disney misfire *Condorman.*

Piccadilly Jim (1936)
The Girl Next Door (1953)
Artists and Models (1955)
That Certain Feeling (1956)
How to Murder Your Wife (1965)
The War Between Men and

Women (1972)
Condorman (1981)
The Hand (1981)
One Crazy Summer (1986)
Slamdance (1987)
Cellar Dweller (1988)
Brenda Starr (1989)

Cassidy, Hopalong

William Boyd, the undisputed king of "B"-movie Westerns, made 66 Hopalong Cassidy movies for Paramount and United Artists between 1935 and 1948. Clarence E. Mulford created the character in 1912 in a series of "old school" novels. But no one took an interest in them until veteran Western producer Harry (Pop) Sherman envisioned a profitable low-budget series for Paramount. Many actors were considered for the lead role (including David Niven, according to one source), but Sherman finally settled on Boyd. A popular silent actor, Boyd was a favorite of Cecil B. DeMille's and appeared in such classics as *King of Kings* (1927). A gambling scandal involving *another* William Boyd contributed to his fading star status in the early 1930s, so he welcomed the opportunity to play Hopalong. *Hop-a-Long Cassidy* (the hypens were later dropped), 1935, was a surprise hit for Paramount and no wonder—the Cassidy Westerns cost less than $100,000 and usually grossed twice that amount. Screenwriter Doris Schroeder whitewashed Mulford's original character considerably, so that the movies' Hoppy never smoked or drank liquor. The first films sometimes ran as long as 88 minutes, but later ones lasted just over an hour, which made for plenty of action. James Ellison played Jimmy Nelson, Hoppy's young sidekick at the Bar 20 ranch, with additional support by Gabby Hayes or Andy Clyde. After producing 41 Hopalong films, Paramount sold the rights to United Artists in 1942, which released 25 more entries. The last 12 UA films were produced by Boyd's own Hopalong Cassidy Productions. Boyd eventually pawned almost everything he owned and bought rights to *all* the Hopalong Cassidy Westerns. He sold these to television and, when the film series ended in 1948, he began making new episodes for his TV program. Edgar Buchanan played Hoppy's TV sidekick during the series' 1949–51 run.

Hop-a-Long Cassidy (1935)
The Eagle's Brood (1935)
Bar 20 Rides Again (1935)
Call of the Prairie (1936)
Three on the Trail (1936)
Heart of the West (1936)
Hopalong Cassidy Returns (1936)
Trail Dust (1936)
Borderland (1937)
Hills of Old Wyoming (1937)
North of the Rio Grande (1937)
Rustler's Valley (1937)
Hopalong Rides Again (1937)
Texas Trail (1937)
Heart of Arizona (1938)
Bar 20 Justice (1938)
Pride of the West (1938)
In Old Mexico (1938)
Sunset Trail (1938)
The Frontiersman (1938)
Partners of the Plains (1938)

Cassidy of Bar 20 (1938)
Range War (1939)
Law of the Pampas (1939)
Silver on the Sage (1939)
The Renegade Trail (1939)
Santa Fe Marshal (1940)
The Showdown (1940)
Hidden Gold (1940)
Stagecoach War (1940)
Three Men from Texas (1940)
Doomed Caravan (1941)
In Old Colorado (1941)
Border Vigilantes (1941)
Pirates on Horseback (1941)
Wide Open Town (1941)
Outlaws of the Desert (1941)
Riders of the Timberline (1941)
Secret of the Wastelands (1941)
Stick to Your Guns (1941)
Twilight on the Trail (1941)
Undercover Man (1942)
Lost Canyon (1942)

Colt Comrades (1943)
Bar 20 (1943)
Hoppy Serves a Writ (1943)
Border Patrol (1943)
The Leather Burners (1943)
False Colors (1943)
Riders of the Deadline (1943)
Mystery Man (1944)
Forty Thieves (1944)
Texas Masquerade (1944)
Lumberjack (1944)
The Devil's Playground (1946)

Fool's Gold (1947)
Hoppy's Holiday (1947)
Marauders (1947)
Unexpected Guest (1947)
Dangerous Venture (1947)
Sinister Journey (1948)
Silent Conflict (1948)
Strange Gamble (1948)
Borrowed Trouble (1948)
The Dead Don't Dream (1948)
False Paradise (1948)

Cats

As befits their nature, felines have maintained a subtle screen profile. While dogs (q.v.) have panted their way through major film series (see **Lassie** and **Rusty**), cats have been content with a pawful of starring roles and a few choice parts. A frisky ginger cat inherited a wretched baseball team in 1951's *Rhubarb* and turned it into a winner (with a little help from motivational publicist Ray Milland). A female cat narrated Disney's *The Three Lives of Thomasina*, a charming Scottish tale spanning but one-third of her nine lives. Other Disney feline features starred: Siamese cats *(That Darn Cat!* and *Lady and the Tramp)*, alien cats *(The Cat from Outer Space)*, and animated cats *(The Aristocats* and *Oliver and Company)*. *Gay Purr-ee* was a non–Disney feature-length cartoon with the voices of Robert Goulet and Judy Garland. Tom, the animated cat of Tom and Jerry fame, danced with Gene Kelly in *Anchors Aweigh* and swam with Esther Williams in *Dangerous When Wet*. For the best supporting feline performance, the nod goes to Art Carney's co-star in 1974's *Harry and Tonto*. This bittersweet comedy about the travels of an elderly man and his cat earned Carney a Best Actor Oscar. James Bond's archnemesis Blofeld had a white Persian kitty for a pet in some of the 007 films, most notably 1971's *Diamonds Are Forever*. Gale Sondergaard played Shirley Temple's self-centered cat Tylette in the 1940 adaptation of the Oz-like fantasy *The Blue Bird*. Humans have transformed into cats (typically not the domestic variety) in the 1942 and 1982 versions of *The Cat People* and *Cat Girl* (1957). A dead girl's soul possessed a cat in 1946's *The Cat Creeps*, while an Egyptian cat goddess possessed human victims in the 1973 TV-movie *The Cat Creature*. The nastiest cats were the ones that unknowingly ate human flesh in *The Corpse Grinders* (1971) and decided they liked the taste. See also **Lions and Tigers**.

Alice in Wonderland (1933)
The Black Cat (1934)
The Blue Bird (1940)
The Black Cat (1941)

Anchors Aweigh (1945)
Alice in Wonderland (1950)
Rhubarb (1951)
Dangerous When Wet (1953)

Lady and the Tramp (1955)
Bell, Book, and Candle (1958)
Gay Purr-ee (1962)
The Three Lives of Thomasina (1963)
The Incredible Journey (1963)
That Darn Cat! (1965)
Eye of the Cat (1969)
The Aristocats (1970)
The Corpse Grinders (1971)
Alice's Adventures in Wonderland (1972)
The Cat Creature (1973 TVM)

Harry and Tonto (1974)
The Blue Bird (1976)
The Cat from Outer Space (1978)
ffolkes (aka Assault Force; North Sea Hijack) (1980)
Cat's Eye (1985)
The Richest Cat in the World (1986 TVM)
Oliver and Company (1988)
Uninvited (1988)
The Adventures of Milo and Otis (1989)

Caution, Lemmy

American actor Eddie Constantine played Peter Cheyney's two-fisted pulp detective in a series of modest French mysteries, beginning in the early 1950s and lasting through the mid-1960s. A bit player in American films, Constantine followed his dancer wife to Paris, where he achieved minor popularity as a singer. His first Caution film, 1953's *Gun Moll*, cost a paltry $50,000, but earned impressive grosses. European audiences responded enthusiastically to his man-of-action image, which naturally transcended language barriers. Interestingly, Constantine's overseas stardom foreshadowed the 1960's European successes of other American actors such as Clint Eastwood, Charles Bronson, and Lee Van Cleef. The hard-drinking, womanizing Caution made little impact in the U.S., although later efforts such as *Attack of the Robots* (1962) and *Your Turn, Darling* (1963) eventually wound up on American television. Acclaimed French director Jean-Luc Godard cast Constantine as Lemmy Caution in his baffling, esoteric, futuristic "thriller" *Alphaville* (1965). It's considered the best of the Caution pictures, although it is certainly not representative of the series.

Gun Moll (aka La Mome Vert-de-Gris) (1953)
This Man Is Dangerous (aka Dangerous Agent; Cet Homme Est Dangereaux) (1953)
Dames Don't Care (aka Les Femmes s'en Balancent) (1954)
You Dig? (aka Vouz Pigez?) (1956)
Women Are Like That (aka Comment qu'elle Est!) (1960)
Attack of the Robots (aka Cards on the Table; Cartes sur la Table) (1962)
Lemmy and the Girls (aka Ladies' Man; Lemmy pour les Dames) (1962)
Your Turn, Darling (aka Lemmy Caution, FBI Agent; You Do It, Cuties; A Toi de Paire, Migonne) (1963)
Alphaville (aka Alphaville, une Etrange Aventure de Lemmy Caution) (1965)

Cave People

Cavewoman to caveman in *When Dinosaurs Ruled the Earth:* "N'dye krasta m'kan neecro tedak." As any film buff with a prehistoric dictionary knows, that translates to: "Come fast. Kill evil flying monster." Those kinds of dialogue limitations have hampered storylines for prehistoric people pictures. The genre's best films have been visually arresting pieces with plots borrowed from silent films and the added excitement of a dinosaur or two (scientific accuracy being a minor concern). Hal Roach's 1940 opus *One Million B.C.* set the standard with its tale of forbidden love between Tumak (Victor Mature) of the violent Rock People and Loana (Carole Landis) of the peaceful Shell People. The dinosaurs were economically created by magnifying living lizards. *Variety* called the picture "corny" at the time of release and, indeed, it inspired no 1940s imitations. In 1950, the low-budget *Prehistoric Women* added a feminist angle and some narration (in addition to character grunts). Roger Corman's *Teenage Caveman* (1958) was obviously targeted toward young adults, which partially explains the rationale for the twist ending of revealing the past to be the future. However, Britain's Hammer Pictures deserves total credit for turning cave people epics into profitably sturdy boxoffice performers. Its 1966 remake *One Million Years, B.C.* brilliantly paired a scantily-clad Raquel Welch with Ray Harryhausen's impressive stop-motion dinosaurs (q.v.), thus appealing to both older and younger male viewers. Hammer followed it with *Prehistoric Women* (1968), *When Dinosaurs Ruled the Earth* (1970), and *Creatures the World Forgot* (1971). *The Tribe* was a 1974 TV-movie along the same lines, only minus the nudity and dinosaurs. Ringo Starr and his wife Barbara Bach spoofed caveman epics in the 1981 hit comedy *Caveman.* Another 1981 release, *Quest for Fire* was a big-budgeted "serious" effort, featuring a cave people language devised by novelist Anthony *(A Clockwork Orange)* Burgess. *Clan of the Cave Bear,* 1985, was a dismal flop despite its best-seller origins and the presence of then-popular star Daryl Hannah. Of course, not all cave people films have been set in prehistoric times. The contemporary caveman has been around since scientists discovered one roaming about modern-day Africa in the 1927 silent comedy *The Missing Link.* Lightning revived a caveman in *Dinosaurus* (1960), Joan Crawford discovered a missing link hiding in an obscure cave in *Trog* (1970), and scientist Timothy Hutton found a Neanderthal frozen in ice in *Iceman* (1984). The overanxious scientists in *The Neanderthal Man* (1953) and *Monster on the Campus* (1958) actually turned themselves into prehistoric men. In the former film, the serum that turned Robert Shayne into a Neanderthal also transformed his kitty into a sabre-toothed tiger. See also **Dinosaurs.**

The Missing Link (1927)	*Dwellers)* (1940)
One Million B.C. (aka *Man*	*Prehistoric Women* (1950)
and His Mate; The Cave	*The Neanderthal Man* (1953)

Monster on the Campus (1958)
Teenage Caveman (aka Prehistoric World) (1958)
Dinosaurus (1960)
Eegah! (1962)
One Million Years B.C. (1966)
The Oldest Profession in the World ("Prehistoric Era" sketch) (1966)
Prehistoric Women (aka Slave Girls) (1967)
Valley of the Dragons (1970)
Trog (1970)
When Dinosaurs Ruled the Earth (1970)
When Women Had Tails (1970)
Skullduggery (1970)

Creatures the World Forgot (1971)
Schlock (aka The Banana Monster) (1971)
The Creeping Flesh (1973)
The Tribe (1974 TVM)
The People That Time Forgot (1977)
Caveman (1981)
Quest for Fire (1981)
History of the World—Part I (1981)
Iceman (1984)
Clan of the Cave Bear (1985)
Cavegirl (1985)
Link (1986)

Centerfolds

Life's been tough for girls posing in the buff. Kim Basinger played a model whose career went into a tailspin after appearing in a girlie magazine in *Katie: Portrait of a Centerfold* (1978). Apparently, the film had little impact on Basinger, who eventually *did* pose in *Playboy* (but not as the centerfold). The sad real-life story of Dorothy Stratten, a Playmate-turned-actress murdered by her former lover, reached the small screen in 1981 and the big screen two years later. Jamie Lee Curtis played Stratten in the TV-movie *Death of a Centerfold: The Dorothy Stratten Story*, while Mariel Hemingway took the lead in Bob Fosse's *Star 80* (1983). In another fact-based story, 1983's *Policewoman Centerfold*, a lady cop lost her job after posing for a nude layout. The movies have yet to exploit the plight of male nude models, once again confirming the industry's chauvinistic tendencies toward women. See also **Strippers**.

The Centerfold Girls (1974)
Katie: Portrait of a Centerfold (1978 TVM)
Death of a Centerfold: The Dorothy Stratten Story (1981 TVM)

Star 80 (1983)
Policewoman Centerfold (1983 TVM)
I Married a Centerfold (1984 TVM)

Chan, Charlie

Sherlock Holmes reigns as cinema's busiest sleuth, but Charlie Chan ranks a surprising—and very strong—second, with over forty mysteries to his credit. Although Earl Derr Bigger's novels were popular in the 1920s, his Hawaiian police detective was relegated to a strictly supporting role in his big-screen debut, 1926's *The House Without a Key*. He fared better in subsequent outings, but didn't make an impact until Warner Oland made the part his own in 1931's *Charlie Chan Carries On*. Although Swedish by birth, Oland specialized in Oriental roles and, at one point in his career, was playing detective Chan and villain Fu Manchu (q.v.) simultaneously. Oland brought warmth and deceiving wit to the role, masterfully phrasing words of wisdom such as: "Alibi, like dead fish, cannot stand test of time." Keye Luke usually played Charlie's #1 son, providing youth appeal and comic support, as did other sons Benson Fong and Victor Sen Yung in later entries. The Oland Chan films are considered the best of the series, with *Charlie Chan at the Opera* (co-starring Boris Karloff and a young Ray Milland) as the highlight. When Oland died in 1938, American-born Sidney Toler assumed the role and continued the 20th Century–Fox series in capable fashion until 1942. Two years later, Toler was back as Chan in a low-budget Monogram series. On his death in 1947, he was replaced by Roland Winters, who made the last Monogram entry in 1949. Eight years later, Chan resurfaced in the form of J. Carrol Naish in a syndicated TV series called "The New Adventures of Charlie Chan." It lasted for only 39 half-hour episodes. Ross Martin, best known as Artemus Gordon on TV's "Wild, Wild West," made an unlikely Chan in the 1973 TV-movie *Happiness Is a Warm Clue* (aka *The Return of Charlie Chan*). Filmed for U.S. television in 1970, this attempt to revive Chan sat on the shelf for three years, showed up on British TV in 1973, and finally made its American debut on the late show in 1979. At least, the 1981 spoof *Charlie Chan and the Curse of the Dragon Queen* received a general release, though to little avail. Critics panned it and audiences proved that they greatly preferred Oland and Toler to a feebly unfunny Peter Ustinov. The Chan character was much better parodied in Neil Simon's *Murder by Death* (1976). Two of the most potentially interesting Chan films were never made. In *The Four Star Murder Case*, Charlie would have teamed up with Philo Vance, Mr. Moto, and Michael Shayne to solve one mighty tough case. *Charlie Chan at College* would have cast the Oriental detective as a visiting professor demonstrating the finer aspects of crime-solving to his students.

The House Without a Key (1926) (George Kuwa)
The Chinese Parrot (1928) (Sojin)
Behind That Curtain (1929) (E.L. Park)
The Black Camel (1931) (Oland)
Charlie Chan Carries On (1931) (Oland)
Charlie Chan's Chance (1932) (Oland)
Charlie Chan's Greatest Case (1932) (Oland)
Charlie Chan's Courage (1934) (Oland)
Charlie Chan in London (1934) (Oland)
Charlie Chan in Egypt (1935) (Oland)
Charlie Chan in Shanghai (1935) (Oland)
Charlie Chan in Paris (1935) (Oland)
Charlie Chan at the Circus

(1936) (Oland)
Charlie Chan at the Opera
(1936) (Oland)
Charlie Chan at the Race Track
(1936) (Oland)
Charlie Chan's Secret (1936)
(Oland)
Charlie Chan on Broadway
(1937) (Oland)
Charlie Chan at the Olympics
(1937) (Oland)
Charlie Chan at Monte Carlo
(1938) (Oland)
Charlie Chan in Honolulu
(1938) (Toler)
Charlie Chan at Treasure Island
(1939) (Toler)
Charlie Chan in Reno (1939)
(Toler)
*Charlie Chan in the City of
Darkness* (1939) (Toler)
*Charlie Chan at the Wax
Museum* (1940) (Toler)
Charlie Chan's Murder Cruise
(1940) (Toler)
Murder Over New York (1940)
(Toler)
Charlie Chan in Panama (1940)
(Toler)
Charlie Chan in Rio (1941)
(Toler)
Dead Men Tell (1941) (Toler)
Castle in the Desert (1942)
(Toler)
Charlie Chan in Black Magic
(aka *Charlie Chan in Meeting
at Midnight; Charlie Chan at*

Midnight; Black Magic)
(1944) (Toler)
*Charlie Chan in the Secret Ser-
vice* (1944) (Toler)
The Chinese Cat (1944) (Toler)
The Jade Mask (1945) (Toler)
The Red Dragon (1945) (Toler)
The Scarlet Clue (1945) (Toler)
The Shanghai Cobra (1945)
(Toler)
*Charlie Chan in Dangerous
Money* (aka *Dangerous
Money*) (1946) (Toler)
Dark Alibi (1946) (Toler)
Shadows Over Chinatown
(1946) (Toler)
The Trap (1947) (Toler)
The Chinese Ring (1947)
(Winters)
*Charlie Chan and the Golden
Eye* (aka *The Golden Eye;
Mystery of the Golden Eye*)
(1948) (Winters)
Docks of New Orleans (1948)
(Winters)
The Feathered Serpent (1948)
(Winters)
The Shanghai Chest (1948)
(Winters)
Sky Dragon (1949) (Winters)
Happiness Is a Warm Clue (aka
The Return of Charlie Chan)
(1973 TVM) (Ross Martin)
*Charlie Chan and the Curse of
the Dragon Queen* (1981)
(Peter Ustinov)

Chess

The game's intensity has been best captured by *Dangerous Moves*, 1985's Best Foreign Film about how two brilliant players eventually become manipulated by their own obsessions. Max Von Sydow played a chess game with Death in Ingmar Bergman's symbolic *The Seventh Seal* (1957). Steve McQueen and Faye Dunaway practically made love over a game board in *The Thomas Crown Affair* (1968). Sherlock Holmes (Basil Rathbone) used people as chess pieces to solve the puzzle of the Musgrave Ritual in 1943's *Sherlock Holmes Faces Death*. Philo Vance (Rathbone again) clashed with a devious murderer who left a chess piece and Mother Goose rhymes as clues in S.S. Van Dine's *The Bishop Murder Case* (1930).

The Bishop Murder Case (1930)	*The Thomas Crown Affair*
Sherlock Holmes Faces Death	(1968)
(1943)	*Dangerous Moves* (1985)
The Seventh Seal (1957)	

Child Custody Disputes

The commercial success 1979's *Kramer vs. Kramer* brought the bitter struggles over child custody into close focus and undoubtedly contributed to public awareness. However, earlier movies periodically visited the same subject, often just as effectively. An obscure 1942 Paramount film, *My Heart Belongs to Daddy*, featured Martha O'Driscoll as a dancer fighting her in-laws, who maintain that her profession is unsuitable for raising her baby. Bing Crosby gave his best non-singing performance as a father fighting desperately to keep his son in 1957's *Man on Fire*. As in *Kramer*, *Man on Fire* painfully depicts a no-win situation, with a young boy caught in the middle. *One Potato, Two Potato*, 1964, injected intriguing controversy, with Barbara Barrie as a woman who marries a black man and then clashes with her ex-husband on custody of her daughter. Another variation cropped up in 1974's *Unwed Father*, in which a young man tries to gain custody of his illegitimate daughter. Post–*Kramer* films include the sensitive Australian import *Careful, He Might Hear You* (1983) and *Ernie Kovacs: Between the Laughter* (1984). The latter real-life story dealt with Kovacs' efforts to retrieve his two daughters, who were kidnapped by their mother after a child custody dispute. Overly-cute Drew Barrymore sued parents Shelley Long and Ryan O'Neal for custody of herself in 1984's *Irreconcilable Differences*.

My Heart Belongs to Daddy	(1983)
(1942)	*Irreconcilable Differences*
Man on Fire (1957)	(1984)
One Potato, Two Potato (1964)	*Ernie Kovacs: Between the*
Unwed Father (1974 TVM)	*Laughter* (1984 TVM)
Kramer vs. Kramer (1979)	*The Good Mother* (1988)
Careful, He Might Hear You	

Children Raised by Animals

This theme dates back to the Roman myth about twin brothers Romulus and Remus, who were abandoned in the woods as infants and left to die, only to be found and nursed by a she-wolf. Unfortunately, this splendid legend was recounted in perfunctory terms in its only major screen version, the 1963 Italian costume epic *Duel of the Titans*. Wolves were parents again in Rudyard Kipling's *Jungle Book*, in which the young boy Mowgli joined a wolfpack after a vicious tiger separated him from his parents. Alexandra Korda produced 1942's *The Jungle Book,* a lavish live action adaptation starring the charismatic child actor Sabu (who made a career of similar roles). The Disney Studios later turned Kipling's book into a 1967 cartoon musical featuring the voices of Phil Harris and George Sanders. The life of Edgar Rice Burroughs' Tarzan (q.v.) has been detailed in many films, although his childhood among the apes was best portrayed in 1984's *Greystoke: The Legend of Tarzan, Lord of the Apes.* François Truffaut's *The Wild Child* (1969) was a fact-based story about a boy who raised himself in the woods and the doctor dedicated to "civilizing" him. The 1976 TV-movie *Stalk the Wild Child* was a thinly-disguised American version about a boy raised by wolves. It was followed by a second TV-movie called *Lucan,* in which a former "wolf child" sets out to find his parents and his own identity. It served as the pilot for the 1977–78 "Lucan" TV series. Howie Mandel played a man raised by wolves in the dismal 1987 comedy *Walk Like a Man.* A parentless youth raised himself and lived in the sewers in another best-forgotten satire, 1987's *Wild Thing.*

The Jungle Book (1942)	TVM)
Zamba (1949)	*Lucan* (1977 TVM)
Duel of the Titans (1961)	*Greystoke: The Legend of Tarzan, Lord of the Apes* (1984)
The Jungle Book (1967)	
The Wild Child (1969)	*Walk Like a Man* (1987)
Stalk the Wild Child (1976	*Wild Thing* (1987)

Christian, Dr. (Paul)

Prior to his screen debut as paternal country doctor Paul Christian, Jean Hersholt had already provided the character's radio voice and starred in a similar role in three 20th Century–Fox films. Daryl Zanuck was the man behind Fox's *The Country Doctor* (1936), a family drama based on the birth of the Dionne Quintuplets (and featuring a brief appearance by star-to-be Tyrone Power). Hersholt scored as the family's rural physician and appeared in two sequels: *Reunion* (1936) and *Five of a Kind* (1938). A year later, Hersholt moved to RKO and initiated a new series with *Meet Dr. Christian.* Christian was the Marcus Welby of his era and, in the span of an hour, could cure an epidemic of spinal meningitis and solve a handful of personal crises for his patients. True to character, Hersholt was a great humanitarian himself and received two special Academy Awards for work with the Motion Picture Relief Fund. In 1956, the year of his death, the Academy of Motion Picture Arts and Sciences created an annual humanitarian award to be given in his name. Other *Christian* series regulars included Dorothy Lovett as the doctor's faithful nurse and Robert Baldwin as her boyfriend, the town druggist. Ring Lardner, Jr., wrote several of the scripts. In 1956, MacDonald Carey played the title role in the syndicated TV series "Dr. Christian."

Meet Dr. Christian (1940)	(1940)
The Courageous Dr. Christian (1940)	*Remedy for Riches* (1940)
	Melody for Three (1941)
Dr. Christian Meet the Women	*They Meet Again* (1941)

Christmas

There was a time when the coming of the yuletide season promised that lesser-known holiday favorites, such as *The Cheaters* and the 1951 *A Christmas Carol* would be pulled from the vaults to air alongside annual classics like *The Bishop's Wife, It's a Wonderful Life,* and *Miracle on 34th Street.* But a glut of recently-produced Christmas fare, mostly made-for-TV movies, has diluted the holiday marketplace and sent the "lesser knowns" back into the film vaults. No fewer than 19 Christmas-oriented TV-movies were broadcast by the major networks between 1977 and 1988. Six theatricals were also released during the same period. Ironically, the networks' heaping servings of Christmas sentiment were undoubtedly inspired by the lasting popularity of holiday classics like *It's a Wonderful Life* (which was remade for TV as 1977's *It Happened One Christmas*). As one would expect, Charles Dickens' *A Christmas Carol* has provided the source material for the most yuletide films: *A Christmas Carol* (1938) with Reginald Owen as Scrooge, *A Christmas Carol* (1951) with Alastair Sim, the musical *Scrooge* (1970) with Albert Finney, *An American Christmas Carol* with Henry Winkler (1979 TVM), *A Christmas Carol* with George C. Scott (1984 TVM), and the 1988 contemporary take-off *Scrooged* with Bill Murray (not to mention the famous cartoon short "Mr. Magoo's Christmas Carol"). Santa Claus has appeared rather less than one would think, notching appearances in *Babes in Toyland* (1961), *Santa Claus Conquers the Martians* (1964), *The Christmas That Almost Wasn't* (1966), *Santa Claus: The Movie* (1985), and *Ernest Saves Christmas* (1988). Art Carney played St. Nick in *The Night They Saved Christmas* (1984), a part he knew well as a result of his 1960 appearance in the touching "Night of the Meek" episode of "The Twilight Zone." He starred as a drunken department store Santa who loses his job, only to find a magic bag of toys and become the real St. Nick. Of course, not everyone in a Santa suit experiences that kind of magic. Christopher Plummer played an unstable murderer who robbed a bank disguised as Santa in *The Silent Partner* (1978). A psychotic killer sported a Santa suit in the tasteless 1984 slasher film *Silent Night, Deadly Night.*

A Christmas Carol (1938)	*Christmas in Connecticut* (aka *Indiscretion*) (1945)
Beyond Tomorrow (1940)	
Holiday Inn (1942)	*It's a Wonderful Life* (1946)
Christmas Holiday (1944)	*The Bishop's Wife* (1947)
The Cheaters (aka *The Castaway*) (1945)	*Christmas Eve* (aka *Sinner's Holiday*) (1947)

Miracle on 34th Street (aka *The Big Heart*) (1947)
A Christmas Carol (aka *Scrooge*) (1951)
The Lemon Drop Kid (1951)
The Holly and the Ivy (1952)
White Christmas (1954)
Babes in Toyland (1961)
Santa Claus Conquers the Martians (1964)
The Christmas That Almost Wasn't (1966)
The Christmas Tree (aka *When Wolves Cry*) (1969)
Scrooge (1970)
The Homecoming—A Christmas Story (1971 TVM)
Home for the Holidays (1972 TVM)
A Dream for Christmas (1973 TVM)
Miracle on 34th Street (1973 TVM)
Black Christmas (aka *Silent, Night, Evil Night; Stranger in the House*) (1975)
Christmas Miracle in Caufield, U.S.A. (aka *The Christmas Coal Mine Miracle*) (1977 TVM)
The Gathering (1977 TVM)
It Happened One Christmas (1977 TVM)
A Christmas to Remember (1978 TVM)
An American Christmas Carol (1979 TVM)
Christmas Lilies of the Field (1979 TVM)
The Man in the Santa Claus Suit (1979 TVM)
A Christmas Without Snow (1980 TVM)
You Better Watch Out (aka *Christmas Evil; Terror in Toyland*) (1980)
A Christmas Story (1983)
The Gift of Love: A Christmas Story (1983 TVM)
A Christmas Carol (1984 TVM)
It Came Upon a Midnight Clear (1984 TVM)
The Night They Saved Christmas (1984 TVM)
Silent Night, Deadly Night (1984)
One Magic Christmas (1985)
Santa Claus: The Movie (aka *Santa Claus*) (1985)
Christmas Eve (1986 TVM)
The Christmas Gift (1986 TVM)
The Christmas Star (1986 TVM)
Christmas Comes to Willow Creek (1987 TVM)
The Christmas Visitor (aka *Bushfire Moon*) (1987 TVM)
I'll Be Home for Christmas (1988 TVM)
Ernest Saves Christmas (1988)
Scrooged (1988)
A Very Brady Christmas (1988 TVM)
National Lampoon's Christmas Vacation (1989)
Prancer (1989)

Cinerama

Former Paramount special effects technician Fred Waller invented this widescreen process, which produces a 165-degree curved image, in the early 1950s. It evolved from an earlier Waller system called Vitarama, which used eleven synchronized projectors to create an illusion of vastness and motion on a curved theater screen. Vitarama was a big hit at the 1937 World's Fair, but its expense and technical requirements made it impractical for common use. Waller refined it over the next two decades and introduced a new version in 1952 with the travelogue film *This Is Cinerama*. The Cinerama process required a film to be shot with three cameras, one facing straight ahead and the other two slightly to the left and right of the middle camera. Three synchronized projectors then projected all three films on a curved screen simultaneously. Like *This Is Cinerama*, the early films shown in the process focused on spectacular visual effects—breathtaking rollercoaster rides and soaring plane flights over the Grand Canyon. Unlike 3-D, Cinerama survived the 1950s, perhaps because its equipment restrictions limited the number of theaters that could show Cinerama films and elevated the process to special event status. The first nontravelogue was 1962's *How the West Was Won*. Occasional films continued to be made in Cinerama throughout the 1960s. However, technical difficulties, specifically problems with keeping the projectors synchronized, drove the development of a one-projector Cinerama process. The "new" Cinerama amounted to little more than projecting a 70mm image on a curved screen. It was abandoned in the 1970s, though expositions and amusement parks continue to exhibit popular Cinerama-like projection systems. See also **3-D; Gimmicks.**

This Is Cinerama (1952)
Cinerama Holiday (1955)
Seven Wonders of the World (1956)
Search for Paradise (1957)
South Seas Adventure (1958)
How the West Was Won (1962)
The Wonderful World of the Brothers Grimm (1962)
It's a Mad, Mad, Mad, Mad

World (1963)
Circus World (1963)
The Best of Cinerama (1964)
Battle of the Bulge (1965)
Grand Prix (1966)
2001: A Space Odysessy (1968)
Ice Station Zebra (1968)
Custer of the West (1968)
Krakatoa, East of Java (aka *Volcano*) (1969)

Circuses

The allure of the big top setting has faded recently, but for four decades, it was an ideal place to find high-wire dramatics, ferocious beasts, incognito killers, and perhaps a troupe of vampires. Laughs, too, as evidenced by the number of comedies set against a circus backdrop. W.C. Fields played a ringmaster in *You Can't Cheat an Honest Man* (1939), the Marx Brothers saved one from bankruptcy in *At the Circus* (1939), and even Dean Martin and Jerry Lewis got into the act with *Three Ring Circus* (1954). Movie murderers have also exhibited a special fondness for circuses, as evidenced in *Charlie Chan at the Circus* (1936), *Circus of Horrors* (1960), *Psycho Circus* (1967), and *Berserk* (1968). On a classier level, James Stewart played a murder suspect hiding out as a mild-mannered clown in Cecil DeMille's 1952 extravaganza *The Greatest Show on Earth*. This multi-character melodrama garnered a Best Picture Oscar and tallied record boxoffice figures for Paramount. The film's successful behind-the-

CIRCUSES

scenes formula was more or less copied in *The Big Circus* (1959), *The Big Show* (1961), and *Circus World* (1964). The life of the world's greatest circus showman was chronicled in 1934's *The Mighty Barnum* and 1986's *Barnum*, with Wallace Beery and Burt Lancaster in the title roles, respectively. Serious European directors have used circuses for symbolic purposes, as in Ingmar Bergman's *Sawdust and Tinsel* (1953), Federico Fellini's *La Strada* (1954), and Wim Wenders' *Wings of Desire* (1987). Four Disney pictures have taken place at least partially under the big top: *Dumbo* (1941), *Toby Tyler* (1960), *A Tiger Walks* (1964), and *The Three Lives of Thomasina* (1964). *Lady in the Dark* (1944) had a musical dream sequence set in a circus, while Rodgers and Hart's *Billy Rose's Jumbo* (1962) revolved around a circus owned by Doris Day. The circus in 1961's *Gorgo* featured a dinosaur as its main attraction. Unfortunately, it turned out to be a baby with a mad mother in hot pursuit. See also **Fairs and Carnivals**.

He Who Gets Slapped (1924)
The Circus (1928)
Dangerous Curves (1929)
Freaks (aka *Nature's Mistakes*) (1932)
Polly of the Circus (1932)
The Big Cage (1933)
The Mighty Barnum (1934)
Circus Clown (1934)
Charlie Chan at the Circus (1936)
At the Circus (1939)
You Can't Cheat an Honest Man (1939)
Chad Hanna (1940)
Dumbo (1941)
Road Show (1941)
Sunny (1941)
The Wagons Roll at Night (1941)
The Dark Tower (1943)
Lady in the Dark (1944) (dream sequence)
Dual Alibi (1947)
Caged Fury (1948)
The Fat Man (1951)
Encore (1952) (segment)
Sawdust and Tinsel (aka *The Naked Night*) (1953)
Man on a Tightrope (1953)
Three Ring Circus (aka *Jerrico, the Wonder Clown*) (1954)
The Greatest Show on Earth (1954)
La Strada (aka *The Road*) (1954)
Carnival Story (1954)
Ring of Fear (1954)
Trapeze (1956)
Invitation to the Dance (1957)
Merry Andrew (1958)
The Big Circus (1959)
The Flying Fontaines (1959)
Circus of Horrors (1960)
Toby Tyler, or Ten Weeks with a Circus (1960)
The Big Show (1961)
Gorgo (1961)
Hippodrome (1961)
Bimbo the Great (1961)
Billy Rose's Jumbo (aka *Jumbo*) (1962)
The Main Attraction (1962)
Circus World (aka *The Magnificent Showman*) (1964)
A Tiger Walks (1964)
The Three Lives of Thomasina (1964)
Rings Around the World (1967)
Psycho Circus (aka *Circus of Fear*) (1967)
Berserk (1968)
Vampire Circus (1971)
The Clowns (1971)
Punch and Jody (1974 TVM)
The Last Circus Show (aka *The Balloon Vendor*) (1974)

The Great Wallendas (1978
  TVM)
*When the Circus Comes to
  Town* (1981)

Side Show (1981 TVM)
Barnum (1986 TVM)
Wings of Desire (1987)
Big Top Pee Wee (1988)

Cisco Kid

The origins of the Cisco Kid separate him from his many rival "B"-movie
Western heroes. The Kid's sound debut was 1929's *In Old Arizona,* which
had the triple distinction of being based on an O. Henry short story,
featuring an Oscar-winning turn by Warner Baxter as Cisco, and introducing the popular song "My Tonia" (recorded by Nic Lucas). The film was a
sizable hit for Fox, chiefly due to the expert direction of Western specialist
Raoul Walsh. Baxter starred in the 1930 semi-sequel *The Arizona Kid*
before officially reprising his Robin Hood-like Mexican outlaw in 1931's
The Cisco Kid. In Old Arizona alumnus Edmund Lowe also returned as
the dedicated Texas Ranger bent on capturing Cisco. After this second
Cisco film, Baxter strove to avoid typecasting and appeared in musicals
(42nd Street), biographical dramas *(Prisoner of Shark Island),* and comedies *(Daddy Long Legs).* However, by 1936, his popularity was declining
and he appeared in the Cisco-like *Robin Hood of El Dorado.* Three years
later, 20th Century–Fox hailed his comeback in *The Return of the Cisco
Kid.* Yet, unlike the earlier films in the series, *Return* was a programmer,
running just 70 minutes and co-starring young performers like Cesar
Romero. In fact, Romero stepped up into the lead role in the follow-up
The Cisco Kid and the Lady and five subsequent films. Fox dumped the
series in 1941, but four years later, Monogram picked it up and installed
former *Three Mesquiteers* (q.v.) supporting player Duncan Renaldo as
Cisco. Renaldo starred in three films, beginning with 1945's *The Cisco Kid
Returns,* before Monogram replaced him with Gilbert Roland, the only
Latin actor to portray the Kid. An affable, sturdy performer, Roland made
six modestly entertaining Cisco entries before Monogram ended its series.
Surprisingly, United Artists revived the series in 1949 and recalled Renaldo
to reprise the Mexican bandit hero. Renaldo made five entries, assisted by
Leo Carillo as his chubby sidekick Pancho. In late 1950, Renaldo and
Carillo transitioned from hour-long theatrical features to a half-hour syndicated TV series. "The Cisco Kid" quickly became the biggest non-
network hit of the 1950s. Its 156-episode run concluded in 1956, although
it is still shown on television today (since the producers were smart enough
to film in color).

In Old Arizona (1929) (Warner
  Baxter)
The Cisco Kid (1931) (Baxter)
Return of the Cisco Kid (1939)
  (Baxter)

The Cisco Kid and the Lady
  (1939) (Cesar Romero)
The Gay Caballero (1940)
  (Romero)
Lucky Cisco Kid (1940) (Romero)

Viva Cisco Kid (1940) (Romero)
Romance of the Rio Grande (1941) (Romero)
Ride On, Vaquero (1941) (Romero)
The Cisco Kid Returns (1945) (Duncan Renaldo)
In Old Mexico (aka *The Cisco Kid in Old Mexico*) (1945) (Renaldo)
South of the Rio Grande (1945) (Renaldo)
The Gay Cavalier (1946) (Gilbert Roland)
South of Monterey (1946) (Roland)
Beauty and the Bandit (1946) (Roland)
King of the Bandits (1947) (Roland)
Riding the California Trail (1947) (Roland)
Robin Hood of Monterey (1947) (Roland)
The Valiant Hombre (1949) (Renaldo)
The Daring Caballero (1949) (Renaldo)
The Gay Amigo (1949) (Renaldo)
Satan's Cradle (1949) (Renaldo)
The Girl from San Lorenzo (1950) (Renaldo)

Clairvoyants and Fortunetellers

The ability to predict the future has been a liability as often as a blessing in the movies. Claude Rains played a phony fortuneteller in 1935's *The Clairvoyant* who discovers that his predictions—including one of his death—are coming true. A similar fate befell Akim Tamiroff in *The Great Gambini* (1937) and Edward G. Robinson in *The Night Has a Thousand Eyes* (1948). Five years earlier, Robinson played a man fatally obsessed with a palm reader's uncanny predictions in the eeriest tale in Julien Duvivier's anthology *Flesh and Fantasy*. Mr. Big forcibly employed the clairvoyant Domino (Jane Seymour) in the 1973 Bond adventure *Live and Let Die*. Alas, 007 put an end to Domino's prophetic powers, since they were somehow tied to her virginity. Clairvoyants capable of predicting murders aided the police in *The Eyes of Charles Sand* (1972), *Man on a Swing* (1974) and *Eyes of Laura Mars* (1978). The 1971 TV-movie *Sweet, Sweet Rachel* spun off the short-lived 1972 series "The Sixth Sense," which starred Gary Collins as a psychic private investigator. Traditional gypsy and roadside fortune tellers have had brief, but memorable, scenes in *The Wizard of Oz*, *The Wolf Man*, and *The Leopard Man*. The finest clairvoyant comedy, Rene Clair's *It Happened Tomorrow* (1944), featured Dick Powell as a reporter who gets tomorrow's newspaper delivered a day early. Other lighthearted fortune-telling tales include Eddie Cantor's *Palmy Days* (1932) and Ealing's *The Oracle* (1952).

The Hole in the Wall (1929)
Palmy Days (1932)
The Clairvoyant (aka *The Evil Mind*) (1935)
The Great Gambini (1937)
The Wizard of Oz (1939)
The Wolf Man (1940)
The Crystal Ball (1943)
Flesh and Fantasy (1943)
The Leopard Man (1943)

It Happened Tomorrow (1944)
Inner Sanctum (1948)
Night Has a Thousand Eyes (1948)
The Oracle (1952)
Dr. Terror's House of Horrors (aka *The Blood Suckers*) (1965)
Sweet, Sweet Rachel (1971 TVM)
The Eyes of Charles Sand (1972 TVM)
Visions... (aka *Visions of Death*) (1972 TVM)
Baffled (1972 TVM)
Live and Let Die (1973)
Man on a Swing (1974)
The Premonition (1976)
Eyes of Laura Mars (1978)
Mind Over Murder (1979 TVM)
The Dead Zone (1983)
Second Sight (1989)

The Cohens and the Kellys

The Jewish Cohens and the Irish Kellys were feuding families in a series of seven Universal comedies that spanned the transition from silent to talking pictures. 1926's *The Cohens and the Kellys* was based on Aaron Hoffman's play *Two Blocks Away,* although the obvious similarities to Anne Nichols' Broadway hit *Abie's Irish Rose* resulted in a lawsuit. This first picture established the framework for the series, with the families being drawn together by the romance between the Kellys' son and the Cohens' daughter and the inheritance of a fortune. Jewish shopkeeper Cohen initially inherited the money, only to discover that it actually belonged to Irish cop Kelly. In the end, they became partners, setting the stage for a series of wild adventures in Africa (buying elephant tusks for a piano company), Scotland (entering the tartan business), and even Atlantic City. In most of the films, George Sidney and Vera Gorden played the Cohens with Charlie Murray and Kate Price as the Kellys. *The Cohens and Kellys in Scotland* is considered the best of the series, although *Hollywood* featured guest bits by Tom Mix, Boris Karloff, and Lew Ayres. Almost forty years after the last *Cohen–Kelly* movie, the premise of feuding Jewish and Irish families popped up again in the TV series "Bridget Loves Bernie."

The Cohens and the Kellys (1926)
The Cohens and the Kellys in Paris (1928)
The Cohens and Kellys in Atlantic City (1929)
The Cohens and Kellys in Scotland (1930)
The Cohens and Kellys in Africa (1930)
The Cohens and Kellys in Hollywood (1933)
The Cohens and Kellys in Trouble (1933)

Color / B&W Features

The dramatic use of color in black and white films (and vice versa) began with 1939's *The Wizard of Oz,* which transported Dorothy from monochrome Kansas into exciting, colorful Oz. The same trick was repeated in *The Blue Bird* (1940), a similar fantasy in which a black and white prologue gave way to a lengthy color dream sequence. The idea of filming reality in black and white and fantasy in color was neatly reversed in 1946's *Stairway to Heaven* (aka *A Matter of Life and Death*). It starred David Niven as a wounded pilot destined to die, but so determined to live that he argues his case in a celestial trial. Because he wants to continue his existence in this world, the earthly segments are shown in color, while the scenes in Heaven are in black and white. Forty-one years later, Heaven reverts to color and reality to b&w in the opening of *Made in Heaven* (later in the movie, the earthly scenes acquire color, too). Less elaborate uses of color are displayed in *Portrait of Jennie*, *The Picture of Dorian Gray*, and *The Moon and Sixpence*, three b&w films in which paintings appear in color. In other films: Judy Holliday drove away in a gold auto in the original b&w print of *The Solid Gold Cadillac*. In William Castle's gimmicky *The Tingler*, there's a brief—but highly effective sequence—in which bright red blood splashes out of a b&w bathroom sink faucet. And in George Romero's *Martin*, a would-be teen vampire has black and white dreams of his earlier life as a bloodsucker.

The Wizard of Oz (1939)
The Blue Bird (1940)
The Moon and Sixpence (1942)
Stairway to Heaven (aka *A Matter of Life and Death*) (1946)
Portrait of Jennie (1948)
I'll Never Forget You (1951)
Jack and the Beanstalk (1953)
The Solid Gold Cadillac (1956)
The Tingler (1959)
The Private Lives of Adam and Eve (1960)

If... (1968)
And Now My Love (1975)
Martin (1978)
Movie Movie (1978)
19/19 (1985)
Kiss of the Spider Woman (1985)
Mishima (1985)
She's Gotta Have It (1986)
Made in Heaven (1987)
Radium City (1987)
Wings of Desire (1988)

Coma

The frightening side effects of unusual comas provided the premise for two exceptionally clever films, 1970's *The Mind of Mr. Soames* and 1983's *The Dead Zone*. Both films effectively balanced science fiction, horror, and reality by concentrating on the personal traumas of the coma victims. *The Dead Zone*, adapted from Stephen King's best-seller, starred Christopher Walken as an accident victim who emerges from a five-year coma with the ability to foresee the future of those he touches. This apparent gift turns out to a liability which drives Walken's character to commit murder to prevent a future disaster. In *The Mind of Mr. Soames*, a scientist revives a man from a 30-year coma—which began with his birth. Thus, he is "born" as an adult with the mind of a baby. More mainstream pictures include 1978's *Coma*, with Genevieve Bujold as a dedicated doctor who discovers that the body parts of comatose patients

are being auctioned in an organ blackmarket. *Patrick* (1978) was a
telekinetic teen, ala *Carrie,* who wrecked havoc while in a comatose state.
Seizure: The Story of Kathy Morris (1980) was the real-life story of a
singer's struggle to recover from a coma. See also **Suspended Animation.**

The Mind of Mr. Soames (1970)	*Morris* (1980 TVM)
Coma (1978)	*Brimstone and Treacle* (1982)
Patrick (1978)	*The Dead Zone* (1983)
Seizure: The Story of Kathy	*Bad Dreams* (1988)

Comic Book Characters

With the notable exceptions of Superman (q.v.) and Batman, few comic
book characters have encountered significant success in feature films. During the 1940s, they thrived in action-packed *serials* like Columbia's *Batman* and *Captain America.* A young Robert Wagner brought Prince
Valiant to life in a 1954 film and the briefly popular 1966–68 TV series
"Batman" spawned a campy feature-length theatrical film. Both movies
were intended for juvenile audiences and no sequels followed. In the
mid–1970s, comic book superheroes achieved minor popularity in the form
of made-for-TV movies (both *The New Original Wonder Woman* and *The
Incredible Hulk* led to TV series). And then in 1978, the big-budgeted
Superman caught the public's fancy and three progressively less interesting, but still profitable, sequels appeared over the next decade.
Meanwhile, a pair of Japanese samurai imports, based on the *Lone Wolf
and Cub* comic book series, acquired a cult following in the U.S. The
films were *Lightning Swords of Death* and *Shogun Assassin* and they
traced the exploits of a hunted warrior who pushes his son around in an
armed baby cart. Comic books, as a literature form, acquired a serious
adult following in the 1980s. This ultimately led to the 1989 brooding
blockbuster version of *Batman,* with Michael Keaton as the Caped
Crusader (sans Robin) and Jack Nicholson hamming it up as The Joker.
See also **Superman; The Incredible Hulk.**

Prince Valiant (1954)	*The Incredible Hulk* (1977 TVM)
Superman and the Mole Men (1951)	*Spider-Man* (1977 TVM)
Batman (1966)	*Dr. Strange* (1978 TVM)
Danger: Diabolik (1968)	*Superman* (1978)
The Adventures of Barry Mc-Kenzie (1972)	*Captain America* (1979 TVM)
Barry McKenzie Holds His Own (1974)	*Mandrake* (1979 TVM)
Wonder Woman (1974 TVM)	*Shogun Assassin* (1981)
Lightning Swords of Death (1974)	*Swamp Thing* (1982)
The New Original Wonder Woman (1975 TVM)	*Howard the Duck* (1986)
	The Spirit (1987 TVM)
	Return of the Swamp Thing (1989)
	Batman (1989)

Comic Book–style Movies

The old E.C. horror comics have inspired four multipart movies: *Tales from the Crypt, Vault of Horror, Creepshow,* and *Creepshow 2.* With its animated introductions and dark quirky humor, *Creepshow* rates as the best of these efforts.

Comic Strip Characters

Comic strips have provided a rich source of film material, serving as the basis for several popular film series. The most influential was undoubtedly Chic Young's "Blondie" (q.v.) strip, which was adapted into a 27-film series that lasted from 1938 to 1951. No other comic strip favorite has matched that level of success, although Dick Tracy, Jiggs and Maggie, Jungle Jim, Red Ryder, Dick Barton, and the Peanuts Gang (all q.v.) also earned their own film series. Surprisingly, other famous funnies' characters have floundered on the screen. Perhaps, filmmakers felt that the 1959–63 "Dennis the Menace" TV series oversaturated viewers with the troublesome youngster, for Dennis' film debut was a throwaway 1987 TV-movie. A similar fate befell *Brenda Starr* (1976) and *Buck Rogers in the 25th Century* (1979), although the latter made-for-TV movie actually received a theatrical distribution. The exploits of Li'l Abner and Little Orphan Annie were adapted into splashy, overblown musicals which sadly lost sight of their characters' charms. Film versions of adult comic strips have been scarce, consisting mostly of a couple of sexy heroines *(Barbarella, Modesty Blaise)* and a sex-obsessed cat *(Fritz the Cat).* See also **Barton, Dick; Blondie; Jiggs and Maggie; Jungle Jim; Peanuts; Ryder, Red; Tracy, Dick.**

Little Orphan Annie (1932)
Joe Palooka (1934)
Reg'lar Fellows (1941)
The Sad Sack (1957)
Li'l Abner (1959)
Dondi (1961)
Modesty Blaise (1966)
Barbarella (aka *Barbarella, Queen of the Galaxy*) (1968)
Fritz the Cat (1972)
The Nine Lives of Fritz the Cat (1975)
Brenda Starr (1976 TVM)
Buck Rogers in the 25th Century (1979)
Flash Gordon (1980)
Annie (1982)
Dennis the Menace (1987 TVM)
Brenda Starr (1989)

Compilation Films (Fictional)

The birth of the "compilation film" can be traced to its widespread use by documentary filmmakers during the two World Wars. Gifted filmmakers such as Frank Capra edited selected newsreel footage to produce historical time capsules and effective propaganda pieces. In the late 1950s, former Pathé News employee Robert Youngson, who had directed the 1950 newsreel compilation *Fifty Years Before Your Eyes,* turned the compilation movie into a tool for preserving—and reviving—fictional films. His

1957 compilation *The Golden Age of Comedy* featured choice clips of silent classics starring Laurel and Hardy, Will Rogers, and Harry Langdon. It revived interest in the great silent comedians, prompting Charlie Chaplin to release *The Chaplin Revue* (1958), which was simply three shorts strung together with some behind-the-scenes footage (actually, earlier Chaplin shorts had been packaged together as early as 1938). The following year, Youngson returned with another superior silent comedy compilation, *When Comedy Was King*. In the 1960s, he raided the studios' vaults and produced: *The Days of Thrills and Laughter* (1961), *Thirty Years of Fun* (1963), *MGM's Big Parade of Comedy* (1964), *Laurel and Hardy's Laughing 20's* (1965), *The Further Perils of Laurel and Hardy* (1967), and *Four Clowns* (1970). Youngson died in 1974, the same year in which Jack Haley, Jr., produced the highly-successful MGM musical compilation *That's Entertainment*. Haley's film was a financial bonanza for MGM, costing next to nothing and providing glamorous publicity for the studio's 50th anniversary. The inevitable sequel *That's Entertainment Part 2* appeared in 1976, this one combining the musical clips with "straight" scenes (e.g. Garbo playing *Camille*). Haley added a belated third installment to his MGM compilation series with 1985's *That's Dancing*. Despite a marvelous selection of dance footage, it failed to attract the young audiences which flocked to the contemporary hit *Flashdance* (1983). Although Youngson and Haley's compilations are the most fondly remembered, other filmmakers have utilized the format effectively. Warner Bros. compiled its best Looney Tunes cartoons and released them into the theatres as *Bugs Bunny, Superstar* (1979), *The Great American Chase* (1979), *Bugs Funny's 3rd Movie: 1001 Rabbit Tales* (1982), and *Daffy Duck's Movie: Fantastic Island* (1983). The funniest segments from Sid Caesar's classic TV series "Your Show of Shows" surfaced in the 1973 compilation *Ten from Your Show of Shows* (1973). A year earlier, skits from British television's "Monty Python's Flying Circus" came stateside as *And Now for Something Completely Different*. Science fiction and horror film retrospectives have reached the screen as *It Came from Hollywood* (1982) and *Terror in the Aisles* (1984). *It's Showtime* (1976) was an enjoyable compilation of animal movie clips, highlighted by a canine rendition of "Singin' in the Rain."

Charlie Chaplin Carnival (1938)	*Laughter* (1961)
Charlie Chaplin Cavalcade (1938)	*Harold Lloyd's World of Comedy* (1962)
Charlie Chaplin Festival (1938)	*Harold Lloyd's Funny Side of Life* (1963)
The Golden Age of Comedy (1957)	*Laugh with Max Linder* (1963)
The Chaplin Revue (1958)	*Thirty Years of Fun* (1963)
When Comedy Was King (1959)	*The Great Chase* (1963)
The Days of Thrills and	*Marilyn* (1963)
	MGM's Big Parade of Comedy

(1964)
The Love Goddesses (1965)
The World of Abbott and Costello (1965)
Laurel and Hardy's Laughing 20's (1965)
The Further Perils of Laurel and Hardy (1967)
The Crazy World of Laurel and Hardy (1967)
Four Clowns (1970)
And Now for Something Completely Different (1972)
Ten Years from Your Show of Shows (1973)
That's Entertainment (1974)

Bugs Bunny, Superstar (1975)
It's Showtime (1976)
That's Entertainment Part 2 (1976)
America at the Movies (1976)
The Great American Chase (aka *The Bugs Bunny/Roadrunner Movie*) (1979)
Bugs Bunny's 3rd Movie: 1001 Rabbit Tales (1982)
It Came from Hollywood (1982)
Daffy Duck's Movie: Fantastic Island (1983)
Terror in the Aisles (1984)
That's Dancing (1985)
The Puppetoon Movie (1987)

Composers (Classical)

Hollywood-produced biographies, supplemented by a handful of imports, have glossed over the history of classical music by focusing almost exclusively on a select number of composers. A French director (Julien Duvivier) made Hollywood's first major composer biography of the sound era with 1938's *The Great Waltz*, the story of Johann Strauss (the Younger) and his unforgettable "The Blue Danube." Co-star/soprano Miliza Korjus and lyricist Oscar Hammerstein II turned two Strauss melodies into the popular hits "I'm in Love with Vienna" and "One Day When We Were Young." Despite the film's success, seven years elapsed before the Chopin biography *A Song to Remember* (1945) made a star of Cornel Wilde and inspired a trio of imitations. Stewart Granger played violinist virtuoso/composer Niccolo Paganini in *The Magic Bow* (1946). *Song of Love* (1947) cast Katharine Hepburn and Paul Henried as Clara and Robert Schumann and Robert Walker as their friend Johannes Brahms. Jean-Pierre Aumont played Rimsky-Korsakov in 1947's campy *Song of Scheherezade*, which dealt primarily with the composer's infatuation with a Spanish-Moroccan dancer (Yvonne De Carlo). Occasional films about classical composers continued to appear during the next two decades. However, a new trend did not emerge until Ken Russell introduced his unconventional biographies in the early 1970s. Russell made his mark on British television in the 1960s with critically-acclaimed documentaries and biographies of Wagner, Debussy, and Elgar. His theatrical films have been greeted less enthusiastically due to his penchant for excess (the descriptive publicity line for his 1971 Tchaikovsky biography *The Music Lovers* was: "The story of a homosexual who married a nymphomaniac"). Russell's rollercoaster style has managed to confuse his critics for years. His 1974 biopic *Mahler* earned praise for its intelligence and restraint, but the director's excesses were on display again in the following year's *Lisztomania*, a rock version of Liszt's life starring The Who's Roger Daltrey. In the post–Russell era, Czech director Milos Forman has made the biggest impact with his splendid 1984 Best Picture *Amadeus*. Peter Shaffer adapted the film from his own play about the conflict between Mozart contemporary Salieri and the Master himself.

The Great Waltz (1938) (Johann Strauss)
The Great Victor Herbert (1939)
The Great Mr. Handel (1942)
A Song to Remember (1945) (Chopin)
The Magic Bow (1947) (Niccolo Paganini)
Song of Love (1947) (Robert Schumann)
Song of Scheherazade (1947) (Rimsky-Korsakov)
The Great Gilbert and Sullivan (aka *The Story of Gilbert and Sullivan*) (1953)
Deep in My Heart (1954) (Sigmund Romberg)
Magic Fire (1956) (Richard Wagner)
Song Without End (1960) (Franz Liszt)
The Magnificent Rebel (1962) (Beethoven)
The Waltz King (1963) (Johann Strauss)
Song of Norway (1970) (Edvard Grieg)
The Music Lovers (1971) (Peter Tchaikovsky)
The Great Waltz (1972) (Johann Strauss)
Ludwig (1973) (Beethoven)
Mahler (1974)
Lisztomania (1975) (Liszt)
Wagner (1983) (Richard Wagner)
Amadeus (1984) (Wolfgang Amadeus Mozart)
Spring Symphony (1984) (Clara Schumann)

Composers (Popular)

Few popular composers have lived long enough (or been famous enough) to see their life stories reach the screen. However, there have been some noteworthy exceptions: Richard Rodgers was in his prime when 1948's *Words and Music* was released and Cole Porter was still composing when Cary Grant played him in *Night and Day* (1945). Jerome Kern died during the filming of *Till the Clouds Roll By* (1945) and George M. Cohan passed away the year that *Yankee Doodle Dandy* was released (1942). Turn-of-the-century songwriters have proven to be popular film subjects, with 20th Century–Fox specializing in them in the 1940s. Victor Mature played Gay '90s Broadway composer Paul Dresser in *My Gal Sal* (1942); singer Dick Haymes was songwriter Ernest R. Ball in Damon Runyon's *Irish Eyes Are Smiling;* and Mark Stevens played Joseph E. Howard in *I Wonder Who's Kissing Her Now* (1947). Many fields of music are represented by merely a movie or two, as evidenced by the biographies of folk songwriter Woody Guthrie *(Bound for Glory)*, minstrel man Dan Emmett *(Dixie)*, and marching band composer John Philip Sousa *(Stars and Stripes Forever)*.

89

Swanee River (1939) (Stephen
Foster)
My Gal Sal (1942) (Paul
Dresser)
Yankee Doodle Dandy (1942)
(George M. Cohan)
Dixie (1943) (Dan Emmett)
Irish Eyes Are Smiling (1944)
(Ernest R. Ball)
Rhapsody in Blue (1945)
(George Gershwin)
Night and Day (1945) (Cole
Porter)
Till the Clouds Roll By (1946)
(Jerome Kern)

I Wonder Who's Kissing Her
Now (1947) (Joe Howard)
Words and Music (1948)
(Rodgers and Hart)
I Dream of Jeannie (1952)
(Stephen Foster)
I'll See You in My Dreams
(1952) (Gus Kahn)
Stars and Stripes Forever (1953)
(John Philip Sousa)
St. Louis Blues (1958) (W.C.
Handy)
Bound for Glory (1976) (Woody
Guthrie)

Computers

The fact that the HAL 9000 remains the best-remembered character from
2001: A Space Odyssey is a testament to the dramatic potential of movie
computers. Given a speaking voice and a significant role, the computer
can effectively dominate his human co-stars in interesting science fiction
films like The Forbin Project (1970). However, the early film appearances
of computers showed little sign of their potential. A nuclear brain called
Novac took control of a secret subterranean laboratory in 1954's Gog. Unfortunately, the computer's "artificial intelligence" turned out to be enemy
agent programming. Humans manipulated the computers in Desk Set
(1957) and The Honeymoon Machine (1961) for comedic purposes. Then
in 1965, the computer took a giant step forward with Jean-Luc Godard's
dense, futuristic thriller Alphaville. Godard presented a bleak world of
emotionless people controlled by a super-computer. Stanley Kubrick made
HAL more human-like in 1968's 2001, giving the computer a warm personality and a friendly voice ("Everything's under control, Dave"). But
HAL nevertheless took a turn for the worse and sought to eliminate his
human colleagues to gain control of a space station. The super-computer
in 1970's The Forbin Project displayed larger-scale ambitions, setting its
sights on world domination. It achieved that goal, too, by linking up with
its Soviet counterpart and thus controlling the defense systems for both
the U.S. and the Soviet Union. Proteus IV, the computer in 1977's
Demon Seed, was more concerned with propagating itself than with controlling the world. To that end, it trapped its creator's wife (Julie Christie)
in her house and "raped" her. Another computer, named Edgar, did not
go that far, but he too found himself attracted to his owner's love interest
in 1984's Electric Dreams. Less interesting computers have played small
parts in many movies. College students used a computer to create a line of
credit for an imaginary man in the 1971 TV-movie Paper Man. An

electrical accident dumped a computer's memory banks into college student Kurt Russell's brain in Disney's *The Computer Wore Tennis Shoes* (1967). George Segal had a small computer surgically implanted into his brain, with horrifying results, in 1974's *The Terminal Man.* Two teens showed the power of the personal computer when they used one to create gorgeous Kelly LeBrock in 1985's *Weird Science.* See also **Robots; Androids and Cyborgs.**

Gog (1954)
Desk Set (aka *His Other Woman*) (1957)
The Honeymoon Machine (1961)
Alphaville (1965)
Billion Dollar Brain (1967)
2001: A Space Odyssey (1968)
The Computer Wore Tennis Shoes (1969)
The Forbin Project (aka *Colossus: The Forbin Project*) (1970)
Paper Man (1971 TVM)
The Terminal Man (1974)
Dark Star (1975)
Demon Seed (1977)
Institute for Revenge (1979 TVM)
Alien (1979)
Tron (1982)
WarGames (1983)
Electric Dreams (1984)
Deadly Impact (1985)
Weird Science (1985)
Jumpin' Jack Flash (1986)

Concert Movies

The filmed rock 'n' roll concert came into vogue in the early 1970s, though technically 1969's *Monterey Pop* ushered in the new genre with lively performances by The Mamas and the Papas, Janis Joplin, and others. *Woodstock* and *Gimme Shelter* are the best-known concert films, both for their music and social commentary. The Rolling Stones have starred in more movies than any other rock act, with *Gimme Shelter, Let's Spend the Night Together, The T.A.M.I. Show,* and *Ladies & Gentlemen, The Rolling Stones.* Surprisingly, the genre has acquired a certain appeal for well-known, contemporary directors—Martin Scorsese directed a documentary about The Band called *The Last Waltz,* while Jonathan Demme helmed the Talking Heads' *Stop Making Sense* (1984). The latter film was one of only a handful made during the 1980s, signalling that young rock fans preferred the free footage provided by MTV. Nevertheless, concert films still appear occasionally, as evidenced by U2's 1988 release *Rattle and Hum.* Rob Reiner's *This Is Spinal Tap* tells the history of a fictitious group and is a hilarious parody of rock documentaries and concert films.

Jazz on a Summer Day (1959)
The T.A.M.I. Show (1964)
The Big T.N.T. Show (1966)
Don't Look Back (1967)
Monterey Pop (1969)
Woodstock (1970)
Gimme Shelter (1970)
Popcorn (1970)
Johnny Cash: The Man, His World, His Music (1970)
Mad Dogs and Englishmen (aka *Joe Cocker: Mad Dogs and*

Englishmen) (1971)
Celebration at Big Sur (1971)
Soul to Soul (1971)
Elvis on Tour (1972)
Fillmore (1972)
Concert for Bangladesh (1972)
Let the Good Times Roll (1973)
Ladies and Gentlemen, The Rolling Stones (1975)
The Song Remains the Same (1976) (Led Zeppelin)
The Last Waltz (1977)
Rust Never Sleeps (1979) (Neil Young)
Divine Madness (1980) (Bette Midler)
Rockshow (1980) (Paul McCartney)
No Nukes (aka *The Muse Concert: No Nukes*) (1980)
Heartland Reggae (1980)
Emerson, Lake and Palmer in Concert (1981)
Let's Spend the Night Together (1982)
Gospel (1982)
Stop Making Sense (1984) (The Talking Heads)
Bring on the Night (1985) (Sting)
Home of the Brave (1986) (Laurie Anderson)
Hail! Hail! Rock 'n' Roll (aka *Chuck Berry Hail! Hail! Rock 'n' Roll*) (1987)
Big Time (1988)
Depeche Mode 101 (1989)

Confessions... Series

Only the first of this feeble series of British sex farces was released in the U.S. Reviews were unkind, with the New York Times commenting that *Confessions of a Window Cleaner* "reeks of something...once called Swinging London." Still, the movies are now shown regularly on pay-cable as "adults-only" features. Actor Robin Askwith was the principal series regular. Sadly, the films also featured faded British stars like Diana Dors *(Confessions of a Driving Instructor)*.

Confessions of a Window Cleaner (1973)
Confessions of a Pop Singer (1975)
Confessions of a Driving Instructor (1976)
Confessions from a Holiday Camp (1977)

Courts Martial

Several fine courtroom dramas have revolved around military courts martial. Stanley Kubrick's chilling *Paths of Glory* detailed the plight of three French soldiers tried for cowardice during World War I after their doomed mission failed. In terms of emotional power, its only rival is the incisive 1979 Australian picture *Breaker Morant*. This potent drama, set during the Boer War, also concerned three soldiers facing court martial as scapegoats. Tom Courtenay played court martial defendants in *Private Potter* (1962) and *King and Country* (1964). In the first film, he portrayed a soldier, accused of cowardice, who claimed to have seen God. In the World War I–set *King and Country*, Dirk Bogarde defended Courtenay of a desertion charge. Richard Basehart and Lee Marvin gave strong performances as soldiers facing courts martial during the Korean War in *Time Limit* (1957) and *Sergeant Ryker* (1968), respectively. Herman Wouk's Pulitzer Prize–winning novel *The Caine Mutiny* (1954) climaxed in a court martial, with Van Johnson and Robert Francis as the naval officers who rebelled against Humphrey Bogart's neurotic Captain Queeg. The fact-based *Sergeant Matlovich vs. the U.S. Air Force* (1978) chronicled a homosexual serviceman's struggle to remain in the military. *The Winslow Boy* (1950) offered a fascinating account of the fight for a young boy's right to a trial after expulsion from a British military academy. The British officers stationed in India in *Conduct Unbecoming* (1975) conducted their own court martial when they suspected one of the group of perverse acts. Bradford Dillman and Peter Graves starred in a 1966 TV series called "Court-Martial," set during World War II.

The Winslow Boy (1950)	*Keller* (1961)
The Caine Mutiny (1954)	*Private Potter* (1962)
Court Martial (aka *Carrington VC*) (1954)	*Billy Budd* (1962)
	King and Country (1964)
The Court Martial of Billy Mitchell (1955)	*The Man in the Middle* (1964)
	Sergeant Ryker (1968)
The Rack (1956)	*Conduct Unbecoming* (1975)
Paths of Glory (1957)	*Sergeant Matlovich vs. the U.S. Air Force* (1978 TVM)
Time Limit (1957)	
Sergeant Rutledge (1960)	*Breaker Morant* (1979)
The Court Martial of Major	

Crabs and Lobsters

Most movie crabs have probably appeared on dinner plates, but there have been a few exceptions. A giant pink crab, animated by special effects wizard Ray Harryhausen, had a choice scene in 1961's *Mysterious Island*. Yet, even it was killed, boiled, and devoured. The title creatures of *Attack of the Crab Monsters* (1956) ate human heads which enabled them to telepathically lure more human prey for supper entrees. Still another giant crab washed ashore in 1982's *Night of the Claw* (aka *Island Claws*). The shadow of an alien crab-like creature accompanied the title visitors to Earth in 1959's *Teenagers from Outer Space*. Edible, normal-sized crabs and lobsters have been the subjects of restaurant business dramas *(King Crab)*, lobster fisherman sagas *(High Tide at Noon)*, and even a Doris Day comedy *(It Happened to Jane)*.

Attack of the Crab Monsters (1956)	*Mysterious Island* (1961)
	The Lost Continent (1968)
High Tide at Noon (1957)	*Night of the Claw* (aka *Island Claws*) (1982)
Teenagers from Outer Space (1959)	
	King Crab (1980 TVM)
It Happened to Jane (aka *Twinkle and Shine*) (1959)	*Lobster Man from Mars* (1989)
	The Little Mermaid (1989)

Crane, Bill

Universal made three Crane mysteries in the late 1930s as part of its "Crime Club" series. The intent was to develop "B" movies from popular, but lesser-known, detectives. Author Jonathan Latimer's Bill Crane certainly fit the bill. A private eye with a drinking problem, Crane wandered through a downbeat world layered with cynicism. Such an existence would make Sam Spade and Philip Marlowe genre legends in later movies. Preston Foster played Crane.

The Westland Case (1937)   *The Last Warning* (1938)
The Lady in the Morgue (1938)

The Creature from the Black Lagoon

The Gill Man (as he's fondly known) was the brainchild of producer William Alland, who was inspired by a vague South American legend about a prehistoric monster that roamed the swamps. Universal Pictures spared no expense on 1954's *Creature from the Black Lagoon*, shooting the film in 3-D (q.v.) and investing $12,000 in the creature suit. The story, another reworking of "Beauty and the Beast," sends a scientific expedition down the Amazon where it discovers a man/fish creature with a fondness for human women. Like Kong, the Creature was a sympathetic monster, who simply asked to be left alone. But Universal had other ideas. The Gill Man was back in 1955's *Revenge of the Creature*, in which he's captured and transported to a Florida aquarium before female trouble again causes his demise. Worse was yet to come. He becomes a land mammal — thanks to unwanted surgery — in 1956's *The Creature Walks Among Us*, the final film in the trilogy. In the movie's closing scene, the Gill Man walks into the ocean, apparently aware that he will drown in the water that was once his home. Ricou Browning played the Creature in all three movies, although Ben Chapman handled the land scenes in the first film and Don Megowan was the "transformed" Creature in the last. A generic Creature (looking suspiciously like a Black Lagoon resident) surfaced in 1987's juvenile adventure *The Monster Squad*.

The Creature from the Black   *The Creature Walks Among Us*
    Lagoon (1954)   (1956)
The Revenge of the Creature   *The Monster Squad* (1987)
    (1955)

The Crime Doctor

Despite a past clouded by amnesia, Dr. Robert Ordway became a leading criminal psychologist — only to discover that he was once a criminal himself. Armed with "insider knowledge" of how the criminal mind works, Ordway repaid society by bringing villains to justice. Such was the premise for this series of slightly offbeat detective films starring Warner Baxter as Ordway. The series originated from Max Marcin's long-running radio program and resulted in ten films over a six-year period. Baxter, an Oscar winner as the Cisco Kid in 1929's *In Old Arizona*, was the only actor ever to play the Crime Doctor.

The Crime Doctor (1943)	*The Crime Doctor's Manhunt* (1946)
The Crime Doctor's Strangest Case (1943)	*Just Before Dawn* (1946)
Shadows in the Night (1944)	*The Millerson Case* (1947)
The Crime Doctor's Courage (1945)	*The Crime Doctor's Gamble* (1948)
The Crime Doctor's Warning (1945)	*The Crime Doctor's Diary* (1949)

Crusoe, Robinson

Daniel Defoe's classic novel about a man's struggle for survival on an isolated island influenced so many books and films that literary critics created a term for the genre — Robinsonnade. Spanish surrealist director Luis Bunuel made the best screen version, a remarkably straightforward, lyrical 1952 film starring Dan O'Herlihy. Douglas Fairbanks updated the tale as a gent whose island existence was the result of a bet in 1932's *Mr. Robinson Crusoe*. Amanda Blake played the title role in 1954's *Miss Robin Crusoe*, an unexceptional female variation, and Dick Van Dyke updated the story for children in Disney's *Lt. Robin Crusoe, USN* (1966). *Man Friday* (1976) gradually reversed the roles of master Crusoe (Peter O'Toole) and manservant Friday (Richard Roundtree). Despite its promising premise, the film deteriorated into an unpleasant affair. A more successful twist was displayed in 1964's *Robinson Crusoe on Mars*, a colorful adventure which substituted a barren planet for the typical remote island. It was remade as *Enemy Mine* in 1986 with Dennis Quaid and Lou Gossett, Jr. *Crusoe* (1989) was a return to Defoe's original story, though Aidan Quinn's hero was younger than his predecessors. Many films, such as *Swept Away* (1975) and *Castaway* (1987), have borrowed the shipwrecked plot. Indeed, Defoe's original even predated Wyss's *The Swiss Family Robinson* and thus indirectly influenced film and TV variations of that novel — to include "Gilligan's Island." See also **Islands.**

Mr. Robinson Crusoe (1932)	*Swept Away* (aka *Swept Away by an Unusual Destiny in the Blue Sea of August*) (1975)
Adventures of Robinson Crusoe (aka *Robinson Crusoe*) (1952)	
Miss Robin Crusoe (1954)	*Man Friday* (1976)
Robinson Crusoe on Mars (1964)	*Enemy Mine* (1986)
	Castaway (1987)
Lt. Robin Crusoe, USN (1966)	*Crusoe* (1989)

Cyclops

These one-eyed mythological Titans who forged thunderbolts for Zeus have been largely misrepresented in their few film appearances. Kirk

Douglas fought one as *Ulysses* (1955) and special effects genius Ray Harryhausen brought one to life with thrilling results in his classic fantasy *The Seventh Voyage of Sinbad* (1958). However, the title creature in Bert I. Gordon's contemporary sci-fi feature *Cyclops* (1957) was just a 50-foot tall man (Dean Parkins) with a flab of skin covering one eye. Parkins played a similar creature in Gordon's *War of the Colossal Beast* (1958). Just to confuse matters, this latter film bore no releation to *Cyclops* (although the creatures look quite similar), but it *was* a sequel to Gordon's non-cyclops picture *The Amazing Colossal Man* (1957). A gentle cyclops warrior, considerably shorter (at about eight feet), aided Ken Marshall on a quest to save his beloved princess in *Krull* (1983). Albert Dekker played the devious *Dr. Cyclops* (1940), a mad scientist obsessed with shrinking humans. The film featured nary a cyclops, its title being simply a reference to the doctor's poor eyesight. See also **Giant People; Gorgons.**

Ulysses (1955)
Cyclops (1957)
The Seventh Voyage of Sinbad (1958)
War of the Colossal Beast (1958)

Atlas Against the Cyclops (aka *Monster from the Unknown World; Maciste nella Terror dei Ciclopi*) (1961)
Krull (1983)

Dancer, Joe

Three years after his "Baretta" series went off the air, Robert Blake returned to star as rugged private detective Joe Dancer in the 1981 TV-movie, *The Big Black Pill,* a pilot for a new show. The movie drew insufficient ratings to warrant a series, but Blake refused to give up. He played Dancer in two additional films. The effort proved fruitless, however, for a regular series still failed to materialize.

The Big Black Pill (aka *Joe Dancer*) (1981 TVM)
The Monkey Mission (1981 TVM)
Murder 1, Dancer 0 (1983 TVM)

Daninsky, Waldemar (El Hombre Lobo)

Paul Naschy, Spain's number one film star of the 1970s, created and portrayed the Polish werewolf Waldemar Daninsky—better known in his homeland as El Hombre Lobo. Naschy's films, like the better Mexican horror movies of the 1960s, stressed atmosphere at the expense of logic. Additionally, Naschy believed in the Mexican adage that horror can be multiplied by increasing the number of monsters. El Hombre Lobo encountered vampires in *Mark of the Werewolf,* Jekyll/Hyde in *Dr. Jekyll and the Werewolf,* and aliens, a mummy, the Frankenstein Monster, and Dracula in the monster all-star epic *The Man Who Came from Ummo.* Despite his European popularity, Naschy (real name Jacinto Molina) has found little fame in the U.S. For its American release, 1968's 3-D *Mark of the Werewolf* was typically shown in 2-D under the misleading title *Frankenstein's Bloody Terror* and minus 45 minutes of footage. See also **Werewolves.**

> *Mark of the Werewolf* (aka *La Marca del Hombre Lobo; Frankenstein's Bloody Terror; Hell's Creatures*) (1968)
> *Nights of the Werewolf* (aka *Las Noches del Hombre Lobo*) (1969)
> *The Werewolf's Shadow* (aka *La Noche de Walpurgis; The Werewolf vs. the Vampire Women*) (1970)
> *The Man Who Came from Ummo* (aka *El Hombre Que Vino de Ummo; Assignment Terror; Dracula vs. Frankenstein*) (1970)
> *Fury of the Wolfman* (aka *La Furia del Hombre Lobo*) (1970)
> *Dr. Jekyll and the Werewolf* (aka *Dr. Jekyll y el Hombre Lobo*) (1971)
> *Curse of the Devil* (aka *El Retorno de la Walpurgis*) (1973)
> *The Werewolf and the Yeti* (aka *La Maldicion de la Bestia; Night of the Howling Beast*) (1976)

Dates in Title

In addition to the eight *Friday the 13th* films (q.v.), there's also been *Saturday the 14th, D-Day the Sixth of June, The Night of January 16th,* and *September 30, 1955.* The latter film dealt with how James Dean's death (on that date) affected a fanatical fan (Richard Thomas). The movie was originally titled *9-30-55* and later retitled *24 Hours of the Rebel* for TV. See also **Years in Title.**

The Daughters of Joshua Cabe

When fur trapper Buddy Ebsen suddenly needs a "family" to hold on to his homestead, he hires a prostitute, a thief, and a pickpocket to pose as his daughters. Karen Valentine, Lesley Ann Warren, and Sandra Dee played the original *Daughters of Joshua Cabe* in this unexpectedly popular 1972 "ABC Movie of the Week." Two subpar sequels followed, each featuring entirely different casts.

> *The Daughters of Joshua Cabe* (1972 TVM)
> *The Daughters of Joshua Cabe Return* (1975 TVM)
> *New Daughters of Joshua Cabe* (1976 TVM)

The Dead End Kids *see* The Bowery Boys

Deafness

The world of the deaf has received little attention in film. Like blindness (q.v.), it has been misused as a plot gimmick in syrupy romances. Opera star Mario Lanza found love with a deaf girl in the massively sentimental *For the First Time.* Loretta Young played a deaf socialite in love with poor physician Alan Ladd in the 1944 romance *And Now Tomorrow*. Five years earlier, Young had portrayed a deaf person with more conviction in *The Story of Alexander Graham Bell*. *Johnny Belinda* (1948) hinted at the unjust prejudice experienced by deaf people. The 1952 British film *The Crash of Silence* opened new vistas with its touching, semidocumentary look into the world of a deaf girl. Few films about deafness have matched its power. *Silent Victory: The Kitty O'Neil Story* (1979) was an inspirational real-life account of a deaf woman who became a successful stunt person (q.v.). The Emmy Award–winning *Love Is Never Silent* (1985) co-starred Phyllis Frelich and Ed Waterstreet, acclaimed performers from the National Theatre for the Deaf. Deaf actress Marlee Matlin won a Best Actress Oscar for 1986's *Children of a Lesser God,* an unsentimental story of the love between an independent-minded deaf woman and a teacher of the deaf (William Hurt). Despite its exploitative title, 1975's *Deafula* was merely the famous vampire story told in sign language.

The Story of Alexander Graham Bell (aka *The Modern Miracle*) (1939)
And Now Tomorrow (1944)
Johnny Belinda (1948)
The Crash of Silence (aka *Mandy*) (1952)
Man of a Thousand Faces (1957)
For the First Time (1959)
The Miracle Worker (1962)
Gigot (1962)
The Heart Is a Lonely Hunter (1965)
Psych-out (1968)
Deafula (1975)
Silent Victory: The Kitty O'Neil Story (1979 TVM)
The Miracle Worker (1979 TVM)
Johnny Belinda (1982 TVM)
Hear No Evil (1982 TVM)
Love Is Never Silent (1985 TVM)
Children of a Lesser God (1986)
Crazy Moon (aka *Huggers*) (1986)
Bridge to Silence (1989 TVM)
See No Evil, Hear No Evil (1989)

Dear Ruth

A teenage girl pens passionate love letters to a soldier and encloses her older sister's photograph. When his leave comes due, he decides to pay her a visit. The casting of William Holden (the soldier), Joan Caulfield (the older sister), and Mona Freeman (the younger sister) propelled the routinely-plotted *Dear Ruth* into one of Paramount's biggest hits of 1947. In the belated sequel, *Dear Wife* (1949), newlyweds Caulfield and Holden encounter family problems when troublesome Freeman sets up Holden as a rival Senatorial candidate to the girls' father (Edward Arnold). Freeman had the spotlight to herself in 1951's *Dear Brat*. Holden had gone on to bigger parts *(Sunset Boulevard)* and Caulfield to television briefly (1953's "My Favorite Husband") and then semiretirement. See also **Letters.**

Dear Ruth (1947)
Dear Wife (1949)
Dear Brat (1951)

Death Incarnate

The personification of Death has been portrayed in various ways, as a lonely romantic, a beautiful temptress, and a hideous skeleton-creature greedy for souls. Fredric March played a curious Death anxious to understand why humans cling so desperately to life in *Death Takes a Holiday* (1934). He takes a vacation to investigate the phenomena and falls in love, while the world suffers during his leave of absence — for dying people can no longer die. Feisty Lionel Barrymore proved more than a match for Cedric Hardwicke's Mr. Brink (aka Death), by literally chasing Death up a tree in the 1939 comedy *On Borrowed Time*. In Ingmar Bergman's *The Seventh Seal* (1956), Max Von Sydow played a 14th century knight who matches wits with Death in a game of chess. Death was among the uninvited guests at evil Prince Prospero's (Vincent Price) masquerade ball in Roger Corman's stylish *Masque of the Red Death.* Jessica Lange made an elegant Death in Bob Fosse's *All That Jazz,* while a dreadful decaying Death swarmed anxiously about John Neville whenever he was about to give up on life in *The Adventures of Baron Munchausen.* On television, Robert Redford played Mr. Death in the memorable 1962 "Nothing in the Dark" episode of "The Twilight Zone."

Death Takes a Holiday (1934)
On Borrowed Time (1939)
Orpheus (1949)
The Seventh Seal (1956)
Masque of the Red Death (1964)
Death Takes a Holiday (1971 TVM)

All That Jazz (1979)
Monty Python's the Meaning of Life (1983)
The Adventures of Baron Munchausen (1989)
Edgar Allan Poe's Masque of the Red Death (1989)

Death Wish

Charles Bronson's biggest hit cast him as a mild-mannered architect transformed into an emotionless vigilante after a gang of punks attacked his wife and daughter. Some critics condemned the film's questionable ethics, with *N.Y. Times* reviewer Vincent Canby writing: "The movie seems to have been made for no reason except to exploit its audiences' urban paranoia and vestigal fascination with violence for its own sake." Even writer Brian Garfield, on whose novel it is based, attacked the film for advocating vigilantism. He later appealed to CBS to not broadcast the film in prime time (which it did). Despite the controversy, *Death Wish* was a blockbuster and some tabloids even claimed that it briefly lowered the crime rate in New York City. Still, Bronson and director Michael Winner avoided making a sequel for eight years. They should have kept it that way. *Death Wish II* was an embarrassing rehash of the original, transplanted to Los Angeles. Two additional Bronson sequels were not much better. See also **Vigilantes**.

99

Death Wish (1974)
Death Wish II (1982)
Death Wish III (1985)

Death Wish IV: The Crack-down (1987)

Dentists

The movie dentist has experienced a checkered career since his extravagant 1923 debut in Erich von Stroheim's nine-hour marathon silent movie *Greed*. Gibson Gowland played von Stroheim's lead, an appropriately greedy lower-class dentist with an illegal practice (a fellow dentist is called "Painless" Potter). However, the bad side of dentistry is better represented by murderer Ralph Bellamy in *Footsteps in the Dark* and Nazi torture specialist Laurence Olivier (who drills holes in healthy teeth) in *Marathon Man*. Sadistic dentists have been played for laughs in both the 1960 and 1986 versions of *The Little Shop of Horrors*. Jack Nicholson was a masochistic patient in the former, while Steve Martin enthusiastically sang "I'm a Dentist" in the latter. Bob Hope played a dentist who accidentally became a gunslinging Western hero in 1948's *The Paleface*. It spawned the Hope sequel *Son of Paleface* (1952) and the Don Knotts remake *The Shakiest Gun in the West* (1968). The murder of a playboy dentist set the mystery into motion in 1985's lighthearted affair *Compromising Positions*. Government agent Peter Falk drafted dentist Alan Arkin into the spy business in *The In-Laws* (1979). And W.C. Fields portrayed cinema's most perverse dentist in his hilarious pre–Hays Code short *The Dentist* (1932). His struggle to pull a tooth results in some very compromising—and funny—positions with a female patient.

Greed (1923)
The Dentist (1932)
Aren't Men Beasts! (1937)
Footsteps in the Dark (1941)
The Strawberry Blonde (1941)
The Great Moment (1944)
One Sunday Afternoon (1948)
The Paleface (1948)
The Fat Man (1951)
Son of Paleface (1952)
Bells Are Ringing (1960)
Dentist in the Chair (1960)
Come Dance with Me (1960)
The Little Shop of Horrors (1960)
Get on With It (aka *Dentist on the Job*; *Carry on TV*) (1961)
The Shakiest Gun in the West (1968)
Cactus Flower (1969)
Marathon Man (1976)
The In-Laws (1979)
Ten (1979)
Straight Through the Heart (1983)
Compromising Positions (1985)
The Little Shop of Horrors (1986)

The Devil

Mr. Scratch, Beelzebub, Mephistopheles, Lucifer, Satan—the Devil has been known by many names throughout history. And on the screen, he has been portrayed in many guises by a diverse group of performers. Walter Huston played a cunning, though admittedly likable, Mr. Scratch in 1941's *All That Money Can Buy,* adapted from Stephen Vincent Benet's 19th century New England variation of *Faust*. Although ultimately out-witted by lawyer Daniel Webster (Edward Arnold), Scratch displayed a sharp talent for turning the tables. When Webster demanded an American jury for his client, Scratch produced 12 of history's worst criminals and then made the point: "Dastard, liar, traitor, knave... Americans all." Peter Cook's George Spiggot (aka The Devil) proved equally adept at crafty tricks in 1967's *Bedazzled,* an hilarious updating of Faust with Dudley Moore as the woeful short-order cook who sells his soul for seven wishes. At one point, Moore's inability to be specific with his wishes results in his transformation into a nun (i.e. he wishes to be in love with a woman in a place where no men are around). The Devil has been played for comedy in less memorable films as well, as portrayed by Vin-cent Price in *The Story of Mankind* (1957), Christopher Lee in *Poor Devil* (1973), Bill Cosby in *The Devil and Max Devlin* (1981), and George Burns (in both title roles) in *Oh God, You Devil!* (1984). The Devil, as the in-carnation of evil, has taken a back seat to his disciples in most horror films. Still, Robert DeNiro made an eerie villain—one Mr. Lou Cipher—in the moody horror/mystery *Angel Heart* (1987). Soap star Susan Lucci proved that the Devil could easily be a woman in the 1984 TV-movie *In-vitation to Hell*. Victor Buono made an unexpected appearance as the Devil beneath a possessed house in 1978's *The Evil*. His scenes were cut from some prints, indicating that the filmmakers were as confused as the audience in regard to his sudden presence in a haunted house movie. Nigel Kneale's intriguing 1967 sci-fi/fantasy *Five Million Years to Earth* (see **Quatermass**) suggested that the Devil's origins were extraterrestrial. The Devil's son—the Antichrist—first gained prominence in 1976's *The Omen* (q.v.).

The Sorrows of Satan (1927)
All That Money Can Buy (aka *The Devil and Daniel Webster*) (1941)
Cabin in the Sky (1943)
Heaven Can Wait (1943)
Angel on My Shoulder (1946)
Alias Nick Beal (1949)
Meet Mr. Lucifer (1953)
The Story of Mankind (1957)
Damn Yankees (1958)
The Private Lives of Adam and Eve (1960)
Bedazzled (1967)
Five Million Years to Earth (aka *Quatermass and the Pit*) (1967)

Doctor Faustus (1968)
The Devil in Love (1968)
The Devil's Daughter (1972 TVM)
Poor Devil (1973 TVM)
The Sentinel (1977)
The Evil (1978)
The Devil and Max Devlin (1981)
Invitation to Hell (1984 TVM)
Oh God, You Devil! (1984)
Crossroads (1986)
Angel Heart (1987)
Hunk (1987)
Prince of Darkness (1987)

Antichrist

The Omen (1976) *The Visitor* (1979)
The Chosen (aka *Holocaust* *Fear No Evil* (1981)
    2000) (1978)

Dinosaurs

The evolution of the cinematic dinosaur begins and ends with Willis
O'Brien. A master of special effects photography, O'Brien perfected the
stop-motion animation technique used in nearly all the memorable
dinosaur sequences. After stints as a cowboy, prize fighter, and sculptor,
O'Brien made his first dinosaur film in 1917, a short called *The Dinosaur
and the Missing Link*. He filmed his brontosaurus (a jointed wooden
skeleton covered by clay) one frame at a time, moving the model slightly
between each picture to create an illusion of motion. O'Brien continued
making other shorts (e.g. *The Ghost of Slumber Mountain*) and eventually landed the job of special effects creator for *The Lost World* (1925),
an adaptation of Arthur Conan Doyle's novel about a journey into a
prehistoric land. O'Brien's brilliant effects shine even today, especially the
final sequence in which an escaped brontosaurus wrecks havoc in London.
O'Brien went on to create his masterpiece in 1933's *King Kong* (q.v.),
which featured a dynamic struggle between Kong and a Tyrannosaurus
Rex. In 1949, he finally won an Oscar for *Mighty Joe Young*, another
giant ape opus. However, his most cherished projects were never realized.
These included two cowboy/dinosaur scripts called *Creation* and *Gwangi*.
O'Brien eventually sold the idea for the former film, which sadly made it
to the screen as the forgotten, low-budget feature *The Beast of Hollow
Mountain* (1957). However, O'Brien protégé Ray Harryhausen created
some superb animation sequences for the 1969 dinosaur Western *The
Valley of Gwangi*. Harryhausen, the modern master of stop-action animation, was also responsible for the dinosaur that trashed the amusement
park in *The Beast from 20,000 Fathoms* (1953) and the pterodactyl that
snatched Raquel Welch in *One Million Years, B.C.* Of Harryhausen's
rivals, Jim Danforth and David Allen have received the highest marks for
their lifelike creatures in, respectively, *When Dinosaurs Ruled the Earth*
(1970) and *Caveman* (1980). The high cost of stop-motion photography
has limited its use over the years and filmmakers have resorted to alternate
methods for creating dinosaurs. In 1940's *One Million, B.C.*, live lizards
were photographed on miniature sets. The effect was convincing enough
to warrant use of that footage in countless low-budget features. In the
1950s, Japan's special effects wizard Eiji Tsuburaya perfected the man-in-a-
monster suit approach with Toho's *Godzilla* films (see separate entries for
Japanese monsters Godzilla, Ghidrah, Rodan, Mothra, and Gamera).
Finally, animated dinosaurs have appeared in *Fantasia* (the creation of the
world segment) and *The Land Before Time*, a children's film about lost
baby dinos searching for their parents. See also **Cave People**.

The Lost World (1925)	*The Lost World* (1960)
The Savage (1926)	*Dinosaurus* (1960)
King Kong (1933)	*Gorgo* (1961)
One Million B.C. (1940)	*Reptilicus* (1962)
Fantasia (1941)	*One Million Years, B.C.* (1966)
Unknown World (1948)	*When Dinosaurs Ruled the*
Two Lost Worlds (1950)	*Earth* (1969)
The Lost Continent (1951)	*The Valley of Gwangi* (1969)
The Beast from 20,000 Fathoms	*The Last Dinosaur* (1977 TVM)
(1953)	*The Crater Lake Monster* (1977)
King Dinosaur (1955)	*Where Time Began* (1978)
The Animal World (1956)	*Baby...Secret of the Lost*
The Beast of Hollow Mountain	*Legend* (1985)
(1956)	*My Science Project* (1985)
The Giant Behemoth (1959)	*The Land Before Time* (1988)

Dionne Quintuplets *see* Christian, Dr. (Paul)

Dirigibles

The motorized gas-filled aircraft known as dirigibles, airships, zeppelins, and blimps have made irregular screen appearances since airplanes replaced them in the 1930s. Howard Hughes' World War I aerial spectacular *Hell's Angels* (1930) confirmed the birth and signalled the death of the movie dirigible. The zeppelin raid over London, although elaborately staged, paled in comparison to the film's classic airplane dogfights. Dirigible crashes occurred at the climaxes of *The Lost Zeppelin* (1929), *Madam Satan* (1930), *Dirigible* (1931) and *Murder in the Air* (1940). The latter film, which starred Ronald Reagan as secret service agent Brass Bancroft (q.v.), was built around actual footage, obtained by industrious producer Bryan Foy, of a dirigible crashing into the ocean. The airship disaster in *Madame Satan* was preceded by a wild onboard party and followed by a happy ending. Over two decades later, a madman named Robur (Vincent Price) set out to conquer the world from his flying airship fortress, The Albatross, in the 1961 Jules Verne fantasy *Master of the World*. Two realistic films about dirigibles were featured in 1971. *Zeppelin* was a World War I tale of intrigue about an attempt to steal secrets from a German zeppelin factory. The fact-based *The Red Tent* chronicled a disasterous 1928 airship flight over the North Pole (a plot reminiscent of 1929's *The Lost Zeppelin*). Another fact-based drama, 1975's *The Hindenberg*, was about the 1937 New York dirigible explosion that claimed the lives of almost half the passengers and crew. Its weak narrative lead up to a chilling climax featuring actual newsreel footage of the Hindenberg. The familiar sight of a blimp hovering over the Super Bowl was played for suspense in 1977's *Black Sunday*, a presidential assassination thriller. James Bond grappled with a villain aboard an airship over the Golden Gate

Bridge in *A View to a Kill* (1985), while Indiana Jones and his father hijacked a Nazi airplane attached to an airborne dirigible in *Indiana Jones and the Last Crusade* (1989). See also **Balloons, Hot Air.**

Zeppelin Attack on New York (1917)	*Master of the World* (1961)
	The Assassination Bureau (1968)
The Lost Zeppelin (1929)	*Zeppelin* (1971)
Hell's Angels (1930)	*The Red Tent* (1971)
Madame Satan (1930)	*Island at the Top of the World* (1974)
Dirigible (1931)	
Murder in the Air (1940)	*The Hindenberg* (1975)
The Fabulous World of Jules Verne (1958)	*Black Sunday* (1977)
	A View to a Kill (1985)
The Fabulous Baron Munchausen (1961)	*Indiana Jones and the Last Crusade* (1989)

The Dirty Dozen

Robert Aldrich's 1967 original was a solid World War II action film about 12 ruthless criminals offered parole in return for participating in a deadly mission behind German lines. Lee Marvin played the tough major who whipped the gang into top-notch soldiers. For the record, the original dozen were played by: John Cassavetes, Jim Brown, Telly Savalas, Donald Sutherland, Charles Bronson, Trini Lopez, Tom Busby, Colin Maitland, Al Mancini, Stuart Cooper, Ben Carruthers, and Clint Walker. Although the film became MGM's number one grosser of the year, a sequel did not appear until 18 years later—and then as a TV-movie. Probably inspired by the runaway success of 1985's *Rambo,* NBC telecast *The Dirty Dozen: The Next Mission* later that year. Lee Marvin reprised his role as the Dozen's leader and Ernest Borgnine and Richard Jaeckel returned in their original supporting roles. Telly Savalas starred in two more TV-movie sequels before the Fox network introduced the very short-lived "Dirty Dozen" TV series. Interestingly, although the original *Dirty Dozen* spawned a host of imitators in the late 1960s (e.g. *The Devil's Brigade, A Reason to Live, a Reason to Die*), the plot was borrowed from Roger Corman's 1964 quickie *The Secret Invasion.*

The Dirty Dozen (1967)	*Mission* (1987 TVM)
The Dirty Dozen: The Next Mission (1985 TVM)	*The Dirty Dozen: The Fatal Mission* (1988 TVM)
The Dirty Dozen: The Deadly	

Dirty Harry

Clint Eastwood created San Francisco police inspector Harry Callahan, a ruthless distributor of justice, in Don Siegel's influential 1971 action picture *Dirty Harry*. Armed with his trademark .357 magnum pistol, Eastwood/Callahan became the perfect anti-hero for the 1970s, reassuring the public that criminals above the law could—and would—be punished. Not surprisingly, the character mellowed as the series progressed, with Harry even teaming up with a female partner (Tyne Daly) in *The Enforcer*. Ironically, the series' weakest entry, *Sudden Impact,* introduced Harry's infamous quote: "Go ahead...Make my day." Imitators, such as Jack Palance in *One Man Jury* (1978), Sylvester Stallone in 1986's *Cobra* and Steven Seagal in 1988's *Above the Law,* have failed to duplicate Eastwood's success—perhaps because they lack his grimacing humor.

> *Dirty Harry* (1971) *Sudden Impact* (1983)
> *Magnum Force* (1973) *The Dead Pool* (1988)
> *The Enforcer* (1976)

Disaster Movies

Films climaxing in disasters date back to the 1930s—with the earthquake that rocked Gable and Tracy in *San Francisco,* the storm sequence in *Hurricane,* and the locusts that stripped the fields in *The Good Earth.* All these were grand spectacles, but mere movie subplots. The disaster film, as a genre, came into vogue in the early 1970s with the releases of *Airport* and *The Poseidon Adventure.* A canny producer named Irwin Allen exploited the latter film, a tale of an upside-down ocean liner, into a box-office smash ("Who will survive?" ads asked) and quickly became known as the King of Disaster Films. He followed it with the fiery all-star opus *The Towering Inferno* and suddenly disaster films were all the rage. Cheap rip-offs and foreign imports filled America's screens with avalanches, volcanic eruptions, and tidal waves. Then Allen's lavish disaster epic about killer bees, 1978's *The Swarm,* crashed at the boxoffice and the fate of the genre went down with it. Allen's follow-ups, including a *Poseidon* sequel and two made-for-TV films, generated little interest. By the time 1979's *Meteor* came hurling toward Earth, moviegoers treated it like a real disaster—avoiding it like the plague while flocking to the parody *Airplane!* Other disaster movie spoofs include *The Big Bus* (1976), a movie-within-a-movie in *Drive-In,* and the "That's Armaggedon!" segment in *Kentucky Fried Movie* (1977). See also **Airport.**

> *Airport* (1970) *Avalanche* (1978)
> *The Poseidon Adventure* (1972) *Gray Lady Down* (1978)
> *Earthquake* (1974) *The Swarm* (1978)
> *The Towering Inferno* (1974) *Beyond the Poseidon Adventure*
> *The Hindenberg* (1975)   (1979)
> *Tidal Wave* (1975) *Meteor* (1979)
> *The Big Bus* (1976) *Airplane!* (1980)
> *Irwin Allen's Flood* (aka *Flood!*) *When Time Ran Out* (aka
> (1976 TVM)   *Volcano*) (1980)
> *Irwin Allen's Fire* (aka *Fire!*) *Airplane 2: The Sequel* (1982)
> (1977 TVM)

Disguises

The cinema's most renowned master of disguises was probably the murderer in John Huston's stylish murder mystery *The List of Adrian Messenger*. The film employed an interesting gimmick too, in that the crafty criminal (Kirk Douglas) was flanked by four heavily-disguised, heavyweight performers (Frank Sinatra, Tony Curtis, Robert Mitchum, and Burt Lancaster). Rod Steiger wore all the disguises himself as the psychotic murderer in *No Way to Treat a Lady*, while Tony Curtis played a nice guy — and a real-life disguise specialist — in 1960's *The Great Impostor*. Several performers have disguised themselves as the opposit sex for extended periods. Ginger Rogers tried to pass for a boy to save on train fare in *The Major and the Minor* (1942), while Barbra Streisand did it to get an education in *Yentl* (1983). Her charade ran into several complications when she became engaged to Amy Irving and fell in love with best friend Mandy Patinkin. Liv Ullmann experienced a worse fate, however, when her male disguise was revealed in *Pope Joan* (1972). As for male performers, Jack Lemmon and Tony Curtis (again) donned skirts, wigs, and high heels and joined an all-girls' band to elude gangsters in Billy Wilder's *Some Like It Hot*. Dustin Hoffman played an unemployed actor who became a popular soap opera actress in *Tootsie* (1982). Several performers have disguised themselves as *Charley's Aunt* in the various screen versions of Brandon Thomas' play. Movie characters noted for their disguises include Sherlock Holmes (q.v.), Inspector Neilson (John Barrymore) in the Bulldog Drummond films (q.v.), and bumbling Inspector Clouseau (see **Pink Panther Series**). It is difficult to single out a *best* disguise, but Marlene Dietrich was hardly recognizable in a key scene in *Witness for the Prosecution* (1958) and Debra Winger fooled a lot of moviegoers playing a male angel named Emmett in 1987's *Made in Heaven*, going unbilled for her performance.

Sylvia Scarlett (1935)	*The Great Impostor* (1960)
The Phantom Strikes Again (aka *The Gaunt Stranger*) (1938)	*The List of Adrian Messenger* (1963)
Hold That Co-ed (aka *Hold That Girl*) (1938)	*No Way to Treat a Lady* (1968)
Charley's Big-Hearted Aunt (1940)	*Pope Joan* (aka *The Devil's Impostor*) (1972)
Charley's Aunt (aka *Charley's American Aunt*) (1941)	*Sleuth* (1972)
The Major and the Minor (1942)	*Triple Echo* (1973)
The Ringer (1952)	*Toma* (1973 TVM)
Where's Charley? (1952)	*Tootsie* (1982)
Some Like It Hot (1959)	*Yentl* (1983)
Witness for the Prosecution (1958)	*Her Life as a Man* (1984 TVM)
	Just One of the Guys (1985)
	Soul Man (1986)
	He's My Girl (1987)
	Too Outrageous! (1987)

District Attorney, Mr.

Like many film series of the 1940s, this one was adapted from a hit radio show. However, Republic Pictures' movies never matched the popularity of the radio programs, which were based on the career of New York D.A. (and future Presidential candidate) Thomas E. Dewey. Dennis O'Keefe played young P. Cadwallader Jones in 1941's *Mr. District Attorney,* which co-starred Peter Lorre. James Ellison replaced O'Keefe in 1941's *The Carter Case* and John Hubbard played the role in 1943's *Secrets of the Underground.* Although the series failed to catch on, O'Keefe revived the role (though the character was now named Steve Bennett) in 1946's *Mr. District Attorney.* Following its failure, radio show creator Edward C. Byron set his sights on television and produced the 1951–52 small-screen series *Mr. District Attorney* starring Jay Jostyn. Following its cancellation, a 1954 syndicated series with David Brian ran for a single season.

Mr. District Attorney (1941)	(1943)
The Carter Case (1941)	*Mr. District Attorney* (1946)
Secrets of the Underground	

Doctor in the House Series

Doctor in the House was a well-done, lightweight 1954 comedy about British medical students featuring rising star Dirk Bogarde, lovely Kay Kendall, and ever-dependable Kenneth More. But character actor James Robertson Justice, as the blusterous chief surgeon Sir Lancelot Spratt, stole the show from them all. Bogarde and Justice teamed again in the follow-up, 1955's *Doctor at Sea,* which cast Dirk as a young ship's physician romancing Brigitte Bardot while tolerating the endless tirades of Captain Hogg (Justice). The third film, *Doctor at Large* (1957), gave Justice (as Spratt again) more screen time and set the pattern for the rest of the series. Whether the handsome male lead was Bogarde, Leslie Phillips, or Michael Craig, the real star was always Justice. He consistently made the *Doctor* films diverting entertainment. A 1970 British TV series "Doctor in the House" lasted for three seasons. See also **Hospitals.**

Doctor in the House (1954)	*Doctor in Distress* (1963)
Doctor at Sea (1955)	*Doctor in Clover* (1966)
Doctor at Large (1957)	*Doctor in Trouble* (1970)
Doctor in Love (1960)	

Dogs

Man's best friend has enjoyed a long and prosperous film career, both as a supporting player and a major star. A German Shepherd named Rin Tin Tin became the first canine boxoffice attraction in silent films such as *The Clash of the Wolves* (1924) and *A Dog of the Regiment* (1930). He died in 1932, although two of his descendants went on to play the lead in the

1954–1959 TV series "The Adventures of Rin Tin Tin." Lassie (q.v.) eventually replaced Rinty as Hollywood's top dog, but other canines have starred in their own film series, including Rusty (q.v.) and Benji. Nick and Nora Charles's little dog Asta stole her share of scenes in *The Thin Man* (q.v.) films, as did Daisy in the *Blondie* (q.v.) movies. Walt Disney Productions seemed to specialize in dog films in the late 1950s and early 1960s. Animated tales paired two unlikely dog lovers in 1955's *Lady and the Tramp* and let loose the cinema's biggest litter in 1961's *101 Dalmations* (although technically, the two Dalmation parents adopted most of those puppies). Mouseketeer Tommy Kirk starred in the sentimental boy-and-dog story *Old Yeller* (1957) and its more upbeat sequel *Savage Sam* (1962). Other Disney dogs include the Irish setter in *Big Red* (1962), the three dogs (two good and one mean) in *The Incredible Journey* (1963), *The Ugly Dachshund* (1966), and the animated sniffer in *The Fox and the Hound* (1981). Some of the screen's most memorable dog pictures were derived from classic canine books like Jack London's *Call of the Wild* (1935), Ouida's *A Dog of Flanders* (1959), Albert Peyton Terhune's *Lad: A Dog* (1962), Richard Adams's *The Plague Dogs* (1982), and, of course, Eric Knight's venerable *Lassie Come Home* (1943). Mongrels easily outnumber any breed as the most popular dogs in the cinema. Still, there have been a lot of German Shepherds—the Rin Tin Tin movies, the Rusty series, *The Littlest Hobo, Kelly and Me, Won Ton Ton, K-9*, and *We Think the World of You*. And Doberman pinschers unexpectedly became the trendy dogs of the early 1970s, appearing in movies like *They Only Kill Their Masters* (1972), *The Doberman Gang* (1972), *The Daring Dobermans* (1973), and *The Amazing Dobermans* (1976). Not all dogs have been portrayed as man's best friend. *Cujo* (1983) was about a rabid Saint Bernard dead set on devouring Dee Wallace, while *Dogs* (1976) and *The Pack* (1977) were remarkably similar thrillers about humans being stalked by wild dogs. James Brolin played a man stranded overnight in a department store—and at the mercy of vicious security dogs—in the 1973 TV-movie *Trapped*. *Devil Dog: The Hound of Hell* (1978) featured an evil, possessed pooch, while a vampire dog distinguished *Dracula's Dog* (1977). David Warner may have encountered the most frightening of all movie dogs when he threatened the safety of the Antichrist in 1976's *The Omen*. Canine fantasies have opted for a lighter tone. An ancient spell periodically turned Tommy Kirk into a lovable sheepdog in 1959's *The Shaggy Dog*. Dean Jones experienced a similar problem in the 1976 sequel *The Shaggy D.A.* A murdered Alsatian returned to Earth as private eye Rex Terrier (Dick Powell) to find his killer in 1951's hilarious *You Never Can Tell*. *Oh, Heavenly Dog!* (1980) reversed the premise and lost the laughs, despite the presence of Chevy Chase and Benji. A cast of humans portrayed the anxious dogs awaiting either new homes or death in Robert Downey's off-the-wall satire *Pound* (1970). A crafty pup named Blood communicated telepathically with his dense human companion (Don Johnson) in the post-apocalypse satire *A Boy and His Dog* (1975). And henpecked husband Walter Abel found solace with a talking dog in *The Fabulous Joe* (1947). See also **Lassie; Rusty; The Shaggy Dog.**

Skippy (1931)
Lucky Dog (1933)
The Kennel Murder Case (1933)
Call of the Wild (1935)
The Voice of Bugle Ann (1936)
Storm in a Teacup (1936)
The Hound of the Baskervilles (1939)
The Biscuit Eater (1940)
It Shouldn't Happen to a Dog (1946)
The Fabulous Joe (1947)
The Emperor's Waltz (1948)
You Never Can Tell (1951)
Behave Yourself! (1951)
Bloodhounds of Broadway (1952)
The Lady and the Tramp (1955)
It's a Dog's Life (aka *Bar Sinister*) (1955)
Goodbye My Lady (1956)
Kelly and Me (1957)
Old Yeller (1957)
The Man Who Wagged His Tail (1957)
The Littlest Hobo (1958)
A Dog of Flanders (1959)
The Hound of the Baskervilles (1959)
The Shaggy Dog (1959)
The Silent Call (1961)
101 Dalmations (1961)
Big Red (1962)
Savage Sam (1962)
Lad: A Dog (1962)
Wild and Wonderful (1963)
The Incredible Journey (1963)
Git (1965)
The Ugly Dachshund (1966)
The Spy with a Cold Nose (1966)
Alexander (1968)
Pound (1970)
They Only Kill Their Masters (1972)
Call of the Wild (1972)
Sounder (1972)
White Fang (1972)
The Doberman Gang (1972)
The Daring Dobermans (1973)
Trapped (1973 TVM)
Where the Red Fern Grows (1974)
Digby—The Biggest Dog in the World (1974)
A Boy and His Dog (1975)
The Great Adventure (1975)
Dogpound Shuffle (aka *Spot*) (1975)
The Omen (1976)
The Call of the Wild (1976 TVM)
Dogs (1976)
Won Ton Ton, the Dog Who Saved Hollywood (1976)
The Amazing Dobermans (1976)
The Shaggy D.A. (1976)
The Pack (aka *The Long Dark Night*) (1977)
Dracula's Dog (aka *Zoltan, Hound of Hell*) (1977)
Devil Dog: The Hound of Hell (1978 TVM)
C.H.O.M.P.S. (1979)
The Black Marble (1980)
The Courage of Kavik, the Wolf Dog (aka *Kavik, the Wolf Dog*) (1980)
The Fox and the Hound (1981)
Rottweiler (aka *Dogs of Hell*) (1981)
The Plague Dogs (1982)
Hear No Evil (1982 TVM)
Skeezer (1982 TVM)
White Dog (1982)
Cujo (1983)
Second Sight: A Love Story

(1984 TVM)
Love Leads the Way (1984 TVM)
Hambone and Hillie (1984)
Gus Brown and Midnight Brewster (1985 TVM)
A Cry in the Dark (1988)
Oliver and Company (1988)
Pound Puppies and the Legend
of Big Paw (1988)
Watchers (1988)
K-9 (1989)
We Think the World of You (1989)
Turner and Hooch (1989)
The Adventures of Milo and Otis (1989)
All Dogs Go to Heaven (1989)

Doinel, Antoine

French director François Truffaut introduced his cinematic alter ego as an imaginative, troublemaking adolescent in 1959's *The 400 Blows*. Ironically, the film also marked Truffaut's feature film debut—an impressive one that earned him a Grand Prix for direction at the Cannes Film Festival and contributed much to the success of the French "New Wave" films of the 1960s. Jean-Pierre Leaud played Antoine, a 14-year-old who steals and lies in defiance of adults, particularly his neglectful parents. He is finally sent to a reform school for his theft of a typewriter, but manages to escape. However, Truffaut and Leaud brought Antoine back and gave him his first girlfriend in the "Antoine and Colette" episode in the 1962 anthology *Love at Twenty*. In 1968's *Stolen Kisses*, Antoine gets kicked out of the Army, becomes a night watchman, gets fired, and joins a detective agency. More importantly, he falls in love with Christine, who rejects him until he becomes interested in an older woman. Their subsequent marriage comes apart, despite the birth of a son, in 1970's *Bed and Board*. They are divorced at the beginning of 1979's *Love on the Run*, a reflective closing episode combining new footage with clips from the four previous films. Leaud was the only actor to portray Antoine Doinel.

The 400 Blows (1959)
Love at Twenty (1962)
Stolen Kisses (1968)
Bed and Board (1970)
Love on the Run (1979)

Dolls

Horror and fantasy filmmakers have found the most imaginative uses for dolls. A dying killer transferred his soul into a happy-looking "Chuckie" doll in Tom Holland's 1988 sleeper hit *Child's Play*. Amazingly, the film's characters—and the movie-going public—readily took to the idea of a little doll running around an apartment wielding a knife and shouting profanities. A living doll also harrassed Karen Black in the most chilling segment of 1975's *Trilogy of Terror*. Other murder-minded dolls stalked human prey in *Cathy's Curse*, a 1977 *Exorcist* clone about a possessed rag doll, and in cult director Stuart Gordon's *Dolls* (1987). Voodoo dolls have cropped up in several films, though none to better effect than in 1962's

Burn, Witch, Burn. Teen nerds Anthony Michael Hall and Ilan Mitchell-Smith turned a Barbie doll into fetching Kelly LeBrock in the 1985 comedy *Weird Science.* The title murderer in *The Psychopath* (1966) left dolls as a calling card at the scene of his crimes. In non-horror films, dolls have been used as unlikely hiding places. Escaped fugitives fought over a doll stuffed with heroin in the 1961 drive-in picture *Wild Youth.* On a more intellectual scale, Robert Mitchum pursued two children and a doll filled with money in 1955's *The Night of the Hunter,* Charles Laughton's haunting fable of good vs. evil. Despite its title, the dolls in Tod Browning's *The Devil-Doll* (1936) were really shrunken people. The most bizarre doll film was also one of the first, 1907's *The Doll's Revenge.* It was about a little boy who destroys his sister's doll, only to have the parts reassemble themselves. The doll then grew to human size, was joined by another doll, and the two of them pulled the wicked boy apart and devoured him. Both *The Incredible Shrinking Man* (1957) and *The Incredible Shrinking Woman* (1981) used doll houses for temporary residences.

The Doll's Revenge (1907)	*Trilogy of Terror* (1975 TVM)
Night of the Hunter (1955)	*Cathy's Curse* (aka *Cauche-*
Wild Youth (aka *Naked Youth*)	*mares*) (1977)
(1961)	*Raggedy Ann and Andy* (1977)
Burn, Witch, Burn (aka *Night*	*The Dollmaker* (1984 TVM)
of the Eagle) (1962)	*Weird Science* (1985)
Jack the Giant Killer (1962)	*River's Edge* (1986)
The Doll (1963)	*Dolls* (1987)
The Psychopath (1966)	*Child's Play* (1988)

Dolphins

Flipper, the biggest dolphin star, made the theatrical features *Flipper* (1963) and *Flipper's New Adventure* (1964) before settling into a 1964–68 TV series. Mitzi the Dolphin (who died of a heart attack in 1971 at the age of 22) played Flipper on the big screen. Suzy the Dolphin replaced her in the TV version. In 1973's *Day of the Dolphin,* George C. Scott and wife Trish Van Devere taught dolphins how to speak rudimentary English ("Fa loves pa!"). Don Knotts played a meek bookkeeper who becomes an animated dolphin and joins the Navy in the charmless 1964 fantasy *The Incredible Mr. Limpet.* A deep sea diver jilted Rosanna Arquette for a pair of playful dolphins in 1988's *The Big Blue.* Given Rosanna's whiny performance, it was the right choice. See also **Whales, Sharks, and Fish.**

Boy on a Dolphin (1957)	*Island of the Blue Dolphins*
Flipper (1963)	(1964)
Flipper's New Adventure (1964)	*Day of the Dolphin* (1973)
The Incredible Mr. Limpet	*The Big Blue* (1988)
(1964)	*Splash Too* (1988 TVM)

Dracula

Although Bram Stoker's immortal vampire novel was published in 1897, a film version was not attempted until F.W. Murnau's *Nosferatu* appeared in 1922. To avoid royalty payments, Murnau never mentioned Dracula by name. Stoker's widow nevertheless sued on the grounds of copyright infringement and some of the prints were destroyed. In 1930, Universal and Tod Browning signed horror great Lon Chaney for the title role in a film version of John Balderston and Hamilton Deane's popular stage play. However, Chaney died unexpectedly and the role went to Bela Lugosi, a screen unknown who had played Count Dracula on stage. Lugosi's compelling presence and Browning's atmospheric direction made *Dracula* a great success (it has dated rather poorly). Although Universal followed it with several popular horror films (*Frankenstein* etc.), a sequel did not appear until 1936's *Dracula's Daughter*. An offbeat love story with some fine performances, this sequel attracted little attention and was Universal's last attempt at a first-class vampire film. Seven years later, Lon Chaney, Jr., turned up as Count Alucard (spell it backwards) in Robert Siomak's lively programmer *Son of Dracula*. Despite Chaney's miscasting, this unusual entry had its share of memorable moments—notably Dracula's transformation into mist as his coffin floated toward the surface in a swamp. The Count's Universal career ended with bit parts in 1944's *House of Frankenstein*, 1945's *House of Dracula* (played by John Carradine in both), and 1948's *Abbott and Costello Meet Frankenstein* (in which Lugosi reprised his interpretation). Except for the 1953 Turkish film *Dracula Istanbulda*, Dracula lay dormant for almost a decade. Then, Hammer Films resurrected him with style with their 1958 classic *Horror of Dracula*. As embodied by tall, imposing Christopher Lee, Dracula was a vicious, powerful, handsome vampire whose cunning was matched only by his brilliant adversary Van Helsing (superbly played by Peter Cushing). The Hammer version was a smash, but Lee (and the Count himself) were oddly missing from the equally-memorable sequel *Brides of Dracula* (1960). Lee was back in 1966's *Dracula, Prince of Darkness,* but his role was brief and, amazingly, he had no dialogue. Despite occasional sparks of interest, the rest of the Hammer Dracula films were run-of-the-mill vampire features. Technically, the last was 1974's *Legend of the Seven Golden Vampires* (aka *The Seven Brothers Meet Dracula*), but Lee's absence and an emphasis on martial arts made this hardly seem like a Dracula picture. In between the Hammer entries, Lee also appeared as Dracula in Jesus Franco's *Count Dracula* (1971), a fairly literal adaptation of Stoker's book, and a French comedy *Dracula and Son* (1976). Although Lee and Lugosi were the screen's most famous Draculas, a host of other actors have essayed the role. The usually vicious Jack Palance emphasized the Count's sympathetic side in Dan Curtis' handsome 1973 TV-movie. PBS's *Count Dracula* (1978) featured Louis Jourdan in an aristocratic, sensual interpretation. Klaus Kinski was disturbing (and quite "unsensual") in Werner Herzog's 1978 remake of *Nosferatu*, while Frank Langella was surprisingly forgettable recreating his Broadway performance in 1979's big-budgeted *Dracula*. See also **Vampires.**

Universal's Dracula Films

Dracula (1931) (Lugosi)
Dracula's Daughter (1936) (Gloria Holden as the daughter)
Son of Dracula (1943) (Chaney, Jr.)
House of Frankenstein (1944) (Carradine)
House of Dracula (1945) (Carradine)
Abbott and Costello Meet Frankenstein (1948) (Lugosi)

Hammer's Dracula Films

Horror of Dracula (aka *Dracula*) (1958) (Lee)
Brides of Dracula (1960) (actually, the Count is never seen)
Dracula, Prince of Darkness (1964) (Lee)
Dracula Has Risen from the Grave (1968) (Lee)
Taste the Blood of Dracula (1970) (Lee)
Scars of Dracula (1970) (Lee)
Dracula A.D. 1972 (aka *Dracula Today*) (1972) (Lee)
The Satanic Rites of Dracula (aka *Count Dracula and His Vampire Bride; Count Dracula Is Alive and Well and Living in London*) (1973) (Lee)
The Legend of the Seven Golden Vampires (aka *The Seven Brothers Meet Dracula*) (1974) (John Forbes Robertson)

Other Dracula Films

Nosferatu (1922) (Max Schreck)
Dracula Istanbulda (1953) (Atif Kaptan)
Curse of Dracula (aka *Return of Dracula; The Fantastic Disappearing Man*) (1958) (Francis Lederer)
Billy the Kid vs. Dracula (1965) (Carradine)
Mad Monster Party (1966) (puppet)
Dracula vs. Frankenstein (aka *Blood of Frankenstein*) (1972) (Zandor Vorkov)
Blacula (1972) (Charles Macaulay)
Dracula's Great Love (aka *El Grande Amore del Conde Dracula*) (1972) (Paul Naschy)
Lake of Dracula (aka *Choisu Me*) (1972) (Mori Kishida)
Dracula (1973 TVM) (Jack Palance)
Lady Dracula (aka *Legendary Curse of Lemora; Lemora, the Lady Dracula*) (1973) (Leslie Gilb)
Blood for Dracula (aka *Andy Warhol's Dracula*) (1974) (Udo Kier)
Vampira (aka *Old Dracula*) (1975) (David Niven)
Nocturna (1978) (Carradine)
Nosferatu (1978) (Klaus Kinski)
Dracula (1979) (Frank Langella)
The True Life of Dracula (1979) (Stefan Sileanu)
Mama Dracula (1980) (Louise Fletcher)

Dracula's Last Rites (1980) (Gerald Fielding)
The Monster Club (1987) (Duncan Regehr)

Dragons

The dragon has made little impact as a cinematic monster, being relegated principally to supporting roles. A splendid animated dragon dominated the fiery climax of Disney's *Sleeping Beauty* (1959), but his screen time was all too short. The same can be said of *The Reluctant Dragon* (1941), a documentary about the Disney Studios which featured a short cartoon version of Kenneth Grahame's story. Special effects genius Ray Harryhausen devised very life-like dragons for 1958's *The Seventh Voyage of Sinbad* and 1963's *Jason and the Argonauts*. After Jason slew the seven-headed hydra in the latter film, its teeth turned into skeleton warriors which promptly attacked the mythological hero. A year earlier, fairytale protagonist Jack battled a sorceror-turned-dragon in the Harryhausen-inspired fantasy *Jack the Giant Killer*. Only two films, both from Disney, have given dragons what could be called leading roles. *Pete's Dragon*, a 1977 live action/animation film, starred a friendly dragon named Elliott (animated) who helped a young boy (live action) find a loving home. Elliott, a rather plump creature with tiny wings, could make himself invisible—a rare trait for his species. In contrast to likable Elliott, Disney's *Dragonslayer* (1981) featured a hideous, fire-breathing dragon appeased only by human sacrifice. The monster and its magnificent lair were created with hi-tech wizardry by George Lucas' Industrial Light and Magic Company. In terms of sheer opulence, *Dragonslayer* rates as the dragon's finest hour. As for contemporary dragons, there really are none. One could argue that *Q the Winged Serpent* (1982) had many dragon-like qualities, but technically he was the ancient bird-god Quetzalcoatl. Likewize, the Japanese monster Ghidrah (q.v.) boasted three heads, breathed fire, and flew. But whether he or any of his Japanese monster companions were dragons or unidentified dinosaurs remains a source of debate. The Philo Vance (q.v.) murder mystery *The Dragon Murder Case* (1934) revolved around a "dragon" pool where a swimmer mysteriously disappeared. Despite the presence of unusual claw prints and much talk about dragons, Vance exposed a human murderer. The medieval dragon in 1986's *Star Knight* turned out to be an alien spaceship. See also **Dinosaurs; Sea Serpents.**

The Niebelungen (1924)	*Goliath and the Dragon* (1960)
The Reluctant Dragon (1941)	*Jack the Giant Killer* (1962)
The Sword and the Dragon (aka *Ilya Mourometz*) (1956)	*The Magic Sword* (1962)
The Seventh Voyage of Sinbad (1958)	*Jason and the Argonauts* (1963)
Sleeping Beauty (1959)	*Ghidrah, the Three Headed Monster* (1965)
	Pete's Dragon (1977)

Jabberwocky (1977)	*Star Knight* (aka *The Knight of*
Dragonslayer (1981)	*the Dragon*) (1986)
The NeverEnding Story (1984)	*Erik the Viking* (1989)

Drew, Nancy

Teenage sleuth Nancy Drew has appeared in countless books by "Carolyn Keene" (a pseudonym for numerous authors who worked for supervising writers Edward Stratemeyer and daughter Harriet Adams). Yet, her screen career was a surprisingly brief one, with Bonita Granville playing her in four formula "B" films. Pamela Sue Martin starred in a 1977–78 TV series "The Nancy Drew Mysteries" and Janet Louise Johnson took over the role when that show merged into "The Hardy Boys Mysteries" during the 1978–79 season.

Nancy Drew, Detective (1938)	*Nancy Drew—Reporter* (1939)
Nancy Drew and the Hidden	*Nancy Drew—Troubleshooter*
Staircase (1939)	(1939)

Drug Addiction

The United States' efforts to curb its drug addiction problems in the late 1980s brought the subject unprecedented attention in the cinema. No fewer than six major 1987–88 films portrayed the dangers of cocaine, crack, and other narcotics. Comedian Michael Keaton turned serious as a successful businessman forced to enter a clinic for treatment in *Clean and Sober* (1988). James Woods tackled a similar role, with his typical intensity, in the same year's *The Boost*. Even Michael J. Fox played against type as a nice guy turned druggie in *Bright Lights, Big City* (1988). Yet, despite the presence of these big-name stars, all three films crashed at the boxoffice, as did *Less Than Zero* (1987) and *Bird* (1988). Faced with grim nightly newscasts of drug-related crimes, it's likely that American moviegoers preferred to avoid seeing their screen favorites as manipulated addicts. Not surprisingly, the track record of earlier drug addiction pictures has been riddled with similar failures. *The Cocaine Fiends* (1936) was ignored upon its initial release and promoted as camp in the early 1970s along with *Reefer Madness* (1936). Yet, *Cocaine Fiends* contained little material that was even unintentionally funny, being a bleak tale of a young girl whose boyfriend hooks her, and eventually her brother too, on dope. Almost two decades later, producer-director Otto Preminger tumbled censorship barriers with his powerful, highly successful *The Man with the Golden Arm* (1955). Frank Sinatra, in his finest performance, played Frankie Machine, a drummer who turns to drugs to escape pressure. A scene of Sinatra "shooting up" was deleted when the film was originally shown in Maryland (a court ruling eventually restored it). In the wake of *Golden Arm*, smaller anti-drug films were released, but with little impact. Cameron Mitchell played boxer-turned-addict Barney Ross in *Monkey on*

My Back (1957). Teen heartthrob James Darren fell in with the wrong crowd south of the border in *The Tijuana Story* (1957). And Peter Graves battled narcotics use among truckers in *Death in Small Doses* (1957). Another wave of addiction movies began in the early 1970s, following the gradual decline of drug culture hits like Roger Corman's *The Trip* (1967). The most effective was the potent 1971 documentary *Dusty and Sweets McGee* (1971), which sadly included Billy Gray of TV's "Father Knows Best" as one of its real-life addicts. Although drug addiction would seem to have little appeal as a comedy subject, cult director Larry Cohen broached the subject in *The Stuff* (1985), an uncomfortable satire about an addictive food. Stand-up comic Richard Pryor discussed his near-death after freebasing in his 1982 concert film *Richard Pryor Live on the Sunset Strip*. A fictionalized version of the incident also came into play in Pryor's semiautobiographical *Jo Jo Dancer, Your Life Is Calling* (1986).

The Cocaine Fiends (1936)	*Sandwich* (1978)
Reefer Madness (aka *Tell Your Children; The Burning Question; The Dope Addict; Doped Youth; Love Madness*) (1936)	*A Cry for Love* (1980)
	Angel Dusted (1981 TVM)
	I'm Dancing as Fast as I Can (1982)
The Man with the Golden Arm (1955)	*Desperate Lives* (1982 TVM)
Death in Small Doses (1957)	*Scarface* (1983)
Monkey on My Back (1957)	*Cocaine: One Man's Seduction* (1983 TVM)
The Tijuana Story (1957)	*Torchlight* (1984)
Corridors of Blood (aka *Doctor of Seven Dials*) (1958)	*The Stuff* (1985)
Believe in Me (1971)	*Jo Jo Dancer, Your Life Is Calling* (1986)
Dusty and Sweets McGee (1971)	*Cracked Up* (1987 TVM)
Panic in Needle Park (1971)	*Deadly Care* (1987 TVM)
Born to Win (1971)	*Less Than Zero* (1987)
Go Ask Alice (1973 TVM)	*The Boost* (1988)
The Death of Richie (aka *Richie*) (1977 TVM)	*Clean and Sober* (1988)
	Bright Lights, Big City (1988)
A Hero Ain't Nothing But a	*Bird* (1988)
	Drugstore Cowboy (1989)

Drummond, Bulldog

Although not a detective by trade, Captain Hugh "Bulldog" Drummond was always more than willing to crack a mystery, particularly if a young attractive woman was involved. The novels (and a play) were written by H.C. (Sapper) McNeile in the 1920s. Carlyle Blackwell and Jack Buchanan portrayed Drummond in the first screen adaptations in 1922 and 1925, respectively. But the ideal Drummond proved to be Ronald Colman, who played the gentleman detective in 1929's *Bulldog Drummond* (adapted from the play) and 1934's *Bulldog Drummond Strikes Back*. The impeccable Colman brought flair and a sense of fun to the part, and was ably assisted by Claud Allister or Charles Butterworth as Drummond's chum Algy. Other notable actors (e.g. Ray Milland and Ralph Richardson) played Drummond on their way to stardom, but an official series did not get underway until 1937. During the next three years, American John Howard made seven fast-moving, but undistinguished series entries with Reginald Denny as Algy and E.E. Clive as his butler. The first three Howard films also featured John Barrymore, whose career was floundering, as a Scotland Yard inspector who specialized in disguises. The Howard series ended with Hugh's marriage to his long-time fiancée Phyllis in *Bulldog Drummond's Bride*. Still, Drummond showed up as a batchelor eight years later in pictures starring Ron Randell and Tom Conway (both detective movie veterans). Walter Pidgeon played a middle-aged Drummond with a prized pig in 1951's *Calling Bulldog Drummond*. And in 1967, dashing Richard Johnson updated the character in the Bondian adventure *Deadlier Than the Male*. Johnson's Drummond bore little resemblance to McNeile's original but the movie did well enough to warrant a 1971 sequel *Some Girls Do*. It performed poorly at the boxoffice and killed off the series. However, *Bullshot*, an unexpected British spoof surfaced in 1982. Its hero, Captain Hugh "Bullshot" Crummond, was played by Alan Shearman, who co-adapted his own stage play.

Bulldog Drummond (1929) (Ronald Colman)
Temple Tower (1930) (Kenneth McKenna)
Bulldog Drummond Strikes Back (1934) (Colman)
The Return of Bulldog Drummond (1934) (Ralph Richardson)
Bulldog Jack (aka *Alias Bulldog Drummond*) (1935) (Atholl
    Fleming)
Bulldog Drummond at Bay (1937) (John Lodge)
Bulldog Drummond Escapes (1937) (Ray Milland)
Bulldog Drummond Comes Back (1937) (John Howard)
Bulldog Drummond's Revenge (1937) (Howard)
Arrest Bulldog Drummond (1938) (Howard)
Bulldog Drummond in Africa (1938) (Howard)
Bulldog Drummond's Peril (1938) (Howard)
Bulldog Drummond's Secret Police (1939) (Howard)
Bulldog Drummond's Bride (1939) (Howard)
Bulldog Drummond Strikes Back (1947) (Ron Randell)
Bulldog Drummond at Bay (1947) (Randell)
The Challenge (1948) (Tom Conway)
Thirteen Lead Soldiers (1948) (Conway)
Calling Bulldog Drummond (1951) (Walter Pidgeon)
Deadlier Than the Male (1967) (Richard Johnson)
Some Girls Do (1971) (Johnson)
Bullshot (1982) (Alan Shearman)

Dupree, Paula (The Ape Woman)

After the Wolf Man's debut in 1941, Universal went two years without introducing a new addition to its gallery of monsters which included Dracula, the Frankenstein Monster and the Invisible Man (all q.v.). Thus, the studio was anxious to come up with a creature of equal popularity. Perhaps inspired by the success of Val Lewton's *The Cat People* (1942), Universal opted for a female monster—an ape woman. So, in 1943's *Captive Wild Woman,* that formidable mad scientist John Carradine employed gland transplants to change Cheela the orangutan into sultry Paula Dupree (Acquanetta). The operation was quite a success until Paula became jealous when Milburn Stone (Doc on "Gunsmoke") failed to return her affections. That's when she turned into a murderous half-ape/half-woman (again, the plotline owes much to *Cat People* and even the earlier *Island of Lost Souls*). Paula gets gunned down during a circus stampede, but she nevertheless appeared in two sequels, played by Acquanetta again in *Jungle Woman* (1944) and by Vicky Lane in *Jungle Captive* (1945). Neither matched the tone of the original, one of Edward Dmytryk's last "B" films before he made his mark with 1944's *Murder, My Sweet.* Sadly, Universal never paired Paula Dupree with the Wolf Man— they would have made an interesting couple. See also **Apes and Monkeys; Humanimals.**

  Captive Wild Woman (1943) *Jungle Captive* (1945)
  Jungle Woman (1944)

Durango Kid

Charles Startlett portrayed this mysterious masked rider in a long-running "B" Western series for Columbia. Often described as a Robin Hood of the West, the Durango Kid used his guns more often than his guitar—thus distinguishing himself from his contemporaries, singing cowboys like Gene Autry, Roy Rogers, and Tex Ritter. Prior to acting, Startlett played football at Dartmouth, where he appeared as an extra in the 1926 Richard Dix film *The Quarterback.* The Durango Kid series ended when Startlett retired in 1953.

The Durango Kid (1940)	*Gunning for Vengeance* (1946)
Return of the Durango Kid (1945)	*Galloping Thunder* (1946)
	Two-Fisted Stranger (1946)
Both Barrels Blazing (1945)	*The Desert Horseman* (1946)
Rustlers of the Badlands (1945)	*Heading West* (1946)
Blazing the Western Trail (1945)	*Landrush* (1946)
	Terror Trail (1946)
Outlaws of the Rockies (1945)	*The Fighting Frontiersman* (1946)
Lawless Empire (1945)	
Frontier Gun Law (1946)	*South of the Chisholm Trail* (1947)
Roaring Rangers (1946)	

The Lone Hand Texan (1947)
West of Dodge City (1947)
Law of the Canyon (1947)
Prairie Raiders (1947)
The Stranger from Ponca City (1947)
Riders of the Lone Star (1947)
Buckaroo from Powder River (1947)
Last Days of Boot Hill (1947)
Six Gun Law (1948)
Phantom Valley (1948)
West of Sonora (1948)
Whirlwind Raiders (1948)
Blazing Across the Pecos (1948)
Trail to Laredo (1948)
El Dorado Pass (1948)
Quick on the Trigger (1948)
Challenge of the Range (1949)
Laramie (1949)
The Blazing Trail (1949)
South of Death Valley (1949)
Bandits of Eldorado (1949)
Desert Vigilante (1949)
Horsemen of the Sierras (1949)

Renegades of the Sage (1949)
Trail of the Rustlers (1950)
Outcast of Black Mesa (1950)
Texas Dynamo (1950)
Streets of Ghost Town (1950)
Across the Badlands (1950)
Raiders of Tomahawk Creek (1950)
Lightning Guns (1950)
Frontier Outpost (1950)
Prairie Roundup (1951)
Ridin' the Outlaw Trail (1951)
Fort Savage Raiders (1951)
Snake River Desperadoes (1951)
Bonanza Town (1951)
Cyclone Fury (1951)
The Kid from Amarillo (1951)
Pecos River (1951)
Smoky Canyon (1952)
The Hawk of Wild River (1952)
Laramie Mountains (1952)
The Rough Tough West (1952)
Junction City (1952)
The Kid from the Broken Gun (1952)

Earthquakes

The climactic crumble experienced by Spencer Tracy and Clark Gable in 1936's *San Francisco* ranks highest on the cinematic scale for impact. However, the California quake in 1974's all-star *Earthquake* was significantly louder, since it was accompanied by a rumbling sound system dubbed "sensurround." Aerial photographers Jackie Cooper and Cleavon Little could not convince townsfolk that an earthquake was on the way in 1974's *The Day the Earth Moved.* Dana Andrews could not figure out how to stop the monsterous quake he initiated with missile tests in *Crack in the World* (1965). And scientists could not figure out what to do with the giant insect released by an Arctic earthquake in *The Deadly Mantis* (1957). Fortunately, Superman knew how to stop an earthquake from dropping California into the Pacific and did so quite effectively in 1978's *Superman.*

San Francisco (1936)
The Sisters (1938)
The Rains Came (1939)
Flame of the Barbary Coast (1945)
Green Dolphin Street (1947)
The Deadly Mantis (1957)

In Search of the Castaways (1962)
The Night the World Exploded (1964)
Crack in the World (1965)
Short Walk to Daylight (1972 TVM)

Earthquake (1974)
The Day the Earth Moved (1974 TVM)

Superman (1978)
Prisoners of the Lost Universe (1983 TVM)

Earth's Core

Science fiction filmmakers have tended to ignore the fact that the earth's core actually consists of molten lava. In 1951's *Unknown World,* a group of scientists used a submarine-tank (called a cyclotram) to burrow their way 1600 miles beneath the earth's surface. Their goal was to find a safe haven from atomic bomb warfare, but instead they found a world where the human race could not reproduce. On their *Journey to the Center of the Earth* (1959), James Mason and friends uncovered a forest of mushrooms, a crystal cavern, a salt vortex, prehistoric monsters, an underground sea, and a lost city. It was a marvelous showcase for the Jules Verne story, especially compared to the cut-rate 1967 Spanish version *Where Time Began.* Peter Cushing played another scientist with a drilling machine in 1976's *At the Earth's Core,* adapted from an Edgar Rice Burroughs non–Tarzan fantasy. *Battle Beneath the Earth* (1967) did not take place at the earth's core, but it was nevertheless set far below the surface. Its imaginative premise concerned a Chinese plot to burrow tunnels from Hawaii to underneath the continental U.S. for the purpose of planting atomic bombs. *The Mole People* (1956) also featured extensive underground footage, but did not involve the earth's core. Dana Andrews set off an atomic bomb near the earth's core, causing *A Crack in the World* (1965). See also **Tunnels.**

Unknown World (1951)
Journey to the Center of the Earth (1959)
Adventure at the Center of the Earth (1964)
A Crack in the World (1965)

Battle Beneath the Earth (1967)
At the Earth's Core (1976)
Where Time Began (aka Trip to the Center of the Earth) (1978)
What Waits Below (1985)

East Side Kids *see* The Bowery Boys

Elephants

Elephants have been steadily employed bit players, having stampeded through dozens of jungle pictures and pranced around numerous three-ring circuses. Starring roles have been relatively scarce, but almost always memorable. Elephants sporting tutus participated in an animated ballet in the "Dance of the Hours" segment in Disney's *Fantasia* (1940). The following year, Disney introduced the world's first flying elephant in the children's classic *Dumbo.* In his only starring role without Stan Laurel, Oliver Hardy played a doctor who treated—and then couldn't get rid of—a chummy elephant in *Zenobia* (1939). Two elephants appeared in the 1942 Lupe Velez vehicle *Mexican Spitfire's Elephant* (see also **Mexican Spitfire**). The first was a toy elephant stuffed with valuable jewels, while the second was a live pink one with green polka dots. Unfortunately, the movie was filmed in black and white. The Italian comedy *Hello, Elephant* (1952) was about a schoolteacher who receives an elephant as a gift from an Indian prince. Few viewers found it funny, although the film's alternate title—*Pardon My Trunk*—still has its admirers. Sabu, who played the Indian prince, starred fifteen years earlier as the *Elephant Boy*. Other children-and-elephant movies include *The Bashful Elephant, Taffy and the Jungle Hunter,* and *Maya* with Jay (Dennis the Menace) North. On the serious side, Trevor Howard embarked on a crusade to save African elephants from greedy ivory hunters in John Huston's *The Roots of Heaven* (1958). A smashing elephant stampede played a critical part in reuniting estranged couple Peter Finch and Elizabeth Taylor in 1954's *Elephant Walk*. Burt Reynolds and Sally Field transported a pregnant elephant cross-country in the feeble 1980 comedy *Smokey and the Bandit II*. Jean de Brunhoff's beloved children's character Babar, the King of the Elephants, made his big-screen debut in animated form in 1989's *Babar: The Movie*.

Elephant Boy (1937)
Zenobia (1939)
Fantasia (1940)
Dumbo (1941)
Mexican Spitfire's Elephant (1942)
Elephant Stampede (aka *Bomba and the Elephant Stampede*) (1951)
Hello, Elephant (aka *Pardon My Trunk*) (1952)
Elephant Walk (1954)
Jupiter's Darling (1955)
The Roots of Heaven (1958)
Elephant Gun (1959)
Hannibal (1960)
The Bashful Elephant (1962)
Billy Rose's Jumbo (aka *Jumbo*) (1962)
Taffy and the Jungle Hunter (1965)
Maya (1966)
Hannibal Brooks (1969)
An Elephant Called Slowly (1970)
The African Elephant (aka *King of the Elephants*) (1972)
Smokey and the Bandit II (1980)
Babar: The Movie (1989)

End of the World / Post-Apocalypse

Pessimism sells few movie tickets, thus making the total destruction of the Earth an unpopular film subject. Nevertheless, planet Earth was wiped out by a streaking star in 1951's *When Worlds Collide*, with only a few survivors escaping to a sister planet to continue the human race. An atomic bomb blew the Earth into dust particles in 1970's *Beneath the Planet of the Apes*. Although no one escaped during that film's climax, the crafty sequel, 1971's *Escape from the Planet of the Apes*, revealed that a trio of intelligent apes had hijacked a rocket and avoided the explosion. The world's fate was left up in the air in the final scene of *The Day the Earth*

Caught Fire (1962). Two newspapers awaited a final verdict before distribution, one with a headline reading "World Saved," the other declaring "World Doomed." Several films such as *On the Beach* (1959) and *Testament* (1983) have ended with the human race facing ultimate extinction as a result of radioactive fallout. In contrast, the "post-apocalypse" genre consists of films in which a handful of humans have survived a near-catastrophic event and built a new world. Former radio writer Arch Oboler pioneered this type of film with 1951's *Five,* a talky tale of conflict among the last five people on Earth. Seen today, it's hard to gauge the film's impact, but at the time of its release, *Variety* called it "intriguing...but depressing in its assumption." *The World, the Flesh, and the Devil* (1959) added gloss to the same theme, but is chiefly remembered for turning Manhattan into a ghosttown. Similar post-apocalypse character dramas include Roger Corman's *The Day the World Ended* (1956), the underrated vampire-plague film *The Last Man on Earth* (1964), and the TV-movie *Where Have All the People Gone?* (1974). Later low-budget films such as *A Boy and His Dog* and *The Ultimate Warrior* (both 1975) injected heavy action elements into their post-apocalypse plotlines. These led to the runaway success of 1982's *The Road Warrior* (aka *Mad Max 2*), which resulted in a slew of repetitive action films set in the barren wastelands of the future. More original views of the post-apocalypse are featured in *The War Game* (1967) and *The Bed Sitting Room* (1969). A bleak favorite at antinuke film showings, *The War Game* employs a vivid documentary style to show the devastating after-effects of an atomic blast on London. On the other hand, *The Bed Sitting Room* makes its point with satire by showing nuclear survivors turning into furniture and pet birds. Many science fiction films have shown the Earth surviving a brush with total apocalypse, although, in a Biblical sense, none can match the close call detailed in 1988's *The Seventh Sign.* See also **Mad Max.**

When Worlds Collide (1951)	*Glen and Randa* (1971)
Five (1951)	*Doomsday Machine* (1973)
The Day the World Ended (1956)	*Where Have All the People Gone?* (1974 TVM)
The World, the Flesh, and the Devil (1959)	*A Boy and His Dog* (1975)
On the Beach (1959)	*The Ultimate Warrior* (1975)
The Day the Earth Caught Fire (1962)	*Damnation Alley* (1977)
Creation of the Humanoids (1962)	*Wizards* (1977)
The Last Man on Earth (1964)	*Mad Max* (1979)
The War Game (1967)	*Quintet* (1979)
The Bed Sitting Room (1969)	*Virus* (1980)
Beneath the Planet of the Apes (1970)	*Testament* (1983)
	The Day After (1983)
	Warlords of the 21st Century (aka *Battletruck*) (1983)
	Warriors of the Wasteland

(1983)	*Radioactive Dreams* (1986)
Stryker (1983)	*World Gone Wild* (1988)
Threads (1984 TVM)	*Badlands 2000* (1988 TVM)
Le Dernier Combat (1984)	*Cherry 2000* (1988)
Def-Con 4 (1985)	*Miracle Mile* (1989)
The Quiet Earth (1985)	

Episode Films *see* Anthologies

Eternal Youth / Rejuvenation

The search for eternal youth has sparked movie explorations into fantastic lands as well as medically-questionable scientific experiments. In 1937's *Lost Horizon*, Ronald Colman and his fellow plane crash survivors found Shangri-La, James Hilton's utopia of eternal youth, quite by accident. H. Rider Haggard's oft-filmed *She* concerned an ageless queen obsessed with exposing her reincarnated lover to the Flame of Eternal Life. Unfortunately, when she re-entered the flame with him, her age caught up with her in a hurry. Oscar Wilde's aristocratic protagonist Dorian Gray sold his soul so that his portrait could age—while he retained his youth—in *The Picture of Dorian Gray* (1945). In the offbeat *Angel on the Amazon* (1948), an elderly woman took on the appearance of a 25-year-old after a frightening encounter with a panther. Industrious individuals have sought everlasting youth through medical means in *The Man in Half-Moon Street* (1944), its remake *The Man Who Could Cheat Death* (1959), *The Leech Woman* (1960), *The Wasp Woman* (1960), and *The Night Strangler* (1972). Alas, the rejuvenation methods employed in these films required their users to obtain fluids, glands, or body parts from living humans. Ingrid Pitt experienced a similar problem as *Countess Dracula* (1972), who retained her youth by bathing in the blood of virgins. This gruesome tale was actually based on the life of murderess Elisabeth Bathory. On a lighter note, children flew to Never-Never Land to avoid adulthood in *Peter Pan* (1953), while a group of old-timers went to another planet to elude death in *Cocoon* (1985). Ponce de Leon never found the Fountain of Youth, but Tarzan did in 1949's *Tarzan's Magic Fountain*. It rejuvenated Cheetah into a baby chimp. Another chimpanzee caused mix-ups in *Monkey Business* (1952) when he poured Cary Grant's experimental rejuvenation formula into a water cooler. Nathaniel Hawthorne's classic Fountain of Youth short story "Dr. Heideggar's Experiment" reached the screen in 1963 as a segment of *Twice Told Tales*.

The Elixir of Life (1911)	(1944)
She (1935)	*The Picture of Dorian Gray*
Lost Horizon (1937)	(1945)
The Corpse Vanishes (1942)	*Angel on the Amazon* (aka
The Man in Half-Moon Street	*Drums Along the Amazon*)

(1948)
Tarzan's Magic Fountain (1949)
Hurricane Island (1951)
Monkey Business (1952)
Peter Pan (1953)
Jungle Moon Men (1955)
The Man Who Could Cheat Death (1959)
The Wasp Woman (1960)
Atom Age Vampire (1961)
Twice Told Tales (1963)
The Fat Spy (1965)
She (1965)
The Immortal (1969 TVM)
Satanik (1969)

Flesh Feast (1970)
The Night Strangler (1972 TVM)
Baron Blood (aka *The Torture Chamber of Baron Blood*) (1972)
Countess Dracula (1972)
Lost Horizon (1973)
The Thirsty Dead (1975)
Tuck Everlasting (1980)
Cocoon (1985)
Evil Spawn (1987)
The Rejuvenator (aka *Rejuvenatrix*) (1988)
Cocoon: The Return (1988)

Fairs and Carnivals

Fairs on film have evoked a nostalgic atmosphere of Americana, as typified by the three film versions of *State Fair*. Will Rogers starred in the original 1933 film about a family's adventures at the Iowa State Fair, but the 1945 version, boasting Rodgers and Hammerstein's only film score, remains the best remembered. The turn-of-the-century musical *Meet Me in St. Louis* (1944) ended with the opening of the 1903 World's Fair and also provided Judy Garland with one of her biggest hits "Have Yourself a Merry Little Christmas." Elvis Presley attended the Seattle World's Fair in 1963's *It Happened at the World's Fair*. A belly dancer caused quite a sensation at the 1890's Chicago Fair in *Little Egypt* (1951). Jean Simmons' brother mysteriously disappeared without a trace at the 1889 Paris Exposition in the intriguing mystery *So Long at the Fair* (1950). And *The World of Tomorrow* (1984) provided a retrospective look at the 1939 New York World's Fair. Less international fairs provided the settings for comedy in *Ma and Pa Kettle at the Fair* (1952) and romance in the Dan Dailey musical *Meet Me at the Fair* (1944). In contrast to frivolous fairs, carnival films have tended to offer a darker view of life. Spencer Tracy played a ruthless carnival promoter who has visions of Hell in the 1935 curio *Dante's Inferno*. Tyrone Power, in a change-of-pace role, was a heartless carny hustler who hits the big time in the spiritualism racket in *Nightmare Alley* (1947). He gets his comeuppance, however, and eventually winds up as a sideshow freak. Linda Lawson played a sideshow mermaid (q.v.) who actually believed herself to be a descendant of the murderous Sea People in Curtis Harrington's minor cult favorite *Night Tide* (1961). A spooky carnival run by the mysterious Mr. Dark invaded a quiet, Midwestern town in the underrated 1983 adaptation of Ray Bradbury's chilling *Something Wicked This Way Comes*. Stupid teenagers got themselves killed one by one after hiding out in a funhouse filled with wackos in Tobe Hooper's dreary 1981 slasher picture *The Funhouse*. Less human monsters seem to prefer amusement parks over carnivals. *The Beast from 20,000 Fathoms* (1953) was toying with the Coney Island Cyclone rollercoaster when Lee Van Cleef shot him up with radioactive isotope. Godzilla (q.v.) battled his archnemesis Ghidrah (q.v.), along with several other creatures, in a children's amusement park in *Godzilla on Monster Island* (1971), one of Toho's sillier pictures. The amusement park in *Gorilla at Large* (1954) featured a murderous ape who turned out to be Anne Bancroft (!) in a gorilla suit. George Segal tracked a madman specializing in sabotaging rollercoasters throughout the nation in 1977's *Rollercoaster*. It was filmed in real amusement parks (e.g. King's Dominion in Virginia) and presented in "Sensurround," a sound system which simulated rumbling vibrations during key scenes. Alfred Hitchcock's 1951 classic *Strangers on a Train* featured several amusement park scenes, including the thrilling merry-go-round climax. Likewise, the famous hall of mirrors showdown in Orson Welles' *Lady from Shanghai* took place in an amusement park crazy house. The cinema's most famous amusement park is Coney Island, which provided the setting for *Sinner's Holiday* (1930), *Coney Island* (1943), its remake *Wabash Avenue* (1950), and the aforementioned *Beast from 20,000 Fathoms* (1953). *The Third Man* featured a tense conversation between Joseph Cotten and Orson Welles atop a ferris wheel, while *Luv* opted for an awkward ferris wheel love scene. The rollercoaster rumbles in *Rollercoaster* may have been deafening, but the most stomach-churning rollercoaster footage still belongs to 1952's *This Is Cinerama* (see **Cinerama**), which projected its speeding dives and turns on a 165-degree curved movie screen. See also **Circuses**.

Sinner's Holiday (1930)	*The Beast from 20,000 Fathoms*
State Fair (1933)	(1953)
Dante's Inferno (1935)	*Gorilla at Large* (1954)
Strike Me Pink (1936)	*The Glass Tomb* (1955)
Coney Island (1943)	*Dance With Me, Henry* (1956)
Meet Me in St. Louis (1944)	*Night Tide* (1961)
State Fair (aka *It Happened*	*State Fair* (1962)
One Summer) (1945)	*It Happened at the World's Fair*
Nightmare Alley (1947)	(1963)
Lady from Shanghai (1948)	*Roustabout* (1964)
Are You With It? (1948)	*Luv* (1967)
The Third Man (1949)	*Rollercoaster* (1977)
Wabash Avenue (1950)	*Kiss Meets the Phantom of the*
So Long at the Fair (1950)	*Park* (1978 TVM)
Texas Carnival (1951)	*The Death of Ocean View Park*
Strangers on a Train (1951)	(1979 TVM)
Little Egypt (1951)	*Carny* (1980)
Ma and Pa Kettle at the Fair	*The Funhouse* (1981)
(1952)	*Something Wicked This Way*
Meet Me at the Fair (1952)	*Comes* (1983)

The World of Tomorrow (1984)   *Funland* (1986)
Slayground (1984)   *Two-Moon Junction* (1988)
Breaking All the Rules (1985)   *Kansas* (1989)

The Falcon

Rarely has a film series been spawned from so little and turned out so different. The Falcon's only appearance in literature was Michael Arlen's "Gay Falcon," a short story about Gay Lawrence, a hardboiled detective ("Lady, be calm...I don't want to get tough with you"). Yet, by the time the Falcon hit the screen in 1941 in the guise of George Sanders, he had become a charming, debonair rascal—very similar to the Saint (q.v.). The transformation was a practical one, since Sanders had just completed a series of five successful Saint features (ironically, RKO made both the Saint and Falcon series). Sometimes, it was difficult to tell if Sanders was supposed to be the Saint or the Falcon—in 1941, he made one of each *(The Saint in Palm Springs* and *The Gay Falcon). Saint* creator Leslie Charteris also took note of the Falcon/Saint similarities and threatened RKO with a lawsuit. But the series still continued with fairly enjoyable programmers like *The Saint Takes Over,* which has the distinction of being the first screen version of Raymond Chandler's Philip Marlowe novel *Farewell, My Lovely.* Yet, after his third Falcon film, Sanders decided he'd had enough of the "B" movie detective life. RKO was determined to save a profitable series, though, and chose to kill off Sanders character and replace him with his brother. Such was the plot of 1942's *The Falcon's Brother,* in which Tom Conway—who *really* was Sanders' brother—played the title role. Conway slipped so smoothly into the role that the series never skipped a beat. Despite suave, British good looks and a Colman-esque voice, Conway never made the leap to stardom. Yet, he made a stalwart "B" movie hero and his Falcon films were a notch above their competitors, with *The Falcon and the Co-eds* rating as a snappy mystery by any standard. Set in a girls' boarding school by a seaside cliff, it evoked a haunting atmosphere which was neatly balanced by low-key humor (pleasantly provided by three young girls instead of the typical wisecracking female reporter). Conway left the series in 1948 and was replaced by John Calvert in three additional entries. Meanwhile, Conway struggled with alcoholism in the 1950s and died of a liver ailment in 1964. Charles McGraw starred in the 1954 TV series "The Adventures of the Falcon," which mysteriously changed the Falcon's name to Mike Waring.

The Gay Falcon (1941) (Sanders)   (Sanders and Conway)
A Date with the Falcon (1941)   *The Falcon and the Coeds*
  (Sanders)   (1943) (Conway)
The Falcon Takes Over (1942)   *The Falcon in Danger* (1943)
  (Sanders)   (Conway)
The Falcon's Brother (1942)   *The Falcon Strikes Back* (1943)

(Conway)
The Falcon in Hollywood (1944)
(Conway)
The Falcon in Mexico (1944)
(Conway)
The Falcon in San Francisco
(1945) (Conway)
The Falcon's Adventure (1946)
(Conway)
The Falcon's Alibi (1946)

(Conway)
The Falcon Out West (1946)
(Conway)
Appointment with Murder
(1948) (Calvert)
The Devil's Cargo (1948)
(Calvert)
Search for Danger (1949) (Calvert)

Film Star Biographies

The cinema's relative youth is largely responsible for the scarcity of pre–1975 movie star screen biographies. Many of the performers that dominated the 1930s and 1940s were still making films in the 1950s and 1960s. Thus, early screen biographies focused on silent film greats like Ruldolph Valentino, Will Rogers, Buster Keaton, Jeanne Eagels, and Lon Chaney *(Man of a Thousand Faces)*. An interesting exception was 1955's *To Hell and Back,* in which then-current star Audie Murphy played himself. The film, though, ignored Murphy's Hollywood career in favor of his World War II adventures as the U.S. Army's most-decorated soldier. Diana Barrymore's screen career consisted of six mediocre films made in the early 1940s. But her life story warranted a 1958 big-screen treatment when her autobiography *Too Much Too Soon* shot up the best-seller charts. The film version dwelled on the sensationalistic aspects of Ms. Barrymore's book (e.g. her struggle with alcoholism) and, in many ways, set the pattern for the exploitative biographical tomes of the 1980s. There was little exploitative—or interesting—about the two 1965 films called *Harlow,* in which Jean Harlow was played by Carroll Baker and Carol Lynley. However, the 1975 TV-movie *Valentino,* while strictly a fan magazine portrait, revived interest in the lives of movie stars. Over the next two years, three movie star biographies reached the theaters: *Gable and Lombard* (1976), *W.C. Fields and Me* (1976), and *Valentino* (1977). All three hit with a thud, chiefly due to miscasting in the principal roles (e.g. James Brolin as Gable, Rod Steiger as W.C. Fields). Concurrently, made-for-TV films continued to thrive, thanks to well-chosen subjects and some genuine craftsmanship. Horror film director John Carpenter and former child star Kurt Russell combined to produce a highly-rated biography of *Elvis!* (1979). Loni Anderson and Arnold Schwarzenneger certainly brought the right physical qualities to their roles of Jayne Mansfield and her husband Mickey Hargitay in 1980's *The Jayne Mansfield Story.* Garson Kanin's nostalgic book *Moviola* inspired biographies of Marilyn Monroe *(This Year's Blonde)* and Greta Garbo and John Gilbert *(The Silent Lovers).* The trend burned out quickly, however, and came to an end with *Mommie Dearest,* the 1981 theatrical version of Christina Crawford's shocking best-seller about her mother Joan and two 1983 films about Frances Farmer *(Will There Ever Be a Morning?* and *Frances).* Performers who have played themselves in film biographies include Audie Murphy, Sophia Loren *(Sophia Loren: Her Own Story),* Shirley MacLaine *(Out on a Limb),* and Ann Jillian *(The Ann Jillian Story).* See also **Autobiographical Films.**

Valentino (1951)
The Story of Will Rogers (1952)
The Eddie Cantor Story (1954)
To Hell and Back (1955)
The Buster Keaton Story (1957)
Man of a Thousand Faces (1957)
Jeanne Eagels (1957)
Too Much Too Soon (1958)
The George Raft Story (aka Spin of a Coin) (1961)
Harlow (1965a)
Harlow (1965b)
Funny Girl (1968) (Barbra Streisand as Fanny Brice)
The Legend of Valentino (1975 TVM)
Funny Lady (1975) (Streisand as Brice)
Gable and Lombard (1976)
W.C. Fields and Me (1976)
Goodbye, Norma Jean (1976)
Valentino (1977)
Bud and Lou (1978 TVM)
Rainbow (1978 TVM) (Andrea McArdle as Judy Garland)
Elvis! (1979 TVM)
Bogie – The Last Hero (aka Bogie) (1980 TVM)
Haywire (1980 TVM)
The Jayne Mansfield Story (1980 TVM)
Marilyn: The Untold Story (1980 TVM)
Sophia Loren: Her Own Story (1980 TVM)
The Silent Lovers (1980 TVM)
This Year's Blonde (aka The Secret Love of Marilyn Monroe) (1980 TVM)
The Patricia Neal Story (1981 TVM)
Mommie Dearest (1981)
Mae West (1982 TVM)
Frances (1983)
Grace Kelly (1983 TVM)
Will There Ever Be a Morning? (1983 TVM)
My Wicked, Wicked Ways... The Legend of Errol Flynn (1985 TVM)
Out on a Limb (1987 TVM)
The Ann Jillian Story (1988 TVM)

Fires and Firefighters

Crackling flames of fate have provided a central premise, an initiating spark, or a climactic turn of events for dozens of films. Chronicles of historical fires have detailed the facts behind the 1666 Great Fire of London *(The Glorious Adventure),* the Great Chicago Fire *(In Old Chicago),* and the deadly turn-of-the-century New York City blaze which changed factory fire regulations forever *(The Triangle Factory Fire Scandal).* Producer Irwin Allen mounted a pair of large-scale fictional films built around out-of-control flames. *The Towering Inferno* (1974) merged the plots of two similar books *(The Tower* and *The Glass Inferno)* into a tense tale of a burning skyscraper occupied by an all-star cast led by Paul

Newman and Steve McQueen. Allen transposed the plot to an outdoor setting for his TV-movie *Fire!* (1977), leaving the character vignette structure intact. Another TV-movie, 1974's *Terror on the 40th Floor,* duplicated *The Towering Inferno's* fiery skyscraper plotline to less effect. Ravaging forest fires cut a path of smoldering destruction in *The Blazing Forest* and *Red Skies of Montana* (both 1952), while providing fiery climaxes to *Ring of Fire* and, most memorably, *Bambi.* An oil blaze required four men to drive two trucks of nitroglycerin over dangerous mountain roads in the classic 1953 French thriller *The Wages of Fear.* Less intense dramas focusing on oil firefighters include the John Wayne picture *Hellfighters* (1969) and the concisely-titled *Oil* (1977). Firefighting of a more general variety has provided the background for slapstick farce *(Fireman Save My Child),* romantic comedy *(Roxanne),* family drama *(The Quinns),* a mediocre TV series pilot *(Firehouse),* and a fact-based biography (*Firefighter,* the story of the L.A.F.D.'s first female member). Oscar Werner played a futuristic fireman who burned books in François Truffaut's 1966 adaptation of Ray Bradbury's *Fahrenheit 451* (the best temperature for book-incinerating). Other firestarters have set plots ablaze in *Violent Playground* (1958), *She Played with Fire* (1958), *Pyro* (1964), and *Playing with Fire* (1985). Even Paul Newman played a character with a reputation for barn-burning in Martin Ritt's *The Long, Hot Summer* (1958). Drew Barrymore played the title role in Stephen King's *Firestarter* (1984), a fanciful thriller about a little girl who inherited the power to will fires to begin. Most movie dragons (q.v.) have possessed flame-inducing breath, with the most impressive scorcher being the creature Vertithrax from Disney's 1981 fantasy *Dragonslayer.* Large-scale fires have climaxed too many movies to mention and yet it's impossible to leave out the elaborately-staged burning of Atlanta in *Gone with the Wind* (1939). Likewise, the burning of Rome, best displayed in 1951's *Quo Vadis,* deserves honorable mention. On the science fiction/fantasy front, 1958's *The Flame Barrier* introduced an alien protoplasm which could melt human flesh. 1981's *Quest for Fire* sent three cave people (q.v.) in search of replacement flames when a wolf attack extinguished their only campfire. Ursula Andress lost her eternal youth (q.v.) when she stepped into the cold Flame of Eternal Life for the second time in *She* (1965). The fate of the world was undecided at the conclusion of 1962's *The Day the Earth Caught Fire,* with our planet hurtling toward the sun for an incinerating destiny.

The Glorious Adventure (1921)
Fireman Save My Child (1932)
In Old Chicago (1938)
The Shining Hour (1938)
Gone with the Wind (1939)
The Forest Rangers (1942)
Fires Were Started (aka *I Was a*

Fireman) (1942)
The Blazing Forest (1952)
Red Skies of Montana (aka
    Smoke Jumpers) (1952)
Inferno (1953)
Fireman Save My Child (1954)
The Flame Barrier (1958)

Maracaibo (1958)
Violent Playground (1958)
The Long, Hot Summer (1958)
She Played with Fire (aka Fortune Is a Woman) (1958)
Ring of Fire (1961)
The Day the Earth Caught Fire (1962)
Pyro (1964)
Harvey Middleman, Fireman (1965)
Fahrenheit 451 (1966)
The Fireman's Ball (1968)
Hellfighters (1969)
Firehouse (1972 TVM)
The Towering Inferno (1974)
Terror on the 40th Floor (1974 TVM)
Bug (1975)
Fire! (1977 TVM)
The Quinns (1977 TVM)

Pine Canyon Is Burning (1977 TVM)
The Storyteller (1977 TVM)
Oil (1977)
The Triangle Factory Fire Scandal (1979 TVM)
City on Fire (1979)
Don't Go in the House (1980)
Quest for Fire (1981)
Code Red (1981 TVM)
Uncommon Valor (1983 TVM)
Firestarter (1984)
The Burning Bed (1984 TVM)
The Long, Hot Summer (1985 TVM)
Playing with Fire (1985 TVM)
Firefighter (1986 TVM)
On Fire (1987 TVM)
Nice Girls Don't Explode (1987)
Roxanne (1987)
Always (1989)

Fish

The movies have been stocked with a small, but diverse, catch of fish—little ones with very sharp teeth, big ones capable of swallowing boats, and even a pair of prehistoric fish. It is one of these latter fish that proved particularly troublesome for college professor Arthur Franz in *Monster on the Campus* (1958). Any animal coming into contact with the dead fish's fluid reversed its evolution process—Franz's dog became a wolf-like creature and the professor turned into a homicidal Neanderthal man. A living, standard-issue prehistoric fish ate vacationers in the *Jaws*-inspired *Up from the Depths* (1979). No one questioned the age of the giant fish that swallowed Baron Munchausen and his mates in *The Adventures of Baron Munchausen* (1989). But judging from the contents of his "stomach," he must have been a pretty old fish. Oddly enough, the cinema's most celebrated horror movie fish is neither oversized nor prehistoric. In fact, the piranha looks rather wimpish, but his sharp teeth and carnivorous appetite has made him a popular villain's pet. Director Joe Dante made him a star with 1978's *Piranha*, a spoof strictly for horror film buffs and drive-in fanatics. The Italian-Brazilian coproduction *Killer Fish* featured a bizarre cast worthy of being fish food: Lee Majors, Karen Black, Margaux Hemingway, James Franciscus, and Marisa Berenson. Prior to hitting the big time with 1984's *The Terminator*, director James Cameron fashioned the 1981 in-name-only sequel *Piranha II: The Spawning*. Kevin Kline won a Best Supporting Actor Oscar as Otto, the inept thief and raw fish eater in the 1988 comedy hit *A Fish Called Wanda*. See also **Sharks; Dolphins; Whales.**

Monster on the Campus (1958)	*Dark*) (1979)
Barracuda (aka *The Lucifer Project*) (1978)	*Up from the Depths* (1979)
	Piranha 2: The Spawning (1981)
Piranha (1978)	*A Fish Called Wanda* (1988)
Killer Fish (aka *Deadly Treasure of the Piranha*) (1979)	*The Adventures of Baron Munchausen* (1989)
Screamers (aka *Isle of the Fishmen; Something Waits in the*	*The Little Mermaid* (1989)

Five Little Peppers

The Peppers, another wholesome family in the Hardy Family (q.v.) mold, were the subject of a brief Columbia film series. 1939's *Five Little Peppers and How They Grew*, which opened to promising reviews, set the flimsy premise: Mrs. Pepper worked at a factory while her oldest daughter Polly attended the other four little Peppers. Subsequent movies attracted little attention and the series came to an abrupt end after four entries. Dorothy Peterson was Mrs. Pepper and her five offspring were played by Edith Fellows (Polly), Charles Peck (Ben), Tommy Bond (Joey), Bobbie Larson (Dave) and Dorothy Ann Seese (Phronsie). Ronald Sinclair played the Pepper kids' rich friend Jasper with veteran character actor Clarence Kolb as his grandfather.

Five Little Peppers and How They Grew (1939)	*Five Little Peppers at Home* (1940)
Out West with the Peppers (1940)	*Five Little Peppers in Trouble* (1940)

Flagg and Quirt

Brawling, patriotic Marines Captain Flagg and Sergeant Quirt first clashed with one another in 1926's *What Price Glory?*, a silent screen adaptation of the Maxwell Anderson–Laurence Stallings play. Romantic lead Edmund Lowe played against type as the roughneck Quirt, with Victor McLaglen more than his match as Flagg. Set in France during World War I, this deft mixture of raucous comedy and realistic adventure found the two Marines at odds over the charms of an irresistible girl named Charmaine. The chemistry between the stars and the nonstop action (expertly directed by Raoul Walsh) made the film immensely popular. McLaglen and Lowe returned as Flagg and Quirt in three lighthearted follow-ups, all directed by Walsh. Whether they were running liquor in South America *(Hot Pepper)* or soldiering in Sweden *(Women of All Nation)*, Flagg and Quirt were almost always quarreling over a woman. John Ford remade *What Price Glory?* in 1952 with James Cagney as Flagg and Dan Dailey as Quirt. The 1942 McLaglen-Lowe vehicle *Call Out the Marines* is sometimes erroneously listed as a Flagg and Quirt film. Actually, the two stars played characters named McGinnis and Curtis and the setting was World War II.

What Price Glory? (1926)   *Hot Pepper* (1933)
The Cockeyed World (1929)   *What Price Glory?* (1952)
Women of All Nations (1931)

Floods

Floods have appeared less frequently than other motion picture disasters (see **Earthquakes; Volcanoes**), despite the increased likelihood of their natural occurrence. The biggest flood, in terms of scope, was the biblical one that set *Noah's Ark* afloat in 1929. The potential love affair between Indian aristocrat Tyrone Power and English socialite Myrna Loy was disrupted by floods, earthquakes, and plague in 1939's *The Rains Came.* In *A Cry in the Wilderness* (1974), George Kennedy had himself locked inside a barn after being bit by a rabid skunk—and then learns a flood is on the way. Not all floods are caused by rain. The gravitational pull of another planet flooded metropolitan cities all over the world—including Manhattan—in *When Worlds Collide* (1951). Enterprising (and cheap) New World Pictures re-edited a 1973 Japanese film called *The Submersion of Japan* into the 1975 disaster-drama *Tidal Wave.*

Metropolis (1925)
The Johnstown Flood (1926)
Noah's Ark (1929)
The Rains Came (1939)
Floods of Fear (1958)
When Worlds Collide (1951)
Heidi and Peter (1955)
Wild River (1960)
In Search of the Castaways

(1962)
Mister Moses (1965)
The Little Ark (1972)
A Cry in the Wilderness (1974 TVM)
Tidal Wave (1975)
Flood! (aka *Irwin Allen's Flood!*) (1976 TVM)
The River (1984)

The Fly

Before *Shogun,* there was *The Fly.* Long before his novels made him a best-selling author, James Clavell penned this 1958 cult favorite about a scientist who transforms himself into a man/fly mutation. Al (David) Hedison played the inventor of an experimental device that broke matter into molecules, transported them from one terminal to another, and then reconstructed the original object. Hedison's obsession with his invention caused him to transport himself—unaware that a house fly had buzzed into the terminal with him. The device merged the human and fly molecules, the result being a man with a fly's head and "arm" (and a fly with the appropriate human parts). The rest of the film focused on the trauma experienced by Hedison's wife (Patricia Neal). Although consistently interesting, *The Fly* does not work as a horror film because the "monster" elicits more sympathy than terror—and there's no villain. *The*

Return of the Fly (1959) introduced some bad guys, but the basic plot remained the same except for an upbeat ending. Made-in-England *Curse of the Fly* (1965) dealt with a matter transmission device, but otherwise bore little resemblance to the first two films. In 1986, Canadian director David Cronenberg directed a stylish re-thinking of *The Fly*, with Jeff Goldblum as a scientist who mutates himself and dreams of creating a new species. It was followed by *The Fly II*, a 1989 sequel which found son Eric Stolz experiencing mutation problems before discovering how to reverse the process. See also **Teleportation.**

The Fly (1958)	*The Fly* (1986)
The Return of the Fly (1959)	*The Fly II* (1989)
The Curse of the Fly (1965)	

Flying People

Flying humans have become all but extinct in the cinema. Superman, and to a lesser extent Supergirl, were common air-bound sights in the late 1970s and early 1980s — but both of them were technically aliens since they hailed from the planet Krypton. Thus, the only major films in the past two decades to feature flying Earthlings have been *Condorman* (1981) and *The Boy Who Could Fly* (1986). Michael Crawford, prior to becoming a Broadway sensation as *The Phantom of the Opera*, played a cartoonist-turned-superhero who attempted a winged flight over Paris in *Condorman*, a dismal Disney secret agent spoof produced during the studio's low point. Nick Castle's *The Boy Who Could Fly* was a tender fantasy about an apparently autistic teen who yearned to fly — and eventually soared into the clouds. Pre–1971 flights of fantasy have featured a unique brand of eccentricity. Bud Cort played a lad obsessed with donning his home-made wings and taking a flight around the Astrodome in Robert Altman's erratic satire *Brewster McCloud* (1970). The French fantasy *Fifi la Plume* (1964) concerned a thief who joined a circus as a "bird-man" and actually learned to fly. Comedian Soupy Sales starred as a "miniscule molecular particle surveillance monitor" (i.e. a janitor) who took to the air after becoming "ionized" in 1966's *Birds Do It*. A decade earlier, the Disney folks brought literature's most famous flying boy to the screen in the animated *Peter Pan* (1953). Schizophrenic Vietnam vet Matthew Modine longed to be a bird and take to the air in 1984's *Birdy*. Floating, not flying, people have also appeared in a handful of films like *Mary Poppins* (1964) and *The Fury* (1978). See also **Superman.**

Peter Pan (1953)	*Superman* (1978)
Fifi la Plume (1964)	*Condorman* (1981)
Birds Do It (1966)	*Supergirl* (1984)
Brewster McCloud (1970)	*The Boy Who Could Fly* (1986)

Football

Baseball may be the national pastime, but football outranks it easily as the movies' favorite team sport. Yet, unlike baseball, football has enshrined few of its legends. Its movie hall of fame has covered the careers of players Jim Thorpe *(Jim Thorpe—All American)*, Brian Piccolo *(Brian's Song)*, Elroy "Crazylegs" Hirsch *(Crazylegs)*, and Rocky Bleier *(Fighting Back)*. To their credit, football-oriented filmmakers have shown equal respect for the men on the sidelines, with profiles of real-life collegiate coaching greats Knute Rockne *(Knute Rockne, All American)*, Bear Bryant *(The Bear)*, and Eddie Robinson *(Grambling's White Tiger)*. On the fictional front, the movies have left no football field untouched. Tom Cruise, Anthony Michael Hall, and Gary Busey played high school gridiron stars in, respectively, *All the Right Moves*, *Johnny Be Good*, and *Blood Sport*. The re-playing of a 20-year-old high school game was the subject of the Robin Williams comedy *The Best of Times* (1986). However, the majority of football pictures have dealt with the college game, often on a comic or musical level. Harold Lloyd starred as a clutzy student transformed into an unlikely football hero in his 1925 classic *The Freshman*. The Marx Brothers' hilarious *Horse Feathers* (1932) pitted their Huxley College team against archrival Darwin U. in one of the screen's more bizarre climactic games. Jack Oakie was the team's star and Bing Crosby a crooning college professor in the 1933 musical *College Humor*. Another gridiron musical, 1936's *Pigskin Parade*, co-starred Judy Garland (in her film debut) and Jack Haley three years before *The Wizard of Oz*. Fictional pro players have experienced more stressful careers. In 1974's *The Longest Yard*, former quarterback Burt Reynolds found himself in prison leading a bunch of fellow cons against the warden's team. Charlton Heston was another quarterback, fighting to stay in the game despite his age, in 1969's *Number One*. A similar problem plagued injury-prone Nick Nolte in *North Dallas Forty* (1979), a perceptive seriocomedy that also addressed the business end of the sport. The most enjoyable film about the realities of professional football was probably *Paper Lion* (1968), based on writer George Plimpton's bestseller about his undercover stint as a rookie for the Detroit Lions. Unpleasant pro games were featured in *Black Sunday* (terrorists planted a bomb in the blimp), *Two Minute Warning* (a sniper in the stadium), and *Superdome* (another killer on the loose). Two TV-movies about the Dallas Cowboy Cheerleaders treated women with minimal respect. However, tough-minded ladies took to the football field in *The Oklahoma City Dolls* (1981) and *Quarterback Princess* (1983). The cinema's most unlikely gridiron stars include the quarterbacking chimp in *Bonzo Goes to College* (1952) and the field goal kicking mule *Gus* (1976).

The Freshman (1925)	*Saturday's Millions* (1933)
Good News (1930)	*College Coach* (1933)
Horse Feathers (1932)	*College Humor* (1933)

Fighting Youth (1935)
Pigskin Parade (1936)
Hold 'Em Navy (1937)
1,000 Dollars a Touchdown (1939)
Knute Rockne, All American (1940)
Rise and Shine (1941)
Good News (1947)
The Spirit of West Point (1947)
Father Was a Fullback (1949)
Saturday's Hero (aka *Idols in the Dust*) (1951)
The Guy Who Came Back (1951)
Jim Thorpe—All American (1951)
The Rose Bowl Story (1952)
Bonzo Goes to College (1952)
The All-American (1953)
Crazylegs (aka *Crazylegs, All American*) (1953)
Son of Flubber (1963)
The Fortune Cookie (1966)
Paper Lion (1968)
Number One (1969)
M*A*S*H (1970)
Brian's Song (1970 TVM)
Footsteps (aka *Footsteps: Nice Guys Finish Last*) (1972 TVM)
A Fan's Note (1972)
Blood Sport (1973 TVM)

The Longest Yard (1974)
Gus (1976)
Two Minute Warning (1976)
Something for Joey (1977 TVM)
Black Sunday (1977)
Semi-Tough (1977)
Heaven Can Wait (1978)
Superdome (1978 TVM)
Dallas Cowboy Cheerleaders (1979 TVM)
North Dallas Forty (1979)
H.O.T.S. (1979)
Dallas Cowboy Cheerleaders II (1980 TVM)
Coach of the Year (1980 TVM)
Fighting Back (1980 TVM)
Grambling's White Tiger (1981 TVM)
The Oklahoma City Dolls (1982 TVM)
All the Right Moves (1983)
Quarterback Princess (1983 TVM)
Off Sides (1984 TVM)
The Bear (1984)
The Best of Times (1986)
Wildcats (1986)
Everybody's All-American (1988)
Johnny Be Good (1988)
Glory Days (1988 TVM)

Foreign Legion

P.C. Wren's 1925 adventure novel *Beau Geste* established a much-copied formula for desert tales of derring-do among soldiers in the French Foreign Legion. It was first filmed as a silent in 1926 with an all-star cast of Ronald Colman, Victor McLaglen, and William Powell. This exciting story of three honor-bound brothers and a ruthless sergeant struck box-office gold for Paramount, who released a hurried sequel two years later. *Beau Sabreur* was based on a Wren novel which took place within the framework of *Beau Geste*. Yet, despite the presence of William Powell and newcomer Gary Cooper, it failed to repeat its predecessor's success. Still, it fared better than another Wren-based sequel, 1931's *Beau Ideal*. Colman and McLaglen returned as Foreign Legion rivals in 1936's *Under Two Flags,* with aristocratic Rosalind Russell and commoner Claudette

Colbert as the women vying for Colman's love. Its pre-*Geste* source novel
had been filmed earlier in 1916 and 1922. Thirteen years after the release
of Colman's 1926 *Beau Geste,* Paramount mounted a lavish scene-for-
scene remake starring *Beau Sabreur* alumnus Gary Cooper, Ray Milland,
and Robert Preston as the brothers. Brian Donlevy outshone the leads,
however, earning an Oscar nomination for his sadistic sergeant. Telly
Savalas played that role in Universal's best-forgotten 1966 *Beau Geste,*
which trimmed the number of brothers to two (Guy Stockwell and Doug
McClure) and tacked on a happy ending. For a change of pace, Dick
Powell played a contemporary American agent who joins the Foreign
Legion to track down Nazis in the World War II adventure *Rogue's Regi-
ment* (1948). Foreign Legion films in general—and *Beau Geste* in
particular—have been spoofed by Laurel and Hardy *(The Flying Deuces),*
Abbott and Costello *(A&C in the Foreign Legion),* and the Carry On
Gang *(Follow That Camel).* Marty Feldman's *The Last Remake of Beau
Geste* (1977) was an uneven affair, basically a one-joke movie about
unlikely twin brothers (!) Feldman and Michael York. That same year saw
the release of *March or Die,* an awkward combination of traditional
Foreign Legion adventure and 1970s–style violence. It died a swift boxoffice death.

Beau Geste (1926)	*Ten Tall Men* (1951)
Beau Sabreur (1928)	*Flesh and the Woman* (1953)
Morocco (1930)	*Desert Legion* (1953)
Beau Ideal (1931)	*Legion of the Doomed* (1958)
Le Grand Jeu (1934)	*Beau Geste* (1966)
Under Two Flags (1936)	*Follow That Camel* (aka *Carry*
Beau Geste (1939)	*On Follow That Camel*)
The Flying Deuces (aka *Flying*	(1967)
Aces) (1939)	*Man of Legend* (1971)
Rogue's Regiment (1948)	*The Last Remake of Beau Geste*
Outpost in Malaya (1949)	(1977)
Abbott and Costello in the	*March or Die* (1977)
Foreign Legion (1950)	*Renegades* (1982 TVM)

Four Daughters Series

Fanny Hurst's story "Sister Act" reached the screen in 1938 as *Four
Daughters,* a vehicle designed to spotlight the Lane Sisters. The movie was
a popular and artistic smash, but the sensation turned out to be a young
actor named John Garfield who played Priscilla Lane's erratic suitor and
eventual husband. Unfortunately, Garfield's character committed suicide,
so that he was limited to a flashback role in the 1939 follow-up *Four
Wives.* Undaunted, Warner Bros. paired Garfield and Lane (along with
Claude Rains who had played her father) in an unrelated, but very similar
picture called *Daughters Courageous* (1941). The studio then picked up
with the original series, now Garfield-less and losing momentum, with

1941's *Four Mothers*. Priscilla, Rosemary, and Lola Lane, along with Gale Page, played the four Lemp sisters in all three films. Claude Rains co-starred with them, while Eddie Albert appeared in the last two entries.

Four Daughters (1938)   *Four Mothers* (1941)
Four Wives (1939)

Francis, the Talking Mule

Chill Wills was the voice behind the mule and Donald O'Connor played the straight man in all but one entry in this popular Universal comedy series. The relationship between the bumbling, sincere human and the crafty (occasionally cruel) mule was established when they met in the Army in 1950's *Francis*. The running gag of the series—Francis would talk only to O'Connor, so that Donald always wound up looking crazy—naturally wore thin as the series progressed. But O'Connor, an underrated comedian, and Wills maintained a delightful rapport. The script writers gave them a fair share of decent material as well, with the funniest bit being when Francis psychoanalyzed an unmotivated race horse in *Francis Goes to the Races* (1952). The series began to show signs of wear when Wills showed up in a *human* supporting role in *Francis Joins the WACs* (1954) and O'Connor played a double role in *Francis Joins the Navy* (1955). The latter film turned out to be the final one for O'Connor and Wills. But Universal was not ready to end its last profitable series. Paul Frees spoke for Francis and Mickey Rooney played the mule's sidekick in 1956's best-forgotten *Francis in the Haunted House*. It ended the series on a down note. However, just five years later, veteran *Francis* director Arthur Lubin proved that talking animals could still be funny when he introduced television audiences to that famous talking horse—"Mr. Ed." See also **Talking Animals**.

Francis (1950)   (1953)
Francis Goes to the Races (1951)   *Francis Joins the WACs* (1954)
Francis Goes to West Point   *Francis in the Navy* (1955)
  (1952)   *Francis in the Haunted House*
Francis Covers the Big Town   (1956)

Frankenstein / The Monster

The cinema's favorite mad scientist, Mary Shelley's Victor Frankenstein, has spent most of his film career in the shadow of his creation: the Frankenstein Monster. Indeed, when most people talk about Frankenstein, they are referring to the Monster—not the man. Yet, both the doctor and his creation rank as two of the movies' most enduring characters. Thomas Edison's film company produced the first version of Shelley's classic, 1910's *Frankenstein*, featuring contract player Charles Ogle as a shaggy, clawed monster. Two other silent versions followed, *Life Without a Soul* (1915) and an obscure Italian picture *The Monster of Frankenstein* (1920).

A decade later, Universal Studios made Frankenstein a household name with the release of James Whale's 1931 horror classic. In Whale's version, Colin Clive played Henry Frankenstein as an intelligent, but definitely ir-rational, man of science (the name change—from Victor to Henry—has never been satisfactorily explained). Boris Karloff's man-made creature elicited both terror and sympathy, giving him a depth of character rare for a movie monster. Director Whale exploited these assets to even greater effect with his 1935 sequel *The Bride of Frankenstein,* considered by many critics as the finest of all Frankensteins. It also holds the distinction of be-ing the only film in the Universal series in which the Monster spoke with his own voice. After *Bride,* Whale and Clive bowed out of the series. Nevertheless, 1939's *Son of Frankenstein* remained a superior outing in which Henry's son Wolf (Basil Rathbone) revives the Monster (Karloff); much to the delight of the mad shepherd Ygor (Bela Lugosi). These first three entries were "A" pictures in every respect, but the series succumbed to the "B" level with 1942's *Ghost of Frankenstein.* Bela Lugosi was still around as the disturbing Ygor, but Lon Chaney, Jr., made a mediocre monster and even reliable Cedric Hardwicke seemed uninspired as Henry's *other* son Ludwig. Universal subsequently paired the Monster with other creatures in its gallery, resulting in 1943's *Frankenstein Meets the Wolf Man* and the monster rallies *House of Frankenstein* (1944) and *House of Dracula* (1945). The Universal series ended with its self-spoof *Abbott and Costello Meet Frankenstein* (1948). However, Britain's Hammer Films revived the Frankenstein name in 1957 with its colorful, gory (for the time) adaptation *Curse of Frankenstein.* The Hammer series wisely shifted its focus from the Monster to the doctor. In a stroke of casting genius, Peter Cushing was chosen to play Victor Frankenstein and his crisp, energetic performance brought him well-deserved fame. As the series con-tinued, Cushing developed his character, gradually becoming more ruthless, but always managing to evoke a measure of pity. The lone Ham-mer picture to star another actor was the ill-fated 1970 satire *Horror of Frankenstein,* which presented Ralph Bates as a younger, more sexually-active Victor. Although Hammer retired its series in 1974, the Franken-stein myth continued to thrive on film. Paul Morrissey directed a 1973 3-D version under the auspices of Andy Warhol called *Flesh for Frankenstein* (aka *Andy Warhol's Frankenstein*). The success of 1972's *Blacula* guaranteed the making of a "blaxploitation" Frankenstein. However, when *Blackenstein* appeared the following year, it lacked the style and polish of its vampire predecessor and vanished quietly. On television, the 1974 TV-movie *Frankenstein: The True Story* was a surprisingly literate adaptation with a very human-looking monster (Michael Sarrazin). It nevertheless strayed from the true story. It did feature a rare female monster (Jane Seymour), as did *Bride of Frankenstein* (Elsa Lanchester), *Frankenstein Created Woman* (Susan Denberg), and *The Bride* (Jennifer Beals). There was no real monster in 1973's *Spirit of the Beehive,* a Spanish film about a child deeply disturbed from watching Whale's original. David Carradine played a futuristic race car drive named Frankenstein in Paul Bartel's offbeat satire *Death Race 2000* (1975). *Gothic* (1986) and *Haunted Summer* (1988) dealt with the incidents surrounding Mary Shelley's writing of her novel. In the following list, the doctor, or his replacement mad scientist, is listed prior to the monster in parentheses after the title:

Universal Series

Frankenstein (1931) (Colin Clive/Boris Karloff)

Bride of Frankenstein (1935) (Clive/Karloff and Elsa Lanchester)

Son of Frankenstein (1939) (Basil Rathbone/Karloff)

The Ghost of Frankenstein (1940) (Cedric Hardwicke/Lon Chaney, Jr.)

Frankenstein Meets the Wolf Man (1943) (Patric Knowles/Bela Lugosi)

House of Frankenstein (aka *Chamber of Horrors*) (1944) (Karloff/Glenn Strange)

House of Dracula (1945) (Onslow Stevens/Strange)

Abbott and Costello Meet Frankenstein (1948) (Lugosi as Dracula/Strange)

Hammer Series

Curse of Frankenstein (1957) (Peter Cushing/Christopher Lee)

Revenge of Frankenstein (1958) (Cushing/Michael Gwynn)

Evil of Frankenstein (1964) (Cushing/Kiwi Kingston)

Frankenstein Created Woman (1967) (Cushing/Susan Denberg)

Frankenstein Must Be Destroyed (1969) (Cushing/Freddie Jones)

Horror of Frankenstein (1970) (Ralph Bates/Dave Prowse)

Frankenstein and the Monster from Hell (1973) (Cushing/Prowse)

Other Frankenstein Films

Life Without Soul (1915) (William Cohill/Percy Standing)

The Monster of Frankenstein (1920) (Luciano Albertini/Umberto Guarracino)

I Was a Teenage Frankenstein (1957) (Whit Bissell/Gary Conway)

Frankenstein's Daughter (1958) (Donald Murphy/Uncredited)

Frankenstein 1970 (1958) (Boris Karloff/Mike Lane)

How to Make a Monster (1960) (Gary Conway as actor in Monster make-up)

Frankenstein Meets the Space Monster (1964) (James Karen/Robert Reilly)

Jesse James Meets Frankenstein's Daughter (1966) (Narda Onyx/Cal Bolder)

Frankenstein Conquers the World (1966) (Nick Adams/Uncredited)

Munster, Go Home! (1966) (Fred Gwynne as Monster-lookalike Herman Munster)

Mad Monster Party? (1967) (puppets)

Dr. Frankenstein on Campus (aka *Flick*) (1970) (Robin Ward as doctor who *was* the Monster)

The Man Who Came from Ummo (aka *El Hombre Que Vino de
   Ummo; Assignment Terror; Dracula vs. Frankenstein*) (1970) (Paul
   Naschy as Monster)
Lady Frankenstein (aka *La Figlia di Frankenstein*) (1971) (Joseph
   Cotten as Dr. Frankenstein)
Dracula vs. Frankenstein (aka *Blood of Frankenstein; They're
   Coming to Get You* (J. Carrol Naish/John Bloom)
Frankenstein (1973 TVM) (Robert Foxworth/Bo Svenson)
Blackenstein (aka *Black Frankenstein*) (1973) (John Hart/Joe DiSue)
Flesh for Frankenstein (aka *Andy Warhol's Frankenstein*) (1973)
   (Udo Kier/Srojan Zelenovic)
Spirit of the Beehive (1973)
Frankenstein: The True Story (1974 TVM) (Leonard Whiting/
   Michael Sarrazin)
Young Frankenstein (1974) (Gene Wilder/Peter Boyle)
Victor Frankenstein (aka *Terror of Frankenstein* (1975) (Leon Vitali/
   Per Oscarsson)
Death Race 2000 (1975)
Frankenstein—Italian Style (1977) (G. Tedeschi/A. Maccione)
Dr. Franken (1980 TVM) (Robert Vaughn/Robert Perault)
The Bride (1985) (Sting/Jennifer Beals and Clancy Brown)
The Vindicator (aka *Frankenstein '88*) (1986) (Richard Cox/David
   McIlwraith)
The Monster Squad (1987) (Tom Noonan as the Monster)

Friday the 13th

This modest 1980 *Halloween* (q.v.) clone has a lot to answer for—chiefly
for inspiring the most successful film series of the 1980s. Who would have
thought that watching teens get bumped off during summer camp would
be so popular? Actually, the series' survival can be attributed to two clever
ideas. It capitalized on 1982's 3-D craze with the gut-wrenching *Friday the
13th Part 3*. Then, after finally disposing of the indestructible killer Jason
in *Friday the 13th—The Final Chapter*, it had *another* character assume
Jason's identity. In 1987, the syndicated TV series "Friday the 13th" made
its debut. However, it owed less to Jason and more to earlier anthology
shows like "Night Gallery." See also **Slasher Movies; Halloween.**

Friday the 13th (1980)
Friday the 13th Part 2 (1981)
Friday the 13th Part 3 (1982)
*Friday the 13th—The Final
   Chapter* (1984)
*Friday the 13th Part V: A New
   Beginning* (1985)
*Friday the 13th Part VI: Jason
   Lives* (1986)
*Friday the 13th Part VII: The
   New Blood* (1988)
*Friday the 13th Part VIII: Jason
   Takes Manhattan* (1989)

Fu Manchu

Warner Oland, best known as Charlie Chan, portrayed Sax Rohmer's evil
Oriental mastermind in three early talkies: *The Mysterious Fu Manchu*,

The Return of Fu Manchu, and *Daughter of the Dragon*. Boris Karloff took over in 1932's *Mask of Fu Manchu*, with Myrna Loy as his equally-dastardly daughter. However, a series did not result again until Christopher Lee essayed the role in 1965's entertaining *Face of Fu Manchu*, co-starring Nigel Green as intrepid archnemesis Nayland Smith. Producer Harry Alan Towers followed it with four additional entries with Lee. Unfortunately, these modest efforts were hampered by poor production values and increasingly dreadful scripts. Towers also made a movie version of Sax Rohmer's *The Million Eyes of Su-Muru* (1967) and a sequel *Rio 70*. Both films starred *Goldfinger* beauty Shirley Eaton as a female Fu called Su-muru. In 1978, Peter Sellers played both Fu and Nayland Smith in the dismal spoof *The Fiendish Plot of Dr. Manchu*. Sadly, it turned out to be Sellers' swan song. A syndicated TV series, "The Adventures of Fu Manchu" starring Glen Gordon, ran briefly in the mid–1950s.

The Mysterious Fu Manchu (1929)
The Return of Fu Manchu (1930)
Daughter of the Dragon (1931)
Mask of Fu Manchu (1932)
Face of Fu Manchu (1965)
Bride of Fu Manchu (1966)
Blood of Fu Manchu (aka *Kiss and Kill*) (1968)
Castle of Fu Manchu (aka *Assignment: Istanbul*) (1968)
Vengeance of Fu Manchu (1968)
The Fiendish Plot of Dr. Fu Manchu (1978)

The Gambler Series

Country singer Kenny Rogers wisely banked on his easygoing charm to carry 1980's *The Gambler*, a TV-movie western inspired by his hit song. The minimal plot starred Rogers as crafty gambler Brady Hawkes who teams up with a cowpoke (Bruce Boxleitner) on the road to lighthearted adventures. Linda Evans joined them for a 1983 sequel and Linda Gray signed on for a third film. All three were big ratings hits, as was another song-inspired Rogers' film *Coward of the County* (1981 TVM). However, movie-goers seemed less impressed with Rogers, brushing off his 1982 theatrical feature *Six Pack* and sending it to the flop pile.

The Gambler (aka *Kenny Rogers as The Gambler*) (1980 TVM)
The Gambler—The Adventure Continues (aka *Kenny Rogers as The Gambler—The Adventure Continues*) (1983 TVM)
The Gambler III, the Legend Continues (1987 TVM)

Gambling

With the roll of a die or the flip of a card, gambling has made fortunes, wrecked relationships, shattered reputations, and led to cold-blooded murder. The most powerful films on the subject are those dealing with compulsive gamblers. Earnest writer Gregory Peck rescued Ava Gardner from the perils of gambling—only to catch the fever himself in 1949's *The Great Sinner*. That same year's *The Lady Gambles* was described by one critic as "a kind of *Lost Weekend* of the gaming tables." Barbara Stanwyck played the woman who sacrificed everything, including husband Robert Preston, after falling under the spell of a roulette table. She nevertheless managed to pull off a happy ending. The gambling addicts of the 1970s were less fortunate. Robert Altman's *California Split* was a depressing comedy about a pair of hopeless losers played convincingly by George Segal and Elliott Gould (the film's title is slang for cutthroat high-low poker). *The Gambler* (1975) presented the same premise, less one character and minus the humor that made *California Split* tolerable. Ladies fared even worse in made-for-TV movies, with bored housewife Shirley Jones catching gambling fever in *Winner Takes All* (1975) and lonely med student's wife Valerie Bertinelli following suit in *The Seduction of Gina* (1984). In contrast to compulsive players unable to control their fate, professional gamblers know when to quit—usually. Pro poker player Steve McQueen had "The Man" (Edward G. Robinson) on the ropes in the marathon stud poker game that climaxed 1965's *The Cincinnati Kid*. But The Kid played his cards wrong and wound up with nothing (except a $5000 debt). Tony Curtis and Matt Dillon knew when to trash the cards and pocket the dice in *Mister Cory* (1957) and *The Big Town* (1987), respectively. However, neither of them hulled in winnings comparable to the loot accumulated by unlikely card shark/con artist Joanne Woodward in *Big Hand for the Little Lady* (1966). Dozens of other movies have featured professional gamblers, though their occupation has not always been of primary importance to the plot. Several films not exclusively about gambling have integrated it cleverly into their story. A crooked card game and a subsequent lynching provoked a series of murders in the mystery–western *Five Card Stud* (1968). Vacationing married couple Julie Haggerty and Albert Brooks stopped in Las Vegas long enough for Haggerty to lose their "nest egg" in the savagely funny *Lost in America* (1985). The scene in which the frantic Brooks tries to convince casino owner Garry Marshall to return the money is a delight. It's almost as funny as the gin rummy game between bubble-headed Judy Holliday and gruff gangster Broderick Crawford in *Born Yesterday* (1950).

The Man Who Broke the Bank at Monte Carlo (1935)	*Mister Cory* (1957)
Lady Luck (1946)	*Queen of Spades* (1960)
The Lady Gambles (1949)	*Who's Got the Action?* (1962)
The Great Sinner (1949)	*Bay of Angels* (1962)
The Queen of Spades (1949)	*The Cincinnati Kid* (1965)
Gambling House (1950)	*Big Hand for the Little Lady*
The Gambler and the Lady (1952)	(aka *Big Deal at Dodge City*) (1966)
Mississippi Gambler (1953)	*Five Card Stud* (1968)
	The Gamblers (1969)

California Split (1974)
The Gambler (1975)
Thursday's Game (1974 TVM)
Winner Take All (1975 TVM)
The Gambler (1980 TVM)
Casino (1980 TVM)
Lookin' to Get Out (1982)

Stacy's Knights (1983)
The Seduction of Gina (1984 TVM)
Lost in America (1985)
Fever Pitch (1985)
The Big Town (1987)
House of Games (1987)

Game Shows

The quintessential game show movie remains 1950's *Champagne for Caesar,* a wry satire starring Ronald Colman as a genius who practically bankrupts quiz show sponsor Vincent Price. Art Linkletter, an ideal choice, played the show's ("Masquerade for Money") obnoxious host. Mary Steenburgen appeared on a quiz show in *Melvin and Howard* and Arnold Schwarzenegger was an unwilling contestant on a futuristic game show in *The Running Man* (a variation on the government-sponsored hunt in 1965's *The Tenth Victim*). *Shock Treatment* (1981), the seldom-seen sequel to *The Rocky Horror Picture Show,* was an appropriately bizarre satire on television quiz programs. Radio contests were the subject of *Christmas in July* (in which Dick Powell spends the money *thinking* he's won the cash), *The Jackpot* (contest winner James Stewart finds his life changing for the worse), and *Ma and Pa Kettle on Vacation.* And in Woody Allen's *Radio Days,* burglars emptying out a house answer a radio quiz show question and win the homeowners new furniture.

Take It or Leave It (1944)
Champagne for Caesar (1950)
Game Show Models (1977)
Three on a Date (1978 TVM)
Melvin and Howard (1980)

Shock Treatment (1981)
For Love or Money (1984 TVM)
The Running Man (1987)
Death Row Game Show (1987)

Gamera [Gammera]

Daiei Studios created this giant, flying, fanged, fire-breathing turtle to compete with rival Toho's Godzilla film series (q.v.). Like Godzilla, Gamera started his career as a bad guy, but turned good in later installments. He was also discovered in a similar fashion, when a plane containing an atomic bomb crashed in the Arctic. The giant turtle's initial appearance was not a total surprise, however, as a scientist in the dubbed version of 1965's *Gamera* confessed: "I heard there were giant turtles that lived on the Arctic continent." Gamera flew by withdrawing into his shell and rotating like a flying saucer.

Gamera (aka *Gamera, the Invincible; Gammera; Daikaiju Gamera*) (1965)
Gamera vs. Guiron (aka *Attack of the Monsters; Gamera tai Guiron*) (1969)

Gamera vs. Outer-Space Monster Virus (aka *Destroy All Planets;
Gamera tai Viras*) (1968)
Gamera vs. Jiger (aka *Gamera vs. Monster X; Gamera tai Daimaju
Jaiga*) (1970)
Gamera vs. Zigra (aka *Gamera vs. the Deep Sea Monster Zigra;
Gamera tai Shinkai Kaiju Jigura*) (1971)
Gamera vs. Gyaos (aka *Return of the Giant Monsters; Gamera tai
Gyaos*) (1967)
Gamera vs. Barugon (aka *War of the Monsters; Gamera tai Barugon*)
(1966)

Gangsters (Real Life)

Although gangsters have been a prominent screen fixture since the 1930s,
the genre's early films focused almost exclusively on fictitious bad guys.
The first major picture to borrow its plot from the nation's headlines was
careful to change names and slightly alter the facts. Nevertheless,
everyone—incuding the censors—recognized that Howard Hawks' *Scarface*
(1932) was the story of Al Capone. In contrast, Paramount promoted the
fact-based aspects of its *Persons in Hiding* series (q.v.), which was based
on a best-seller written by J. Edgar Hoover. This series of four "B" movies
introduced to moviegoers the blood-splattered crime careers of Bonnie
Parker and Clyde Barrow (1939's *Persons in Hiding*) and Ma Barker (1940's
Queen of the Mob). Four years later, 20th Century–Fox produced *Roger
Touhy—Gangster* starring Preston Foster as Capone's henchman. Fox
hyped the fact that it was made in cooperation with the FBI and partially
filmed at the Illinois State Penitentiary. The following year, poverty row
studio Monogram mounted one of its finest films, *Dillinger,* a slick
biography starring Lawrence Tierney as the 1930s most popular gangster.
In a way, *Dillinger* established the gangster biopic formula for a wave of
late 1950s films chronicling the careers of Machine Gun Kelly, Baby Face
Nelson, Bonnie Parker, and Pretty Boy Floyd. Fact-based gangster movies
declined in popularity in the mid–1960s, but shot back with a vengeance
with Arthur Penn's 1968 blockbuster *Bonnie and Clyde.* The success of
1972's *The Godfather* further fueled interest in gangster films of any type.
Subsequently, television jumped into the genre with a quartet of snappy
pictures based on the careers of the 1930s most famous gangsters. Dale
Robertson played FBI agent Melvin Purvis in two of these films, battling
Machine Gun Kelly in *Melvin Purvis: G-Man* (1974) and then the Dillinger gang in *The Kansas City Massacre* (1975). The 1970's gangster film
cycle ended with the theatrical boxoffice bomb *Capone* (1975). However,
real-life gangster films were on the rise again in the late 1980s, thanks to
the blockbuster hit *The Untouchables* (1987) and the publicity surrounding the opening of Al Capone's secret vault (alas, the contents turned out
to be rather dull). The most popular real-life gangsters on films are: Al

Capone *(Scarface, The Scarface Mob, The St. Valentine's Day Massacre, Capone, The Untouchables, The Revenge of Al Capone);* John Dillinger *(Dillinger, Young Dillinger, Dillinger, The Lady in Red);* Pretty Boy Floyd *(Pretty Boy Floyd, A Bullet for Pretty Boy, The Story of Pretty Boy Floyd);* Ma Barker *(Queen of the Mob, Ma Barker's Killer Brood, Bloody Mama);* and Bonnie Parker *(Persons in Hiding, The Bonnie Parker Story, and Bonnie and Clyde).*

Scarface (aka *Scarface, the Shame of a Nation*) (1932)
Persons in Hiding (1939)
Queen of the Mob (1940)
Roger Touhy, Gangster (1944)
Dillinger (1945)
Baby Face Nelson (1957)
Machine Gun Kelly (1958)
The Bonnie Parker Story (1958)
The Scarface Mob (1958)
The FBI Story (1959)
Pretty Boy Floyd (1960)
The Rise and Fall of Legs Diamond (1960)
Ma Barker's Killer Brood (1960)
Portrait of a Mobster (1961)
Mad Dog Coll (1961)
King of the Roaring 20's — The Story of Arnold Rothstein (aka *The Big Bankroll*) (1961)
Young Dillinger (1965)
Bonnie and Clyde (1967)
The St. Valentine Day's Massacre (1967)
Bloody Mama (1970)

A Bullet for Pretty Boy (1971)
The Valachi Papers (1972)
Dillinger (1973)
The FBI Story — Alvin Karpis (aka *The FBI Story — The FBI versus Alvin Karpis, Public Enemy Number One*) (1974 TVM)
Melvin Purvis: G-Man (aka *The Legend of Machine Gun Kelly*) (1974 TVM)
Crazy Joe (1974)
The Story of Pretty Boy Floyd (aka *Pretty Boy Floyd*) (1974 TVM)
Lepke (1975)
The Kansas City Massacre (1975 TVM)
Capone (1975)
The Lady in Red (1979)
The Untouchables (1987)
Nitti (1988 TVM)
The Revenge of Al Capone (1989 TVM)

Genies

Genies have been common fixtures in Arabian Nights fantasy-adventures, such as *The Wonders of Aladdin* (1961), *A Thousand and One Nights* (1968), and, of course, 1940's splendid *The Thief of Bagdad,* which featured Rex Ingram as the cinema's most resourceful, intimidating, and ultimately dependable genie. However, genies and magic lamps have also found their way into contemporary-set films. In the 1945 musical *Where Do We Go from Here?,* Army reject Fred MacMurray found a magic lamp and asked its bumbling genie (Gene Sheldon) to get him into the armed forces. The genie complied, but somehow kept putting Fred into the wrong army — in Valley Forge with Washington, on the Santa Maria with Columbus. Eric Blore was a grumpy genie in 1955's *Bowery to Bagdad,* but who wouldn't be with those overaged Bowery Boys Sach (Huntz Hall) and Slip (Leo Gorcey) around to cause trouble? Burl Ives donned the genie attire for 1964's *The Brass Bottle*, which co-starred Tony Randall and Barbara Eden. Eden went on to become the most famous of all genies in the 1965–70 TV sitcom "I Dream of Jeannie" and its 1985 made-for-TV reunion movie *I Dream of Jeannie: 15 Years Later*. Not all genies are nice — the evil one in 1987's *The Outing* was out to get some teens trapped in a museum overnight. The most interesting wish granted by a genie was in the 1963 "I Dream of Genie" episode of TV's "The Twilight Zone," in which a man given only *one wish* wishes to become a genie.

The Thief of Bagdad (1924)
The Thief of Bagdad (1940)
A Thousand and One Nights (1945)
Where Do We Go from Here? (1945)
Bowery to Bagdad (1955)
The Boy and the Pirates (1960)
The Wizard of Baghdad (1960)
The Wonders of Aladdin (1961)
The Brass Bottle (1964)
A Thousand and One Nights (1968)
Aladdin (1981)
I Dream of Jeannie: 15 Years Later (1985 TVM)
The Outing (1987)

Ghidrah

A giant, winged dragon with three (count 'em) fire-breathing heads, Ghidrah was "hatched" when a meteorite exploded in *Ghidrah the Three-Headed Monster* (1965). He has been the most consistently vicious Japanese monster and a formidable opponent — his three heads can battle Godzilla, Rodan, and Mothra simultaneously. He was created by master monster-maker Eiji Tsuburaya.

Monster Zero (aka *Invasion of the Astro-Monsters; Kaiju Daisenso*) (1965)
Ghidrah the Three-Headed Monster (aka *The Greatest Battle on Earth; Sandi Kaiju Chikyu Saidai No Kessen*) (1965)
Destroy All Monsters (aka *Operation Monsterland; Kaiju Soshingeki*) (1968)
Godzilla on Monster Island (aka *Godzilla vs. Gigan; Gojira tai Gaigan*) (1971)

Ghosts

Although ghost films have never been in short supply, serious ghostly dramas have been few and far between. The ghost, unlike his supernatural peers the vampire (q.v.) and the werewolf (q.v.), became strongly associated with comedy early in his career. This resulted in a stigma that has been hard to erase. Nevertheless, several of those comedies have served the ghost well, resulting in semi-classics like *The Ghost Goes West* (1936), *Topper* (1937), and *The Ghost Breakers* (1940). Robert Donat played the title role in *The Ghost Goes West*, in which gravel-voiced Eugene Pallette purchased a castle and, unknowingly, the spirit doomed to haunt it. Cary

Grant and Constance Bennett starred as the ghostly, fun-loving Kerby couple in 1937's *Topper* (q.v.). They became quite a headache for meek banker Cosmos Topper (Roland Young), who also grappled with ghosts in two sequels. A haunted house and voodoo trappings provided the atmospheric setting for *The Ghost Breakers,* a successful stage play transformed into one of Bob Hope's finest vehicles. Most comedy teams have encountered real or would-be ghosts, including Olsen and Johnson in *Ghost Catchers* (1944), Martin and Lewis in *Scared Stiff* (a 1953 remake of *The Ghost Breakers*), the Bowery Boys in *Ghost Chasers* (1951), and Abbott and Costello in *The Time of Their Lives* (1946). The latter film proved to be one of Abbott and Costello's best, with Lou and Marjorie Reynolds as a pair of frustrated Revolutionary ghosts and Bud as a mortal who tries to help them escape their earthly prison. The popularity of ghostly comedies has remained surprisingly steady over the years. In the 1980s, for example, boxoffice duds like *Kiss Me Goodbye* (1982) and *High Spirits* (1988) were counterbalanced and overshadowed by unexpected hits like *Ghostbusters* (1984) and *Beetlejuice* (1988). Alas, serious ghost films have not fared nearly as well. *The Scoundrel* (1935) remains an obscure melodrama, despite the magnetic presence of Noel Coward as a cynical writer who returns to Earth after his death. (Its lack of success may have inspired Coward's sophisticated ghostly farce *Blithe Spirit,* which appeared first as a 1941 stage play and then a 1945 movie.) In the 1940s, Hollywood made a rare excursion into ghostly horror with *The Uninvited* (1944). It featured Ray Milland, a creepy house overlooking rhythmic waves, a haunting theme by Victor Young, and a pervading odor of mimosa. Strangely, it turned out to be an isolated success (there was nary a ghost in Paramount 1945's follow-up *The Unseen*). Sixteen years later, British director Jack Clayton ushered in the era of the intellectual ghost film with *The Innocents* (1961), a chilling adaptation of Henry James' *The Turn of the Screw.* This eerie tale of an unstable governess and her manipulative charges left its ghostly element up to the viewer's imagination. One could effectively argue that Deborah Kerr's governess was a little insane from the beginning or that she was driven to madness by a ghost. This same type of ambiguity could also be applied to Robert Wise's *The Haunting* (1963) and Stanley Kubrick's *The Shining* (1980). *The Legend of Hell House* (1973) was a more conventional horror film, but nevertheless a scary yarn about a nasty spirit harrassing parapsychologists investigating a spooky house. *The Entity* (1983) claimed to be a fact-based story of a woman sexually assaulted repeatedly by a ghost. On a more pleasant note, mortal/ghost romances have been the subject of *The Ghost and Mrs. Muir, Sandcastles,* and *Kiss Me Goodbye.* That master of gimmicks, William Castle, also produced a ghost movie. During the theatrical run of 1960's *13 Ghosts,* viewers were given cardboard glasses which allowed them to see "invisible" ghosts in the film. The ever-industrious Castle dubbed this

GHOSTS

gimmick "Illusion-O." Naturally, many ghost movies have settled for logical explanations in lieu of supernatural ones. *The Ghost of St. Michaels* (1941), for example, turned out to be a very mortal enemy agent. See also **Poltergeist.**

The Ghost Train (1927)
The Ghost Train (1931)
The Scoundrel (1935)
The Return of Peter Grimm (1935)
The Ghost Goes West (1936)
Topper (1937)
A Christmas Carol (1938)
Happy Landing (1938)
The Ghost Breakers (1940)
Earthbound (1940)
The Ghost of St. Michael's (1941)
Hold That Ghost (1941)
The Ghost Train (1941)
The Remarkable Andrew (1942)
The Man in the Trunk (1942)
The Canterville Ghost (1944)
Ghost Catchers (1944)
The Uninvited (1944)
A Place of One's Own (1944)
Don't Take It to Heart (1945)
Wonder Man (1945)
Blithe Spirit (1946)
The Time of Their Lives (1946)
The Ghost and Mrs. Muir (1947)
The Ghosts of Berkeley Square (1947)
The Cockeyed Miracle (1948)
Cardboard Cavalier (1949)
A Christmas Carol (aka *Scrooge*) (1951)
Ghost Ship (1952)
Scared Stiff (1953)
Brigadoon (1954)
The Headless Ghost (1958)
The Ghost of Dragstrip Hollow (1959)
The Invisible Creature (aka *The House on Marsh Road*) (1959)
13 Ghosts (1960)
The Innocents (1961)
The Haunting (1963)

The Ghost and Mr. Chicken (1966)
The Ghost in the Invisible Bikini (1966)
Blackbeard's Ghost (1968)
Ghosts—Italian Style (1969)
The Extraordinary Seaman (1969)
Sole Survivor (1970)
The Amazing Mr. Blunden (1972)
Sandcastles (1972 TVM)
The Legend of Hell House (1973)
Madhouse Mansion (aka *Ghost Story*) (1974)
Reflections of Murder (1974 TVM)
The Haunting of Julia (aka *Full Circle*) (1976)
Death at Love House (1976 TVM)
Empire of Passion (1978)
The Ghost of Flight 401 (1978)
Dominique (aka *Dominique Is Dead*) (1978)
The Changeling (1979)
An American Christmas Carol (1979 TVM)
The Shining (1980)
Beyond Evil (1980)
Poltergeist (1981)
Ghost Story (1981)
Don't Go to Sleep (1982 TVM)
O'Hara's Wife (1982)
Kiss Me Goodbye (1982)
The House Where Evil Dwells (1982)
The Entity (1983)
The Haunting Passion (1983 TVM)
Somewhere Tomorrow (1983)
Ghostbusters (1984)
Haunted Honeymoon (1986)

Ghouls

According to Moslem folklore, a ghoul is an evil spirit that robs graves and feasts upon dead flesh. Horror movies have modified that definition over the years and produced a loose variation of the term, defining a ghoul as a dead person who eats the flesh of the living. (For a discussion of noncarnivorous living dead, see **Zombies**.) Though less well-known than vampires and werewolves, ghouls have been around for awhile. Boris Karloff starred in the once-lost 1933 British film *The Ghoul*. Yet, while he rose from the dead to recover a stolen jewel, he was not—technically—a ghoul. Ten years later, *The Mad Ghoul* cast the delightful George Zucco as a mad scientist whose experiments with an ancient gas turn his nice assistant, David Bruce, into a creature who feeds on fresh human hearts. However, George Romero's 1968 cult shocker *Night of the Living Dead* (q.v.) set the gory standard by which most ghoul movies are judged. Shot near Pittsburgh for a paltry $118,000, Romero's downbeat chiller centered around seven people trapped in a farmhouse surrounded by hungry resurrected dead people. It made little impact on its initial release, but by the early 1970s, it had emerged as a midnight movie staple and a critics' favorite. A trio of interesting ghoulish pictures appeared between 1972 and 1974, but only a few drive-in patrons saw them. Bob Clark *(A Christmas Story)* directed 1972's *Deathdream,* a reworking of "The Monkey's Paw" in which a dead Vietnam soldier returned home to eat his loved ones. The year after they produced *American Graffiti,* Gloria Katz and Willard Huyck made 1974's *Dead People,* which was reissued as *Return of the Living Dead* to capitalize on Romero's film. Italy's *Don't Open the Window* was an intriguing variation whereby a government device to kill insects transformed the dead into ghouls. By 1979, Romero had found the capital to make his long-awaited sequel *Dawn of the Dead.* This lengthy, gory, overly symbolic tale made a profit in the U.S. (where it was unrated), but performed exceptionally well overseas. Italian director Lucio Fulci subsequently made two Romero-inspired rip-offs: 1979's *Zombie* and 1980's *City of the Living Dead.* Meanwhile, *Night of the Living Dead* cowriter John Russo clashed with Romero on the rights to a Living Dead sequel. The two settled out of court, allowing Russo to make his 1985 ghoul satire *Return of the Living Dead.* Its surprise boxoffice success overshadowed Romero's *Day of the Dead* (1985), which, prior to its commercial and critical failure, was intended as the final chapter of Romero's ghoul trilogy. Romero has since indicated a fourth film might be on the drawing board. Bill Hinzman, who played the *first* ghoul in Romero's

Living Dead original, made an amateurish 1989 tribute dubbed *Revenge of the Living Zombies*. See also **Cannibalism; Night of the Living Dead; Zombies.**

The Mad Ghoul (1943)
Night of the Living Dead (1968)
Deathdream (aka *The Night Walk; Dead of Night*) (1972)
Children Shouldn't Play with Dead Things (1973)
Dead People (aka *Return of the Living Dead; Messiah of Evil; Revenge of the Screaming Dead*) (1974)
Don't Open the Window (aka *Breakfast at the Manchester Morgue*) (1974)
Dawn of the Dead (aka *Zombie*) (1979)

Zombie (aka *Zombie 2; Zombie Flesh-Eaters*) (1979)
Bloodeaters (1980)
City of the Living Dead (aka *Gates of Hell*) (1980)
Night of the Zombies (1983)
City of the Walking Dead (aka *Nightmare City*) (1983)
Return of the Living Dead (1985)
Day of the Dead (1985)
Return of the Living Dead II (1988)
Redneck Zombies (1989)
Revenge of the Living Zombies (1989)

Giants

Bigger has not meant better for humans of gigantic proportions. In the science fiction genre, hardly anyone has grown big because they *wanted* to. *The Amazing Colossal Man* was a victim of a plutonium explosion, while an alien caused the *Attack of the 50-Foot Woman*. Neither of those title characters dealt with their new-found size very well and both eventually went crazy. A major problem that plagued them, along with *The 30 Foot Bride of Candy Rock* (1958), was their wardrobe. Embarrassingly, the Colossal Man wound up wearing big diapers, while the 30-Foot Bride made a nice-looking toga out of a parachute. Producer-director Bert I. Gordon, a major proponent of rear-screen projection, specialized in giant people movies. In addition to *The Amazing Colossal Man* (1957), he produced its sequel *War of the Colossal Beast* (1958), the very similar *Cyclops* (1957), and *Village of the Giants* (1965). The latter film, a very loose adaptation of H.G. Wells' *Food of the Gods,* starred little Ronnie Howard as a whiz kid who turns a bunch of teenagers into rowdy giants. Buddy Baer (whose nephew Max Jr. played Jethro on "The Beverly Hillbillies") portrayed a gigantic conquistador in 1958's *Giant from the Unknown* and Abbott and Costello's oversized nemesis in 1952's *Jack and the Bean Stalk*. In Costello's only film sans Abbott, he turned his girlfriend Dorothy Provine into the aforementioned *30 Foot Bride of Candy Rock* (1958). See also **Little People.**

Alice in Wonderland (1951)
Jack and the Bean Stalk (1952)
Cyclops (1957)

The Amazing Colossal Man (1957)
War of the Colossal Beast (1958)

Attack of the 50-Foot Woman
   (1958)
Giant from the Unknown
   (1958)

The 30 Foot Bride of Candy
   Rock (1959)
Village of the Giants (1965)

Gidget

The original beach party teen was played by Sandra Dee in the 1959 eponymous opus. It was semiserious, with Gidget getting somewhat involved with an older man, a beachcomber played by Cliff Robertson. The follow-ups were more lighthearted, with the spunky teen being portrayed by five different actresses. The films spawned two TV series: Sally Field's 1965–66 version and a syndicated series that cropped up in the mid–1980s. See also **Beach Party.**

Gidget (1959) (Sandra Dee)
Gidget Goes Hawaiian (1961)
   (Deborah Walley)
Gidget Goes to Rome (1963)
   (Cindy Carol)
Gidget Grows Up (1969 TVM)

(Karen Valentine)
Gidget Gets Married (1972
   TVM) (Monie Ellis)
Gidget's Summer Reunion
   (1985 TVM) (Caryn Richman)

Gildersleeve, The Great

Portly, baritone-voiced comedian Harold Peary played Throckmorton P. Gildersleeve ("Gildy") in this short-lived RKO series inspired by a hit radio show. The character first appeared in the 1941 comedy *Look Who's Laughing,* which brought together radio favorites Bergen and McCarthy and Fibber McGee and Molly. After additional appearances as Gildy in *Here We Go Again* and *Seven Days Leave* (both 1942), Peary launched his own series with 1943's *The Great Gildersleeve.* He played the unlikely "custodian" of his teenage niece Margie (Nancy Gates) and enterprising nephew Leroy (Freddie Mercer). Jane Darwell, just three years after winning an Oscar as Ma Joad in 1939's *The Grapes of Wrath,* provided maternal support as Aunt Emma. The movies never rose above program filler and usually cast Gildy as an unlikely hero — clashing with gangsters, avoiding marriage-minded spinsters, and encountering ghostly ancestors. When Gildy got into a jam (e.g. zipped in a sleeping bag with a cat and dog), he typically responded with a bellowing "Oh, Leeeeroy!" When things were going well, though, one could count on hearing his trademark giggle.

Look Who's Laughing (1941)
Here We Go Again (1942)
Seven Days Leave (1942)
The Great Gildersleeve (1943)

Gildersleeve's Bad Day (1943)
Gildersleeve on Broadway
   (1943)
Gildersleeve's Ghost (1944)

Gilligan's Island

During its original 1964–66 telecasts, "Gilligan's Island" scored reasonably well in the ratings opposite "The Lawrence Welk Show" and then "The Donna Reed Show." But the series' juvenile audience eventually spelled its doom on the network. Ironically, those same viewers turned the syndicated reruns of "Gilligan's Island" into a very profitable money-making machine. The series gradually built a large broad-based following which persuaded NBC to reunite the cast members for 1978's *Rescue from Gilligan's Island*. With the exception of Tina Louise as Ginger, all the original castaways returned. Time had not been kind to some of the performers, but the show's fans still enjoyed watching the Minnow's passengers finally get home — only to go on a reunion cruise and land back on the island. The movie performed very well in the ratings and there was talk of reviving the series. However, dwindling audiences for two additional films put that idea to rest.

> *Rescue from Gilligan's Island* (1978 TVM)
> *The Castaways on Gilligan's Island* (1979 TVM)
> *The Harlem Globetrotters on Gilligan's Island* (1981 TVM)

Gimmicks

When television entered American homes in the early 1950s, Hollywood panicked. Convinced that families would stay at home to watch the small screen, filmmakers sought innovative ideas to make theatrical films different. 3-D was revived (see separate entry), widescreen processes were introduced, and William Castle lured moviegoers with gimmicks that would make a carny barker jealous. A prolific "B"-movie director from 1943, Castle made his first horror feature in 1958. *Macabre* was a decent low-budget picture about a man trying to find his kidnapped daughter, who had been buried alive. However, Castle turned it into a surprise moneymaker by issuing viewers a $1000 life insurance policy from Lloyds of London — in case anyone died of fright while watching the movie. Castle followed up with 1958's *House on Haunted Hill,* starring Vincent Price and a gimmick called "emergo." Not quite as clever as its name, "emergo" was simply a skeleton on a wire which projectionists dropped over unsuspecting viewers during the film's big shock scene. *The Tingler* followed the same year and if there's a classic gimmick, this is it. Price stars again, this time as a doctor who discovers a crustacean-like creature that grows at the base of the spine during moments of intense fright. When you scream, the creature reduces in size and becomes harmless. However, if you're too afraid to scream, the Tingler snaps your spine, causing instant death. At the highlight of the film, Price surgically removes a Tingler, which subsequently escapes to a movie theatre below him. The screen goes black and Price urges the real movie audience to: "Scream! Scream for your lives!"

To heighten the effect, some patrons at selected movie theatres received mild electric shocks (yes, Castle had actually wired some of the seats!). Castle's next two gimmicks were far less elaborate. For *13 Ghosts* (1960), he provided viewers with filtered glasses which allowed them to see the movie's "invisible" ghosts (he called this "Illusion-O"). And in his 1961 psycho thriller *Homicidal,* he interrupted the film with a "fright break," which told viewers that "all those too timid to take the climax will be welcomed to the Coward's Corner." Although Castle was the King of Gimmicks, others have resorted to similar tactics to draw audiences. See also **3-D; Cinerama.** Some of the more memorable gimmicks:

Scent of Mystery (1960). In selected theatres, over 30 aromas were piped in via plastic tubes. This was dubbed "Smell-O-Vision."

Psycho (1960). During its first run, theatres refused to admit patrons once the film started.

Ten Little Indians (1965). Featured a "murder minute" at the climax, informing viewers they had all the clues — and 60 seconds — to solve the mystery.

Chamber of Horrors (1966). Sounded the "horror horn" and showed the "fear flasher" before every murder.

Wicked, Wicked (1973). The entire movie was shown in a split-screen, process the producers touted as "Duovision."

Earthquake (1974). First of the "Sensurround" movies, whereby the soundtrack was amplified in certain scenes to cause a rumbling sensation. It also caused headaches. Other "sensurround" movies were *Midway* (1976) and *Rollercoaster* (1977).

The Beast Must Die (1974). A "werewolf break" gave viewers time to guess the werewolf's identity.

Polyester (1981). "Odorama" provided patrons with scratch-and-sniff cards with instructions on when to scratch during the flick.

Dead Men Don't Wear Plaid (1982). Steve Martin "acted" with stars from Hollywood's golden days by intercutting footage from famous films.

Clue (1985). Released with three endings, each one identifying a different character as the murderer.

Million Dollar Mystery (1987). Viewers could win a million dollars themselves by piecing together clues provided in the film.

Godzilla

Japan's biggest star, both literally (400 feet tall, 2 million tons) and in terms of popularity, Godzilla has starred in 15 films since his 1954 debut. The first, and best, was *Godzilla, King of the Monsters,* in which H-bomb tests revive the prehistoric creature and equip him with radioactive breath. He leaves his native Oto island and topples most of Tokyo before an "oxygen destroyer" spells his doom. Raymond Burr co-starred as a wheelchair-ridden reporter (shades of "Ironside"). The film was a smash hit in Japan and fared very well when imported to the U.S. in 1956. Its sequel,

Godzilla Raids Again (1955), has caused infinite nightmares for film historians. Besides sporting the alternate titles *Godzilla's Counterattack* and *The Return of Godzilla,* it was released in the U.S. as *Gigantis, the Fire Monster.* Confusingly, the title monster was not a Godzilla rival, but the Big G himself. After two more movies as a baddie, Godzilla turned good monster in 1965's *Monster Zero.* He continued to soften as the series progressed: He was a single parent in *Son of Godzilla* and taught a human boy about courage in *Godzilla's Revenge.* By the early 1970s, he was a shadow of his ruthless self and the series appeared to end with *Terror of Godzilla* (aka *Terror of Mechagodzilla*). But—just to show you can't keep a good dragon down—he attempted a comeback with *Godzilla 1985,* a semiremake of the original. It was a tremendous flop in the U.S. and retirement for the big guy seemed imminent. However, Toho Studios announced another comeback, *Godzilla vs. Biollante,* in 1989.

> *Godzilla, King of the Monsters* (aka *Godzilla; Gojira*) (1954)
> *Gigantis, the Fire Monster* (aka *The Return of Godzilla; Godzilla Raids Again; Godzilla's Counterattack; Gojira no Gyakushu*) (1955)
> *King Kong vs. Godzilla* (aka *Kingukongu tai Gojira*) (1963)
> *Godzilla vs. The Thing* (aka *Godzilla vs. Mothra; Godzilla tai Mothra*) (1964)
> *Monster Zero* (aka *Invasion of the Astro-Monsters; Kaiju Daisenso*) (1965)
> *Ghidrah the Three-Headed Monster* (aka *The Greatest Battle on Earth; Sandai Kaiju Chikyu Saidai No Kessen*) (1965)
> *Godzilla vs. the Sea Monster* (aka *Ebriah—Terror of the Deep; Nankai no Dai Ketto*) (1966)
> *Destroy All Monsters* (aka *Operation Monsterland; Kaiju Soshingeki*) (1968)
> *Son of Godzilla* (aka *Gojira no Musuko*) (1968)
> *Godzilla's Revenge* (aka *Ord Kaiju Daishingeki*) (1969)
> *Godzilla on Monster Island* (aka *Godzilla vs. Gigan; Gojira tai Gaigan*) (1971)
> *Godzilla vs. the Smog Monster* (aka *Gojira tai Hedora*) (1971)
> *Godzilla vs. Megalon* (aka *Gojira tai Megaro*) (1973)
> *Godzilla vs. the Bionic Monster* (aka *Godzilla vs. the Cosmic Monster; Gojira tai Meka-Gojira*) (1974)
> *Terror of Godzilla* (aka *Terror of Mechagodzilla; Meka-Gojira no Gyakusyu*) (1975)
> *Godzilla 1985* (1985)

(Note: Godzilla's foot also appears in the memorable animated short *Bambi Meets Godzilla* and Bob Goldthwait dons a Godzilla suit and blunders through a miniature city in 1986's *One Crazy Summer.*)

Golf

Golf seldom ranks with its peers as a television sport—the ball being too small to follow and the game devoid of blue-collar suspense. That same handicap applies to its big screen career, resulting in but a handful of golf films. *Banning* (1967) examined (somewhat superficially) the country club set obsessed with golfing. It starred Robert Wagner as a washed-up pro who regains his self-respect and teaches the snobs a lesson. One of the stories in *Dead of Night* (1945) concerned a pair of golfing buddies who make a wager—with one of them winding up a ghost. In 1964's *Goldfinger*, James Bond introduced himself to villain Auric Goldfinger by cheating in a golf game. The President was kidnapped on a golf course in the spy spoof *In Like Flint*. And Bing Crosby and Bob Hope engaged in their favorite pastime in a sketch for 1947's Paramount all-star extravaganza *Variety Girl*. The only real-life golfer to have his story reach the silver screen was Ben Hogan, the subject of 1951's *Follow the Sun*.

The Cohens and Kellys in Scotland (1930)	*Goldfinger* (1964)
You're Telling Me (1934)	*Banning* (1967 TVM)
Carefree (1938)	*In Like Flint* (1967)
Dead of Night (1945)	*Once You Kiss a Stranger* (1969)
Variety Girl (1947)	*Enter the Dragon* (1973)
Follow the Sun (1951)	*Caddyshack* (1980)
Pat and Mike (1952)	*Caddyshack II* (1988)
The Caddy (1953)	*Dead Solid Perfect* (1988 TVM)

Gorgons

In Greek mythology, the gorgons were female creatures who had snakes for hair and eyes which could turn men into stone. There were three sisters: Stheno and Euryale, who were immortal, and Medusa, their well-known sibling, whose fame stems from her death at the hands of Perseus (he used a reflecting shield and a decapitating sword). Hammer Studios, Britain's "House of Horror" (and never one to worry about tradition), added a fourth sister named Magaera in its 1964 chiller *The Gorgon*. Medusa, though, still reigns as cinema's most noteworthy gorgon. Ray Harryhausen brought her to life via stop-motion animation in 1981's *Clash of the Titans*. Tony Randall played Medusa, along with several other characters, in George Pal's juvenile fantasy *The Seven Faces of Dr. Lao* (1964). And she made a brief, and very fakey, appearance in the low-budget sand-and-sandal epic *Medusa vs. the Son of Hercules* (1962). See also **Cyclops**.

Medusa vs. the Son of Hercules (1962)	*The Seven Faces of Dr. Lao* (1964)
The Gorgon (1964)	*Clash of the Titans* (1981)

Governesses and Nannies

Deborah Kerr heads an impressive group of actresses who have played governesses. She matched wits with the King of Siam (Yul Brynner) in

The King and I (1946), fought would-be ghosts while losing her grip on sanity in *The Innocents* (1961), and "cured" troublesome teen Hayley Mills in *The Chalk Garden* (1964). However, references being what they are (and the *Innocents* episode being rather disturbing), one must recommend Julie Andrews over Ms. Kerr for employment as a governess. Ms. Andrews was a cheery, lyrical nanny who brought out the best in her charges in both *Mary Poppins* (1964) and *The Sound of Music* (1965). Bette Davis also proved capable in *All This and Heaven Too* (1940), but she was at her nastiest as *The Nanny* (1965). Other notable actresses to perform nanny duties include Ingrid Bergman *(Adam Had Four Sons)* and Katharine Hepburn *(Flame Over India)*. Disney's animated *Peter Pan* (1953) featured the immortal Nana, the St. Bernard nanny. Juliet Mills (Hayley's sister) portrayed a governess with a magic touch in the 1970–71 TV series "Nanny and the Professor." See also **Babysitters.**

All This and Heaven Too (1940)	*west Frontier)* (1959)
Adam Had Four Sons (1941)	*The Innocents* (1961)
Jane Eyre (1944)	*The Chalk Garden* (1964)
The Unseen (1945)	*Mary Poppins* (1964)
Anna and the King of Siam	*The Sound of Music* (1965)
(1946)	*The Nanny* (1965)
Blanche Fury (1948)	*Jane Eyre* (1970 TVM)
Peter Pan (1953)	*The Nightcomers* (1971)
The King and I (1956)	*Blue Blood* (1973)
Flame Over India (aka *North-*	*Miss Mary* (1986)

Grave Robbers

The grisly real-life duo of William Burke and William Hare have been the subject of four films. These 19th-century Edinburgh grave robbers sold cadavers to medical students for purposes of dissection. When the supply of fresh corpses dried up, Burke and Hare turned to murder. Burke was accused of over a dozen murders and was hanged in 1829. Hare, who had testified against his partner, served a prison term and was later freed. On the screen, Burke was first portrayed by Boris Karloff (though the character was called Gray) in Val Lewton's 1945 adaptation of Robert Louis Stevenson's *The Body Snatcher.* Fifteen years later, Burke returned, with Hare this time, in *The Flesh and the Fiends,* a Hammer-style horror picture starring Peter Cushing. *Burke and Hare* (1971) elevated the gruesome twosome from supporting to principal characters, but lacked the style of Freddie Francis' handsome 1985 version *The Doctor and the Devils.* Other grave diggers have turned up frequently in horror films, most notably James Whale's original *Frankenstein.* Jacques Tourneur's 1964 horror spoof *A Comedy of Terrors* starred Vincent Price and Peter Lorre as budget-minded morticians who dug up graves to recover their coffins. In *Invisible Invaders,* creatures from outer space occupied the dead bodies of Earthlings and then dug themselves out of their graves.

Frankenstein (1931)
The Body Snatcher (1945)
The Greed of William Hart (1948)
The Abductors (1957)
Invisible Invaders (1959)
The Flesh and the Fiends (aka *Mania*) (1960)
The Anatomist (1961)

Corridors of Blood (aka *Doctor of Seven Dials*) (1962)
A Comedy of Terrors (1964)
Burke and Hare (1971)
Dr. Jekyll and Sister Hyde (1971)
The Doctor and the Devils (1985)

Great Gildersleeve, The *see* Gildersleeve, The Great

Gypsies

The victims of movie stereotyping, gypsies have too often been portrayed as ominous fortunetellers or hotblooded vagabonds. Maria Ouspenskaya created the most famous celluloid gypsy, as Maleva the fortune teller who first informs Lon Chaney, Jr.: "Even a man who is pure in heart and says his prayers by night, can become a wolf when the wolfbane blooms and the autumn moon is bright." Alas, that's exactly what happened to Lon in 1941's *The Wolf Man,* following a bite from Maleva's gypsy-werewolf son (Bela Lugosi). Although father Claude Rains put his werewolf son out of his misery, both the Wolf Man and Maleva the gypsy returned two years later for *Frankenstein Meets the Wolf Man.* The talented Ouspenskaya lost her Russian nationality in gypsy guise, but other performers have looked downright out of place. The intentional miscasting was part of the fun in 1936's *The Bohemian Girl,* which featured Stan Laurel and Oliver Hardy as unlikely gypsies. However, Jane Russell made a silly gypsy temptress in *Hot Blood* (1955), while Marlene Dietrich chewed the scenery (in entertaining fashion) in *Golden Earrings* (1947). Frank Sinatra, in heavy make-up and sporting an earring, had a gypsy cameo in John Huston's gimmicky 1963 mystery *The List of Adrian Messenger.* Few films have focused on the plight of present-day gypsies. One that did was 1978's *King of the Gypsies,* an adaptation of Peter Maas' bestseller about a dying gypsy ruler (Sterling Hayden) who passes the tribe's leadership to his grandson (Eric Roberts), ignoring the birth rights of his son (Judd Hirsch). Actor Robert Duvall directed *Angelo, My Love* (1983), a curious mixture of fact and fiction set in New York City and starring a former gypsy child (Angelo Evans).

Caravan (1934)
Vanessa, Her Love Story (1935)
The Bohemian Girl (1936)
Wings of the Morning (1937)
The Hunchback of Notre Dame

(1939)
The Wolf Man (1941)
Frankenstein Meets the Wolf Man (1943)
Gypsy Wildcat (1944)

Cry of the Werewolf (1944)
House of Dracula (1945)
Caravan (1946)
Madonna of the Seven Moons (1946)
Golden Earrings (1947)
Jassy (1947)
The Loves of Carmen (1948)
Gypsy Fury (1951)
Charge of the Lancers (1954)
Hot Blood (1955)
The Gypsy and the Gentleman (1957)

Babes in Toyland (1961)
The List of Adrian Messenger (1963)
From Russia with Love (1963)
Los Tarantos (1964)
Gypsy Girl (aka *Sky West and Crooked*) (1965)
The Virgin and the Gypsy (1970)
Alex and the Gypsy (1970)
King of the Gypsies (1978)
Angelo, My Love (1983)

Halloween

The most influential horror film of the late 1970's, this well-made psycho thriller inspired a rash of "slasher" movies (q.v.). Unfortunately, its imitators failed to realize that *Halloween* (1978) worked because of its suspense—not gore. The thin plot concerned a babysitter and her friends, who are terrorized by an emotionless telepath on Halloween night. Donald Pleasance and Jamie Lee Curtis contributed effective performances, but the true star was John Carpenter, whose tour-de-force direction created some classic frights. Carpenter produced, but did not direct, 1981's pallid sequel *Halloween II*. *Halloween III: Season of the Witch* (1983) ignored the plot of the earlier films and opted for a clever tale about a diabolical Halloween mask manufacturer. It bombed with critics and movie-goers. Five years later, the series resumed with *Halloween IV: The Return of Michael Myers* (1988) and *Halloween V: The Revenge of Michael Myers,* (1989) non–Carpenter entries with Pleasance returning to confront the original killer. They ignored the second and third films and picked up where the original *Halloween* left off. See also **Friday the 13th; Slasher Movies.**

Halloween (1978)
Halloween II (1981)
Halloween III: Season of the Witch (1983)

Halloween IV: The Return of Michael Myers (1988)
Halloween V: The Revenge of Michael Myers (1989)

Hammer, Mike

Mickey Spillane's rough and tough private eye has had a checkered screen career. Biff Elliott played the movies' first Hammer in the 1953 3-D flick *I, the Jury,* a pedestrian adaptation of Spillane's 1946 best-seller. Ralph Meeker also missed the mark as Hammer in Robert Aldrich's *Kiss Me Deadly* (1955), but the picture nevertheless remains a stylish film noir with a loyal cult following. Spillane took a shot at the role himself in 1963's *The Girl Hunters,* but he quickly abandoned his acting career to return to writing. To date, the most successful Hammer has been Stacy Keach, who played Hammer in the 1983 TV-movie *Murder Me, Murder You,* and the subsequent series "Mickey Spillane's Mike Hammer" (later retitled "The New Mike Hammer"). In the earlier days of television, Darren McGavin starred in a 1957–58 syndicated TV series called "Mickey Spillane's Mike Hammer."

I, the Jury (1953) (Biff Elliott)
Kiss Me Deadly (1955) (Ralph Meeker)
My Gun Is Quick (1957) (Robert Bray)
The Girl Hunters (1963) (Mickey Spillane)
Mickey Spillane's Margin for Murder (1981 TVM) (Kevin Dobson)

I, the Jury (1982) (Armand Assante)
Murder Me, Murder You (1983 TVM) (Stacy Keach)
The Return of Mickey Spillane's Mike Hammer (1986 TVM) (Keach)
Murder Takes All (1989 TVM) (Keach)

Happy Hooker Series

Xaviera Hollander's best-seller about her experiences as New York City's premiere madam served as the inspiration for three ill-conceived features. *The Happy Hooker* (1975) had pretensions of being a sly, naughty satire. But a leaden script and a miscast, red-headed Lynn Redgrave resulted in a major misfire. Blonde Joey Heatherton replaced Redgrave in *The Happy Hooker Goes to Washington* (1977), a sex-and-politics comedy that was sexually boring and politically unfunny. Brunette Martine Beswicke finished the series with *The Happy Hooker Goes Hollywood* (1980). The Brits proved that a funny movie could be made from the confessions of a real-life madam with 1987's *Personal Services,* an honest, sharply-etched portrait of Cynthia Payne (played by Julie Walters).

The Happy Hooker (1975)
The Happy Hooker Goes to Washington (1977)
The Happy Hooker Goes to Hollywood (1980)

Hardy, Andy

For a decade, the Hardys reigned as America's favorite family and Mickey Rooney, as Andy Hardy, captured the public's affection as no other teenager. His growing pains were chronicled in 15 highly successful films released during 1937–1946. The MGM series made a modest debut with *A Family Affair,* Louis Mayer's attempt to duplicate the popularity of Eugene O'Neill's family comedy-drama *Ah, Wilderness.* Mayer even reunited three stars from the 1935 film version of O'Neill's play: Lionel Barrymore, Cecilia Parker, and 17-year-old Mickey Rooney. To MGM's surprise, *A Family Affair* was a solid hit, prompting an immediate sequel. In *You're Only Young Once,* Lewis Stone replaced Lionel Barrymore, with Rooney and Parker (as Andy's older sister Marian) remaining as the Hardy children. Other series regulars included British actress Fay Holden as Ma, Sara Haden as Aunt Millie, and Ann Rutherford as Andy's sometime girlfriend. The cast clicked immediately, especially the chemistry between stern, but understanding, Judge Stone and his unpredictable son Andy. The popularity of Rooney's character became evident in the third film, 1938's *Judge Hardy's Children,* and the series shifted its focus to Andy. The plots typically centered on Andy's love life and this afforded MGM the opportunity to build up rising stars like Judy Garland, Donna Reed, Lana Turner, Esther Williams, and Kathryn Grayson. The series lost momentum during World War II, with its star in the Army, and never fully recovered. Mickey was growing up, too — he was 24 when college student Andy encountered a pair of vivacious twins in *Andy Hardy's Blonde Trouble.* The series apparently ended in style with 1946's *Love Laughs at Andy Hardy.* However, 12 years later, *Andy Hardy Comes Home* tried to turn Rooney into an understanding father figure. This one-time revival didn't work, due to the absence of Lewis Stone (he died in 1953) and the growing popularity of television family comedies.

A Family Affair (1937)	(1941)
You're Only Young Once (1938)	*Life Begins for Andy Hardy* (1941)
Judge Hardy's Children (1938)	*Andy Hardy's Double Life* (1942)
Love Finds Andy Hardy (1938)	
Out West with the Hardys (1938)	*The Courtship of Andy Hardy* (1942)
The Hardys Ride High (1939)	*Andy Hardy's Blonde Trouble* (1944)
Judge Hardy and Son (1939)	
Andy Hardy Gets Spring Fever (1939)	*Love Laughs at Andy Hardy* (1946)
Andy Hardy Meets Debutante (1940)	*Andy Hardy Comes Home* (1958)
Andy Hardy's Private Secretary	

Having Babies Series

Title tells all in this TV-movie series about couples experiencing childbirth. The second film introduced Susan Sullivan as Dr. Julie Farr, who became the principal character in the third film. Sullivan subsequently starred in a 1978 TV series known both as "Having Babies" and "Julie Farr, M.D." Less than three years after the show's demise, Ms. Sullivan showed up as Maggie on the long-running soap opera "Falcon Crest." See also **Babies.**

Having Babies (aka *Giving Birth*) (1976 TVM)	*Having Babies II* (1977 TVM)
	Having Babies III (1978 TVM)

Heaven

The cinema's view of heaven has tended to rely on soft focus and swirling mist. The most visually arresting conception along these lines is probably Michael Powell and Emeric Pressburger's *Stairway to Heaven* (1946), with its neverending staircase projecting itself from colorful Earth to black-and-white heaven. On the other hand, heaven looked very much like this world in *Made in Heaven*. In 1985's *The Heavenly Kid,* it was an ugly place filled with crowded trains and angels in frumpy clothes—no wonder the title character returned to Earth. *The Adding Machine* (1968) offered a bleak view of heaven with hellish overtones. It sent a clerk, who had murdered his boss after being replaced by a machine, to a heaven where he worked constantly with a similar machine. More humane heavenly activities have included celestial trials *(Stairway to Heaven* and *The Story of Mankind)*, plans for armageddon *(The Horn Blows at Midnight)*, and preparation of children about to be born *(The Blue Bird* and *Made in Heaven)*. Some of the most prominent heavenly authority figures include Rex Ingram's "de Lawd" in *Green Pastures* (1930), Lionel Barrymore's "Heavenly General" in *A Guy Named Joe* (1943), and Abraham Sofaer as the judge in *Stairway to Heaven.* Peter Cook as the Devil went to heaven to tell God he had won the battle for souls in the irreverent comedy *Bedazzled* (1967). Actress Diane Keaton edited movie clips and interviews into her offbeat documentary *Heaven* (1987). Purgatory has been glimpsed in 1944's *Between Two Worlds* and 1985's *Impure Thoughts.* See also **Angels.**

Liliom (1930)
Green Pastures (1936)
The Blue Bird (1940)
Here Comes Mr. Jordan (1941)
A Guy Named Joe (1943)
Heaven Can Wait (1943)
The Horn Blows at Midnight (1945)
Down to Earth (1947)
Stairway to Heaven (aka *A Matter of Life and Death*) (1946)
The Bad Lord Byron (1948)

You Never Can Tell (1951)
Carousel (1956)
The Flight That Disappeared (1961)
The Story of Mankind (1957)
Bedazzled (1967)
The Adding Machine (1968)
Heaven Can Wait (1978)
Resurrection (1980)
The Heavenly Kid (1985)
Made in Heaven (1987)
Heaven (1987)
All Dogs Go to Heaven (1989)

Hell

No one wants to go to hell—and filmmakers have been no exception. Director Harry Lachman offered the most elaborate view, a striking 10-minute sequence of writhing souls in 1935's *Dante's Inferno.* Italian horror specialist Mario Bava created an atmospheric Hades for 1961's *Hercules in the Haunted World* (apparently, the producers decided against the title *Hercules in Hell*). Christopher Lee, as one of Pluto's disciples, kept the seas of lava flowing and the naked girls chained. Surprisingly, the 1972 TV-movie *Haunts of the Very Rich* offered an interesting variation, whereby seven people trapped on a paradise island come to realize they are in hell. See also **The Devil**.

Dante's Inferno (1935)	*Haunts of the Very Rich* (1972
Heaven Can Wait (1943)	TVM)
Angel on My Shoulder (1946)	*The Sentinel* (1977)
Huis Clos (1954)	*Invitation to Hell* (1984 TVM)
Hercules in the Haunted World	*The Gate* (1987)
(1961)	

Helm, Matt

Dean Martin, playing a third-rate James Bond, fumbled his way through four Helm pictures, all made between 1966 and 1968. Tony Franciosa reprised the role for the 1975 TV-movie *Matt Helm* and a short-lived series. Franciosa's Helm was a private eye, though, instead of a secret agent.

The Silencers (1966)	*The Ambushers* (1968)
Murderer's Row (1967)	*The Wrecking Crew* (1969)

Henry Series

Character actor Raymond Walburn played Henry Latham, a rascally cheapskate with good intentions, in this minor Monogram series. The plots frequently hinged on Henry's outraged reactions to rising prices. In *Father Makes Good,* he bought a cow to avoid a milk tax. He refused to pay the butcher and took up hunting in *Father's Wild Game.* In other series entries, Henry bumbled routine jobs (e.g. accidentally burned up a toll bridge), but somehow managed to straighten things out in the end. Walter Catlett was Henry's pal Mayor Colton.

Henry the Rainmaker (1949)	*Father's Wild Game* (1951)
Leave It to Henry (1949)	*Father Takes the Air* (1951)
Father Makes Good (1950)	

Herbie, the Love Bug

Disney's longest-running film series starred a lovable Volkswagen Beetle with a mind of its own. *The Love Bug* and *Herbie Rides Again* did brisk business, but the later Herbie movies were released when Disney Productions was struggling to recapture its youthful audience. Dean Jones played Herbie's human sidekick in the first and third films and revived his role for the hour-long (!) CBS television series "Herbie, the Love Bug." It premiered in 1982 and lasted just one month before being cancelled.

The Love Bug (1969)	(1977)
Herbie Rides Again (1974)	*Herbie Goes Bananas* (1980)
Herbie Goes to Monte Carlo	

Hercules

Super distributor Joseph E. Levine transformed *Hercules,* a modest Italian sword-and-sandal epic, into one of the biggest international hits of 1957. Steve Reeves, a former Mr. World and Mr. Universe, starred as the mythical muscle man who undertakes a series of perilous quests to win the hand of a beautiful princess (the worthy Sylva Koscina). Reeves repeated the role in the sequel *Hercules Unchained,* but bowed out after that. Since then, a succession of muscular hunks have essayed the role: Reg Park, Mark Forest, Alan Steel (real name Sergio Ciani), Gordon Scott, Arnold Schwarzenegger, and most recently Lou *(Incredible Hulk)* Ferrigno. Even muscle builder Mickey Hargitay played Herc in *The Loves of Hercules*—with wife Jayne Mansfield in support in a double role! None of these cheap programmers were particularly distinguished, although horror director Mario Bava's *Hercules in the Haunted World* presented an atmospheric view of Hell. Hercules clones have proliferated, too, especially during the mid–1960s. Maciste (q.v.) and Goliath both had their own series, though it was often difficult to tell who was who. *Maciste e la Regina di Samar* wound up as *Hercules Against the Moonmen* when shown on American TV. The 1974 United Artists release *Hercules vs. Kung Fu* (aka *Mr. Hercules Against Karate*) had nothing to do with Hercules, being just another Kung Fu school "chop socky" picture. See also **Maciste.**

> *Hercules* (aka *The Labors of Hercules; Le Fatiche di Ercole*) (1957) (Steve Reeves)
> *Hercules Unchained* (aka *Ercole e la Regina di Lidia*) (1959) (Reeves)
> *The Loves of Hercules* (aka *Hercules and the Hydra*) (1960) (Mickey Hargitay)
> *Ulysses Against Hercules* (aka *Hercules vs. Ulysses; Ulysses Against the Son of Hercules; Ulisse contro Ercole*) (1961) (Georges Marchal)
> *The Fury of Hercules* (aka *La Furia di Ercole*) (1961) (Brad Harris)
> *Hercules in the Vale of Woe* (aka *Hercules Against Maciste in the Vale of Woe*) (1962) (Kirk Morris)
> *The Three Stooges Meet Hercules* (1962) (Samson Burke)
> *Hercules and the Captive Women* (aka *Hercules and the Haunted Women; Ercole alla Conquista della Atlantide*) (1963) (Reg Park)
> *Hercules, the Invincible* (aka *Ercole l'Invincibile*) (1963) (Dan Vadis)
> *Jason and the Argonauts* (1963) (Nigel Green)
> *Conquest of Mycene* (aka *Hercules Attacks; Hercules vs. Moloch; Ercole contro Moloch*) (1963) (Gordon Scott)
> *Hercules vs. the Giant Warriors* (aka *Triumph of Hercules; Hercules and the Ten Avengers; Il Trionfo di Ercole*) (1964) (Vadis)
> *Hercules Against Rome* (aka *Ercole contro Roma*) (1964) (Alan Steel)
> *Samson and the Mighty Challenge* (aka *Hercules, Maciste, Samson, and Urus vs. the Universe; Ercole, Sansone, Maciste, Ursus gli Invincili*) (1964) (Steel)
> *Hercules Against the Sons of the Sun* (aka *Ercole contro i Figli del*

Sole) (1964) (Mark Forest)
Hercules and the Tyrants of Babylon (aka *Ercole contro i Tiranni di Babilonia*) (1964) (Rock Stevens)
Hercules in the Haunted World (aka *Hercules vs. the Vampires; Hercules at the Center of the Earth; Ercole al Centro Delle Terra*) (1964) (Park)
Hercules of the Desert (aka *La Valle dell'Eco Tonante*) (1964) (Morris)
Hercules, Samson, and Ulysses (aka *Ercole Sfida Sansone*) (1965) (Morris)
Hercules, Prisoner of Evil (aka *Terror of the Kirghiz*) (1967) (Park)
Hercules in New York (aka *Hercules: The Movie*) (1970) (Arnold Schwarzenegger)
Hercules (1983) (Lou Ferrigno)
Hercules II (aka *Adventures of Hercules*) (Ferrigno)

Hickok, Wild Bill, Series

Frontier marshal James Butler Hickok, aka Wild Bill, has been portrayed by many actors—but only one was popular enough to borrow his nickname permanently. Gordon Elliott became Wild Bill Elliott after trail blazing his way to fame in Columbia's 1938 serial *The Great Adventures of Wild Bill Hickock*. Two years later, Columbia resurrected Wild Bill as Wild Bill and produced an eight film Hickok series. The series came to an end when Elliott signed with Republic in 1943 and went on to achieve his greatest success as Red Ryder (q.v.).

Prairie Schooner (aka *Through the Storm*) (1940)
Beyond the Sacramento (aka *The Power of Justice*) (1941)
The Wildcats of Tucson (aka *Promise Unfulfilled*) (1941)
Across the Sierras (aka *Welcome Stranger*) (1941)
North from the Lone Star (1941)
Hands Across the Rockies (1941)
Lone Star Vigilantes (aka *The Devil's Price*) (1942)
Bullets for Bandits (1942)

The Higgins Family

With MGM's Hardy Family (q.v.) and 20th Century–Fox's Jones Family (q.v.) riding high in the late 1930s, it was inevitable that low-budget Republic Pictures would initiate its own family affair. Thus, the Higgins Family series was born. For the first seven films, it was indeed a family affair with James, Lucille, and son Russell Gleason portraying Joe, Lillian, and Sidney Higgins. The early entries centered on conflicts between Joe and Lillian. They wound up in divorce court in *The Higgins Family*, but a happy ending prevailed. However, they were at odds again in *Should Husbands Work?*, with Lillian taking over Joe's job and leaving him the housework. The Gleasons, along with Harry Davenport as Grandpa, bowed out of the series after 1940's *Grandpa Goes to Town*. Roscoe Karns (Joe), Ruth Donnelly (Lil), George Ernest (Sidney), and Spencer Charters (Grandpa) took over the roles for the last two films. Interestingly, George Ernest and Russell Gleason both appeared in the Jones Family series. Ernest played young Roger Jones, while Gleason was Bonnie Jones' boyfriend and eventual husband Herbert Thompson. Russell Gleason's acting career ended suddenly when he fell from a hotel window in 1945. He was 37.

The Higgins Family (1938)	*Earl of Puddlestone* (1940)
The Covered Trailer (1939)	*Grandpa Goes to Town* (1940)
Money to Burn (1939)	*Meet the Missus* (1940)
My Wife's Relations (1939)	*Petticoat Politics* (1941)
Should Husbands Work? (1939)	

The High Schoolers

The forerunner of AIP's *Beach Party* movies (q.v.), this Monogram series mixed energetic teens with popular music. Freddie Stewart and June Preisser played the main characters, bland high school lovers Freddie Trimball and Dodie Rogers. However, the series is best remembered for featuring supporting performers which TV would turn into familiar faces. Fellow student Noel Neill went on to become Lois Lane in the hit "Superman" TV series. College professor Frank Cady became Sam Drucker on "Green Acres." And Alan Hale, Jr., the Marine-turned-student in 1947's *Sarge Goes to College,* wound up spending several years as the Skipper on "Gilligan's Island." If the series' entries featured dull, stereotypical plots (a big football game, class elections, etc.), the music made up for it. In addition to boasting offbeat tunes like "Jungle Rhumba" and "Sherwood's Forest," the High Schooler films captured captivating performances by bands like the Gene Krupa Orchestra.

High School Hero (1946)	*Vacation Days* (1947)
Junior Prom (1946)	*Campus Sleuth* (1948)
Sarge Goes to College (1947)	*Smart Politics* (1948)

Hitchhiking

Hitchhiking has come into play in dozens of "road" movies, such as 1985's *The Sure Thing* and, most memorably, 1934's *It Happened One Night.* The latter featured the now-classic scene in which Clark Gable, after trying futilely to attract a ride via the traditional thumb method, receives instruction from Claudette Colbert on how to use one's legs to better effect. The dangers of picking up hitchhikers have been explored in subtle thrillers like *Hitchhike!* and gory horror pictures like *The Hitcher.* The horror anthology *Creepshow 2* spawned the most memorable hitchhiking line, with a walking corpse following Lois Chiles around and moaning repeatedly: "Thanks for the ride, lady!" The 1972 *Thumb Tripping* rates the most hitchhiking scenes per movie with its plot about two hippies (Michael Burns and Meg Foster) hitching across the country. Many movies have revolved around characters picked up from the roadside, including *Detour* (1945), *Three Into Two Won't Go* (1969), and *Ginger in the Morning* (1973).

It Happened One Night (1934)	*Hitchhike!* (1974 TVM)
The Devil Thumbs a Ride (1947)	*Diary of a Hitchhiker* (1979 TVM)
The Hitch-Hiker (1953)	*Road Games* (1981)
Knife in the Water (1962)	*Vagabond* (1985)
Nightmare in the Sun (1964)	*The Hitcher* (1986)
Thumb Tripping (1972)	*Creepshow 2* (1987)

Hitler

The role of Adolf Hitler has frustrated more than one good actor. Alec Guinness gave one of his lesser performances as the Nazi dictator in *Hitler: The Last Ten Days* (1973). Anthony Hopkins overplayed the part (but nevertheless won an Emmy) in the 1981 TV-movie *The Bunker*. Even reliable Richard Basehart could not overcome his basic miscasting in the low-key 1962 biography *Hitler*. Derek Jacobi probably gave the best star turn as Hitler in the epic two-part TV-movie *Inside the Third Reich* (1982). In the 1940s, character actor Robert Watson specialized in playing Hitler. In addition to starring in 1943's *The Hitler Gang,* he did cameos as Hitler in *The Devil with Hitler* (1942), *The Miracle of Morgan's Creek* (1944), *The Story of Mankind* (1957), and many others. Plots to assassinate Hitler provided the premise for *Man Hunt* (1941), its remake *Rogue Male* (1976), *Hitler—Dead or Alive* (1943), *The Strange Death of Adolf Hitler* (1943), *The Plot to Assassinate Hitler* (1955), and the fact-based *Jackboot Mutiny* (1955). Luther Adler played an impersonator who *did* kill Hitler and take his place in 1951's fanciful *The Magic Face.* Veronica Lake played a mad scientist who dumps a swarm of maggots on Hitler's faced in the obscure gorefest *Flesh Feast* (1970). Another deranged scientist managed to keep Hitler's head alive atop a table in 1963's dreadful *They Saved Hitler's Brain.* Ira Levin fashioned an ingenius plot about Hitler cloning in 1978's *The Boys from Brazil.* The same year's *The Lucifer Complex* found Robert Vaughn investigating another Hitler cloning plot. Charlie Chaplin treated Hitler comically in his topical farce *The Great Dictator* (1940). Indiana Jones got Hitler's autograph in *Indiana Jones and the Last Crusade* (1989), while Woody Allen's *Zelig* (1983) turned up in newsreel footage with the German dictator. Mel Brooks' *The Producers* (1968) featured a stage musical called "Springtime for Hitler."

The Great Dictator (1940)	*Hitler: Dead or Alive* (1943)
Man Hunt (1941)	*The Strange Death of Adolf Hitler* (1943)
To Be or Not to Be (1942)	

The Hitler Gang (1944)
The Magic Face (1951)
Canaris Master Spy (1954)
The Plot to Assassinate Hitler (1955)
Jackboot Mutiny (1955)
The Last Ten Days (aka The Last Ten Days of Adolf Hitler) (1956)
Hitler (1962)
The Black Fox (1962)
They Saved Hitler's Brain (aka Madmen of Mandoras) (1963)
The Producers (1968)
Flesh Feast (1970)
Adolf Hitler: My Part in His Downfall (1972)

Hitler: The Last Ten Days (1973)
Undercovers Hero (aka Soft Beds, Hard Battles) (1973)
Rogue Male (1976 TVM)
The Boys from Brazil (1978)
The Lucifer Complex (1978)
Our Hitler, a Film from Germany (1980)
The Bunker (1981 TVM)
To Be or Not to Be (1983)
Hitler's S.S.: Portrait in Evil (1985 TVM)
Dirty Dozen: The Next Mission (1985 TVM)
Indiana Jones and the Last Crusade (1989)

Hockey

This game's reputation for violence would seem to make it ideal subject matter for a movie. But even during the bloody 1970s, when *The Longest Yard* (1974) and *Rollerball* (1975) glorified sports violence, hockey made little impact. Its big shot at stardom came with 1977's *Slap Shot,* which cast Paul Newman as the desperate coach of a bush-league hockey team. The film fared well at the boxoffice, but its returns failed to inspire even a "B"-movie rip-off. ABC capitalized on the game's temporary popularity following the USA team's stunning upset of the Russians in the 1980 Olympics by producing a movie version titled *Miracle on Ice.* Five years later, Michael Keaton and Rob Lowe took to the ice in *Touch and Go* and *Youngblood,* respectively. Keaton's film sat on the shelf for over a year and then barely got released. Lowe's picture fizzled as well, signalling either a lack of public interest in hockey or the game's inability to attract serious filmmakers. Hockey also played a minor role in *Love Story* — Oliver (Ryan O'Neal) had a passion for playing it. *Friday the 13th's* popular killer Jason made hockey masks fashionable for psychopaths.

King of Hockey (1936)
It's a Pleasure (1945)
Love Story (1970)
Paperback Hero (1973)
Slap Shot (1977)
The Deadliest Season (1977 TVM)

The Boy Who Drank Too Much (1980 TVM)
Miracle on Ice (1981 TVM)
Hockey Night (1984)
Generation (1985 TVM)
Touch and Go (1986)
Youngblood (1986)

Holmes, Sherlock

Literature's most renowned detective is certainly one of the screen's busiest. Only Charlie Chan rivals him in number of film appearances in the sound era and, even at that, the Baker Street sleuth has been played by more actors than any detective. The first recorded screen appearance of Arthur Conan Doyle's fictional mastermind was in a 1903 silent short (very short, about a minute) called *Sherlock Holmes Baffled.* The Conan Doyle mysteries made popular silent film subjects, but a definitive Holmes interpretation did not emerge until William Gillette made *Sherlock Holmes* in 1916. The screenplay was based on Gillette's own stage play, originally performed in 1899. Ellie Norwood was the most prolific silent Holmes, appearing in seven films between 1921 and 1923. British screen veteran Clive Brook introduced Holmes to the "talkies" in 1929's *The Return of Sherlock Holmes,* an updated mystery about a retired Holmes lured into detecting again by Watson's grown daughter(!). Four other actors played Conan Doyle's sleuth from 1931–1937, with Arthur Wontner garnering the most praise. Already in his mid-fifties, Wontner played an older Holmes, ably assisted by Ian Fleming (not the author) as Dr. Watson in all but one case (*The Sign of Four* with Ian Hunter). It's interesting to note that the five Wontner films were based on Conan Doyle works. Despite his success, Wontner's Holmes interpretation was eclipsed in 1939, when, in a stroke of casting genius, Basil Rathbone was signed to play Holmes in 20th Century– Fox's lavish *The Hound of the Baskervilles.* Rathbone's crisp, energetic performance was delightfully balanced by Nigel Bruce's bumbling, but endearing, Watson (who in no way resembled Conan Doyle's intelligent physician/companion). The *Hound* was a rousing success and Fox quickly followed it with *The Adventures of Sherlock Holmes,* pitting Holmes against archvillain Professor Moriarty (superbly played by the menacing George Zucco). It rates as the finest of all Holmes films. Unfortunately, Fox let the series die and when Rathbone and Bruce reappeared as Holmes and Watson, it was for budget-minded Universal. Consisting of 12 movies shot between 1942 and 1946, the Universal series boasted updated story lines and shorter running times. Holmes battled Nazis, spies, and famous murderers with sinister names like The Creeper. The series peaked with *The Scarlet Claw,* an eerie, atmospheric puzzler featuring a marsh phantom and a murderous master of disguises. Roy William Neill produced and directed most of the entries and series regulars included Dennis Hoey as a frustrated Inspector Lestrade and Mary Gordon as the kindly housekeeper Mrs. Hudson. When Rathbone put his violin case away for good in 1946, other actors were hesitant to take up the role. Then in 1959, Hammer Films—England's foremost horror film factory—starred Peter Cushing in a colorful adaptation of *The Hound of the Baskervilles.* It was more violent than its predecessors, but handsomely mounted and boasting an excellent Watson in Andre Morell. Hammer could not secure rights for future films, although Cushing went on to play Holmes again on British television. With the Rathbone barrier broken, Holmes became a popular screen fixture again. John Neville played a dashing Holmes who encountered Jack the Ripper in *A Study in Terror* (1965), a film produced in association with Conan Doyle's son Adrian. Robert Stephens offered a complex, offbeat portrait in Billy Wilder's sly satire *The Private Life of Sherlock Holmes* (1970). Jack the Ripper reappeared to match wits with Christopher Plummer's sleuth in *Murder by Decree* (1979). The 1988 *Without a Clue* proposed the novel twist that Watson (Ben Kingsley) was the brains behind the duo and that Holmes was just an actor hired to play a part. On television, many performers have essayed the role, including Jeremy Brett, whose long-running series still appears on PBS's "Mystery!"

Rathbone/Bruce

The Hound of the Baskervilles (1939)
The Adventures of Sherlock Holmes (1939)
Sherlock Holmes and the Voice of Terror (1942)
Sherlock Holmes and the Secret Weapon (1942)
Sherlock Holmes in Washington (1943)
Sherlock Holmes Faces Death (1943)
Crazy House (1943) (cameo appearance)
The Scarlet Claw (1944)
Sherlock Holmes and the Spider Woman (aka *Spider Woman*)
  (1944)
The House of Fear (1945)
The Woman in Green (1945)
Pursuit to Algiers (1945)
Terror by Night (1946)
Dressed to Kill (aka *Sherlock Holmes and the Secret Code*) (1946)

Others

The Return of Sherlock Holmes (1929) (Clive Brook)
Paramount on Parade (1930) (cameo by Brook)
Sherlock Holmes' Fatal Hour (aka *The Sleeping Cardinal*) (1931)
  (Arthur Wontner)
The Speckled Band (1931) (Raymond Massey)
The Hound of the Baskervilles (1931) (Robert Rendel)
The Missing Rembrandt (1932) (Wontner)
The Sign of Four (1932) (Wontner)
Sherlock Holmes (1932) (Brook)
A Study in Scarlet (1933) (Reginald Owen)
The Triumph of Sherlock Holmes (1935) (Wontner)
Silver Blaze (1937) (Wonter)
The Hound of the Baskervilles (1959) (Peter Cushing)
Sherlock Holmes and the Deadly Necklace (1962) (Christopher Lee)
A Study in Terror (1965) (John Neville)
The Private Life of Sherlock Holmes (1970) (Robert Stephens)
The Hound of the Baskervilles (1972 TVM) (Stewart Granger)
The Adventures of Sherlock Holmes' Smarter Brother (1975)
  (Douglas Wilmer, Gene Wilder as the brother)
Sherlock Holmes in New York (1976 TVM) (Roger Moore)
The Seven-Per-Cent Solution (1976) (Nicol Williamson)

Murder by Decree (1979) (Christopher Plummer)
The Sign of Four (1983) (Ian Richardson)
The Hound of the Baskervilles (1983) (Ian Richardson)
Young Sherlock Holmes (aka *Sherlock Holmes and the Pyramid of Fear*) (1985) (Nicholas Rowe)
The Great Mouse Detective (1986)
The Return of Sherlock Holmes (1987 TVM) (Michael Pennington)
Without a Clue (1988) (Michael Caine as Reginald Kincaid as Holmes)

(Note: George C. Scott portrayed a man who believed himself to be Sherlock Holmes in 1971's *They Might Be Giants*. His psychiatrist, played by Joanne Woodward, was naturally named Dr. Watson. The plot was reworked in a 1976 TV-movie *The Return of the World's Greatest Detective*.)

Hood, Robin

Although five silent films appeared between 1909 and 1913, this legendary outlaw did not become a hot movie property until Douglas Fairbanks portrayed him in 1922. Since then, Robin Hood has never gone a decade without being featured in at least one movie. Errol Flynn was the definitive Robin in the 1939 classic *The Adventures of Robin Hood*. Apparently to avoid comparison with Flynn, no other major actor essayed the role until Richard Todd in Disney's 1952 *The Story of Robin Hood*. In the meantime, John Derek, Cornel Wilde, and June Laverick played the outlaw's offspring in, respectively, *Rogues of Sherwood Forest, Bandits of Sherwood Forest,* and *Son of Robin Hood* (actually daughter). Richard Greene leapt from his successful 1955–58 "Adventures of Robin Hood" TV series into a big-screen version, 1960's *The Sword of Sherwood Forest*. A few years later, Disney offered an animated *Robin Hood*, depicting the characters as animals (Robin was a fox). Sean Connery appeared as an older, wearier outlaw opposite Audrey Hepburn's Maid Marian in the "realist" version *Robin and Marian* (1976). Frank Sinatra and Bing Crosby headed an all-star cast in a musical gangster variation called *Robin and the Seven Hoods* (1964). Robin has been parodied in *Time Bandits* (1981), *The Zany Adventures of Robin Hood* (1984), and in Mel Brooks' short-lived 1975 TV-series "When Things Were Rotten."

Robin Hood (1922)	*The Story of Robin Hood* (1952)
The Adventures of Robin Hood (1938)	*Ivanhoe* (1952)
Bandits of Sherwood Forest (1946)	*Men of Sherwood Forest* (1954)
The Prince of Thieves (1948)	*Son of Robin Hood* (1959)
Rogues of Sherwood Forest (1950)	*Sword of Sherwood Forest* (1961)
Tales of Robin Hood (1951)	*Robin and the Seven Hoods* (1964)

A *Challenge for Robin Hood*
  (1968)
Robin Hood (1973)
Robin and Marian (1976)
Time Bandits (1981)

*The Zany Adventures of Robin
  Hood* (1984 TVM)
Robin Hood and the Sorcerer
  (1984 TVM)

Horse Racing / Equitation

Mickey Rooney is the undisputed champ of horse racing sagas with a track career spanning half a century. He played the son of a disgraced jockey in *Down the Stretch* (1936), Wallace Beery's jockey protégé in *Stablemates* (1937), a young jockey involved with crooks (and teamed with Judy Garland for the first time) in *Thoroughbreds Don't Cry* (1937), Elizabeth Taylor's young mentor in *National Velvet* (1944), the trainer of *The Black Stallion* (1979), and a horse owner in *Lightning, the White Stallion* (1986). Surprisingly, Rooney never made a race track comedy. However, horse racing hijinks seem to be a requirement for most comedians. The Marx Brothers produced the most memorable, 1937's *A Day at the Races,* which featured Groucho at his best as horse doctor Hugo Z. Hackenbush. Abbott and Costello raced a steed named Tea Biscuit in *It Ain't Hay* (1943). It was called *Money for Jam* in Great Britain, which one shouldn't confuse with *Money from Home* (1953), another stateside horse race comedy with Dean Martin and Jerry Lewis. Hope and Crosby never raced horses in the *Road* movies, but Bob gambled on them in *Sorrowful Jones* (1949) and *The Lemon Drop Kid* (1951), while Bing backed one in Frank Capra's *Riding High* (1950). Donald O'Connor and his talking mule sidekick Francis could have made a fortune in *Francis Goes to the Races* (1951), since the race horses told Francis that they always determined the winner before the race even began. A little boy's ability to predict horse race results with amazing accuracy ended in tragedy in *The Rocking Horse Winner,* a 1949 adaptation of the D.H. Lawrence short story. Filmmakers have deemed few real-life horse racing champions worthy of film biographies. The exceptions include a pair of exceptional horses in *The Story of Seabiscuit* (1949) and *Phar Lap* (1983), the latter being Australia's most famous racing champ. Although most horse races are of the Triple Crown variety, a handful have explored other horse racing events: Elizabeth Taylor entered *National Velvet* in the Grand National Steeplechase; father and daughter Charles Coburn and Peggy Cummins raced trotting horses in *The Green Grass of Wyoming* (1948); Tatum O'Neal and Melissa Gilbert set their sights on equestrian championships in, respectively, *International Velvet* (1978) and *Sylvester* (1985); and Gene Hackman and James Coburn were two of the riders in the grueling cross-country horse race in *Bite the Bullet* (1975). Other films featuring memorable horse racing sequences include *My Fair Lady* (1964) and the carousel horse race in *Mary Poppins* (1964). Film critics have pondered for years whether the title of *Million Dollar Legs* (1939) refers to the film's race horse or its star Betty Grable.

Broadway Bill (aka *Strictly Confidential*) (1934)
Little Miss Marker (aka *The Girl in Pawn*) (1934)
Down the Stretch (1936)
Three Men on a Horse (1936)
Charlie Chan at the Race Track (1936)
A Day at the Races (1937)
Thoroughbreds Don't Cry (1937)
Stablemates (1938)
Come on George (1939)
Million Dollar Legs (1939)
The Lady's from Kentucky (1939)
It Ain't Hay (aka *Money for Jam*) (1943)
National Velvet (1944)
Home in Indiana (1944)
The Great Mike (1944)
She Went to the Races (1945)
My Brother Talks to Horses (1946)
The Homestretch (1947)
Black Gold (1947)
The Green Grass of Wyoming (1948)
The Story of Seabiscuit (aka *Pride of Kentucky*) (1949)
The Great Dan Patch (1949)
Sorrowful Jones (1949)
Under My Skin (1949)
The Rocking Horse Winner (1949)
Boy from Indiana (1950)

Blue Grass of Kentucky (1950)
Riding High (1950)
Francis Goes to the Races (1951)
Blue Blood (1951)
The Galloping Major (1951)
The Lemon Drop Kid (1951)
The Rainbow Jacket (1951)
Boots Malone (1952)
Four Against Fate (aka *Derby Day*) (1952)
A Girl in Every Port (1952)
Money from Home (1953)
Fast Company (1953)
Pride of the Blue Grass (1954)
The Fighting Chance (1955)
Dry Rot (1956)
Glory (1956)
Photo Finish (1957)
Just My Luck (1957)
The Sad Horse (1959)
Mary Poppins (1964)
My Fair Lady (1964)
Bite the Bullet (1975)
International Velvet (1978)
Casey's Shadow (1978)
Run for the Roses (aka *Thoroughbred*) (1978)
My Old Man (1979 TVM)
Little Miss Marker (1980)
On the Right Track (1981)
Phar Lap (1983)
Sylvester (1985)
The Longshot (1986)
Lightning, the White Stallion (1986)
Hot to Trot (1988)

Horses

The horse has been a favorite film subject since Eadweard Muybridge used photography to study a horse in motion (allegedly to settle a $5000 bet) in 1872. Early horse roles were principally supporting ones, though Tom Mix's horse Tony attracted enough admirers to star in his own film, 1922's *Just Tony*. However, most early talkies either relegated horses to a mere means of transportation for cowboys or revolved around horse racing (see separate entry for a detailed discussion and list). *Kentucky* (1938) strayed from the race track long enough to offer a story of rival horse-breeding families. Yet, it lacked the horse appeal inherent in *My Friend Flicka* (1943), a heartwarming tale of the love between a young boy (Roddy McDowell) and a mare with madness in her bloodline (Flicka is the Swedish word for girl). McDowell and cast returned two years later with *Thunderhead, Son of Flicka,* a picturesque sequel in which McDowell set his horse free at the end. The following year, the same studio, 20th Century–Fox, released *Smoky,* Will James' classic horse story about the friendship between a wild stallion and a drifting cowboy (Fred MacMurray). *Smoky* and *Flicka* turned out to be highly influential films, establishing the pattern for other non-racing, person-loves-horse plots. Even John Steinbeck's *The Red Pony* (1949) offered only a minor variation, giving equal time to a purely human subplot about a boy confused over love for his father and affection for a hired hand. Two superior children-and-horse films, *Misty* (1961) and *The Black Stallion* (1979), were set partially on islands and adapted from popular juvenile novels (by Marguerite Henry and Walter Farley, respectively). *The Appaloosa* (1966) was a horse film for adults, with brooding Marlon Brando stalking the bandits that stole his steed. The only horse in *The Horse Without a Head* (1963) was a toy one hiding stolen loot. The most colorful stallion was the famous Horse of a Different Color that pranced around the Emerald City in 1939's *The Wizard of Oz*. Pegasus, the mythological winged horse, took to the air with Harry Hamlin aboard in the 1981 fantasy *Clash of the Titans*. Finally, for the record, the most famous cowboy horses were: Trigger (Roy Rogers), Champion (Gene Autry), Topper (Hopalong Cassidy), White Flash (Tex Ritter), Fritz (William S. Hart), Tarzan (Ken Maynard), and Blackjack (Allan Lane). Lane, in his post-cowboy days, provided the voice for TV's famous talking horse "Mr. Ed" (1961–65).

Just Tony (1922)
Kentucky (1938)
Sergeant Murphy (1938)
The Wizard of Oz (1939)
Florian (1940)
My Friend Flicka (1943)
Thunderhead — Son of Flicka (1945)
Smoky (1946)
Black Beauty (1946)
The Red Stallion (1947)
King of the Wild Horses (1947)
Stallion Road (1947)
The Red Pony (1949)
Flame of Araby (1951)
The Lion and the Horse (1952)
Gypsy Colt (1954)

Black Horse Canyon (1954)
The Courage of Black Beauty (1957)
Tonka (aka *A Horse Named Comanche*) (1958)
King of the Wild Stallions (1959)
The Misfits (1961)
Misty (1961)
The Horse Without a Head (1963)
The Miracle of the White Stallions (1963)
Mary Poppins (1964)
Indian Paint (1964)
The Appaloosa (aka *Southwest to Sonora*) (1966)

Smoky (1966)
The Horse in the Gray Flannel
    Suit (1968)
Black Beauty (1971)
The Red Pony (1973 TVM)
Running Wild (1973)
Mustang Country (1976)
The Littlest Horse Thieves (aka
    Escape from the Dark) (1976)
Equus (1977)

The Black Stallion (1979)
Eagle's Wing (1979)
The Electric Horseman (1979)
Wild Horse Hank (1979)
Clash of the Titans (1981)
A Rare Breed (1981)
The Man from Snowy River
    (1982)
Danger Down Under (1988
    TVM)

Hospitals

Film series about the medical profession, particularly the *Dr. Kildare*
(q.v.) movies and the British *Doctor in the House* (q.v.) comedies, have
made extensive use of hospital settings. Non-series hospital dramas
reached their peak during the 1960s, their production fueled by the success of popular TV series like "Dr. Kildare" and "Ben Casey." However,
by the early 1970s, filmmakers had begun to view hospitals with increasing
cynicism. Peter Sellers played a money-minded hospital administrator in
the smutty comedy *Where Does It Hurt?* (1972). It lacked the bite of Pad-
dy Chayefsky's *The Hospital,* a black comedy about a metropolitan
medical establishment run by incompetents and housing a killer. Still, either of those was easier to digest than Frederick Wiseman's potent documentary *Hospital* (1970). A decade later, director Lindsay Anderson ripped
into the British medical community with his irreverent hit-and-miss satire
Britannia Hospital (1982). Other hospital-set comedies have been less ambitious, preferring to generate medical gags instead of social commentary.
Nevertheless, the sight of the Carry On Gang carousing through a hospital
is almost as frightening as it is funny. The hospital, as a setting for fright
films, has been employed in *Halloween II* (1982), *Visiting Hours* (1982),
and *Terminal Choice* (1985). The hospital in *Halloween II* rates as the
creepiest—a cheap administrator's dream come true, where the staff is virtually nonexistent and the lights are turned off at every opportunity. In
1958's *Revenge of Frankenstein,* Dr. Frankenstein ran a clinic for the poor
(which allowed him to amass spare body parts). Genevieve Bujold discovered a scheme in which patients were killed and their body parts sold in
Michael Crichton's hospital thriller *Coma* (1978). Alastair Sim, as the
witty, droll Inspector Cockrill, investigated multiple murders in a World
War II hospital in the delightful 1946 mystery *Green for Danger.*

Green for Danger (1946)
The Sleeping City (1950)
White Corridors (1951)
Emergency Hospital (1956)
Behind the Mask (1958)
Carry On Nurse (1960)

The Young Doctors (1961)
The Interns (1962)
A Stitch in Time (1963)
The New Interns (1964)
U.M.C. (aka Operation Heart-
    beat) (1969 TVM)

Hospital (1970)	*Doctors' Private Lives* (1978)
The Hospital (1971)	*House Calls* (1978)
The Carey Treatment (1972)	*Halloween II* (1982)
Where Does It Hurt? (1972)	*Visiting Hours* (1982)
The Young Nurses (1973)	*Young Doctors in Love* (1982)
The Healers (1974 TVM)	*Britannia Hospital* (1982)
Medical Story (1975 TVM)	*Emergency Room* (1983 TVM)
One of Our Own (1975 TVM)	*Terminal Choice* (1985)
Coma (1978)	*Critical Condition* (1987)

Hotels

The hotel setting has registered as a favorite among filmmakers ever since *Grand Hotel*'s impressive guest roster made multicharacter dramas fashionable. This 1932 Best Picture, set in a Berlin hotel, featured Greta Garbo as a lonely ballerina, John Barrymore as a down-on-his-luck thief, Wallace Beery as a cold-hearted businessman, Lionel Barrymore as a dying man, and Joan Crawford as an ambitious secretary. It was officially remade with an American setting as 1945's *Weekend at the Waldorf,* but there have been dozens of unofficial copies which have borrowed the format. *Hotel Berlin* (1944), based on a novel by *Grand Hotel* author Vicki Baum, was a thinly-disguised reworking bolstered by an all-star Warner Bros. cast. *Separate Tables* (1958) was set at a seaside resort and earned Oscars for Best Actor David Niven and Best Supporting Actress Wendy Hiller. The 1933 *International House* brought an eclectic group of comedians (W.C. Fields, Burns & Allen, etc.) together at an Oriental hotel in a wild plot about early television. Other all-star hotel pictures have included Arthur Hailey's *Hotel* (1967) and the Neil Simon comedies *Plaza Suite* (1971) and *California Suite* (1978). Deserts seem like unsuitable locations for hotels, but Field Marshal Rommel (Erich von Stroheim) visited one in Billy Wilder's *Five Graves to Cairo* (1943) and Yvonne DeCarlo operated one in *Hotel Sahara* (1951). Despite the scorching sun, those hotels offered life-saving rates strictly unavailable at cheaper, horrorific places like the Bates Motel of *Psycho* fame. While the Bates has a corner on the terror motel market, it has received some competition from the Overlook Hotel in *The Shining* (1980), *Horror Hotel* (1960), and *Motel Hell* (1980). Jean Simmons' brother—and his hotel room—mysteriously disappeared in 1950's *So Long at the Fair.* Jean's frustration increased significantly when the hotel staff refused to acknowledge existence of the room or her brother. More pleasant hotels have provided the settings for musicals and comedies. Bing Crosby's *Holiday Inn* (1942) opened only on holidays, but still attracted quite a crowd due to Bing's crooning, Fred Astaire's dancing, and Irving Berlin's catchy tunes. Bing and Danny Kaye put on a big show to save their old Army general's hotel in 1954's *White Christmas.* Groucho played a desk clerk who had to deal with rowdy guests like Chico and Harpo in the 1929 Marx Brothers comedy *The Cocoanuts.* Nine years later, *Room Service* found Groucho and the boys sidestepping eviction from their hotel suite, while desperately trying to salvage a stage play.

The Cocoanuts (1929)
Grand Hotel (1932)
International House (1933)
Hollywood Hotel (1937)
Room Service (1938)
Hotel for Women (aka *Elsa Maxwell's Hotel for Women*) (1939)
Holiday Inn (1942)
Five Graves to Cairo (1943)
Hotel Reserve (1944)
Step Lively (1944)
Escape in the Desert (1945)
Hotel Berlin (1945)
Weekend at the Waldorf (1945)
So Long at the Fair (1950)
Hotel Sahara (1951)
White Christmas (1954)
The Girl Rush (1955)
The Green Man (1957)
Separate Tables (1958)
The Bellboy (1960)
Psycho (1960)
Horror Hotel (aka *The City of the Dead*) (1960)
Wake Me When It's Over (1960)
Man at the Carlton Tower (1961)
The Inn on the River (1962)
Tiara Tahiti (1962)
Honeymoon Hotel (1964)
Hotel (1967)
Nightmare Hotel (1970)
Plaza Suite (1971)
Snowball Express (1972)
Inn of the Damned (1974)
California Suite (1978)
Motel Hell (1980)
The Shining (1980)
Somewhere in Time (1980)
Experience Preferred...But Not Essential (1983 TVM)
Pink Motel (1983)
The Hotel New Hampshire (1984)
Private Resort (1985)
Bates Motel (1987 TVM)

The Howling

This loosely-connected werewolf series continued the 1980s trend of milking a decent horror film for as many sequels as possible (see also **Halloween, Friday the 13th,** and **Nightmare on Elm Street**). Joe *(Gremlins)* Dante directed 1981's *The Howling,* an affectionate mixture of gruesome horror and dark humor (peppered with inside jokes). Dee Wallace played the television newscaster who encounters a werewolf, suffers trauma, and goes to a retreat to recover. Alas, the place turns out to be crawling with bloodthirsty werewolves and Wallace unwillingly joins the pack. The Wallace character (played by another actress) appeared fleetingly in 1984's *The Howling II: Your Sister Is a Werewolf,* a U.S.-European coproduction. This cheap-looking sequel featured a tasteless werewolf lovemaking session and excessive footage of Sybil Danning's cleavage. Wit, style, and adequate werewolf makeup were conspicuously missing. Philippe Mora's *The Howling III* shifted the locale to Down Under and introduced two tribes of Aussie "werewolves" (who carry their offspring in pouches). The tongue-in-cheek premise strove to prove that werewolves are people, too. It even featured a defected Russian ballerina who transforms into a werewolf while on stage. *Howling IV* (1988) was lensed on a shoestring budget in South Africa. Instead of pursuing another interesting tangent, it chose to rehash the original film by sending an emotionally unstable novelist to a retreat once again populated by werewolves. See also **Werewolves.**

The Howling (1981)	*Marsupials* (1987)
The Howling II: Your Sister Is a Werewolf (1984)	*Howling IV:...The Original Nightmare* (1988)
The Howling III: The	

Huggetts Family

Described by film critic Leslie Halliwell as "Britain's answer to the Hardys," the Huggetts appeared in four features for Gainsborough. They were not even top-billed in their debut film, 1947's *Holiday Camp* (Jack Warner as Mr. Huggett was listed third in the cast). This charming comedy-drama, set at a highly-regimented holiday resort, interwove the story of several characters. But British moviegoers favored the Huggetts and they were given their own vehicle with 1948's *Here Come the Huggetts.* The next year, they became involved in politics and then concluded the series with a trip to Africa and an encounter with smugglers. Jack Warner and Kathleen Harrison, who played parents Joe and Ethel Huggett, continued to make films together (e.g. 1951's *A Christmas Carol*). Hazel Court played their widowed daughter Joan in *Holiday Camp.* Other Huggett children included Susan Shaw as Susan and 15-year-old Petula Clark as Pet. Diana Dors and David Tomlinson, who both became familiar faces to British film fans, also appeared in supporting roles.

Holiday Camp (1947)	*Vote for Huggett* (1948)
Here Come the Huggetts (1948)	*The Huggetts Abroad* (1949)

Hulot, Monsieur

Writer-director Jacques Tati introduced his alter-ego in 1954's *Monsieur Hulot's Holiday,* a highly visual comedy about a middle-aged bachelor with a knack for unintentionally causing disruptions at a summer resort. The film featured minimal dialogue, inviting critics to compare Hulot to Chaplin's Tramp. Tati's later films expanded on his theme of man trapped in a technology-heavy, time-conscious world. A combination of financial problems and Tati's pursuit of perfection has severely limited his output. In addition to the four Hulot movies, he has produced only one other feature-length film, 1949's *Jour de Fete.* Tati did a cameo as Mr. Hulot in François Truffaut's *Bed and Board* (1970).

Monsieur's Hulot's Holiday (1953)	*Playtime* (1967)
Mon Oncle (1958)	*Traffic* (1971)

Humanimals

Not quite human, not quite animal, and not just a werewolf—that's an apt description of a humanimal. The phrase was coined in the 1951 comedy-fantasy *You Never Can Tell* to describe animals reincarnated as humans (Dick Powell played ex-dog Rex Terrier). More loosely defined, "humanimal" includes all creatures that are animal-turned-human, human-turned-animal, or a combination of species (see **Werewolves** entry for lycanthropes and were-cats). In both *Island of Lost Souls* (1933) and *The Island of Dr. Moreau* (1977), mad scientist Moreau (Charles Laughton and Burt Lancaster, respectively) medically transformed animals into men. It was obviously not a pleasant process, as the animal-men referred to the operating room as the House of Pain. Another mad scientist (John Carradine) turned a female ape into a beautiful woman in 1943's *Captive Wild Woman* (see **Dupree, Paula**), while George Zucco tried a monkey-to-man experiment in 1942's *Dr. Renault's Secret*. Malcolm McDowell accidentally discovered a pig-man in an experimental hospital in the 1973 satire *O Lucky Man!* Similar medical experiments yielded disappointing results in bottom-of-the-barrel horror pictures like *Terror Is a Man* and *Twilight People*. Not all humanimals were produced by science or reincarnation. Puppet boy Pinocchio fell in with a crowd of naughty kids on Pleasure Island and they were all transformed into donkeys in Disney's version of the famous fairy tale. Two children had the power to transform themselves into bears at night in the offbeat fable *The Two Little Bears* (1961). See also **Dupree, Paula; Werewolves.**

A Blind Bargain (1922)	*Atlantis, the Lost Continent* (1961)
Island of Lost Souls (1933)	
Pinocchio (1940)	*The Reptile* (1966)
Dr. Renault's Secret (1942)	*The Vulture* (1967)
The Mad Monster (1942)	*Twilight People* (1972)
Captive Wild Woman (1943)	*O Lucky Man!* (1973)
You Never Can Tell (1951)	*The Island of Dr. Moreau* (1977)
Terror Is a Man (aka *Blood Creature*) (1959)	*Oh, Heavenly Dog* (1980)
The Two Little Bears (1961)	*Ladyhawke* (1985)

Hunchbacks

The most famous, of course, is that charismatic bellringer Quasimodo, created by Victor Hugo in his classic *The Hunchback of Notre Dame* and portrayed on the screen by a bevy of fine actors, most notably: Lon Chaney, Sr. (1923), Charles Laughton (1939), Anthony Quinn (1957), and Anthony Hopkins (1981). Quasimodo's only rival for film popularity has been Ygor, the hunchbacked once-hanged shepherd immortalized by Bela Lugosi in *Son of Frankenstein* (1939) and *Ghost of Frankenstein* (1940) and parodied by Marty Feldman in *Young Frankenstein* (1974).

The Hunchback of Notre Dame
  (1923)
Son of Frankenstein (1939)
The Hunchback of Notre Dame
  (1939)
The Ghost of Frankenstein
  (1940)
House of Frankenstein (1944)
House of Dracula (1945)
Phantom from Space (1953)
Richard III (1956)
The Hunchback of Notre Dame
  (1957)
Revenge of Frankenstein (1958)
Mad Monster Party? (1967)
Candy (1968)

Ryan's Daughter (1970)
The Hunchback of the Morgue
  (1972)
Terror in the Wax Museum
  (1973)
Captain Kronos: Vampire
  Hunter (1974)
Young Frankenstein (1974)
Mr. Quilp (aka The Old
  Curiosity Shop) (1975)
The Hunchback of Notre Dame
  (1981 TVM)
Alsino and the Condor (1982)
Jean de Florette (1986)
The Name of the Rose (1986)
The Secret Garden (1987 TVM)

Hunting Parties

A favorite pasttime of the movies' idle rich, hunting parties served as social allegories in *The Shooting Party* (1984) and Jean Renoir's *The Rules of the Game* (1939). In Renoir's masterpiece, a rabbit hunt involving wealthy guests at a French chateau forms the center of the movie's structure. The hunters wait patiently, rifles in hand, for servants to beat the brush and scare rabbits from their hiding place. Then, they take part in a cruel, vivid massacre of dozens of rabbits. The death of these innocent animals — by a society they cannot comprehend — is mirrored later in the film by the accidental murder of a naive romantic. The death of a young boy during a fox hunt in 1988's *A Handful of Dust* signals the disintegration of his affluent parents' marriage. Bored European aristocrats Brigitte Bardot and Stephen Boyd visited the American West to mount a hunting expedition in Louis L'Amour's *Shalako* (1969). They found little game, but a lot of restless Apaches and an unlikely cowboy hero in Sean Connery. Errol Flynn saved an Indian chieftain during a tiger hunt in *The Charge of the Light Brigade* (1936) and lived to regret it. John Huston's gimmicky mystery *The List of Adrian Messenger* (1963) opened and closed with a fox hunt. The film's murderer, a master of disguises, plots a young boy's death, but meets his own demise in the heat of the climactic hunt. Hunting parties of a different kind, led by men obsessed, comprised the plots to *Moby Dick* (1930, 1956) and *The White Buffalo* (1977).

Moby Dick (1930)
The Charge of the Light
  Brigade (1936)
Rules of the Game (1939)
Moby Dick (1956)
The List of Adrian Messenger

  (1963)
The Hunt (1966)
Shalako (1969)
The White Buffalo (1977)
The Shooting Party (1984)
A Handful of Dust (1988)

Hypnosis

The hypnotist's unnerving stare, his piercing eyes aglow with flaming intensity, has been a trademark shot in almost all movies involving hypnosis. In 1909, film pioneer D.W. Griffith made *The Criminal Hypnotist,* one of the first movies in which hypnosis played a key role. A decade later, German director Robert Wiene made the highly expressionistic *The Cabinet of Dr. Caligari,* a macabre tale about a hypnotist who sends a somnambulist to commit murders. Two years later, fellow countryman Fritz Lang introduced Dr. Mabuse (q.v.), a criminal mastermind and hypnotist extraordinaire. The Mabuse character appeared in eight additional films, making him the screen's most enduring hypnotist. His fame has been equalled only by George du Maurier's *Svengali,* a mad Russian hypnotist whose mind-controlling eyes turned the beautiful, but untalented, Trilby into a singing sensation. Du Maurier's story has been filmed at least six times, with the 1931 version starring John Barrymore generally considered the finest. Jose Ferrer used hypnosis to manipulate Gene Tierney and implicate her in murder in Otto Preminger's *Whirlpool* (1949). A mesmerist employed it to control the Frankenstein Monster in *The Evil of Frankenstein* (1964). In 1953's *Invasion U.S.A.,* a man induced mass hypnosis on the patrons of a neighborhood bar so they could experience the effects of a Communist invasion. Count Dracula (q.v.) used a hypnotic look to great advantage in many of his films, although much of the effect could be attributed to his vampire charms. Hypnotism has played a major role in several reincarnation (q.v.) films, most notably *The Search for Bridey Murphy* (1956), *Spell of the Hypnotist* (1956) and the Barbra Streisand musical *On a Clear Day You Can See Forever* (1970). See also **Brainwashing.**

The Criminal Hypnotist (1909)
The Cabinet of Dr. Caligari (1919)
Dr. Mabuse, the Gambler (aka *The Great Gambler — Image of a Generation*) (1921)
Dr. Mabuse, King of Crime (aka *Inferno — People of a Generation*) (1922)
Running Wild (1927)
Svengali (1931)
Hypnotized (1933)
The Garden Murder Case (1936)
Night Monster (aka *House of Mystery*) (1942)
Calling Dr. Death (1943)
Shadows in the Night (1944)
The Frozen Ghost (1945)
The Woman in Green (1945)
Bewitched (1945)
The Mask of Dijon (1946)
Fear in the Night (1947)
Road to Rio (1947)
Whirlpool (1949)
Invasion U.S.A. (1953)
Svengali (1954)
The Hypnotist (1956)
Nightmare (1956)
The Search for Bridey Murphy (1956)
The She Creature (1956)
Spell of the Hypnotist (1956)
Hold That Hypnotist (1957)
I Was a Teenage Werewolf (1957)
Blood of Dracula (1957)

Curse of the Demon (aka *Night of the Demon*) (1958)
The Hypnotic Eye (1960)
Hypnosis (aka *Dummy of Death*) (1963)
The Evil of Frankenstein (1964)
The Misadventures of Merlin Jones (1964)
Creature of Destruction (1968)
On a Clear Day You Can See Forever (1970)
Let's Do It Again (1975)
Svengali (1983 TVM)

I Love a Mystery

Columbia Pictures produced this belated entry into the detective series sweepstakes of the 1940s. Based on Carleton E. Morse's hit radio show, the *I Love a Mystery* trilogy starred Jim Bannon as investigator Jack Packard and Barton Yarborough as his crony Doc Long. Their 1946 debut film was also their best, a strange little mystery about a secret Oriental society intent on securing a businessman's head because he resembled their dead founder. The story had been previously produced on the radio program as "The Head of Jonathan Monk." Despite offbeat plotlines, the film series failed to catch on and ended in 1946. Universal Pictures tried to revive the series with the made-for-TV film *I Love a Mystery*, which featured Les Crane as Packard and David Hartman as Long. A campy spoof of the radio series, it sat on the studio's shelf for six years before being televised in 1973.

I Love a Mystery (1945)
The Devil's Mask (1946)
The Unknown (1946)
I Love a Mystery (1973 TVM)

If . . .

If. . . (1968), *O Lucky Man!* (1973), and *Britannia Hospital* (1982) comprise director Lindsay Anderson's loosely-connected, savagely satirical trilogy about rebellions against society. In *If. . .*, the most critically acclaimed of the trilogy, three boys revolt against their highly-structured, often cruel, British public school. Yet, unlike Jean Vigo's 1933 classic *Zero for Conduct,* this rebellion goes to the extreme, complete with Malcolm McDowell and his fellow revolters gunning down authority figures in attendance at Speech Day. The film's surrealistic tones—is it real or fantasy?—is heightened by Anderson's alternating use of color and black & white (an economical necessity according to him). *O Lucky Man!* narrowed the focus to an individual, an ambitious young coffee salesman (McDowell again), trying to fit into society—to be wealthy, successful, and powerful. But he is manipulated by his own ambition and by those he aspires to be like. His wealthy employer frames him for a crime, he goes to prison, gets re-educated and released, tries to "help" others as he was, gets mugged by ungrateful tramps, and finally does something because *he wants* to do it. This, too, becomes an act of rebellion against a society of manipulators. The third film, *Britannia Hospital,* opted for a broader view and a more obvious target in one of society's standard institutions. McDowell and other alumni from the first two films appeared in brief roles, but *Britannia Hospital*'s heavily-episodic structure made it very hit-or-miss. It has failed to achieve the faithful followings of *If. . .* and *O Lucky Man!*

    If. . . (1968)   *Britannia Hospital* (1982)
    O Lucky Man! (1973)

In Search of. . .

Budget-minded film company Sunn Classics pioneered the pseudo-documentary with this brief 1970s series. Its first release was its best, a faithful adaptation of Erich Von Daniken's bestseller *Chariots of the Gods?* (1974). Actually, the film had been made in Germany in 1969 and excerpts had been aired on American TV as the one-hour TV special *In Search of Ancient Astronauts*. Sunn picked the film up in 1974 and marketed it using a system called "four walling." This consisted of saturating the market with TV previews, renting theaters for limited runs (one or two weeks), and then keeping all boxoffice receipts. The system worked amazingly well, with Sunn receiving large returns on minimal investments. Subsequently, it produced "documentaries" about Noah's Ark, the Shroud of Turin, mysterious "monsters" like the Yeti and Nessie and life and death. "Real" footage was frequently intercut with fictional reenactments. And one could always count on the narrator to add some sensationalism ("Would you like to see what it's like to enter that region between life and death?"). *In Search of Dracula* (1971) was produced by another company, though it was very much in the Sunn-style. Leonard Nimoy hosted a syndicated television program along the same lines. Dubbed "In Search of. . . ," it consisted of 144 episodes broadcast during 1976–82.

    Chariots of the Gods? (1974)   *Beyond and Back* (1978)
    In Search of Noah's Ark (1976)   *In Search of Historic Jesus*
    The Mysterious Monsters (1976)   (1979)

The Incredible Hulk

Comic book legend Stan Lee created the Incredible Hulk, an interesting Jekyll and Hyde (q.v.) variant, in 1962. Lee's protagonist was Dr. Bruce Banner, a scientist accidentally altered by a massive dosage of radiation. The outcome was that, when overcome with anger, the normally reserved Banner transformed into a greenish, super-strong Hulk with the dimensions of a Mr. Universe. Eventually, the Hulk would change back to Banner, who would remember nothing about his alter ego's activities. CBS brought the comic book character to TV in 1977 first in a couple of pilot movies and then as a "Fugitive"-styled series with a clever casting twist. Mild mannered Bill Bixby played Banner, with bodybuilder Lou Ferrigno replacing him as the Hulk. The show enjoyed a modest four-year run on the basis of its juvenile audience. There have been two revival movies, the first one pairing the Hulk with Thor, another comic book superhero. See also **Comic Book Characters.**

The Incredible Hulk (1977 TVM)	*The Incredible Hulk Returns* (1988 TVM)
The Return of the Incredible Hulk (aka *The Return of the Hulk*) (1977 TVM)	*The Trial of the Incredible Hulk* (1989 TVM)

Inner Sanctum

Lon Chaney, Jr. starred in this generally undistinguished low-budget mystery film series, which occasionally hinted at horror. The highlights were 1944's *Weird Woman,* the first film version of Fritz Leiber's *Conjure Wife* (later remade as the superior *Burn, Witch, Burn*) and an intriguing little puzzler titled *Calling Dr. Death.* In the latter film, Chaney plays a neurologist who uses hypnotism to determine if he unconsciously murdered his unfaithful wife. Inspired by a hit radio series, each movie was preceded by a warped head in a crystal ball who welcomed viewers to the Inner Sanctum (a mild version of "The Twilight Zone"). *Strange Confession* (1945) is frequently confused with Julien Duvivier's 1944 film of the same title, which is known as *The Impostor.* Oddly enough, the 1948 feature *Inner Sanctum* was not part of this series.

Calling Dr. Death (1943)	*The Frozen Ghost* (1945)
Dead Man's Eyes (1944)	*Pillow of Death* (1945)
Weird Woman (1944)	*Stranger Confession* (1945)

Insects

Be they little specks or large enough to crush a man, insects have long been a big screen pest. Indeed, the only insect of purely noble intentions was Jiminy Cricket of *Pinocchio* fame. He was also the best six-legged singer. In most films, however, insects have been portrayed as unthinking machines of destruction. A plague of locusts stripped the wheat fields in the climax to *The Good Earth* (an effect achieved by superimposing coffee grounds over oil-covered wheat). An army of soldier ants destroyed a South American plantation in 1954's *The Naked Jungle,* although the crisis served to mend Charlton Heston and Eleanor Parker's shaky marriage. That same year introduced a colony of 12-foot-high ants in *Them!,* the finest giant insect picture ever made. It was also the first to imply that nature was rebelling against man's misuse of radiation. Imitations quickly followed, featuring giant grasshoppers *(The Beginning of the End)* and a preying mantis *(The Deadly Mantis).* A single, regular-sized fly proved the culprit in 1958's *The Fly* (q.v.) when it interrupted an experiment and merged atomic particles with an affable scientist. Nine years later, *The Deadly Bees* started an insect film subgenre with its lively shock scenes of swarming bees stinging nice people to death. Variations gained popularity in the next decade, amid real-life rumors of killer bees flying up from South America. A popular TV-movie, *The Savage Bees,* was followed by *The Bees,* Irwin Allen's big-budget bust *The Swarm,* and *Terror Out of the Sky.* In other notable insect-related features: The Devil (Peter Cook) turned Dudley Moore into a fly in one of the episodes of *Bedazzled;* the Academy Award-winning pseudodocumentary *The Hellstrom Chronicle* explored the premise that insects will inherit the Earth one day; a government device designed to kill insects raised dead humans in *Don't Open the Window* and turned them into flesh-eating ghouls; a colony of intelligent ants bred humans to create a new super race in *Phase IV;* and the moon's inhabitants were discovered to be the insect-like Selenites in *First Men in the Moon.* See also **The Fly.**

The Good Earth (1937)
Pinocchio (1940)
Hoppity Goes to Town (aka *Mr. Bug Goes to Town*) (1941)
Once Upon a Time (1944)
Them! (1954)
The Naked Jungle (1954)
The Deadly Mantis (1957)
The Beginning of the End (1957)
The Fly (1958)
The Wasp Woman (1960)
Mysterious Island (1961)
First Men in the Moon (1964)
The Deadly Bees (1967)
Bedazzled (1967)
The Hellstrom Chronicle (1971)
Invasion of the Bee Girls (1973)
Phase IV (1974)
Don't Open the Window (aka *Breakfast at the Manchester Morgue*) (1974)
Killer Bees (1974 TVM)
Locusts (1974 TVM)
Bug (1975)
The Savage Bees (1976 TVM)
Empire of the Ants (1977)
Damnation Alley (1977)
Sinbad and the Eye of the Tiger (1977)
It Happened at Lake Wood Manor (aka *Panic at Lake Wood Manor; Ants*) (1977 TVM)
The Exorcist II: The Heretic (1977)
Terror Out of the Sky (1978 TVM)
The Bees (1978)
The Swarm (1978)
The Beast Within (1982)
Creepshow (1982)
Creepers (1985)
The Nest (1988)
Honey, I Shrunk the Kids (1989)

Invasions/Takeovers of the U.S.

The cinema has rarely dealt with the end of U.S. democracy, viewing it as a sobering premise with limited commercial appeal. Arch Oboler's *Strange Holiday* (1942) was about a businessman (Claude Rains) who returns from an isolated vacation spot to discover that American Nazis have gained control of the country. The film was originally produced in 1940 for General Motors employees. GM shelved it, however, and later sold it to MGM. The film sat in MGM's vaults until Rains and Oboler bought it back and released it in 1945 through a small independent company. After *Strange*

Holiday's fate, it's easy to see why the enemy invasion in 1953's *Invasion U.S.A.* was framed by a plot device explaining its events as being induced by mass hypnosis. Still, the film's opening scene is undeniably powerful, with a television broadcaster reporting that an enemy task force has taken over Alaska and set off atomic bombs in Washington state. Rod Serling's *Seven Days in May* (1964) internalized the takeover attempt, focusing on a military coup to oust the U.S. President. The Russians seized an Alaskan pipeline in retaliation for a U.S. grain embargo in the two-part TV-movie *World War III* (1982). John Mulius's *Red Dawn* (1984) was a pre-*glasnost* adventure about a successful Communist invasion of the U.S. and a subsequent guerilla counterattack staged by patriotic teenagers. The 1987 television miniseries "Amerika" expanded the same premise into a week's worth of TV viewing. The villainous Kryptonites of *Superman II* (1981) humbled the President and thrashed the White House before receiving their comeuppance from the Man of Steel.

Strange Holiday (1942)	*Superman II* (1981)
Invasion U.S.A. (1953)	*World War III* (1982)
Seven Days in May (1964)	*Red Dawn* (1984)

Invisibility

The father of modern movie invisibility was John P. Fulton, a special effects photographer who engineered the ingenius optical tricks in Universal's *Invisible Man* series. The original 1933 film set a standard that was difficult even for Fulton to better. How can anyone forget the eerie scene in which Jack Griffin (Claude Rains) unwraps the bandages covering his face—only to reveal an apparently headless man? Employing double exposure and masked negatives, Fulton displayed his superb invisibility effects in six other Universal films (denoted in list with *). Although no one has rivaled Fulton's trickwork, invisibility has shown up in movies with regularity since the late 1950s. The otherwise forgettable *Phantom from Space* (1953) introduced an invisible alien, a premise explored with more imagination in *Fiend Without a Face* (1958) and *Invisible Invaders* (1959). The murderous creature in 1956's *Forbidden Planet* could not be seen with the naked eye either. However, its invisibility status remains in question, since it turned out to be a "mental force" generated by Walter Pidgeon. Invisible criminals proliferated in the 1960s with Edgar G. Ulmer's *The Amazing Transparent Man* (1960) and the German series entry *The Invisible Dr. Mabuse* (1961). But gradually, invisibility became nothing more than a comedy gimmick in films like Disney's *Now You See Him, Now You Don't* (1971), the 3-D *Man Who Wasn't There* (1983), and *The Invisible Kid* (1988). Two TV-movies served as pilots for "serious" series. David McCallum played an invisible scientist on the run in 1975's *The Invisible Man* and its subsequent 1975-76 series. NBC cancelled the show after half a season, but still had faith in the concept. So, another pilot film *Gemini Man* was made with Ben Murphy as a government agent who could turn invisible for 15 minutes a day. The show debuted in September 1976—and went off the air in one month. An earlier TV series of "The Invisible Man" ran on CBS during 1958–60. The actor playing the lead role was never revealed.

The Invisible Man (1933)
The Invisible Man Returns (1940)
The Body Disappears (1941)
The Invisible Woman (1941)
The Invisible Agent (1942)
The Invisible Man's Revenge (1944)
Abbott and Costello Meet Frankenstein (cameo) (1948)
Abbott and Costello Meet the Invisible Man (1951)
Phantom from Space (1953)
Forbidden Planet (1956)
The Invisible Boy (1957)
The New Invisible Man (aka H.G. Wells' Invisible Man) (1957)
Fiend Without a Face (1958)
The Invisible Avenger (aka Bourbon St. Shadows) (1958)
Invisible Invaders (1959)
The Amazing Transparent Man (1960)
The Invisible Dr. Mabuse (aka The Invisible Horror) (1961)
The Invisible Terror (1963)
Mad Monster Party? (1967)
Mr. Superinvisible (aka The Invincible Invisible Man) (1967)
Now You See Him, Now You Don't (1971)
The Invisible Man (1975 TVM)
Gemini Man (aka Code Name: Minus One) (1976 TVM)
The Invisible Woman (1983 TVM)
The Man Who Wasn't There (1983)
The Invisible Kid (1988)

Islands

Tropical islands have long been a favorite movie setting—and with good reason. Where else is one apt to find cannibals, wild jungle animals, pirates, buried treasure, and erupting volcanoes? Monsters, too. King Kong lived on Skull Island, Godzilla visited Monster Island, Japan's favorite giant caterpillar, Mothra, was hatched on Infant Island, and an oversized pink crab harrassed hungry humans on *The Mysterious Island*. Human monsters are no exception, with Count Zaroff hunting human prey in *The Most Dangerous Game* and Dr. Moreau creating disfigured humans out of innocent animals in *The Island of Lost Souls*. On the other hand, islands have also brought unlikely lovers together, as in *The Blue Lagoon, Her Jungle Love, Return to Paradise,* and *Mutiny on the Bounty*. Island politics, as established by shipwrecked victims, are usually pretty simple, as portrayed in *Swiss Family Robinson, Robinson Crusoe,* and *Tempest*. But they can also get wildly out of hand, as in *Lord of the Flies,* William Golding's political parable about young shipwrecked boys who create their own civilization. Some of the more unique uses of island

settings occur in the following: *And Then There Were None* (1945),
Agatha Christie's classic whodunit about nine guests trapped on an island
mansion with a murderer; *The Challenge* (1970), which pits two men,
each representing his country, against one another to fight World War III
on an island; and Val Lewton's *Isle of the Dead* (1945), an eerie horror
tale about passengers quarantined on a Greek island where a dead woman
seems to be alive. One unique aspect to island-set films is that they can
end without warning. You never know when a volcano *(Atlantis, the Lost
Continent)* or a tropical storm *(Hurricane)* is going to wipe out the whole
place. See also **Crusoe, Robinson.**

Island of Lost Souls (1932)
The Most Dangerous Game (1932)
King Kong (1933)
Hurricane (1937)
The Edge of the World (1937)
Her Jungle Love (1938)
Road to Singapore (1940)
Beyond the Blue Horizon (1942)
Isle of the Dead (1945)
On an Island with You (1948)
The Blue Lagoon (1949)
Tight Little Island (aka *Whiskey Galore*) (1949)
Return to Paradise (1953)
Attack of the Crab Monsters (1957)
Island in the Sun (1957)
Swiss Family Robinson (1960)
Atlantis, the Lost Continent (1961)
The Mysterious Island (1961)
No Man Is an Island (aka *Island Escape*) (1962)
The Island (1962)
Donovan's Reef (1963)
Lord of the Flies (1963)
Island of the Blue Dolphins (1964)
Island of Terror (1966)
Hawaii (1966)
Island of the Burning Doomed (aka *Island of the Burning Damned*) (1967)
Godzilla on Monster Island (aka *Godzilla vs. Gigan*) (1971)
Papillon (1973)
Terminal Island (1973)
The Savage Is Loose (1974)
Islands in the Stream (1976)
Island of Dr. Moreau (1977)
Rescue from Gilligan's Island (1978 TVM)
The Blue Lagoon (1980)
The Island (1980)
Tempest (1982)
Pascali's Island (1988)

It's Alive

Larry Cohen's 1974 low-budget shocker about a killer baby has attracted a
strong cult following, chiefly due to its dual-sided view of modern morals.
When his wife gives birth to a murderous mutant baby, John Ryan em-
barks on a personal crusade to destroy the creature. His wife pleads for the
life of their "child," but Ryan feels socially responsible for all the deaths.
However, when he finally confronts his son, he realizes that "it" is an innocent. He watches helplessly as the police brutally murder it. In the 1978
sequel *It Lives Again,* Ryan's character has evolved into an obsessed man
fighting against a closed society that's unwilling to accept anything it cannot understand (e.g. the mutant children). Ryan dies, but converted

parent Frederic Forrest carries on the crusade. Cohen returned to the theme nine years later in the barely-released *It's Alive III: Island of the Alive*. A reworking of the second film, it once again portrayed the children as helpless victims of a cruel, prejudiced society.

It's Alive (1974)	*It's Alive III: Island of the*
It Lives Again (aka *It's Alive II*)	*Alive* (1987)
(1978)	

Jack the Ripper

This unidentified murderer of at least five prostitutes in London's Whitechapel distinct in 1888, the Ripper has been a screen fixture since the 1920s. He appeared briefly in a nightmare sequence in *Waxworks* (1924), in which his wax figure comes to life. And in G.W. Pabst's *Pandora's Box,* he popped up at the film's climax to deal retribution to a sinner. However, the first movie to feature Jack in a starring role was Alfred Hitchcock's 1926 adaptation of Marie Belloc Lowndes's chilling novel *The Lodger.* Unfortunately, when matinee idol Ivor Novello was cast in the title role, the ending was altered so that the Lodger turned out not to be the Ripper after all. The film was remade twice, in 1932 with Novello repeating his role (this version aka *The Phantom Fiend*) and in 1944 with Laird Cregar. The latter film was a gripping, atmospheric yarn, faithful to the book, and sporting a fine, frenzied performance from Cregar. (In fact, its success resulted in Cregar playing a psychotic murderer again in 1945's *Hangover Square.*) Over the next decades, the Ripper continued to appear in "B" films such as *The Curse of the Wraydons* (1946) and *Room to Let* (1950). However, the Terror of Whitechapel regained the spotlight with the release of 1959's *Jack the Ripper.* Scripted by horror veteran Jimmy Sangster (who also wrote *Room to Let*), this ordinary thriller offered no new variations. Yet, in the hands of super-producer Joseph E. Levine, it was exploited into a sensational worldwide hit that paved the way for more serious "psycho" films like *Peeping Tom* and *Psycho.* Six years later, Jack encountered Sherlock Holmes in the stylish pastiche *A Study in Terror.* It was produced in association with Arthur Conan Doyle's son Adrian. A similar fictional confrontation occurred in 1979's *Time After Time,* in which the Ripper (memorably played by David Warner) steals H.G. Wells' time machine and escapes to present-day San Francisco—where his acts of violence fit right in. In 1988's underrated *Jack's Back,* a modern-day killer replicated the Ripper's crimes in honor of Jack's 100th anniversary.

The Lodger (1926)	(1946)
The Lodger (aka *The Phantom*	*Room to Let* (1950)
Field) (1932)	*Man in the Attic* (1953)
The Lodger (1944)	*Jack the Ripper* (1958) (four-
The Curse of the Wraydons	part anthology with one

episode about the Ripper)
Jack the Ripper (1959)
A Study in Terror (1965)
Hands of the Ripper (1972)
(Jack's daughter)
The Ruling Class (1972)
Knife for the Ladies (1973) (a
Western variation)
Black the Ripper (1975)

Jack the Ripper (1976)
Murder by Decree (1979) (Jack
meets Holmes again)
Time After Time (1979)
Bridge Across Time (aka *Arizona Ripper*) (1985 TVM)
Jack's Back (1988)
Jack the Ripper (1988 TVM)

Jaws

Despite a hefty $12 million price tag and production difficulties, 1975's *Jaws* was pegged for blockbuster status from the start. Audiences had been carefully primed by Peter Benchley's thrilling bestseller and a publicity campaign that beached a Great White shark on the cover of *Time* magazine. The simple story of an East Coast resort transformed into a hunting ground for an insatiable shark went on to gross $133 million. Discounting ticket inflation, that made it the boxoffice champ of all time until *Star Wars* (and eventually *E.T.*) displaced it. The inevitable sequel, *Jaws 2*, followed in 1978, with local police chief Roy Scheider, his wife Lorraine Gary, and mayor Murray Hamilton returning from the original. Journeyman director Jeannot Szwarc replaced Steven Spielberg as helmer in what was basically a rehash of the original. The shark was a female this time (spouse of the first one), but she was scary enough to earn $82.5 million in domestic rentals. No one seemed interested in making a second sequel, though a National Lampoon–style spoof *Jaws 3 People 0* sat on the drawing boards for awhile. Finally, in 1983, at the height of the 3-D craze (q.v.), Universal released *Jaws 3-D*. A sequel in name only, it pitted Sea World staffers Dennis Quaid and Bess Armstrong against another human-devouring shark. The 3-D effects were excellent, but the profit figures were disappointing and apparently ended the series. Unfortunately, however, *Jaws: The Revenge* unexpectedly surfaced in 1987. Lorraine Gary returned as Roy Scheider's widow, who has become convinced that another shark (the son of the first one?) has a personal vendetta against her family. It was nonsense from start to finish with the entire cast, including Michael Caine, looking thoroughly embarrassed. No one went to see it, either, hopefully ending the series for good. See also **Sharks.**

Jaws (1975)
Jaws 2 (1978)

Jaws 3 (aka *Jaws 3-D*) (1983)
Jaws: The Revenge (1987)

Jekyll, Dr., and Mr. Hyde

Robert Louis Stevenson's dual-sided doctor has been one of the most active characters in cinema. Undoubtedly, much of his popularity stems from the challenge the double role affords actors, allowing them to run the gamut from good Dr. Jekyll to vile Mr. Hyde. Prior to 1920, no fewer than 12 silent versions appeared, ranging from Gene Gauntier's 1908 film to the comedy *Dr. Jekyll and Mr. Hyde Done to a Frazzle* (1914) to the offbeat *Miss Jekyll and Madame Hyde* (1915). Sheldon Lewis received good reviews as Jekyll/Hyde in a 1920 version for Louis B. Mayer. However, that same year, he was eclipsed by John Barrymore, whose flamboyant performance would remain the standard for the next decade. Barrymore's interpretation took a back seat, though, to Fredric March's Oscar-winning portrayal in Rouben Mamoulian's *Dr. Jekyll and Mr. Hyde* (1932). This remains the definitive adaptation of Stevenson's work with March still the only performer to win an Academy Award for a horror film. Spencer Tracy wore minimal make-up in MGM's lavish 1941 version, trying to emphasize Jekyll's emotional (as opposed to physical) transformation into Hyde. Tracy and the film received mixed reviews, inviting less-than-favorable comparisons to the March version. Subsequently, a major Jekyll/Hyde film was not made until Jean Renoir's French variation *The Testament of Dr. Cordelier* (1959). Nevertheless, Jekyll remained a popular character in lesser films. Abbott and Costello met the good doctor (as played by Boris Karloff) in 1951. In the film's funniest scene, Lou drinks Jekyll's potion and is transformed into a giant talking mouse. Louis Hayward played Jekyll's son and Gloria Talbott his daughter in a pair of unexceptional "B" horror films (although Talbott's movie confused matters by making Jekyll a werewolf!). Hammer Films remade Stevenson's tale as 1960's *House of Fright* (aka *The Two Faces of Dr. Jekyll*). Naturally, the British studio stressed the story's sexual elements, but it also included a refreshing twist, presenting Henry Jekyll as a dull wimp and Hyde as a dashing, handsome devil. Hammer also deserves credit for another interesting variation, 1971's *Dr. Jekyll and Sister Hyde,* in which Ralph Bates drinks the serum and turns into Martine Beswick. Dozens of movies have featured dual-personality themes or paid homage to Stevenson's story, such as 1942's *Before I Hang, The Nutty Professor,* Jean-Luc Godard's *Alphaville* (which featured two characters named Jekyll and Hyde), and Ken Russell's *Altered States* (1980).

> *Dr. Jekyll and Mr. Hyde* (1920) (Lewis)
> *Dr. Jekyll and Mr. Hyde* (1920) (Barrymore)
> *Dr. Pyckle and Mr. Pride* (1925) (parody with Stan Laurel)
> *Dr. Jekyll and Mr. Hyde* (1932) (March)
> *Dr. Jekyll and Mr. Hyde* (1941) (Tracy)
> *Abbott and Costello Meet Dr. Jekyll and Mr. Hyde* (1951)
> *Son of Dr. Jekyll* (1951)
> *Daughter of Dr. Jekyll* (1957)
> *The Testament of Dr. Cordelier* (aka *The Doctor's Horrible Experiment*) (1959)
> *House of Fright* (aka *The Two Faces of Dr. Jekyll*) (1960)
> *Mad Monster Party?* (1967)

Dr. Jekyll and Sister Hyde
   (1971)
Dr. Jekyll and the Werewolf
   (1971)
I, Monster (1971)
Twisted Brain (aka Horror
   High) (1974)

Dr. Black and Mr. Hyde (aka
   The Watts Monster; Dr.
   Black and Mr. White) (1976)
Dr. Heckyl and Mr. Hype
   (1980)
Jekyll and Hyde... Together
   Again (1982)

Jesus

The film industry's concern for reverence and its aversion to controversy
have severely limited screen portraits of Jesus. In many biblical films,
Christ's hand is shown or his voice is heard (as in 1959's *Ben Hur*), but
full figure shots are carefully avoided. Cecil B. DeMille mounted a tasteful
story of Jesus' life with 1927's *King of Kings,* starring H.B. Warner in the
title role. Nicholas Ray remade it to less effect in 1961 with 36-year-old
(but still youthful-looking) Jeffrey Hunter as Christ. Unkind critics
promptly dubbed it *I Was a Teenage Jesus.* George Stevens recruited
solemn Swedish actor Max Von Sydow to play Jesus in his excessively
lavish production of *The Greatest Story Ever Told* (1965). Originally
released at over four hours in length, it was cut to 141 minutes—but still
flopped. However, it did receive Harvard Lampoon's Please-Don't-Put-Us-
Through-DeMille-Again Award for being the movie "which best embodied the pretentions, extravagance and blundering ineffectiveness of the
traditional screen spectacular." The following year, Marxist filmmaker Pier
Paolo Pasolini received the praise of both film critics and Roman Catholic
leaders for his low-key, amateur-cast *The Gospel According to St. Matthew.* Other straightforward, reverent versions of Christ's life include
Franco Zeffirelli's two-part, 6½-hour TV-movie *Jesus of Nazareth* (1977),
the Israeli-made *Jesus* (1979), and another TV-movie *The Day Christ Died*
(1980). In 1973, the popular stage musicals *Jesus Christ, Superstar* and
Godspell reached the screen, but neither found an eager audience. *In
Search of Historic Jesus* (1979) purported to be a documentary about the
Shroud of Turin, but was less than enlightening. Two films of significantly
greater interest surfaced in 1988. *The Seventh Sign* mixed elements of
mystery and fantasy into its plot about Jesus' (Jurgen Prochnow) return to
Earth to prepare the human race for the forthcoming Apocalypse. Despite
an intriguing theme, it attracted little attention, especially when compared to the exaggerated controversy surrounding Martin Scorsese's *The
Last Temptation of Christ.* Fundamentalist groups tried to stop—sight
unseen—this adaptation of Nikos Kazantzakis' novel, chiefly due to a
dream sequence where Jesus (Willem Dafoe) was tempted by desires of
the flesh. Monty Python's *Life of Brian* (1979) incurred less wrath, despite
presenting a satirical tale about a poor bloke who is mistaken for Jesus and
crucified (it ends with a song-and-dance number on the cross). Christ's life

has been told in allegorical terms in a number of films, such as *El Topo* (1971) and *Greaser's Palace* (1972). Peter O'Toole and Peter Boyle played lunatics who believed they were Christ in, respectively, *The Ruling Class* (1971) and *The Dream Team* (1989).

Intolerance (1916)	*Jesus Christ, Superstar* (1973)
King of Kings (1927)	*The Passover Plot* (1976)
Ben Hur (1959)	*Jesus of Nazareth* (1977 TVM)
King of Kings (1961)	*In Search of Historic Jesus*
Barabbus (1962)	(1979)
The Greatest Story Ever Told	*Jesus* (1979)
(1965)	*The Day Christ Died* (1980)
The Gospel According to St.	*The Inquiry* (1987)
Matthew (1966)	*The Last Temptation of Christ*
The Milky Way (1969)	(1988)
Godspell (1973)	*The Seventh Sign* (1988)
The Gospel Road (1973)	

Jiggs and Maggie

George McManus created this comic strip in 1916 about a nouveau riche Irish couple with social aspirations. Comedian Johnny Ray played Jiggs in a series of silent two-reelers produced by Pathé Studios. The characters also appeared in a successful 1921 stage play called *Bringing Up Father*. That play served as the basis for a 1928 MGM film starring J. Farrell McDonald as the badgered Jiggs and Marie Dressler as society-minded Maggie. However, a series did not appear until budget-conscious Monogram re-introduced the characters in 1946 with another version of *Bringing Up Father*. Joe Yule (Mickey Rooney's father) and Renie Riano starred as Jiggs and Maggie in that film and four subsequent entries. Yule died in 1950, shortly after completing *Jiggs and Maggie Out West*. For sheer silliness, *Jiggs and Maggie in Society* rates as the series highlight, with Maggie taking dancing lessons from Arthur Murray and Jiggs learning etiquette from Dale Carnegie. Neil O'Malley and Agnes Moorehead also played the couple on a 1941 radio program.

Bringing Up Father (1928)	*Jiggs and Maggie in Jackpot*
Bringing Up Father (1946)	*Jitters* (aka *Jackpot Jitters*)
Jiggs and Maggie in Court	(1949)
(1948)	*Jiggs and Maggie Out West*
Jiggs and Maggie in Society	(1950)
(1949)	

Jones, Indiana

Steven Spielberg on *Raiders of the Lost Ark:* "The film's like popcorn, it doesn't fill you and it's easy to digest and it melts in your mouth and it's the kind of thing you can just go and chow down over and over again." That's precisely what moviegoers did with 1981's blockbuster homage to the days of serial thrills. Director Spielberg and executive producer George

Lucas (who cowrote the story) received most of the credit, with the witty screenplay by Lawrence Kasdan (pre–*Big Chill*) being largely ignored. Harrison Ford, playing a part not dissimilar from Han Solo in the *Star Wars* (q.v.) films, created the whip-carrying archaeologist/adventurer who battled Nazis for the Ark of the Covenant circa 1936. For some reason, the 1984 follow-up *Indiana Jones and the Temple of Doom,* turned out to be a *prequel* (q.v.) set three years before *Raiders.* The plot sent Indiana to India to fetch a magical jewel and rescue some enslaved children. The film made tons of money, but incurred a surprising amount of wrath. It was criticized for being racist toward Indians, antifeminist, and overly violent for its intended audience composed largely of children. The last complaint eventually led the Motion Picture Association of America to assign the PG-13 film rating. Spielberg and Lucas set the series on track with what they claimed would be the final entry, 1989's *Indiana Jones and the Last Crusade.* Although *Batman* eclipsed it as the year's top money-maker, the *Last Crusade* received an overwhelming thumbs up from both critics and the public. The teaming of Ford and Sean Connery as his father turned out to be pure magic—which set the rumor mill about a fourth film into motion.

> *Raiders of the Lost Ark* (1981)   *Indiana Jones and the Last*
> *Indiana Jones and the Temple*   *Crusade* (1989)
>   *of Doom* (1984)

The Jones Family

While the Hardy's (q.v.) are still fondly remembered, the Jones' have been all but forgotten. Yet, 20th Century–Fox's Jones Family series actually came first and set the pattern for the wholesome family comedy/dramas of the late 1930s and 1940s. For the first film, 1936's *Every Saturday Night,* the family's last name was Evers. It switched to Jones that same year in *Educating Father,* the entry that set the tone for the rest of the series by putting Pa Jones in the spotlight. This emphasis on a none-too-perfect father figure is what distinguishes the Jones comedies from the Hardy pictures, which clearly belong to teenager Andy Hardy (Mickey Rooney). Veteran character actor Jed Prouty played bespeckled Pa Jones and Spring Byington, who made a career of maternal roles, was Ma. The principal Jones kids were played by Shirley Deane (oldest daughter Bonnie), Kenneth Howell (Jack), George Ernest (Roger), and June Carlson (Lucy). Bonnie Jones married her boyfriend Herbert Thompson (Russell Gleason) and became a mother in 1938's *Love on a Budget.* But stagestruck little sister Lucy remains the best remembered of the children, stealing scenes with her impersonations of Katharine Hepburn and Greta Garbo. Typical plots involved Pa's candidacy for mayor *(Hot Water),* a family vacation in Yosemite *(Back to Nature),* and an oil swindle *(Big Business).* Despite its modest popularity, the Jones Family series ended in

1940, while the Hardys lasted well into the decade. Many of the cast members, though, continued in similar movies, with Russell Gleason even appearing in the rival Higgins Family series (q.v.).

Educating Father (1936)	*Down on the Farm* (1938)
Every Saturday Night (1936)	*The Jones Family in Hollywood*
Back to Nature (1936)	(1939)
Big Business (aka *The Jones*	*Too Busy to Work* (1939)
Family in Big Business)	*Quick Millions* (aka *The Jones*
(1937)	*Family in Quick Millions*)
Off to the Races (1937)	(1939)
Hot Water (1937)	*Everybody's Baby* (1939)
Borrowing Trouble (1937)	*Too Busy to Work* (1939)
A Trip to Paris (1938)	*On Their Own* (1940)
Love on a Budget (1938)	*Young as You Feel* (1940)
Safety in Numbers (1938)	

Josser, Jimmy

British vaudeville comedian Ernie Lotinga played the "much put upon" Jimmy Josser on the stage and in a series of shorts before making the transition to feature-length films. *P.C. Josser* (1931), an adaptation of Lotinga's play "The Police Force," was a minor comedy about Josser's attempts to regain his job as a policeman. It pretty much set the pattern for the rest of the series, which briefly enjoyed minor popularity in its native country.

P.C. Josser (1931)	*Josser on the River* (1932)
Dr. Josser KC (1931)	*Josser in the Army* (1932)
Josser Joins the Navy (1932)	*Josser on the Farm* (1934)

Judges

While lawyers have garnered most of the courtroom limelight, judges have proven themselves to be more versatile outside the typical legal settings. In *The Life and Times of Judge Roy Bean* (1972), the legendary Western judge (Paul Newman) appointed himself to his post and heard cases in the local saloon. The judges in 1983's *The Star Chamber* moonlighted as vigilantes who executed criminals that avoided sentencing due to legal loopholes. Robert Van Gulick's Judge Dee, a seventh-century oriental detective, solved his only celluloid case in the engaging 1974 TV-movie *Judge Dee and the Monastery Murders*. Female judges have been represented by Susan Hayward in *The Bachelor and the Bobby-Soxer* (1948) and Jill Clayburgh in *First Monday in October* (1981). The latter film, based on a play pre-dating Sandra Day O'Connor's appointment, cast Clayburgh as the first woman on the Supreme Court. Arthur Hill may have played the screen's most courageous judge, as the real-life official who battled a racially-prejudiced town in *Judge Horton and the Scottsboro Boys* (1976), a vivid account of the trial of nine blacks accused of raping a white woman. As Judge Hardy in the Andy Hardy series (q.v.), stern but fair Lewis Stone played a judge more often than any other performer. On the small screen, Judge Wapner still listens to plaintiffs and dishes out decisions on a weekday basis on "The People's Court."

Ann Vickers (1933)
Judge Priest (1934)
Angel on My Shoulder (1946)
Cass Timberlane (1947)
The Bachelor and the Bobby-
    Soxer (aka Bachelor Knight)
    (1947)
An Act of Murder (aka Live for
    Tomorrow) (1948)
The Judge Steps Out (1949)
The Judge and Jake Wyler
    (1972 TVM)
The Life and Times of Judge

Roy Bean (1972)
Judge Dee and the Monastery
    Murders (1974 TVM)
Jury of One (aka The Verdict)
    (1974)
The Judge and the Assassin
    (1975)
Judge Horton and the Scotts-
    boro Boys (1976 TVM)
First Monday in October (1981)
The Star Chamber (1983)
Crime of Innocence (1985 TVM)

Jungle Jim

Johnny Weissmuller hung up his loincloth after 1948's *Tarzan and the Mermaids,* but he didn't stay out of the jungle for long. That same year, he moved from RKO to Columbia and kicked off a series of low-budget action pictures for producer Sam Katzman. Weissmuller's *Jungle Jim,* although based on a comic strip and radio program, was clearly inspired by Tarzan (q.v.). Sure, Jungle Jim wore clothes and spoke in complete sentences (most of the time), but the fast-paced plots (which got progressively sillier) were pure Burroughs. In the first film, Jim had a pet crow and a little dog. These "unjungle" denizens were later traded for a trusty chimp sidekick. The *Jungle Jim* films never rose above the level of backlot juvenile features, but the supporting cast sometimes included a surprising face or two, such as "B"-movie faves Buster Crabbe and Ray "Crash" Corrigan. The outrageousness of the plots deserve special mention, too. Jim battled "man monsters" *(Jungle Jim in the Forbidden Land),* pesky pygmies *(Jungle Moon Men),* and Nazis *(Voodoo Tiger).* In the last three films, Weissmuller dropped the Jungle Jim monicker and went by his real name. When the series ended in 1955, he moved to television and made the half-hour "Jungle Jim" syndicated series. It lasted for 26 episodes and co-starred Martin Huston.

Jungle Jim (1948)
The Lost Tribe (1949)
Mark of the Gorilla (1950)
Pygmy Island (1950)
Captive Girl (1950)
Fury of the Congo (1951)
Jungle Manhunt (1951)

Jungle Jim in the Forbidden
    Land (1952)
Voodoo Tiger (1952)
Killer Ape (1953)
Savage Mutiny (1953)
Valley of the Headhunters (1953)
Jungle Maneaters (1954)

As Johnny Weissmuller (but still considered part of Jungle Jim series):

Cannibal Attack (1954)   *Jungle Moon Men* (1955)
Devil Goddess (1955)

The Karate Kid

Critics dubbed it a junior-league *Rocky,* but the 1984 sleeper hit *The Karate Kid* had its own winning formula built around the friendship between a gawky teen (Ralph Macchio) and a janitor/philosopher/martial artist (Noriyuki "Pat" Morita). Okay, it *was* directed by *Rocky* veteran John Avildsen and did climax with a dramatic fight in the ring—but there were no characters named Adrienne, Mick, or Apollo. In 1986 *The Karate Kid Part II* took Morita and Macchio to the Orient with predictable results, being notable only for spawning Peter Cetera's number one song "The Glory of Love." Audiences snubbed a second sequel, released in 1989, which basically rehashed the original.

The Karate Kid (1984)   *The Karate Kid Part III* (1989)
The Karate Kid Part II (1986)

Karnstein Trilogy

Hammer Films, the "House of Horror" in the 1960s, saw its once-loyal audience dwindling rapidly in the early 1970s. To attract new horror fans, it updated its Christopher Lee *Dracula* (q.v.) films and introduced a new series about lesbian vampire Mircalla Karnstein. Based on Sheridan Le Fanu's novel *Carmilla,* 1970's *The Vampire Lovers* pitted veteran vampire hunter Peter Cushing against buxom Ingrid Pitt as Mircalla. In the end, she lost her head—and was staked as well. She was resurrected in the form of Yutte Stensgaard for 1971's *Lust for a Vampire,* a lively sequel directed by horror veteran Jimmy Sangster. The series concluded with 1971's *Twins of Evil,* in which Mircalla (now played by Katya Keith) takes a back seat to a tale about twin village girls—one an innocent and one a vicious vampire. Again, Peter Cushing was around to provide the necessary heroics, although his character died in the process. Hammer was gasping for its dying breath, too. It produced its last theatrical film in 1974. See also **Vampires.**

The Vampire Lovers (1970)   *Love a Vampire*) (1971)
Lust for a Vampire (aka *To*   *Twins of Evil* (1971)

Kettle, Ma and Pa

Marjorie Main and Percy Kilbride made their debut as Ma and Pa Kettle in the 1947 Universal comedy *The Egg and I.* Adapted from Betty McDonald's bestseller, the picture featured Claudette Colbert as a Bostonian lass introduced to chicken farming by new hubby Fred MacMurray. The Kettles were merely supporting characters, but they were responsible for the film's funniest scenes. Universal reteamed Main and Kilbride the following year in the cornpone Donald O'Connor comedy *Feudin', Fussin' and A-Fightin'* and then turned them into stars with 1949's *Ma and Pa Kettle*. Produced for $200,000 to $400,000 each, the Kettle movies earned tidy profits for Universal through the mid–1950s. The simple series formula usually found lazy, laidback Pa getting into unintentional mischief, while Ma ruled the Kettle brood of 15 kids. Several entries derived humor by moving the Kettles (temporarily) to big cities. Thus, the Kettle clan visited New York *(Back at Home)*, Paris *(Vacation)*, and Hawaii *(Waikiki)*. Richard Long played Tom, the Kettles' oldest son, and other children included Lori Nelson (Rosie) and Brett Halsey (Elwin). Pa's Indian cohort Crowbar was played by four actors: Vic Potel, Chief Yowlachie, Teddy Hart, and Zachary Charles. After seven films in as many years, Percy Kilbride quit the series. There was no Pa Kettle in 1956's *The Kettles in the Ozarks,* although Arthur Hunnicutt's Uncle Sedge was mighty similar. Pa was back, though, in the guise of character actor Parker Fennelly in 1957's *The Kettles on Old MacDonald's Farm.* It turned out not only to be the last Kettle film, but also Marjorie Main's final screen role. She retired from acting and died in 1975.

The Egg and I (1947)
Ma and Pa Kettle (1949)
Ma and Pa Kettle Go to Town (1950)
Ma and Pa Kettle Back on the Farm (1951)
Ma and Pa Kettle at the Fair (1952)
Ma and Pa Kettle on Vacation (1953)
Ma and Pa Kettle at Home (1954)
Ma and Pa Kettle at Waikiki (1955)
The Kettles in the Ozarks (1956)
The Kettles on Old MacDonald's Farm (1957)

Kildare, Dr.

The year after Joel McCrea introduced Dr. James Kildare in Paramount's *Interns Can't Take Money* (1937), MGM launched an immensely popular Kildare film series starring Lew Ayres. The supporting cast at Blair General Hospital was a potent one, featuring wheelchair-bound Lionel Barrymore as Dr. Gillespie, Laraine Day as Mary Lamont, and Nell Craig as Nurse Parker. Ayres and company made nine movies, dealing efficiently with daily medical crises and topical subjects like insulin shock. Then, in 1941, the series stunned moviegoers with *Dr. Kildare's Wedding Day,* in which Day's character was killed off. That same year, Ayres elicited a wave of bad publicity by refusing to enter the army on the grounds he was a conscientious objector. MGM promptly dropped Ayres from the Kildare series, although the actor eventually enlisted and served in combat. Rather than casting a new Kildare, MGM shifted the series focus to Barrymore with 1942's *Calling Dr. Gillespie.* Later that year, Van Johnson was introduced as *Dr. Gillespie's New Assistant,* a role he continued in four of the final five Gillespie pictures. Throughout the Kildare/Gillespie series, MGM introduced up-and-coming stars like future "Marcus Welby" Robert Young, Donna Reed, and child star Margaret O'Brien. "Dr. Kildare" came to television in 1961 with Richard Chamberlain in the lead and Raymond Massey as Dr. Gillespie. It enjoyed high ratings and a five-year run. A half-hour syndicated program, "Young Dr. Kildare," lasted for 24 episodes in 1972. See also **Hospitals.**

Interns Can't Take Money (aka You Can't Take Money) (1937) (McCrea)

Young Dr. Kildare (1938) (Ayres)

Calling Dr. Kildare (1939) (Ayres)

The Secret of Dr. Kildare (1939) (Ayres)

Dr. Kildare Goes Home (1940) (Ayres)

Dr. Kildare's Crisis (1940) (Ayres)

Dr. Kildare's Strange Case (1940) (Ayres)

The People vs. Dr. Kildare (aka My Life Is Yours) (1941) (Ayres)

Dr. Kildare's Wedding Day (aka Mary Names the Day) (1941) (Ayres)

Dr. Kildare's Victory (aka The Debutante and the Doctor) (1941) (Ayres)

Calling Dr. Gillespie (1942) (Barrymore as Gillespie)

Dr. Gillespie's New Assistant (1942) (Barrymore)

Dr. Gillespie's Criminal Case (aka Crazy to Kill) (1943) (Barrymore)

Between Two Women (1944) (Barrymore)

Three Men in White (1944) (Barrymore)

Dark Delusion (aka Cynthia's Secret) (1947) (Barrymore)

King Kong

"The Eighth Wonder of the World," as showman Carl Denham proclaimed Kong in the 1933 original, was actually a three-foot model brought to life by master stop-motion animator Willis O'Brien. The marvelous O'Brien had previously performed his camera trickery on the dinosaurs (q.v.) in 1925's *The Lost World.* His post–*Kong* work included some excellent effects in the seldom-shown 1933 sequel *Son of Kong* and another giant friendly ape opus, 1949's *Mighty Joe Young.* But O'Brien's contribution accounts for just part—albeit a crucial one—of *King Kong's* enduring success. The other critical ingredients are the film's simplistic beauty-and-the-beast theme and its capability to make Kong a *character* audiences can identify with. Subsequent Kong films have floundered drastically on both counts. Japan monster movie-maker Inoshira Honda revived Kong after a 29-year hiatus for "the colossal clash of all time," 1963's *King Kong vs. Godzilla.* Featuring a man in an ape suit as Kong, it was a dull affair, of interest only in that Kong won the fight in U.S. prints and Godzilla won in the Japanese version. Honda mounted a sequel of sorts with 1968's *King Kong Escapes,* which pitted the giant ape against a robotic replica called Mechani-Kong. At least, Honda did not dare compare it to the original *Kong.* Unfortunately, Dino De Laurentiis did just that with his $24 million man-in-ape-suit 1976 remake. *Variety* dubbed it "a brilliant remake," but most critics drubbed it and plans for an immediate sequel were temporarily scrapped. However, that sequel finally reached the screen in 1986 as *King Kong Lives.* Kong, its turns out, had survived his fall from the World Trade Center, but required a blood transfusion. Enter Mrs. Kong. This ludicrous picture turned the giant ape into a giant turkey at the boxoffice. Nevertheless, it introduced star Linda Hamilton to the beauty and the beast angle—excellent training for her 1987 TV series "Beauty and the Beast." See also **Apes and Monkeys.**

King Kong (1933)	*King Kong Escapes* (aka
Son of Kong (1933)	*Kingukongu No Gyakushu)*
King Kong vs. Godzilla (aka	(1968)
Kingukongu tai Gojira)	*King Kong* (1976)
(1963)	*King Kong Lives* (1986)

Kojak, Theo

The fact-based *The Marcus-Nelson Murders* (1973) introduced bald, lollipop-licking police lieutenant Theo Kojak to TV audiences. The film was adapted from Selwyn Rabb's book *Justice in the Back Room,* an account of the 1963 Wylie-Hoffert murders which played a major role in the Supreme Court's Miranda decision. Savalas's Emmy-nominated portrayal resulted in the popular 1973–78 "Kojak" TV series. After a vacation from the role, Savalas revived Kojak in two TV-movies before returning on a regular basis in 1989 as a revolving character on "The ABC Saturday Mystery."

The Marcus-Nelson Murders	TVM)
(aka *Kojak and the Marcus-*	*Kojak: The Price of Justice*
Nelson Murders) (1973 TVM)	(1987 TVM)
Kojak: The Belarus Files (1985	

Korean War

If not for the escapades of TV's Hawkeye Pierce and the rest of the "M*A*S*H" unit, the Korean War might have slipped into relative obscurity. And yet, during the days when American forces fought in Korea, the war was a popular film subject. Significantly, these war films of the 1950s differed in tone from their World War II counterparts of the 1940s. While escapist entertainment and glossy romances still drew crowds, many of these new pictures were grim, realistic adventures uninterested in glorifying war. Cult movie favorite Samuel Fuller produced two violent, powerful Korean War adventures in 1951: *The Steel Helmet* and *Fixed Bayonets.* The first film dealt with the war's brutal ironies, beginning with a sergeant whose unit is wiped out, while he alone survives because of his helmet. The horror of war dominated *Fixed Bayonets,* as evidenced by a chilling scene where soldiers put their feet together to avoid frostbite—and one foot, already without feeling, is left out. Similar tough-minded films like *Retreat, Hell!* (1952) and *Men in War* (1957) substituted sturdy stars (e.g. Frank Lovejoy, Robert Ryan) for big-name draws. Nevertheless, Hollywood favorites like Humphrey Bogart *(Battle Circus)* and Robert Mitchum *(One Minute to Zero)* donned fatigues long enough to fight a skirmish or two. William Holden starred as a jet pilot in love with Grace Kelly in the popular hit *Bridges at Toko-Ri* (1954) and then romanced Jennifer Jones in Hong Kong during the war in *Love Is a Many Splendored Thing* (1955). Lower-budgeted Korean War pictures provided roles for an impressive crop of rising young stars, such as Lee Marvin *(The Glory Brigade),* Charles Bronson *(Target Zero),* Robert Redford *(War Hunt),* and Michael Caine and Robert Shaw (both in *Hell in Korea*). Future best-selling author Tom Tryon *(Harvest Home)* played a soldier on shore leave from Korea in *Marines, Let Go!* (1961). Veteran Western character actor L.Q. Jones and Alvy Moore (Mr. Kimble on "Green Acres") had supporting roles in, respectively, *Target Zero* and *The Glory Brigade.* Two decades later, these two would team to produce and direct the science fiction cult hit *A Boy and His Dog* (1975). The effects of the Korean War back home in the states was a rare film subject, although 1951's *I Want You* dealt with it sensitively. On the other hand, 1953's *Take the High Ground* was a routine boot camp picture about soldiers undergoing intensive training prior to being shipped to Korea. The horror of war lasted beyond the battlefield for the soldiers tried for treason in gripping court martial dramas like *The Rack* (1956), *Time Limit* (1957), and *Sergeant Ryker* (1968). With exceptions like the latter film, Korean War pictures became increasingly scarce after Gregory Peck closed out the 1950s with the frightening, realistic *Pork Chop Hill.* The 1963 Kirk Douglas picture *The Hook* was a brutally effective portrait of combat. John Frankenheimer's political thriller *The Manchurian Candidate* (1962) turned a Korean vet into a brainwashed assassin. Robert Altman's film version of *M*A*S*H* (1970) showed battlefield physicians acting crazy in order to maintain their sanity in the face of war's atrocities. It made a successful transition to television in 1972, where it enjoyed an 11-year run.

Fixed Bayonets (1951)	*Combat Squad* (1953)
I Want You (1951)	*The Glory Brigade* (1953)
The Steel Helmet (1951)	*Sabre Jet* (1953)
A Yank in Korea (1951)	*Torpedo Alley* (1953)
Battle Circus (1952)	*Take the High Ground* (1953)
Battle Zone (1952)	*Bridges at Toko-Ri* (1954)
One Minute to Zero (1952)	*Dragonfly Squadron* (1954)
Retreat, Hell! (1952)	*Flight Nurse* (1954)
Mission Over Korea (1953)	*Men of the Fighting Lady* (1954)

Prisoner of War (1954)
Battle Taxi (1955)
Hell's Horizon (1955)
Love Is a Many Splendored
  Thing (1955)
Target Zero (1955)
Hell in Korea (aka A Hill in
  Korea) (1956)
Hold Back the Night (1956)
The Rack (1956)
Strange Intruder (1956)
Men in War (1957)
Time Limit (1957)
The Hunters (1958)
Jet Attack (1958)
Pork Chop Hill (1959)
Battle Flame (1959)

All the Young Men (1960)
Marines, Let Go! (1961)
Sniper's Ridge (1961)
War Hunt (1961)
The Manchurian Candidate
  (1962)
The Nun and the Sergeant
  (1962)
War Is Hell (1963)
The Hook (1963)
Sergeant Ryker (1968)
M*A*S*H (1970)
The Reluctant Heroes (1971
  TVM)
Collision Course (1975 TVM)
Inchon (1982)

Ku Klux Klan

Controversy has stalked the KKK from its inception and has naturally overflowed into its sporadic film appearances. D.W. Griffith's landmark 1915 film *Birth of a Nation* continues to incur the wrath of racial rights groups for its glorification of the KKK. Based on Thomas Dixon, Jr.'s *The Clansmen*, Griffith's film ends with a Southern family being rescued from marauding black men by heroic members of the KKK. The National Association for the Advancement of Colored People (NAACP) mounted an effective boycott of the film on its initial release. That inspired Griffith to write a defense of his film, a pamphlet entitled "The Rise and Fall of Free Speech in America." The 1936 film *Black Legion* never referred to the KKK, but the racist organization which recruited Humphrey Bogart was obviously patterned after the Ku Klux Klan. *The Texans* (1938), a post–Civil War Western, featured a subplot involving the KKK. It was not until 1950's *Storm Warning* that another film dealt exclusively—and frankly—with the Ku Klux Klan. Ginger Rogers starred as a woman who sought help from liberal D.A. Ronald Reagan after learning that her sister (Doris Day) has married a racist, and possibly murderous, Klansman. It was far superior to the 1974 fiasco *The Klansman*, an unlikely all-star mishmash starring Richard Burton, Lee Marvin, O.J. Simpson, and Linda Evans. The 1979 TV-movie *Attack on Terror: The FBI vs. the Ku Klux Klan* was an engrossing fact-based drama about the murder of three civil rights workers in Mississippi in 1964. The same case provided the basis for another fine film, 1988's Oscar-nominated picture *Mississippi Burning*. Another 1988 release, *Betrayed*, cast Debra Winger as an agent investigating a white supremist terrorist group, a topic previously addressed in the 1987 TV-movie *In the Homeland*.

Birth of a Nation (1915)
Black Legion (1936)
The Texans (1938)
Storm Warning (1950)
The FBI Story (1959)
The Klansmen (1974)
Attack on Terror: The FBI vs.
   the Ku Klux Klan (1975
   TVM)

Undercover with the KKK (aka
   The Freedom Riders; My
   Undercover Years) (1979
   TVM)
In the Homeland (1987 TVM)
Betrayed (1988)
Mississippi Burning (1988)
Unconquered (1989 TVM)
Cross of Fire (1989 TVM)

Labor Unions and Strikes

The sight of defiant workers and waving picket signs can form powerful images capable of transcending the themes of even mediocre films. In the hands of a Sergei Eisenstein, the result can be chilling, as was the case with *Strike* (1924), the famed director's gripping account of a 1912 revolt against working conditions in Czarist Russia. Equally compelling was John Sayles' *Matewan* (1987), the fact-based story of a West Virginia coal mine labor dispute circa 1920 which erupted into violence and blood-letting. British films, such as 1944's *The Agitator* and 1960's *The Angry Silence*, have best explored the roles played by powerful individuals on both sides of the picket fence. The latter film concerned a worker ostracized by his peers for refusing to join the walkout. The British even satirized its labor problems with 1960's cunning farce *I'm All Right, Jack*. It was much more adroitly handled than 1958's *Never Steal Anything Small*, an uncomfortable American musical starring James Cagney as a crooked labor leader.

Strike (1924)
Metropolis (1925)
The Guns of Loos (1927)
The Agitator (1944)
The Whistle at Eaton Falls (aka
   Richer than the Earth) (1951)
Inside Detroit (1956)
The Garment Jungle (1957)
Never Steal Anything Small
   (1958)
The Angry Silence (1960)
I'm All Right, Jack (1960)
Flame in the Streets (1961)

Jessica (1962)
Adalen 31 (1969)
Ramparts of Clay (1971)
Harlan County, U.S.A. (1977)
Sleeping Dogs (1977)
Blue Collar (1978)
F.I.S.T. (1978)
Norma Rae (1979)
Keeping On (1981)
Power (1980 TVM)
A Matter of Sex (1984 TVM)
The Killing Floor (1984)
Matewan (1987)

Lassie

The caring collie made her debut in 1943's *Lassie, Come Home,* one of the finest of all dog (q.v.) movies. Eric Knight wrote the original novel about a family forced to part with its cherished collie, which manages to overcome all obstacles and return to them. The MGM cast was an exceptional one: established child star Roddy McDowell, promising 11-year-old

Elizabeth Taylor, plus adults Donald Crisp, Nigel Bruce, and Elsa Lan-
chester. Pal, a male collie, played Lassie. Donald Crisp, Nigel Bruce, and
Pal returned in the 1945 follow-up *Son of Lassie,* with Peter Lawford and
June Lockhart (shades of déjà vu) playing adult versions of McDowell and
Taylor. Elizabeth Taylor was back, however, for the following year's
Courage of Lassie, a confusing entry in which the dog (played by Pal
again) was actually called Bill, not Lassie. Fortunately, Lassie was Lassie in
1948's *The Hills of Home,* a colorful entry which reunited Crisp and the
collie and featured the always enjoyable Edmund Gwenn and a young
Janet Leigh. MGM's last three Lassie entries were unremarkable programmers, although 1948's *The Sun Comes Up* was notable as Jeanette Mac-
Donald's final film appearance. In 1954, Lassie embarked on a long-
running, immensely popular TV series. During the original 1954–71
"Lassie" run, the collie was paired with an assortment of owners, including
Jeff (Tommy Rettig), Timmy and his Mom (Jon Provost and June
Lockhart), and Corey the forest ranger (Robert Bray). The collie's lasting
popularity can be attested by the periodic appearances of new Lassie pictures and interest in a new 1989 TV series reuniting Provost and Lassie.

Lassie, Come Home (1943)	*The Painted Hills* (1951)
Son of Lassie (1945)	*Lassie's Great Adventure* (1963)
Courage of Lassie (1946)	*The Magic of Lassie* (1978)
The Hills of Home (1948)	*Lassie: The New Beginning*
Challenge for Lassie (1949)	(1978)
The Sun Comes Up (1949)	

Lemon Popsicle Series

Former Cannon Films moguls Menahem Golan and Yorum Globus produced this Israeli series of nostalgic teen sex comedies. The films proved to
be immensely popular in Europe, inspiring Cannon to produce an
Americanized version in 1981, appropriately titled *The Last American
Virgin.* Boaz Davidson directed this variation as well as the first four *Pop-
sicle* films.

Lemon Popsicle (1978)	*Lemon Popsicle IV* (aka *Private*
Lemon Popsicle II (aka *Greasy*	*Popsicle*) (1982)
Kids Stuff) (1979)	*Lemon Popsicle V* (aka *Baby*
Lemon Popsicle III: Let's Go to	*Love*) (1983)
Paris (aka *Hot Bubblegum*)	*Lemon Popsicle VI* (aka *Up*
(1980)	*Your Anchor*) (1984)
The Last American Virgin	*Lemon Popsicle VII* (aka *Young*
(1981)	*Love*) (1987)

Letters

Letters have brought lovers together, torn marriages apart, incriminated
the innocent, blackmailed the guilty, and caused endless misunderstandings. Pen pals James Stewart and Margaret Sullivan fell in love through

LETTERS

their letters, not realizing they were coworkers in *The Shop Around the Corner* (1940). A little girl sent her mother's photo to her lonely soldier pen pal in *Never Say Goodbye* (1946), never suspecting that he would come visiting. Similar pen pal deceptions occurred in 1945's *A Letter for Evie* and the 1947 hit comedy *Dear Ruth* (q.v.). One cannot always be certain of the identity of a letter's author. Cyrano de Bergerac (Jose Ferrer) wrote poignant love letters to the beautiful Roxanne, but signed the name of his hapless friend Christian in the 1950 adaptation of Edmund Rostand's celebrated play. Jennifer Jones suffered amnesia in *Love Letters* (1945) after learning that her wartime love letters were not written by her fiancé. The deceiving letters penned by the devious Marquise de Merteuil (Glenn Close) in *Dangerous Liaisons* (1988) eventually led to the death of her lover (John Malkovitch). Celeste Holm provided the voice of the authoress of *A Letter to Three Wives* (1949), in which three ladies learn that one of their husbands has run off with Holm's character. Paul Lukas played a converted Nazi incriminated by false letters sent by a former friend in *Address Unknown* (1944). Loretta Young tried to retrieve another incriminating letter, one framing her for murder, in 1951's *Cause for Alarm*. Pat Boone was similarly panic-stricken over a hard-to-retrieve letter in the British comedy *Never Put It in Writing* (1964). An unsigned love note dropped into a high school locker revealed numerous hidden feelings in the pleasant 1985 comedy *Secret Admirer*. Misdirected letters reaching their destination after a year-long delay provided the premise for the three-part TV-movie *The Letters* and its sequel *Letters from Three Lovers* (both 1973). *84 Charing Cross Road* (1987) traced the charming 20-year letter-writing relationship between a New York book lover (Anne Bancroft) and a British book dealer (Anthony Hopkins). See also **Dear Ruth**.

The Strong Man (1926)
Poison Pen (1939)
The Shop Around the Corner (1940)
The Letter (1940)
Address Unknown (1944)
Love Letters (1945)
A Letter for Evie (1945)
Never Say Goodbye (1946)
The Captive Heart (1946)
Dear Ruth (1947)
The Lost Moment (1947)
Letter from an Unknown Woman (1948)
A Letter to Three Wives (1949)
Cyrano de Bergerac (1950)
Cause for Alarm (1951)

The 13th Letter (1951)
Demoniaque (1958)
Fate Takes a Hand (1961)
Never Put It in Writing (1963)
Dear Brigitte (1965)
The Go-Between (1971)
The Letters (1973 TVM)
Letters from Three Lovers (1973 TVM)
No Sex Please, We're British (1973)
Dirty Tricks (1980)
Touched by Love (aka *To Elvis, With Love*) (1980)
The Letter (1982 TVM)
Love Letters (aka *My Love Letters*) (1983)

204

A Letter to Three Wives (1985
    TVM)
Secret Admirer (1985)

84 Charing Cross Road (1987)
Dangerous Liaisons (1988)

Librarians

It has been difficult for movie librarians to move away from their stereotyped image as shy, conservative bookworms. Despite their star power,
Greer Garson *(Adventure)*, June Allyson *(Good News)*, Shirley Jones *(The
Music Man)*, and Barbara Eden *(The Seven Faces of Dr. Lao)* did little to
alter the stereotyping. In contrast, Bette Davis portrayed a fiery librarian
fired for her refusal to censor a book on communism in 1956's *Storm
Center*. Jewish college dropout-turned-librarian Richard Benjamin ignored
social conventions in his pursuit of country club heiress Ali MacGraw in
the film version of Philip Roth's frank best-seller *Goodbye, Columbus*
(1969). Meek librarian Jason Robards, Jr., turned out to be the only person in town with enough courage and will power to confront the mysterious Mr. Dark in Ray Bradbury's chilling, turn-of-the-century fantasy
Something Wicked This Way Comes (1983). In the 1974 oddity *Mr.
Sycamore*, Robards played a mailman with a crush on librarian Jean Simmons and a bizarre desire to become a tree.

Scandal Street (1938)
Adventure (1945)
Good News (1947)
Katie Did It (1951)
Storm Center (1955)
The Music Man (1962)
Only Two Can Play (1962)

The Seven Faces of Dr. Lao
    (1964)
Goodbye, Columbus (1969)
Mr. Sycamore (1974)
Something Wicked This Way
    Comes (1983)
Off Beat (1986)

Lighthouses

Not surprisingly, horror and fantasy films have made the best use of
lighthouse settings. Adrienne Barbeau operated a lighthouse radio station
in John Carpenter's *The Fog* (1980) — at least until pirate ghosts with grap-
pling hooks forced her to abandon the broadcast booth and seek refuge
on the top of the cylindrical structure. People-eating plants harrassed
lighthouse resident Janette Scott in 1963's *Day of the Triffids*. She
discovered that, like most plants, triffids don't care for salt water. In fantasy films, a lighthouse played a prominent role during the climactic storm
in *Portrait of Jennie* (1948) and Michael Redgrave's life changed for the
better after experiencing ghostly visions in his lighthouse home in
Thunder Rock (1942). The dull side of lighthouse living was displayed in
The Light at the Edge of the World (1971), in which lighthouse keeper
Kirk Douglas fights boring pirates (led by Yul Brynner) for the affections
of boring Samantha Eggar. The sweet side found Shirley Temple brighten-
ing up lighthouse-keeper Guy Kibbee's life in *Captain January* (1936).

Lighthouse by the Sea (1925)
Captain January (1936)
Sh! The Octopus (1938)
Thunder Rock (1942)
Seven Miles from Alcatraz (1942)
A Stolen Life (1946)
Portrait of Jennie (1948)
The Monster of Piedras Blancas (1958)
A Summer Place (1959)
Day of the Triffids (1963)
The Light at the Edge of the World (1971)
Pete's Dragon (1977)
The Fog (1980)
Eye of the Needle (1981)

Lions and Tigers

The big cats have alternated effectively between roles as cuddly, playful felines and vicious, merciless maneaters. In the former category, one must begin with Bert Lahr's lovable Cowardly Lion from *The Wizard of Oz* (1939), who was too afraid to be ferocious ("I'm just a dandy lion"). In the wonderful screwball comedy *Bringing Up Baby* (1938), Katharine Hepburn "lost" Baby, her pet leopard. This required Cary Grant and her to roam through the woods singing the big cat's favorite tune: "I can't give you anything but love—Baby." *Fluffy* and *Clarence, the Cross-Eyed Lion* (both 1965) were harmless pets, too, though their tendency to frighten strangers provided much of the films' humor. Clarence was even popular enough to warrant his own 1966–69 TV series "Daktari." However, as its title suggests, the series devoted more time to Clarence's veterinarian owner Marshall Thompson. Lions peaked in popularity with the release of 1966's family hit *Born Free*, the engrossing true story of a husband and wife's efforts to train their domesticated lioness to fend for herself in the wilds of Africa. A belated sequel, *Living Free*, followed in 1972, accompanied two years later by a short-lived "Born Free" TV series. In contrast to these friendly lions, other features, such as 1981's *Savage Harvest*, have portrayed big cats as powerful, silent killers stalking their prey. Escaped animals in urban settings have proven to be a continuing problem ever since a black leopard slipped away from Jean Brooks during a publicity stunt in 1943's *The Leopard Man*. Films employing a similar premise include 1964's *A Tiger Walks* and two 1978 TV-movies, *Maneaters Are Loose!* and *The Beasts Are on the Streets*. The 1953 jungle adventure *Bwana Devil* introduced the cinema's first 3-D cat and promised to "put a lion in your lap." Stop-action animator Ray Harryhausen created a saber-toothed tiger for his colorful fantasy *Sinbad and the Eye of the Tiger* (1977). No discussion of big cats would be complete without mentioning the animated pencil-thin panther with the pink skin that hams his way through the opening credits of Blake Edwards' *Pink Panther* (q.v.) films. See also **Cats.**

East of Java (1935)
Bringing Up Baby (1938)
The Wizard of Oz (1939)
The Jungle Book (1942)

The Leopard Man (1943)
Maneater of Kumaon (1948)
Samson and Delilah (1949)
Androcles and the Lion (1952)
Fearless Fagan (1952)
The Horse and the Lion (1952)
Track of the Cat (1954)
The African Lion (1955)
The Flute and the Arrow (1957)
Harry Black and the Tiger (aka
   Harry Black) (1958)
Jungle Cat (1960)
The Lion (1962)
Rampage (1963)
A Tiger Walks (1964)
Fluffy (1965)
Clarence, the Cross-Eyed Lion
   (1965)
Born Free (1966)
The Cat (aka *Cat!*) (1966)

The Jungle Book (1967)
Charlie, the Lonesome Cougar
   (1968)
Living Free (1972)
Napoleon and Samantha (1972)
Maneater (1973 TVM)
When the North Wind Blows
   (1974)
Christian the Lion (1976)
Maneaters Are Loose! (1978
   TVM)
The Beasts Are on the Streets
   (1978 TVM)
Night Creature (aka *Out of the
   Darkness*) (1978)
Savage Harvest (1979)
The White Lions (1981)
A Tiger's Tale (1987)
Cheetah and Friends (aka
   Cheetah) (1989)

Little House on the Prairie

Michael Landon executive produced and starred in the 1974 TV-movie *Little House on the Prairie,* a wholesome drama about a pioneer family based on the writings of Laura Ingalls Wilder. The telefilm spawned a very successful 1974–83 TV series which featured Landon as Charles Ingalls, Karen Grassle as his wife Caroline, and Melissa Gilbert and Melissa Sue Anderson as daughters Laura and Mary. Twins Lindsay and Sidney Greenbush alternated as the youngest child Carrie. The show's characters evolved significantly over the years (e.g. Mary went blind; daughter Grace was born) and Landon left the series in 1982 (the title changing to "Little House: A New Beginning"). Without Landon, the series folded—only to be revived in the form of three TV-movie "specials." Landon directed and appeared in the first and third postseries pictures. The town of Walnut Grove was blown up in *The Last Farewell,* leaving Landon free to play an angel in his "Highway to Heaven" series.

Little House on the Prairie
   (1974 TVM)
*Little House on the Prairie:
   Look Back to Yesterday* (1983
   TVM)

*Little House: Bless All the Dear
   Children* (1984 TVM)
Little House: The Last Farewell
   (1984 TVM)

Little People

They come in all sizes—they may be as minute as an atom or as tall as four feet. So, in that aspect, little people is a pretty big category. The tiniest person was probably *The Incredible Shrinking Man*. At the conclusion of Richard Matheson's philosophical 1957 sci-fi film, the hero continues to shrink until he can literally see atomic particles. In both *Fantastic Voyage* and *Innerspace*, people are reduced in size until they can be injected into the bloodstreams of normal-sized folks. Considerably bigger, say around three or four inches in height, are the scientists in *Dr. Cyclops*, the Liliputians in film adaptations of *Gulliver's Travels*, and the title character in *tom thumb*. *Dr. Cyclops* has evolved into something of a cult classic, being the first picture in which little people are harrassed by a cat, a chicken, raindrops, and the like. Finally, there are the "little people" of folklore—leprechauns, gnomes, and mischievous dwarfs. They have appeared in numerous movies, typically in charming, playful roles. Of course, not all movies involving little people are fantastic in nature. In *The Tin Drum*, a child injures himself (becoming a dwarf) so that he can never grow up. Dwarf-sized killers figure prominently in Nicholas Roeg's *Don't Look Now* and David Cronenberg's bizarre chiller *The Brood*. See also **Giant People**.

Minute-sized People

Fantastic Voyage (1966)	*Innerspace* (1987)

Under Five Inches

Bride of Frankenstein (1935)	*Babes in Toyland* (1961)
The Devil Doll (1936)	*Mothra* (1962)
Gulliver's Travels (1939)	*Ghidrah, the Three-Headed*
Dr. Cyclops (1940)	*Monster* (1965)
Peter Pan (1953)	*Help!* (1965)
Girl in His Pocket (1957)	*The Borrowers* (1973 TVM)
The Incredible Shrinking Man	*Don't Be Afraid of the Dark*
(1957)	(1973 TVM)
Attack of the Puppet People	*The Incredible Shrinking*
(1958)	*Woman* (1981)
The Seventh Voyage of Sinbad	*Here Come the Littles* (1985)
(1958)	*Willow* (1988)
tom thumb (1958)	*Honey, I Shrunk the Kids*
The Three Worlds of Gulliver	(1989)
(1960)	*Wicked Stepmother* (1989)

Leprechauns, Gnomes, Dwarfs, Midgets

Snow White and the Seven	*Finian's Rainbow* (1968)
Dwarfs (1938)	*Don't Look Now* (1973)
The Terror of Tiny Town (1938)	*Little Cigars* (1973)
The Luck of the Irish (1948)	*The Brood* (1979)
It's a Small World (1950)	*The Tin Drum* (1979)
Darby O'Gill and the Little	*Under the Rainbow* (1981)
People (1959)	*Time Bandits* (1981)
Jack the Giant Killer (1962)	*Dance of the Dwarfs* (aka
The Gnomemobile (1967)	*Jungle Heat*) (1983)
Even Dwarfs Started Small (1968)	*Willow* (1988)

The Little Tough Guys *see* The Bowery Boys

The Living Dead *see*
Ghouls; Night of the Living Dead

The Lone Wolf

Michael Lanyard, better known as the Lone Wolf, was a jewel thief turned detective created by Louis Joseph Vance in 1914. The character led a lively screen life, being played by eight actors over a span of 29 years. Bert Lytell (a one-time Boston Blackie) starred as Lanyard in five silent films, starting with 1917's *The Lone Wolf*. Other actors followed in his footsteps, including Jack Holt and Henry B. Walthall. However, it was Lytell who returned to the role one last time for the first Lone Wolf "talkie," 1930's *Last of the Lone Wolf*. Five years later, Melvyn Douglas made a promising debut as Lanyard in Columbia's *The Lone Wolf Returns*. With Douglas too much in demand for other roles, Czech import Francis Lederer took over for 1938's *The Lone Wolf in Paris*. He was replaced the following year by Warren William in *The Lone Wolf Spy Hunt*. William, a veteran "gentleman detective," had previously played both Philo Vance (q.v.) and Perry Mason (q.v.). He was an actor in search of a role to call his own — and he found it with Michael Lanyard. William made eight Lone Wolf films, with Eric Blore providing reliable comedy relief as his valet/sidekick. The series was a showcase for promising Columbia starlets and William's leading ladies included Rita Hayworth and Ida Lupino. William retired from the series after 1943's *Passport to Suez*. Gerald Mohr played Lanyard in three films during 1946–47 and ex–Bulldog Drummond (q.v.) Ron Randell starred in the series finale, 1949's *The Lone Wolf and His Lady*. Like most "B"-movie detectives, the Lone Wolf found a home on television, where Louis Hayward played him in a 39-episode 1953 series known as both "The Lone Wolf" and "Streets of Danger."

The Lone Wolf (1917) (Lytell)
False Faces (1919) (Lytell)
The Lone Wolf Returns (1926) (Lytell)
Alias the Lone Wolf (1927) (Lytell)
The Lone Wolf's Daughter (1929) (Lytell)
Last of the Lone Wolf (1930) (Lytell)
Cheaters at Play (1932) (Thomas Meighan)
The Lone Wolf Returns (1935) (Douglas)

The Lone Wolf in Paris (1938) (Lederer)
The Lone Wolf Spy Hunt (1939) (William)
The Lone Wolf Meets a Lady (1940) (William)
The Lone Wolf Strikes (1940) (William)
The Lone Wolf Keeps a Date (1941) (William)
The Lone Wolf Takes a Chance (1941) (William)
Secrets of the Lone Wolf (1941) (William)

Counter-Espionage (1942)
(William)
One Dangerous Night (1943)
(William)
Passport to Suez (1943)
(William)
The Notorious Lone Wolf

(1946) (Mohr)
The Lone Wolf in London
(1947) (Mohr)
The Lone Wolf in Mexico
(1947) (Mohr)
The Lone Wolf and His Lady
(1949) (Randell)

Long Running Times

United States–released theatrical features with running times longer than three hours have been rare, especially prior to the 1950s. Erich von Stroheim's original, unreleased version of his 1924 silent classic *Greed* fitted onto 42 reels (approximately nine hours' worth of film). MGM production head Irving Thalberg insisted on cuts and von Stroheim and friend Rex Ingram deleted six reels of footage. Still not satisfied, Thalberg hired June Mathis to cut eight more reels. By the time it was released, *Greed* boasted a scant 150 minutes. Existing prints run even shorter at 110 minutes. Amazingly, just four years later, von Stroheim made *The Wedding March,* which clocked in at 196 minutes. It was released in two parts and failed miserably at the box office. Leni Riefenstahl's *Olympia,* an epic documentary of the 1936 Olympic Games in Berlin, was also released in two parts (118 minutes and 107 minutes). However, MGM released all 179 minutes of 1936's *The Great Ziegfeld* in one lump sum. This biopic of legendary showman Flo Ziegfeld ranked as Hollywood's longest talkie film until *Gone with the Wind* (yet another MGM release) topped it by 41 minutes in 1939. Despite *GWTW*'s success, Hollywood refrained from overwhelming wartime audiences with lengthy films. Short features cost less and made tidy profits. The studios' perspective changed, though, in the 1950s when television was seen as a growing threat to theatrical movies. Gimmicks such as 3-D (q.v.) and Cinemascope came into vogue — and so did lengthy theatrical epics. In 1956 alone, *The Ten Commandments, Giant,* and *War and Peace* were released. If a viewer watched them on a triple feature (thankfully they never billed together), he'd be watching movies for over ten hours! This trend of long running times continued through the mid–1960s, with an average of two or three epic films being released yearly. No one genre dominated the releases, though Biblical pictures like *The Ten Commandments, Ben-Hur,* and *The Greatest Story Ever Told* seemed to hold an edge. Still, there were long war films *(The Longest Day),* long comedies *(It's a Mad, Mad, Mad, Mad World),* and long musicals *(Star!).* The number of lengthy releases gradually decreased through the 1970s and 1980s, as budget-minded theater owners realized longer movies meant fewer showings and therefore less profit. Television's ability to broadcast multiple-part movies on successive nights also made it a desirable viewer alternative to sitting in a movie theatre for over three hours. Thus, as the miniseries thrived, the long movies faded. A final note: Many long films were trimmed after preview showings or their original releases, and thus now exist in multiple versions. Various cuts of 1970's *Ryan's Daughter* run 206 minutes, 192 minutes, and 176 minutes. Only the original running times are listed below:

Greed (1924) 570m (approximately)

Napoleon (1927) 235m

The Wedding March (1928) 196m

Olympia (aka *Olympische Spiele*) (1936) 225m

The Great Ziegfeld (1936) 179m

Gone with the Wind (1939) 220m

Children of Paradise (1944) 195m

Aan (aka *Savage Princess*) (1952) 190m

The Seven Samurai (1954) 200m

A Star Is Born (1954) 181m

The Ten Commandments (1956) 220m

Giant (1956) 201m

War and Peace (1956) 208m

Raintree County (1957) 187m

Les Miserables (1957) 210m

Ben Hur (1959) 212m

The Big Fisherman (1959) 180m

The Alamo (1960) 192m

Knights of the Teutonic Order (1960) 180m

Exodus (1960) 213m

Pepe (1960) 195m

Rocco and His Brothers (1960) 180m

Spartacus (1960) 196m

El Cid (1961) 184m

Judgment at Nuremberg (1961) 190m

The Longest Day (1962) 180m

Mutiny on the Bounty (1962) 185m

Cleopatra (1962) 243m

Lawrence of Arabia (1962) 222m

It's a Mad, Mad, Mad, Mad World (1963) 192m

The Leopard (1963) 195m

The Fall of the Roman Empire (1964) 187m

The Greatest Story Ever Told (1965) 225m

Hawaii (1966) 189m

The Sand Pebbles (1966) 193m

Camelot (1967) 180m

Star! (1968) 194m

War and Peace (1968) 373m

Ryan's Daughter (1970) 206m

Nicholas and Alexander (1971) 183m

Fiddler on the Roof (1971) 181m

Ludwig (1972) 246m

The Iceman Cometh (1973) 239m

The Godfather, Part II (1974) 200m

Barry Lyndon (1975) 183m

The Memory of Justice (1976) 278m

The Sorrow and the Pity (1976) 260m

1900 (1976) 243m

Mohammed, Messenger of God (aka *The Message*) (1977) 180m

Renaldo and Clara (1978) 232m

The Deer Hunter (1978) 183m

Heaven's Gate (1980) 225m

Reds (1981) 199m

Gandhi (1982) 188m

Fanny and Alexander (1983) 197m

The Right Stuff (1983) 193m

Once Upon a Time in America (1984) 227m
Shoah (1985) 570m

Little Dorrit (1988) 360m (aka *Nobody's Fault* 182m; *Little Dorrit's Story* 178m)

Long Titles

Long movie titles (ten words or more) have posed nightmarish problems to film publicists and theater owners. Imagine trying to get the complete 24-world title to Peter Brooks's *Marat/Sade* on a marquee at a multiscreen complex! To solve this obvious dilemma, most long-titled films have been given shorter alternate names. Thus, Lina Wertmuller's *Swept Away by an Unusual Destiny in the Blue Sea of August* (1975) is more commonly referred to as simply *Swept Away*. Indeed, Wertmuller fans may be the only ones who know the film's full title. Not surprisingly, the reasons behind most long titles remain an ambiguous mystery. However, schlockmeister Roger Corman offers a simple explanation for the first 17-word American film title, 1957's *The Saga of the Viking Women and Their Voyage to the Waters of the Great Sea Serpent*. In *The Films of Roger Corman,* he claims that he came up with "the longest title in the history of motion pictures" because he was unable to think up a one or two word title to describe his film's plot. Corman's tongue-in-cheek attitude toward the title was evidenced by his opening shot of a book's front page reading "The Saga of the Viking Women, etc." If Corman pioneered the long title, Stanley Kubrick made it fashionable by subtitling 1964's *Dr. Strangelove* as *Or, How I Learned to Stop Worrying and Love the Bomb*. Subsequently, alternate titles appeared on major studio pictures like Roman Polanski's *The Fearless Vampire Killers* (1967) and *Those Magnificent Men in Their Flying Machines* (1969). The banner year for long titles was 1967, with three lengthy ones averaging out to 17.7 words each. Long titles have been rare since Lina Wertmuller turned more conventional in the late 1970's.

The Saga of the Viking Women and Their Voyage to the Waters of the Great Sea Serpent (aka *The Viking Women and the Sea Serpent*) (1957)

The Incredibly Strange Creatures Who Stopped Living and Became Mixed Up Zombies (aka *The Teenage Psycho Meets Bloody Mary*) (1963)

Dr. Strangelove; or, How I Learned to Stop Worrying and Love the Bomb (1964)

A Funny Thing Happened on the Way to the Forum (1966)

The Fearless Vampire Killers; or Pardon Me, But Your Teeth Are in My Neck (aka *Dance of the Vampires*) (1967)

Oh Dad, Poor Dad, Mama's Hung You in the Closet and I'm Feeling So Sad (1967)

Persecution and Assassination of Jean-Paul Marat as Performed by the Inmates of the Asylum of Charenton Under the Direction of the Marquis de Sade (aka *Marat/Sade*) (1967)

Those Magnificent Men in Their Flying Machines, or How I Flew from London to Paris in 25 Hours and 11 Minutes (1969)
Can Hieronymus Merkin Ever Forget Mercy Humpe and Find True Happiness? (1969)
Gas-s-s-s (aka *Gas-s-s-s...Or, It May Be Necessary to Destroy the World in Order to Save It*) (1970)
Who Is Harry Kellerman and Why Is He Saying Those Terrible Things About Me? (1971)
Everything You Always Wanted to Know About Sex (But Were Afraid to Ask) (1972)
The Effect of Gamma Rays on Man-in-the-Moon Marigolds (1976)
I Could Never Have Sex with Anyone Who Has So Little Respect for My Husband (1973)
Swept Away by an Unusual Destiny in the Blue Sea of August (aka *Swept Away*) (1975)
Buffalo Bill and the Indians, or Sitting Bull's History Lesson (1976)
The End of the World in Our Usual Bed in a Night Full of Rain (aka *A Night Full of Rain*) (1978)
Come Back to the Five and Dime, Jimmy Dean, Jimmy Dean (1982)
A Joke of Destiny in Wait Around the Corner Like a Bandit (1984)
The Return of the Six Million Dollar Man and the Bionic Woman (1987 TVM)
The Decline of Western Civilization Part II: The Metal Years (1988)

Lookalikes

Although very similar to twins (q.v.), this category addresses movies with characters that look alike, but remain distinctly unrelated. The two most famous sets of movie lookalikes were adapted from Anthony Hope's *The Prisoner of Zenda* and Mark Twain's *The Prince and the Pauper*. In the oft-filmed *Prisoner of Zenda*, a gallant gentleman—a dead ringer for a recently kidnapped king—impersonates the monarch in order to save a Ruritanian country. *Moon Over Parador* (1988) borrowed the plot and updated it to contemporary Latin America. Twain's tale of a young prince who playfully trades places with a lookalike pauper has been filmed many times. The best adaptation was the rousing 1937 Errol Flynn version, but Disney fashioned an adequate remake and an all-star rendition appeared in 1978 under the deceiving title of *Crossed Swords*. In other films, lookalikes have been played for laughs or as part of devious espionage plots. Danny Kaye played lookalikes in both *On the Double* and *On the Riviera*, while comedian Bob Hope was the spitting image of a clever secret agent in *My Favorite Spy*. Yul Brynner had dual roles in the overly-complicated thriller *The Double Man*, playing an East German mole who underwent plastic surgery and special grooming to replace a CIA agent. Sometimes, the government convinces actors (or ordinary lookalikes) to double for VIP's. Thus, the real Winston Churchill was not assassinated in *The Eagle Has Landed* and an actor was persuaded to pose as General

LOOKALIKES

Montgomery for diversion purposes in the World War II action picture *I Was Monty's Double*. That's also how space officials tried to cover up the death of an astronaut in the 1972 TV-movie *The Astronaut*. An interesting variation on the lookalike premise is the "Döppelganger." Literally translated from the German as "double-goer," a Döppelganger is often a ghostly double of a living person. In the "William Wilson" segment of 1968's *Spirits of the Dead*, the protagonist murders the mysterious stranger who has been following him—only to find out it was himself. In the 1969 science fiction puzzler *Journey to the Far Side of the Sun*, Roy Thinnes played an astronaut who landed on a parallel Earth and thereby exchanged places with an exact duplicate of himself (see also **Parallel Worlds**). While Döppelgangers may be lookalikes who are *the same person*, clones are lookalikes derived from the same genes but nonetheless separate entities. Laurence Olivier tracked down little Hitler clones in Ira Levin's ingenious *The Boys from Brazil*. Robert Forster cloned himself and ran into all kinds of trouble in *The Darker Side of Terror*. Additional clones turned up in 1978's *The Clone Master* and 1983's *Anna to the Infinite Power*. Kim Novak played a lookalike in Hitchcock's *Vertigo* who turned out not to be a lookalike after all. See also **Twins**.

The Phantom President (1932)
All the King's Horses (1934)
The Whole Town's Talking (1935)
Honolulu (1937)
The Prince and the Pauper (1937)
So You Won't Talk (1940)
The Saint's Double Trouble (1940)
Berlin Correspondent (1942)
Pardon My Past (1945)
The Forbidden Street (aka *Britannia Mews*) (1948)
The Man with My Face (1950)
Callaway Went Thataway (1951)
My Favorite Spy (1951)
The Man with My Face (1951)
On the Riviera (1951)
The Prisoner of Zenda (1952)
The Brigand (1952)
Stolen Face (1952)
The Four-Sided Triangle (1953)
Flesh and the Woman (1953)
The Most Wanted Man in the World (aka *The Most Wanted Man*) (1953)
Mad About Men (1954)
Invasion of the Body Snatchers (1956)
I Was Monty's Double (1958)
The Square Peg (1958)
Vertigo (1958)
The Scapegoat (1959)
On the Double (1961)
The Double Man (1967)
Spirits of the Dead (The "William Wilson" segment) (1968)
It's Your Move (1968)
Journey to the Far Side of the Sun (aka *Doppelganger*) (1969)
The Man Who Haunted Himself (1970)
Diamonds Are Forever (1971)
The Astronaut (1972 TVM)
The Stranger (1973 TVM)
Royal Flash (1975)
Obsession (1976)
Casanova and Co. (1976)
The Eagle Has Landed (1977)
End of the World (1977)
Crossed Swords (1978)

214

The Boys from Brazil (1978)
Parts: The Clonus Horror (1978)
The Clone Master (1978 TVM)
The Darker Side of Terror
  (1979 TVM)
The Wild, Wild West Revisited
  (1979 TVM)

The Prisoner of Zenda (1979)
Anna to the Infinite Power
  (1983)
Dark Mansions (1986 TVM)
Double Switch (1987 TVM)
Moon Over Parador (1988)
Julia and Julia (1988)

Lottery

Lottery tickets have brought lovers together, torn friends apart, and led to contemplations of murder. Strangers Ronald Colman and Ginger Rogers purchased a ticket together in 1940's *Lucky Partners* and, after a court dispute, wound up confessing their love to each other. David Niven played a film star who agreed to be a lottery prize in 1953's *The Love Lottery*, as did Jeanette MacDonald in 1930's *The Lottery Bride*. Misplaced or stolen lottery tickets caused frantic confusion of the comedy kind in *Uptown Saturday Night* (1974) and Rene Clair's *Le Million* (1931). In *Babette's Feast* (1987), cook extraordinaire Stephane Audran used lottery winnings to show her gratitude to her employers for giving her a home. She spent all the money on a lavish feast—which also provided her with a final chance to practice her culinary art. In the 1966 black comedy *The Wrong Box*, John Mills and family sought to murder Ralph Richardson, thereby winning a tontine, a form of lottery in which the surviving player wins all the money. Michael Keaton uncovered a crooked lottery run by John Davidson in the 1987 flop *The Squeeze*.

The Lottery Bride (1930)
Le Million (1931)
La Belle Equipe (1936)
Lucky Partners (1940)
Three Strangers (1945)
Dual Alibi (1947)
The Love Lottery (1953)

The Wrong Box (1966)
Uptown Saturday Night (1974)
Fox and His Friends (1975)
Lots of Luck (1985 TVM)
Babette's Feast (1987)
The Squeeze (1987)

Lumberjacks

With the trademark crack of falling trees and shouts of "timber!," films about the rugged men who run lumber camps have tended toward sprawling outdoor melodrama. Howard Hawks and William Wyler fashioned a reliable formula with 1936's *Come and Get It*, Edna Ferber's tale of conflict between lumber tycoon Edward Arnold, his son Joel McCrea, and the woman they both loved (Frances Farmer). The 1938 *Valley of the Giants* offered the now-familiar tale about a ruthless lumber man attempting to strip California of its redwood forests. The same story was previously filmed in 1919 and 1927 and remade as the 1952 Kirk Douglas vehicle *The Big Trees*. Wayne Morris, the man who thwarted Charles Bickford in

Valley of the Giants, fought to save a lumber camp in 1950's *The Tougher They Come.* Paul Newman's *Sometimes a Great Notion* focused on the hardships endured by a family of lumberjacks after they defied a local strike.

Come and Get It (aka *Roaring Timber*) (1936)
God's Country and the Woman (1936)
Valley of the Giants (1938)
Moon Over Burma (1940)
The Tougher They Come (1950)
The Blazing Forest (1952)
The Big Trees (1952)
Timberjack (1955)
Spoilers of the Forest (1957)

Girl in the Woods (1958)
Guns of the Timberland (aka *Stampeded*) (1960)
Freckles (1960)
Sometimes a Great Notion (aka *Never Give an Inch*) (1971)
Trouble in High Timber Country (1980 TVM)
The Journey of Natty Gann (1985)

Lupin, Arsene

In Maurice Leblanc's short stories, this French jewel thief was a product of the Parisian streets. However, he became quite a polished gentleman on the screen, especially as portrayed by John Barrymore in 1932's *Arsene Lupin.* Brother Lionel Barrymore starred as Lupin's detective nemesis and Karen Mortley turned up naked in Lupin's bed (pre–Hays Code) as an undercover police agent. Melvyn Douglas played Lupin in the belated MGM sequel, 1938's entertaining *Arsene Lupin Returns.* Interestingly, both Douglas and costar Warren William also played thief-turned-detective The Lone Wolf (q.v.). Although a Lupin film series never materialized, a French television program did appear in the 1970s.

Arsene Lupin (1932)
Arsene Lupin Returns (1938)
Enter Arsene Lupin (1944)

The Adventures of Arsene Lupin (1957)

Lynching

Fritz Lang's *Fury* (1936) rattled Depression Era moviegoers with its powerful depiction of contemporary mob violence. Spencer Tracy portrayed the innocent stranger locked up in a small jail after being charged with kidnapping a young girl. When an incensed mob's lynching effort fails, it burns the jail. However, Tracy's character escapes unseen and lives to administer his own justice/revenge. William Wellman's *The Ox-Bow Incident* (1943), based on Walter Van Tilburg Clark's Western novel, shifted the emphasis from the victim to the lynchers. Again, a mob (in this case, a posse) passes judgment based on weak circumstantial evidence. However, those who oppose the lynching, like drifters Henry Fonda and Harry Morgan, are too passive to make their arguments convincing. Despite these fine films, the most powerful statement against mob violence remains 1950's underrated *The Sound of Fury*. Based on Joe Pagano's novel *The Condemned*, it followed the first half of *Fury*'s plotline before developing into a chilling morality tale. In this case, the accused—Frank Lovejoy and Lloyd Bridges—really are guilty. In fact, Bridge's character murdered a boy in cold blood. But after whipping the townspeople into a frenzy, even journalist Richard Carlson is shocked to see the two criminals hanged in the town square. Other films about lynching lack the conviction of these three, although *The Hanging Tree* (1959) effectively proposes that greed can quench even the bloodthirstiest mob. Of course, not all lynchings result in deaths, as evidenced by Clint Eastwood surviving his own hanging and setting out on a path of revenge in the 1968 Western *Hang 'Em High*.

> *Fury* (1936)
> *Young Mr. Lincoln* (1939)
> *The Ox-Bow Incident* (1943)
> *The Sound of Fury* (aka *Try and Get Me*) (1950)
> *The Woman They Almost*
>
> *Lynched* (1953)
> *The Young Land* (1957)
> *The Hanging Tree* (1959)
> *Five Card Stud* (1968)
> *Hang 'Em High* (1968)

Mabuse, Dr.

Norbert Jacques' criminal mastermind was the subject of three motion picture classics and an offbeat, low-budget film series. Famed director Fritz Lang and his screenwriter wife Thea Von Harbou introduced Mabuse to German audiences in 1921 with *Dr. Mabuse, the Gambler*. Rudolf Klein-Rogge, Von Harbou's ex-husband, starred as the crazed genius and master hypnotist bent on world domination. The same team completed a "second part," titled *Dr. Mabuse, King of Crime*, the following year. The two parts were intended to be shown on consecutive evenings and are frequently listed as one film. For their 1927 U.S. release, the films were heavily cut and edited into a single feature *The Fatal Passions*. Lang and Von Harbou resurrected Mabuse for 1932's *The Testament of Dr. Mabuse*, which was banned for its anti–Hitler statements. Lang subsequently left Germany, while Von Harbou stayed behind. Following a successful career in the U.S., Lang returned to Germany (West Germany) in 1960 to make *The Thousand Eyes of Dr. Mabuse*, his directorial swan song, for producer Artur Brauner. Even without Lang, Brauner continued the series for five more films starring Wolfgang Preiss as Mabuse.

> *Dr. Mabuse, the Gambler* (aka *The Great Gambler—Image of a Generation; Dr. Mabuse, der Spieler*) (1921)
> *Dr. Mabuse, King of Crime* (aka *Inferno—People of a Generation; Inferno—Menschen der Zeit*) (1922)
> *The Testament of Dr. Mabuse* (aka *The Last Will of Dr. Mabuse; The Crimes of Dr. Mabuse; Das Testament des Dr. Mabuse*) (1932)
> *The Thousand Eyes of Dr. Mabuse* (aka *Eyes of Evil; Die Tausend Augen des Dr. Mabuse*) (1960)

The Invisible Dr. Mabuse (aka *Die Unsichtbaren Krallen des Dr. Mabuse*) (1961)
The Return of Dr. Mabuse (aka *Phantom Fiend; Im Stahlnetz des Dr. Mabuse*) (1961)
The Testament of Dr. Mabuse (aka *The Terror of Dr. Mabuse; Das Testament des Dr. Mabuse*) (1962)
Dr. Mabuse vs. Scotland Yard (aka *Scotland Yard Hunts Dr. Mabuse; Scotland Yard Jagt Dr. Mabuse*) (1963)
The Secret of Dr. Mabuse (aka *Dr. Mabuse's Ray of Death; Die Todesstrahlen des Dr. Mabuse*) (1964)

Maciste

A muscular Italian hero in the Hercules (q.v.) mold, Maciste remains anonymous in this country although over a dozen films about him have received U.S. release. The culprits behind this unintentional conspiracy have been American distributors, which changed the original Maciste titles (and subsequently dubbed the dialogue) to misrepresent the films' hero as more widely-known musclemen like Hercules, Goliath, or Samson. Thus, *Maciste alla Corte del Gran Khan* became *Samson and the Seven Miracles of the World,* while *Maciste e la Regina di Samar* became *Hercules Against the Moon Men.* One of the few imports to retain Maciste in its title was 1964's sand-and-sandal spoof *Hercules Against Maciste in the Vale of Woe.* Not surprisingly, that film was later retitled *Hercules in the Vale of Woe,* thus dropping Maciste into anonymity again. Just to confuse matters even further, brawny actors Mark Forest, Reg Park, Kirk Morris, and Alan Steel (aka Sergio Ciani) all played Hercules as well as Maciste.

Maciste in Hell (aka *Maciste all'Inferno*) (1926) (Umberto Guarra-cino)
Son of Samson (aka *Maciste the Mighty; Maciste nella Valle dei Re*) (1960) (Mark Forest)
The Witch's Curse (aka *Maciste all'Inferno*) (1960) (Kirk Morris)
Molemen vs. the Son of Hercules (aka *The Strongest Man in the World; Maciste l'Uomo Più Forte del Mondo*) (1961) (Forest)
Atlas Against the Cyclops (aka *Monster from the Unknown World; Maciste nella Terror dei Ciclopi*) (1961) (Mitchell Gordon)
Colossus and the Headhunters (aka *Maciste Contro i Cacciatori de Teste*) (1962) (Morris)
Death in the Arena (aka *Colossus of the Arena; Maciste il Gladiatore Più Forte del Mondo*) (1962) (Forest)
Fire Monsters Against the Son of Hercules (aka *Colossus of the Stone Age; Maciste Contro i Monstri*) (1962) (Reg Park)
Triumph of the Sons of Hercules (aka *El Trionfo di Maciste*) (1962) (Morris)
Goliath and the Sins of Babylon (aka *Maciste l'Eroe Più Grande del Mondo*) (1963) (Forest)

Samson and the Slave Queen (aka *Zorro Contro Maciste*) (1963)
(Alan Steel)

Samson vs. the Giant King (aka *Giant of the Lost Tomb; Maciste alla Corte dello Zar*) (1963) (Morris)

Samson and the Seven Miracles of the World (aka *Maciste alla Corte del Gran Khan*) (1963) (Gordon Scott)

Goliath and the Vampires (aka *The Vampires; Maciste Contro il Vampiro*) (1964) (Scott)

Hercules in the Vale of Woe (aka *Maciste Against Hercules in the Vale of Woe*) (1964)

Maciste and the King of Samar (aka *Maciste e la Regina di Samar*) (1964) (Steel)

Maciste, Spartan Gladiator (aka *Maciste, Gladiatore di Sparta*) (1964) (Forest)

Hercules of the Desert (aka *La Valle dell'Eco Tonante*) (1964) (Morris)

Samson and the Mighty Challenge (aka *Hercules, Maciste, Samson, and Ursus Against the Universe; Ercole, Sansone, Maciste, Ursus: gli Invincibli*) (1964)

Samson in King Solomon's Mines (aka *Maciste nelle Miniere de Re Salomone*) (1964) (Park)

Hercules Against the Moon Men (aka *Maciste Contro gli Uomini della Luna*) (1964) (Steel)

Hercules Against the Barbarians (aka *Maciste nell'Inferno di Genghis Khan*) (1964) (Forest)

Mad Max

The Australian-imported *Mad Max* movies not only made a star of Mel Gibson, but they also managed to make the near-impossible transition from drive-in cult status into mainstream major hits. The 1979 *Mad Max* starred Gibson as the title character, a futuristic cop who patrols a postapocalyptic world populated with motorcycle gangs and other riff-raff. When his partner and family are murdered, Max becomes a one-man vigilante force and wipes out the "Glory Riders." From the beginning, director/cowriter George Miller's film found favor with science fiction and action fans, but it attracted little critical attention. Undoubtedly, the release of some *dubbed* prints (in which even Gibson spoke with someone else's voice) limited its appeal. That all changed with the superior sequel, 1982's *The Road Warrior* in which Gibson and Miller transformed Max into a mythic warrior. Critics jumped on the bandwagon ("Apocalypse Pow!" proclaimed *Time*) and Gibson's career began to ascend rapidly. He was an established star when he returned to his homeland for 1985's *Mad Max Beyond Thunderdome*. This slick rehash of *Road Warrior,* bolstered by the presence of rock queen Tina Turner, racked up impressive boxoffice figures—but nevertheless lacked the enduring popularity of *Road Warrior*. See also **End of the World/Post-Apocalypse.**

>*Mad Max* (1979)
>*The Road Warrior* (aka *Mad Max 2*) (1981)

>*Mad Max Beyond Thunderdome* (1985)

Magicians

Even though its running time was a scant two minutes, 1896's *Conjuring a Lady at the Robert-Houdin's* holds a unique double distinction among magician films. In addition to containing one of the first filmed magic tricks, it spotlighted the moviemaking talents of former conjuror and cinema pioneer Georges Méliès. Unlike this landmark work, other magician movies have often forgotten that the cinema is a magical medium. They have been largely content to pass off the magician as a devious trickster or bland do-gooder. In 1946's *The Strange Mr. Gregory,* Edmund Lowe played a magician/hypnotist who pretended to be dead to win the affections of Jean Rogers. Vincent Price was a 19th century illusionist who went mad in the well-titled *The Mad Magician* (1954). He sought revenge on his cheating wife (Eva Gabor) and other magicians by murdering them with his famous tricks (the imaginative murder angle was repeated in later Price films like *The Abominable Dr. Phibes* and *Theatre of Blood*). Satanic cult leader Niall MacGinnis performed Halloween magic shows for the kiddies in the classic *Curse of the Demon* (1957) and then explained to Dana Andrews the critical distinctions between black and white magic. On the other hand, heroic magicians have been far less interesting. *Chandu the Magician,* culled from a 1932 serial, sent Edmund Lowe (again) against Beli Lugosi's evil Roxor (oddly, Bela showed up as *Chandu* two years later in another serial). In TV-movies, Christopher George's escape artist in *Escape* (1970) and Bill Bixby's illusionist in *The Magician* (1973) both helped people in trouble—that's TV talk for detective work. Bixby's film served as the pilot for a shortlived 1973–74 TV series. Neither Laurel and Hardy nor Jerry Lewis could mix magic and comedy to much effect in, respectively, *A-Haunting We Will Go* (1942) and *The Geisha Boy* (1958). However, Tommy Smothers had some amusing scenes in *Get to Know Your Rabbit* (1972) and Woody Allen lost his mother at a magic show in his *New York Stories* segment (1989). Tony Curtis and Paul Michael Glaser played the famous magician/escape artist Harry Houdini in 1953 and 1976 films. Ingmar Bergman explored the mystical side of magic in *The Magician* (1958), a haunting tale about an illusionist detained by villagers unconvinced by his magical powers.

>*Conjuring a Lady at the Robert-Houdin's* (1896)
>*The Phantom of Paris* (1931)
>*Chandu, the Magician* (1932)

>*Lady in Distress* (aka *A Window in London*) (1939)
>*A-Haunting We Will Go* (1942)
>*The Strange Mr. Gregory* (1946)

Houdini (1953)
The Mad Magician (1954)
Curse of the Demon (aka Night of the Demon) (1958)
The Geisha Boy (1958)
The Magician (1959)
Two on a Guillotine (1965)
The Mysterious Magician (1965)
Escape (1970 TVM)
Get to Know Your Rabbit (1972)
The Golden Voyage of Sinbad (1973)
The Magician (1973 TVM)
The Great Houdinis (1976 TVM)
The Magician of Lublin (1979)
Mandrake (1979 TVM)
The Escape Artist (1982)
Bagdad Cafe (1988)
New York Stories (1989)

The Magnificent Seven

John Sturges' 1960 remake of the Japanese classic *Seven Samurai* has grown in popularity over the years, becoming—according to *TV Guide*—one of the most frequently shown movies on television. The original seven gunfighters hired to protect a Mexican village were (and this is a great "list" question in its own right): Yul Brynner, Steve McQueen, James Coburn, Robert Vaughn, Charles Bronson, Brad Dexter, and Horst Buchholz. Only Yul returned for the first sequel, 1964's *Return of the Seven*. But Elmer Bernstein's great music score (best known as the Marlboro theme) was used in all four "Seven" films. The original plot has been recycled extensively and transplanted to contemporary Arizona (the 1985 TVM *Command 5*), the Middle East (1968's *The Invincible Six*), and outer space (1980's *Battle Beyond the Stars*). *The Adventures of the Magnificent 6½* (1988) was a children's variation.

The Magnificent Seven (1960)
Return of the Seven (1966)
Guns of the Magnificent Seven (1969)
The Magnificent Seven Ride (1972)

Maisie

The year 1939 was a banner year for MGM, featuring the releases of *Gone with the Wind, The Wizard of Oz,* and *Goodbye, Mr. Chips.* So it's no wonder that no one remembers it as the year Ann Sothern made her debut as Maisie, a tough, spunky girl with a heart of gold. At age 30, Sothern was already a "B" movie veteran, having played similar roles for both Columbia and RKO. Robert Young (as a ranch hand!) co-starred with her in the first series entry, *Maisie.* A few months later, Sothern was back in *Congo Maisie,* a revamped version of the Clark Gable–Jean Harlow sizzler *Red Dust.* Eight more Maisie adventures appeared between 1940 and 1947, making the title character the busiest single woman in the movies. She was a maid in *Maisie Was a Lady,* a police detective in *Undercover Maisie,* and an aircraft factory worker in *Swing Shift Maisie.* Sothern's film career slacked off during the 1950s and she turned to television, experiencing modest success with *Private Secretary* and *The Ann Sothern Show.*

Maisie (1939)	*Swingshift Maisie* (aka *The Girl in Overalls*) (1943)
Congo Maisie (1939)	
Gold Rush Maisie (1940)	*Maisie Goes to Reno* (aka *You Can't Do That to Me*) (1944)
Maisie Was a Lady (1940)	
Ringside Maisie (aka *Cash and Carry*) (1941)	*Up Goes Maisie* (aka *Up She Goes*) (1945)
Maisie Gets Her Man (aka *She Got Her Man*) (1942)	*Undercover Maisie* (1947)

A Man Called Horse

Richard Harris starred in this offbeat Western about an English aristocrat captured by Sioux Indians in 1825. He suffers torture, learns to live with his captors, grows to understand them, and becomes their leader. It was based on Dorothy M. Johnson's 1950 *Collier's* story and featured the harrowing Sun Vow ritual, which required Indian males to be suspended by clamps inserted in their pectoral muscles. Although Harris' character returned to civilization at the film's end, he came back to help his Indian friends in 1976's *The Return of a Man Called Horse.* This sequel lacked the box office zip of its predecessor, but that did not deter the belated release of a third film, 1983's *Triumphs of a Man Called Horse,* which starred Harris and Michael Beck as his son.

A Man Called Horse (1970)	*Triumphs of a Man Called Horse* (1983)
The Return of a Man Called Horse (1976)	

The Man from U.N.C.L.E.

NBC introduced this lighthearted spy TV series in 1964, shortly after the third James Bond thriller, *Goldfinger,* struck the mother lode at the national boxoffice. U.N.C.L.E. stood for United Network Command for Law and Enforcement and was run by gruff, fatherly Mr. Waverly (Leo G. Carroll). The agency's top two agents were American Napoleon Solo (Robert Vaughn) and Russian Illya Kuryakin (David McCallum). (The fact that Americans and Russians were fighting together for world peace makes "The Man from U.N.C.L.E." the first *glasnost* TV series.) The show was an immediate hit, especially with the younger set, and inspired MGM to release a big-screen feature, *To Trap a Spy,* in 1966. Actually, it had been originally shown as a 1964 TV episode called "The Vulcan Affair," but fans didn't seem to mind that they had seen it before. Seven additional movies were released between 1965–68. Meanwhile, the television edition spun off the short-lived series "The Girl from U.N.C.L.E." (starring Stefanie Powers) and dropped in the ratings after peaking at No. 13 for the year in the 1965–66 season. The series was cancelled in January 1968 and replaced by "Rowan and Martin's Laugh-in." A reunion TV movie, *The Return of the Man from U.N.C.L.E.*, surfaced in 1983.

To Trap a Spy (1966)	*The Spy in the Green Hat*
One of Our Spies Is Missing	(1967)
(1966)	*The Helicopter Spies* (1968)
One Spy Too Many (1966)	*How to Steal the World* (1968)
The Spy with My Face (1966)	*The Return of the Man from*
The Karate Killers (1967)	*U.N.C.L.E.* (1983 TVM)

The Man with No Name

Clint Eastwood first portrayed this laconic gunslinger in 1964's *A Fistful of Dollars,* Sergio Leone's spaghetti-Western version of Akira Kurosawa's samurai epic *Yojimbo.* Although it's not actually specified, Eastwood apparently played the same character in Leone's follow-up *For a Few Dollars More* and *The Good, the Bad, and the Ugly* (Clint was the Good, Lee Van Cleef the Bad, and Eli Wallach the Ugly). Clint may have played the role in other Westerns, too (e.g. *High Plains Drifter, Pale Rider*). Given his subtle acting style, it's hard to tell.

Marlowe, Philip

The screen exploits of Raymond Chandler's tough, cynical private eye make for fascinating trivia. The first adaptation of a Marlowe mystery *(Farewell, My Lovely)* was tailored for George Sanders as 1942's *The Falcon Takes Over,* an entry in the long-running Falcon (q.v.) film series. That same year, the Philip Marlowe novel *The High Window,* was adapted for detective Michael Shayne (q.v.) as *Time to Kill.* Two years later, Marlowe finally reached the screen in the guise of Dick Powell, who made the switch from crooner to tough guy in *Murder, My Sweet,* another version of *Farewell, My Lovely.* Powell was terrific as Marlowe, setting a standard that even Bogart couldn't surpass in 1946's *The Big Sleep.* Later that year, actor-director Robert Montgomery filmed *The Lady in the Lake* in first-person, showing audiences everything as Marlowe saw it. It was a novel experiment (e.g. kisses filled the screen, the camera rocked back after a punch to Marlowe's face), but ultimately it was more irritating than interesting. George Montgomery (no relation to Robert) played Marlowe in 1947's *The Brasher Doubloon,* the second version of Chandler's *The High Window.* There were no Marlowe films in the 1950s, but James Garner played the part in 1969's *Marlowe* (which featured Bruce Lee as a minor villain). Elliott Gould played an unrecognizable Marlowe in Robert Altman's 1973 *The Long Goodbye.* And in the late 1970s, a weary-looking Robert Mitchum played the detective in *Farewell, My Lovely* (set in the '40s) and *The Big Sleep* (updated to the present). Ironically, the only Marlowe novel never filmed was *Playback,* which was originally an unsold Chandler screenplay.

Murder, My Sweet (1944)	Marlowe (1969)
The Big Sleep (1946)	The Long Goodbye (1973)
The Lady in the Lake (1946)	Farewell, My Lovely (1975)
The Brasher Doubloon (1947)	The Big Sleep (1978)

Marple, Miss Jane

Agatha Christie's sharp-witted spinster enjoyed modest success in the 1960s when Margaret Rutherford's *Murder, She Said* sparked a four-film series. Rutherford also made a cameo appearance as Miss Marple opposite Tony Randall's Hercule Poirot (q.v.) in 1966's *The Alphabet Murders*. In 1980, Angela Lansbury (pre–"Murder, She Wrote") made a delightful Jane Marple in *The Mirror Crack'd*, but sadly did not return for an encore. That made it possible for Helen Hayes to star as Miss Marple in a pair of entertaining, if easily-forgotten, made-for-TV mysteries.

Murder, She Said (1962)	A Caribbean Mystery (1983
Murder at the Gallop (1963)	TVM)
Murder Ahoy! (1964)	Murder with Mirrors (1985
Murder Most Foul (1965)	TVM)
The Mirror Crack'd (1980)	

The Marseilles Trilogy

The characters of Marcel Pagnol's French trilogy of *Marius, Fanny,* and *Cesar* have maintained universal appeal ever since their first appearances. Thus, in addition to the trilogy, they have appeared (sometimes under different names) in German, Italian, and American features based on Pagnol's works. Pagnol was a rising French playwright when Paramount expressed interest in filming his 1929 hit play *Marius.* The movie version, with Alexander Korda directing from a Pagnol screenplay, was released in 1931. Pierre Fresnay played Marius, who dreams of a life at sea although he has fallen in love with Fanny (Orane Demazis). Fanny tries to make Marius jealous by flirting with the rich, middle-aged Panisse, a friend of Marius' father Cesar (Raimu). Eventually, she and Marius make love, but even that cannot cure Marius' wanderlust. Fanny sacrifices her own happiness and Marius leaves for the sea. Marc Allegret directed the second chapter, 1932's *Fanny,* which Pagnol again adapted from his play. Fanny, who has become pregnant with Marius' child, agrees to marry Panisse. Cesar becomes upset with this arrangement, but eventually agrees to be the child's godfather. After two years at sea, Marius returns and wants Fanny and the child. Panisse won't give the child up and Fanny, although she still loves Marius, again sacrifices her own happiness—this time for her son. Pagnol wrote an original screenplay and directed the final installment, 1936's *Cesar.* Set 17 years later, it opens with the death of Panisse. Fanny tells her 18-year-old son Cesariot that Marius, not Panisse, was his father. With Cesar's help, Cesariot seeks out his father and eventually reunites Fanny, Marius, and Cesar. While film critics preferred the first and last films, *Fanny* attained the greatest popularity at the time of its release. It was remade in Italy in 1933, in Germany in 1934 (with Emil Jannings), and in the U.S. in 1937 as *Port of Seven Seas*. The latter film made little impression despite a solid cast of Wallace Beery, Frank Morgan, and Maureen O'Sullivan. In 1961, producer Joshua Logan condensed the trilogy into *Fanny*, a colorful, but overlong reworking. It reunited *Gigi* stars Leslie Caron (as Fanny) and Maurice Chevalier (as Panisse) and added Charles Boyer (Cesar) and Horst Buccholz (Marius). Unfortunately, Logan's ownership of the rights to *Fanny* prevented Pagnol's trilogy from being shown outside France for several years. Jacques Demy's charming musical *The Umbrellas of Cherbourg* (1964) borrowed and updated *Fanny's* plot.

Marius (1931)	*Cesar* (1936)
Fanny (1932)	*Port of Seven Seas* (1938)
Fanny (1933) (Italian remake)	*Fanny* (1961)
Fanny (1934) (German remake)	

Mason, Perry

Raymond Burr *is* Perry Mason for millions of mystery fans, but Erle Stanley Gardner's lawyer/detective hit the big screen 20 years before the long-running TV series. Warren William was a sharp-witted, gourmet-minded Mason in four Warner Bros. films, beginning with 1934's *The Case of the Howling Dog*. Williams seemed a natural for the part, having already played that urbane sleuth Philo Vance (q.v.) and destined to play the Lone Wolf (q.v.), a jewel thief and detective. In fact, Williams' Mason did so much detection that it was easy to forget he was a lawyer and some entries were devoid of courtroom scenes. Two of Williams' films are of special interest. *The Case of the Curious Bride* featured superstar-to-be Errol Flynn as a murder victim and Donald Woods, a future Perry Mason, in another supporting role. *The Case of the Velvet Claws* found Mason and secretary Della Street (Claire Dodd) married and trying to take a honeymoon! Comic actor Allen Jenkins played Perry's detective assistant Spudsie (*not* Paul) Drake. In 1936, former Sam Spade Ricardo Cortez replaced Williams in *The Case of the Black Cat* and Donald Woods finished the Warner series with 1937's *The Case of the Stuttering Bishop*. The "Perry Mason" TV series debuted in 1957 and enjoyed a nine-year run on CBS. Burr played the lead, of course, with Barbara Hale as Della Street, William Hopper as detective Paul Drake, William Talman as prosecuting attorney Hamilton Burger, and Ray Collins as police Lieutenant Arthur Tragg (Collins died prior to the 1965–66 season). In 1973, CBS revived the show as "The New Adventures of Perry Mason" starring Monte Markham, but it folded after half a season. Then, in 1985, NBC brought back Burr in the TV-movie *Perry Mason Returns*, reuniting him with Hale and introducing William Katt (Hale's real-life son) as Paul Drake's son. The film's ratings went through the roof and a series of equally high-rated made-for-TV movies quickly evolved.

The Case of the Howling Dog (1934) (William)
The Case of the Curious Bride (1935) (William)
The Case of the Lucky Legs (1935) (William)
The Case of the Black Cat (1936) (Cortez)
The Case of the Velvet Claws (1936) (William)
The Case of the Stuttering Bishop (1937) (Woods)
Perry Mason Returns (1985 TVM) (Burr)
Perry Mason: The Case of the Notorious Nun (1986 TVM) (Burr)
Perry Mason: The Case of the Shooting Star (1986 TVM) (Burr)
Perry Mason and the Case of the Sinister Spirit (1987 TVM) (Burr)
Perry Mason: The Case of the Lost Love (1987 TVM) (Burr)
Perry Mason: The Case of the Murdered Madam (1987 TVM) (Burr)
Perry Mason: The Case of the Scandalous Scoundrel (1987 TVM) (Burr)
Perry Mason: The Case of the Avenging Ace (1988 TVM) (Burr)
Perry Mason: The Case of the Lady in the Lake (1988 TVM) (Burr)
Perry Mason: The Case of the Lethal Lesson (1989 TVM) (Burr)
Perry Mason: The Case of the Musical Murder (1989 TVM) (Burr)
Perry Mason: The Case of the All-Star Assassin (1989 TVM) (Burr)

Matadors / Bullfights

Blood and Sand reigns as the best-remembered bullfight film, chiefly because the 1922 and 1941 versions provided screen favorites Rudolph Valentino and Tyrone Power with one of their best roles. Vicente Blanco Ibáñez wrote the original story in 1908 and Tom Cushing adapted it for the stage in 1921. The following year, Valentino starred as the young matador who rises from poverty to stardom in the bullring, only to fall victim to the charms of an irresistible temptress (Nita Naldi). The matador died in the Ibáñez story, but the Valentino version was altered so that his faithful wife nursed him to recovery from near-death. The Tyrone Power remake followed the original closely (with Rita Hayworth as the seducer), but restored the climactic death scene in the bullring. Ex-matador Budd Boetticher, a technical advisor on the Power film, subsequently became a director and made three films about the perils of the bullring and the lifestyles of those who enter it. His semiautobiographical *The Bullfighter and the Lady* (1951) starred Robert Stack as an American (like Boetticher) in Mexico who convinces a famous matador (Gilbert Roland) to help him become a bullfighter. Boetticher followed it with 1955's *The Magnificent Matador*, which cast Anthony Quinn as an aging matador who trains his illegitimate son for the ring despite premonitions of death. Boetticher left Hollywood in 1960 to make a documentary in Mexico about the legendary bullfighter Carlos Arruza. The venture proved disasterous, with the pro-

ducer/director facing endless personal and production problems. The film
was finally completed in 1967 and released in 1972 as *Arruza*. Not surprisingly, bullfighting has been played for laughs in a number of films. In the
1945 comedy *The Bullfighters*, bumbling detectives Laurel and Hardy
discover that Stan resembles a famous matador. Naturally, he winds up
facing an unpleasant-looking bull in the ring. A similar fate befell Lou
Costello in the 1948 Abbott and Costello comedy *Mexican Hayride*. In one
of the livelier scenes in 1957's *The Sun Also Rises*, Errol Flynn and Eddie
Albert played rompish drunks who posed the dangerous question: "Bully,
bully, where's the bull?" Esther Williams (!) played an unlikely-looking
female matador in the 1947 musical *Fiesta*. Still, she looked at ease compared to the Volkswagen-turned-matador in *Herbie Goes Bananas*.

Blood and Sand (1922)	*The Magnificent Matador* (aka
The Kid from Spain (1932)	*The Brave and the Beautiful*)
The Bullfighters (1945)	(1955)
Fiesta (1947)	*The Sun Also Rises* (1957)
Blood and Sand (1941)	*Fun in Acapulco* (1963)
Masquerade in Mexico (1945)	*The Bobo* (1967)
Mexican Hayride (1948)	*Arruza* (1972)
The Bullfighter and the Lady	*Herbie Goes Bananas* (1980)
(1951)	*Bolero* (1984)
The Brave Bulls (1951)	*Matador* (1986)

Meatballs

Five years before 1984's *Ghostbusters* lined their pockets with gold, comedian Bill Murray and director Ivan Reitman made this Canadian sleeper
about life in a summer camp. Despite an abundance of teen comedy
stereotypes, it was ranchy, occasionally schmaltzy, and pretty funny when
Murray was around. Wisely, Murray went on to bigger roles and avoided
further association with Camps North Star and Sasquatch in *Meatballs II*
and *Meatballs III*. John Laroquette, Sally Kellerman, and Patrick Dempsey
were not as selective.

Meatballs (1979)	*Meatballs III* (1987)
Meatballs II (1983)	

Mermaids

Mermaid movies seem to come in waves, with 1947's *Miranda* sparking the
first volley. It starred Glynis Johns as a comely mermaid who rescues a
drowning physician on a Cornwall holiday. To show his gratitude, the
doctor takes the mermaid back to London, where she moves in with him
and his wife and decides that she prefers the sophisticated land-life. This
light comedic concoction inspired a 1954 sequel, *Mad About Men*, in
which mermaid Johns trades places with a lookalike (q.v.) human. In the
meantime, producer-writer Nunnally Johnson mounted an American

imitation of *Miranda* with 1948's *Mr. Peabody and the Mermaid.* William Powell played a man in the midst of a midlife crisis who hooks mermaid Ann Blyth while on a fishing trip. Complications ensue when he takes her back and deposits her into a fish pond near his beach house. A gap of five years separated *Mad About Men* from the next group of mermaid movies. *Mermaids and Sea Robbers* (1959), a Japanese import, and *The Mermaids of Tiburon* (1962) were low-grade fantasies with no redeeming traits. Curtis Harrington's *Night Tide* (1961) was an atmospheric yarn about a sailor (Dennis Hopper) who meets an odd girl (Linda Lawson) who plays a mermaid in a carnival sideshow. She claims to be a descendant of the "sea people," who must kill during a full moon. Far less compelling was 1965's *Beach Blanket Bingo,* which featured a subplot involving a mermaid played by Marta Kristen (the oldest daughter in TV's "Lost in Space"). Almost 20 years later, a mermaid subplot in Bill Forsyth's charming Scottish fantasy *Local Hero* (1983) initiated another round of mermaid movies. The following year's *Splash* was a solid sleeper hit about a young man (Tom Hanks) reunited with the fetching mermaid (Daryl Hannah) who rescued him from drowning as a boy. Ariel the mermaid also fell in love with the human prince she rescued in Disney's 1989 animated version of Hans Christian Andersen's *The Little Mermaid.*

Miranda (1947)
Mr. Peabody and the Mermaid (1948)
Hans Christian Andersen (the "Little Mermaid" sequence) (1952)
Peter Pan (1953)
Mad About Men (1954)
Mermaids and Sea Robbers
(1959)
Night Tide (1961)
The Mermaids of Tiburon (aka *The Aqua Sex*) (1962)
Beach Blanket Bingo (1965)
Local Hero (1983)
Splash (1984)
Splash Too (1988 TVM)
The Little Mermaid (1989)

Mexican Spitfire

By the time she was 30, spicy Latin American actress Lupe Velez had experienced a flirtation with stardom (opposite Douglas Fairbanks in 1927's *The Gaucho*), a scandalous romance with Gary Cooper, and an unhappy marriage to Johnny Weissmuller. Her career was in a slow tailspin when she made a lightweight 1939 comedy called *The Girl from Mexico.* Donald Woods starred as a young advertising executive who falls for a fiery Latin entertainer (Velez), while dealing with his own devious Uncle Matt (Leon Errol). To everyone's surprise, the movie's success spawned a Mexican Spitfire series. Although Velez was the star, Errol stole the show at every turn—playing both Uncle Matt and a delightful drunken Englishman named Lord Epping. Sometimes, the antics got a wee silly—one entry featured a live pink elephant with green polka dots. Sadly, the series ended abruptly in 1944 with Velez's elaborately staged sleeping-pill suicide. (Note: Although both Velez and Errol appeared in 1941's *Six Lessons from Madame La Zonga*, it was not a *Spitfire* entry.)

The Girl from Mexico (1939)
Mexican Spitfire (1939)
Mexican Spitfire Out West (1940)
Mexican Spitfire at Sea (1941)
Mexican Spitfire's Baby (1941)
Mexican Spitfire Sees a Ghost (1942)
Mexican Spitfire's Elephant (1942)
Mexican Spitfire's Blessed Event (1943)

Military Academies

As one would expect, the United States Military Academy—better known as West Point—has provided the bulk of military school settings. West Point stories have ranged from inspirational sport sagas *(The Spirit of West Point)* to musical revues *(West Point Story)* to true-life dramas *(The Silence* and *Dress Gray).* Ask any cadet about his favorite West Point film and he will probably answer *The Long Gray Line,* a sentimental tale about an athletic trainer (Tyrone Power) and his wife (Maureen O'Hara) who become an institution at the school. West Point comedies have been rare, though Francis the Talking Mule tutored Donald O'Connor in 1952's *Francis Goes to West Point* and females invaded the academy in the 1979 TV-movie *Women of West Point.* An "illegal" woman caused Eddie Albert quite a bit of trouble at the Virginia Military Institute in the 1940 comedy *Brother Rat.* The woman turned out to be his pregnant wife (Jane Bryan)—a fact he had hidden from school officials who did not accept married cadets. It was remade as the musical *About Face* with Eddie Bracken in 1952. Not surprisingly, controversial dramas have taken place in fictitious military schools. Ben Gazarra played a sadistic cadet with a dominating hold over classmates in 1957's *The Strange One,* adapted from Calder Willingham's novel *End as a Man.* (Ironically, *Sorority Girl,* a female version of the same novel, was also released in 1957.) In 1981's *Taps,* Timothy Hutton led a group of fellow cadets, including Sean Penn and Tom Cruise, in a revolt against school officials trying to turn their beloved academy into a condominium. David Keith battled modern-day prejudice at a Southern military academy in 1983's *The Lords of Discipline.* The most unlikely military school is the one run by an order of nuns in the Charlton Heston picture *The Private War of Major Benson.* See also **Boarding Schools.**

Tom Brown of Culver (1932)
Flirtation Walk (1934)
Dinky (1935)
Navy Blue and Gold (1937)
The Duke of West Point (1938)
Spirit of Culver (1939)
Brother Rat (1940)
They Died with Their Boots On (1941)
Ten Gentlemen from West Point (1942)
Best Foot Forward (1943)
The Spirit of West Point (1947)
Beyond Glory (1948)
West Point Story (aka *Fine and Dandy*) (1950)

About Face (1952)
Francis Goes to West Point (1952)
The Long Gray Line (1955)
The Private War of Major Benson (1955)
The Strange One (aka End as a Man) (1957)
The Silence (1975 TVM)

Women of West Point (1979 TVM)
Up the Academy (1980)
Taps (1981)
Evilspeak (1982)
The Lords of Discipline (1983)
Hard Knox (1984 TVM)
Dress Gray (1986 TVM)
Combat High (1986 TVM)

Mirrors

Employed principally in fantasy films, mirrors have also been used effectively in comic sequences and climactic confrontations. An imaginary mirror was the gimmick in *Duck Soup,* in which Harpo Marx posed as Groucho's reflection, mimicking perfectly his brother's every movement. Errol Flynn and Donald Woods, both attired in Santa suits, repeated the "no mirror" trick in 1946's *Never Say Goodbye* (as did Lucille Ball and Harpo Marx in TV's "I Love Lucy"). A man's reflection stepped out of a mirror to offer advice to his owner in the 1936 comedy *The Man in the Mirror.* Orson Welles confronted murderess Rita Hayworth in a carnival hall of mirrors in the tense climax of Welles' *Lady from Shanghai* (1948). In a similar fashion, Bruce Lee outdueled villain Shih Kien in a chamber of mirrors in the 1973 martial arts classic *Enter the Dragon.* However, fantasy films have used mirrors most imaginatively, beginning with the Wicked Witch's magic mirror in Disney's *Snow White and the Seven Dwarfs* (1937). In 1945's *Dead of Night,* an antique mirror haunted a happy husband by reflecting the room of its previous owner — a jealous gent who strangled his wife. Another old mirror allowed Bradford Dillman to return from the dead to visit fiancée Linda Day George in the 1969 TV-movie *Fear No Evil.* On a more intellectual scale, a mirror provided the door between Earth and the Zone (a sort of Heaven/Hell) in Jean Cocteau's eerie classic *Orpheus* (1949). For the most bizarre use of mirrors, it's hard to beat *The Boogeyman,* a 1980 sleeper about a shard of a broken mirror which turned people into killers. Finally, mirrors have exposed quite a few vampires, for those smart enough to know that the bloodsuckers cast no reflection.

Duck Soup (1933)
The Man in the Mirror (1936)
Snow White and the Seven Dwarfs (1937)
Dead of Night (1945)
Never Say Goodbye (1946)
Fear in the Night (1947)
Lady from Shanghai (1948)
Orpheus (1949)

Nightmare (1956)
The Witch's Mirror (1960)
The Devil's Bride (aka The Devil Rides Out) (1968)
Fear No Evil (1969 TVM)
Enter the Dragon (1973)
The Boogeyman (aka The Boogey Man) (1980)
The Mirror Crack'd (1980)

| *Come Back to the Five and* | *Dean* (1982) |
| *Dime, Jimmy Dean, Jimmy* | *Big Business* (1988) |

Missing in Action

This 1984 Chuck Norris action picture cashed in on the public's "new patriotism" and shot to the top of the boxoffice charts. In many ways, it paved the way for 1985's *Rambo: First Blood Part II*, with a plot that sent Colonel Norris back into Vietnam to rescue some buddies imprisoned in a POW camp. It was followed by a prequel and then a sequel. *Missing in Action 2: The Beginning* (1985), which was actually filmed *before* the earlier film, focused on Norris' POW escape. *Braddock: Missing in Action III* (1988) had Norris returning to Vietnam again, this time to save his own son. Neither of these two films matched the popularity of the original. See also **Vietnam War.**

Missing in Action (1984)	*Braddock: Missing in Action III*
Missing in Action II: The	(1988)
Beginning (1985)	

Mobile Homes

Not many movie residents have lived in mobile home parks. Dick Powell and Rhonda Fleming called the Clover Trailer Park home in *Cry Danger,* but their place of residence had little to do with the plot. The same can be said of mobile home dwellers Jamie Lee Curtis *(Grandview U.S.A.),* John Travolta and Debra Winger *(Urban Cowboy),* Bette Midler *(Jinxed),* and Holly Hunter and Nicholas Gage *(Raising Arizona).* The first half of 1984's delightful *The Last Starfighter* took place in an atmospheric trailer park where an ugly alien tried to liquidate a teen video game expert. Two wonderful comedies have dealt with couples who have taken their trailers on the road. In *The Long, Long Trailer* (1954), Lucille Ball and Dezi Arnaz went on their honeymoon in a particularly troublesome trailer. Yuppies Albert Brooks and Julie Haggerty gave up the "rat race" for an enlightening life on the road in *Lost in America* (1985). However, they didn't count on Haggerty's losing their nest egg on their first stop—at a casino in Las Vegas.

Monks

In comparison to priests and nuns, monks have been poorly represented in films. The only ones to achieve celebrity status have been Friar Tuck of Robin Hood (q.v.) fame and Rasputin, the Russian monk whose alleged healing powers gained him influence over the Imperial family. This colorful character has attracted many performers, most notably Christopher Lee *(Rasputin—the Mad Monk),* Tom Baker *(Nicholas and Alexandra),* Edmund Purdom *(Nights of Rasputin),* and, in the definitive performance,

Lionel Barrymore *(Rasputin and the Empress)*. The portly frame of Friar Tuck has been inhabited by even more actors, though Eugene Pallette's portrayal in 1938's *The Adventures of Robin Hood* outshines all others. With the exception of Rasputin, other film biographies of monks have been of the saintly variety. Both Franco Zeffirelli's *Brother Sun, Sister Moon* (1973) and the earlier *Francis of Assisi* (1961) told how St. Francis of Assisi founded the Franciscan order of monks. The 1974 *Luther* was a straightforward adaptation of John Osborne's play about the founder of Protestantism. In fictional films, Harrison Ford and Sean Connery encountered an ancient monk who guarded the Holy Grail in the 1989 blockbuster *Indiana Jones and the Last Crusade*. Three years earlier, Connery uncovered a devious murder plot in a 13th century Italian monastery in *The Name of the Rose*. It was not, however, the first monastery mystery. That distinction belongs to the offbeat 1974 TV-movie *Judge Dee and the Monastery Murders*, which was set in seventh century China. Another Chinese monastery appeared briefly in another TV-movie, 1972's *Kung Fu*, the pilot for the 1972–75 series about a fugitive Buddhist monk in the American West. The most unusual monks have been played by Charles Boyer (opposite Marlene Dietrich in *The Garden of Allah*), Marty Feldman *(In God We Trust)*, and Edward G. Robinson (as a gangster who reforms in *Brother Orchid*). Contrary to its title, the 1969 TV-movie *The Monk* had nothing to do with monks. George Maharis played a private eye named Gus Monk. See also **Nuns; Popes and Cardinals.**

Rasputin and the Empress (1932)
The Garden of Allah (1936)
The Adventures of Robin Hood (1938)
Brother Orchid (1940)
Nights of Rasputin (1960)
Francis of Assisi (1961)
Rasputin—the Mad Monk (1966)
I Killed Rasputin (1967)
Nicholas and Alexandra (1971)
Kung Fu (1972 TVM)
Brother Son, Sister Moon (1973)
Luther (1974)
Judge Dee and the Monastery Murders (1974 TVM)
In God We Trust (1980)
The Name of the Rose (1986)
Indiana Jones and the Last Crusade (1989)

Mothra

Toho Studios, the home of Godzilla, introduced this giant female caterpillar (and occasional moth) in 1962. Her debut film marked a turning point in the studio's Japanese monster series: It was the first movie to be shot in color and feature a sympathetic creature. Of course, Mothra wreaked plenty of havoc, just like her predecessors Godzilla (q.v.) and Rodan (q.v.). However, the carnage was a justified response to the kidnapping of two fairies, the Alilenas (q.v.), from Mothra's home island. Mothra's next appearance was in 1964's *Godzilla vs. the Thing*, in which the radioactive "King of Monsters" destroyed the giant caterpillar. However, an egg hatched to unleash two baby giant caterpillars which wove a web of silk around Godzilla and rendered him helpless. Thus, the Mothras that appeared in subsequent films are either children or grandchildren of the original Mothra—it's never made clear. The giant caterpiller's film appearances decreased after Godzilla made the switch from bad guy to good in 1965's *Monster Zero* (aka *Invasion of the Astro-Monster*).

Mothra (aka Mosura) (1962)

Godzilla vs. the Thing (aka Godzilla vs. Mothra; Gojira tai Mothra) (1964)

Ghidrah the Three-Headed Monster (aka The Greatest Battle on Earth; Sandai Kaiju Chikyu Saidai No Kessen) (1965)

Destroy All Monsters (aka Operation Monsterland; Kaiju Soshingeki) (1968)

Godzilla's Revenge (aka Ord Kaiju Daishingeki) (1969)

Moto, Mr.

J.P. Marquand's Japanese sleuth was a brilliant thinker, a master of disguises, and a martial arts expert. That description does not exactly bring Peter Lorre to mind, but he nevertheless made a fine movie Moto. He made eight films in a two-year period, beginning with 1937's *Think Fast, Mr. Moto*. The series ended abruptly in 1939, its demise usually attributed to the U.S.'s growing disenchantment with Japan's World War II activities. In 1965, an unexpected update, *The Return of Mr. Moto,* appeared with movie heavy Henry Silva as Moto. This new Moto bore little resemblance to Marquand's detective and the movie died at the boxoffice. The only other "actor" to play Mr. Moto was Porky Pig in the 1939 cartoon "Porky's Movie Mystery."

Think Fast, Mr. Moto (1937)

Mr. Moto's Gamble (1938)

Mr. Moto Takes a Chance (1938)

The Mysterious Mr. Moto (1938)

Thank You, Mr. Moto (1938)

Mr. Moto on Danger Island (1939)

Mr. Moto's Last Warning (1939)

Mr. Moto Takes a Vacation (1939)

The Return of Mr. Moto (1965)

Motorcycle Gangs

Sheriff's daughter to motorcycle gang leader Marlon Brando: "What are you rebelling against?" Brando: "What ya got?" That simple line of dialogue from 1953's *The Wild One* summarizes the attitude of pointless rebellion that would eventually spark the motorcycle gang films of the late 1960s and early 1970s. Considering the popularity of Brando's film with youth audiences of the 1950s, it's amazing that the genre was not born earlier. In all likelihood, however, audiences were not yet prepared to accept antiestablishment criminals as their idols. Thus, the teen bikers in

1957's *Motorcycle Gang* were presented as a "bad crowd" to be avoided by nice teens. Likewise, Oliver Reed and his fellow "Teddy Boys" had no redeeming features in Joseph Losey's science fiction cult film *These Are the Damned* (1962). Harvey Lembeck brought a little humanity—and a disarming ridiculousness—to his role of gang leader Eric Von Zipper in 1963's *Beach Party* (q.v.) and its subsequent sequels. Three years later, the biker antihero roared onto the screen in the guise of leather-clad, joint-smoking, Hell's Angel leader Peter Fonda in Roger Corman's *The Wild Angels,* about which Hollis Alpert of the *Saturday Review* wrote: it "strings together such incidents as the invasion of a hospital and the rape of a Negro nurse, a gang fight, and an orgy in a church...the film is faulty, and in a sense, irresponsible." Still, many mid–1960s teenagers identified with the angry, ultimately pessimistic attitudes of Fonda's Heavenly Blues and Bruce Dern's Loser. Cheaper, cruder biker films filled drive-in screens in the wake of *Wild Angels's* success. At their best, these exploitation films provided steady work for rising talents like Jack Nicholson *(Hell's Angels on Wheels, Rebel Rousers),* Harry Dean Stanton *(The Miniskirt Mob),* Tyne Daly *(Angel Unchained),* Bruce Dern *(The Cycle Savages, Rebel Rousers),* and disc jockey Casey Kasem *(Wild Wheels).* The worst films were the ones that capitalized on returning Vietnam veterans, such as *Angels from Hell* and *The Angry Breed.* An interesting exception was 1967's *Born Losers,* which introduced a peace-loving, former Green Beret named Billy Jack (Tom Laughlin). Four years later, Laughlin revived the character for the influential, nonbiker sleeper hit *Billy Jack* (q.v.). Still, few motorcycle gang films strayed from the *Wild Angels's* violence-drugs-orgy formula, although female bikers took charge effectively in *The Miniskirt Mob, She-Devils on Wheels,* and *Angels' Wild Women* and supernatural twists livened up *Werewolves on Wheels* and *Psychomania* (the latter concerning bikers revived from the dead). In 1973, the motorcycle gang movie craze gave way to other blossoming, low-budget genres like the martial arts imports and blaxploitation (q.v.) pictures. Ironically, the most influential biker film of the 1966–72 period turned out to be Dennis Hopper and Peter Fonda's 1967 sleeper smash *Easy Rider*—and it was not about motorcycle gangs. Post–1972 film appearances by biker gangs have been rare. A hapless gang incurred the wrath of Clint Eastwood in his comedy hit *Every Which Way But Loose.* Don Murray reunited his own gang to get rid of some contemporary punks in the 1981 TV-movie *Return of the Rebels.* Ed Harris played King Arthur to a travelling group of jousting bikers in George Romero's heavyhanded parable *Knightriders* (1981). On television, "Monty Python's Flying Circus" presented an hilarious skit about a gang of vicious, motorcycle-riding grannies.

The Wild One (1953)
Motorcycle Gang (1957)
These Are the Damned (aka *The Damned*) (1962)

Beach Party (1963)
Motor Psycho (1965)
The Wild Angels (1966)
Born Losers (1967)
Hell's Angels on Wheels (1967)
Rebel Rousers (1967)
The Glory Stompers (1967)
Angels from Hell (1968)
Girl on a Motorcycle (aka
  Naked Under Leather) (1968)
The Miniskirt Mob (1968)
She-Devils on Wheels (1968)
The Savage Seven (1968)
The Angry Breed (1969)
The Cycle Savages (1969)
Wild Wheels (1969)
Angels Die Hard (1970)
Hell's Bloody Angels (aka The
  Fakers; Smashing the Crime
  Syndicate) (1970)
Angel Unchained (1970)
The Black Angels (1970)

C.C. and Company (1971)
Chrome and Hot Leather (1971)
Psychomania (1971)
The Hard Ride (1971)
The Peace Killers (1971)
The Jesus Trip (1971)
Werewolves on Wheels (1971)
Angels' Wild Women (1972)
The Dirt Gang (1972)
Hex (1973)
Every Which Way But Loose
  (1978)
Dawn of the Dead (1979)
Hog Wild (1980)
Return of the Rebels (1981
  TVM)
The Loveless (1981)
Knightriders (1981)
Hear No Evil (1982 TVM)
Hell's Angels Forever (1983)
Eye of the Tiger (1986)
Nam Angels (1989)

Mountain Climbing

No fictional film has been able to match 1953's *Conquest of Everest* in terms of portraying the awesome beauty and never-ending danger of mountain climbing. Sadly, this gripping chronicle of Edmund Hillary's Everest expedition lost the Best Documentary Oscar to Disney's *The Living Desert*. On the dramatic front, Glenn Ford led a group of climbers intent on scaling the Swiss Alps in *The White Tower* (1950). James MacArthur played a young man intent on conquering a peak called the Citadel (actually the Matterhorn) in the 1959 Disney adventure *Third Man on the Mountain*. *Five Days One Summer* and *The Mountain* ended with mountain climbing tragedies. In the latter film, Spencer Tracy followed greedy brother Robert Wagner up the slopes to prevent the looting of plane wreckage. Numerous films have boasted extensive mountain climbing footage, ranging from the scaling of the German fortress in *The Guns of Navarone* to the Clint Eastwood spy adventure *The Eiger Sanction* to the James Bond picture *For Your Eyes Only*.

The White Tower (1950)
Conquest of Everest (1953)
The Mountain (1956)
The Abominable Snowman of
  the Himalayas (1958)
Third Man on the Mountain
  (1959)
The Guns of Navarone (1961)

Climb on Angry Mountain
  (1972 TVM)
The Eiger Sanction (1975)
High Ice (1980 TVM)
The Constant Factor (1980)
For Your Eyes Only (1981)
Five Days One Summer (1982)
A Breed Apart (1984)

Mounties

Television has treated the Royal Canadian Mounted Police far more generously than the cinema. "Sergeant Preston of the Yukon" and "Dudley Doright" may have done little for Mountie prestige, but they still accounted for some brief popularity. On the big screen, Mountie musicals and a handful of modest adventures have attracted little attention. Cecil DeMille saluted the Royal Mounted with his lavish *Northwest Mounted Police* (1940), starring Gary Cooper and Robert Preston. Critic Otis Ferguson called it "two hours of colour, killing, kindness and magnificent country" (Oregon and Hollywood, not Canada). Despite racking up Paramount's biggest grosses of the year, DeMille's film inspired no imitations. Instead, Warner Bros. offered Errol Flynn as a contemporary Mountie tracking a Nazi across Canada in *Northern Pursuit* (1943). *Death Hunt* (1981) followed a similar plotline, with Mountie Lee Marvin hunting down trapper–murder suspect Charles Bronson. The gentle side of married Mountie life was covered in the 1949 Dick Powell–Evelyn Keyes vehicle *Mrs. Mike.* The only true Mountie musical remains *Rose Marie,* which was first filmed without the music as a 1928 silent picture. In 1936, Nelson Eddy and Jeanette MacDonald lent their voices to the operatic songs and enjoyed one of their biggest hits. Howard Keel and Ann Blyth remade *Rose Marie,* with less success, in 1954. Shirley Temple sang a bit as *Susannah of the Mounties* (1937) and "B"-movie series Mountie *Renfrew* (q.v.) could always be counted on for a song if the bad guys were behind bars. The most offbeat casting for a Mountie belongs to Tom Smothers, who played one in the *Friday the 13th* spoof *Pandemonium* (1982). See also **Renfrew of the Mounties.**

Rose Marie (1936)
King of the Royal Mounted (1936)
O'Malley of the Mounted (1936)
Renfrew of the Royal Mounted (1937)
The Girl of the Golden West (1938)
Susannah of the Mounties (1939)
Northwest Mounted Police (1940)
Northern Pursuit (1943)
Mrs. Mike (1949)
R.C.M.P. and the Treasure of

Genghis Khan (aka Dangers of the Canadian Mounted) (1948)
Pony Soldier (aka MacDonald of the Canadian Mounted) (1952)
Fort Vengeance (1953)
Missile Base at Taniak (aka Canadian Mounties vs. Atomic Invaders) (1953)
Rose Marie (1954)
The Canadians (1961)
Alien Thunder (aka Dan Candy's Law) (1973)
Death Hunt (1981)
Pandemonium (1982)

Movie Theaters

Films about movie theaters fall into three general categories: cinemas, projectionists, and drive-ins. Cinemas have been the principal subject of only a handful of films. A young couple inherits, and subsequently manages, a run-down theater in the 1957 British comedy *The Smallest Show on Earth*. A projectionist and a concession girl try to save a closed theater by raising mushrooms in it and selling them in *Coming Up Roses* (1986). Movie characters stray from the screenplay—and one walks off the screen—in Woody Allen's *The Purple Rose of Cairo* (1985). And in Lamberto Bava's *Demons* (1985), a movie prop on display in the lobby unleashes a horde of nasty demons on a theater of unsuspecting patrons. The men that show the movies have been the subject of *Merton of the Movies* (1947), *The Projectionist* (1971), *The Picture Show Man* (1977), and Buster Keaton's classic *Sherlock Jr.* (1924). In the latter film, Buster runs down the aisle in one scene and steps into the movie on the screen, obviously serving as the inspiration for Woody Allen's reverse trick in *Purple Rose*. Drive-in theaters served as the principal setting for two cult favorites, *Targets* (1968) and *Dead End Drive-in* (1986). The low-budget *Targets* starred Boris Karloff as a has-been horror star promoting his latest picture at a drive-in where a mentally unstable sniper begins randomly killing moviegoers. The Australian oddity *Dead End Drive-in* takes place at a futuristic drive-in where patrons are not allowed to leave once they enter. Their tires are stolen during the movies. Drive-in owner Todd Tomorrow (Tab Hunter) specialized in showing esoteric triple-features in John Waters' campy *Polyester* (1981). Films which feature movie theaters in key scenes:

Sherlock Jr. (1924)
The Good Fairy (1935)
Sabotage (1936)
Contraband (aka *Blackout*) (1940)
Merton of the Movies (1947)
White Heat (1949)
Singin' in the Rain (1952)
The Smallest Show on Earth (aka *Big Time Operators*) (1957)
The Blob (1958)
The Tingler (1959)
Crime Does Not Pay (aka *The Gentle Art of Murder*) (1962)
Targets (1968)
The Last Picture Show (1971)
The Projectionist (1971)
Drive-in (1976)

Drive-In Massacre (1976)
Ruby (1977)
The Picture Show Man (1977)
Grease (1978)
The Meateater (1978)
Something Short of Paradise (1979)
Polyester (1981)
Night of the Comet (1984)
Demons (1985)
The Purple Rose of Cairo (1985)
Desperately Seeking Susan (1985)
Coming Up Roses (1986)
Dead End Drive-in (1986)
Anguish (1987)
Who Framed Roger Rabbit? (1988)

Movies About Movies

The film industry's love affair with itself has been a long-term relationship, though frequently a stormy one. The inhabitants of Tinseltown have stereotypically portrayed themselves as ruthless producers, crazed directors, alcoholic actors, and ambitious starlets. Still, the best of these movies have provided an entertaining behind-the-scenes look at filmmaking and/or the gossip scene. An occasional film has actually delved into the psyche of movie makers. The first talking picture to seriously tackle the subject was 1932's *What Price Hollywood?*, George Cukor's tragic tale of a director who transforms a waitress into a star while he slides into alcoholism. The same plot, with Fredric March as an established star and Janet Gaynor as a promising newcomer, surfaced in 1937 as the now-classic *A Star Is Born*. Joel McCrea played a film director who felt he had lost touch with his audience, so he set out to learn about them in Preston Sturges' seriocomic *Sullivan's Travels* (1941). World War II kept the movies about movies lighthearted, leaving it to the 1950s to introduce a bitter view of Hollywood. Gloria Swanson was overpowering as a faded star desperate for public adoration in Billy Wilder's wry *Sunset Boulevard* (1950). Kirk Douglas portrayed an ambitious producer with a bad habit of stepping on people in Vincente Minnelli's hugely entertaining *The Bad and the Beautiful* (1952). Still, even Hollywood insiders liked the film, honoring it with five Oscars, including Best Supporting Actress for Gloria Grahame. The 1954 remake of *A Star Is Born* was even more effective than the original, thanks to James Mason's searing performance as a washed-up star. *The Goddess* (1958), a downbeat, thinly-disguised biography of Marilyn Monroe, signalled the continuation of "realistic" films about Hollywood, a trend which blossomed in the 1960s. That decade produced a line of trashy, but often enjoyable, fare about filmmaking: *Two Weeks in Another Town* (1962) with Kirk Douglas again, *The Carpetbaggers* (1964), *The Oscar* (1966), and *The Movie-Maker* (1967 TVM). "Serious" movies about the industry decreased over the next two decades, though even satiric features like *The Stunt Man* (1980) and *S.O.B.* (1981) offered darkly cynical views of Hollywood. More mainstream comedies have poked gentle fun at the people behind the movies. A host of deft comedians have employed film studio settings, including: Buster Keaton in *Movie Crazy* (1932), W.C. Fields in *The Bank Dick* (1940), Olsen and Johnson in *Hellzapoppin!* (1941), Red Skelton in *Merton of the Movies* (1947), Bud and Lou in *Abbott and Costello Meet the Keystone Kops* (1955), and Jerry Lewis in *The Errand Boy*. Woody Allen's *The Purple Rose of Cairo* (1985) was about a movie character who stepped off the screen and caused all kinds of complications. The early days of filmmaking were remembered fondly in *Singin' in the Rain* (1952) and *Nickelodeon* (1976). On the other side of the Atlantic, England produced *The Magic Box* (1951), an all-star biography of film pioneer William Friese-Greene. Joseph Losey's *Finger of Guilt* (1956) offered a rare look inside a British film studio. French New Wave directors Jean-Luc Godard and François Truffaut paid homage to their craft with *Contempt* (1963) and *Day for Night* (1973). Federico

238

MOVIES ABOUT MOVIES

Fellini's semiautobiographical *8½* (1963) explored the mind of fantasy-ridden director Marcello Mastroianni. The title was a reference to the number of movies Fellini had previously made. See also **Film Star Biographies**.

The Studio Murder Mystery (1929)
Movie Crazy (1932)
What Price Hollywood? (1932)
Once in a Lifetime (1932)
Bombshell (aka *Blonde Bombshell*) (1933)
The Death Kiss (1933)
A Star Is Born (1937)
Stand-In (1937)
Hollywood Cavalcade (1939)
The Bank Dick (aka *The Bank Detective*) (1940)
Sullivan's Travels (1941)
Hellzapoppin! (1941)
The Reluctant Dragon (1941)
World Premiere (1941)
Crazy House (1943)
The Falcon in Hollywood (1944)
Merton of the Movies (1947)
It's a Great Feeling (1949)
You're My Everything (1949)
Sunset Boulevard (1950)
The Magic Box (1951)
Hollywood Story (1951)
The Bad and the Beautiful (1952)
Singin' in the Rain (1952)
A Star Is Born (1954)
Susan Slept Here (1954)
Abbott and Costello Meet the Keystone Kops (1955)
Finger of Guilt (aka *The Intimate Stranger*) (1956)
The Goddess (1958)
Paradise Alley (aka *Stars in the Back Yard*) (1961)
The Errand Boy (1961)
Two Weeks in Another Town (1962)
Contempt (1963)
8½ (1963)
The Carpetbaggers (1964)

The Oscar (1966)
After the Fox (1966)
The Movie Maker (1967 TVM)
Everything for Sale (1968)
The Legend of Lylah Clare (1968)
David Holzman's Diary (1968)
Alex in Wonderland (1970)
Bombay Talkie (1970)
The Movie Murderer (1970 TVM)
The Last Movie (aka *Chinchero*) (1971)
Day for Night (1973)
The Sex Symbol (1974 TVM)
Day of the Locust (1975)
Hollywood Boulevard (1976)
The Last Tycoon (1976)
Nickelodeon (1976)
Evening in Byzantium (1978 TVM)
The Users (1978)
An Almost Perfect Affair (1979)
The Stunt Man (1980)
The Dream Merchants (1980 TVM)
Loose Shoes (aka *Coming Attractions*) (1980)
S.O.B. (1981)
Burden of Dreams (1982)
Passion (1982)
The Last Horror Film (1984)
The Purple Rose of Cairo (1985)
Means and Ends (1985)
Malice in Wonderland (1985 TVM)
I Hate Actors (1986)
Overnight (1986)
Smart Alec (aka *The Movie Maker*) (1986)
Sweet Liberty (1986)
Good Morning, Babylon (1987)

Movies Without Dialogue

Since the advent of "talkies," movies without dialogue have been screen oddities. Charlie Chaplin, who felt uncomfortable with dialogue, resisted making a talking picture until 1940's *The Great Dictator*. Thus, his two classic comedies of the 1930s, *City Lights* and *Modern Times,* were both sans dialogue, their soundtracks consisting solely of sounds and music. Given Chaplin's success as a silent filmmaker, these "nontalkies" were taken in stride. That was not the case with 1952's *The Thief,* an unusual mainstream experiment devised by producer Clarence Greene and director Russell Rouse. This dialogueless film cast Ray Milland as an enemy spy pursued by the FBI. Initially intriguing, *The Thief*'s gimmick grows tiresome and becomes a forced irritation. A similar fate befell Gene Kelly's *Invitation to the Dance* (1957), an ambitious attempt to tell three stories completely in dance. Obviously, the movie puzzled MGM's head brass, who delayed its release for five years. A handful of foreign films have bypassed all language barriers by telling their plots completely in visuals. Poetic visual splendor replaced dialogue in Kaneto Shindo's *The Island* (1961), the low-key story of a solitary family inhabiting a tiny isle. *Le Bal* (1982) told the story of a ballroom through 50 years of dancing. French director-writer-star Jacques Tati's *Mr. Hulot's Holiday* (1953) contained background dialogue, but still charms international audiences with its winning visual humor. Back in the U.S., Mel Brooks spoofed Hollywood of the 1920s in his wacky 1976 comedy *Silent Movie* (in which mime Marcel Marceau had the film's single line of dialogue). Many movies have employed minimal dialogue to great effect, such as Cornel Wilde's thrilling adventure film *The Naked Prey* (1966).

City Lights (1931)	*Shima*) (1961)
Modern Times (1936)	*Silent Movie* (1976)
The Thief (1952)	*Le Bal* (1982)
Mr. Hulot's Holiday (1953)	*Le Dernier Combat* (1984)
Invitation to the Dance (1956)	*Sidewalk Stories* (1987)
The Island (aka *Hadaka no*	*Missing Link* (1989)

Multiple Personalities

Schizophrenia resulting in multiple personalities has enabled several fine performers to display their acting versatility. Ronald Colman won his only Oscar as a psychologically unstable Shakespearean actor who begins to play Othello for real in 1947's *A Double Life*. Joanne Woodward also won an Oscar for her career-breakthrough performance as a woman with three personalities in 1957's *The Three Faces of Eve*. Almost two decades later, Woodward played the psychiatrist to Sally Field's *Sybil* in the fact-based story of a young woman plagued by 17 distinct personalities. The film also provided Field with her acting breakthrough, proving her TV days as "The Flying Nun" were behind her. Hitchcock's *Psycho* (1960) ended with the once-shocking revelation that Norman Bates was *also* his mother. In the seldom-shown 1945 thriller *Bewitched,* Phyllis Thaxter murdered a man as one personality, but remembered nothing about it as her other self. And in *Three Nuts in Search of a Bolt* (1964), three neurotics hired an unemployed actor to visit a psychiatrist for them. When he acts out all their neuroses, the psychiatrist diagnoses him as a victim of multiple personalities! See also **Psychiatrists.**

Bewitched (1945)	(1964)
A Double Life (1947)	*The Boston Strangler* (1968)
Lizzie (1957)	*Sybil* (1976 TVM)
The Three Faces of Eve (1957)	*The Strange Possession of Mrs.*
Psycho (1960)	*Oliver* (1977 TVM)
Three Nuts in Search of a Bolt	*The Five of Me* (1981 TVM)

Multiple Roles

The challenge of playing three or more roles in the same film has appealed to very few performers. It is also likely that the profession's more serious actors have viewed the ploy as mere gimmickry. For whichever reason, it has been a rare screen occurrence. Peter Sellers has played at least three roles in each of three movies. He first performed the trick for the 1959 comedy sleeper *The Mouse That Roared* (1959), appearing as the picture's hero, a count, and the Grand Duchess of Fenwick. Five years later, he landed his most famous triple role as U.S. President Muffey, Captain Mandrake, and Nazi scientist Dr. Strangelove in Stanley Kubrick's cold war satire *Dr. Strangelove; or, How I Learned to Stop Worrying and Love the Bomb* (1964). In the twilight of his career, Seller took on six roles in the barely-released comedy *Undercovers Hero* (1975). Second to Sellers is America's own Jerry Lewis, who must have decided he was ready for bigger numbers after his double role in *The Nutty Professor* (1963). Lewis played five roles in 1966's *Three on a Couch* and seven roles in 1965's *The Family Jewels.* The latter film was obviously patterned after the droll British classic *Kind Hearts and Coronets* (1949), which featured marvelous Alec Guinness as eight murder victims. Except for Malcolm McDowell, the principal cast of the sparkling British satire *O Lucky Man!* (1973) appeared in multiple roles. In a similar vein, the members of the Monty Python comedy troupe have essayed a variety of roles in their pictures, particularly *Monty Python and the Holy Grail* (1974) and *The Life of Brian* (1979).

> *Kind Hearts and Coronets* (1949) (Alec Guinness)
> *Watch the Birdie* (1950) (Red Skelton)
> *The Mouse That Roared* (1959) (Peter Sellers)
> *Dr. Strangelove; or, How I Learned to Stop Worrying and Love the Bomb* (1964) (Peter Sellers)
> *The Seven Faces of Dr. Lao* (1964) (Tony Randall)
> *Three on a Couch* (1966) (Jerry Lewis)

Arabella (1969) (Terry-Thomas)
O Lucky Man! (1973)
Undercovers Hero (aka *Soft Beds and Hard Battles*) (1975) (Peter
  Sellers)
Monty Python and the Holy Grail (1974) (Monty Python Troupe)
Hot Lead and Cold Feet (1978) (Jim Dale)
The Man in the Santa Claus Suit (1978 TVM) (Fred Astaire)
Circle of Iron (aka *The Silent Flute*) (1978) (David Carradine)
The Life of Brian (1979) (Monty Python Troupe)
Cracking Up (aka *Smorgasbord*) (1983) (Jerry Lewis)
Cheech and Chong's Corsican Brothers (1984) (Cheech and Chong)

The Mummy

With facial features swathed in bandages (or wrinkles) and a vocabulary
limited to growls, the Mummy has lacked the personality of his cinematic
peers: Dracula, the Frankenstein Monster, and the Wolf Man. For most of
his career, he has been used as a slow-moving killing machine. He did not
start out that way, though. Karl Freund's *The Mummy* (1932) was a
haunting film about reincarnation and eternal love. As the mummified
priest Imhotep, Boris Karloff appeared only briefly in Jack Pierce's famous
Mummy makeup. He spent most of the film in his reincarnated form,
playing a menacing Egyptian archaeologist. In a fitting climax, he was
reduced to dust when the heroine calls upon the ancient god Isis. Oddly,
the Mummy was not revived until 1941, when former cowboy star Tom
Tyler replaced Karloff in *The Mummy's Hand,* the first of a low-budget
series. Lon Chaney, Jr., took over the role (the Mummy having undergone
a name change, from Imhotep to Kharis) for three additional installments.
None of these films rose above the routine, although *The Mummy's Curse*
offered a different setting (the Louisiana Bayou) and the heroine actually
turned into a mummy in *The Mummy's Ghost.* The official Universal
series ended in 1944, although the studio brought back the Gauzed One
(played by Eddie Powell) for one final fling in 1955's *Abbott and Costello
Meet the Mummy,* one of the comedy duo's last efforts. After laying dormant for a couple years, the Mummy turned up in Mexico and Britain
almost simultaneously. Like most Mexican horror films of the late 1950s,
Rafael Portillo's *The Aztec Mummy* (1957) boasted fine black-and-white
photography and, despite an absurd plot, recalled the eerie atmosphere of
Universal's 1940s features. The title mummy, named Popoca, did well
enough to inspire a series of Aztec Mummy movies, which still crop up on
television today. Meanwhile, fresh on the heels of its *Dracula* success, Britain's Hammer Studios produced a colorful remake of *The Mummy*
(1959). Transplanting the story in England in 1895, this version profitted
from Peter Cushing's steady performance as an intrepid archaeologist and
Christopher Lee's imposing presence as the movies' quickest-footed

Mummy. Despite good notices, Hammer waited five years before continuing the series. It was hardly worth the effort, since two of the three sequels were cheap programmers. The other, however, was 1972's *Blood from the Mummy's Tomb,* an adaptation of Bram Stoker's story "Jewel of the Seven Stars" and a welcome return to the literate approach of Freund's original film. The same story served as the basis for 1980's *The Awakening,* an expensive — but less effective — version starring Charlton Heston and Stephanie Zimbalist. Spanish horror star Paul Naschy, who has played more monsters than anybody, took his turn in the bandages for *The Mummy's Revenge* (1973). And in 1982's ridiculous *Timewalker,* a nasty mummy is revealed to be a misunderstood alien who just wanted to go home. Shades of *E.T.*

Universal's Mummy

The Mummy (1932)	*The Mummy's Ghost* (1944)
The Mummy's Hand (1940)	*Abbott and Costello Meet the*
The Mummy's Tomb (1942)	*Mummy* (1955)
The Mummy's Curse (1944)	

The Aztec Mummy

The Aztec Mummy (aka *La Momia; La Momia Azteca*) (1957)	*Curse of the Aztec Mummy* (aka *La Maldicion de la Momia Azteca*) (1959)
Robot vs. the Aztec Mummy (aka *La Momia Azteca contra el Robot Humano*) (1959)	*Wrestling Women vs. the Aztec Mummy* (aka *La Luchadoras contra la Momia*) (1964)

Hammer's Mummy

The Mummy (1959)	*The Mummy's Shroud* (1967)
Curse of the Mummy's Tomb (1964)	*Blood from the Mummy's Tomb* (1972)

Others

The Egyptian Mummy (1914)	(1963)
The Pharoah's Curse (1956)	*The Mummy's Revenge* (1973)
Curse of the Faceless Man (1958) (very Mummy-like)	*The Awakening* (1980)
Attack of the Mayan Mummy	*Timewalker* (1982)
	The Monster Squad (1987)

The Muppets

Kermit the Frog and Miss Piggy were established television stars and pop icons when they and their furry friends made the leap to the big screen in 1979's *The Muppet Movie.* Film industry watchers expected a guaranteed audience of loyal children, but the film's widespread success surprised even them. The 1981 sequel *The Great Muppet Caper* pitted the gang against jewel thieves who had stolen the Fabulous Baseball Diamond. It outperformed its predecessor at domestic boxoffices, earning a nifty $16 million. Muppet creator Jim Henson interrupted the series in 1982 to produce *The Dark Crystal,* a more conventional "quest fantasy" with puppets. He returned to the Muppets with 1984's *The Muppets Take Manhattan*, in which Kermit took his college musical to the Great White Way. Its box-office receipts were disappointing and Henson turned his attention back to television where "The Muppet Show" had enjoyed a five-year run. Henson coined the phrase "muppet" in the 1950s to describe a combination of "marionette" and "puppet." See also **Puppets.**

> *The Muppet Movie* (1979)   *The Muppets Take Manhattan*
> *The Great Muppet Caper* (1981)   (1984)

Neutron

Neutron was one of three Mexican wrestler superheroes to enjoy South-of-the-Border popularity in the 1960s. The silver-masked Santo (q.v.) was the undisputed king, but Neutron held his own against latecomer rival The Blue Demon (q.v.). Mexico's America Studios shot the first three Neutron films in 1960, starting with *Neutron, the Black Masked*. This introductory effort pitted the wrestler against evil Dr. Caronte and his neutron bomb. Caronte returned in both *Neutron vs. the Amazing Dr. Caronte* and *Neutron Against the Robots*. In the U.S., the films were released out of order and sometimes shown as serials. This latter oddity occurred because the films were originally made in three parts and edited together later. This was a necessity for the filmmakers, since Mexican labor agreements allowed America Studios to produce short features only. See also **Blue Demon; Santo; Wrestling.**

> *Neutron, the Black Masked* (aka *Neutron el Enmascarado Negro*) (1960)
> *Neutron vs. the Amazing Dr. Caronte* (aka *Neutron Contra el Doctor Caronte*) (1960)
> *Neutron Against the Death Robots* (aka *Los Automatas de la Muerte*) (1961)
> *Neutron Battles the Karate Assassins* (1962)
> *Neutron vs. the Maniac* (aka *Neutron and the Cosmic Bomb*) (1962)
> *Neutron Traps the Invisible Killers* (1963)

Night of the Living Dead

On commenting on the scenes of "ghouls" devouring human flesh in 1968's *Night of the Living Dead*, director George Romero once wrote: "I was delighted when one of our investors, who happened to be in the meat packing business, turned up on the set one day with a sackful of animal innards which made the sequences seem so real." The film was shot outside of Pittsburgh over a span of nine months for the rock-bottom price of $118,000. *Night* was panned by the few critics who saw it during its original 1968 release. However, Romero and the film gained some recognition after a glowing *Village Voice* review in 1969 and a 1970 screening at the Museum of Modern Art. Theaters began screening it as a midnight feature in 1971 and its status as a cult classic grew quickly. Romero's subsequent films made little money and he experienced difficulty in financing a sequel. However, with the help of Italian horror filmmaker Dario Argento, he produced 1979's *Dawn of the Dead.* Not surprisingly, the film was hailed by some critics as a brilliant analogy of our times and condemned by others as a violent, pretentious time waster. Both *Night* and *Dawn* dealt with the resurrection of dead people who feed upon the flesh of the living. The former film confined the action to seven people trapped in an isolated farmhouse. They *all* die. *Dawn* began in an urban setting before moving its four central characters to an abandoned shopping mall (the scene of many obvious analogies). Although *Dawn of the Dead* was released without a rating (Romero feared it would be given an "X"), it performed well both in the U.S. and abroad (interestingly, as part of their deal, Argento recut the film for its European release). Romero's long-awaited final installment, *Day of the Dead,* appeared in 1985 and was greeted with much disappointment. Rather than concluding the trilogy (either plotwise or thematically), it opted for a 1950s-style story of understanding scientists trying to prevent the military from killing all the ghouls. It naturally left plenty of room for a fourth *Dead* picture. See also **Ghouls.**

> *Night of the Living Dead*   *Dawn of the Dead* (1979)
> (1968)   *Day of the Dead* (1985)

Nightmare on Elm Street

With a black felt hat, a red-and-green striped sweater, and a right-hand glove with steel "finger knives," Freddy Kreuger can hardly be considered a stylish dresser. Still, that has not deterred him from overtaking Jason (see **Friday the 13th**) as the 1980s most popular killer of teens. The 1984 *Nightmare on Elm Street* introduced Mr. Kreuger (Robert Englund), a janitor at Springwood High with a special interest in kidnapping and murdering teens. The law finally caught up with him, but a court freed him on a technicality. This inspired some vigilante parents to track him down and fry him in a boiler room. In revenge, he invades the dreams of the parents' children and dispenses with them in ghastly fashion. In a *Time* interview, director Wes Craven offered his explanation for the film's unexpected popularity among teens: "Freddy is the most ruthless primal father. The adult who wants to slash down the next generation." The films' flippant humor may have also contributed to "Freddymania." In one scene, Freddy bashes an aspiring teen actress's head into a TV set and then quips: "This is it, Jennifer, your big break in TV." Englund has been the only performer to appear in all four entries, though Heather Langenkamp played the heroine in the first and third films. A syndicated hour-long TV anthology dubbed "Freddy's Nightmares" debuted to impressive ratings in September 1988. Englund introduced the stories and occasionally appeared in them (including the first, a prequel to the original film, directed by

Tobe Hooper). Naturally, the *Nightmare* series has inspired imitations, the most obvious being 1988's *Bad Dreams.* See also **Slasher Movies.**

Nightmare on Elm Street (1984)
Nightmare on Elm Street II:
   Freddy's Revenge (1986)
Nightmare on Elm Street III:
   The Dream Warriors (1987)
Nightmare on Elm Street IV:
   The Dream Master (1988)
Nightmare on Elm Street V:
   The Dream Child (1989)

North Pole / South Pole

The North Pole may be best known as Santa's home, but, in movies, it's been home to a variety of unpleasant creatures. An atomic explosion in the Arctic awoke *The Beast from 20,000 Fathoms.* Both *Frankenstein: The True Story* and the Swedish *Terror of Frankenstein* (aka *Victor Frankenstein*) restored the original ending of Mary Shelley's novel, in which the Monster was stranded in the frozen wastelands. And in Howard Hawks' 1951 sci-fi classic *The Thing (from Another World),* an unfriendly alien tried to devour a group of scientists at an Arctic research station. On the plus side, the North Pole was also where Superman built his personal fortress (and "honeymooned" with Lois Lane) in *Superman II.* The South Pole, despite having a continental advantage in terms of mass, has been the setting for fewer movies. *Scott of the Antarctic* chronicled the exploits of real-life explorer Robert Scott. George Maharis and Bobby Morse explored ways to get women to their isolated residence in *Quick Before It Melts.* John Carpenter transplanted his 1982 remake of *The Thing* from the North Pole to the South Pole. Only two scientists survived in this version, with the fate of the alien (he may be one of the survivors) left unanswered.

North

S.O.S. Iceberg (1933)
She (1935)
The Thing (1951)
The Beast from 20,000 Fathoms (1953)
The Perfect Furlough (aka *Strictly for Pleasure*) (1958)
The Atomic Submarine (1959)
Voyage to the Bottom of the Sea (1961)
Ice Station Zebra (1968)

Frankenstein: The True Story (1973 TVM)
Island at the Top of the World (1974)
Victor Frankenstein (aka *Terror of Frankenstein*) (1975)
Superman II (1980)
Cook and Peary: The Race to the Pole (1983 TVM)
Santa Claus, the Movie (1985)

South

The Secret Land (1948)
Scott of the Antarctic (1948)
The Land Unknown (1957)
Quick Before It Melts (1964)
Cry of the Penguins (aka *Mr. Forbush and the Penguins*) (1971)
The Thing (1982)
Antarctica (1983)

Nostradamus

Mexican horror movie veteran German Robles played a descendant of the prophet Nostradamus (now a vampire) in a ten-part South-of-the-Border serial. In the U.S., it was edited into four feature films, dubbed in English, and released directly to television. The prophecies of the original Nostradamus reached the screen in exploitative splendor with the 1974 Japanese import *The Last Days of Planet Earth* (aka *Prophecies of Nostradamus: Castrophe 1999*).

    Blood of Nostradamus (aka *La Sangre de Nostradamus*) (1960)
    Curse of Nostradamus (aka *La Maldición de Nostradamus*) (1960)
    The Monster Demolisher (aka *Nostradamus y el Destructor de Monstruos*) (1960)
    The Genii of Darkness (aka *Nostradamus, el Genio de las Tinieblas*) (1960)

Nurses Series

"B" movie mogul Roger Corman developed this "R"-rated, loosely-connected film series for the drive-in crowd. After leaving American International Pictures in the late 1960s, Corman started his own production/distribution company, New World Pictures. He served as executive producer on New World's first movie, 1970's *The Student Nurses*. Directed by drive-in cult favorite Stephanie Rothman, this surprisingly unexploitative picture featured strong female characters and even some topical issues (e.g. abortion). One of its stars, Elaine Giftos, used it as a stepping stone for the 1970–71 TV series *The Interns*. Neither Corman nor Rothman had a hand in the other series films, which dealt with nothing more topical than waterbeds. The casts changed from film to film, although Corman movie veteran Dick Miller appeared in the last three entries. Future Oscar nominee Sally *(Anna)* Kirkland starred in *The Young Nurses.*

    The Student Nurses (1970)   *The Young Nurses* (aka *Emer-*
    Private Duty Nurses (1972)   *gency Nurses*) (1973)
    Night Call Nurses (1972)   *Candy Stripe Nurses* (1974)

Nuns

The call of the convent and life within its walls have provided filmmakers with a wealth of varied plotlines. Young would-be nuns have been frequently forced to choose between the convent and the man they love, a problem confronted by Helen Hayes in *The White Sister* (1933), Julie Andrews in *The Sound of Music* (1965), and Mary Tyler Moore in *Change of Habit* (1969). Deborah Kerr and her fellow nuns faced a crisis of faith at a remote Himalayan mission in Powell and Pressburger's hypnotic *Black Narcissus* (1947). Vanessa Redgrave's deranged nun in Ken Russell's *The Devils* (1971) provided the testimony necessary to burn outspoken priest

Oliver Reed for practicing witchcraft. More conventional nuns have dealt with more humane problems: Rosalind Russell played the real-life nurse who initiated treatment for polio in *Sister Kenny* (1946); Celeste Holm and Loretta Young earned Oscar nominations as French nuns trying to build a children's hospital in *Come to the Stable* (1949); and Bonnie Franklin founded a home for women prison parolees in *Sister Margaret and the Saturday Night Ladies* (1986). Movie nuns have been often paired with unruly types, whom they typically reform. These unlikely pairings include nun Deborah Kerr and soldier Robert Mitchum in *Heaven Knows, Mr. Allison* (1957), Robert Webber and Anna Sten in *The Nun and the Sergeant* (1962), detective David Janssen and Susannah York in *The Golden Gate Murders* (1979), and gunfighter Clint Eastwood and Shirley MacLaine in *Two Mules for Sister Sara* (1970). In the latter film, however, MacLaine turned out to be a prostitute disguised as a nun. Although not disguised, Dudley Moore wound up in a nun's habit in the fiendishly funny Faust spoof *Bedazzled* (1967). Tricked by the Devil (Peter Cook), Moore was transformed into a sister in the Order of the Leaping Nuns. The serious side of being a nun has been examined vividly by Fred Zinnemann in *The Nun's Story* (1959) and French director Alain Cavalier in *Therese* (1986). The most troubled nun was the one played by Meg Tilly in *Agnes of God* (1985), the story of a young nun accused of killing a child she claims was immaculately conceived. See also **Monks; Popes and Cardinals.**

The White Sister (1933)
Song of Bernadette (1943)
Till We Meet Again (1944)
The Bells of St. Mary's (1945)
Sister Kenny (1946)
Black Narcissus (1947)
Come to the Stable (1949)
Thunder on the Hill (aka
  Bonaventure) (1951)
Appointment with Danger (1951)
Anna (1951)
Heaven Knows, Mr. Allison
  (1956)
The Miracle (1959)
The Nun's Story (1959)
Conspiracy of Hearts (1960)
The Devil and the Nun (aka
  Mother Joan of the Angels)
  (1960)
Viridiana (1961)
The Nun and the Sergeant
  (1962)
Lilies of the Field (1963)

The Little Nuns (1965)
The Nun (1965)
The Sound of Music (1965)
The Singing Nun (1966)
The Trouble with Angels (1966)
Bedazzled (1967)
*Where Angels Go, Trouble
  Follows* (1968)
Change of Habit (1969)
Two Mules for Sister Sara (1970)
Weekend of Terror (1970 TVM)
Madron (1970)
The Devils (1971)
The Weekend Nun (aka *Matter
  of the Heart*) (1972 TVM)
In This House of Brede (1975
  TVM)
Nasty Habits (1976)
The Golden Gate Murders (aka
  Specter on the Bridge) (1979
  TVM)
Dixie: Changing Habits (1983
  TVM)

Choices of the Heart (aka *In December the Roses Will Bloom Again*) (1983 TVM)
Dark Habits (1983)
September Gun (1983 TVM)
Shattered Vows (1984 TVM)

Agnes of God (1985)
Sacred Hearts (1985)
Therese (1986)
Sister Margaret and the Saturday Night Ladies (1987 TVM)
Angel in Green (1987)

Octopuses and Squids

The first octopus film of note, 1938's *Sh! The Octopus,* was ironically an adaptation of the stage play *The Gorilla.* That typifies the lack of respect shown to these homely creatures throughout most of their screen careers. A giant squid made a memorable splash in Cecil B. DeMille's *Reap the Wild Wind* (1942). Twelve years later, an even bigger squid attacked the submarine *Nautilus* during an intense storm sequence in Disney's *20,000 Leagues Under the Sea.* This was the squid's finest hour, its memorable death coming at the hands of Kirk Douglas (who harpooned it in the eye). Deep sea diver Bob Hope wrestled an oversized squid for laughs in *The Road to Bali* (1952). Special effects wizard Ray Harryhausen created a giant "octopus" for *It Came from Beneath the Sea.* Due to budget constraints, Harryhausen trimmed off two tentacles and subsequently dubbed his creation a "sexopus." The submarine Seaview electrocuted another giant octopus in *Voyage to the Bottom of the Sea.* Killer whales rescued a seaside resort from a similar menace in 1976's low-budget, *Jaws*–inspired rip-off *Tentacles.* Lovely Maud Adams kept a venomous octopus for a pet in the 1983 James Bond adventure *Octopussy,* while Esther Williams swam an underwater ballet with an animated octopus in 1953's *Dangerous When Wet.*

Sh! The Octopus (1938)
Reap the Wild Wind (1942)
The Road to Bali (1952)
Dangerous When Wet (1953)
The Magic Voyage of Sinbad (aka *Sadlow*) (1952)
Beneath the Twelve Mile Reef (1953)
20,000 Leagues Under the Sea (1954)
Monster from the Ocean Floor (1954)
It Came from Beneath the Sea

(1955)
The Bride of the Monster (1956)
The Fabulous World of Jules Verne (1958)
Mysterious Island (1961)
Voyage to the Bottom of the Sea (1961)
King Kong vs. Godzilla (1962)
Octaman (1971)
Tentacles (1976)
Warloads of Atlantis (1978)
Octopussy (1983)
The Little Mermaid (1989)

Oh, God

It took George Burns 81 years to find the role he will best be remembered for, but it was a heavenly part as the unlikely incarnation (complete with trademark cigar) of the Deity in *Oh, God!* (1977). This gentle, uplifting fantasy blossomed into a substantial hit and ultimately begat two sequels. *Oh, God! Book II* (1980) rehashed the original film and added a little girl and globs of sentiment. *Oh God! You Devil* (1984) was a contemporary version of *Faust* with Ted Wass as a singer who sells his soul and Burns in a dual role as God and the Devil.

Oh, God! (1977)

Oh, God! Book II (1980)

Oh God! You Devil (aka *Oh, God, Book III*) (1984)

Oil Wells

The sight of thick, black fluid gushing forth from the ground was a familiar one on the theater screens of the 1950s. How can anyone forget the classic scene where ecstatic, oil-soaked James Dean strikes black gold in 1956's *Giant?* Yet, even before *Giant*, viewers in the 1950s had the option of pulling for nice guy James Stewart to strike oil off the Louisiana Coast *(Thunder Bay)*, hooting against oily villains like Gene Barry *(The Houston Story)*, or simply pondering what former elephant-boy Sabu was even doing on an oilfield *(Jaguar)*. Pre–1950s fare offered more typical wildcatter heroes in the guise of Spencer Tracy, Clark Gable (both in *Boom Town*) and Richard Arlen *(Wildcat)*. A notable exception was 1937's *High, Wide, and Handsome*, a nostalgic Hammerstein-Kern musical with Randolph Scott as an oil driller. Oil women have been scarce, though Faye Dunaway (with a little help from George C. Scott) proved more than tough enough to handle nasty Jack Palance in 1973's *Oklahoma Crude*. John Wayne fought oil fires for a living in *The Hellfighters* (1969), as did Cornel Wilde in *Maracaibo* (1958). A blazing oil fire sends four drifters on a deadly journey over mountainous roads in trucks carrying nitroglycerine in Henri Clouzot's *The Wages of Fear* (1952) and its remake *Sorcerer* (1977).

Oil for the Lamps of China (1935)

High, Wide, and Handsome (1937)

Boom Town (1940)

Flowing Gold (1940)

Wildcat (1942)

Black Gold (1947)

The Big Gusher (1951)

The Wages of Fear (1952)

Thunder Bay (1953)

Blowing Wild (1953)

Lucy Gallant (1955)

The Houston Story (1956)

Giant (1956)

Jaguar (1956)

The Magnificent Roughnecks (1956)

Joe Dakota (1957)

Maracaibo (1958)

Black Gold (1963)

The Hellfighters (1969)

Five Easy Pieces (1970)

Oklahoma Crude (1973)

Oceans of Fire (1976 TVM)

Oil (1977)

Sorcerer (1977)

Roughnecks (1980 TVM)

The Intruder Within (1981 TVM)

Dallas: The Early Years (1986)

Olympics

Documentaries, fact-based dramas, and fictitious tales of inspiring athletic feats have revolved around the greatest event in international sports. Leni Riefenstahl's *Olympia* (1936), a vivid record of the 1936 Berlin games, remains an unparalleled tribute to the athletes and the spirit of the games—all this despite an underlying theme praising Nazism. Kon Ichikawa's mesmersizing *Tokyo Olympiad* (1966) was trimmed from 170 minutes to 93 for its U.S. release, though the shortened version still included the dynamic volleyball match between the women of Japan and the Soviet Union. *Visions of Eight* (1973) featured segments by eight international directors (including Ichikawa again). Most critics found it disappointing, except for John Schlesinger's dramatic feature on the grueling marathon. Film biographies of inspirational Olympic athletes have been devoted to runner Jim Thorpe *(Jim Thorpe—All American)*, decathlete Bob Mathias *(The Bob Mathias Story)*, track star Wilma Rudolph *(Wilma)*, the 1980 U.S. hockey team *(Miracle on Ice)*, runner Billy Mills *(Running Brave)*, gymnast Nadia Comaneci *(Nadia)*, and Jesse Owens *(The Jesse Owens Story)*. The 1976 TV-movie *21 Hours at Munich* recreated the tragic terrorist killings that cast a dark cloud over the 1972 Olympics. Another TV-movie, *The First Olympics—Athens 1896* (1984), chronicled the events that led up to the first modern-day games. The 1962 *It Happened in Athens* offered a fictitious view of the same events, placing special emphasis on Jayne Mansfield as an actress who agrees to marry the winner of the marathon. Earl Derr Bigger's proverb-quoting detective Charlie Chan (q.v.) uncovered a murder plot at the Berlin Games in 1937's *Charlie Chan at the Olympics*. Charlie's No. 1 son (Keye Luke) was even a member of the U.S. swimming team. Jim Hutton played an Olympic walker in the 1966 romantic comedy *Walk, Don't Run*, which found him in overcrowded Tokyo sharing an apartment with Samantha Eggar and matchmaker Cary Grant. A 90-pound weakling sent off for a weight-lifting program and grew up to be a muscular Olympic hammer-thrower in 1956's charming British film *Wee Geordie*. *The Golden Moment: An Olympic Love Story* (1980) found an American decathlete (David Keith) falling in love with a Russian gymnast (Stephanie Zimbalist) at the 1980 Moscow Games—which the U.S. boycotted after this TV-movie was made. The 1980 *Special Olympics* was a heartwarming story of a mentally retarded youngster who finds fulfillment playing sports and enters the Special Olympics.

Million Dollar Legs (1932)
Olympia (aka *Olympische Spiele*) (1936)
One in a Million (1936)
Charlie Chan at the Olympics (1937)

Jim Thorpe—All American (aka *Man of Bronze*) (1951)
The Bob Mathias Story (aka *The Flaming Torch*) (1954)
Wee Geordie (1956)
It Happened in Athens (1962)

Tokyo Olympiad (1966)
Walk, Don't Run (1966)
Downhill Racer (1969)
The Games (1970)
Visions of Eight (1973)
21 Hours at Munich (1976 TVM)
The Loneliest Runner (1976 TVM)
Wilma (1977 TVM)
Special Olympics (aka *A Special Kind of Love*) (1978 TVM)
Analympics (1979)
The Top of the Hill (1980 TVM)
Swan Song (1980 TVM)
The Golden Moment: An Olympic Love Story (1980)
Miracle on Ice (1981 TVM)
Personal Best (1982)
Running Brave (1983)
Nadia (1984 TVM)
The Jesse Owens Story (1984 TVM)
The First Olympics — Athens 1896 (1984 TVM)
16 Days of Glory (1986)

The Omen

This 1976 movie about the coming of the "antichrist" was a slick, well-done chiller, bolstered by crisp performances by Gregory Peck and David Warner. Yet, despite its merits and boxoffice popularity, it hardly warranted a series—even a short-lived one. *Damien — Omen II* was a predictable follow-up, showing Damien coping with teen problems by killing people. The series ended, mercifully, with *The Final Conflict,* which had an adult Damien dabbling in politics. See also **The Devil.**

The Omen (1976)
Damien — Omen II (1978)
The Final Conflict (1981)

Outlaws (Real-Life Western)

Jesse James and Billy the Kid easily outdistance their peers as the most oft-filmed outlaws in American cinema. In James' case, his celluloid fame is deserved, since his legendary exploits are backed up with the famous ill-fated Northfield, Minnesota, bank robbery. Billy the Kid, however, was a minor bandit gunned down in an ambush at the age of 21. His real name was Henry McCarty, though he was also known as William H. Bonney. On the screen, Billy has been portrayed as a wronged hero, a psychopath, and a vampire killer. Western veteran Johnny Mack Brown starred as the talkies' first Kid in 1930's *Billy the Kid,* a lavish MGM production originally shown in 70mm. It was remade a decade later in Technicolor with Robert Taylor, dumping his romantic image, in the title role. In contrast to these big-budget efforts, Billy was also the subject of a minor 1939 Roy Rogers picture *(Billy the Kid Returns)* and 1940's *Billy the Kid Outlawed,* the first of a PRC series starring Bob Steele and later Buster Crabbe (see **Billy the Kid** series). Jane Russell's cleavage overshadowed Billy's story in Howard Hughes' much-publicized, long-delayed *The Outlaw* (1943). It was the Kid's last prestigious picture until Paul Newman played him in Arthur Penn's psychological Western *The Left-Handed Gun* (1958), based on a TV play by Gore Vidal (which was remade for cable-TV in 1989). Billy the Kid's subsequent film appearances have ranged from ambitious to awful. Sam Peckinpah's *Pat Garrett and Billy the Kid* (1973) promised to examine the relationship between lawman Garrett and ex-crony Billy. However, miscasting (Kris Kristofferson as Billy) and an over-emphasis on violence spelled boxoffice and critical doom. Billy discovered his girlfriend's uncle (John Carradine) was a vampire in *Billy the Kid vs. Dracula* (1966), a movie not as dreadful as its title — but close. Emilio Estevez made Billy a romantic antihero in the 1988 "brat pack" Western *Young Guns,* which drew audiences despite an abundance of critical pans. Yet, despite these frequent appearances, Billy still rates second to Jesse James in number of films. James' career first received the lavish treatment with 20th Century–Fox's colorful *Jesse James* (1939), starring Tyrone Power as Jesse and Henry Fonda as brother Frank. Fonda reprised his role in Fritz Lang's superior 1940 sequel *The Return of Frank James,* one of the finest outlaw pictures. Jesse was a common fixture in the programmer Westerns of the 1950s. He was portrayed by Dale Robertson *(Fighting Man of the Plains),* Audie Murphy *(Kansas Raiders),* Willard Parker *(The Great Jesse James Raid),* Robert Wagner *(The True Story of Jesse James),* Ray Stricklyn *(Young Jesse James),* and others. Even Bob Hope was mistaken for the famous outlaw in *Alias Jesse James* (1959), one of his funniest comedies. In 1966, while Billy fought Dracula on one half of a double bill, Jesse saw a pal turned into a bald monster in *Jesse James Meets Frankenstein's Daughter.* Writer-director Philip Kaufman stressed factual detail over interesting narrative in 1972's *The Great Northfield, Minnesota Raid,* which featured Robert Duvall as Jesse and Cliff Robertson as Cole Younger. Both characters also appeared in Walter Hill's stylish outlaw saga *The Long Riders* (1980), a family affair starring: Stacy and James Keach as Jesse and Frank James; David, Keith, and Robert Carradine as the Younger Brothers; and Dennis and Randy Quaid as the lesser-known Mills Brothers. The Younger Brothers were paired with the James' in other pic-tures as well, such as *The Great Missouri Raid* (1950) and *The Intruders* (1970). It's interesting to note that Audie Murphy is the only actor to have played both Billy the Kid and Jesse James and he did it in the same year, starring in 1950's *The Kid from Texas* and *Kansas Raiders.* Belle Starr, the only female outlaw to achieve notoriety, has been portrayed by Gene Tierney *(Belle Starr),* Jane Russell *(Montana Belle),* and Elizabeth Mont-gomery *(Belle Starr).* Paul Newman and Robert Redford brought fame to a couple of minor outlaws with their 1969 smash *Butch Cassidy and the Sundance Kid.* William Katt and Tom Berenger starred in a 1979 prequel *Butch and Sundance: The Early Days.* In made-for-TV movies, the Sun-dance Kid's woman was played by Elizabeth Montgomery in 1974's *Mrs. Sundance* and Katharine Ross (recreating her role from the Newman-Redford picture) in 1976's *Wanted: The Sundance Woman.* Other outlaw gangs appearing in multiple features include the Clantons *(Law and*

Order, Gunfight at the O.K. Corral, Hour of the Gun) and the Daltons *(The Last Day, The Last Ride of the Dalton Gang).* On the small screen, Clu Gulager played Billy the Kid opposite Barry Sullivan's Pat Garrett in the 1960–62 series "The Tall Man," while Christopher Jones starred in 1965–66's "The Legend of Jesse James." In the following, the outlaw's name is listed in parentheses unless specified in the title.

Billy the Kid (aka *The Highwayman Rides*) (1930)
Law and Order (1932) (Clantons)
Jesse James (1939)
Billy the Kid Returns (1939)
Billy the Kid (1940)
Billy the Kid Outlawed (1940)
Belle Starr (1941)
The Return of Frank James (1940)
The Outlaw (1943) (Billy the Kid)
My Darling Clementine (1946) (Clantons)
Belle Starr's Daughter (1947)
Fighting Man of the Plains (1949) (Jesse James)
The Younger Brothers (1949)
I Shot Jesse James (1949)
The Kid from Texas (1950) (Billy the Kid)
Kansas Raiders (1950) (Jesse James)
The Great Missouri Raid (1950) (James and Younger Brothers)
Best of the Badmen (1951) (Jeff Clanton)
Montana Belle (1952) (Belle Starr)
The Great Jesse James Raid (1953)
Jesse James vs. the Daltons (1954)
Jesse James' Women (1954)
The Law vs. Billy the Kid (1954)
The Parson and the Outlaw (1955) (Billy the Kid)
The True Story of Jesse James (1956)

Hell's Crossroad (1957) (Jesse James)
Gunfight at the OK Corral (1957) (Clantons)
The Dalton Girls (1957)
Alias Jesse James (1958)
Badman's Country (1958) (Butch Cassidy)
The Left-Handed Gun (1958) (Jesse James)
Young Jesse James (1960)
Billy the Kid Meets Dracula (1966)
Jesse James Meets Frankenstein's Daughter (1966)
Hour of the Gun (1967) (Clantons)
Butch Cassidy and the Sundance Kid (1969)
The Intruders (1970 TVM) (James and Youngers)
Chisum (1970) (Billy the Kid)
Doc (1971) (Clantons)
Dirty Little Billy (1972)
The Great Northfield, Minnesota Raid (1972) (James and Youngers)
Pat Garrett and Billy the Kid (1973)
Mrs. Sundance (1974 TVM)
The Last Day (1975 TVM) (Daltons)
Wanted: The Sundance Woman (aka *Mrs. Sundance Rides Again*) (1976 TVM)
Go West, Young Girl (1978 TVM) (Billy the Kid)
Butch and Sundance: The Early Days (1979)
The Last Ride of the Dalton Gang (1979 TVM)
Cattle Annie and Little Britches

(1980) (Daltons)
The Long Riders (1980) (James and Youngers)
Belle Starr (1980 TVM)
The Grey Fox (1982) (Bill Miner)

The Last Days of Frank and Jesse James (1986 TVM)
Young Guns (1988) (Billy the Kid)
Billy the Kid (aka *Gore Vidal's Billy the Kid*) (1989 TVM)

Painted People

Covering one's body with paint is not exactly a healthy thing to do. In fact, it resulted in the death of one of the asylum inmates in *Bedlam* (1946), though the institution's vicious director (Boris Karloff) seemed rather undisturbed. Bond villain Auric Goldfinger killed 007's girlfriend (Shirley Eaton) by covering her in his trademark gold in 1964's *Goldfinger*. In contrast, partially painted people have led healthier lives. Marlene Dietrich sported a pair of painted legs for her famous dance scene in *Kismet* (1944). On the kinkier side, Britt Ekland exposed her painted breasts in *Scandal* (1989), while jungle natives dipped Bo Derek in an ugly shade of off-white in *Tarzan, the Ape Man* (1981). See also **Tattoos.**

Kismet (aka *Oriental Dream*) (1944)
Bedlam (1946)

Goldfinger (1964)
Tarzan, the Ape Man (1981)
Scandal (1989)

Painters

The postimpressionists of the late 19th century dominate film biographies of painters, primarily due to the influences of Vincent Van Gogh and Paul Gaugin. The 1956 *Lust for Life,* based on an Irving Stone book, was a colorful portrait of Van Gogh's tormented life. Kirk Douglas played the Dutch painter, with Anthony Quinn earning a Best Supporting Actor Oscar as his friend Gaugin. The unusual 1987 Australian tribute, *Vincent,* consisted mostly of Van Gogh's paintings accompanied by John Hurt's affective readings of his letters. Gaugin's life provided Somerset Maugham with the basis for his novel *The Moon and Sixpence,* which was filmed in 1942. George Sanders played the stockbroker who left his family to pursue painting and wound up dying of leprosy on a South Seas island. The Hays Office, the film industry's censorship watchdog, required that some of the film's nude paintings be toned down by adding leaves or flowers to cover appropriate body parts. Two Gaugin biographies surfaced in the 1980s. The 1980 TV-movie *Gaugin the Savage* boasted fine production values, including on-location footage of France and Tahiti, but a miscast David Carradine doomed the venture. Donald Sutherland made an appropriately passionate Gaugin in 1987's *Wolf at the Door,* a slow-moving account of Gaugin's final days following his return from Tahiti. Aside from Gaugin and Van Gogh, biographies of painters have been scarce and sporadic. Alexander Korda produced 1936's *Rembrandt,* an opulent version of the

Dutch painter's life featuring a classic Charles Laughton performance.
John Huston's *Moulin Rouge* (1953) fictionalized the life of dwarfish
French painter Toulouse-Lautrec (Jose Ferrer). Yet, the film remains
fondly remembered for its atmospheric 19th century Montmartre setting
and an elaborate can-can sequence. A Picasso biography has somehow
eluded filmmakers, although the Cubist painter created a canvas on screen
for French director Henri-Georges Clouzot in 1955's *The Mystery of
Picasso*. *The Picasso Summer* in 1969 starred Albert Finney and Yvette
Mimieux as a vacationing couple who set off in search of the famous artist.
It sat on the studio shelf for some time before debuting in the U.S. as a
late-night network movie. Despite its promising title, *The Adventures of
Picasso* was a 1978 oddball Swedish comedy. In addition to providing biographical material for filmmakers, painters have contributed to the behind-the-scenes art of cinema. Spanish artist Salvador Dalí designed a
haunting, surrealistic dream sequence for Alfred Hitchcock's *Spellbound*
(1945). The special effects crew of 1947's *The Private Affairs of Bel Ami*
claimed that Van Gogh's canvas *The Garden of the Vicarage at Nuenen*
gave them the idea of using plastic to create "dry rain." See also **Paintings**.

Rembrandt (1936)
The Moon and Sixpence (1942)
(Paul Gaugin)
Kitty (1945) (Cecil Kellaway as
Gainsborough in bit role)
Moulin Rouge (1953)
(Toulouse-Lautrec)
The Mystery of Picasso (1955)
Lust for Life (1956) (Van Gogh
and Gaugin)
The Lovers of Montparnasse
(aka *Montparnasse 19*) (1957)
(Modigliani)
The Naked Maja (1959) (Fran-
cisco Goya)

The Agony and the Ecstasy
(1965) (Michaelangelo)
El Greco (1966)
The Picasso Summer (1969)
Savage Messiah (1972) (Henri
Gautier)
The Adventures of Picasso
(1978)
Gaugin the Savage (1980 TVM)
The Rothko Conspiracy (1983
TVM) (Mark Rothko)
Wolf at the Door (1987) (Paul
Gaugin)
Vincent (1988)

Paintings

Canvases have figured prominently in an odd assortment of horror films,
fantasies, mysteries, and comedies. At least three films have been based
on Oscar Wilde's wickedly clever *Picture of Dorian Gray*, the story of a
vile Victorian rake whose portrait ages while he retains his youth. The
1945 version remains the best-remembered, with the portrait appearing in
color in an otherwise black-and-white film. Joseph Cotten played a struggling artist who paints a masterpiece after falling in love with a ghost in
the marvelous 1948 fantasy *Portrait of Jennie*. Again, the film reverted to
color for the closing shot of Cotten's painting. Dana Andrews fell in love
with the portrait of Gene Tierney hanging over her mantle in Otto

Preminger's stylish 1944 mystery *Laura*. That perceptive sleuth Sherlock Holmes cracked the case of *The Hound of the Baskervilles* by examining a painting of Sir Hugo Baskerville and deducing that an unlikely suspect was actually a murderous relative. A theft of a painting provided the excuse for the 1930 Marx Brothers romp *Animal Crackers*. In the 1942 British comedy *Much Too Shy*, George Formby played an unfortunate handyman whose paintings of his clients wound up at an advertising agency—with nude bodies added to them. A demonic portrait hanging in a museum required New York City to call for Bill Murray, Dan Aykroyd, and Harold Ramis in 1989's blockbuster comedy **Ghostbusters II**. See also **Painters**.

Animal Crackers (1930)
The Hound of the Baskervilles (1939) (see **Sherlock Holmes** for other versions)
Much Too Shy (1942)
Laura (1944)
The Picture of Dorian Gray (1945)
Portrait of Jennie (1948)
The Fake (1958)
Now You See It, Now You Don't (1967 TVM)
The Picture of Dorian Gray (1973 TVM)
The Sins of Dorian Gray (1983 TVM)
Hot Paint (1988 TVM)
Ghostbusters II (1989)

Palmer, Harry

Michael Caine played Len Deighton's Cockney thief-turned-disenchanted-spy three times, beginning with 1965's *The Ipcress File*. While other spy movies strove to imitate the Bond films (q.v.), the Palmer series played up its differences. Harry wore thick glasses, enjoyed cooking, and complained about his dirty profession. However, like 007, he had a weak spot for the ladies. Guy Doleman played Palmer's blackmailing superior, while Oscar Homolka was memorable as a Russian officer in the last two films. Fans argue over which entry was the best, though everyone agrees that *Billion Dollar Brain* (directed by maverick Ken Russell) was the weakest. Deighton's character remained nameless in the novels.

The Ipcress File (1965)
Funeral in Berlin (1966)
The Billion Dollar Brain (1967)

Parallel Worlds

Few filmmakers have been attracted to the complex concept of a character floating back and forth between two mirrored worlds. Astronaut Roy Thinnes discovered a twin Earth on his *Journey to the Far Side of the Sun* (1969). It took him awhile to figure out that he had exchanged places with his exact duplicate. The 1971 TV-movie *The Stranger* was an unofficial remake with Glenn Corbett as the baffled astronaut. Kathleen Turner's trips between two parallel worlds left her so confused that she murdered the wrong man in 1987's *Julia and Julia*. Tom Bell's journey into another dimension, courtesy of an explosion, enabled him to save a dying girl's life in *Quest for Love* (1971). A more common variation on the parallel world theme incorporates time travel, as when Lindsay Wagner transported herself into another age whenever she put on an old dress in 1979's *The Two Worlds of Jennie Logan*. See also **Lookalikes; Time Travel.**

Journey to the Far Side of the	*The Stranger* (1973 TVM)
Sun (aka *Doppelganger*)	*The Two Worlds of Jennie*
(1969)	*Logan* (1979 TVM)
Quest for Love (1971)	*Julia and Julia* (1987)

Peanuts

Charles Schulz's lovable "Peanuts" characters leapt from the comic pages to theater screens with 1969's *A Boy Named Charlie Brown*, a full-length animated feature with songs by Rod McKuen. After three more films, Charlie, Snoopy, Lucy, Linus, and the rest of the gang gave up their screen careers and concentrated on their long-running, apparently never-ending series of TV specials. See also **Animated Movies; Comic Strip Characters.**

A Boy Named Charlie Brown	*Brown* (1977)
(1969)	*Bon Voyage, Charlie Brown*
Snoopy, Come Home (1972)	*(and Don't Come Back)*
Race for Your Life, Charlie	(1980)

Penitentiary Series

The 1979 film *Penitentiary* was the first installment in the saga of Too Sweet, an unjustly imprisoned black convict reformed by boxing. Written, produced, and directed by Jamaa Fanaka, the film earned a reputation as a minor league *Rocky* (q.v.), although its gritty approach was praised. Fanaka and star Leon Isaac Kennedy continued with two disappointing sequels, *Penitentiary 2* (1982) and *Penitentiary 3* (1987). The *Rocky* similarities became blatant in these films, right down to the presence of *Rocky III* alumnus Mr. T. in *Penitentiary 2*. Kennedy and his then-wife, sportscaster/model Jayne Kennedy, also made a 1981 remake of the 1947 boxing classic *Body and Soul*. See also **Boxing.**

Penitentiary (1979)	*Penitentiary 3* (1987)
Penitentiary 2 (1982)	

Penrod

Booth Tarkington wrote three books about Penrod Schofield, "The Worst Boy in Town," who consistently stirred up trouble in a quiet, Midwestern town circa 1914. Gordon Griffith appeared in a 1922 version and Ben Alexander took over as Penrod in the following year's *Penrod and Sam*. The latter film was remade by Warner Bros. in 1931 with Leon Janney in the lead and Dorothy Peterson (later Mrs. Pepper in the *Five Little*

Peppers series) as his mother. However, Warner's official Penrod series began in 1937 with the third version of *Penrod and Sam,* with Bobby Mauch as a much nicer boy. This movie also updated the setting, making Penrod the head of a Junior G-Men Club (which met in a barn just like Our Gang). Bobby's twin brother, Billy, joined the cast for the last two films: *Penrod and His Twin Brother* and *Penrod's Double Trouble* (both 1938). The Mauch Twins, who had their greatest success in Errol Flynn's *The Prince and the Pauper* (1937), virtually disappeared from films in the 1940s. However, Penrod showed up again—in diluted form—in two Doris Day musicals: *Moonlight Bay* (1951) and *By the Light of the Silvery Moon* (1953). These films restored the earlier setting, but relegated Penrod to a supporting character and changed his name to Wesley. He was played by Billy Gray, best known as Bud on TV's "Father Knows Best."

Penrod (1922)	(1938)
Penrod and Sam (1923)	*Penrod's Double Trouble* (1938)
Penrod and Sam (1931)	*Moonlight Bay* (1951)
Penrod and Sam (1937)	*By the Light of the Silvery*
Penrod and His Twin Brother	*Moon* (1953)

People Hunters/Human Prey

The premise of hunting human prey for sport was explored vividly in Richard Connell's famous short story *The Most Dangerous Game.* Connell's story about ruthless hunter Count Zaroff has been filmed "officially" as *The Most Dangerous Game* (1932), *A Game of Death* (1946), *Run for the Sun* (1956), and *Blood Lust* (1966). The 1932 version is best remembered, chiefly for Leslie Banks' campy, despicable villain. Future nice guy Alan Alda played a mad, crippled Vietnam veteran who tracked down a harmless couple trapped on his island in *To Kill a Clown.* In the 1973 TV-movie *Maneater,* Richard Basehart portrayed a deranged animal trainer who unleashed two hungry tigers on four visitors. One of the more interesting variations on Connell's plot has people stalking each other as part of a socially acceptable pasttime, a twist featured in *The Tenth Victim* (1965) and Stephen King's *The Running Man* (1987). Perhaps the finest film about people hunters was Cornel Wilde's gripping 1966 adventure *The Naked Prey.* Director Wilde played a safari guide, the only survivor of a native ambush, who is freed by his captors and then methodically tracked down. No other film matches this one for showing how self-survival can force a man to evolve into a killer as brutal as his pursuers.

The Most Dangerous Game (1932)	*The Naked Prey* (1966)
	Blood Lust (1966)
A Game of Death (1946)	*Woman Hunt* (1972)
Johnny Allegro (1949)	*To Kill a Clown* (1972)
Run for the Sun (1956)	*Maneater* (1973 TVM)
The Tenth Victim (1965)	*Open Season* (1974)

Savages (1974 TVM)	(1981)
Escape 2000 (aka *Turkey Shoot*)	*The Running Man* (1987)

Personal Ads

Filmmakers have typically used personal ad columns to bring unlikely lovers together. After reading the personals and suffering amnesia, bored yuppie housewife Rosanna Arquette wound up with practical projectionist Aidan Quinn in *Desperately Seeking Susan* (1985). Recently-divorced Bill Schuppert thought he had found the perfect companion in *The Personals*—until she turned out to be married. In 1981's *I Sent a Letter to My Love,* a lonely woman discovered romance by taking up correspondence with a man listed in the personals. In a bittersweet twist, he turns out to be her paralyzed brother. Police detective Al Pacino used personals to track down a murderer in the 1989 thriller *Sea of Love.*

The Personals (1981)	(1985)
I Sent a Letter to My Love	*The Perfect Match* (1987)
(1981)	*Classified Love* (1987 TVM)
Desperately Seeking Susan	*Sea of Love* (1989)

Persons in Hiding Series

J. Edgar Hoover's nonfiction best-seller *Persons in Hiding* provided the basis for this modest Paramount four-film gangster series. Actually, Courtney Riley Cooper ghostwrote the book, but the FBI director's name sold the copies and gave the series what marquee value it possessed. The best entries were the first and last, tight thrillers featuring a potent combination of rising and veteran stars (e.g. Richard Denning, William Frawley, J. Carrol Nash, Robert Ryan, Ralph Bellamy, Jack Carson, and Hedda Hopper). The 1939 *Persons in Hiding* traced the exploits of Bonnie Parker (later of *Bonnie and Clyde* fame), while 1940's *Queen of the Mob* was based on the career of Ma Barker. See also **Gangsters (Real-Life).**

Persons in Hiding (1939)	*Parole Fixer* (1940)
Undercover Doctor (1939)	*Queen of the Mob* (1940)

Peyton Place

Grace Metalious' cynical, small-town exposé made quite an impact when released in 1957. Its 1961 sequel, *Return to Peyton Place,* was a more conventional soap opera, but it did well enough to inspire a television series. The show premiered in 1964 and became an immediate runaway hit. It ran two or three times weekly for five years, thanks largely to an all-star cast featuring Dorothy Malone, Mia Farrow, Ryan O'Neal, and Ruth Warrick (pre-"All My Children"). *Murder in Peyton Place,* a 1977 made-for-TV-movie killed off Allison MacKenzie and Rodney Harrington (Farrow and O'Neal in the TV series), but reunited regulars Malone and Ed

Nelson. *Peyton Place: The Next Generation,* another TV-movie, was a feeble attempt to drum up interest for a new series.

Peyton Place (1957)
Return to Peyton Place (1961)
Murder in Peyton Place (1977

TVM)
Peyton Place: The Next
Generation (1985 TVM)

Photographers

News photographers, Army photographers, fashion photographers, amateur shutterbugs—photography is a wide field that has interested filmmakers on a regular basis. Photo journalists in volatile environments played key supporting roles in the 1983 films *Under Fire* and *The Year of Living Dangerously.* The latter film featured Linda Hunt in a Best Supporting Oscar performance as a philosophizing *male* photographer in 1965 Indonesia. Nick Nolte played a photojournalist in contemporary Nicaragua in *Under Fire,* while 1986's *Salvador* starred James Woods as a cynical freelance photographer unable to distance himself from his subjects. *84 Charlie Mopic* is the Army job classification for a motion picture cameraman. This 1989 film showed viewers the Vietnam War through his eyes—or rather, his camera. The photographer is glimpsed only when he hands his motion picture camera to someone else to engage in a little horseplay. Most female camera clickers in the movies have been fashion photographers, such as Faye Dunaway in *The Eyes of Laura Mars* and Pam Grier in *Friday Foster.* Photographer Claudette Colbert unexpectedly fell in love with subway digger Fred MacMurray in the 1943 comedy *No Time for Love.* In other comic escapades, Buster Keaton starred in the classic 1928 comedy *The Cameraman.* It was remade, much less effectively, with Red Skelton as 1950's *Watch the Birdie.* Allegedly, an uncredited Keaton supervised many of the gags. Bob Hope played a photographer-turned-detective in *My Favorite Brunette* (which was Dorothy Lamour, of course). The source of Bob's trouble was not Dorothy, but a valuable picture taken with his "keyhole camera." Photographers have not fared well in horror films. David Warner was one of the first to realize that little Damien was not an angelic child in 1976's *The Omen.* Unfortunately, that knowledge lost him his head in the film's goriest sequence. In Michael Powell's cult classic *Peeping Tom* (1960), Carl Boehm played a deranged photographer obsessed with capturing his murder victims on film at the precise moment of their deaths. Scientist Robert Stephen invented a camera that could capture one's spirit as it leaves the body in 1972's intriguing *The Asphyx.* Michaelangelo Antonioni's *Blow-Up* (1966) remains the most overrated movie about a photographer. It took a promising premise (David Hemmings unintentionally photographs what may be a murder) and burdens it with heavyhanded symbolism.

The Cameraman (1928)
Picture Snatcher (1933)

Murder in Greenwich Village
(1937)

Dust Be My Destiny (1939)
China Girl (1942)
Escape from Crime (1942)
Hit the Ice (1943)
No Time for Love (1943)
Double Exposure (1944)
Lover Come Back (aka When
   Lovers Meet) (1946)
My Favorite Brunette (1947)
Watch the Birdie (1950)
I Love Melvin (1953)
Rear Window (1954)
Joe Butterfly (1957)
Funny Face (1957)
Peeping Tom (1960)
A Girl Named Tamiko (1962)
Blow-Up (1966)
Negatives (1968)

Live a Little, Love a Lot (1968)
La Prisonniere (1969)
Little Murders (1971)
The Asphyx (1972)
Friday Foster (1975)
The Omen (1976)
Eyes of Laura Mars (1978)
Georgia, Georgia (1982)
Under Fire (1983)
The Year of Living Dangerously
   (1983)
No Small Affair (1984)
Salvador (1986)
The Girl in the Picture (1986)
Double Exposure (1989)
84 Charlie Mopic (1989)
Margaret Bourke-White (1989
TVM)

Pianists

While movie violinists (q.v.) have been limited to classical settings and trumpet players (q.v.) to jazz scenes, movie pianists have crossed all musical boundaries. The film appearances of a divergent group of real-life musicians confirm this point: Ignace Jan Paderewski and Liberace played the classics in, respectively, *Moonlight Sonata* (1937) and *Sincerely Yours* (1955); Ray Charles opted for the blues in *Blues for Lovers* (1964); and contemporary singer/pianist Charles Aznavour mixed jazz and popular music in *Shoot the Piano Player* (1960), as did Barry Manilow in *Copacabana* (1985). A wide variety of physical impairments and emotional problems have plagued pianists. Liberace went deaf in *Sincerely Yours,* while blind piano players were the subject of *Night Song* (1947), *Torch Song* (1953), and Charles' *Blues for Lovers.* Jack Nicholson abandoned a promising career as a concert pianist to become an aimless drifter in *Five Easy Pieces* (1970). The pianists in *Shoot the Piano Player* and *Fingers* (1978)—the first a washed-up concert performer, the second a promising star—both became involved with gangsters. A dying concert pianist tried to possess Alan Alda's body in the Satanic thriller *The Mephisto Waltz* (1971). That was a mild problem, however, compared to Peter Lorre's struggles with the severed hand of a piano player in *The Beast with Five Fingers* (1946). Still, the incredibly weird Dr. Seuss fantasy *The 5,000 Finger of Dr. T* (1953) rates as the most terrifying pianist film. Little Tommy Rettig starred as a boy who dreams that his vicious piano teacher has imprisoned him and 499 other boys in a castle where they play a giant piano all day long. In comparison, the troubled young piano players of *Madame Sousatzka* and *Running on Empty* (both 1988) had it easy.

Richard Dreyfuss and Amy Irving played young adults going for the same career-making prize, while falling in love in *The Competition* (1980). Two teenage groupies stalked pianist Peter Sellers wherever he went in *The World of Henry Orient* (1964). No discussion of piano players would be complete without at least mentioning Dooley Wilson as Sam in *Casablanca* (1942). Although they were not pianists, Tom Hanks and Robert Loggia danced out a catchy rendition of "Chopsticks" on a giant piano in *Big* (1988).

Moonlight Sonata (1937)
When Tomorrow Comes (1939)
The Great Lie (1941)
That Uncertain Feeling (1941)
Casablanca (1942)
The Constant Nymph (1943)
Love Story (aka *A Lady Surrenders*) (1944)
The Beast with Five Fingers (1946)
Detour (1946)
Carnegie Hall (1947)
Night Song (1947)
Letter from an Unknown Woman (1948)
A Kiss in the Dark (1949)
Strange Fascination (1952)
The 5,000 Fingers of Dr. T (1953)
Torch Song (1953)
Rhapsody (1954)
Sincerely Yours (1955)
The Eddy Duchin Story (1956)

Julie (1956)
Shoot the Piano Player (aka *Shoot the Pianist*) (1960)
The Hands of Orlac (aka *Hands of the Strangler*) (1960)
The World of Henry Orient (1964)
Blues for Lovers (aka *Ballad in Blue*) (1964)
The Battle of the Villa Fiorita (aka *Affair at the Villa Fiorita*) (1964)
The Story of a Woman (1969)
Five Easy Pieces (1970)
The Mephisto Waltz (1971)
Autumn Sonata (1978)
Fingers (1978)
Practice Makes Perfect (1978)
The Competition (1980)
Copacabana (1985 TVM)
Ghost of a Chance (1987 TVM)
Madame Sousatzka (1988)
Running on Empty (1988)

Pigs

Leading roles for pigs have been few and far between—and limited to animated features. The principal characters in the 1955 British adaptation of George Orwell's satire *Animal Farm* were two pigs named Napoleon and Snowball. E.B. White's children's classic *Charlotte's Web* (1973) focused on a friendship between a matronly spider and a shy pig. In supporting roles, real-life pigs have stolen their fair share of scenes. A frollicking contraband porker upstaged Maggie Smith and Michael Palin in the deft food-rationing comedy *A Private Function* (1985). A talking pig popped up opposite Pee Wee Herman in 1988's *Big Top Pee Wee*. In the horror genre, a giant killer boar stalked the Australian countryside in 1984's *Razorback,* while an add for 1982's *Pigs* proclaimed: "They'll eat anything so she had the perfect method to dispose of her victims." Bizarre man/pig love relationships were explored in *Futz* and Pier Paolo Pasolini's

Pigsty (both 1969). People were transformed into pigs in *Ulysses* (1955), *O Lucky Man!* (1973), and *Elvira—Mistress of the Dark* (1988). Hugh "Bulldog" Drummond (Walter Pidgeon) retired from sleuthing to raise pigs in 1951's *Calling Bulldog Drummond.* Animated shorts have featured Pooh's friend Piglet and that world-famous stuttering pig Porky. There's a 1911 silent short boasting the interesting title *The Electrified Pig.* On television, no pig has been able to compete with Arnold Ziffel of "Green Acres" fame.

Calling Bulldog Drummond (1951)	*Pigs* (1982)
Animal Farm (1955)	*Evilspeak* (1982)
Ulysses (1955)	*Razorback* (1984)
Pigsty (aka *Pig Pen; Porcile*) (1969)	*A Private Function* (1985)
Futz (1969)	*Elvira—Mistress of the Dark* (1988)
Charlotte's Web (1973)	*The Milagro Beanfield War* (1988)
O Lucky Man! (1973)	*Big Top Pee Wee* (1988)

Pinball/Video Games

Brooke Shields as a pinball player? The movie was 1978's *Tilt* and Shields, age 13, played a wandering pinball wizard who mounted a challenge against champ Charles Durning. The "tension-filled" pinball matches bore no resemblance to Paul Newman's pool scenes in *The Hustler* or Steve McQueen's poker games in *The Cincinatti Kid.* Three years prior to *Tilt,* flamboyant director Ken Russell brought The Who's rock opera *Tommy* to the screen. The rock group's lead singer Roger Daltry recreated his stage role as "the deaf, dumb, and blind kid who sure plays a mean pinball." Elton John appeared as his opponent, the Pinball Wizard. The ultimate video game movie was Disney's *Tron* (1982), a visually marvelous, but dramatically empty, hi-tech adventure. Jeff Bridges starred as a computer genius sucked into a computer and forced to play a "real" video game for his survival. Emilio Estevez also wound up inside a video game in one of the segments of the 1983 horror anthology *Nightmares.* In 1984's *The Last Starfighter,* aliens used an Earth-bound video game to test fighter-pilot skills to assist in recruiting warriors to save their dying planet.

Tommy (1975)	*Tron* (1982)
Tilt (1978)	*Nightmares* (1983)
Pick-Up Summer (aka *Pinball Summer, Pinball Pick-up*) (1981)	*The Last Starfighter* (1984)
	The Wizard (1989)

The Pink Panther

Blake Edwards' 1964 comedy *The Pink Panther* was a mildly amusing allstar farce about a jewel thief called the Phantom trying to steal the famous Pink Panther diamond. It starred David Niven, Claudia Cardinale,

Robert Wagner, and introduced Peter Sellers as that classic bumbling detective Inspector Clouseau. Thanks to Sellers' hilarious performance, the movie was a hit and he and Edwards reteamed for the 1964 sequel *A Shot in the Dark*. It's the best of all Clouseau movies and marked the debuts of eventual series regulars Herbert Lom (as Clouseau's boss/nemesis) and Burt Kwouk (as the kung fu–minded valet Kato). Surprisingly, another Sellers/Clouseau comedy did not appear for a decade. In the meantime, Alan Arkin starred in *Inspector Clouseau*, a 1968 flop *not* directed by Edwards. But Sellers and Edwards revived both their careers with *The Return of the Pink Panther*, the surprise hit of summer 1975. After two more popular entries, Sellers died in 1980. Nevertheless, outtakes of him were edited into the shoddily-constructed *Trail of the Pink Panther*. It was a well-deserved boxoffice disaster, as was *Curse of the Pink Panther* with Ted Wass following in Sellers' footsteps.

> *The Pink Panther* (1964)
> *A Shot in the Dark* (1964)
> *The Return of the Pink Panther* (1975)
> *The Pink Panther Strikes Again* (1976)
>
> *The Revenge of the Pink Panther* (1978)
> *The Trail of the Pink Panther* (1982)
> *The Curse of the Pink Panther* (1983)

Pirates

The jolly roger has been a screen fixture since before Douglas Fairbanks, Sr., took to the high seas in 1926's colorful *The Black Pirate*. In fact, Robert Louis Stevenson's immortal pirate Long John Silver appeared in an adaptation of *Treasure Island* six years earlier. In the talking film era, Errol Flynn probably logged the most appearances as a pirate. He played Rafael Sabatini's gentlemanly buccaneer in 1935's *Captain Blood*—the role that made him an overnight star. Flynn also played a queen's privateer in *The Sea Hawk*, a British spy among pirates in *Against All Flags*, and a Scottish nobleman-turned-temporary pirate in *The Master of Ballantrae*. Long John Silver easily outdistances his closest rival, Sabatini's Peter Blood, as the screen's busiest pirate. He has been portrayed most memorably by Wallace Beery (1934), Robert Newton (1950 and 1954), and Orson Welles (1972). Female pirates have been scarce, but Maureen O'Hara proved a fiery match for Flynn in *Against All Flags*. Other lady pirate captains were featured in *Anne of the Indies*, *The Pirate Queen*, and *Queen of the Pirates*. Pirate musicals have proven to be dismal box-office failures, despite the presence of some heavyweight talent. RKO's *Dancing Pirate* (1936) was an early Technicolor film (as was the aforementioned *Black Pirate*) featuring a music score by Rodgers and Hart. The 1948 Gene Kelly-Judy Garland musical *The Pirate* is fondly remembered for its fancy footwork (courtesy of Kelly and the Nicholas Brothers) and catchy tunes like "Be a Clown." *The Pirate Movie*, 1982, was an inept rip-off of Gilbert and Sullivan's operetta *The Pirates of Penzance,* which reached the screen itself the following year. To the astonishment of music lovers, it fared little better than its predecessor. Pirate comedies have included the obvious *(Abbott and Costello Meet Captain Kidd),* the offbeat *(Blackbeard's Ghost)* and the inane *(Yellowbeard).* Modern-day pirates harrassed David Warner in *The Island* and futuristic pirates sought water, not treasure, in *Ice Pirates.*

The Black Pirate (1926)
Old Ironsides (1926)
Treasure Island (1934)
Captain Blood (1935)
The Dancing Pirate (1936)
The Buccaneer (1938)
The Sea Hawk (1940)
The Black Swan (1942)
The Princess and the Pirate
  (1944)
Captain Kidd (1945)
The Spanish Main (1945)
Pirates of Monterey (1947)
The Pirate (1948)
Old Mother Riley's Jungle
  Treasure (1949)
Buccaneer's Girl (1950)
Fortunes of Captain Blood
  (1950)
Last of the Buccaneers (1950)
Treasure Island (1950)
Anne of the Indies (1951)
Double Crossbones (1951)
The Pirate Queen (1951)
Abbott and Costello Meet
  Captain Kidd (1952)
Against All Flags (1952)
Blackbeard the Pirate (1952)
Captain Pirate (1952)
Caribbean (aka Caribbean
  Gold) (1952)
The Crimson Pirate (1952)
Yankee Buccaneer (1952)
Peter Pan (1953)
The Master of Ballantrae (1953)
Prince of Pirates (1953)

Raiders of the Seven Seas (1953)
Yankee Pasha (1954)
His Majesty O'Keefe (1954)
Long John Silver (1954)
Pirates of Tripoli (1955)
The Buccaneer (1958)
Queen of the Pirates (1960)
The Boy and the Pirates (1960)
Morgan the Pirate (1961)
Pirate and the Slave Girl (1961)
Pirates of Tortuga (1961)
The Son of Captain Blood
  (1962)
Tiger of the Seven Seas (1962)
Pirates of Blood River (1962)
Hero's Island (1962)
Fury at Smugglers Bay (1963)
Devil-Ship Pirates (1964)
A High Wind in Jamaica (1965)
The King's Pirate (1967)
The Rover (1967)
Blackbird's Ghost (1968)
When Eight Bells Toll (1971)
Treasure Island (1972)
Ghost in the Noonday Sun
  (1973)
Scalawag (1973)
Swashbuckler (aka The Scarlet
  Buccaneer) (1976)
The Island (1980)
The Pirate Movie (1982)
Pirates of Penzance (1983)
Yellowbeard (1983)
Ice Pirates (1984)
Pirates (1986)
The Princess Bride (1987)

Planet of the Apes

In its 1968 review, *Variety* called *Planet of the Apes* an "intriguing blend of chilling satire, a sometimes ludicrous juxtaposition of human and ape mores, optimism and pessimism." It's a fitting description for an unusual series that featured both brilliant plot twists and incredibly dull science fiction. Rod Serling wrote the original film, adapting Pierre *(Bridge Over the River Kwai)* Boulle's satirical novel. Charlton Heston starred as an astronaut hurled into a time warp and landing on a planet where intelligent apes are masters over men. In the film's climactic closing scene, Heston finds the remains of the Statue of Liberty and realizes that he has seen man's future on planet Earth. Critics raved over Serling's witty screenplay, but most of the publicity centered on John Chamber's brilliant ape makeup (which won a special Oscar). Two years later, a dull sequel, *Beneath the Planet of the Apes,* ended with the detonation of an atomic bomb which destroyed the world—and apparently the series. However, when it scored at the box office, producer Arthur P. Jacobs and screenwriter Paul Dehn revived the series with a crafty twist. *Escape from the Planet of the Apes* revealed that two nice apes (Roddy McDowall and Kim Hunter) escaped from the exploding Earth in a spaceship and entered into the same time warp that Heston encountered. They land on Earth circa 1971 and run afoul of human prejudice. However, before they are murdered, they smuggle their infant son to safety. He grows up and, in the fourth film *Conquest of the Planet of the Apes,* leads an ape revolt. In the final series entry, 1973's mediocre *Battle for the Planet of the Apes,* the time line comes full circle and ends where *Planet of the Apes* began. A year later, an hour-long TV series was launched, with McDowall repeating his original role. It bombed in the ratings and became a midseason casualty, although the pilot episode, *Back to the Planet of the Apes,* was later released as a TV-movie. A Saturday morning cartoon version also surfaced during the 1975–76 TV season.

Planet of the Apes (1968)
Beneath the Planet of the Apes (1970)
Escape from the Planet of the Apes (1971)
Conquest of the Planet of the Apes (1972)
Battle for the Planet of the Apes (1973)
Back to the Planet of the Apes (1974 TVM)
Forgotten City of the Planet of the Apes (1974 TVM culled from series episodes)

Plants

Perhaps because of their decorative and unthinking nature, plants have been greatly ignored by filmmakers. In fact, prior to the 1950s, they were restricted to bit roles—nothing they could really sink their roots into. A rare flower, which bloomed only in the moonlight, was featured prominently in 1935's *Werewolf of London.* Called the marifesa, it could cure lycanthropy, but—ironically—Henry Hull was bitten by a werewolf while searching for the flower. In the 1940s, Egyptian high priests used a brew made from tana leaves to periodically revive the Mummy. But the first

abnormal plants of note appeared in *The Wizard of Oz* (1939), in which
Dorothy and the Scarecrow encountered a grove of apple trees who didn't
like their fruit to be picked. Later in the film, they experienced the effects
of sleep-inducing poppies. Arguably, the most renowned plant movie is
1951's *The Thing from Another World* (subsequently shortened to *The
Thing*). It starred an alien frequently described (even in the movie) as a
giant carrot (actually, his shape seemed inspired by the Frankenstein
Monster). He was electrocuted—one could say "cooked"—at the film's
climax. Alien pods invaded a small California community and system-
atically replaced its residents with lookalikes in Don Siegel's *Invasion of
the Body Snatchers* (1956). Less memorable vegetation movies of the 1950s
included *From Hell It Came,* in which radiation created a silly-looking
tree monster, and *Voodoo Island,* which featured a woman-eating cobra
plant. B-movie mogul Roger Corman gave the screen its most charismatic
plant with his campy cult classic *The Little Shop of Horrors* (1960). It was
about a nerd named Seymour Krelboin who crossbreeds a plant that grows
to human size and periodically craves people for dinner, screaming: "Feed
me! Feed me! I'm hungry!" It spawned an Off–Broadway musical in 1982
and a big-budget remake in 1986. The plants in John Wyndham's *The
Day of the Triffids* couldn't talk, but they could communicate via shrill
sounds. In many ways, *Triffids* is the ultimate plant movie. At a height of
10 feet, the poisonous, people-eating Triffids were a menacing crop, indeed. And unlike in other plant pictures, there wasn't just one monster in
Triffids—it was a large-scale invasion. Talking trees appeared in *Babes in
Toyland* (1961) and *Monty Python and the Holy Grail* (1974). A meteorite
caused Stephen King to turn into a plant in 1982's *Creepshow.* And a
mad scientist crossbred humans and plants to create *The Mutations*
(1973).

The Werewolf of London (1935)
The Wizard of Oz (1939)
The Thing (1951)
Fury of the Congo (1951)
Invasion of the Body Snatchers
 (1956)
From Hell It Came (1957)
Voodoo Island (1957)
The Woman Eater (1959)
The Little Shop of Horrors
 (1960)
Babes in Toyland (1961)
The Day of the Triffids (1963)
Dr. Terror's House of Horrors
 (1964)
Maneater of Hydra (aka *Island
 of the Doomed*) (1966)

Navy vs. the Night Monsters
 (1966)
Please Don't Eat My Mother
 (1972)
The Mutations (1973)
*Monty Python and the Holy
 Grail* (1974)
Mr. Sycamore (1974)
The Kirlian Witness (aka *The
 Plants Are Watching*) (1978)
Nick Carter in Prague (aka
 *Dinner for Adele; Adele
 Hasn't Had Her Supper Yet*)
 (1978)
Invasion of the Body Snatchers
 (1978)
Attack of the Killer Tomatoes

(1978)
Creepshow (1982)
The Little Shop of Horrors

(1986)
Return of the Killer Tomatoes
(1988)

Plastic Surgery

Movie surgeons have wasted little time on routine facelifts and nose jobs (though Steve Martin pleaded for a nose alteration in 1987's *Roxanne*). Instead, they have concentrated far more on extensive plastic surgery, frequently resulting in horror movie plots. In 1935's *The Raven*, Bela Lugosi played a Poe-reciting surgeon who turned gangster Boris Karloff's face into a hideous mass of scar tissue. Karloff exacted his revenge by escorting Lugosi to the torture chamber in the film's climax. However, the most common plastic surgery plot involves the scientist who murders innocent bystanders in order to rebuild the facial features of a loved one. Georges Franju's chilling *The Horror Chamber of Dr. Faustus* is considered the classic example of this type. Rock Hudson probably underwent the most elaborate make-over in John Frankenheimer's *Seconds*. He played an elderly millionaire who emerged from high-tech surgery as a new, younger man—only to find out later that the price was too steep. *The Girl Most Likely to...* uncovered a vein of dark humor in its story of a mistreated ugly duckling (Stockard Channing) transformed into a revenge-minded beauty. A car accident, plastic surgery, and a mean mother kept lovers Kathleen Quinlan and Stephen Collins apart in *The Promise*, a rare change-of-face romance.

The Raven (1935)
A Woman's Face (1941)
Black Dragons (1942)
Dark Passage (1948)
Stolen Face (1952)
Jail Bait (1954)
The Face of Terror (1959)
The Mirror Has Two Faces (1959)
Circus of Horrors (1960)
The Awful Dr. Orloff (1961)
The Horror Chamber of Dr. Faustus (aka *Eyes Without a Face*) (1962)
Seconds (1966)
Corruption (1968)
The Groundstar Conspiracy (1972)

The Girl Most Likely to... (1973 TVM)
Ash Wednesday (1973)
Who? (1974)
Scalpel (aka *False Face*) (1976)
Rabid (1977)
The Promise (1978)
Mirror, Mirror (1979 TVM)
The Man with Bogart's Face (aka *Sam Marlowe, Private Eye*) (1980)
Looker (1981)
The Jigsaw Man (1984)
Why Me? (1984 TVM)
Perfect People (1988 TVM)
Batman (1989)
Johnny Handsome (1989)

Poirot, Hercule

Agatha Christie's Belgian sleuth was brought to the screen in the guise of

British actor Austin Trevor in the early 1930s in mysteries like *Alibi* and *Lord Edgware Dies*. Decades later, Tony Randall *(The Alphabet Murders)* and Albert Finney *(Murder on the Orient Express)* took shots at playing Poirot. However, Christie fans quibbled with those interpretations and an acceptable Poirot was not discovered until Peter Ustinov made the role his own, beginning with 1978's *Death on the Nile*. Sadly, the quality of the Ustinov/Poirot films declined gradually after his second film *Evil Under the Sun* (1982). But Ustinov remained entertaining in spite of the progressively worse conditions. David Suchet played The Belgium Sleuth on British TV in the 1980s. Finally, Hercule Poirot was also among the many detectives spoofed in Neil Simon's *Murder by Death* (1976).

Alibi (1931)
Lord Edgware Dies (1934)
The Alphabet Murders (aka *The ABC Murders*) (1966)
Murder on the Orient Express (1974)

Death on the Nile (1978)
Evil Under the Sun (1982)
Thirteen at Dinner (1985 TVM)
Dead Man's Folly (1986 TVM)
Appointment with Death (1988)

Police Academy

An unexpected commercial success, the *Police Academy* series has proven to be the 1980s answer to Britain's *Carry On* comedies (q.v.) of the 1960s. Both series manufactured low-brow humor which moviegoers thrived on and critics found distasteful. The 1984 *Police Academy* naturally set the tone for the rest, focusing on a class of unlikely police recruits led by smart guy Steve Guttenberg, former football player Bubba Smith, and human noise machine Michael Winslow. Unpredictable stand-up comic Bobcat Goldthwait joined the series for entries #3 and #4. After the fourth film, Guttenberg graduated to bigger roles (1987's monster hit *Three Men and a Baby*) and Smith bowed out temporarily. Only Winslow remained for all six entries. The 1985 *Night Patrol* was a worthless rip-off boasting a bizarre cast headed by Linda Blair, Pat Paulsen, and Billy Barty.

Police Academy (1984)
Police Academy 2 (1985)
Police Academy 3: Back in Training (1986)
Police Academy 4: Citizens on Patrol (1987)
Police Academy 5: Assignment Miami Beach (1988)
Police Academy 6: City Under Siege (1989)

Pool

Paul Newman's second tour through the world of smoke-filled pool halls finally resulted in his first Academy Award, as Best Actor for 1986's *The Color of Money*. Newman played Eddie Felson, a smooth veteran pool shark he introduced as an ambitious youth fifteen years earlier in *The Hustler*. Eddie's match against the legendary Minnesota Fats (Jackie

Gleason) in the 1961 picture easily ranks as pool's finest moment in the movies. But other actors have also taken their shot at the eighth ball: James Coburn in *The Baltimore Bullet*, Whoopi Goldberg in *Kiss Shot*, and Johnny Cash in *The Baron and the Kid*, a TV-movie inspired by his country hit "The Baron."

The Hustler (1961)	TVM)
The Baltimore Bullet (1980)	*The Color of Money* (1986)
The Baron and the Kid (1984	*Kiss Shot* (1989 TVM)

Popes and Cardinals

Cardinal Richelieu, who virtually ruled France from 1624–1642, has been the cinema's most prominent senior church figure. George Arliss portrayed him as an unscrupulous scoundrel in *Cardinal Richelieu* (1935), while others who have donned the red robe include Nigel du Brulier in *The Three Musketeers* (1935) and *The Man in the Iron Mask* (1939), Raymond Massey in *Under the Red Robe* (1937), Christopher Logue in *The Devils* (1971), and Charlton Heston in *The Three Musketeers* (1974) and *The Four Musketeers* (1975). *Guilty of Treason* (1949) was a fact-based account of the trial of Cardinal Mindszenty, while *The Cardinal* (1963) offered a fictitious tale of a young American's (Tom Tryon) rise to prominence within the church. Few actors have portrayed popes, although Albert Finney had the lead in the 1984 TV-movie *Pope John Paul II* and Anthony Quinn ruled from the Vatican in *Shoes of a Fisherman* (1968). The 1964 documentary *A Man Named John* traced the accomplishments of Pope John XXIII. A plot to assassinate the Pope lurked behind the comedy bits in Chevy Chase's *Foul Play* (1978). Finally, Liv Ullmann disguised herself as a man to reach the papacy in 1972's *Pope Joan*. See also **Monks; Nuns.**

Cardinal Richelieu (1935)	*The Devils* (1971)
The Three Musketeers (1935)	*Pope Joan* (aka *The Devil's*
Under the Red Robe (1937)	*Impostor*) (1972)
The Man in the Iron Mask	*Brother Sun, Sister Moon* (1973)
(1939)	*The Abdication* (1974)
Guilty of Treason (1949)	*The Three Musketeers* (1974)
Never Take No for an Answer	*The Four Musketeers* (1975)
(1951)	*Foul Play* (1978)
The Cardinal (1963)	*From a Far Country: Pope John*
A Man Named John (1964)	*Paul II* (1981 TVM)
Becket (1964)	*Pope John Paul II* (1984 TVM)
Shoes of a Fisherman (1968)	

Porky's

Shortly before he made the delightful family favorite *A Christmas Story*, director Bob Clark filmed this 1982 Canadian-made comedy smash about horny teens in Florida circa 1954. The majority of the action centered around the establishment of the title, a bar/brothel located just across the county line. Most critics called it smutty and pointless, but a *lot* of teens saw it. Perhaps it was the timing, for the 1983 sequel, *Porky's II: The Next Day,* lacked the box office fire despite reteaming teen leads Dan Monahan, Mark Herrier, and Wyatt Knight. The same trio showed up in a third installment which attracted little attention.

> *Porky's* (1982)   *Porky's Revenge* (1985)
> *Porky's II: The Next Day* (1983)

Prequels

A prequel is the opposite of a sequel, in that its narrative takes place earlier than the original film. For example, German filmmaker Paul Wegener destroyed the Golem, a stone statue brought to life, in 1914's *The Golem: Monster of Fate.* However, six years later, Wegener went back and told the story of the Golem's origin in *The Golem: How He Came to Be.* Hollywood's first prequel was 1948's *Another Part of the Forest,* which depicted the early days of the ruthless Hubbard family first introduced in 1941's *The Little Foxes.* Dan Duryea (as Leo Hubbard) was the only holdover from the original film's cast. In 1966's *Nevada Smith,* a supporting character in the screen version of Harold Robbins' sprawling novel *The Carpetbaggers* (1964) was given his own film. Steve McQueen played the young revenge-minded drifter in *Nevada Smith,* while Alan Ladd (in his last role) portrayed an easy-going middle-aged Nevada in *The Carpetbaggers.* However, it was not until the sequel-crazy early 1980s that the prequel attracted much attention. Even then, however, prequels typically performed poorly at the boxoffice, as evidenced by flops such as *Butch and Sundance: The Early Days* (1979). A noteworthy exception, of course, was *Indiana Jones and the Temple of Doom* (1984), a blockbuster prequel to *Raiders of the Lost Ark* (1981). Ken Russell's adaptation of D.H. Lawrence's *The Rainbow,* a prequel to his own 1970 film *Women in Love,* allowed Glenda Jackson to play the mother of the character she played in *Women in Love.* The longest gap between prequel and original is the 23 years which separated the 1977 adaptation of Henry Handel Richardson's *The Getting of Wisdom* from the 1954 version of his later novel *Rhapsody.* Sometimes, the distinction between prequel and original becomes a bit confusing. The Chuck Norris action picture *Missing in Action II: The Beginning* (1985) was actually filmed before *Missing in Action* (1984). It became a prequel only when the producers decided to release the second film first. (Note: The 1986 TV-movie *Dallas: The Early Years* was similar to a prequel, in that it took place chronologically prior to the television series "Dallas.") In the following list, the prequel is listed in the left column, with the original film listed to the right.

> *The Golem: How He Came to*   *The Golem: Monster of Fate*
> *Be* (aka *Der Golem, Wie Er*   (aka *Der Golem* (1914)
> *in die Welt Kam*) (1920)

Another Part of the Forest (1948)	The Little Foxes (1941)
Nevada Smith (1966)	The Carpetbaggers (1964)
The Nightcomers (1972)	The Innocents (1961)
The Getting of Wisdom (1977)	Rhapsody (1954)
Butch and Sundance: The Early Days (1979)	Butch Cassidy and the Sundance Kid (1969
Hungarians (1979)	Bálint Fábián's Encounter with God (1980)
Amityville II: The Possession (1982)	The Amityville Horror (1979)
Indiana Jones and the Temple of Doom (1984)	Raiders of the Lost Ark (1981)
Missing in Action II: The Beginning (1985)	Missing in Action (1984)
On Valentine's Day (1986)	1918 (1984)
The Rainbow (1989)	Women in Love (1970)

Presidents (U.S.)

The cinema has not treated all presidents equally, but then neither has American history. Abraham Lincoln, according to Guinness, has appeared as a character in over 150 films, far more than any other president. Actor Frank McGlynn specialized in portraying Lincoln for most of his career, beginning with 1915's *The Life of Abraham Lincoln* and continuing in bit roles in films like *The Littlest Rebel* (1935), *The Prisoner of Shark Island* (1936), and *The Plainsman* (1937). Most Lincoln biographies have been reverant sagas starring distinguished performers such as Walter Huston (1930's *Abraham Lincoln*), Henry Fonda *(Young Abe Lincoln)*, and Raymond Massey *(Abe Lincoln in Illinois)*. In 1951 *The Tall Target* offered a suspenseful change of pace, with Dick Powell as a detective (named John Kennedy!) trying to thwart an 1861 assassination attempt on Lincoln. In an even greater fictional elaboration, *The Lincoln Conspiracy* (1977) proposed that assassin John Wilkes Booth was conspiring with members of the U.S. Senate. Ronald Reagan ranks second to Lincoln in number of film appearances—but only because he really was an actor. More legitimate screen appearances have been logged by Andrew Jackson and John F. Kennedy, both of whom have been the subjects of several film biographies. Jackson's exploits in the War of 1812 played a major role in both versions of *The Buccaneer* (1938 and 1958). The scandal surrounding his alleged adulterous affair with future-wife Rachel Robards formed the basis for *The Gorgeous Hussy* (1936) and *The President's Lady* (1953). Interestingly, Charlton Heston played Jackson in both *The President's Lady* and *The Buccaneer* (1958). William Holden befriended Jackson's ghost in the unremarkable 1942 fantasy *The Remarkable Andrew*. Kennedy's pre-presidential adventures as a patrol torpedo boat commander were played for escapist entertainment in 1963's *PT 109,* with Cliff Robertson in the lead. The 1977 TV-movie *Johnny, We Hardly Knew Ye* dealt with Kennedy's first try for public office, while 1984's *Prince Jack* was an inconsequential chronicle about the Kennedy clan. Other Kennedy-related pictures include the documentary *John F. Kennedy: Years of Lightning, Day of Drums* (1966), the assassination thriller *Executive Action* (1973), *Jacqueline Bouvier Kennedy* (1982), and *Hoover vs. the Kennedys: The Second Civil War* (1987). Fictional presidents have been portrayed in many films, several of which have cast our nation's leader into intriguing situations. President Henry Fonda ordered the destruction of New York City in order to avoid a war with the Soviet Union in 1964's *Fail Safe.* That same year, military officer Burt Lancaster plotted a coup to overthrow President Fredric March in *Seven Days in May.* In 1971 TV-movies, a top presidential advisor disappeared in *Vanished,* which more or less prepared viewers for *The President's Plane Is Missing.* The President has also been kidnapped by lethal ladies *(In Like Flint),* terrorists *(The Kidnapping of the President),* and futuristic New York City convicts *(Escape from New York).* Polly Bergen played the country's first female commander-in-chief in the 1964 comedy *Kisses for My President.* James Earl Jones portrayed a black senator thrust into the Oval Office when the President is killed in *The Man* (1964). The following list includes only films specifically about presidents or featuring them in prominent roles (for instance, although George Washington has been a *minor* character in over a dozen movies, those films are not listed). The president's name is shown in parentheses if it is not apparent from the title; some are about fictitious presidents.

Abraham Lincoln (1930)
The Phantom President (1932)
Gabriel Over the White House (1933)
The Gorgeous Hussy (1936) (Jackson)
First Lady (1937)
This Is My Affair (aka *His Affair*) (1937) (McKinley)
The Buccaneer (1938) (Jackson)
Young Mr. Lincoln (1939)
Abe Lincoln in Illinois (1940)
Tennessee Johnson (aka *The Man on America's Conscience*) (1942) (Andrew Johnson)
The Remarkable Andrew (1942) (Jackson)
Wilson (1944)
Magnificent Doll (1946)
(Madison)
The Tall Target (1951) (Lincoln)
The President's Lady (1953) (Jackson)
Suddenly (1954)
The Buccaneer (1958) (Jackson)
Sunrise at Campobello (1960) (Franklin Roosevelt)
Advise and Consent (1962)
PT 109 (1963) (Kennedy)
The Best Man (1964)
Kisses for My President (1964)
Seven Days in May (1964)
Fail Safe (1964)
The Eleanor Roosevelt Story (1965)
John F. Kennedy: Years of Lightning, Day of Drums (1966)
In Like Flint (1967)

The Virgin President (1968)
(Fillmore spoof)
The Great Man's Whiskers
(1971 TVM) (Lincoln)
Vanished (1971 TVM)
The President's Plane Is Missing
(1971 TVM)
The Man (1972)
Hail to the Chief (aka *Hail;
Washington, B.C.*) (1973)
Executive Action (1973)
(Kennedy)
Collision Course (1975 TVM)
(Truman)
Give 'Em Hell, Harry! (1975)
(Truman)
The Wind and the Lion (1975)
(Theodore Roosevelt)
The Lincoln Conspiracy (1977)
Johnny, We Hardly Knew Ye
(1977 TVM) (Kennedy)
Eleanor and Franklin (1976
TVM) (Franklin Roosevelt)
F.D.R. — The Last Year (1980
TVM)

First Family (1980)
*The Kidnapping of the
President* (1980)
Escape from New York (1981)
Jacqueline Bouvier Kennedy
(1982 TVM)
*Eleanor Roosevelt, First Lady of
the World* (1982 TVM)
*The Indomitable Teddy
Roosevelt* (1983)
Prince Jack (1984) (Kennedy)
*Secret Honor: The Last Testa-
ment of Richard M. Nixon*
(1984 TVM)
The Betty Ford Story (1977
TVM)
Assassination (1987)
*Hoover vs. the Kennedys: The
Second Civil War* (1987 TVM)
LBJ: The Early Years (1987
TVM)
Gore Vidal's Lincoln (1988
TVM)
The Final Days (1989 TVM)
(Nixon)

Presley, Elvis

It used to be that the cinema endured a waiting period before spinning off biographical films about deceased personalities. The FDR biography *Sunrise at Campobello* (1960) did not appear until 15 years after the former president's death. Evidently, the film industry deemed Elvis Presley's life more marketable. Less than two years after Presley's death, ABC ushered in *Elvis*, the made-for-TV story of his life. Over the next ten years, five additional Presley-related films appeared amid rumors that the "King" still lived. None of these films surpassed ABC's *Elvis*, a solid picture directed by talented horror specialist John Carpenter and starring an effective Kurt Russell in the title role. North Carolina filmmaker Earl Owensby's *Living Legend* (1980) made no claims about being based on Elvis' life. But the plot similarities and the presence of Elvis' last girlfriend, Ginger Alden, left little doubt as to the picture's intent. The same year's *Touched by Love* was a fact-based story about the pen-pal relationship between a young girl with cerebral palsy and Presley. Don Johnson made an unlikely Elvis in the 1981 TV-movie *Elvis and the Beauty Queen*, the story of Presley's five-year relationship with Linda Thompson (Stephanie Zimbalist). Elvis' only wife, Priscilla Presley, executive-produced 1988's *Elvis and Me*, the TV version of her bestseller. David

Keith was Elvis in 1989's boxoffice bomb *Heartbreak Hotel,* a lighthearted, fictionalized account of Presley's friendship with a teenaged boy.
Presley also played himself in his final two screen appearances: the
behind-the-scenes documentary *Elvis: That's the Way It Is* (1970) and the
concert film *Elvis on Tour* (1972).

Elvis: That's the Way It Is (1970)	*with Love*) (1980)
Elvis on Tour (1972)	*Elvis and the Beauty Queen* (1981 TVM)
Elvis (1979 TVM)	*Elvis and Me* (1988 TVM)
Living Legend (1980)	*Heartbreak Hotel* (1989)
Touched by Love (aka *To Elvis,*	

Prisoners of War

POW films fall into three basic camps: German, Japanese, and Vietnamese. Each of these groups features an Oscar winner of some sort.
William Holden won Best Actor for his portrayal of a cynical prisoner
wrongly tagged an informer in Billy Wilder's *Stalag 17* (1953). Although
not among the first POW films, Wilder's movie combined humor,
suspense, and an assortment of motley characters to create a much-
imitated formula. *The Password Is Courage,* one of several mid–1960s
POW pictures, was based on the real-life exploits of Sergeant-Major
Charles Coward, who made a military career out of escaping from German
camps. *Von Ryan's Express* (1965) opened in a POW camp, but expanded
into a perilous train journey through Nazi-occupied territory. Allied
prisoners escaped during a climactic soccer game with a Nazi team in *Victory* (1981), while less athletic prisoners built a glider in the 1971 TV-
movie *Birdmen. The Great Escape* (1963) made a star of Steve McQueen,
while rolling up enough ticket receipts to make it the most profitable
POW film of the last three decades. It was co-written by James *(Shogun)*
Clavell, whose novel *King Rat* reached the screen in 1965. Set in a
Japanese POW camp, it chronicled the rise and fall of a manipulating con
artist (George Segal). However, the best-remembered Japanese-set POW
film remains David Lean's *The Bridge on the River Kwai* (1957). It earned
Oscars for Best Picture, Best Director, and Best Actor, the latter honoring
Alec Guinness's portrayal of a stubborn, manipulated British officer. Other
Japanese prison camp films include *The Purple Heart* (1944), *Escape to
Mindinao* (1968), *Merry Christmas, Mr. Lawrence* (1983), and *Empire of
the Sun* (1987). *The Deer Hunter,* the 1978 Oscar winner for Best Picture,
was partially set in a Vietnamese POW camp where prisoners were sub-
jected to a chilling game of Russian roulette. *When Hell Was in Session*
(1979) was a grim account of a Navy officer held prisoner for seven years in
North Vietnam. However, *Missing in Action II* (1985), *P.O.W. The
Escape* (1986), and *The Hanoi Hilton* (1987) used Vietnamese prison
camps strictly for their topical exploitation value. A handful of films have

PRISONS

dealt with female POW camps, most notably *Two Thousand Women*
(1944), *Three Came Home* (1950), *A Town Like Alice* (1956), and *Women
of Valor* (1986). Although most movie POWs seem to be American or
British, there have been exceptions. Jean Renoir's anti-war classic *Grand Illusion* (1937) focused on French prisoners during World War I. *Until Hell
Is Frozen* (1950) was set in a Russian camp and *The McKenzie Break*
(1970) had captured Germans escaping from a Scottish POW camp!
Television introduced the infamous POW camp sitcom "Hogan's Heroes"
in 1965. It enjoyed a six-year run and a profitable after-life in syndication.
See also **Prisons.**

Everything Is Thunder (1936)
Grand Illusion (aka *La Grande
Illusion*) (1937)
The Cross of Lorraine (1943)
Two Thousand Women (1944)
The Purple Heart (1944)
The Captive Heart (1948)
Act of Violence (1949)
The Wooden Soldier (1950)
Three Came Home (1950)
Stalag 17 (1953)
Break to Freedom (aka *Albert
RN*) (1953)
The Bamboo Prison (1954)
Prisoner of War (1954)
A Town Like Alice (aka *Rape of
Malaya*) (1956)
The Bridge on the River Kwai
(1957)
The Colditz Story (1957)
The Camp on Blood Island
(1958)
Breakout (aka *Danger Within*)
(1958)
Until Hell Is Frozen (1960)
A Coming-Out Party (aka *A
Very Important Person*)
(1961)
The Manchurian Candidate
(1962)
The Great Escape (1963)
The Password Is Courage (1963)
Von Ryan's Express (1965)
King Rat (1965)
Escape to Mindinao (1968)
The McKenzie Break (1970)
Birdmen (aka *Escape of the
Birdmen*) (1971 TVM)
The Deer Hunter (1978)
Escape to Athena (1979)
When Hell Was in Session
(1979 TVM)
Victory (1981)
Merry Christmas, Mr. Lawrence
(1983)
*Missing in Action II: The
Beginning* (1985)
Women of Valor (1986 TVM)
Opposing Force (aka *Hellcamp*)
(1986)
P.O.W. The Escape (aka
Behind Enemy Lines) (1986)
Empire of the Sun (1987)
The Hanoi Hilton (1987)

Prisons

The most engrossing accounts of life behind bars are those based on real-
life exploits. Robert Stroud, a prisoner who became a leading ornitholo-
gist, was portrayed in Oscar-nominated fashion by Burt Lancaster in *Bird-
man of Alcatraz* (1962) and by Art Carney in *Alcatraz: The Whole Shocking Story* (1980). The appeals to prevent the execution of Caryl Chessman,
a rapist/murderer known as the "Lover's Lane Bandit," was the subject of
1955's *Cell 2455, Death Row* and 1977's *Kill Me If You Can*. *Papillon*

chronicled Henri Charrière's thrilling escape from Devil's Island. *Escape from Alcatraz* (1979) was inspired by a daring 1962 breakout engineered by convict Frank Norris (Clint Eastwood). As the aforementioned films indicate, Alcatraz rates as the cinema's busiest real-life prison. Other actual penitentiaries which have provided movie settings include Sing Sing *(20,000 Years in Sing Sing, Castle on the Hudson)*, San Quentin *(Duffy of San Quentin, Women of San Quentin)*, and Folsom *(Inside the Walls of Folsom Prison)*. Foreign prisons have proven to be harrowing places, especially as depicted in *Midnight Express* (1978), *Kiss of the Spider Woman* (1985), *Jacobo Timerman: Prisoner Without a Name, Cell Without a Number* (1983), and *Dadah Is Death* (1988). Not all movie prisons have been surrounded by four walls. Futuristic New York City was envisioned as a prison in John Carpenter's *Escape from New York* (1981). A similar premise was explored earlier in 1973's *Terminal Island,* which was set in a futuristic coed penal colony off the coast of California. An entire planet was used as a prison in 1985's *Space Rage*. Women prison pictures date back to 1931, although 1950's *Caged* remains the best remembered. However, its most disturbing scene (a prisoner gets her head shaved) seems tame by today's standards. Since Jonathan Demme's drive-in feature *Caged Heat* earned critical cudos in 1974, exploitative "women in prison" films have proliferated. Linda Blair was lusted after by both fellow female inmates and male guards in *Chained Heat* (1983) after being sexually assaulted with a broom handle in the 1974 made-for-TV film *Born Innocent.* Other women prison movies include *The Weak and the Wicked* (1953), *School for Unclaimed Girls* (1969), *The Concrete Jungle* (1982) and *Reform School Girls* (1986). Although most inmates have concentrated solely on escaping from prison, Peter Sellers was concerned with how to break out and then back into one in the 1960 comedy *Two Way Stretch*. Convict Noel Coward led a luxurious prison life—and even masterminded elaborate crimes—in 1969's *The Italian Job*. See also **Penitentiary Series.**

The Big House (1930)	*San Quentin* (1946)
Ladies of the Big House (1931)	*Brute Force* (1947)
The Criminal Code (1931)	*White Heat* (1949)
The Last Mile (1932)	*Caged* (1950)
Hold 'Em Jail (1932)	*Inside the Walls of Folsom*
20,000 Years in Sing-Sing	*Prison* (1951)
(1933)	*Hellgate* (1952)
Ladies They Talk About (1933)	*The Weak and the Wicked*
San Quentin (1937)	(1953)
Alcatraz Island (1937)	*Riot in Cell Block Eleven* (1954)
King of Alcatraz (1938)	*The Steel Cage* (1954)
Blackwell's Island (1939)	*Duffy of San Quentin* (1954)
The Big Guy (1939)	*Betrayed Women* (1955)
Castle on the Hudson (aka	*Cell 2455, Death Row* (1955)
Years Without Days) (1940)	*Women's Prison* (1955)

Gang Busters (1955)
Hold Back Tomorrow (1955)
Unchained (1955)
Behind the High Wall (1956)
Girls in Prison (1956)
Jailhouse Rock (1957)
Escape from San Quentin (1957)
The Last Mile (1958)
Two Way Stretch (1960)
Birdman of Alcatraz (1962)
The Concrete Jungle (1962)
Convicts Four (aka Reprieve) (1962)
House of Women (1962)
The Hill (1965)
Cool Hand Luke (1967)
99 Women (1969)
School for Unclaimed Girls (aka The Smashing Birds I Used to Know; House of Unclaimed Women) (1969)
Riot (1969)
Breakout (1970)
There Was a Crooked Man (1970)
The Glass House (aka Truman Capote's The Glass House) (1972 TVM)
The Hot Box (1972)
Sweet Sugar (aka Chaingang Girls) (1972)
Papillon (1973)
Caged Heat (aka Renegade Girls) (1974)
Terminal Island (1973)
Breakout (1975)
Short Eyes (aka Slammer) (1977)

Kill Me If You Can (1977 TVM)
Midnight Express (1978)
Escape from Alcatraz (1979)
Penitentiary (1979)
Alcatraz: The Whole Shocking Story (1980 TVM)
Attica (1980 TVM)
Brubaker (1980)
Stir Crazy (1980)
Inmates: A Love Story (1981 TVM)
Escape from New York (1981)
The Concrete Jungle (1982)
Love Child (1982)
Dangerous Company (1982 TVM)
Bad Boys (1983)
Women of San Quentin (1983 TVM)
Chained Heat (1983)
Jacobo Timerman: Prisoner Without a Name, Cell Without a Number (aka Prisoner Without a Name, Cell Without a Number) (1983 TVM)
Beyond the Walls (1984)
Mrs. Soffel (1984)
Kiss of the Spider Woman (1985)
Space Rage (1985)
Star Slammer: The Escape (aka Prison Ship) (1986)
Vendetta (1986)
The Naked Cage (1986)
Reform School Girls (1986)
Prison for Children (1987 TVM)
Weeds (1987)
Prison (1988)
Lock Up (1989)

Psychiatrists

Sympathetic, homicidal, crazy—psychiatrists (and the occasional psychologist) have run the gamut of screen characters. Michael Caine played a murderous shrink in desperate need of psychiatric help himself in *Dressed to Kill*. Surprisingly, women psychiatrists have proven even more adept at murder. Psychology professor Loretta Young accidentally killed a student and then covered up her crime in 1949's *The Accused*. Manipulated psychiatrist Lindsay Crouse went over the edge in the final scene of *House of Games* (1987) and unexpectedly shot Joe Mantegna. In Hitchcock's *Spellbound,* Gregory Peck played an amnesiac who *thought* he was a prominent psychiatrist. Dan Aykroyd was a patient masquerading as a radio talk show psychiatrist in *The Couch Trip.* The world's most famous psychiatrist, Sigmund Freud, had his life chronicled in 1962's *Freud* (with Montgomery Clift in the lead role). Alan Arkin played Freud to Nicol Williamson's Sherlock Holmes in the stylish 1976 adaptation of Nicholas Meyers' *The Seven-Per-Cent Solution.* And Alec Guinness took his turn as Freud, having imaginary conversations with contemporary psychiatrist Dudley Moore in *Lovesick.* Fred Astaire made a most unlikely psychiatrist in the Astaire-Rogers musical *Carefree.* Brian Cox played the cinema's creepiest psychologist in 1986's *Manhunter,* as a criminal mastermind who communicates with a serial killer from his prison cell. John Vernon had the best line as a psychiatrist in 1982's *Airplane II: The Sequel.* When a lawyer asked him to give his impression of the defendant, he replied: "I'm sorry, I don't do impressions. My expertise is in psychiatry." See also **Hypnosis; Multiple Personalities.**

Carefree (1938)
The Cat People (1942)
Lady in a Jam (1942)
She Wouldn't Say Yes (1945)
The Dark Past (1948)
The Accused (1949)
The Astonished Heart (1950)
Bedtime for Bonzo (1951)
Teresa (1951)
Sleeping Tiger (1954)
The Cobweb (1955)
Three Faces of Eve (1957)
The Undead (1957)
Oh Men! Oh Women! (1957)
Stop Me Before I Kill! (aka *The Full Treatment*) (1961)
Mix Me a Person (1961)
The Couch (1962)
Pressure Point (1962)
Freud (1962)
David and Lisa (1962)
Tender Is the Night (1962)
Captain Newman, M.D. (1963)
Blindfold (1965)
Three on a Couch (1966)
The President's Analyst (1967)
The Impossible Years (1968)
Coming Apart (1969)
Dial Hot Line (1969)
The Psychiatrist: God Bless the Children (aka *Children of the Lotus Eater*) (1970 TVM)
They Might Be Giants (1971)
Klute (1971)
Dark Places (1972)
Diagnosis: Murder (1975)
One Flew Over the Cuckoo's Nest (1975)
The Seven-Per-Cent Solution (1976)
Sybil (1976 TVM)
Face to Face (1976)
Equus (1977)
High Anxiety (1977)
Dressed to Kill (1980)
Simon (1980)
Ordinary People (1980)
Phobia (1980)
Zelig (1983)
Lovesick (1983)
Private Sessions (1985 TVM)
Manhunter (1986)
Beyond Therapy (1987)
A Different Affair (1987 TVM)
House of Games (1987)
The Couch Trip (1988)
Jack's Back (1988)
The Dream Team (1989)

Psycho

In François Truffaut's 1967 interview book *Hitchcock,* Hitch offered this explanation for making *Psycho:* "I think that the thing that appealed to me and made me decide to do the picture was the suddenness of the murder in the shower, coming, as it were, out of the blue. That was about all." Shot on a backlot with Hitchcock's TV series crew, *Psycho* was a clever shocker about meek hotel owner Norman Bates (Anthony Perkins), who periodically assumed his dead mother's identity and became a jealous murderess. This inexpensive picture made its famed director a wealthy man and eventually became Hitch's best-known film to a generation of baby boomers. Yet, even when his film career began to decline after failures like *Torn Curtain* (1966) and *Topaz* (1969), Hitchcock resisted a *Psycho* sequel. Yet, just three years after Hitchcock's death, the inevitable *Psycho II* was released. In an attempt to out-twist its predecessor, this sequel revealed that, despite dual personalities, alleged murderer Norman Bates (Perkins) was not as mad as most people thought. Perkins directed and starred in the 1986 follow-up *Psycho III,* which proved to be an uneasy mixture of dark humor and studio-inserted gore. The 1987 TV-movie *Bates Motel* strove for a lighter touch, but failed to find one. It starred Bud Cort (Harold in *Harold and Maude*) as a former mental patient who inherited the motel from fellow ex-inmate Norman Bates.

Psycho (1960)	*Psycho III* (1986)
Psycho II (1983)	*Bates Motel* (1987 TVM)

Puppets

Puppetry, as the sole means of telling a story, has garnered little interest in the cinema. Except for Jirí Trnka's *A Midsummer Night's Dream* (1958), most all-puppet features have been aimed strictly at juveniles. Early efforts, such as *Willy McBean and His Magic Machine* (1965) and *Mad Monster Party* (1967), were viewed as low-cost alternatives to animation. The James Bond-style 1966 British TV puppet series *Thunderbirds* attracted a more sophisticated audience. It inspired two theatrical features, *Thunderbirds Are Go* (1966) and *Thunderbird 6* (1968). American puppeteer Jim Henson hit boxoffice gold in the early 1980s with three movies using characters from his television series "The Muppet Show" (q.v.). However, his elaborate 1983 non–Muppet, puppet fantasy *The Dark Crystal* baffled Miss Piggy fans and was only modestly successful. Charming puppet sequences have graced a handful of films, most notably the Cary Grant/Katharine Hepburn romantic comedy *Holiday* (1938) and the family musicals *The Sound of Music* (1965) and *Lilli* (1953). In the latter film, Leslie Caron sang "Hi Lilli, Hi Lo" with a quartet of puppets and later danced a semi-ballet with life-size puppet replicas. In the 1931 Marx

Brothers comedy *Monkey Business,* Harpo pretended to be a puppet. A
good fairy transformed a puppet-boy into a real boy in Disney's classic
Pinocchio (1940). The TV-movie *Special People* (1984) told the true-life
story of a puppet troupe composed of mentally handicapped young people. Master mime Marcel Marceau played a puppeteer who could revive
the dead in the disturbing 1974 fantasy *Shanks.* Murderous puppeteers
have appeared in *The Falcon Strikes Back* (1943) and *Bluebeard* (1944). A
crazy scientist reduced humans to puppet size in schlockmeister Bert I.
Gordon's *Attack of the Puppet People* (1958). See also **The Muppets.**

Monkey Business (1931)	*The Sound of Music* (1965)
Pinocchio (1940)	*Willy McBean and His Magic*
The Falcon Strikes Back (1943)	*Machine* (1965)
Bluebeard (1944)	*Thunderbirds Are Go* (1966)
The Forbidden Street (aka	*Mad Monster Party?* (1967)
Britannia Mews) (1948)	*Thunderbird 6* (1968)
Lilli (1953)	*Shanks* (1974)
A Midsummer Night's Dream	*Side Show* (1981 TVM)
(1951)	*The Dark Crystal* (1983)
Attack of the Puppet People	*Special People* (1984 TVM)
(1958)	*Puppet Master* (1988)

Quatermass, Professor

The intrepid, brilliant, sometimes eccentric scientist Bernard Quatermass
made his initial appearance on TV in Nigel Kneale's 1954 three-hour BBC
serial *The Quatermass Experiment.* The program, about an astronaut who
returns to Earth and evolves into a "vegetable monster," was phenom-
enally successful. A big-screen version was naturally in order and it came
in 1955, courtesy of a struggling studio called Hammer Films. Hammer
promptly replaced Reginald Tate, TV's Quatermass, with American Brian
Donlevy—the biggest star it could afford—and dubbed the film *The
Creeping Unknown* for its American showings. Despite Donlevy's
lackluster performance, the movie was a hit and a sequel *Enemy from
Space* (aka *Quatermass II*) was released in 1957. It was also based on a
Kneale TV serial and Donlevy again ousted the small-screen lead (John
Robinson). A ten-year hiatus followed, before Hammer revived the series
in grand fashion with 1967's *Five Million Years to Earth* (aka *Quatermass
and the Pit*). A unique blend of science fiction and gothic horror, it
boasted a fine lead performance by Scottish actor Andrew Keir and an ingenious premise ("Gentlemen," announces Quatermass emphatically, "we
are the Martians."). Quatermass' next and final appearance was in the
1979 serial *Quatermass.* Distinguished actor John Mills took his turn as
Quatermass, whose demise at the end of the film signalled an end to the
series. This 200-minute TV miniseries was trimmed to 107 minutes and
given a limited theatrical release as *The Quatermass Conclusion.*

The Creeping Unknown (aka *The Quatermass Experiment; The
   Quatermass Xperiment*) (1955)
Enemy from Space (aka *Quatermass II*) (1957)
Five Million Years to Earth (aka *Quatermass and the Pit*) (1967)
The Quatermass Conclusion (aka *Quatermass*) (1979)

Queen, Ellery

A unique literary creation, Ellery Queen is famous as both a fictional
detective and a best-selling "author" (as a pseudonym for cousins Frederic
Dannay and Manfred B. Lee). His film career, however, has been an un-
equivocal disaster. Donald Cook made an uninspired Queen in 1935's *The
Spanish Cape Mystery*. A year later, he was followed by comedian Eddie
Quillan in *The Mandarin Mystery*. Columbia launched an official series in
1940 by casting Ralph Bellamy as *Ellery Queen, Master Detective*. Charley
Grapewin played Ellery's police inspector father, Richard Queen. These
movies relied heavily on comic relief and Bellamy's clumsy detective
resembled the literary Queen in name only. After four mysteries, sturdy
William Gargan replaced Bellamy for three additional films. In the 1950s,
four actors played Queen on television. Richard Hart was Ellery in 1950's
"The Adventures of Ellery Queen." He died in 1951 and was replaced by
Lee Bowman until the series was cancelled in 1952. In 1954, Hugh
Marlowe starred in a syndicated TV series also titled "The Adventures of
Ellery Queen" (aka "Mystery Is My Business"). George Nader popped up
as Queen in a 1958–59 series called "The Further Adventures of Ellery
Queen" (aka "Ellery Queen"). Peter Lawford made the screen's worst
Queen in the 1971 TV-movie *Ellery Queen: Don't Look Behind You,*
while Jim Hutton and David Wayne played Ellery and Inspector Queen,
respectively, in another made-for-TV mystery, 1975's *Ellery Queen* (aka
Too Many Suspects). Hutton's film evolved into an entertaining weekly
series that lasted a year. Queen's story "Ten Days Wonder" (which did not
feature Queen the detective) was made into a 1972 film starring Orson
Welles and Anthony Perkins.

The Spanish Cape Mystery (1935) (Cook)
The Mandarin Mystery (1936) (Quillan)
Ellery Queen, Master Detective (1940) (Bellamy)
Ellery Queen and the Murder Ring (1941) (Bellamy)
Ellery Queen and the Perfect Crime (1941) (Bellamy)
Ellery Queen's Penthouse Mystery (1941) (Bellamy)
A Close Call for Ellery Queen (1942) (Gargan)
Enemy Agents Meet Ellery Queen (1942) (Gargan)
A Desperate Chance for Ellery Queen (1942) (Gargan)
Ellery Queen: Don't Look Behind You (1971 TVM) (Lawford)
Ellery Queen (aka *Too Many Suspects*) (1975 TVM) (Hutton)

Rabbits

Despite their ability to reproduce in massive numbers, bunnies have been pretty scarce in the cinema. The Disney children's classic *Bambi* made a star out of Thumper the rabbit. Another animated feature, 1978's *Watership Down*, offered a literary fable about a warren of rabbits seeking a new home. Bugs Bunny, the cinema's only Oscar-winning rabbit, has a few theatrical cartoon compilations (q.v.) to his name. And, naturally, one must not forget James Stewart's six-foot, invisible rabbit chum in *Harvey*. A 1965 spy spoof called *The Nasty Rabbit* featured the unforgettable song "The Jackrabbit Shuffle." The picture's plot revolved around virus-carrying rabbits. Still, they were bunnies without malice, unlike the nasty ones—standing four feet tall and weighing 150 pounds—that terrorized Janet Leigh in 1972's *Night of the Lepus* (surely a movie she'd like to forget). *Rabbit Run*, *The Rabbit Trap*, *Bunny Lake Is Missing*, and *Bunny O'Hare* were rabbit films in name only. Ditto for *A Bunny's Tale*, which was about Gloria Steinem's undercover stint as a Playboy bunny.

Alice in Wonderland (1933)	*Night of the Lepus* (1972)
The Rules of the Game (1939)	*Monty Python and the Holy*
Bambi (1942)	*Grail* (1974)
Song of the South (with Brer	*The Bugs Bunny/Roadrunner*
Rabbit) (1946)	*Movie* (1979)
Harvey (1950)	*Watership Down* (1978)
Alice in Wonderland (1951)	*The Adventures of the Ameri-*
The Nasty Rabbit (aka *Spies a*	*can Rabbit* (1986)
Go Go) (1965)	*Jean de Florette* (1986)
Get to Know Your Rabbit	*Who Framed Roger Rabbit?*
(1972)	(1988)

Racing *see* Auto Racing; Horse Racing

Radio

During the Great Depression, movies ranked as the second most popular form of entertainment—with radio firmly entrenched in the number one position. Surprisingly, the film industry promoted its rival, with dozens of films set behind the scenes of radio programs. Many of these films were built around the era's big radio singing stars, such as Dick Powell in *Twenty Million Sweethearts* (1934) and Bing Crosby in the series-inspiring *The Big Broadcast* (1932). On the dramatic side, *Two Against the World* (1936) starred Humphrey Bogart as a moralistic radio station manager. Mystery radio shows provided the background for real murders in the Abbott and Costello comedy *Who Done It?* (1942) and the Claude Rains vehicle *The Unsuspected* (1947). Few films have been principally about radio stations. Paul Newman played a drifter-turned-d.j. who gains fame broadcasting on the right-wing radio station *WUSA* (1970). A rock station's management rebelled against its uptight parent company in the 1978 satire *FM*, which laid the groundwork for the broader 1978–82 TV sitcom "WKRP in Cincinnati." Disc jockeys have appeared as principal characters in the guise of Clint Eastwood *(Play Misty for Me)*, Adrienne Barbeau *(The Fog)*, Wolfman Jack *(American Graffiti)*, Bill Paterson *(Comfort and Joy)*, Robin Williams *(Good Morning, Vietnam)*, and Tim McIntire *(American Hot Wax)*. The latter two movies chronicled the lives of real-life d.j.'s Adrian Cronauer and rock 'n' roll legend Alan Freed. Oliver Stone's *Talk Radio* (1988) was practically a one-man show about a controversial radio talk show host, but it was not the first film on the subject. Call-in radio programs were integral to the plots of Jack Nicholson's *The King of Marvin Gardens* (1972) and George Romero's vampire chiller *Martin* (1978). Of course, not all radio broadcasts have originated from Earth. *Orpheus* (1949) and *Christine* (1983) both featured cars equipped with radios that picked up otherworldly signals. Celestial broadcasts were the subject of *Red Planet Mars* (1952) and *The Next Voice You Hear* (1950), which co-starred Nancy Davis Reagan. Both these films conveyed optimistic religious messages, although their heavyhanded approach limited their showings. Radio's subtler influence on its listening audience was explored in *Music Hath Charms* (1935) and Woody Allen's *Radio Days* (1987). The former film showed how a dance band's music played different roles in the lives of those listening to it. In contrast, radio's ability to incite hysteria was powerfully displayed in 1975's *The Night That Panicked America*, a fact-based drama about Orson Welles' 1938 "War of the Worlds" broadcast.

The Big Broadcast (1932)
Death at Broadcasting House (1934)
Music Hath Charms (1935)
Two Against the World (aka *One Fatal Hour; The Case of Mrs. Pembroke*) (1936)
Love Is on the Air (1937)
The Great American Broadcast (1940)
Wake Up and Live (1942)
Who Done It? (1942)
I'll Tell the World (1945)
Where There's Life (1947)
The Unsuspected (1947)
Orpheus (1949)
The Next Voice You Hear (1950)
Red Planet Mars (1952)

WUSA (1970)
Play Misty for Me (1971)
The King of Marvin Gardens (1972)
The Night That Panicked America (1975 TVM)
American Hot Wax (1978)
FM (1978)
Martin (1978)
On the Air Live with Captain Midnight (aka *Captain Midnight*) (1979)
Radio On (1979)
The Fog (1980)
Christine (1983)
Comfort and Joy (1984)
Radio Days (1987)
Good Morning, Vietnam (1987)
Talk Radio (1988)

Rambo

Rambo named after a poet? University of Iowa professor David Morrell, who created one-man-army John Rambo in his novel *First Blood,* claims that he derived his hero's name from 19th century symbolist poet Arthur Rimbaud. But when Morrell sold the film rights to his book for $90,000, it's doubtful if he envisioned bare-chested, muscle-rippling Sylvester Stallone as his character. Stallone, though, was anxious to break away from his *Rocky* image when he was offered the chance to do *First Blood.* The 1982 film introduced Rambo as a misunderstood drifter, a former Green Beret, who runs afoul of a redneck sheriff in a small town. Despite substituting explosions for punches, Rambo and Rocky are very much alike — two underdogs fighting apparently insurmountable odds to make a point. The picture proved to be Stallone's first non–*Rocky* hit. His 1985 sequel, *Rambo: First Blood Part II,* sent its hunky hero into Cambodia in search of POWs. Stallone brilliantly capitalized on a new wave of patriotism and the sequel's grosses went through the roof. Again, the actor portrayed Rambo as a soldier betrayed at every turn and yet still patriotic to his country. That tone changed with 1988's *Rambo III,* which paired Rambo with his trusty ex-commander (Richard Crenna) and made him less of a loner fighting the establishment. The public noticed the difference. It made a lot of quick cash, but failed to follow the profitable path of its predecessors.

First Blood (1982)	(1985)
Rambo: First Blood Part II	*Rambo III* (1988)

The Range Busters

Monogram Pictures launched this low-budget Western series in an effort to duplicate rival Republic's successful Three Mesquiteers (q.v.) films. John "Dusty" King joined former Mesquiteers Ray "Crash" Corrigan and Max Terhune to form Monogram's cowboy trio. Their adventures followed the Mesquiteers closely, even to the point of mixing Old West stories with contemporary adventures (e.g. the boys clashed with Nazis in 1943's *Cowboy Commandos* and Japanese in *Texas to Bataan*). A more interesting series might have focused on the stars' varied backgrounds: Corrigan was a stunt daredevil, Terhune a former ventriloquist, and King a band vocalist.

The Range Busters (1940)	*Saddle Mountain Roundup*
Trailing Double Trouble (1940)	(1941)
West of Pinto Basin (1940)	*Tonto Basin Outlaws* (1941)
Trail of the Silver Spurs (1941)	*Underground Rustlers* (1941)
The Kid's Last Ride (1941)	*Thunder River Feud* (1942)
Tumbledown Ranch in Arizona	*Boot Hill Bandits* (1942)
(1941)	*Texas Trouble Shooters* (1942)
Wrangler's Roost (1941)	*Texas to Bataan* (1942)
Fugitive Valley (1941)	*Trail Riders* (1942)

Two Fisted Justice (1943)   *Cowboy Commandos* (1943)
The Haunted Ranch (1943)   *Black Market Business* (1943)
Land of Hunted Men (1943)   *Bullets and Saddles* (1943)

Rats *see* Rodents

Reincarnation

The definitive film on this intriguing subject has yet to be made. In the past, reincarnation has been chiefly employed in comedies and low-budget efforts which emphasized its sensationalistic values. The best known of these latter films was 1956's *The Search for Bridey Murphy,* an adaptation of Morey Bernstein's allegedly fact-based best-seller about a housewife who reveals under hypnosis that she led another life 200 years earlier. This dreary, uninvolving tale captured the public's fancy and imitations followed in rapid succession. *Spell of the Hypnotist* (1956), Roger Corman's *The Undead* (1957), and the Bowery Boys' *Hold That Hypnotist* (1957) all concerned people who learned of previous existences through hypnotism. Corman's movie, shot in a refurbished supermarket, was the best of the bunch, mixing witch trials and time travel elements with its reincarnation plot. Hypnotism also played a prominent role in the only reincarnation musical comedy, Barbra Streisand's *On a Clear Day You Can See Forever.* Finally, no discussion on celebrity reincarnation would be complete without mentioning Shirley MacLaine, who espoused her beliefs in *Out on a Limb,* a TV-movie based on her autobiographical bestseller. See also **The Mummy.**

She (1935)   *She* (1965)
Corridor of Mirrors (1948)   *On a Clear Day You Can See*
You Never Can Tell (1951)   *Forever* (1970)
The Search for Bridey Murphy   *The Reincarnation of Peter*
   (1956)   *Proud* (1975)
I've Lived Before (1956)   *Audrey Rose* (1977)
Hold That Hypnotist (1957)   *Oh, Heavenly Dog!* (1980)
The She Creature (1957)   *All of Me* (1984)
Spell of the Hypnotist (1957)   *Deja Vu* (1985)
The Undead (1957)   *Out on a Limb* (1987 TVM)
Goodbye, Charlie (1964)   *Chances Are* (1989)

Remakes of Foreign Films

The problems inherent in remaking foreign films into English-language pictures have both intrigued and frustrated filmmakers. No rule of thumb has met with steady success. John Sturges translated Akiro Kurosawa's classic *The Seven Samurai* (1954) into the enduringly popular American Western *The Magnificent Seven* (1960). Likewise, Italian "spaghetti-Western" king Sergio Leone also exploited the samurai/Western link and turned Kurosawa's *Yojimbo* (1961) into Clint Eastwood's breakthrough film, *A Fistful of Dollars* (1964). But Martin Ritt's *The Outrage* (1964), a philosophical Western remake of Kurosawa's *Rashomon* (1951), missed the tone of the Japanese original and bored audiences and critics equally. Although Kurosawa's films have been popular targets for remakes, American and British filmmakers have shown a special fondness for the French cinema. Julien Duvivier's *Pepe Le Moko* (1937) was remade as *Algiers* just a year after its release. The remake incorporated the same setting and plot and even cast a Frenchman in the lead — Charles Boyer as the charming gangster originally created by Jean Gabin. French thrillers from the 1940s and 1950s have been turned into little films *(Midnight Episode)* and costly bombs *(Sorcerer)*. The popularity of French light comedies in the 1970s and 1980s inspired a slew of Americanized versions. Most of these state-side remakes compared poorly with their continental counterparts and fizzled at the boxoffice. Big name stars did not help either. Walter Matthau and Jack Lemmon looked out of place in *Buddy, Buddy* (1981), while Richard Pryor floundered in *The Toy* (1982). However, the surprise successes of 1986's *Down and Out in Beverly Hills,* 1987's *Three Men and a Baby* and, to a lesser degree, 1989's *Cousins,* have ensured that the French cinema will continue to be raided for remake properties. Interestingly, not all remakes have gone the direct route of foreign film into English-language film. Bergman's *Smiles of a Summer Night* (1955) and Fellini's *Nights of Cabiria* (1957) stopped at Broadway long enough to be transformed into the hit musicals *A Little Night Music* and *Sweet Charity.* Thus, the film versions of these musicals are indirect remakes of the original movies. Along similar lines, one could argue that Fritz Lang's *Human Desire* (1954) was based solely on Emile Zola's novel *La Bête Humaine* and not on Jean Renoir's 1938 adaptation of Zola's book. Occasionally, this question of whether a film is or is not a remake becomes a matter of opinion. Many critics consider Curtis Harrington's *Games* (1967) a remake of Clouzot's *Les Diaboliques,* although the films differ substantially in setting and premise (perhaps, it's more a variation than a remake). Likewise, Claude LeLouch's *Another Man, Another Chance* (1977) is often listed as a Western remake of his own contemporary romance *A Man and a Woman* (1966) since the plots of both films are about a widow and widower falling in love. That's a pretty common plot, allowing one to argue that 1968's *With Six You Get Eggroll* was an earlier remake of Lelouch's original. Occasionally, foreign countries have remade American films, as in the case of 1957's *The Burglar* and 1971's *La Casse* (aka *The Burglars*). In the following list, the remakes are listed chronologically on the left with the original films shown on the right.

Port of Seven Seas (1938)	*Fanny* (1932)
Algiers (1938)	*Pepe Le Moko* (1937)
Scarlet Street (1945)	*La Chienne* (1931)

The Unfinished Dance (1947)	*Ballerina* (1938)
The Long Night (1947)	*Le Jour se Leve* (aka *Daybreak*) (1939)
Midnight Episode (1951)	*Monsieur le Souris* (aka *Midnight in Paris*) (1947)
The Thirteenth Letter (1951)	*Le Corbeau* (aka *The Raven*) (1948)
Human Desire (1954)	*Le Bête Humaine* (aka *The Human Beast; Judas Was a Woman*) (1938)
The Magnificent Seven (1960)	*The Seven Samurai* (aka *Shichinin no Samurai*) (1954)
The Outrage (1964)	*Rashomon* (1951)
A Fistful of Dollars (1964)	*Yojimbo* (1961)
Games (1967)	*Les Diaboliques* (aka *Diabolique*) (1955)
Cop-Out (1968)	*Les Inconnus dans la Maison* (aka *Strangers in the House*) (1949)
Sweet Charity (1969)	*Nights of Cabiria* (aka *Le Notti di Cabiria*) (1957)
Another Man, Another Chance (1977)	*A Man and a Woman* (aka *Un Homme et une Femme*) (1966)
Sorcerer (1977)	*The Wages of Fear* (aka *La Salaire de la Peur*) (1953)
Which Way Is Up? (1977)	*The Seduction of Mimi* (aka *Mimi Metallurgico Ferita nell'Onore*) (1974)
A Little Night Music (1978)	*Smiles of a Summer Night* (aka *Sommarnattens Leende*) (1955)
Dear Detective (1979 TVM)	*Dear Detective* (aka *Tendre Poulet; Dear Inspector*) (1978)
Willie and Phil (1980)	*Jules and Jim* (aka *Jules et Jim*) (1961)
Buddy, Buddy (1981)	*A Pain in the A--* (aka *L'Emmerdeur*) (1974)
Kiss Me Goodbye (1982)	*Dona Flor and Her Two Husbands* (aka *Dona Flor e Seurs Dois Maridos*) (1977)
The Toy (1982)	*Le Jouet* (1976)
Breathless (1983)	*A Bout de Souffle* (aka *Breathless*) (1960)
The Lost Honor of Kathryn Beck (aka *Act of Passion*) (1984 TVM)	*The Lost Honor of Katharina Blum* (aka *Die Verlorene Ehre der Katharina Blum*) (1975)

Crackers (1984)	*Big Deal on Madonna Street* (1958)
The Woman in Red (1984)	*Pardon Mon Affaire* (aka *Un Elephant ça Troupe Enormement*) (1976)
Happy New Year (1987)	*Happy New Year* (aka *La Nonne Année; The Happy New Year Caper*) (1973)
Down and Out in Beverly Hills (1986)	*Boudu Saved from Drowning* (aka *Boudu Sauvé des Eaux* (1932)
Three Men and a Baby (1987)	*Three Men and a Cradle* (aka *Trois Hommes et un Couffin*) (1985)
Three Fugitives (1989)	*Les Fugitifs* (1986)
Cousins (1989)	*Cousin, Cousine* (1975)
Baby Cakes (1989 TVM)	*Zuckerbaby* (aka *Sugarbaby*) (1985)

Renfrew of the Royal Mounted

Renfrew the singing Mountie had already appeared in Laurie York Erskine's books and on the radio before Monogram gave him his own film series. James Newill, a singer on the Burns and Allen radio show, played Sergeant Renfrew and always found time to sing a sturdy tune or two like "Mounted Men." Lightning the Dog accompanied him on his first trek, but Dave O'Brien became Renfrew's regular sidekick Kelly beginning with 1939's *Crashing Thru*. The plots were naturally action-oriented and somewhat lacking in plausibility (in *Sky Bandits*, the bad guys hijacked a plane carrying an experimental death ray). Newill later became one of the *Texas Rangers* (q.v.), creating the role that Tex Ritter would later play. A syndicated "Renfrew" TV series ran briefly in 1953. See also **Mounties.**

Renfrew of the Royal Mounted (1937)	*Crashing Thru* (1939)
	Fighting Mad (1939)
On the Great White Trail (aka *Renfrew of the Royal Mounted on the Great White Trail; Renfrew on the Great White Trail*) (1938)	*Danger Ahead* (1940)
	Yukon Flight (1940)
	Murder on the Yukon (1940)
	The Sky Bandits (1940)

Revere, Johnny

John Paul (Johnny) Revere was another sturdy Western hero in the typical Republic Pictures mold. Eddie Dew played him in the first two films, getting comic support from Gene Autry's usual sidekick Smiley Burnette. Robert Mitchum played a bit part in 1943's *Beyond the Last Frontier*, but Dew's second entry, *Raiders of Sunset Pass*, was much more interesting. A sort of feminist Western, it pitted a group of tough ladies (dubbed the Women's Army of the Plains, or WAPs) against some male rustlers during World War II. Western series veteran Bob Livingston (see **Lone Rider; Three Mesquiteers**) replaced Dew in the final two entries.

    Beyond the Last Frontier (1943)   *Pride of the Plains* (1944)
    Raiders of Sunset Pass (1943)   *Beneath Western Skies* (1944)

Riley, Old Mother

Donning a gray wig, a frumpy dress, and a plaid-colored shaw, British comedian Arthur Lucan transformed himself into Old Mother Riley, a spunky Irish washerwoman, in 14 features between 1937 and 1952. Katie MacShane, Lucan's wife, played Old Mother Riley's daughter. The two had created the characters in a vaudeville sketch called "Bridget's Night Out." Despite their popularity in Britain, the movies never caught on in the U.S., although 1952's *My Son, the Vampire* (aka *Old Mother Riley Meets the Vampire*) finally showed up on American screens in 1963. By then, Lucan had been dead for nine years and co-star Bela Lugosi for seven.

    Old Mother Riley (1937)
    Old Mother Riley in Paris (1938)
    Old Mother Riley in Business (1939)
    Old Mother Riley MP (1939)
    Old Mother Riley's Ghosts (1940)
    Old Mother Riley's Circus (1941)
    Old Mother Riley in Society (1942)
    Old Mother Riley Detective (1943)
    Old Mother Riley at Home (1944)
    Old Mother Riley Headmistress (1945)
    Old Mother Riley's New Venture (1947)
    Old Mother Riley's Jungle Treasure (1949)
    My Son, the Vampire (aka *Old Mother Riley Meets the Vampire; Vampires Over London*) (1952)

Road Movies

The Road to Singapore (1940) was originally written for George Burns and Gracie Allen. When they turned it down, it was revamped as a "buddy comedy" for Fred MacMurray and Jack Oakie. But prior commitments kept MacMurray and Oakie tied up, so Paramount—in a stroke of casting magic—paired Bing Crosby and Bob Hope for their musical comedy debut. Their initial *Road* picture *(Singapore)* was a huge success, but, when seen today, it clearly lacks the wacky humor that made the series memorable. Everyone has their favorite *Road* picture, but it's hard to top the bizarre Alaskan outing, *Road to Utopia*—which featured animated fish, the Paramount mountain, and the only ending in which Bob got the girl (well, sort of). Dorothy Lamour co-starred in all but *Hong Kong,* in which she made only a cameo appearance, leaving the female lead to a young Joan Collins.

Road to Singapore (1940)	*Road to Rio* (1947)
Road to Zanzibar (1941)	*Road to Bali* (1952)
Road to Morocco (1942)	*Road to Hong Kong* (1962)
Road to Utopia (1945)	

Robin Hood *see* Hood, Robin

Robots

For purposes of categorization, robots are defined as machines requiring guidance to function *and* which look distinctively different from humans. Human-like machines capable of independent thought are discussed under the **Androids and Cyborgs** entry. Although it is a difficult distinction to draw, there are obvious differences between *Forbidden Planet's* Robbie the Robot and the androids played by Rutger Hauer and Daryl Hannah in *Blade Runner*. The robot's origin in film can be traced back to early silent films like *The Electric Servant* (1909). Yet, while the Golem thrived in the early 1920s and the Frankenstein Monster ruled in the 1930s, robots were restricted to sporadic appearances in serials such as *The Phantom Empire* and *The Undersea Kingdom*. The robot's relative anonymity finally ended with 1951's *The Day the Earth Stood Still*. This superior science fiction saga worked on many levels, but remains fondly remembered for introducing the first robot "star": Gort. Standing 12 feet tall with no facial features nor visible joints, Gort was a rather imposing "mechanical man," especially when he opened his visor and unleashed his disintegration ray on a helpless tank. Gort could not talk, however, and that certainly placed some constraints on his personality. MGM corrected that quirk with its contribution to the robotic race, the ever-helpful — and talking — Robby the Robot. After his popular debut in 1956's *Forbidden Planet*, Robby turned up again in a larger role in *The Invisible Boy* (1957), in which a computer temporarily converted him to evil. Robby retired after *The Invisible Boy*, although a robot bearing an amazing resemblance to him later joined the cast of TV's 1965–68 "Lost in Space" series. No other robotic stars emerged until 1977, when George Lucas' *Star Wars* introduced that charismatic robotic pair: C3PO and R2D2. Their skyrocketing popularity, especially among the young set, revitalized interest in robots and accounted for their major supporting roles in films like *The Black Hole* and *Buck Rogers in the 25th Century* (both 1979). In other robot films of interest: The robot "drones" Huey and Dewey in 1972's *Silent Running* appear to be the forerunners to R2D2's design. Lightning struck a meek little robot, No. 5, and brought him "alive" in *Short Circuit* (1986). Both King Kong (q.v.) and Godzilla (q.v.) fought robot versions of themselves in, respectively, *King Kong Escapes* (1968) and *The Terror* *of Godzilla* (1975). *Tobor, the Great* (1954) had the catchiest robot name (spell it backwards). See also **Androids and Cyborgs; Computers.**

The Electric Servant (1909)	*Star Wars* (1977)
The Day the Earth Stood Still (1951)	*Buck Rogers in the 25th Century* (1979)
Robot Monster (1953)	*The Black Hole* (1979)
Gog (1954)	*C.H.O.M.P.S.* (1979)
Target Earth (1954)	*Runaway* (1984)
Tobor the Great (1954)	*Chopping Mall* (1986)
Forbidden Planet (1956)	*Short Circuit* (1986)
The Invisible Boy (1957)	*Space Camp* (1986)
Attack of the Robots (1962)	*Robot Holocaust* (1987)
King Kong Escapes (1968)	*Too Much* (1987)
Silent Running (1971)	*Short Circuit 2* (1988)
The Terror of Godzilla (1975)	

Rocky

In 1976, an unknown character actor named Sylvester Stallone wrote a script (in three-and-a-half days, reputedly) about a mediocre, small-time boxer who gets a shot at the world championship. Producers Irwin Winkler and Robert Chartoff offered Stallone $300,000 for the screenplay, but the actor held out for $75,000, a percentage of the profits, and the lead role. He got what he wanted—and the rest is history. A simple picture, *Rocky* boasted a memorable cast: Talia Shire as Rocky's shy girlfriend, Burt Young as her obnoxious, hustling brother, Burgess Meredith as Rocky's grizzled manager, and Carl Weathers as cocky heavyweight champion Apollo Creed. Rocky lost the title bout (in a split decision), but audiences loved the film's old-fashioned emotion. It went on to gross $55 million and win an Academy Award for Best Picture. Subsequently, Stallone tried his hand at other movies, but none approached the success of *Rocky.* Thus, the inevitable sequel, *Rocky II,* appeared in 1979. A rehash of the original, it had Rocky winning a rematch with Creed and almost losing his wife due to medical complications. Although it was a boxoffice smash, Stallone vowed it would be the last *Rocky* picture. Nevertheless, no one was surprised when *Rocky III* was released in 1982. Probably the cleverest film in the series, it traced Rocky's decline as a champion, capped by a humiliating defeat at the hands of ruthless Clubber Lang (Mr. T) and the death of faithful manager Meredith. Encouraged by former opponent and new-found friend Apollo Creed, Rocky recaptured that "eye of the tiger" and beat Clubber into a pulp. Again, Stallone insisted this was the last of the series, but again the boxoffice receipts led him to a different decision. The dismal *Rocky IV* followed in 1985, with Rocky avenging Creed's death at the hands of a heartless Russian "fighting machine" (Dolph Lundgren). Stallone then "retired" his character—only to announce plans for 1990's *Rocky V.* As sports fans know, boxers never retire. See also **Boxing.**

Rocky (1976)   *Rocky III* (1982)
Rocky II (1979)   *Rocky IV* (1985)

Rodan

This pterodactyl-like creature with supersonic wing speed made an il-
lustrious debut in 1956's *Rodan*. However, he never achieved the popularity of Godzilla (q.v.) or even Mothra (q.v.) and was quickly relegated to a
supporting player in the mid–1960s Japanese "monsteramas." One of the
reasons for Rodan's lesser fame might have been his weapon arsenal.
While Godzilla boasted fiery breath and Mothra a cocoon-producing fluid,
Rodan dispensed with foes (and buildings) by simply flapping his gigantic
wings.

> *Rodan* (1956)
> *Monster Zero* (aka *Invasion of the Astro-Monsters; Kaiju Daisenso*)
> (1965)
> *Ghidrah the Three-Headed Monster* (aka *The Greatest Battle on
> Earth; Sandai Kaiju Chikyu Saidai No Kessen*) (1965)
> *Destroy All Monsters* (aka *Operation Monsterland; Kaiju Soshingeki*)
> (1968)

Rodents

Rats have had an image problem in the movies, typically being pictured as
untrustworthy. There have been exceptions, of course, such as the lovable
rat family in the animated feature *The Secret of NIMH* (1982). And
technically, the people-killing rats in *Willard* (1971) and *Ben* (1972) did
not dispose of anyone who didn't deserve it. In fact, *Ben* was basically a
heartwarming story of the friendship between a boy and his rat (and, lest
we forget, this film featured Michael Jackson's popular hit "Ben"). Giant
rats have populated horror films such as *Food of the Gods* (1976) and
Deadly Eyes (1982). Sondra Locke's *Ratboy* (1986) was a sympathetic film
about a disfigured boy who resembled a rat, while the Russian import *The
Redeemer* (1977) was about rat people disguising themselves in order to
infiltrate the human race. Chuck Norris killed a rat with his teeth in *Missing in Action 2* (1985), while people have tramped through rat-infested
chambers in *Inferno* (1978) and *Indiana Jones and Last Crusade* (1989).
On the other hand, mice on film have been portrayed as cute, charming
creatures, especially in animated form. Thoughtful mice helped Cinderella
get ready for the ball in Disney's 1951 version of the fairy tale. Adven-
turous mice formed The Mouse Rescue Aid Society in *The Rescuers* (1977).
A sleuthing mouse resembling Sherlock Holmes matched wits with a
devious rat (Professor Ratigan) in 1986's *The Great Mouse Detective*.
Finally, one of the biggest holiday hits of 1986, *An American Tail,* concerned the plight of two immigrant mice children in turn-of-the-century
New York City.

Cinderella (1950)
Lady and the Tramp (1955)
The Pied Piper of Hamlin (1957 TVM)
Willard (1971)
The Rats Are Coming, the Werewolves Are Here (1972)
Ben (1972)
The Pied Piper (1972)
The Missing Are Deadly (1974 TVM)
Food of the Gods (1976)
The Mouse and His Child (1987)
The Redeemer (1977)
The Rescuers (1977)
Inferno (1978)

Rock 'n' Roll High School (1979)
Deadly Eyes (aka The Rats) (1982)
The Secret of NIMH (1982)
Of Unknown Origin (1983)
Nightmares (1983)
Missing in Action 2 – The Beginning (1985)
An American Tail (1986)
Ratboy (1986)
The Great Mouse Detective (1986)
Indiana Jones and the Last Crusade (1989)
Gnaw: Food of the Gods II (1989)

Rodeos

Few filmmakers seemed interested in the rodeo setting prior to the 1970s. A handful of "B" films, including the 3-D effort Arena, emerged in the 1950s. However, the rodeo gained more exposure through a bit part in 1956's Bus Stop, in which Don Murray played a naive rodeo star visiting the big city for the first time and struggling to understand urban conventions. Thirteen years later, The Wild Bunch, and its theme of the aging cowboy as a symbol of social change, revived interest in the contemporary cowboy. Subsequently, four features about aging rodeo stars appeared in 1972, all starring veteran performers well into their forties or older: Richard Widmark (age 58 in When the Legends Die), Cliff Robertson (47 in J.W. Coop), James Coburn (44 in The Honkers), and Steve McQueen (42 in Junior Bonner). The latter film was made by Wild Bunch director Sam Peckinpah. The plight of the younger rodeo wrangler was explored in Riding Tall, yet another 1972 release. It starred Andrew Prine as a rodeo rider coping with conventional love problems. The 1980 TV-movie Rodeo Girl was the true story of world champion rodeo star Sue Pirtle. The 1974 documentary The Great American Cowboy told the story of rodeo legend Larry Mahan.

The Cowboy and the Lady (1938)
A Lady Takes a Chance (aka The Cowboy and the Girl) (1943)
Rodeo (1952)
The Lusty Men (1952)
Bronco Buster (1952)
Arena (1953)

Bus Stop (aka The Wrong Kind of Girl) (1956)
Born Reckless (1959)
Stay Away Joe (1968)
Black Rodeo (1971)
The Honkers (1972)
Junior Bonner (1972)
J.W. Coop (1972)
When the Legends Die (1972)

Riding Tall (aka *Squares*) (1972)   *Goldenrod* (1977 TVM)
The Great American Cowboy   *Rodeo Girl* (1980 TVM)
  (1974)

Rohmer's Comedies and Proverbs

Eric Rohmer initiated this new series in 1980 after completing his "Six Moral Tales" (q.v.) and two nonseries excursions, *The Marquis of O* and *Perceval.* Although less thematically linked than the "Moral Tales," Rohmer's "Comedies and Proverbs" extended the filmmaker's views on love, loneliness, and irony. In *The Aviator's Wife* (1980), a man pining for the title character forgets her after falling for an attractive student — whom he later discovers in the arms of another man as well. In *The Perfect Marriage* (1982), a woman tries to persuade a man that she will make the perfect wife and he will make the perfect husband — only to find out the man has been engaged to another all along. As with his "Moral Tales" series, critics ignored the early entries, while heaping praise on later ones like the international hit *Pauline at the Beach* (1982), *Boyfriends and Girlfriends* (1988), and *Summer* (1986). The original title of the latter film was *Le Rayon Vert*, which actually translates as *The Green Ray*, referring to a "flash of green" seen in rare sunsets in Southern climates. Keeping with the series' theme, it opened with a proverb from Rimbaud: "Ah, let the season start/ When fancy takes the heart."

>*The Aviator's Wife* (aka *La Femme de l'Aviateur*) (1980)
>*The Perfect Marriage* (aka *Le Beau Marriage*) (1982)
>*Pauline at the Beach* (aka *Pauline à la Plage*) (1982)
>*Full Moon in Paris* (aka *Les Nuits de la Pleine Lune*) (1984)
>*Summer* (aka *Le Rayon Vert; The Green Ray*) (1986)
>*Boyfriends and Girlfriends* (aka *L'Ami de Mon Amie; My Girl-friend's Boyfriend*) (1988)

Rohmer's Moral Tales

Eric Rohmer was best known as a writer and editor for the prestigious cinema journal *Cahiers du Cinéma* when he set out to make a series of films linked by a common theme. His initial effort, the 1962 short *La Boulangère de Monceau*, established the premise for what would eventually comprise a six-film series. A young man about to commit to one woman meets a second woman who causes him to question his original choice. Rohmer expanded on that premise in 1963's hour-long *Suzanne's Profession*, but the series attracted little attention until his fourth entry, 1969's *My Night at Maud's*, garnered international raves. Rohmer completed his "Six Moral Tales" in 1972 with *Chloe in the Afternoon*. In the 1980s, he embarked on his "Comedies and Proverbs" (also referred to as "Parables") series. See also **Rohmer's Comedies and Proverbs.**

>*La Boulangère de Monceau* (1962)

Suzanne's Profession (aka *La Carrière de Suzanne*) (1963)
La Collectioneuse (1967)
My Night at Maud's (aka *Ma Nuit chez Maud*) (1969)
Claire's Knee (aka *Le Genou de Claire*) (1970)
Chloe in the Afternoon (aka *L'Amour, l'après-midi; Love in the Afternoon*) (1972)

Roller Skating / Skateboards

On the silver screen, roller skating has never enjoyed the popularity of ice skating, although trendy filmmakers have tried to capitalize on both roller derby and roller disco fads. At the height of the roller derby craze in the early 1970s, Raquel Welch donned knee pads and a helmet for her rough-and-tumble title role in *Kansas City Bomber* (1972), the saga of a derby queen. A more enlightening look at those roller skating ladies was provided in the previous year's documentary *Derby*. James Caan participated in a futuristic, and even more violent, variation of roller derby in *Rollerball* (1975). The most unlikely champion roller skater was probably Mickey Rooney, who strapped on skates for 1950's *The Fireball*. The most graceful skaters were Fred Astaire and Ginger Rogers, who performed a roller skate dance number to "Let's Call the Whole Thing Off" in 1937's *Shall We Dance*. Later dancers have naturally lacked their polish. Scott Baio and Dorothy Stratten took to the disco dance floor on roller skates in *Skatetown, U.S.A.*, as did Linda Blair in *Roller Boogie* (1979). Mercifully, both movies slid out of theaters in no time. More interesting uses of roller skates can be found in *Return to Oz* (1985) and *Solarbabies* (1986). In the former film, a gang of skating humanoids pestered Dorothy. The futuristic teens in *Solarbabies* used skates as their primary means of transportation. Movies featuring skateboards include *Skateboard, Thrashin', Gleaming the Cube,* and even *Back to the Future*. Bill Murray's *Loose Shoes* included a trailer for the make-believe movie "Skateboarders from Hell."

Shall We Dance (1937)	*Xanadu* (1980)
The Fireball (1950)	*Loose Shoes* (aka *Coming*
It's Always Fair Weather (1955)	*Attractions*) (1980)
Derby (1971)	*The Personals* (1981)
Kansas City Bomber (1972)	*Return to Oz* (1985)
Unholy Rollers (1972)	*Back to the Future* (1985)
Roll, Freddy, Roll (1974 TVM)	*Roller Blade* (1986)
Rollerball (1975)	*Solarbabies* (1986)
Rollerbabies (1976)	*Thrashin'* (1986)
Skateboard (1977)	*Madame Sousatzka* (1988)
Skatetown U.S.A. (1977)	*Gleaming the Cube* (1989)
Roller Boogie (1979)	*Back to the Future II* (1989)

Room at the Top

This dour 1958 drama is best remembered for its frank attitude toward sex, its depressing northern England setting, and Simone Signoret's Oscar-winning performance as an ambitious young man's mistress. Laurence Harvey played Joe Lampton, the working-class lad determined to get to the top at all costs—even the death of his lover. Harvey returned to the role in 1965's *Life at the Top*, his character's ambition now replaced by disillusion. Kenneth Haigh starred as Lampton in a popular 1971–73 British TV series called "Man at the Top." It subsequently led to a third film, 1975's *Man at the Top*, the dramatics now transformed into big business soap opera. John Braine wrote the original novel.

> *Room at the Top* (1958)   *Man at the Top* (1975)
> *Life at the Top* (1965)

The Rough Riders

Despite its title, this Monogram series had nothing to do with the early days of Teddy Roosevelt. Instead, it was just another Western series starring veteran screen cowboy Buck Jones. Jones had been Universal's major Western hero in the 1930s, but he was fading when Monogram cast him with Tim McCoy and Raymond Hatton as The Rough Riders. The trio played U.S. marshals with a penchant for infiltrating outlaw gangs. The series ended abruptly in 1942 when Jones died in the Cocoanut Grove nightclub fire while on a U.S. Savings Bonds campaign. Jones had actually escaped from the building, but was overcome by the flames when he returned to help others.

> *Arizona Bound* (1941)   *Ghost Town Law* (1942)
> *The Man from Bodie* (1941)   *Down Texas Way* (1942)
> *Forbidden Trails* (1941)   *Riders of the West* (1942)
> *Below the Border* (1942)   *West of the Law* (1942)

Running

The melodic strains of the *Chariots of Fire* theme automatically bring to mind the vision of barefoot runners gliding across a sandy beach. That, plus the fact it won the 1981 Best Picture Oscar, makes *Chariots* the most well-known running film, but other pictures have covered the sport with equal depth. The 1962 *Loneliness of the Long Distance Runner* made Tom Courtenay a star for his portrayal of a lonely lad who finds solace in pounding a cross-country course. *See How She Runs* (1978), *Running* (1979), and *On the Edge* (1985) were more conventional examinations of the runner's psyche, dealing with the obsession and motivation that make some athletes push themselves to the limit. Olympic runners have been profiled in the documentary *Visions of Eight*, the biographies *Running Brave* (Billy Mills), *Babe* (Babe Didrikson), and *The Jesse Owens Story*, and the fictional features *The Loneliest Runner*, *The Games*, *Goldengirl*, and *Personal Best*.

> *Loneliness of the Long Distance*   *Billie* (1965)
>   *Runner* (1962)   *The Games* (1970)

Visions of Eight (1973)
Babe (1975 TVM)
Marathon Man (1976)
The Loneliest Runner (1976 TVM)
See How She Runs (1978 TVM)
Goldengirl (1979)
Running (1979)
The Jericho Mile (1979 TVM)
Chariots of Fire (1981)

Personal Best (1982)
Running Brave (1983)
The Terry Fox Story (1983 TVM)
Courage (aka *Raw Courage*) (1984)
The Jesse Owens Story (1984 TVM)
On the Edge (1985)
China Run (1987)

Rusty

Rusty was Columbia's answer to canine rival Lassie in this affable boy-and-dog series of the late 1940s. Al Martin wrote the series opener, 1945's *Adventures of Rusty,* which introduced Ted Donaldson as young Danny Mitchell and Rusty as his faithful German Shepherd, a former police dog. John Litel, best known as Henry Aldrich's (q.v.) dad, played Danny's father in the first three films before being replaced by Tom Powers. Ann Doran was Danny's stepmother. The stories usually centered on Danny's personal problems (e.g. misunderstandings with Dad in *For the Love of Rusty*), but it was Rusty who consistently saved the day. See also **Dogs.**

Adventures of Rusty (1945)
The Return of Rusty (1946)
Son of Rusty (1947)
For the Love of Rusty (1948)

My Dog Rusty (1948)
Rusty Leads the Way (1948)
Rusty Saves a Life (1949)
Rusty's Birthday (1950)

Ryder, Red

Republic Pictures first brought Fred Harmon's comic strip Western hero to the screen in the 1940 serial *The Adventures of Red Ryder.* Star Don Barry took the nickname "Red" and kept it for the rest of his career—but he was not Republic's choice to headline a Red Ryder film series. That distinction went to Wild Bill Elliott, a veteran "B" Western star Republic lured away from Columbia in 1943. Elliott had acquired *his* nickname "Wild Bill" while playing Wild Bill Hickock (q.v.) in an earlier serial and series. Gabby Hayes played Elliott's grizzled sidekick in the first two Ryder pictures, 1944's *Tucson Raiders* and *Marshal of Reno.* But he was eventually dropped, allowing young Bobby Blake (Robert Blake of TV's "Baretta") to assume the sidekick role as the Indian boy Little Beaver. After 16 films, Republic promoted Elliott to bigger pictures and signed Allan "Rocky" Lane to play Red. Lane had been a contract player since 1929 at Fox, Warners, and RKO before joining Republic as a serial star in 1940. His transition into the Ryder films went smoothly, assisted by Blake who provided continuity as Little Beaver. Lane played Red seven times before the Ryder series moved to Eagle Lion in 1949. After his acting career ended in 1961, Lane provided the voice of TV's "Mr. Ed." The Eagle Lion pictures starred Jim Bannon, best known as detective Jack Packard in Columbia's shortlived *I Love a Mystery* series (q.v.). Don Reynolds co-starred as Little Beaver. Plagued by legal problems involving rights to the source comic strip, the Eagle Lion *Red Ryder* series folded within a year.

> *Tucson Raiders* (1944) (Bill Elliott)
> *Marshal of Reno* (1944) (Elliott)
> *Vigilantes of Dodge City* (1944) (Elliott)
> *Cheyenne Wildcat* (1944) (Elliott)
> *The San Antonio Kid* (1944) (Elliott)
> *Sheriff of Las Vegas* (1944) (Elliott)
> *Marshal of Laredo* (1945) (Elliott)
> *Lone Texas Ranger* (1945) (Elliott)
> *The Great Stagecoach Robbery* (1945) (Elliott)
> *Phantom of the Plains* (1945) (Elliott)
> *Colorado Pioneers* (1945) (Elliott)
> *Wagon Wheels Westward* (1945) (Elliott)
> *Sun Valley Cyclone* (1946) (Elliott)
> *Sheriff of Redwood Valley* (1946) (Elliott)
> *California Gold Rush* (1946) (Elliott)
> *Conquest of Cheyenne* (1946) (Elliott)
> *Santa Fe Uprising* (1946) (Allan Lane)
> *Stagecoach to Denver* (1946) (Lane)
> *Homesteaders of Paradise Valley* (1947) (Lane)
> *Rustlers of Devil's Canyon* (1947) (Lane)
> *Vigilantes of Boom Town* (1947) (Lane)
> *Marshal of Cripple Creek* (1947) (Lane)
> *Oregon Trail Scouts* (1947) (Lane)
> *The Fighting Redhead* (1949) (Jim Bannon)
> *The Cowboy and the Prizefighter* (1949) (Bannon)
> *Roll, Thunder, Roll* (1949) (Bannon)
> *Ride, Ryder, Ride* (1949) (Bannon)

Sabata

A spaghetti-Western antihero in the mold of Clint Eastwood's Man with No Name (q.v.), Sabata was played by Lee Van Cleef and Yul Brynner. Interestingly, Van Cleef created the character for 1970's *Sabata,* gave way to Brynner for 1971's *Adios, Sabata,* and then returned for 1972's final entry *Return of Sabata.*

The Saint

Leslie Charteris' dapper adventurer Simon Templar walked a thin line between crime and the law. His calling card featured a stick figure with a halo, thus explaining his moniker, the Saint. The movies never alluded much to the Saint's criminal tendencies—he was strictly a good guy with a mischievous streak. George Sanders was the screen's busiest Saint, although Louis Hayward and Hugh Sinclair each starred in two movies. Jean Marais played the upper class sleuth on the French screen. In the 1960s, Roger Moore made the role his own with a highly successful TV series, which even spawned a theatrical film (composed of two episodes). Although Moore's show ended in 1969, fellow Brit Ian Ogilvy starred in a revival series, "The Return of the Saint," in 1978. Eleven years later, the Saint popped up again as a revolving character in a syndicated series called "The Mystery Wheel of Adventure."

> *The Saint in New York* (1938) (Hayward)
> *The Saint in London* (1939) (Sanders)
> *The Saint Strikes Back* (1939) (Sanders)
> *The Saint's Double Trouble* (1940) (Sanders)
> *The Saint Takes Over* (1940) (Sanders)
> *The Saint in Palm Springs* (1941) (Sanders)
> *The Saint Meets the Tiger* (1941) (Sinclair)
> *The Saint's Vacation* (1941) (Sinclair)
> *The Saint's Girl Friday* (1953) (aka *The Saint Returns*) (Hayward)
> *The Fiction-Makers* (1968 TVM) (Moore)
> *The Saint and the Brave Goose* (1981 TVM) (Ogilvy)

St. Trinian's

An unruly girls' school where young ladies spent more time studying betting sheets than history, St. Trinian's provided the setting for a popular series of British farces spanning 26 years. The director-writing team of Frank Launder and Sidney Gilliat created the series, but it was droll comic genius Alastair Sim who made the first entries consistently entertaining. Actually, Launder, Gilliat, and Sim had teamed up earlier for 1950's *The Happiest Days of Your Life,* a riotous comedy about a girls' school (St. Swithin) which was accidentally "displaced" into a boys' school (Nutbourne). Sim and Margaret Rutherford played the respective heads of the schools, but they generously devoted screen time to their youthful, mischievous co-stars. *The Belles of St. Trinian's* (1954) initiated the series proper and introduced a swarm of rebellious girls which made St. Swithin's look like a charm school. Sim was doubly delightful as both the headmistress (in drag, of course) and her brother. Sim also appeared, albeit too briefly, in 1958's follow-up *Blue Murder at St. Trinian's,* in which a jewel thief on the lam wishes he had never stumbled into the "perfect hiding place." Launder and Gilliat produced two additional lackluster entries without Sim. The series apparently ended with 1966's *The Great St. Trinian's Train Robbery.* However, Launder returned to the school 14 years later for *The Wildcats of St. Trinian's,* a time-capsule comedy that failed to find an audience. Gilliat served as a production consultant, but did not have an active role in the writing chores. Launder and Gilliat broke into the movies as writers in the 1930s. They penned the screenplay for Hitchcock's classic *The Lady Vanishes* (1937). See also **Boarding Schools.**

The Belles of St. Trinian's (1954)
Blue Murder at St. Trinian's (1958)
The Pure Hell of St. Trinian's (1961)
The Great St. Trinian's Train Robbery (1966)
The Wildcats of St. Trinian's (1980)

Santo

The origin of this Mexican wrestling superhero remains somewhat hazy, though it may date as far back as 1952's *El Enmascarado de Plata* (aka *The Silver Mask*). Irregardless, Santo has appeared in some forty-odd feature films, making his series the longest-running in Mexican cinema. The series peaked in popularity during the 1960s, a decade in which the Silver-Masked wrestler fought a plethora of vampires, zombies, witches, man-made monsters, and other wrestlers. Originally, the "movies" were made as serials for Mexican television. But due to the scarce number of television markets, they were ultimately edited into features and released to neighborhood theaters. The actor behind Santo's silver mask was never billed, although Rodolfo Guzman Huerta and Eric del Castillo are generally credited as the principal Santos. Yet, with the wrestler's facial features hidden, one could never be certain about his real-life identity. Rival wrestlers The Blue Demon (q.v.) and Neutron (q.v.) were introduced in the early 1960s. Neutron made little impact, but the Blue Demon eventually co-starred with Santo in 1968's *Santo Against Blue Demon in Atlantis.* Its success led to additional wrestler pairings, culminating in the Mexican monster e vaganza *Santo and Blue Demon vs. the Monsters*—which pitted the tag team against three vampires, a mummy, a cyclops, a Frankenstein monster, a mad doctor, and a robot double of the Blue Demon. The Santo films never strayed from their juvenile plotlines, despite gradually stressing sexual content until nude scenes had become obligatory by the late 1960s. Santo remained relatively unknown in the U.S. until cable networks gave him new exposure in the 1980s. See also **Blue Demon; Neutron; Wrestling.**

Santo Contra Hombres Infernales (1958)
Santo vs. the Zombies (aka *Invasion of the Zombies; Santo Contra los Zombies*) (1961)
Samson vs. the Vampire Women (aka *Santo Contra las Mujeres Vampiro*) (1961)
Santo vs. the King of Crime (aka *Santo Contra el Rey de Crimen*) (1963)
Santo in the Hotel of the Dead (aka *Santo en el Hotel de la Meurte*) (1963)
Santo Against the Diabolical Brain (aka *Santo contra el Cerebro Diabólico; El Cerebro del Mal*) (1963)

Samson in the Wax Museum (aka *Santo en el Museo de Cera*) (1963)
Santo Attacks the Witches (aka *The Witches Attack; Santo Ataca; Atacan las Brujas*) (1965)
Santo vs. Baron Brakola (aka *Santro Contra el Baron Brakola*) (1966)
Santo vs. the Strangler (aka *Santo Contra el Estrangulador*) (1966)
Profanadores de Tumbas (1966)
The Ghost of the Strangler (aka *Espectro del Estrangulador; Santo Contra el Espectro*) (1967)
Santo vs. the Martian Invasion (aka *Santo vs. Invasion de los Marcianos*) (1967)
Santo Against Blue Demon in Atlantis (aka *Santo Contra Blue Demon en la Atlántida*) (1968)
The Diabolical Hatchet (aka *El Hacha Diabólica*) (1968)
The World of the Dead (aka *El Mundo de los Muertos*) (1969)
Santo in the Revenge of the Vampire Women (aka *Santo en la Venganza de las Mujeres Vampiro*) (1969)
Santo and Dracula's Treasure (aka *The Vampire and Sex; El Vampiro y el Sexo*) (1969)
Santo and Blue Demon vs. the Monsters (aka *Santo y Blue Demon Contra los Monstruos*) (1971)
Murderers from Other Worlds (aka *Asesinos de Otros Mundos*) (1971)
Suicide Mission (aka *Misión Suicida*) (1971)
Santo Against the Daughter of Frankenstein (aka *The Daughter of Frankenstein; Santo Contra la Hija de Frankenstein*) (1972)
Santo in the Mummy's Revenge (aka *Santo en la Venganza de la Momia*) (1972)
Santo Against the Black Magic (aka *Santo Contra la Magia Negra*) (1972)
Santo vs. Capulina (1972)
Santo and Blue Demon vs. Dracula and the Wolf Man (aka *Santo y Blue Demon Contra Dracula y el Hombre Lobo*) (1973)
Pafnucio Santo (1976)

Sea Serpents

Judging from their reluctance to be photographed, one might assume that sea serpents are shy creatures. Filmmakers have certainly honored the creatures' privacy. *The Secret of the Loch,* a mild 1934 British comedy, may be the only feature film exclusively about the Loch Ness Monster. Holmes encountered "Nessie" in *The Private Life of Sherlock Holmes* (1970), but he revealed "the serpent" to be a mechanical trick. Nessie was one of *The Mysterious Monsters* (1976) addressed in the exploitative Sunn Classics "documentary." And a tiny fish grew into Nessie in one of the magical moments in George Pal's 1964 fantasy *The Seven Faces of Dr. Lao.* Some of the suspects in *The Dragon Murder Case* (1934) pointed to murder evidence which suggested a sea serpent, but Philo Vance knew better and later identified a human culprit. Quests for sea serpents opened *20,000 Leagues Under the Sea* (1954), *The Viking Women and the Sea Serpent* (1957), and, quite naturally, *The Quest* (1986). Timothy Bottoms and Ray Milland found what they were looking for in *The Sea Serpent* (1986), a film they would surely like to forget.

The Secret of the Loch (1934)	*The Seven Faces of Dr. Lao*
The Dragon Murder Case (1934)	(1964)
20,000 Leagues Under the Sea	*The Private Life of Sherlock*
(1954)	*Holmes* (1970)
The Viking Women and the	*The Sea Serpent* (1986)
Sea Serpent (1957)	*The Quest* (1986)

Secret Service Series *see* Bancroft, Brass

Serials into Features

The practice of condensing movie serials into feature films was pioneered in the 1930s by a small company called Mascot Pictures. A major producer of early serials, Mascot discovered it could get twice the value out of its serials by also re-releasing highlights as feature films. Thus, the 1933 John Wayne Western serial *The Three Musketeers* was recut and released as *Desert Command*. A rival studio, Principal, squeezed *two* feature films out of its Bela Lugosi serial *The Return of Chandu* (1934). The first four chapters were condensed into the film *The Return of Chandu*, while the last eight chapters were edited into another feature called *Chandu on Magic Island*. In a unique reversal, Burroughs-Tarzan Enterprises edited its 1935 feature film *The New Adventures of Tarzan* (aka *Tarzan and the Green Goddess*) into a 12-chapter serial in a desperate attempt to compete with MGM's Tarzan (q.v.). The company reasoned that theater owners uninterested in showing the feature version might be induced to play the serial version. The ploy did not work. In 1936, Universal released its first *Flash Gordon* serial, an expensive ($350,000 according to most sources) space opera that earned a fervent following. Inspired by Orson Welles' famous "War of the Worlds" radio broadcast and the success of the serial sequel *Flash Gordon's Trip to Mars,* Universal released two Flash Gordon feature versions in 1938. *Trip to Mars* was condensed into *Mars Attacks the World,* while the original *Flash Gordon* became *Rocketship.* Confusingly, the footage from these serials, a third Flash Gordon entry, and a Buck Rogers serial have been re-edited into other feature versions as well. For example, *Trip to Mars* can be viewed as the 99-minute *Deadly Ray from Mars* in addition to the aforementioned 101-minute *Mars Attacks the World.* Although Universal encountered great success with its Flash Gordon serials, little Republic Pictures eventually became the most popular producer of serials. Throughout the 1940s and midway through the 1950s, Republic filled matinee screens with exciting chapters of *Spy*

304

Smasher (1942), *Captain America* (1944), and *Panther Girl of the Kongo* (1955). The television series format contributed greatly to the death of theatrical serials in the mid–1950s. However, in 1965, Columbia revived interest in serials by mounting a limited release of its 1943 *Batman* serial. This, along with the 1966 "Batman" TV series, inspired Republic to condense 26 of its best serials and release them directly to television. In the following list, the serials are listed chronologically on the left, with the feature versions shown on the right.

The Three Musketeers (1933)	*Desert Command*
The Return of Chandu (1934)	*Chandu on Magic Isle; The Return of Chandu*
The New Adventures of Tarzan (1935)	*The New Adventures of Tarzan*
Darkest Africa (1936)	*Batmen of Africa* (aka *King of Jungleland*)
Undersea Kingdom (1936)	*Sharad of Atlantis*
Robinson Crusoe of Clipper Island (1936)	*Robinson Crusoe of Mystery Island*
Flash Gordon (1936)	*Rocketship; Spaceship to the Unknown; Space Soldiers; Atomic Rocketship*
Zorro Rides Again (1937)	*Zorro Rides Again*
Fighting Devil Dogs (1938)	*Torpedo of Doom*
Flash Gordon's Trip to Mars (1938)	*Mars Attacks the World; Deadly Rays from Mars*
Hawk of the Wilderness (1938)	*Lost Island of Kioga*
Buck Rogers (1939)	*Planet Outlaws; Destination Saturn*
Flash Gordon Conquers the Universe (1940)	*Purple Death from Outer Space; Perils from the Planet Mongo; Space Soldiers Conquer the Universe*
The Mysterious Dr. Satan (1940)	*Dr. Satan's Robot*
Spy Smasher (1940)	*Spy Smasher Returns*
The Perils of Nyoka (1942)	*Nyoka and the Lost Secrets of Hippocrates*
G-Men vs. the Black Dragon (1943)	*Black Dragon of Manzanar*
The Masked Marvel (1943)	*Sakima and the Masked Marvel*
The Tiger Woman (1944)	*Jungle Gold*
Manhunt of Mystery Island (1945)	*Captain Mephisto and the Transformation Machine*
Federal Operator 99 (1945)	*FBI 99*
The Purple Monster Strikes (1945)	*D-Day on Mars*
The Crimson Ghost (1946)	*Cyclotrode "X"*

The Black Widow (1947)	*Sombra, the Spider Woman*
G-Men Never Forget (1948)	*Code 645*
Dangers of the Canadian Mounted (1948)	*R.C.M.P. and the Treasure of Genghis Khan*
Federal Agents vs. Underworld, Inc. (1948)	*Golden Hands of Kurigal*
King of the Rocket Men (1949)	*Lost Planet Airmen*
The Invisible Monster (1950)	*Slaves of the Invisible Monster*
Flying Disc Man from Mars (1951)	*Missile Monsters*
Radar Men from the Moon (1952)	*Retik, the Moon Menace*
Zombies of the Stratosphere (1952)	*Satan's Satellites*
Jungle Drums of Africa (1952)	*U-238 and the Witch*
Canadian Mounties vs. Atomic Invaders (1953)	*Missile Base at Taniak*
Trader Tom of the China Seas (1954)	*Target: Sea of China*
Panther Girl of the Kongo (1955)	*The Claw Monsters*

Sewers

Until olfactory films can be refined (see "Smellovision" under **Gimmicks**), sewer settings will be underappreciated. Still, the dark catacombs that lurk beneath urban areas have served the horror film well, providing an atmospheric retreat for people-shy monsters. *The Phantom of the Opera* played piano and plotted murder in his tastefully-decorated sewer lair. To his dismay, Christine, the unwilling object of his affections, found it a loathsome place. Rats are a common sight in sewers, so naturally 1972's *Ben,* a tale about a misunderstood rodent and his young human friend, featured extensive sewer footage. Other more horrorific sewer residents include the giant ants in *Them!* (1954), the killer baby in *It's Alive* (1974), the title creatures in *Alligator* (1980), and the 1988 remake of *The Blob.* The 1984 *C.H.U.D.* (that's Cannibalistic Humanoid Underground Dwellers) was about a mutant race that lived in the sewers by day and sought surface victims at night. It was obviously inspired by the H.P. Lovecraft short story "Pickman's Model," which was adapted into a chilling segment on Rod Serling's 1970–73 TV series "Night Gallery." *The Third Man* (1949) featured a memorable scene in which Harry Lime (Orson Welles) is chased through a Vienna sewer. Lex Luthor's sewer lair in *Superman* (1978) looked very posh, possibly setting a new standard for screen supervillains. And a band of Christians trekked through the Caesar Augustus Memorial Sewer in Monty Python's *Life of Brian* (1979).

The Phantom of the Opera
  (1943)
The Third Man (1949)
Them! (1954)
Kanal (aka *They Loved Life;*
  Sewer) (1956)
Who's Minding the Mint?
  (1967)
Ben (1972)
It's Alive! (1974)

Superman (1978)
Life of Brian (1979)
Alligator (1980)
The Blues Brothers (1980)
C.H.U.D. (1984)
Wild Thing (1987)
Something Is Out There (1988)
The Blob (1988)
Cyborg (1989)
Ghostbusters II (1989)

Sex Change

Exploitation films have frequently tackled subjects considered taboo even by serious filmmakers. Thus, it is not surprising that the first films to address men undergoing surgical operations to become women (and vice versa) were drive-in second features. Edward J. Woods, Jr., director of the infamous *Plan Nine from Outer Space,* broached the subject back in 1953 with *Glen or Glenda?* A shoddily-constructed film (like most of Woods'), it told the stories of transvestite Glen and ex-marine Alan who becomes Ann. Although undoubtedly inept, the film was nevertheless ahead of its time in terms of subject matter. Seventeen years later, United Artists released the low-budget filler *The Christine Jorgensen Story* (1970), the alleged facts behind "the world's first sex change operation." That same year, Gore Vidal's satiric sex-change novel *Myra Breckinridge* reached the screen, with film critic Rex Reed as Myron who becomes surprisingly transformed into Raquel Welch as Myra! The film drowned in its own tastelessness despite a memorable cast and a decent budget. The obscure British picture *I Want What I Want* (1972) treated the subject with much greater respect. Both critics and audiences responded well to 1975's *Dog Day Afternoon,* the story of a man who stages a bank robbery to pay for his male lover's sex-change operation. Karen Black shocked her dinner companions by revealing she was once a man in *Come Back to the Five and Dime, Jimmy Dean, Jimmy Dean* (1982). The 1986 TV-movie *Second Serve* was the biography of surgeon Richard Raskins who became tennis player Renee Richards (Lynn Redgrave played both roles). Two other movies have dealt with non-surgical change of sexes. Young Dr. Jekyll (Ralph Bates) downed his formula and transformed into an evil woman (Martine Beswicke) in Hammer Films' sly 1972 variation *Dr. Jekyll and Sister Hyde.* A 14-year-old girl wished to become a boy—and did—in the 1986 fantasy *Something Special.*

Glen or Glenda? (aka *I*
  Changed My Sex; I Led Two
  Lives; He or She?) (1953)
The Christine Jorgensen Story
  (1970)

Myra Breckinridge (1970)
I Want What I Want (1971)
Dr. Jekyll and Sister Hyde
  (1972)
Dog Day Afternoon (1975)

*Come Back to the Five and
    Dime, Jimmy Dean, Jimmy
    Dime* (1982)
The World According to Garp
    (1982)

Second Serve (1986 TVM)
Something Special (aka *Willy /
    Milly; I Was a Teenage Boy*)
    (1986)

The Shadow

"Who knows what evil lurks in the hearts of men?" The Shadow knew—
and this mysterious do-gooder dealt out his own brand of justice in a
series of immensely popular pulp novels, a radio program, and a handful
of films. Created by Maxwell Grant (real name Walter Gibson) in 1931,
the Shadow sent his agents into the underworld to infiltrate the ganglords.
When they got into trouble, the Shadow—revolvers blazing at his side—
came out of the darkness to rescue them. Grant established in an early
novel that the Shadow *was not* wealthy socialite Lamont Cranston. Nevertheless, both on radio and in the movies, Cranston and the Shadow were
synonymous. Former silent film star Rod La Rocque brought the Shadow
to the screen in 1937's *The Shadow Strikes* and 1938's *International Crime.*
La Rocque retired from acting in the early 1940s and entered into a successful real estate career. Monogram Pictures revived the Shadow for a
1946 three-film series starring serial star Kane ("Spy Smasher") Richmond.
Released in 1946, the titles were: *Behind the Mask, The Shadow Returns,*
and *The Missing Lady.* The Shadow's last film appearance was in
Republic's 1958 picture *The Invisible Avenger,* a New Orleans–set mystery
re-released in 1962 as *Bourbon Street Shadows.* Richard Derr played the
lead.

The Shadow Strikes (1937) (Rod
    La Rocque)
International Crime (1938)
    (La Rocque)
Behind the Mask (1946) (Kane
    Richmond)
The Shadow Returns (1946)

(Richmond)
The Missing Lady (1946) (Rich-
    mond)
The Invisible Avenger (aka
    Bourbon Street Shadows)
    (1958) (Richard Derr)

Shaft

A slick, violent action picture about a supercool black private eye, 1971's
Shaft ignited the "blaxploitation" craze (q.v.) while enjoying its own
mainstream success. Ernest Tidyman's screenplay practically turned John
Shaft into a black male stereotype (a tough dude described in the theme
song as a "sex machine"). But Richard Roundtree's rugged performance
and Gordon Parks' gritty direction gave the film a new look much copied
by other black filmmakers. Isaac Hayes' hit theme won an Oscar (despite
having minimal words) and eventually landed him a starring role in the
1974 movie *Truck Turner.* Roundtree appeared in both *Shaft* sequels and

then made the jump to television. His 90-minute "Shaft" TV series rotated with *The CBS Tuesday Night Movie* and a James Stewart lawyer show called "Hawkins." The TV version whitewashed the Shaft character (less violence, no sex) and caught the cancellation axe after one season.

Shaft (1971)   *Shaft in Africa* (1973)
Shaft's Big Score (1972)

The Shaggy Dog

An ancient curse and a magical ring made Tommy Kirk his own best friend as the boy-turned-dog in 1959's *The Shaggy Dog*. This amusing variation on the werewolf theme established a juvenile formula that worked very well for Disney during the 1960s (e.g. *Son of Flubber, The Misadventures of Merlin Jones*). The film also provided major roles for future child superstars Annette Funicello and Tommy Kirk, while co-starring Fred MacMurray and Tim Considine a year before "My Three Sons." Dean Jones portrayed Kirk's character as an adult in 1976's *The Shaggy D.A.* The 1987 TV-movie *The Return of the Shaggy Dog* ignored the second film, being a direct sequel to the 1959 original.

The Shaggy Dog (1959)   *The Return of the Shaggy Dog*
The Shaggy D.A. (1976)   (1987 TVM)

Sharks

Except for bit parts, sharks had a hard time finding movie roles prior to 1975's *Jaws* (q.v.). *Killer Shark* (1950) put Roddy McDowell aboard a shark-hunting vessel, but offered little excitement. Victor Mature became concerned about the way sharks gobbled up Navy flyers in 1956's *The Sharkfighters*. He eventually devised a shark repellent, derived from octopus ink, that turned away even the hungriest underwater predator. *Blue Water, White Death* was a striking 1971 documentary about the Great White shark. It failed to find an audience until four years later after the release of *Jaws*. Naturally, the phenomenal success of Steven Spielberg's blockbuster inspired a host of imitators. The 1982 *Great White* was so similar to *Jaws* that Universal Pictures went to court and acquired an injunction to remove the rip-off from circulation. *Mako: The Jaws of Death* offered a refreshing twist on the post–*Jaws* shark genre, with Richard Jaeckel as a man trying to protect sharks from people who would exploit them. See also **Dolphins; Fish; Jaws; Whales.**

Killer Shark (1950)   *Jaws* (1975)
The Sharkfighters (1956)   *Mako: The Jaws of Death* (aka
Tiko and the Shark (1965)   *The Jaws of Death*) (1976)
Shark! (aka *Maneater*) (1969)   *Shark Kill* (1976 TVM)
Blue Water, White Death   *Tintorera — Bloody Waters*
    (1971)   (1977)
Shark's Treasure (1974)   *Great White* (1982)

Shayne, Michael

Brett Halliday's two-fisted private eye made his film debut with 1941's *Michael Shayne, Detective.* Lloyd Nolan, a veteran tough guy, starred as Shayne in seven films from 1941–42. Hugh Beaumont, best known as Ward Cleaver on TV's "Leave It to Beaver," reprised Shayne for five additional features in 1946–47. Although these fast-paced mysteries never rose above the programmer level, they paved the way for more serious private eye films, such as the 1944 Philip Marlowe vehicle *Murder, My Sweet.* Ironically, the Shayne movie *Time to Kill* was based on the Marlowe novel *The High Window.* Richard Denning starred in the "Michael Shayne" TV series in 1960–61.

Michael Shayne, Detective (1941) (Nolan)
Blue, White, and Perfect (1941) (Nolan)
Dressed to Kill (1941) (Nolan)
Sleepers West (1941) (Nolan)
Just Off Broadway (1942) (Nolan)
The Man Who Would Not Die (1942) (Nolan)
Time to Kill (1942) (Nolan)
Blonde for a Day (1946) (Beaumont)
Larceny in Her Heart (1946) (Beaumont)
Murder Is My Business (1946) (Beaumont)
Three on a Ticket (1947) (Beaumont)
Too Many Winners (1947) (Beaumont)

Six Million Dollar Man

Martin Caidin's novel *Cyborg* inspired the 1973 TV-movie and subsequent 1974–78 TV series "The Six Million Dollar Man." Lee Major starred as Steve Austin, a critically injured astronaut who had certain body parts replaced by "atomic-powered electromechanical devices." The end result was a superhero—part human, part machine (but not nearly as interesting as *Robocop*). He acquired a bionic girlfriend in 1975, when tennis pro Jaime Sommers (Lindsay Wagner) met with a sky-diving accident. She proved too popular for just one man, so she got her own show, "The Bionic Woman," in 1976. It went off the air in 1978, a few months after the final telecast of "The Six Million Dollar Man." However, just to show you can't keep a bionic pair down for good—and in the wake of the hit movie *Robocop*—Steve and Jaime were reunited for 1987's *The Return of the Six Million Dollar Man and the Bionic Woman.* It proved to be a ratings hit, thus inspiring a second post-series movie pitting the twosome against a bionic villain. See also **Androids and Cyborgs.**

The Six Million Dollar Man (1973 TVM)
The Return of the Six Million Dollar Man and the Bionic Woman (1987 TVM)
Bionic Showdown: The Six Million Dollar Man and the Bionic Woman (1989 TVM)

Skiing

Fictional Olympic skiers have been portrayed in the movies as obsessive, self-centered types, as evidenced by Robert Redford's character in *Downhill Racer* (1969) and Wayne Rogers in *The Top of the Hill* (1980). Real-life Olympic skiers-turned-actors have chosen more likable roles, though that's done little to extend their brief film careers. Olympic great Jean-Claude Killy starred in the 1972 heist film *Snow Job*, earning high marks for his slalom skills and low ones for his thesping. Suzy ("Chapstick") Chaffee's role was strictly a supporting one in the 1978 TV-movie *Ski Lift to Death*. Non–Olympic real-life skiers have appeared in the documentaries *Last of the Ski Bums* (1969) and *The Man Who Skied Down Everest* (1976). The latter film, which chronicled the exploits of Japanese skier Yuichiro Miura, won an Oscar for Best Documentary. *Ski Bum* was a less serious affair about the joys of skiing, produced by the makers of the classic surfing documentary *The Endless Summer*. The James Bond spy thrillers have exhibited a special flair for ski scenes. A lengthy, breathtaking ski sequence, among the finest chases in the entire series, forms the centerpiece of 1969's *On Her Majesty's Secret Service*. A shorter chase opened 1977's *The Spy Who Loved Me*, ending with Bond skiing off a cliff and releasing a parachute. Bond was back on the slopes, to less effect, in 1985's *A View to a Kill*. The fact-based drama *Going for the Gold: The Bill Johnson Story* (1985) chronicled the life of the 1984 Olympic downhill champion. A life-threatening accident ended the career of 1956 Olympic hopeful Jill Kilmont in *The Other Side of the Mountain* (1975). On a cheerier note, the Beatles frollicked on the slopes to the tune of "Ticket to Ride" in Richard Lester's hectic 1965 farce *Help!*

The Man Who Knew Too Much (1934)
I Met Him in Paris (1937)
Two-Faced Woman (1941)
The Duchess of Idaho (1950)
Ski Troop Attack (1960)
The Pink Panther (1964)
Help! (1965)
Ski Party (1965)
Caprice (1967)
The Double Man (1967)
Ski on the Wild Side (1967)
Last of the Ski Bums (1969)
On Her Majesty's Secret Service (1969)
Ski Fever (1969)
Downhill Racer (1969)
The Ski Bum (1971)
The Ski Raiders (1972)
Snow Job (1972)
Snowball Express (1972)
The Other Side of the Mountain (aka *A Window to the Sky*) (1975)
The Man Who Skied Down Everest (1976)
The Spy Who Loved Me (1977)
The Deadly Triangle (aka *Crisis in Sun Valley*) (1977 TVM)
Ski Lift to Death (1978 TVM)
Lost and Found (1979)
The Top of the Hill (1980 TVM)
Swan Song (1980 TVM)
Hot Dog…The Movie (1984)
Just the Way You Are (1984)
Better Off Dead (1985)
A View to a Kill (1985)

Going for the Gold: The Bill   *Fire and Ice* (1987)
    Johnson Story (1985 TVM)

Slasher Movies

A subgenre of the psycho thriller, the slasher movie enjoyed tremendous popularity among young adults during the 1978–83 period. John Carpenter's *Halloween* (1978) is generally considered the prototype, introducing what would become the mandatory ingredients: sexually active teenage protagonists, a conspicuous absence of adults, gory murders (the higher the body count, the better), and a seemingly indestructible killer. Despite a low budget and frail storyline, Carpenter's incredibly tense direction brought *Halloween* (q.v.) critical acclaim as well as boxoffice millions. Amazingly, imitations were slow to follow (although the grisly-titled *Driller Killer* was released the next year). Then in 1980, Sean S. Cunningham exploited a routine thriller called *Friday the 13th* (q.v.) into a boxoffice smash. (Nine years earlier, Cunningham had produced the infamous shocker *Last House on the Left.*) Unlike Carpenter's movie, *Friday the 13th* garnered few favorable reviews, but its lucrative grosses did not go unnoticed by low-budget filmmakers. Slasher films flooded the nation's screens during 1981, exhibiting a special fondness for titles involving holidays. Yet, with the exception of the *Friday the 13th* series, slasher films began to fade temporarily in 1983, primarily a victim of their own lack of originality. The genre was practically dead in its grave when Wes Craven (who directed *Last House on the Left*) introduced a razor-fingered killer named Freddy Krueger in 1984's *Nightmare on Elm Street* (q.v.). The *Elm Street* and *Friday the 13th* movies continue to reap huge profits and both have spawned anthology television series and numerous imitations. See also **Friday the 13th; Halloween; Nightmare on Elm Street.**

Halloween (1978)
The Driller Killer (1979)
Friday the 13th (1980)
Mother's Day (1980)
Prom Night (1980)
Silent Scream (1980)
Terror Train (1980)
The Burning (1981)
Final Exam (1981)
The Final Terror (1981)
Funhouse (1981)
Graduation Day (1981)
Happy Birthday to Me (1981)
My Bloody Valentine (1981)
New Year's Evil (1981)
Night School (1981)

Road Games (1981)
Student Bodies (1981)
Slumber Party Massacre (1982)
The House on Sorority Row (1983)
Silent Night, Deadly Night (1984)
April Fool's Day (1986)
Hello, Mary Lou: Prom Night II (1987)
Bad Dreams (1988)
Sleepaway Camp 2: Unhappy Campers (1988)
Cheerleader Camp (aka *Bloody Pom Poms*) (1988)

Smithee, Allen / Alan

When a director or writer wishes his name to be withdrawn from a movie — for whatever reason — he must petition the Director's or Writer's Guild of America (providing he's a member, of course). If the Guild grants his request, his credit is assigned to a fictitious person named Allen (or Alan) Smithee. At least, this has been the standard practice since 1967, when Smithee "replaced" Robert Totten and Don Siegal as directors of *Death of a Gunfighter*. In that instance, both Totten and Siegel alleged that star Richard Widmark had interfered with their creative control of the picture. Prior to the "Smithee rule," George Cukor had his name removed from 1947's *Desire Me*. Its credits simply did not list a director.

> *Death of a Gunfighter* (1967) (directors: Totten and Siegel)
> *Fade-in* (1968) (director: Jud Taylor)
> *The Challenge* (1970) (director unknown)
> *City in Fear* (1980) (director: Jud Taylor)
> *Fun and Games* (1980 TVM) (director unknown)
> *Student Bodies* (1981) (producer: Michael Ritchie)
> *Moonlight* (1982 TVM) (directors: Jackie Cooper and Rod Holcomb)
> *Dune* — TV version (1984) (director David Lynch)
> *Stitches* (1985) (director: Rod Holcomb)
> *Let's Get Harry* (1986) (director: Stuart Rosenberg)
> *Dalton: Code of Vengeance II* (1986 TVM) (director unknown)
> *Ghost Fever* (1987) (director: Lee Madden)
> *Morgan Stewart's Coming Home* (1987) (director: Paul Aaron)
> *Riviera* (1987) (director: John Frankenheimer)
> *The Horror Show* (1989) (writer unknown)

Smokey and the Bandit

Burt Reynold's star power peaked with this 1977 road company in which he, then-girlfriend Sally Field, and Jackie Gleason seem to be having *more* fun than the audience. Burt played a bootlegger who spends the entire film eluding redneck sheriff Gleason, while having a good ol' time with chum Jerry Reed and perky passenger Field. The humor was so tongue-in-cheek that Burt almost seemed to be winking at the audience after every line. The formula provided more of the same with 1980's *Smokey and the Bandit II,* only this time it tasted a little stale, despite the presence of a baby elephant. *Smokey and the Bandit III* (1983) was a misguided attempt to make a Burt Reynolds film without Burt. Initially, Jackie Gleason played a double role, as the pursued and the pursuer. When this confused preview audiences, it was reshot with sheriff Gleason chasing Jerry Reed. By that point, no one really cared either way.

> *Smokey and the Bandit* (1977)
> *Smokey and the Bandit II* (1980)
> *Smokey and the Bandit III* (1983)

Snakes

Snakes have led a charismatic screen existence, often stealing pictures on the basis of a scene or two. A wispy snake made a brief guest appearance in the 1931 Sherlock Holmes mystery *The Speckled Band,* but the picture nevertheless remained named after the viper. Likewise, the snake pit scene in *Raiders of the Lost Ark* (1981) made a lasting impression despite its brevity. A solitary snake, such as the Black Mambo in *Venom* (1982), has wrecked as much havoc as a slew of them slithering rampantly throughout a submarine, as in *Fer-de-Lance* (1974). A shy teenager conjured up giant snakes to kill her thoughtless classmates in 1978's *Jennifer. Stanley* (1972) used his influence on regular-sized snakes, with just as much effect. A Mayan curse turned a Cornish lass into a snake-woman in 1966's *The Reptile,* while Strother Martin's experiments slowly transformed Dirk Benedict into a king cobra in 1973's *Ssssss* ("Don't say it, hiss it!" said the ads). Amanda Donohoe boasted some ugly-looking fangs in *Lair of the White Worm* (1988), but the film's real monster turned out to be the hideous snake god she worshiped. Bob Fosse played a hissing snake in the 1974 fantasy *The Little Prince.* The only one of *The Seven Faces of Dr. Lao* (1964) *not* played by Tony Randall was the animated serpent.

The Speckled Band (1931)	*Fer-de-Lance* (1974 TVM)
The Lady Eve (1941)	*Jennifer* (aka *Jennifer, the*
Cobra Woman (1944)	*Snake Goddess*) (1978)
Cult of the Cobra (1955)	*The Little Prince* (1974)
The Seven Faces of Dr. Lao	*Raiders of the Lost Ark* (1981)
(1964)	*Venom* (1982)
The Reptile (1966)	*Jaws of Satan* (aka *King Cobra*)
Snake People (aka *Isle of the*	(1982)
Snake People) (1968)	*Spasms* (1983)
Stanley (1972)	*Lair of the White Worm* (1988)
Ssssss (1973)	

Soccer

Probably the most popular sport worldwide, soccer has only recently made strides in endearing itself to American athletes and fans. The shortage of English-language soccer films reflects the game's relative obscurity in the U.S. prior to the 1980s. Great Britain produced soccer films like *The Winning Goal* (1920) and *The Ball of Fortune* (1926) in the days of silent cinema. A few other scattered British releases surfaced in the 1930s and 1950s. However, in countries like Czechoslovakia and Brazil, where soccer reigns supreme, a flood of soccer films reached the public in the decades following World War II. None of these films received a major U.S. release. However, the game gained some American exposure when Sylvester Stallone headed an all-star cast, including former soccer great Pele, in the 1981 POW/soccer adventure *Victory.* That same year saw the release of Bill Forsyth's charming Scottish comedy *Gregory's Girl,* in which an incompetent goalie pursues a hot-shot female soccer teammate. An animated animal soccer game was played in the 1969 Disney fantasy *Bedknobs and Broomsticks.*

The Winning Goal (1920)
The Ball of Fortune (1926)
The Great Arsenal Stadium
  Mystery (1939)
The Great Game (1953)
Small Town Story (1953)
Bloomfield (1969)
Bedknobs and Broomsticks

(1971)
The Hero (1972)
Yesterday's Hero (1979)
Victory (aka *Escape to Victory*)
  (1981)
Gregory's Girl (1981)
Hotshot (1987)

Somewhere Series

War-weary British audiences of the 1940s found the *Somewhere* films agreeably silly in spite of their nonexistent plots and sloppy production values. The movies consisted mostly of old, loosely-connected vaudeville sketches performed by dancehall veterans like Frank Randle, Harry Korris, and Robbie Vincent. The low-brow humor frequently bordered on tasteless, making the *Somewhere* films the forerunners of the *Carry On* (q.v.) comedies of the late 1950s and 1960s. Ironically, Randle made a 1949 non–*Somewhere* film called *What a Carry On.*

Somewhere in England (1940)
Somewhere in Camp (1942)
Somewhere on Leave (1942)

Somewhere in Civvies (1943)
Somewhere in Politics (1949)

South Pole *see* North Pole/South Pole

Star Trek

The road from cancelled TV series to phenomenally-successful film series is a bizarre one traveled only by the *Starship Enterprise.* Gene Roddenberry's science fiction TV series debuted on NBC in 1966. Sci-fi fans embraced it, but it was a consistent ratings loser opposite veteran series like "My Three Sons" and "Bewitched." An enthusiastic write-in campaign saved it from cancellation after its second season, but the series was axed after its third year in 1969. Shortly thereafter, its 78 episodes went into syndication and began playing almost daily on local TV stations. By 1974, the show had developed a dizzyingly loyal cult following (dubbed "trekkies"), who honored stars William Shatner (Kirk) and Leonard Nimoy (Spock) at national conventions and urged Roddenberry to revive the series. Roddenberry tried just that. He had laid the groundwork for a "Star Trek" made-for-TV movie (and pilot for a new series) when George Lucas' *Star Wars* went through the boxoffice roof in 1977. Eager to duplicate *Star Wars's* receipts, Paramount decided to turn its *Star Trek* movie into a lavish theatrical space opera. The $40-million *Star Trek — The Motion Picture* was rushed into theaters just in time for Christmas 1979. Trekkies made it a hit, but the reviews were mixed, with critics and fans complaining of an overemphasis on special effects. However, bestselling writer-turned-director Nicholas Meyer set the film series on track with the 1982 sequel *Star Trek II: The Wrath of Khan.* Jack Soward's script resurrected supervillain Khan (Ricardo Montalban) from the TV episode "Space Seed" and climaxed with Spock's "death." Leonard Nimoy took over the directing reins for *Star Trek III: The Search for Spock* (1984) and *Star Trek IV: The Voyage Home* (1986), both of which were praised for capturing the flavor of the series. After helming the non–*Trek* smash *Three Men and a Baby* (1987), Nimoy handed over *Star Trek* directing chores to his co-star. William Shatner directed and co-wrote the story for 1989's *Star Trek V: The Final Frontier,* which opened strongly enough to temporarily oust *Indiana Jones and the Last Crusade* from number one on *Variety*'s box-office charts. Its popularity was shortlived however, as even faithful fans found it a plodding, unexciting trek with old friends. Roddenberry launched "Star Trek: The Next Generation," a new syndicated TV series with a different cast, in 1987.

Star Trek — The Motion Picture (1979)
Star Trek II: The Wrath of Khan (1982)
Star Trek III: The Search for Spock (1984)
Star Trek IV: The Voyage Home (1986)
Star Trek V: The Final Frontier (1989)

Star Wars

George Lucas' tremendously popular space adventure trilogy has developed its own mythos in an amazingly short period of time. When *Variety* predicted a "huge outlook" for *Star Wars* back in 1977, it turned out to be the venerable newspaper's grossest understatement. But the film's greatest impact was not in dollars, but in influencing the near-future of American cinema. Like another late 1970's hit, *Halloween* (q.v.), *Star Wars* fostered dozens of imitations, such as *Battle Beyond the Stars* (1980), *Spacehunter* (1983), *The Ice Pirates* (1984), and the Mel Brooks spoof *Spaceballs* (1986). However, whereas *Halloween* impacted on a specific genre, Lucas' mixture of adventure and morals carried over into non–science fiction films — most notably his and Steven Spielberg's *Indiana Jones* (q.v.) movies. Curiously, Lucas' interest in the *Star Wars* films seemed to diminish as the series progressed. He turned over the directing reins to Irvin Kershner on 1980's *The Empire Strikes Back* (arguably the best) and to Richard Marquand on 1983's *Return of the Jedi.* Despite insisting that the trilogy was the middle three chapters of a longer series, Lucas has shown no intention of making additional, framing films. He did, nonetheless, give the furry little friendly Ewoks (introduced in

Return) two TV-movie adventures. Although oriented toward the juvenile audience, these small-screen sequels boasted the usual excellent production values and a reasonable amount of charm. The major theatrical stars—Harrison Ford, Mark Hamill, Carrie Fisher—were naturally missing.

Star Wars (1977)
The Empire Strikes Back (1980)
Return of the Jedi (1983)
The Ewok Adventure (1984

TVM)
Ewoks: The Battle for Endor
(1985 TVM)

Statues Come to Life

German director/actor Paul Wegener gave the cinema its first living statue with his 1914 horror classic *The Golem: Monster of Fate* and its 1920 prequel *The Golem: How He Came to Be*. These films were based on a Jewish myth about a Rabbi who brought to life a giant man of clay to protect persecuted Jews. However, when the Rabbi lost control of his creation, a young girl destroyed it by removing the Star of David from its chest. The same story served as the basis for Julian Duvivier's *Golem* (1936), the French television film *Le Golem* (1966), and an updated British version called *It* (1966) starring Roddy McDowell. An interesting Japanese variation, *Majin, Monster of Terror* (1966) told the story of a giant stone god summoned to wreak vengeance on those who displaced a kingdom's rightful rulers. Two sequels, *The Return of Majin* and *Majin Strikes Again,* also appeared in 1966. Bill Murray, Dan Aykroyd, and Harold Ramis used "positive slime" to bring the Statue of Liberty to life to battle evil in 1989's *Ghostbusters II*. Not all living statues have been of the giant variety nor have they been necessarily human-like. Ava Gardner played a storefront statue of Venus who became a living mortal in 1948's *One Touch of Venus*. Yet another Venus statue came to life in the form of game show hostess Vanna White in the 1988 TV-movie *The Goddess of Love*. A contemporary witch sent a giant stone eagle to dispense with a college professor and his wife in the intelligent 1962 fantasy *Burn, Witch, Burn*. Statues turned into people and people into statues in Jean Cocteau's stylized *Blood of a Poet* (1930). See **Gorgons** for other movies where people have been transformed into statues.

The Golem: Monster of Fate (aka *Der Golem*) (1914)
The Golem: How He Came to Be (aka *Der Golem, Wie Er in die Welt Kam*) (1920)
Blood of a Poet (aka *Le Sang d'un Poète*) (1930)
One Touch of Venus (1948)
The Miracle (1959)
Burn, Witch, Burn (aka *Night of the Eagle*) (1962)

Jason and the Argonauts (1963)
It (1966)
Majin, Monster of Terror (aka *Majin, the Hideous Monster; Daimajin*) (1966)
Majin Strikes Again (aka *Daimajin Gyakushu*) (1966)
The Return of Majin (aka *The Return of Giant Majin; Daimajin Ikaru*) (1966)
The Golden Voyage of Sinbad

(1973)
Mannequin (1987)
Creepshow 2 (1987)

The Goddess of Love (1988 TVM)
Ghostbusters II (1989)

Strippers

Strippers have appeared in the background of many films, but have been the subject of few. Celebrated stripper/actress/author Gypsy Rose Lee had a hand in four films about strippers. Her mystery novel *The G-String Murders* was adapted for the screen as the 1943 Barbara Stanwyck vehicle *Lady of Burlesque*. This potentially grisly story about a backstage strangler wisely mixed in comedy elements. In Britain, it sported the more exploitative title *Striptease Lady*. Lee's play *Doll Face*, about a burlesque queen with Broadway ambitions, was turned into a 1945 film. Likewise, her autobiography *Gypsy* spawned a hit Broadway musical and a 1962 movie version. Finally, she appeared in a supporting role in 1963's *The Stripper*. Based on William Inge's play *A Loss of Roses*, it starred a miscast Joanne Woodward as a former stripper seeking a new life and becoming involved with a 19-year-old. Danish actress Britt Ekland played an Amish girl-turned-stripper in William Friedkin's fond homage to old-time burlesque *The Night They Raided Minsky's* (1968). The serious side of striptease was explored in 1986's *Stripper*, a surprisingly straightforward, nonexploitative documentary about three professional strippers entering a Las Vegas contest. The fact-based *Blaze* (1989) was a behind-the-headlines look at the scandalous love affair between Louisiana governor Earl K. Long and famed stripper Blaze Starr. Naturally, "B"-movie directors have exploited striptease for its cheesecake value. Drive-in filler of this kind has ranged from disgusting tripe like 1987's *Stripped to Kill* to modestly amusing fodder like Stephanie Rothman's *The Working Girls*. Male strippers have not received equal time, although Christopher Atkins played one in 1983's best-forgotten *A Night in Heaven*. His leading lady was Lesley Ann Warren, an ecdysiast herself in 1982's *Portrait of a Stripper*.

Lady of Burlesque (aka *Striptease Lady*) (1943)
Delightfully Dangerous (1945)
Lady Godiva Rides Again (1951)
Sex Kittens Go to College (aka *The Beauty and the Robot*) (1960)
A Cold Wind in August (1961)
Danger by My Side (1962)
Gypsy (1962)
The Stripper (aka *Woman of Summer*) (1963)
The Night They Raided

Minsky's (1968)
The Working Girls (1973)
Portrait of a Stripper (1982 TVM)
A Night in Heaven (1983)
Little Treasure (1985)
Stripper (1986)
Kandyland (1987)
Stripped to Kill (1987)
Ladykillers (1988)
Dance of the Damned (1989)
Stripped to Kill 2 (1989)
Blaze (1989)

Stunt People

Films about stunt people naturally tend to emphasize action over intellect, as in 1977's *Hooper,* an easy-going Burt Reynolds vehicle about an aging stuntman contemplating one last death-defying feat. In both *Stunt Seven* (1979) and *Stunts Unlimited* (1980), the government sent stunt experts on top-secret rescue missions. No one bothered to question the logic behind substituting Hollywood union men for military-trained specialists. The engrossing real-life story of a deaf stuntwoman was the subject of *Silent Victory: The Kitty O'Neil Story* (1979). The 1980 *The Stunt Man* was a thought-provoking yarn about a desperate fugitive (Steve Railsback) hired by a crazy film director (Peter O'Toole) to perform dangerously real stunts. On television, Lee Majors played a stuntman who tracked down bail jumpers on the side in "The Fall Guy." A lunatic casting director somehow concluded that the Dave Clark Five would be just right as the fun loving stuntmen in 1965's *Having a Wild Weekend.*

Lucky Devils (1932)
Having a Wild Weekend (aka *Catch Us If You Can*) (1965)
Stuntman (1968)
Hollywood Boulevard (1976)
Stunts (aka *Who Is Killing the Stuntmen?*) (1977)
Hooper (1978)
Texas Detour (1978)
Silent Victory: The Kitty O'Neil Story (1979 TVM)
Stunt Seven (1979 TVM)
Stunts Unlimited (1980 TVM)
The Stunt Man (1980)

Submarines

Tense war melodramas and fanciful science fiction adventures have made the most effective use of submarine settings. The 1938 *Submarine Patrol* was a routine World War I actioner that unknowingly paved the way for later World War II star-studded efforts. In 1943 alone: Cary Grant navigated a submarine into Japanese waters in *Destination Tokyo;* Humphrey Bogart took on the Germans in *Action in the North Atlantic;* John Mills helmed a British sub in *We Dive at Dawn;* and Tyrone Power clashed with Dana Andrews in *Crash Dive.* The popularity of sub war dramas decreased in the 1950s, but big name stars still kept them afloat at the boxoffice. Sub officers Clark Gable and Burt Lancaster engaged in a bitter conflict in 1958's *Run Silent, Run Deep.* That same year, Glenn Ford was given a mission to destroy a Japanese ship carrying his family in *Torpedo Run.* Most of the World War II films which survived into the 1960s were epic-scale features like *The Longest Day* (1962) and *Battle of the Bulge* (1965). Thus, the submarine war film disappeared into obscurity until the German-made *Das Boot (The Boat)* unexpectedly surfaced to wow arthouse audiences in 1981. An incredibly tense, claustrophobic thriller, it traced the final days of a doomed *German* submarine during World War II. In contrast to the realism of war, futuristic submarines have appeared principally in escapist entertainment. Two Jules Verne novels have provided the basis for the best-known submarine fantasies. Disney's 1954 adaptation of *20,000 Leagues Under the Sea* remains a splendid spectacle for children of all ages, highlighted by a thrilling attack by a giant squid. Verne's sequel *Mysterious Island* has been filmed twice, first as a loose adaptation in 1929 and later as a compact 1961 adventure (which actually contained little footage of the famous submarine *Nautilus*). Irwin Allen, prior to his "disaster movie" days, produced 1961's *Voyage to the Bottom of the Sea*, which starred Walter Pidgeon as commander of the submarine *Seaview*. The wild plot pitted the *Seaview* against a giant octopus, onboard saboteurs, and a radiation belt threatening to burn the Earth to a crisp. The *Seaview*, with Richard Basehart replacing Pidgeon, transitioned to television as the 1964–68 series "Voyage to the Bottom of the Sea." The most elaborate submarine was probably the supership featured in the 1963 Japanese fantasy *Atragon* — it could travel underwater, on land, or in the air! Animated Beatles sailed aboard 1968's *The Yellow Submarine* (which is where they all lived). In 1966's *Batman*, the Penguin, the Riddler, the Joker, and the Cat Woman plotted mischief from within a penguin-shaped submarine. James Bond used a minisub in *Thunderball* (1965), while a full-size submarine was stolen in the 1977 Bond adventure *The Spy Who Loved Me*. Herpephobes should try to avoid *Fer-de-Lance*, a 1974 TV-movie about snakes slithering rampantly about a damaged submarine.

Mysterious Island (1929)
The Devil and the Deep (1932)
Hell Below (1933)
Submarine D-1 (1937)
Submarine Patrol (1938)
Escape to Glory (aka *Submarine Zone*) (1940)
Crash Dive (1943)
Destination Tokyo (1943)
We Dive at Dawn (1943)
Action in the North Atlantic (1943)
The Damned (1947)
Operation Disaster (aka *Morning Departure*) (1950)
Hell and High Water (1954)
20,000 Leagues Under the Sea (1954)
Above Us the Waves (1956)
The Deep Six (1958)
Run Silent, Run Deep (1958)
The Silent Enemy (1958)
Torpedo Run (1958)
Atomic Submarine (1959)
On the Beach (1959)
Operation Petticoat (1959)
Up Periscope (1959)
Atlantis, the Lost Continent (1960)
The Mysterious Island (1961)
Voyage to the Bottom of the Sea (1961)
Mystery Submarine (aka *Decoy*) (1962)
The Bedford Incident (1965)
Around the World Under the Sea (1966)
The Russians Are Coming, the Russians Are Coming (1966)
Batman (1966)
Assault on the Wayne (1970 TVM)
Yellow Submarine (1968)
Submarine X-1 (1968)
Nobody's Perfect (1968)
Ice Station Zebra (1969)
Latitude Zero (1969)
The Land That Time Forgot

(1974)   *Das Boot* (aka *The Boat*) (1981)
Fer-de-Lance (1974 TVM)   *The Fifth Missile* (1986)
The Spy Who Loved Me (1977)   *The Abyss* (1989)
Gray Lady Down (1978)

Subways

Underground trains have been underutilized as film settings, principally because their frequent stops and passenger turnover prohibit the development of an involved plot. Nevertheless, French director Luc Bresson fashioned a stylish tale about contemporary underground denizens in 1985's *Subway.* The underrated horror film *Raw Meat* was about the trapped survivors of a London subway disaster and their descendants—who evolve into cannibals. Vicious Robert Shaw and cronies hijacked a NYC subway and held the passengers for ransom in the 1974 thriller *The Taking of Pelham One Two Three.* The difficulties of getting a seat on the morning subway were explored in the 1950 comedy *Pretty Baby.* Youth gangs harrassed subway passengers in *The Warriors* (1979) and *We're Fighting Back* (1981). Subway workers figured prominently in the plots of *No Time for Love* (1943) and *Sugarbaby* (1985). The remains of an alien spaceship were unearthed during a subway station excavation in the clever sci-fi fantasy *Five Million Years to Earth* (1967). See also **Trains.**

No Time for Love (1943)
Pretty Baby (1950)
Dutchman (1966)
Five Million Years to Earth (aka
   Quatermass and the Pit)
   (1967)
The Incident (1967)
Short Walk to Daylight (1972
   TVM)
Raw Meat (aka *Deathline*)
   (1973)
*The Taking of Pelham One
   Two Three* (1974)
The Warriors (1979)
We're Fighting Back (1981)
Subway (1985)
Sugarbaby (1985)

Suicide

Although suicide has played an integral role in dozens of features, films expressly about it fall into two general categories. The first includes movies in which someone attempts to thwart a potential suicide. In 1951's *Fourteen Hours,* Richard Basehart spent the better part of a day on a skyscraper's ledge as likable policeman Paul Douglas and others (including Grace Kelly) tried to talk him out of taking the plunge. While Basehart's character fell into a net and lived, Sissy Spacek succeeded in killing herself in 1986's *'night, Mother,* despite desperate pleas from parent Anne Bancroft. An angel named Clarence dissuaded James Stewart from suicide in Frank Capra's perennial holiday offering *It's a Wonderful Life* (1946). Paralyzed Richard Dreyfuss fought a hospital staff for his right to die in the powerful *Whose Life Is It Anyway?* (1981). The second category of suicide films revolves around how a loved one's suicide affects the living. Families and friends dealt with devastating teenage suicides in *Silence of the Heart* (1984), *Surviving* (1985), and *Permanent Record* (1988). Angie Dickinson played a woman trying to rebuild her life after her husband took his in *The Suicide's Wife* (1979). On the lighter side, suicide has been played for laughs in a handful of offbeat comedies. After tightening a noose around his neck in *Reuben, Reuben,* poet Tom Conti changed his mind — only to have a dog burst into the room and knock his chair out from under him. Bud Cort delighted in staging elaborate fake suicides in the cult classic *Harold and Maude* (1971). In 1978's *The End,* a dying man unable to commit suicide decides he needs professional help with his death. Would-be suicide victims met and fell in love in *Paris in Spring* (1935) and *Tulips* (1981). And four middled-aged men decided to commit group suicide by eating themselves to death in the French farce *La Grande Bouffe* (1973). Several films have climaxed in shocking suicides. *Guyana Tragedy: The Story of Jim Jones* (1980) ended with the bizarre mass suicide staged in the late 1970s by the Rev. Jones and his cult followers. A murderess (Jean Simmons) rejected by her lover (Robert Mitchum) backed their car off a cliff in Otto Preminger's *Angel Face* (1953). In 1948's *The Red Shoes,* a ballerina confronted with choosing between art and love plunges to her death. Ship steward Edmund Gwenn explained the ultimate fate of suicide victims to his fellow dead passengers in 1944's *Between Two Worlds:* suicides can never get off the ship.

Dangerous Corner (1934)	*Guyana Tragedy: The Story of*
Paris in Spring (aka *Paris Love*	*Jim Jones* (1980 TVM)
Song) (1935)	*Tulips* (1981)
Between Two Worlds (1944)	*Whose Life Is It Anyway?* (1981)
It's a Wonderful Life (1946)	*The Eyes, the Mouth* (1982)
The Red Shoes (1948)	*Reuben, Reuben* (1983)
Fourteen Hours (1951)	*Right of Way* (1983 TVM)
Angel Face (1953)	*Silence of the Heart* (1984
The Slender Thread (1965)	TVM)
The Art of Love (1965)	*A Reason to Live* (1985 TVM)
Harold and Maude (1971)	*Mishima* (1985)
La Grande Bouffe (1973)	*Surviving* (1985 TVM)
The End (1978)	*'night Mother* (1986)
Leap into the Void (1979)	*Permanent Record* (1988)
The Suicide's Wife (aka *A New*	*Retribution* (1988)
Life) (1979 TVM)	

Summer Camp

Summer camp settings seem to foster rivalries, love affairs, and pranks among their teen residents. Rivals Kristy McNichol and Tatum O'Neal wagered each other on who would lose her virginity first at the summer camp in *Little Darlings* (1980). On a broader scale, the boys and girls of

Camp North Star challenged the rich kids' camp across the river to an absurd athletic contest in *Meatballs* (q.v.) (1979). And the Peanuts Gang (q.v.) got involved in a river race in *Race for Your Life, Charlie Brown* (1977). Michael J. Fox and Nancy McKeon found summer camp love in the 1975 TV-movie comedy *Poison Ivy*. A more honest relationship, between a disfigured teenage boy and a blind girl, took place at the summer camp in *Mask* (1985). The 1987 *Ernest Goes to Camp* dispensed with any pretensions of plot and focused on the antics of a bumbling counselor and his practical joke–prone charges. Hayley Mills played a pair of twins who meet accidentally at a summer camp and wound up reuniting their divorced parents in *The Parent Trap* (1961). *The Acorn People* (1981) was a heartwarming story about a camp for severely handicapped youngsters. Murders galore took place at the isolated summer camps in the *Friday the 13th* films (q.v.), *The Burning* (1981), and *Summer Camp Nightmare* (1987).

Make a Wish (1937)	*Meatballs* (1979)
The Under-Pup (1939)	*Friday the 13th* (1980)
There's Magic in Music (1941)	*Little Darlings* (1980)
Summer Love (1958)	*Gorp* (1980)
Beware of Children (1961)	*The Burning* (1981)
The Parent Trap (1961)	*The Acorn People* (1981 TVM)
Please Sir (1971)	*Mask* (1985)
Poison Ivy (1975 TVM)	*Ernest Goes to Camp* (1987)
Race for Your Life, Charlie Brown (1977)	*Summer Camp Nightmare* (1987)

Superman

"You'll believe a man can fly!" proclaimed the ads when *Superman* was released in 1978. Millions of moviegoers did just that, making the Man of Steel's celebrated screen return the first of a profitable series. Actually, Superman made his first feature-length movie appearance in 1951 in the guise of stocky George Reeves. *Superman and the Mole Men* (1951) was a low-budget independent feature aimed at the juvenile trade. It would have likely remained a "B"-movie oddity, except that its minor success resulted in a phenomenal, syndicated TV series "The Adventures of Superman." In all, 104 half-hour episodes were broadcast originally between 1952 and 1957. Reeves starred as Clark Kent/Superman, with Phyllis Coates and later Noel Neill as Lois Lane, Jack Larson as Jimmy Olsen, and John Hamilton as Perry White. Despite obvious budget limitations, the series made the most of its special effects. Later episodes were even filmed in color, a television rarity in the 1950s. Sadly, Reeves became typecast by the role and had difficulty finding work, a fact that may have attributed to his 1959 suicide. The Superman character, created by writer Jerry Siegel and artist Joe Shuster, first appeared in comic book form in 1939. Bud Collyer provided the voice of Superman for a 1940–1951 radio series. Kirk

Allyn also played the Man of Steel in 1948 and 1950 serials (and can be seen as Lois Lane's father in the TV-expanded version of 1978's *Superman*). But with the smash success of *Superman,* Christopher Reeve made the role his own for a generation of comic book lovers. Much of the 1981 sequel *Superman II* was filmed simultaneously with the first film, partially accounting for the original's $55 million price tag. Whereas *Superman* dealt with the Man of Steel's origin and introduced the supporting characters, *Superman II* promptly pitted our hero against three vicious outlaws from his own planet. The romance between Lois Lane (Margot Kidder) and Clark Kent/Superman was also developed, to the extent that they consummated their relationship. The series took an inexplicable turn for the worse with 1983's *Superman III,* which boasted the additional marquee value of Richard Pryor. Margot Kidder made a brief appearance as Lois Lane, but Superman's love interest was old flame Lana Lang (Annette O'Toole). Reeve balked at starring in a fourth film, so executive producers Ilya and Alexander Salkind brought *Supergirl* to the screen in 1984. Casting an unknown (as they did with Reeve), the Salkinds failed to create another star in girl-next-door Helen Slater. The silly plot and Faye Dunaway's hammy villainess was a far cry from *Superman II.* The only cast holdover from the *Superman* films was Marc McClure as Jimmy Olsen. The failure of *Supergirl* apparently ended the series. However, Cannon Films acquired distribution rights from Warner Bros. and lured Reeve back into the fold. The actor wrote the story and directed some scenes in 1987's *Superman IV: The Quest for Peace.* Despite the presence of Gene Hackman (returning as Lex Luthor) and a token appearance by Kidder, *Superman IV* was a victim of shoddy special effects and a pretentious plot. It sent Superman packing for an indefinite vacation from the movies. See also **Comic Book Characters.**

Superman and the Mole Men (1951)	*Superman III* (1983)
	Supergirl (1984)
Superman (1978)	*Superman IV: The Quest for*
Superman II (1981)	*Peace* (1987)

Surfing

The quest for the Big Wave was a constant teenage concern in the lightweight *Gidget* (q.v.) and *Beach Party* (q.v.) movies of the 1960s. However, serious surfers had little opportunity to promote their sport prior to Bruce Brown's 1966 documentary *The Endless Summer.* This lyrical homage to the beauties and dangers of surfing earned critical raves and a loyal cult following. Dramatic films have been far less interesting. The 1978 *Big Wednesday* traced the lives of surfing buddies Jan-Michael Vincent, William Katt, and Gary Busey from the mid–1960s to the late 1970s. *Shimmering Light* (1978) sent Beau Bridges to Australia in search of the Big Wave. The 1987 *North Shore* starred Matt Adler as a cocky surfer eager to challenge the famed Oahu waves in Hawaii. David Dukes played a man permanently paralyzed by a surfing accident in the 1979 TV-movie *Some Kind of Miracle*. The 1987 *Beach Party* reunion film *Back to the Beach* featured Frankie Avalon staging a surfing duel against a wonderfully tacky rear-screen wave. Australian filmmaker-star Yahoo Serious had Albert Einstein inventing the first surfboard and riding a few waves into the offbeat 1989 comedy *Young Einstein*.

The Endless Summer (1966)	*Some Kind of Miracle* (1979
Pacific Vibrations (1971)	TVM)
Big Wednesday (aka *Summer of*	*North Shore* (1987)
Innocence) (1978)	*Back to the Beach* (1987)
Shimmering Light (1978 TVM)	*Aloha Summer* (1988)
California Dreaming (1979)	*Young Einstein* (1989)

Surrogate Motherhood

Television movies have frequently borrowed their stories from the headlines, with no better example than the four films about surrogate motherhood broadcast between 1979 and 1988. The celebrated case of *Baby M* garnered the most attention, but earlier efforts explored the same territory with less fanfare. In fact, *The Seeding of Sarah Burns* (1979) was a fictional drama with remarkable similarities to *Baby M*. Kay Lenz played the woman who undergoes an embryo transplant and then has second thoughts about giving up the baby. Two 1982 TV-movies covered the same ground, with Susan Dey and Stephanie Zimbalist as the surrogate mothers in *The Gift of Life* and *Tomorrow's Child*. The 1984 theatrical release *The Surrogate* dispensed with emotional crises in favor of a whodunit plot. *Private Practices: The Story of a Sex Surrogate* (1986) was a detailed documentary on the subject. Along similar lines, a sterile wife and her spouse hired a young woman to conceive a child with the husband in 1970's *The Baby Maker*.

The Baby Maker (1970)	*The Gift of Life* (1982 TVM)
The Seeding of Sarah Burns	*The Surrogate* (1984)
(1979 TVM)	*Private Practices: The Story of a*
Tomorrow's Child (aka *Genesis*)	*Sex Surrogate* (1986)
(1982 TVM)	*Baby M* (1988 TVM)

Suspended Animation

If one is to believe science fiction cinema, the most popular method for inducing suspended animation is to freeze living cells. The Frankenstein Monster was discovered frozen in ice, and subsequently revived to full strength, in both *The House of Frankenstein* (1944) and *The Evil of Frankenstein* (1964). Likewise, a Neanderthal Man encased in ice was thawed in Fred Schepisi's heavyhanded social parable *Iceman* (1984). Warped scientist Dana Andrews tried to bring back frozen Nazis in 1967's

The Frozen Dead. And a man frozen through cryogenic means returned to life as a killer in Wes Craven's offbeat 1985 TV-movie *Chiller.* *Star Trek* creator Gene Roddenberry produced three TV pilot films about a 20th century man awakened from suspended animation to find himself in the future. Alex Cord starred in *Genesis II* (1973), with John Saxon playing the lead in both *Planet Earth* (1974) and *Strange New World* (1975). None of these TV-movies resulted in a weekly series. Actually, the 1939 *Buck Rogers* serial was probably the first "film" to use suspended animation as a means of placing contemporary man into the future. It was re-edited into two feature films (1953's *Planet Outlaws* and 1965's *Destination Saturn*) and later remade as 1979's *Buck Rogers in the 25th Century.* Woody Allen borrowed the basic premise for comedic purposes in 1973's *Sleeper.* Other interesting uses of suspended animation have appeared in *This Island Earth* (1954) and *In Like Flint* (1967). The aliens in the former film were among the first to use suspended animation as a method for enabling living beings to endure unbearably long space voyages. The villains in *Flint* suspended a golf game long enough to replace the real president with a lookalike substitute. On television, the 1967–68 sitcom "The Second Hundred Years" was about a 33-year-old man who was frozen in a glacier in 1933, only to thaw out 101 years later and encounter his now middle-aged son. See also **Coma.**

The House of Frankenstein (1944)	*Genesis II* (1973 TVM)
This Island Earth (1954)	*Planet Earth* (1974 TVM)
Dinosaurus! (1960)	*Live Again, Die Again* (1974 TVM)
Frozen Alive (1964)	*Strange New World* (1975 TVM)
The Evil of Frankenstein (1964)	*Buck Rogers in the 25th Century* (1979)
Kiss the Girls and Make Them Die (1966)	*Iceman* (1984)
In Like Flint (1967)	*Chiller* (1985 TVM)
The Frozen Dead (1967)	
Sleeper (1973)	

Swamps

Sun-baked bodies trudging slowly through murky waters. Bloodsucking leeches clinging to human flesh. The crisp snap of an alligator's jaws. These are familiar sights and sounds in movie swamps, which have been used chiefly as convenient hideouts, treacherous short-cuts, and unlikely long-term residences. In Jean Renoir's *Swamp Water* (1941), Dana Andrews chased his dog into a Georgia swamp and discovered the secret hiding place of an alleged murderer (Walter Brennan). He also discovered Brennan's lonely daughter Ann Baxter and, eventually, the real murderers (who met their fate in a pit of quicksand). Brennan repeated his role for the 1952 remake *Lure of the Wilderness.* Richard Gere and Kim Basinger took a short-cut through the Louisiana swamps to elude pursuers in 1986's *No Mercy*. In contrast, Michael Beck and hostage Lee Remick took a Carolina swamp route to avoid the law in the 1984 TV-movie *Rearview Mirror*. Barbara Hershey won a Cannes Best Actress Award in 1987's *Shy People* as a Bayou widow whose life is disrupted by an unexpected visit from city relative Jill Clayburgh. Hershey's swampy residence reflected her character's internal strength and emotional isolation. No hidden meanings were behind the swamp setting in *Gator Bait*, a drive-in quickie about a Cajun girl (former playmate Claudia Jennings) navigating a zippy launch to avoid lusty Bayou males. Nine National Guardsmen wound up fighting unfriendly Cajuns in the *Deliverance*-inspired *Southern Comfort* (1981). The Mouse Rescue Aid Society ventured into a threatening swamp to find a helpless child mouse in Disney's 1977 animated feature *The Rescuers*. The 1982 *Swamp Thing*, based on a cult comic book, was about a good scientist transformed into a half-man, half-plant monstrosity. He ventured out of the marshy waters to periodically rescue girlfriend Adrienne Barbeau from the clutches of evil scientist Louis Jourdan. The plot was essentially repeated in the 1989 sequel *Return of the Swamp Thing*, with Jourdan returning as the villain and Heather Locklear replacing Barbeau.

Swamp Water (aka *The Man Who Came Back*) (1941)	(1966)
	Frogs (1972)
Swamp Fire (1946)	*Live and Let Die* (1973)
Lure of the Wilderness (1952)	*Gator Bait* (1976)
Cry of the Hunted (1953)	*The Rescuers* (1977)
Swamp Women (aka *Swamp Diamonds; Cruel Swamp*) (1955)	*Southern Comfort* (1981)
	Swamp Thing (1982)
Lure of the Swamp (1957)	*Rearview Mirror* (1984 TVM)
Attack of the Giant Leeches (aka *The Giant Leeches*) (1959)	*No Mercy* (1986)
	Down by Law (1986)
	Shy People (1987)
Curse of the Swamp Creature	*Return of the Swamp Thing* (1989)

Sword and Sorcery

Although its literary basis dates back to the 1930s, the sword and sorcery genre of the 1980s probably owes its cinematic inspiration to George Lucas' *Star Wars* (1977) and *The Empire Strikes Back* (1980). Han Solo and Luke Skywalker, while lacking the physical attributes of muscular heroes, together form the basic mold of an ironic adventurer sent forth on a preordained quest. However, the genre proper—complete with muscle-bulging hunks and heavy swords—began with 1982's *Conan the Barbarian*. Robert E. Howard wrote 17 Conan stories, which appeared in *Weird Tales* pulp magazine between 1932–36 (four others were published post-humously). John Milius' film version offered little more than a straight-forward telling of Conan's beginnings, but it made a star of Arnold

Schwarzenegger and inspired a sequel as well as a rash of imitators. One rip-off, *The Sword and the Sorcerer,* starring TV stars-to-be Lee Horsley ("Matt Houston") and Kathleen Beller ("Dynasty"), actually beat *Conan* to the theaters. More typical imitations included an ineptly-made Italian series starring former *Tarzan* Miles O'Keefe as a silly beefcake hero named Ator (q.v.). Despite attempts to infuse the genre with good-natured camp (Don Coscarelli's *Beastmaster*) or elaborate production design (Peter Yates' *Krull*), the sword and sorcery craze died softly in 1985 with *Red Sonja,* a boxoffice failure despite the potentially potent pairing of Arnold Schwarzenegger and Brigitte Nielsen. See also **Ator.**

The Sword and the Sorcerer (1982)	*Future* (1983)
Conan the Barbarian (1982)	*Ator the Fighting Eagle* (1983)
Sorceress (1982)	*Fire and Ice* (1983)
Beastmaster (1983)	*Deathstalker* (1984)
Krull (1983)	*Conan the Destroyer* (1984)
Yor — the Hunter from the	*Red Sonja* (1985)
	Iron Warrior (1987)

Talking Animals

Talking animals have been a screen oddity, with the exceptions of Francis the Talking Mule (q.v.) and various animated critters. Bing Crosby and Bob Hope's wacky *Road* comedies featured a talking fish in *Road to Utopia* and a pair of conversing camels in *Road to Morocco.* Another talking camel made a cameo in the adventure spoof *Slave Girl* (1947). Walter Abel had a talking dog in *The Fabulous Joe* (1947), Mickey Rooney a conversant duck in *Everything's Ducky* (1961), Bob Goldthwait a chattering horse in *Hot to Trot* (1988), and Pee Wee Herman a prose-producing pig in *Big Top Pee Wee* (1988). Don Johnson could speak telepathically with his dog Blood in Harlan Ellison's science fiction satire *A Boy and His Dog* (1975). No discussion of talking animals would be complete without mentioning TV's famous talking horse "Mr. Ed." See also **Francis the Talking Mule.**

Road to Morocco (1942)	*Everything's Ducky* (1961)
Road to Utopia (1945)	*A Boy and His Dog* (1975)
Slave Girl (1947)	*Hot to Trot* (1988)
The Fabulous Joe (1947)	*Big Top Pee Wee* (1988)

Tammy

A wholesome backwoods teenager, Tammy managed to charm the socks off of everyone she met. Her adventures were mild, to say the least, but nevertheless influential. They set the stage for similar fodder such as Gidget (q.v.) and thus proved there was a lucrative market for teen-oriented, nonhorror pictures (a fact exploited by AIP's *Beach Party* series). Twenty-five-year-old Debbie Reynolds, already an established star, created the role in 1957's *Tammy and the Bachelor*. She also sang the memorable title tune, which hit #1 on *Billboard*'s pop chart in July 1957. Sandra Dee, after introducing Gidget in 1959, played Tammy in two sequels, with John Gavin and Peter Fonda as her love interests. A half-hour sitcom starring Debbie Watson debuted in September 1965 and lasted a single season. Four of its episodes were edited into an 87-minute movie and released theatrically as *Tammy and the Millionaire*.

Tammy and the Bachelor (aka *Tammy*) (1957) (Reynolds)	*Tammy and the Doctor* (1963) (Dee)
Tammy Tell Me True (1961) (Dee)	*Tammy and the Millionaire* (1967) (Watson)

Tarzan

Edgar Rice Burroughs' muscular jungle hero has shown remarkable endurance since his film debut in 1918. He has survived ill-conceived character changes, gross miscastings, and cheap-looking backlot jungles. Elmo Lincoln, a D.W. Griffith player who had appeared in *Birth of a Nation*, was the first actor to don the loincloth in 1918's *Tarzan of the Apes*. From the beginning, Burroughs stressed that he wanted the film to be a faithful adaptation. Yet, despite his presence during filming, the plot strayed slightly from the book—a problem that would plague Burroughs on a much larger scale in future Tarzan pictures. The movie performed well at the boxoffice and a less successful sequel, *Romance of Tarzan*, came out later that year. Burroughs reaped little profit off these films and sold the rights to subsequent novels to other producers. During the silent era: Goldwyn distributed *The Revenge of Tarzan* (1920), National Film Corporation turned *Son of Tarzan* (1921) into a serial, Elmo Lincoln reprised the role for another serial *The Adventures of Tarzan* (1921), and Film Booking Offices (later RKO Radio) released *Tarzan and the Golden Lion* (1927). The star of the latter picture, Jim Pierce, married Burroughs' daughter Joan and they later played Tarzan and Jane in a radio series. Following two more Tarzan serials in the early 1930s, Irving Thalberg acquired series rights for MGM. *Tarzan the Ape Man* (1932) was a lavish jungle epic. It made a film star of former Olympic swimming champion Johnny Weissmuller, but also unfortunately dispensed with Burroughs' conception of Tarzan as an educated man. Weissmuller's Tarzan spoke in broken English ("Tarzan—Jane") and never strayed from his beloved jungle in his series debut. Still, audiences loved the wild animal thrills and the romance between primitive Tarzan and civilized Jane (Maureen O'Sullivan). MGM mounted an even more impressive sequel in 1934's *Tarzan and His Mate*, which most critics consider Weissmuller's finest Tarzan epic. The studio produced four more Tarzan entries, introducing Johnny Sheffield as Boy in 1939's *Tarzan Finds a Son* and concluding the series with 1942's *Tarzan's New York Adventure*. Although the MGM Tarzan films dominated the 1930s, other independent efforts competed against them. Sol Lesser, who had acquired an option from Burroughs through a third party, signed Buster Crabbe for *Tarzan the Fearless* (1933). It was edited into two different versions, so theater owners could show it as a 71-minute feature or as a serial. The same fate befell 1935's *The New Adventures of Tarzan*. This historic oddity was produced by Burroughs' own company, thus ensuring that Tarzan acted like an educated man. Herman Brix, later known as Bruce Bennett, played the lead. Initially available as a feature or serial, the film was recut *again* in 1938 and released with a new title *Tarzan and the Green Goddess*. A third non–MGM effort, 1938's *Tarzan's Revenge,* offered minimal backlot thrills and a lackluster hero as played by Glenn Morris. MGM may have felt these low-budget rivals weakened the boxoffice attraction of their films. However, RKO did not hesitate to grab Weissmuller and launch its own Tarzan series in 1943. Johnny Sheffield accompanied Weissmuller to RKO, but Maureen O'Sullivan bowed out as Jane. There was no Jane—but lots of Nazis—in RKO's first entry *Tarzan Triumphs.* The film marked Sol Lesser's return as a Tarzan producer and he eventually instilled Brenda Joyce as the series' new Jane. Although relying heavily on stock footage, the RKO films drew steady business. Johnny Sheffield, eventually outgrew his role as Boy and left the series after 1947's *Tarzan and the Huntress.* Monogram immediately signed him to play Bomba, the Jungle Boy (q.v.). Weissmuller turned in his loincloth the following year, after Lesser refused to give him a percentage of the profits. Producer Sam Katzman grabbed Weissmuller for the lead in his Jungle Jim (q.v.) series. Bland Lex Barker replaced Weissmuller for the five remaining RKO pictures, beginning with 1949's *Tarzan's Magic Fountain.* When Barker balked at signing a multi-picture contract, Lesser dropped him in favor of muscular Gordon Scott, a former lifeguard with no acting experience. Scott's first Tarzan picture, *Tarzan's Hidden Jungle* (1955) was RKO's last. Unperturbed, industrious producer Lesser took Scott and the series to MGM and unleashed the first Technicolor Tarzan adventure with 1957's *Tarzan and the Lost Safari.* Lesser and Scott also did *Tarzan's Fight for Life* (1958) for MGM and then made three TV pilots which were edited into *Tarzan and the Trappers* (1958). The latter films fared poorly and Lesser sold his film and TV series rights to Sy Weintraub in 1959. Weintraub produced four superior Tarzan films, the first two starring Scott and the last two introducing stunt man and veteran actor Jock Mahoney. The Mahoney films featured exotic locales, vibrant colors, and a literate interpretation by the star. Unfortunately, Mahoney stepped aside after his second film and the Weintraub series took a turn for the worse. Mahoney's replacement, former Rams linebacker Mike Henry had the right physique, but his performance doomed 1966's *Tarzan and the Valley of Gold* and two sequels. Henry turned down Weintraub's TV series, allowing Ron Ely to became the small screen's first Tarzan. The series debuted in 1966 and enjoyed a two-year run. In 1970, unsuspecting movie-goers were lured to the theaters to see *Tarzan's Jungle Rebellion* and *Tarzan's Deadly Silence,* two features compiled from TV series episodes. Except for an "R"-rated cartoon spoof *Shame of the Jungle* (1975), the 1970s was a quiet decade for Tarzan. In 1981, John and Bo Derek produced the unintentionally funny *Tarzan, the Ape Man,* devoting more screen time to Bo's frequently nude Jane than to Miles O'Keefe's hunky Tarzan. In contrast, 1984's *Greystoke: The Legend of Tarzan, Lord of the Apes* made a legitimate stab at transferring Burrough's novel to the screen intact. Tarzan's childhood in the jungle was depicted splendidly, but his eventual trip to England brought the picture to a standstill. Christopher Lambert made a fine Tarzan, while Andie McDowell's voice as Jane was dubbed by actress Glenn Close. Five years later, Tarzan unexpectedly reappeared in *Tarzan in Manhattan,* an ill-conceived TV-movie with Jane as a taxi driver. It was funnier, in a sad sort of way, than Jimmy Durante's appearance as "Schnarzan" in the 1934 movie industry spoof *Hollywood Party.*

Tarzan of the Apes (1918) (Elmo Lincoln)
Romance of Tarzan (1918) (Lincoln)
The Revenge of Tarzan (1920) (Gene Pollar)
Tarzan and the Golden Lion (1927) (Jim Pierce)
Tarzan the Ape Man (1932) (Weissmuller)
Tarzan the Fearless (1933) (Buster Crabbe)
Tarzan and His Mate (1934) (Weissmuller)
The New Adventures of Tarzan (aka *Tarzan's New Adventure;* re-edited in 1938 as *Tarzan and the Green Goddess*) (1935) (Herman Brix aka Bruce Bennett)
Tarzan Escapes (1936) (Weissmuller)
Tarzan's Revenge (1938) (Glenn Morris)
Tarzan Finds a Son! (1939) (Weissmuller)
Tarzan's Secret Treasure (1941) (Weissmuller)
Tarzan's New York Adventure (1942) (Weissmuller)
Tarzan Triumphs (1943) (Weissmuller)
Tarzan's Desert Mystery (1943) (Weissmuller)
Tarzan and the Amazons (1945) (Weissmuller)
Tarzan and the Leopard Woman (1946) (Weissmuler)
Tarzan and the Huntress (1947) (Weissmuller)
Tarzan and the Mermaids (1948) (Weissmuller)
Tarzan's Magic Fountain (1949) (Lex Barker)
Tarzan and the Slave Girl (1950) (Barker)
Tarzan's Peril (aka *Tarzan and the Jungle Queen*) (1951) (Barker)
Tarzan's Savage Fury (1952) (Barker)
Tarzan and the She-Devil (1953) (Barker)
Tarzan's Hidden Jungle (1955) (Gordon Scott)
Tarzan and the Lost Safari (1957) (Scott)
Tarzan's Fight for Life (1958) (Scott)
Tarzan and the Trappers (1958) (Scott)
Tarzan's Greatest Adventure (1959) (Scott)

Tarzan the Ape Man (1959) (Denny Miller)
Tarzan the Magnificent (1960) (Scott)
Tarzan Goes to India (1962) (Jock Mahoney)
Tarzan's Three Challenges (1963) (Mahoney)
Tarzan and the Valley of Gold (1966) (Mike Henry)
Tarzan and the Great River (1967) (Henry)
Tarzan and the Jungle Boy (1968) (Henry)
Tarzan's Jungle Rebellion (1970) (Ron Ely)
Tarzan's Deadly Silence (1970) (Ely)
Shame of the Jungle (1975) (voice of Johnny Weissmuller, Jr.)
Tarzan the Ape Man (1981) (Miles O'Keefe)
Greystoke: The Legend of Tarzan, Lord of the Apes (1984) (Christopher Lambert)
Tarzan in Manhattan (1989 TVM) (Joe Lara)

Tattoos

The most tattooed characters in cinema history are probably *The Illustrated Man* (1969) and Queequeg of *Moby Dick* (1956) fame. As to which of these has the *most* tattoos, well, that's difficult to determine, although Queequeg may get the edge on the basis of his tattooed face. Still, one could make an argument in favor of the Illustrated Man. His face may have been unmarked, but his tattoos did move and tell stories. In other films: Burt Lancaster sported *The Rose Tattoo* (1955) on his chest, symbolizing his "sexual prowess" and also reminding widow Anna Magnani of her deceased husband. Bruce Dern played a wacko artist in 1981's *Tattoo* who kidnaps Maud Adams so he can tattoo her entire body. It was written by Joyce Buñuel, Luis' daughter. Tattoos have been used less dramatically for concealing treasure maps, as in *The Stranger and the Gunfighter* (1976). See also **Painted People.**

The Rose Tattoo (1955)	*Get Charlie Tully* (1976)
Moby Dick (1956)	*The Stranger and the Gun-*
The Illustrated Man (1969)	*fighter* (1976)
The Golden Voyage of Sinbad	*Tattoo* (1981)
(1973)	*Double Exposure* (1989)

Taxi Drivers

Colorful cabbies have appeared as memorable supporting characters in dozens of movies and have been played by an impressive group of veteran character actors. James Gleason drove Loretta Young and angel Cary Grant to a frozen lake in *The Bishop's Wife* (1947) and wound up ice skating with them. Streetwise cabbie Ernest Borgnine navigated Kurt Russell through the hazardous ruins of futuristic Manhattan in the sci-fi adventure *Escape from New York* (1981). Yaphet Kotto played the unfortunate cab driver stuck with taking self-confessed murderer David Janssen to Mexico in the suspense-drama *Night Chase* (1971). Ricardo Cortez was one of the first actors to play a taxi driver in a leading role, starring opposite Barbara Stanwyck in 1931's *Ten Cents a Dance* (a rare directorial effort by Lionel Barrymore). Other star performers who have played cabbies include George Raft *(Pick-up)*, Red Skelton *(The Yellow Cab Man)*, and Fred Astaire *(The Purple Taxi)*. In the respective boxoffice bombs *Rhinestone* (1984) and *Die Laughing* (1980), Sylvester Stallone and Robby Benson proved that taxi drivers can't sing professionally. Lady cabbies have been represented on-screen by Beulah Bondi in *She's a Soldier Too* (1944) and Sophia Loren in *Aurora* (1984). In the 1989 TV-movie *Tarzan in Manhattan*, Jane turned out to be a cab driver! Britain's long-running *Carry On* comedy film series (q.v.) featured the appropriately-titled entry *Carry On, Cabby* (1963). The 1981 animated feature *Heavy Metal* included a segment about a futuristic N.Y.C. cab driver. *D.C. Cab* (1983) was an episodic comedy about a cab company, obviously inspired by the 1978-83 "Taxi" TV series. The best-remembered cabbie performance is probably Robert DeNiro's splendid portrait of unbalanced Vietnam vet Travis Bickle in Martin Scorsese's *Taxi Driver* (1976).

Ten Cents a Dance (1931)
Taxi (1932)
Pick-up (1933)
The Big City (aka *Skyscraper Wilderness*) (1937)
She's a Soldier Too (1944)
Two Guys from Milwaukee (1946)
The Bishop's Wife (1947)
The Yellow Cab Man (1950)
Taxi (1953)
99 River Street (1953)
The Catered Affair (aka *Wedding Breakfast*) (1956)
Carry On, Cabby (1963)
Night Chase (aka *The Man in the Back Seat*) (1970 TVM)
Pigeons (aka *The Sidelong Glances of a Pigeon Kicker*) (1971)
Law and Disorder (1974)

Taxi Driver (1976)
Adventures of a Taxi Driver (1976)
The Purple Taxi (1977)
Love in a Taxi (1980)
Die Laughing (1980)
The Princess and the Cabbie (1981 TVM)
Escape from New York (1981)
Heavy Metal (1981)
Chan Is Missing (1982)
Hit and Run (aka *Revenge Squad*) (1982)
D.C. Cab (1983)
Signal 7 (1983)
Rhinestone (1984)
Aurora (1984 TVM)
Tarzan in Manhattan (1989 TVM)
Wired (1989)
Look Who's Talking (1989)

Telekinesis [Psychokinesis, or PK]

Movie teenagers have displayed a special knack for acquiring telekinesis, the power to move objects with the mind. Sissy Spacek showed just how much havoc a mistreated, revenge-minded, telekinetic teen could wreak in the 1976 adaptation of Stephen King's *Carrie*. She veered cars off course, sent knives flying through the air, and demolished a high school gym with

a fire hose. Imitations were bound to follow and Brian De Palma produced an interesting one with 1978's *The Fury*, which offered two
telekinetic teens — one good (Amy Irving) and one gone bad (Andrew
Stevens). In contrast, the telekinetic teen comedy *Zapped!* (1982) offered a
trite plot about a horny guy (Willie Aames) who takes a perverse interest
in friend Scott Baio's newly-acquired talent. A young boy and a teenage
girl used their telekinetic powers to battle a demon and knife-fingered
Freddy Krueger, respectively, in the 1988 films *Cameron's Closet* and *Friday the 13th Part VII — The New Blood*. As for adults, some playful gods
endowed meek Roland Young with temporary telekinetic powers in the
H.G. Wells fantasy *The Man Who Could Work Miracles*. In George Pal's
underrated 1968 thriller *The Power*, scientist George Hamilton tracked
down a mysterious telekinetic killer capable of changing his appearance by
controlling people's minds (which made him devilishly difficult to find).
Chevy Chase explored the frivolous side of telekinesis as an air traffic con-
troller in the mild 1981 comedy *Modern Problems*. Richard Burton played
the most destructive — and lazy — telekinetic villain by causing all sorts of
disasters from his hospital bed in *The Medusa Touch* (1978).

The Man Who Could Work Miracles (1936)	*Modern Problems* (1981)
	Zapped! (1982)
The Power (1968)	*Firestarter* (1984)
Carrie (1976)	*Cameron's Closet* (1988)
The Man with the Power (1977 TVM)	*Friday the 13th Part VII — The New Blood* (1988)
The Fury (1978)	
The Medusa Touch (1978)	

Telephones

Although telephones have played bit parts in thousands of movies,
a few particularly memorable roles are called to mind. A foreign
agent used the telephone (and a Robert Frost poem) to activate brainwashed killers in *Telefon*. A party line brought Doris Day and Rock
Hudson together in *Pillow Talk*. Judy Holliday ran a telephone answer-
ing service called Susanswerphone in the otherwise forgettable musical comedy *Bells Are Ringing*. And Barbara Stanwyck inadvertently
learned of her own proposed murder via the phone in *Sorry, Wrong
Number*. Telephone numbers have been played for drama in the fact-
based *Call Northside 777* and for strained chuckles in the goofy *Tran-
sylvania 6-5000*. James Coburn was almost killed in a phone booth
in *The Carey Treatment*, while Christopher Reeve used booths for
dressing rooms in the *Superman* movies. Telephones were employed
as spur-of-the-moment murder weapons in *The Naked Kiss* and *The
Stepfather*. Clever premeditated murderers found ingenius uses for
phones in *The Invisible Killer* and *Murder by Phone*. Devious

Vincent Price bumped off a victim with a spiked telephone receiver in *Dr. Phibes Rises Again.*

The Invisible Killer (1940)	*When Michael Calls* (1972
Call Northside 777 (aka *Calling*	TVM)
Northside 777) (1948)	*The Secret Night Caller* (1975
For the Love of Mary (1948)	TVM)
Sorry, Wrong Number (1948)	*Telefon* (1977)
Southside 1-1000 (1950)	*When a Stranger Calls* (1979)
Chicago Calling (1951)	*Don't Answer the Phone* (1980)
Dial M for Murder (1954)	*Murder by Phone* (aka *Bells*)
Pillow Talk (1959)	(1980)
Bells Are Ringing (1960)	*E.T. The Extra-Terrestrial*
The Naked Kiss (1964)	(1982)
I Saw What You Did (1965)	*Hotline* (1982 TVM)
The Slender Thread (1965)	*Transylvania 6-5000* (1985)
Boy, Did I Get a Wrong	*The Stepfather* (1987)
Number! (1966)	*Call Me* (1988)
Dial Hot Line (1969)	*The Telephone* (1988)
The Day the Hot Line Got Hot	*976-EVIL* (1989)
(1969)	*Party Line* (1989)
Dr. Phibes Rises Again (1972)	*Dial: Help* (1989)

Teleportation

Science fiction buffs have defined teleportation as the process of almost instantaneously transmitting matter from one place to another. This is usually accomplished by breaking down an animal or object into its molecules, transporting the molecules through space, and then reassembling them. Edward Page Mitchell may have been the first writer to describe the process in his 1877 short story "The Man Without a Body." In the *Star Trek* (q.v.) TV series and films, the crew of the Starship Enterprise used a teleporter as a routine mode of travel. The Delambre and Brundle families had a terrible time with teleportation experiments in *The Fly* (q.v.) movies. Andre Delambre initiated the problems by unknowingly allowing a fly to sneak into the teleportation booth with him. Their molecules merged—resulting in a disgusting combination of man/fly (and also fly/man). Bryant Halliday encountered a slightly different problem in 1966's *The Projected Man.* His "projection device" transported him successfully, but it also charred half his face and endowed him with a deadly electric touch.

Television

Even before television's success threatened the popularity of theatrical movies, the big screen all but ignored the little screen. The 1933 comedy *International House* used an early television experiment as the premise for jamming an all-star cast into a Chinese hotel. The stars included W.C.

Fields, George Burns and Gracie Allen, Bela Lugosi, and—appearing in a
TV broadcast—Rudy Vallee and Cab Calloway. On a smaller scale, comedians operated a pirate TV station out of a castle in 1939's *Band Waggon,*
which was inspired by a hit British radio series. Amazingly, this
lighthearted comedy was considerably ahead of its time, for pirate TV
broadcasts were not further explored until 1983's *Videodrome* and 1986's
Riders of the Storm. During the 1950s, the early days of network TV provided the setting for fluffy comedies like *Two Gals and a Guy* and *Simon
and Laura.* A noteworthy exception was 1956's *The Great Man,* a scathing
look at a much-loved TV personality revealed by Jose Ferrer to have been
an unscrupulous, egotistical heel. The decade also produced Arch Obler's
The Twonky (1953), a bizarre satire that remains an oddity after almost
three decades. The title creature was a futuristic robot which begins running Hans Conried's life after becoming accidentally trapped inside the
man's TV set. The sarcastic *Variety* review commented that the "thought is
posed that Twonky can reduce mankind to automatons"—a charge television is still facing today. Indeed, by the mid–1970s, television was ingrain-
ed as an integral part of American society, prompting renewed interest in
movies about TV. *The Groove Tube* (1974) was the first of several movies
consisting of loosely-connected comedy sketches built around television.
The Front (1976) and *My Favorite Year* (1982) evoked nostalgia toward the
early days of television. The former film skillfully covered a dark period in
TV history—the blacklisting of writers accused of Communist activities.
Ethics in the television industry have been addressed principally in films
about network TV news. News broadcasts were packaged as entertainment
in 1976's *Network,* while news reporter William Hurt faked an emotional
tear for the camera in 1987's *Broadcast News.* The 1983 TV-movie *Special
Bulletin* looked just like a news broadcast, with anchors Ed Flanders and
Kathryn Walker keeping viewers informed about a terrorist group
threatening to destroy Charleston, S.C., with a nuclear bomb. The film
simulated the feel of a real broadcast so well that the final outcome carried a shattering, terrifying jolt. Horror filmmakers have used television to
temporarily house transient ghosts, demons, and extraterrestrials in
Poltergeist, Demons 2, and *Terrorvision,* respectively. None of those was
nearly as frightening as David Cronenburg's powerful horror/satire
Videodrome, which cast James Woods as a broadcast executive metamor-
phosed into a television/man (at one point, he slips a videotape into a
newly-formed slot in his stomach). This overly complex film (was it all an
hallucination?) disgusted most moviegoers and died quickly at the boxoffice. The 1985 *Explorers,* while not a movie about television, featured
aliens who learned everything they knew about humans from watching
Earth TV—a frightening premise when one thinks about it. The 1985
comedy-drama *Static* was about a young man who claimed to have invented a television capable of tuning in Heaven.

International House (1933)
Murder by Television (1935)
Band Waggon (1939)
Two Gals and a Guy (1951)
The Twonky (1953)
Meet Mr. Lucifer (1953)
The Glass Web (1953)
Simon and Laura (1955)
The Great Man (1956)
A Face in the Crowd (1957)
The Gazebo (1959)
The Thrill of It All (1963)
Panic Button (1964)
The Barefoot Executive (1971)
The Love Machine (1971)
The Groove Tube (1974)
The Front (1976)
Network (1976)
Tunnelvision (1976)
Telethon (1977 TVM)
KGOD (aka Pray TV) (1980)
Deathwatch (1980)
My Favorite Year (1982)

This Is...Kate Bennett (1982 TVM)
Wrong Is Right (1982)
Poltergeist (1982)
Videodrome (1983)
Special Bulletin (1983 TVM)
The Record (1984)
The Ratings Game (1984 TVM)
Static (1985)
Reckless Disregard (1985 TVM)
Ginger and Fred (1985)
America (1986)
News at Eleven (1986 TVM)
Terrorvision (1986)
Riders of the Storm (aka The American Way) (1986)
Broadcast News (1987)
Pass the Ammo (1988)
Switching Channels (1988)
Demons 2 (1988)
The Brain (1988)
UHF (1989)

Television-Expanded Films

Television has long practiced the "art" of dicing up theatrical films to fit a specified time period or to deleting material its censors deemed unacceptable. However, the equally offensive practice of expanding theatrical films for television showings did not gain widespread popularity with the networks until the mid–1970s. That's when network executives realized that it was cheaper to add leftover footage to an existing film than to pay for new programming. Thus, instead of one night of *Superman*, they could add enough footage to stretch its impressive ratings over two nights. In the case of *Superman*, the new scenes did allow film buffs to glimpse Kirk Allyn (Superman in the movie serials) and Noel Neill (Lois in the TV series) as Lois Lane's parents. However, other TV expansions have been less thoughtful. The James Bond adventure *On Her Majesty's Secret Service* was expanded by simply tacking the climactic ski chase onto the front of the film, adding a voiceover, and repeating the same scene (in its proper sequence) later in the broadcast. Director Gene Palmer shot almost an hour of new footage, complete with new cast, for the network TV broadcast of the already-inflated *Two Minute Warning*. Alas, one cannot blame the networks alone. Director David Lynch had his name removed from the credits of *Dune* when the movie was lengthened for its syndicated showing. On the other hand, Francis Ford Coppola played a central role in altering his *Godfather* films for a special television broadcast. He intercut scenes from the 175-minute *The Godfather* (1972) and 200-minute *The Godfather, Part II* (1974), added footage from the cutting room floor, and produced the mammoth 475-minute *The Godfather Saga*.

Requiem for a Heavyweight (1962)	*Two Minute Warning* (1976)
Secret Ceremony (1968)	*The Godfather Saga* (1977)
On Her Majesty's Secret Service (1969)	*The Concorde: Airport '77* (aka *Airport '77*) (1977)
Jeremy (1973)	*The Deep* (1977)
Earthquake (1974)	*Superman* (1978)
	Dune (1984)

Television Movie Sequels to Theatrical Films

ABC-TV pioneered the concept of the television movie sequel with 1974's *Mrs. Sundance*, a small-screen continuation of 1969's *Butch Cassidy and the Sundance Kid*. Elizabeth Montgomery replaced Katharine Ross in the role of Etta Place, the Sundance Kid's widow and the new quarry of ruthless bounty hunters. Although produced by 20th Century–Fox, who made the original, *Mrs. Sundance* caused no confusion in regard to its origin — it looked and played like a made-for-TV movie, right down to the perfectly-timed commercial breaks. Interestingly, just two years later, 20th Century–Fox convinced Katharine Ross to recreate the role for *Wanted: The Sundance Woman*, another TV sequel. This version ignored *Mrs. Sundance* (which no doubt confused some meticulous viewers) and involved Etta with Mexican rebel Pancho Villa. Ross is one of four performers to play the same role in both a theatrical film and its TV-movie sequel. George C. Scott repeated his Oscar-winning 1970 portrayal of General George Patton for the 1986 TV film *The Last Days of Patton*. Lee Marvin returned as the leader of *The Dirty Dozen* in *The Dirty Dozen: Next Mission*. And Barry Newman played lawyer Tony Petrocelli on the big screen in *The Lawyer* (1970) and on the small screen in *Night Games* (1974). The latter served as a pilot for Newman's short-lived series "Petrocelli." Other TV-movie sequels have also doubled as pilots for prospective series, such as *Matt Helm, Nevada Smith, True Grit, Serpico: The Deadly Game,* and *Our Man Flint: Dead on Target*. In some of these features, the only connection with the original feature was the name of the main character. Dean Martin's Matt Helm was a boozing super secret agent, while Tony Franciosa's TV incarnation was a wisecracking private eye with a steady girlfriend. The longest gap between a theatrical film and a made-for-TV sequel is 28 years — from 1952's *High Noon* to 1980's *High Noon II: The Return of Will Kane*. The casting of Lee Majors in the Gary Cooper role still rankles some Cooper fans. *The Dirty Dozen* has spawned the most TV sequels: three and still counting. In the following list, the TV-movies are listed chronologically in the left column with the theatrical film on the right (if a theatrical series, the last series entry is shown):

338

Mrs. Sundance (1974 TVM)	*Butch Cassidy and the Sundance Kid* (1969)
Sidekicks (1974 TVM)	*Skin Game* (1971)
Night Games (1974 TVM)	*The Lawyer* (1970)
Nick and Nora (1975 TVM)	*Song of the Thin Man* (1947)
Matt Helm (1975 TVM)	*The Wrecking Crew* (1969)
Nevada Smith (1975 TVM)	*Nevada Smith* (1966)
Look What's Happened to Rosemary's Baby (aka *Rosemary's Baby II*) (1976 TVM)	*Rosemary's Baby* (1968)
Wanted: The Sundance Woman (aka *Mrs. Sundance Rides Again*) (1976 TVM)	*Butch Cassidy and the Sundance Kid* (1969)
Our Man Flint: Dead on Target (1976 TVM)	*Our Man Flint* (1966)
Serpico: The Deadly Game (1976 TVM)	*Serpico* (1973)
A Matter of Wife . . . and Death (1976 TVM)	*Shamus* (1973)
True Grit (1978 TVM)	*True Grit* (1969)
A Real American Hero (1978 TVM)	*Final Chapter—Walking Tall* (1973)
Christmas Lilies of the Field (1979 TVM)	*Lilies of the Field* (1963)
High Noon II: The Return of Will Kane (1980 TVM)	*High Noon* (1952)
Revenge of the Stepford Wives (1980 TVM)	*The Stepford Wives* (1975)
Trackdown: Finding the Goodbar Killer (1983 TVM)	*Looking for Mr. Goodbar* (1977)
The Jerk Too (1984 TVM)	*The Jerk* (1979)
The Dirty Dozen: The Next Mission (1985 TVM)	*The Dirty Dozen* (1967)
Popeye Doyle (1986 TVM)	*The French Connection II* (1975)
The Return of the Shaggy Dog (1987 TVM)	*The Shaggy D.A.* (1976)
The Parent Trap II (1986 TVM)	*The Parent Trap* (1961)
The Last Days of Patton (1986 TVM)	*Patton* (1970)
Bates Motel (1987 TVM)	*Psycho III* (1986)
The Dirty Dozen: The Deadly Mission (1987 TVM)	*The Dirty Dozen* (1967)
If It's Tuesday, This Still Must Be Belgium (1987 TVM)	*If It's Tuesday, This Must Be Belgium* (1969)
The Stepford Children (1987 TVM)	*The Stepford Wives* (1975)
The Dirty Dozen: The Fatal	*The Dirty Dozen* (1967)

339

Mission (1988 TVM)

The Great Escape II: The   *The Great Escape* (1963)
Untold Story (1988 TVM)

Amityville: The Evil Escapes   *Amityville 3-D* (1983)
(1989 TVM)

Note: The 1989 TV-movie *Get Smart, Again* was obviously intended as a television series reunion movie (q.v.) and thus is not listed as a sequel to 1980's *The Nude Bomb* (aka *The Return of Maxwell Smart*).

Television Series Reunion Movies

A wave of nostalgia washed over television viewers of the 1980s, making small screen movies based on old television series the most significant TV-movie trend of the decade. The nostalgia went beyond mere revival of a TV show's premise, for, in almost all cases, the made-for-TV movies reunited some of the series' original cast members. The 1969 *Dragnet* could lay claim to being the first TV series reunion film. It was based on the then-running 1967–70 "Dragnet" series which was an updated revival of the original 1952–59 "Dragnet." Jack Webb starred as police sergeant Joe Friday in the movie and both runs of the series. *The New Maverick* (1978) reunited James Garner and Jack Kelly as free-wheeling brothers Bret and Bart Maverick, roles they originated in the popular 1957–62 Western series. However, the purpose of the 1978 TV-movie was to launch a new show starring Charles Frank as their nephew Ben (the series "Young Maverick" ran very briefly in 1979). On the other hand, 1977's *Father Knows Best Reunion* and 1978's *Rescue from Gilligan's Island* offered nothing new, just pure nostalgia with the original cast members returning (except for Tina Louise as Ginger Grant in the latter film). Their successful ratings (*Gilligan* resulted in two sequels) initiated a steady growth in the number of TV series reunion films. Interestingly, the "Gilligan's Island" TV series was only a modest hit during its 1964–67 run, cracking the top 20 shows only once. The series gained tremendous popularity, especially among young viewers, through syndicated repeats running on local stations. Subsequently, syndication success became a criteria for determining if a series had potential as a reunion film, thus accounting for TV-movies based on "The Brady Bunch," "The Munsters," and "I Dream of Jeannie." Indeed, hit series have not always resulted in hit movies. *The Return of the Beverly Hillbillies* (1981) was a painful reunion highlighted by the absence of series regulars Irene Ryan (Granny), Max Baer (Jethro), and Raymond Bailey (Mr. Drysdale). Without the 1960s spy movie genre to spoof, 1983's *The Return of the Man from U.N.C.L.E.* came across as dry and dated, despite the presence of stars Robert Vaughn and David McCallum. In contrast, Raymond Burr's triumphant *Perry Mason Returns* (1985) was a well-conceived update that inaugurated a series of highly-rated Perry Mason (q.v.) TV-movies. The longest gap between a series' last year and its reunion film is the 25 years separating the 1959–63 series "The Many Affairs of Dobie Gillis" from 1988's *Bring Me the Head of Dobie Gillis*. Twenty-seven years separated the series "Peter Gunn" from the 1989 TV-movie—however, the TV-movie *Peter Gunn* was a reunion only in that Blake Edwards produced and directed both movie and show. Peter Strauss and an all new cast replaced Craig Stevens and the other series regulars. Michael Landon, Jr., was the only link between his father's "Bonanza" series and 1988's *Bonanza: The Next Generation*. The 1987 *Police Story: The Freeway Killing* was an oddity—a revival of an anthology TV show. See also **Theatrical Films Based on Television Series**. In the following list, only the first reunion film is shown (e.g. see **Gilligan's Island** for a list of other movies based on the series):

Dragnet (1969 TVM)
Father Knows Best Reunion (1977 TVM)
The New Maverick (1978 TVM)
Rescue from Gilligan's Island (1978 TVM)
The Return of the Mod Squad (1979 TVM)
The Wild, Wild West Revisited (1979 TVM)
The Return of Frank Cannon (1980 TVM)
The Brady Girls Get Married (1981 TVM)
The Munsters' Revenge (1981 TVM)
The Return of the Beverly Hillbillies (1981 TVM)
A Day for Thanks on Walton's Mountain (1982 TVM)
The Return of the Man from U.N.C.L.E. (1983 TVM)
Still the Beaver (1983 TVM)
The Return of Marcus Welby (1984 TVM)
I Dream of Jeannie: 15 Years Later (1985 TVM)
Kojak: The Belarus File (1985 TVM)
Perry Mason Returns (1985 TVM)
Kung Fu: The Movie (1986 TVM)
Return to Mayberry (1986 TVM)
Eight Is Enough: A Family Reunion (1987 TVM)
Gunsmoke: Return to Dodge (1987 TVM)
The Return of the Six Million Dollar Man and the Bionic Woman (1987 TVM)
Police Story: The Freeway Killing (1987 TVM)
Still Crazy Like a Fox (1987 TVM)
Bonanza: The Next Generation (1988 TVM)
Bring Me the Head of Dobie Gillis (1988 TVM)
The Incredible Hulk Returns (1988 TVM)
The Return of Ben Casey (1988 TVM)
Get Smart Again (1989 TVM)
Peter Gunn (1989 TVM)
The Return of Sam McCloud (1989 TVM)

Tennis

Tennis and golf (q.v.) have failed to interest many filmmakers, perhaps because the two sports were once viewed as leisurely activities reserved for the country club set. Director Ida Lupino lent a feminist slant to 1951's *Hard, Fast and Beautiful*, an overwrought drama about a domineering mother who pushed her daughter toward tennis stardom. The 1978 TV biography *Little Mo* told the story of teen Grand Slam champion Maureen Connelly, who died after a long struggle with cancer. Two theatrical tennis movies were releasing the following year and both flopped badly. *Racquet* starred Bert Convey as a tennis pro who used sex to get what he wanted, while *Players* featured Dean Paul Martin as a promising player forced to choose between the game and a woman (Ali MacGraw). Real-life tennis stars Pancho Gonzalez *(Players)* and Bobby Riggs *(Racquet)* lent the movies a touch of credibility. *Spring Fever* (1983) simply recruited a real player to play the lead role, but teenaged Carling Bassett showed no promise as an actress (of course, neither did the rest of the cast, which included Susan Anton as the girl's mother). The 1986 *Second Serve* examined the fascinating real-life saga of Richard Raskins, the male surgeon who underwent a sex-change operation and became tennis player Renee Richards. Tennis games have served as memorable set pieces in several movies. Monsieur Hulot (q.v.) experienced a great deal of trouble with the game in one of the funniest scenes in *Monsieur Hulot's Holiday*. A troupe of mimics played an imaginary game of tennis in the symbolic denouement of *Blow-Up*. And in Alfred Hitchcock's *Strangers on a Train*, tennis player Farley Granger rushes through a big match so he can stop psychopath Robert Walker from murdering again.

You Can't Cheat an Honest Man (1939) (table tennis)
Come to the Stable (1949)
Hard, Fast and Beautiful (1951)
Strangers on a Train (1951)
Monsieur Hulot's Holiday (1953)
Dial M for Murder (1954)
Blow-Up (1966)
The High Commissioner (aka *Nobody Runs Forever*) (1968)
The Christian Licorice Store (1971)
Little Mo (1978 TVM)
Racquet (1979)
Players (1979)
Spring Fever (1983)
Second Serve (1986 TVM)
Jocks (aka *Road Trip*) (1987)

The Texas Rangers

This was another routine Western series (once again built around three lawmen) until Tex Ritter joined the cast in 1944. The original lineup consisted of Dave O'Brien, Guy Wilkerson, and James Newill, best known as the singing Mountie of the *Renfrew* series (q.v.). Ritter replaced Newill after *Brand of the Devil* and distinguished the films with his familiar voice. Ironically, Ritter's biggest hit song occurred in a Western in which he did not star—1952's *High Noon*. Eagle Lion reissued the Texas Ranger pictures, with different titles, in the late 1940s.

Rangers Take Over (1943)
Bad Men of Thunder Gap (aka *Thundergap Outlaws*) (1943)
West of Texas (aka *Shootin'*
Irons) (1943)
Border Buckaroos (1943)
Fighting Valley (1943)
Trail of Terror (1944)

The Return of the Rangers (1944)
Boss of the Rawhide (1944)
Gunsmoke Mesa (1944)
Outlaw Roundup (1944)
Guns of the Law (1944)
The Pinto Bandit (1944)
Spook Town (1944)
Brand of the Devil (1944)

Gangsters of the Frontier (1944)
Dead or Alive (1944)
The Whispering Skull (1944)
Marked for Murder (1945)
Enemy of the Law (1945)
Three in the Saddle (1945)
Frontier Fugitives (1945)
Flaming Bullets (1945)

Theatrical Films Based on TV Series

The reasons why some TV series have been developed into theatrical films, while others have not, defines logic. Surprisingly, television ratings have rarely been used as criteria. The 1964–66 sitcom "The Munsters" was hardly a ratings hit, but that did not deter Universal from releasing a 1966 theatrical version dubbed *Munster, Go Home*. Likewise, the Saturday morning kiddie show "H.R. Pufnstuf" seemed an odd choice for a big-screen musical when 1970's *Pufnstuf* appeared in theaters. Ironically, both the "Pufnstuf" and "Munsters" TV series were cancelled almost simultaneously with the release of their feature film versions. Cult television shows have fared far better as theatrical films. The gothic soap opera "Dark Shadows" had a built-in audience of loyal fans when the movie *House of Dark Shadows* premiered in 1967. It did well enough to inspire a second picture, 1971's *Night of Dark Shadows*. The classic TV series "Star Trek" performed dismally in the ratings (ranking 52 in its best season) during its original 1966–69 run. However, by the time an expensive big-screen version was mounted in 1979, the show had turned into a national phenomenon thanks to syndicated showings on local TV stations. The *Star Trek* (q.v.) film series initiated by *Star Trek – The Motion Picture* easily outdistances all other TV series-inspired films in terms of both box-office and popularity. Its closest competition comes from Jim Henson's Muppets (q.v.), which used the syndicated "Muppet Show" as a springboard for three theatrical features beginning with 1979's *The Muppet Movie*. On British television, three of the Quatermass (q.v.) science fiction serials were remade as theatrical movies and the 1970–75 comedy series "On the Buses" inspired a 1971 big screen version. The longest span between a series' last season and its theatrical version was the 18 years that separated "The Twilight Zone" (1959–1965) from *Twilight Zone – The Movie* (1983). The most successful movie based on a television flop was 1988's *The Naked Gun*, which evolved from the very short-lived comedy series "Police Squad" (1982). *The Man from U.N.C.L.E.* movies (q.v.) were not "new" theatrical films, but merely episodes of the TV series edited together.

Here Come the Nelsons (1952)   *Our Miss Brooks* (1956)

The Lone Ranger (1956)
The Creeping Unknown (aka
   The Quatermass Experiment)
   (1956)
The Lineup (based on TV series
   "San Francisco Beat") (1958)
McHale's Navy (1964)
Munster, Go Home (1966)
A Man Called Flintstone (1966)
Batman (1966)
Gunn (1967)
Dark Shadows (1967)
Pufnstuf (1970)
On the Buses (1971) (from a
   British series)
Dad's Army (1971) (from a
   British series)
Callan (1974) (from a British

series)
Star Trek — The Motion Picture
   (1979)
The Muppet Movie (1979)
The Blues Brothers (1980) (from
   the TV series "Saturday
   Night Live")
The Gong Show Movie (1980)
The Nude Bomb (aka *The
   Return of Maxwell Smart*)
   (1980)
Twilight Zone — The Movie
   (1983)
Smurfs and the Magic Flute
   (1984)
Dragnet (1987)
Masters of the Universe (1987)
The Naked Gun (1988)

The Thin Man

In the 1930s and 1940s, one detective film series stood above all the others. With two big stars in the leads and plenty of MGM gloss, the six Thin Man mysteries clearly separated themselves from their "B"-movie competitors. These were "A" efforts and marketed as such, with new entries released only at two or three-year intervals. The first film, based on Dashiell Hammett's novel, cast William Powell and Myrna Loy as wealthy, amateur detectives Nick and Nora Charles. Powell already had extensive detective film experience, having played Philo Vance (q.v.) in four films for Paramount and Warner Brothers. But unlike the urbane Vance, Nick Charles afforded Powell the opportunity to display his gift for light comedy. Myrna Loy provided the perfect foil, becoming a role model for spunky film heroines. The third family member was Asta, Nick and Nora's faithful, and mischievous, fox terrier. Nick, Jr., made his series debut in the third entry, *Another Thin Man* (actually the title made little sense since the "thin man" was a murder victim played by Edward Ellis in the first film). The quality of the mysteries declined as the series progressed, but the films remained popular due to the Charles' sophisticated relationship, a natural blend of good-natured insults and honest affection. As with the Hardy series (q.v.), MGM used the Thin Man films as a training ground for its brightest acting prospects: James Stewart (playing against type) in *After the Thin Man*, Donna Reed in *Shadow of the Thin Man*, and Gloria Grahame and Dean Stockwell (as Nick, Jr.) in *Song of the Thin Man*. Peter Lawford and Phyllis Kirk played Nick and Nora on television, enjoying a modest two-year run with their 1957 series "The Thin Man." Craig Stevens (TV's "Peter Gunn") and Jo Ann Pflug tried to

344

update the characters in the charmless 1975 TV-movie *Nick and Nora*. The Charleses were among the detectives spoofed in Neil Simon's *Murder by Death* (1976).

The Thin Man (1934)	*The Thin Man Goes Home* (1944)
After the Thin Man (1936)	
Another Thin Man (1939)	*Song of the Thin Man* (1947)
Shadow of the Thin Man (1941)	*Nick and Nora* (1975 TVM)

3-D

Three-dimensional, or stereoscopic, films create an illusion of depth by separating the right eye's field of view from the left eye's. This is usually accomplished by requiring viewers to wear cardboard glasses with clear polarized lenses or lenses tinted red and blue-green (the latter process is called anaglyphic 3-D). Although experimental 3-D films date back to 1915, the depth process was largely ignored until the early 1950s. Faced with the growing popularity of television, movie moguls felt that something new was needed to lure patrons back to the theaters. The astonishing success of Arch Obler's low-budget, three-dimensional jungle adventure *Bwana Devil* ("A lion in your lap!" proclaimed the poster) convinced Hollywood that 3-D was the answer to its problems. Over 40 stereoscopic films were released between 1953 and 1954. Arguably, the finest was 1953's *House of Wax,* which launched Vincent Price's horror career by casting him as a mad sculptor who makes wax figures from his murder victims. Unfortunately, quality efforts like *House of Wax* and *It Came from Outer Space* were quickly overshadowed by technically inept, let's-make-a-buck features like *Robot Monster* and *Cat Women of the Moon*. By 1955, the 3-D craze had ended, brought to an early death by the popularity of less expensive wide-screen processes like Cinemascope (which also offered something TV couldn't). Attempts to revive 3-D proved fruitless for almost two decades. Then in 1969, the unexpected success of *The Stewardesses,* a low-budget sex picture, inspired a fleeting interest in 3-D again. However, as in the 1950s, poor quality 3-D movies flooded the market and snuffed out the chances of a big comeback. But just to prove you can't keep a good idea down, 3-D surfaced once more in the early 1980s with the release of a ludicrous Italian Western dubbed *Comin' at Ya*. This time, the major studios jumped on the bandwagon and produced big-budget features like *Jaws 3* and *Metalstorm*. Despite a few legitimate hits (e.g. *Friday the 13th Part III*), the idea of 3-D never really captured the public's fancy and it faded within a year. Nevertheless, the 1980s craze did produce the first 3-D feature-length cartoon, 1985's *Starchaser: The Legend of Orin*. See also **Cinerama; Gimmicks.**

Bwana Devil (1952)	(1953)
Arena (1953)	*Devil's Canyon* (1953)
The Charge at Feather River	*Fatal Desire* (1953)

Money from Home (1953)
The Moonlighter (1953)
Fort Ti (1953)
Flight to Tangier (1953)
Hondo (1953)
House of Wax (1953)
I, the Jury (1953)
It Came from Outer Space
 (1953)
Invaders from Mars (1953)
Inferno (1953)
Kiss Me Kate (1953)
Man in the Dark (1953)
Miss Sadie Thompson (1953)
The Maze (1953)
Outlaw Territory (aka Hannah
 Lee) (1953)
Robot Monster (1953)
Sangaree (1953)
Wings of the Hawk (1953)
Second Chance (1953)
The Stranger Wore a Gun
 (1953)
Cat Women of the Moon (aka
 Rocket to the Moon) (1954)
Creature from the Black Lagoon
 (1954)
Dial M for Murder (1954)
Drums of Tahiti (1954)
The French Line (1954)
Gog (1954)
Gorilla at Large (1954)
The Mad Magician (1954)
Phantom of the Rue Morgue
 (1954)
Taza, Son of Cochise (1954)
Son of Sinbad (1954)
Eyes of Hell (aka The Mask)

(1961)
The Bubble (aka Fantastic In-
 vasion of Planet Earth) (1966)
The Mark of the Werewolf (aka
 Frankenstein's Bloody Terror)
 (1968)
The Stewardesses (1969)
Three Dimensions of Greta
 (1972)
The Flesh and Blood Show (aka
 Asylum of the Insane) (1972)
Andy Warhol's Frankenstein
 (aka Flesh for Frankenstein)
 (1973)
The Playmates (1973)
A*P*E (1976)
The Surfer Girls (1980)
Comin' at Ya! (1981)
Rottweiler (aka Dogs of Hell)
 (1981)
Friday the 13th Part 3 (1982)
Treasure of the Four Crowns
 (1982)
Parasite (1982)
Jaws 3 (aka Jaws 3-D) (1983)
The Man Who Wasn't There
 (1983)
Metalstorm: The Destruction of
 Jared-Syn (1983)
Spacehunter: Adventures in the
 Forbidden Zone (1983)
Tales of the Third Dimension
 (1984)
Silent Madness (aka Omega
 Factor; Night Killer) (1984)
Hit the Road Running (1984)
Starchaser: The Legend of Orin
 (1985)

The Three Mesquiteers

Popular Western novelist William Colt MacDonald created these three Dumas-inspired do-gooders: Stony Brooke, the trio's hot-tempered leader; Tucson Smith, his more rational friend and frequent romantic rival; and Lullaby Joslin, the easy-going comedian of the group. Law of the 45's (1935) was the first Mesquiteer novel to reach the screen, but it did not feature all three Mesquiteers. That distinction belongs to RKO's Powdersmoke Range (1935), which starred Harry Carey, Hoot Gibson, and

Big Boy Williams as, respectively, Tucson, Stony, and Lullaby. The following year, little Republic Pictures snatched up the property and launched the *official* Three Mesquiteers series. Republic's original Mesquiteer line-up featured Ray "Crash" Corrigan as Tucson, Robert Livingston as Stony, and Syd Saylor as Lullaby. Max Terhune replaced Saylor in the second film and it's this cast—Corrigan, Livingston, and Terhune—that's best remembered. Other performers, though, also spent time in the saddle. Ralph Temp temporarily replaced Livingston and an upcoming actor named John Wayne played Stony for awhile. A cowboy singer named Dick Weston had a musical number in 1937's *Wild Horse Rodeo*. Weston later became a Western star in his own right—after changing his name to Roy Rogers. Duncan Renaldo, best known as the Cisco Kid (q.v.) joined the cast in 1939 for a brief stint as a new character named Rico. Meanwhile, Corrigan, Livingston, and Terhune moved to other studios and launched new series. Corrigan and Terhune joined John "Dusty" King to form *The Range Busters* (q.v.) for Monogram. Livingston teamed up with Al "Fuzzy" St. John in PRC's *The Lone Rider* movies. These series and many similar ones owe much to the "Western trio" premise fostered by the first Mesquiteer pictures.

Law of the 45's (1935)
Powdersmoke Range (1935)
The Three Mesquiteers (1936)
Ghost Town Gold (1936)
Roarin' Lead (1936)
Riders of the Whistling Skull (1937)
Hit the Saddle (1937)
Gunsmoke Ranch (1937)
Come On, Cowboys (1937)
Range Defenders (1937)
Heart of the Rockies (1937)
The Trigger Trio (1937)
Wild Horse Rodeo (1937)
The Purple Vigilantes (1938)
Call the Mesquiteers (1938)
Outlaws of Sonora (1938)
Riders of the Black Hills (1938)
Heroes of the Hills (1938)
Pals of the Saddle (1938)
Overland Stage Raiders (1938)
Santa Fe Stampede (1938)
Red River Range (1938)
The Night Riders (1939)
Three Texas Steers (1939)
Wyoming Outlaws (1939)
New Frontier (1939)

The Kansas Terrors (1939)
Cowboys from Texas (1939)
Heroes of the Saddle (1940)
Pioneers of the West (1940)
Covered Wagon Days (1940)
Rocky Mountain Rangers (1940)
Oklahoma Renegades (1940)
Under Texas Skies (1940)
The Trail Blazers (1940)
Lone Star Raiders (1940)
Prairie Pioneers (1941)
Saddlemates (1941)
Gangs of Sonora (1941)
Outlaws of the Cherokee Trail (1941)
Gauchos of El Dorado (1941)
West of Cimarron (1941)
Code of the Outlaw (1942)
Raiders of the Range (1942)
Westward Ho (1942)
The Phantom Plainsmen (1942)
Shadows on the Sage (1942)
Valley of Hunted Men (1942)
Thundering Trails (1943)
The Blocked Trail (1943)
Santa Fe Scouts (1943)
Riders of the Rio Grande (1943)

Three Mothers

Stephen King once confessed that 1977's *Suspiria*, the first of this would-be horror trilogy, was one of his "guilty pleasures, in part because it treated us to an entire girls' school being bombarded by a rain of maggots at dinner...good stuff." Italian horror stylist Dario Argento allegedly based the films on an essay by Thomas De Quincey entitled "Levana and Our Ladies of Sorrow." The "ladies" are the three wicked sisters who produce the sorrows of the world: Mater Suspiriorum (Mother of Sighs); Mater Tenebrarum (Mother of Darkness); and Mater Lachrymarum (Mother of Tears). Although its English-language title suggests that *Tenebrae* (1982) is part of the "trilogy," there is strong evidence to suggest otherwise. The plot features no supernatural elements, focusing on a murderer replicating crimes from author Tony Franciosa's novel (which is titled *Tenebrae*). Thus, Argento fans still await a third film to conclude the trilogy.

Suspiria (1977)	*Tenebrae* (aka *Tenebres;*
Inferno (1980)	*Unsane*) (1982)

Three Smart Girls

Teen star Deanna Durbin made her feature film debut in 1936's *Three Smart Girls,* a sentimental comedy about the efforts of three sisters to reunite their separated parents. Nan Grey and Barbara Read played the other two sisters. Helen Parrish replaced Read in the 1939 follow-up *Three Smart Girls Grow Up,* which focused on Deanna's plans to marry off her older sisters. This fluffy sequel gave the 18-year-old Durbin one of her biggest recording hits with "Because." She reprised the Penelope Craig character one more time, as an adult, in the more serious World War II romance *Hers to Hold* (1943).

Three Smart Girls (1936)	(1939)
Three Smart Girls Grow Up	*Hers to Hold* (1943)

Tibbs, Virgil

An urbane black detective from Philadelphia, Tibbs first appeared as a fish out of water in the 1967 Best Picture *In the Heat of the Night* (1967), a mystery set in a racially prejudiced Southern town. Rod Steiger won a Best Actor Oscar as the town's sheriff, but it was Tibbs, as portrayed by Sidney Poiter, who came back for a sequel. *They Call Me MISTER Tibbs* (1970) sent Tibbs to San Francisco to solve a homicide. He was still there in 1971, working with a vigilante group to crack a drug ring in *The Organization.* That was the last Tibbs film, except for a 1988 TV version (and series pilot) of *In the Heat of the Night* starring Howard Rollins as Virgil Tibbs.

In the Heat of the Night (1967)	*The Organization* (1971)
They Call Me MISTER Tibbs (1970)	*In the Heat of the Night* (1988 TVM)

Time Travel

The subject of time has long fascinated filmmakers, as evidenced by 1910's *The Times Are Out of Joint,* an obscure sci-fi feature about a clock that manipulates time by accelerating motion. Generally, however, movies about time travel fall into three categories: traveling into the past, traveling into the future, and traveling from the future back to present day. The first category is by far the most common, dating back to Mark Twain's *A Connecticut Yankee in King Arthur's Court.* Twain's novel alone has been filmed four times, as a silent film, a Will Rogers comedy, a Bing Crosby musical, and a Disney feature (mysteriously titled *Unidentified Flying Oddball*). Leslie Howard traveled back to 18th century England in *Berkeley Square,* as did Tyrone Power in the remake *I'll Never Forget You,* while Christopher Reeve willed himself back to turn-of-the-century America in *Somewhere in Time.* All three fell in love with beautiful ladies, lost them temporarily, and then were reunited in one way or another. Spacecrafts accidentally stumbled through time warps in *World Without End* (1956) and *Planet of the Apes* (1968). In 1986's *Star Trek IV: The Voyage Home,* the Enterprise used warp speed to go back in time to save some whales. Curious scientists have naturally preferred to travel to the future, as in *The Time Travelers* (1964) and George Pal's 1960 adaptation of H.G. Wells' *The Time Machine.* A cornered Jack the Ripper used Wells' time machine to make a quick escape to modern-day San Francisco in Nicholas Meyer's stylish thriller *Time After Time* (1979). Finally, inhabitants of the future have sought to change their course of events by traveling back to present day in *Cyborg 2087* (1966) and its partial remake *The Terminator* (1984). The former film, an underrated cheapie, cast Michael Rennie as a cyborg assigned to stop the creation of his own "race." Other time-related movies of interest include: 1944's *It Happened Tomorrow* (a reporter acquires tomorrow's newspaper today), 1947's *Repeat Performance* (two people live a year over again), 1956's *The Atomic Man* (a scientist moves 7.5 seconds ahead of everyone else), and *The Jetty* (a man remembers his own future death).

Berkeley Square (1933)
Time Flies (1944)
Fiddlers Three (1944)
Where Do We Go from Here? (1945)
Repeat Performance (1947)
A Connecticut Yankee in King Arthur's Court (1949)
I'll Never Forget You (aka The House in the Square) (1951)
The Atomic Man (aka Timeslip) (1956)
World Without End (1956)
The 30 Foot Bride of Candy Rock (1959)
Beyond the Time Barrier (1960)
The Time Machine (1960)
The Jetty (aka: La Jette; The Pier) (1963)
The Time Travelers (1964)
Dr. Who and the Daleks (1965)
Willy McBean and His Magic Machine (1965)
Cyborg 2087 (1966)
Daleks—Invasion Earth 2150 A.D. (aka Invasion Earth

2150 A.D.) (1966)
Journey to the Center of Time (1967)
The Planet of the Apes (1968)
A Witch Without a Broom (1968)
Hu-Man (1975)
Time Travelers (1976 TVM)
The Time Machine (1978 TVM)
Jubilee (1978)
Time After Time (1979)
Unidentified Flying Oddball (1979)
The Day Time Ended (aka Time Warp) (1980)
The Final Countdown (1980)
Somewhere in Time (1980)
Time Bandits (1981)
Through the Magic Pyramid (1981 TVM)
Timerider (1983)
The Philadelphia Experiment (1984)
The Terminator (1984)

The Cold Room (1984 TVM)
Arthur the King (1985 TVM)
The Blue Yonder (aka Time Flyer) (1985 TVM)
Trancers (aka Future Cop) (1985)
My Science Project (1985)
Back to the Future (1985)
Biggles: Adventures in Time (aka Biggles) (1986)
Peggy Sue Got Married (1986)
Star Trek IV: The Voyage Home (1986)
Timestalkers (1987 TVM)
Out of Time (1988 TVM)
Earth*Star Voyager (1988 TVM)
Bill and Ted's Excellent Adventure (1989)
Quantum Leap (1989 TVM)
Time Trackers (1989)
Millenium (1989)
Back to the Future II (1989)
Turn Back the Clock (1989 TVM)

Titanic

Both *Titanic* and *A Night to Remember* chronicled the human drama surrounding the 1912 luxury liner disaster. The 1979 *S.O.S. Titanic* was a made-for-TV rehash, while *Raise the Titanic* was a dull adaptation of Clive Cussler's best-seller about salvaging the sunken ship. The *Titanic* returned as a ghost ship, complete with spooky passengers, in 1989's *Ghostbusters II*.

Titanic (1953)
A Night to Remember (1958)
S.O.S. Titanic (1979 TVM)

Raise the Titanic! (1980)
Ghostbusters II (1989)

Topper

George and Marion Kerby were a fun-loving couple until a car crash put a premature end to their earthy existence. Required to perform a good deed to earn admittance into Heaven, the ghostly Kerbys turned their attention to meek banker Cosmo Topper. Cosmo's subsequent problems with George and Marion generated most of the laughs in 1937's *Topper*. The film was a guaranteed success, with Cary Grant, Constance Bennett, and Roland Young in the principal roles. Bennett and Young returned for the 1939 sequel *Topper Takes a Trip,* which found Marion badgering Cosmo on his Riviera vacation. Only Young (and Billie Burke as Mrs. Topper) remained for 1941's *Topper Returns*. It drew poor comparisons with the first two films, but has since come to be regarded as a first-rate haunted house comedy. It also gave Burke a chance to shine with some wacky dialogue: "My, my, it's strange how it's always cold in the winter and warm in the summer, isn't it?" Leo G. Carroll played Cosmo in the 1953–56 TV series "Topper," with Robert Sterling and Anne Jeffreys as the Kerbys. Kate Jackson and then-husband Andrew Stevens produced and starred (as the Kerbys) in a lackluster 1979 TV-movie, co-starring Jack Warden as Cosmo Topper. In 1983's *Somewhere Tomorrow*, a lonely teenage girl watched *Topper,* bumped her head, and then met a boy ghost. See also **Ghosts.**

Topper (1937)   *Topper Returns* (1941)
Topper Takes a Trip (1939)   *Topper* (1979 TVM)

Tracy, Dick

Chester Gould's comic strip police detective had been the subject of four 1937–41 Republic serials before RKO decided he had potential as a "B" film series hero. Former tough guy Morgan Conway brought Tracy alive in 1946's *Dick Tracy* and 1947's *Dick Tracy vs. Cueball,* a pair of lively action pictures balanced nicely by a sense of humor. The scripts stayed close to the comic strip characters, with Anne Jeffreys as Tess Truehart, Esther Howard as Filthy Flora of the Dripping Dagger Inn, and Ian Keith as Vitamin Flintheart. Ralph Byrd, who had played the detective for Republic, took over the role in the last two films in the series. Since they appeared when film series were declining in popularity, the Tracy films are but forgotten today. That's a shame, for they featured some very colorful villains: Mike Mazurki's Spitface *(Dick Tracy),* Dick Wessel's Cueball, and Boris Karloff's Gruesome. In 1989, Warren Beatty announced plans to film a lavish *Dick Tracy* starring Madonna and himself.

Dick Tracy (aka *Spitface*) (1946)   *Dick Tracy Meets Gruesome*
Dick Tracy vs. Cueball (1947)   (aka *Dick Tracy's Amazing*
Dick Tracy's Dilemma (aka   *Adventure*) (1947)
  Mark of the Claw) (1947)

The Trail Blazers

Monogram Pictures was the home of the "B" Western in the 1940s. The budget-minded studio was already producing The Rough Riders (q.v.) and The Range Busters (q.v.) films when it introduced the Trail Blazers series in 1943. Monogram signed the three biggest names available (at budget price) and wound up with cowboy greats Hoot Gibson, Ken Maynard, and Bob Steele. Gibson and Maynard had retired in the 1930s, but Monogram lured them back to the screen even though they were 51 and 48, respectively. After just seven pictures, the series came to an end and Gibson and Maynard closed out their film careers except for occasional appearances.

Blazing Guns (1943)
The Law Rides Again (1943)
Wild Horse Stampede (1943)
Arizona Whirlwind (1944)

Death Valley Rangers (1944)
Outlaw Trail (1944)
Westward Bound (1944)

Trailers *see* Mobile Homes

Trains

Trains have long been a favorite setting for tense dramas and mysteries, primarily since the close confines force character interaction by restricting movement beyond a limited area. Mysteries which take place almost entirely on trains include the Basil Rathbone Sherlock Holmes entry *Terror by Night* and the 1974 all-star adaptation of Agatha Christie's *Murder on the Orient Express.* Two of Alfred Hitchcock's most famous works are set aboard trains: A little old lady who's really a spy (Dame May Whitty) gets kidnapped in *The Lady Vanishes,* while Robert Walker and Farley Granger swap murders in a chilling scene in *Strangers on a Train.* Trains are hijacked and used as getaway vehicles in *Runaway Train* (Jon Voight and Eric Roberts as convicts) and *Von Ryan's Express* (with Frank Sinatra and fellow escaped POWs speeding through Germany to freedom). A thawed-out primeval monster and a demented Cossack (Telly Savalas) wreak havoc aboard the *Horror Express!* However, that's nothing compared to the deadly virus threatening Sophia Loren and Burt Lancaster as they race through Europe in *The Cassandra Crossing.* It is enough to make one revel in fluffier (and far more entertaining) outings like the Gene Wilder–Richard Pryor action-comedy *The Silver Streak.* See also **Subways.** The following movies either take place on trains or feature memorable train scenes:

The Iron Horse (1924)
Number Seventeen (1932)
The Phantom Express (1932)
Shanghai Express (1932)
Rome Express (1932)
Union Depot (1932)
The Silver Streak (1934)
Twentieth Century (1934)
Streamline Express (1935)
Florida Special (1936)
Night Mail (1936)
California Straight Ahead (1937)
La Bête Humaine (aka *The Human Beast*) (1938)
The Lady Vanishes (1938)
Union Pacific (1939)

Night Train to Munich (aka *Night Train*) (1940)
Broadway Limited (1941)
Lady on a Train (1945)
One Way to Love (1945)
Terror by Night (1946)
Sleeping Car to Trieste (1948)
Berlin Express (1948)
Train of Events (1949)
Peking Express (1951)
Strangers on a Train (1951)
Diplomatic Courier (1952)
The Narrow Margin (1952)
Terror on a Train (aka *Time Bomb*) (1952)
The Titfield Thunderbolt (1953)
The Paris Express (aka *The Man*

Who Watched the Trains Go By) (1953)
Human Desire (1954)
The Great Locomotive Chase (aka *Andrews' Raiders*) (1956)
Flame Over India (aka *North West Frontier*) (1959)
Night Train (1959)
Train Robbery Confidential (1962)
From Russia with Love (the most memorable of several James Bond train scenes) (1963)
Stop Train 349 (1964)
Dr. Terror's House of Horrors (1965)
The Sleeping Car Murders (1965)
The Train (1965)
Von Ryan's Express (1965)
Closely Watched Trains (1966)
The Great St. Trinian's Train Robbery (1966)
Trans-Europe Express (1966)
The Great British Train Robbery (1967)
Istanbul Express (1968)
Boxcar Bertha (1972)
Horror Express (aka *Panic on the Trans-Siberian Express*) (1972)
Emperor of the North (aka *Emperor of the North Pole*) (1973)
The Train Robbers (1973)
Hijack (1973 TVM)
Runaway! (aka *The Runaway Train*) (1973 TVM)
Breakheart Pass (1976)
The Silver Streak (1976)
The Cassandra Crossing (1977)
The Stationmaster's Wife (1977)
Julia (1977)
The Great Train Robbery (aka *The First Great Train Robbery*) (1979)
Avalanche Express (1979)
Disaster on the Coastliner (1979 TVM)
Hanging by a Thread (1979 TVM)
Cafe Express (1980)
Terror Train (1980)
Chattanooga Choo Choo (1984)
The Lady Vanishes (1979)
Murder on the Orient Express (1974)
Romance on the Orient Express (1985 TVM)
Runaway Train (1985)
Stand by Me (1986)
Planes, Trains, and Automobiles (1987)
Throw Momma from the Train (1987)

Traveling Salespersons

The exploits of those who earn their living selling door-to-door have been played mostly for laughs. Lady vendors have proven to be far more adept than their male counterparts at peddling products: Joan Blondell sold booze-flavored toothpaste in *The Traveling Saleslady* (1935); Joan Davis tried to convince Westerners they needed soap in *The Traveling Saleswoman* (1950); Ginger Rogers marketed girdles in *The First Traveling Saleslady* (1956); Phyllis Diller pushed pianolas in *Did You Hear the One About the Traveling Saleslady?* (1968); and Lucille Ball specialized in cosmetics as *The Fuller Brush Girl* (1950). Red Skelton had one of his best roles as *The Fuller Brush Man* (1948), the hit which inspired Ball's similarly-titled sequel. Lou Costello played an incompetent vacuum cleaner salesman in 1946's *Little Giant,* as did Jimmy Durante and Phil Silvers in *You're in the Army Now* (1941). Both comedies featured the patented scene in which dirt is dumped on a clean carpet for an unsuccessful vacuum demonstration. Serious films about traveling salesmen include the 1951 and 1985 adaptations of Arthur Miller's searing stage play *Death of a Salesman.* The 1960 *Never Let Go* was about a salesman victimized by car thieves. Steve Martin played a Depression-era sheet-music salesman in the offbeat dramatic musical *Pennies from Heaven* (1981).

The Traveling Saleslady (1935)
You're in the Army Now (1941)
Little Giant (aka *On the Carpet*) (1946)
The Emperor Waltz (1948)
The Fuller Brush Man (aka *That Mad Mr. Jones*) (1948)
The Traveling Saleswoman (1950)
The Fuller Brush Girl (aka *The Affairs of Sally*) (1950)
Death of a Salesman (1951)
The Bigamist (1953)
The First Traveling Saleslady (1956)
Never Let Go (1960)
Did You Hear the One About the Traveling Saleslady? (1968)
O Lucky Man! (1973)
Naughty Wives (1974)
Pennies from Heaven (1981)
Death of a Salesman (1985 TVM)
Tin Men (1987)
Traveling Man (1989 TVM)

Truck Drivers

Truckers have been stereotyped as macho men of action, particularly during the 1970s. Typical roles featured country singer Jerry Reed playing a good ol' boy trucker in *High-Ballin'* (1978), Claude Akins and Frank Converse as no-nonsense truck drivers in *In Tandem* (1974), and Kris Kristofferson as the leader in charge of a *Convoy* (1978). Lady truckers have been virtually ignored, although a few females have nevertheless proven themselves as tough as their male counterparts. Kim Darby and Annie Potts played spunky women truckers in *Flatbed Annie and Sweetie Pie: Lady Truckers* (1979), as did Deborah Raffin in *Willa* (1979) and Helen Shaver in *High-Ballin'.* Few big-name stars have been attracted to truck-driving roles, although Humphrey Bogart was behind a rig's wheel in *They Drive by Night* (1940). James Cagney, while still on the road to stardom, drove a truck as the *St. Louis Kid* (1934). The most existential truckers were the ones driving nitroglycerin over dangerous mountain roads in 1953's *Wages of Fear* and its 1977 remake *Sorcerer.* The most mysterious one was the unseen rig driver who tried to run Dennis Weaver off the road in Steven Spielberg's 1971 TV-movie *Duel.* The TV series' *Movin' On* and *B.J. and the Bear* both evolved from made-for-TV movies. In the latter series, the "Bear" was a mischievous truck-ridin' chimpanzee.

Quick Millions (1931)
St. Louis Kid (1934)
California Straight Ahead (1937)
They Drive by Night (aka *The Road to Frisco*) (1940)

Desperate (1947)	*Sorcerer* (1977)
Thieves' Highway (1949)	*F.I.S.T.* (1978)
The Wages of Fear (1953)	*High-Ballin'* (1978)
Death in Small Doses (1957)	*Steel Cowboy* (1978 TVM)
The Long Haul (1957)	*Convoy* (1978)
The Big Gamble (1960)	*B.J. and the Bear* (1978 TVM)
Moonfire (1970)	*Flatbed Annie and Sweetiepie:*
Duel (1971 TVM)	*Lady Truckers* (aka *Flatbed*
Deadhead Miles (1972)	*Annie*) (1979 TVM)
In Tandem (aka *Movin' On*)	*Willa* (1979 TVM)
(1974 TVM)	*Coast to Coast* (1980)
White Line Fever (1975)	*Road Games* (1981)
The Great Smokey Roadblock	*Brothers-in-Law* (1985 TVM)
(aka *The Last of the Cow-*	*Big Trouble in Little China*
boys) (1976)	(1986)
Breaker! Breaker! (1977)	*Killing Machine* (1986)
Handle with Care (aka *Citi-*	*Rolling Vengeance* (1987)
zen's Band) (1977)	

Trumpet Players

Young trumpet players have been portrayed as brash, compulsive musicians by Kirk Douglas in *Young Man with a Horn* (1950) and Steve McQueen in *Love with the Proper Stranger* (1963). Burt Young was a down-on-his-luck trumpeteer who befriended a terminally-ill youth in the maudlin *Uncle Joe Shannon* (1978). Carole Lombard rescued Fred Mac-Murray from the skids in 1937's *Swing High, Swing Low*. Danny Kaye played real-life bandleader/trumpet player Red Nichols in *The Five Pennies*. He even played a duet with Louis Armstrong, whose story reached the TV screen in 1976's *Louis Armstrong—Chicago Style*. Ben Vereen starred as "Satchmo." See also **Pianists; Violinists.**

Swing High, Swing Low (1937)	*A Man Called Adam* (1966)
Young Man with a Horn (1950)	*Louis Armstrong—Chicago*
The Five Pennies (1959)	*Style* (1976 TVM)
Love with the Proper Stranger	*Uncle Joe Shannon* (1978)
(1963)	

Tunnels

Tunnels have been a common fixture in POW (q.v.) sagas like *The Wooden Horse* (1950) and, of course, *The Great Escape* (1963). The Germans built secret tunnels, too, though a British spy thwarted their efforts in *The W Plan* (1930). John Garfield masterminded a tunnel through a cemetery to assassinate a Cuban official in 1949's *We Were Strangers*. On a considerably larger scale, the 1933 German film *The Tunnel* was about the construction of a tunnel connecting Europe and the U.S. It was remade in Britain in 1935's *Transatlantic Tunnel*. A Chinese army tried to "burrow" its way into the U.S. to mount an invasion in *Battle Beneath the Earth* (1968). Several films have featured "tunnels of love," while TV even offered a 1966–67 "Time Tunnel" series.

The W Plan (1930)	*The Wooden Horse* (1950)
The Tunnel (aka *Der Tunnel*) (1933)	*Stalag 17* (1953)
	The Hole (1959)
Transatlantic Tunnel (aka *The Tunnel*) (1935)	*The Great Escape* (1963)
	Battle Beneath the Earth (1968)
We Were Strangers (1949)	*Berlin Tunnel 21* (1981 TVM)

Twins

The most frequent use of twins has been to portray good and evil, as in *Dead Ringer* and *The Dark Mirror* (featuring Bette Davis and Olivia de Havilland, respectively, in double roles). But comedies of mistaken identities have been popular, too. Hayley Mills swapped places with her sister (Hayley Mills, too) and reunited their divorced parents in *The Parent Trap*. In a neat technical trick, the two Hayley's even sang a duet. Two sets of twins separated at birth caused all kinds of confusion in *Start the Revolution Without Me* and *Big Business*. Horror movies such as Brian De Palma's *Sisters* and cult favorite *Basket Case* have featured Siamese twins in murderous roles. And in *The Miracle of Morgan's Creek*, Betty Hutton gave birth to septuplets, which certainly seems to fit this category in spirit. See also **Lookalikes.**

Freaks (aka *Nature's Mistakes*) (1932)	*Wonder Man* (1945)
	A Stolen Life (1946)
Strangers in Love (1932)	*The Guilty* (1947)
The Sphinx (1933)	*Dual Alibi* (1947)
The Black Room (1935)	*Chained for Life* (1950)
Our Relations (1936)	*I Cover the Underworld* (1955)
Man of Affairs (aka *His Lordship*) (1936)	*House of Numbers* (1957)
	The Girl in the Kremlin (1957)
A Stolen Life (1938)	*Duel of the Titans* (1961)
The Man in the Iron Mask (1939)	*The Parent Trap* (1961)
	Dead Ringer (aka *Dead Image*) (1964)
The Boys from Syracuse (1940)	
Among the Living (1941)	*Open the Door and See All the People* (1964)
Two-Faced Woman (1941)	
Keep 'Em Flying (1941)	*Cat Ballou* (1965)
The Corsican Brothers (1941)	*Start the Revolution Without Me* (1970)
The Dark Mirror (1942)	
Nazi Agent (1942)	*Twins of Evil* (vampires, to be exact) (1972)
Dead Men Walk (1943)	
Cobra Woman (1944)	*The Other* (1972)
Here Come the Waves (1944)	*Sisters* (1973)
Miracle of Morgan's Creek (1944)	*Twin Detectives* (1976 TVM)
	The Man in the Iron Mask

(1977 TVM)
Zorro, the Gay Blade (1981)
Basket Case (1982)
The Dark Mirror (1984 TVM)
Cheech and Chong's The Corsican Brothers (1984)
Brotherly Love (1985 TVM)
Deceptions (1985 TVM)
The Covenant (1985 TVM)
Killer in the Mirror (1986 TVM)

Double Agent (1987 TVM)
Nightmare at Shadow Woods (1987)
Big Business (1988)
Dead Ringers (1988)
Dominick and Eugene (1988)
Take Two (1988)
Jack's Back (1988)
Twins (1988)

Two-Headed Creatures

The old adage that two heads are better than one has never held true for the movies. The first two-headed monster movie of note, 1959's U.S./Japanese co-production *The Manster* (aka *The Split*), concerned a reporter who grew a second head after a mad scientist injected him with an experimental serum. Eventually, the man/beast split apart totally and the parts fought each other. Bruce Dern transplanted a head onto a new body in the aptly-titled *The Incredible Two-Headed Transplant* (1971). That film was quickly eclipsed by the following year's *The Thing with Two Heads*—the heads belonging to Ray Milland and Rosey Grier. The theme of two men—one white, one black—connected to each other was better explored in the Tony Curtis–Sidney Poitier chase drama *The Defiant Ones*. But, on strictly visual terms, the sight of Milland and Grier jammed together in one big suit remains a whole lot more fun to watch. An ad man working on a pimple cream campaign grew an obnoxious second head in Bruce Robinson's black comedy *How to Get Ahead in Advertising* (1989). Finally, *Ghidrah, the Three-Headed Monster* (q.v.) deserves special mention since, he sported the minimum requirement of two heads.

The Seventh Voyage of Sinbad (1958)
The Manster (1959)
The Magic Sword (1962)
Jack the Giant Killer (1962)
The Incredible Two-Headed Transplant (1971)

The Thing with Two Heads (1972)
Monty Python and the Holy Grail (1974)
Willow (1988)
How to Get Ahead in Advertising (1989)

U.N.C.L.E. *see* The Man from U.N.C.L.E.

Uptown Saturday Night

Sidney Poitier directed Bill Cosby and himself in this silly 1974 comedy about two friends, a stolen lottery ticket, and a *Godfather*-like gangster (Harry Belafonte). In the 1985 follow-up *Let's Do It Again,* they used hypnosis to turn Jimmie Walker (from TV's "Good Times") into an unlikely boxer. The final installment, 1977's *A Piece of the Action,* balanced the laughs with a more serious plot about ghetto kids.

Uptown Saturday Night (1974)   *A Piece of the Action* (1977)
Let's Do It Again (1975)

Vampires

With his sexuality, air of mystery, and aristocratic manners, the vampire has long been a favorite subject of filmmakers. Count Dracula and his descendants dominated the 1930s and 1940s (see **Dracula** entry for details). However, there were some notable exceptions, such as 1932's *Vampyr* (aka *The Strange Adventure of David Gray*) and 1943's *Return of the Vampire.* Directed by Carl Dreyer, *Vampyr* is a wonderfully atmospheric, but slow moving, classic, while *Return* is of interest solely because it features Bela Lugosi as a very Dracula-like character stalking victims in World War II England. The vampire was generally ignored through the mid–1950s, although *Old Mother Riley Meets the Vampire* (aka *My Son, the Vampire*) sadly marked Lugosi's last appearance as one of the undead. However, vampire movies made a resounding comeback in 1957–58. Herman Cohen, the man responsible for *I Was a Teenage Frankenstein,* made 1957's teen-oriented *Blood of Dracula* (in which a young girl is made to believe she's a vampire). That same year, German Robles made his debut as Count Lavud in the Mexican movie *The Vampire* and John Beals took pills to grow fangs in *Mark of the Vampire* (not to be confused with Lugosi's 1935 film of the same title). In 1958, Jimmy Sangster wrote two vampire films—the competent *Blood of the Vampire* and Hammer Films' landmark *Horror of Dracula* (aka *Dracula*), arguably the most influential of all vampire movies. The Hammer approach, with its blatant emphasis on Dracula's sexual attraction, put vampirism in a new light. Hammer continued that trend with 1960's *Brides of Dracula,* another fine effort in which Baron Meinster (not the Count) preys upon a girls' boarding school. French director Roger Vadim offered *Blood and Roses* in 1960, a less subtle variation of the sexuality theme featuring a lesbian vampire. Naturally, other countries tried to cash in on the vampire's new-found popularity. The U.S. contributed a vampire Western *Curse of the Undead* (1959), Italy produced *The Vampire and the Ballerina* (1960), and Mexico added *World of Vampires* (1960). Hammer returned to its favorite subject in 1963 with *Kiss of Evil,* a well-acted, though unsurprising, bloodsucking tale. A year later, Vincent Price fought a world infected by a vampire plague in Italy's *The Last Man on Earth,* an underrated adaptation of Richard Matheson's chilling novel *I Am Legend.* Yet, despite these lively efforts, the vampire was becoming anemic at the box office by the late 1960s. Hence, some new twists were introduced to draw back the dwindling audience. Hammer Studios resurrected lesbian vampires with its 1970–71 Karnstein trilogy (q.v.) *The Vampire Lovers, Lust* *for a Vampire,* and *Twins of Evil.* Robert Quarry played a contemporary vampire confronted by hippies in 1971's *Count Yorga.* And in another contemporary-set tale, William Marshall played a black African prince who is bit by Dracula and becomes *Blacula.* Despite modest success, these films failed to ignite a major revival and the vampire sank quietly into his grave, except for occasional trips to the blood bank (e.g. Dan Curtis's high-rated 1971 TV-movie *The Night Stalker* and the 1979 spoof *Love at First Bite*). By the early 1980s, the vampire was lost amid the slasher films made in the wake of *Halloween* and *Friday the 13th.* But, just to show you can't keep a good bloodsucker down, he was revived yet again in a rash of youth-oriented pictures like *Fright Night* (1985), *The Lost Boys,* and *After Dark* (both 1987). These movies prove that the vampire, although clearly not the boxoffice champ he once was, remains a force to be reckoned with. The villainous ladies in *Lair of the White Worm* and *The Kiss* (both 1988), while technically not vampires, exhibited similar traits. See also **Dracula; Karnstein Trilogy.**

Vampyr (aka *The Strange Adventure of David Gray*) (1932)

The Return of the Vampire (1943)

The Vampire's Ghost (1943)

Dead Men Walk (1943)

My Son, the Vampire (aka *Old Mother Riley Meets the Vampire; Vampires Over London*) (1952)

Mark of the Vampire (aka *The Vampire*) (1957)

Blood of Dracula (1957)

The Vampire (aka *El Vampiro*) (1957)

The Vampire's Coffin (aka *El Ataud del Coffin*) (1958)

Blood of the Vampire (1958)

Uncle Was a Vampire (1959)

Curse of the Undead (1960)

The World of Vampires (aka *El Mundo de los Vampiros*) (1960)

Blood and Roses (1960)

The Vampire and the Ballerina (1960)

Kiss of Evil (aka *Kiss of the Vampire*) (1963)

The Last Man on Earth (1964)

Goliath and the Vampires (aka *The Vampires*) (1964)

Planet of the Vampires (aka *The Demon Planet*) (1965)

Munster, Go Home! (1966)

Planet of Blood (aka *Queen of Blood*) (1966)

Track of the Vampire (aka *Blood Bath*) (1966)

The Fearless Vampire Killers (or Pardon Me, But Your Teeth Are in My Neck) (1967)

House of Dark Shadows (1970)

Vampire Men of the Lost Planet (1970)

The House That Dripped Blood (1970)

Count Yorga, Vampire (1971)

The Velvet Vampire (aka *Cemetery Girls*) (1971)

The Return of Count Yorga (1971)

The Bloodsuckers (aka *Incense for the Damned*) (1971)

The Night Stalker (1971 TVM)

Daughters of Darkness (1971)

Vampire Circus (1971)

Blacula (1972)

The Bloody Vampire (1972)

The Deathmaster (1972)

Scream, Blacula, Scream (1973)

Captain Kronos: Vampire

Hunter (aka *Kronos*) (1974)	*Once Bitten* (1985)
Spermula (1975)	*Vamp* (1986)
Martin (1978)	*After Dark* (1987)
Love at First Bite (1979)	*The Lost Boys* (1987)
Vampire (1979 TVM)	*Vampire's Kiss* (1988)
Last Rites (aka *Dracula's Last Rites*) (1980)	*My Best Friend Is a Vampire* (1988)
I, Desire (1982 TVM)	*Fright Night Part 2* (1989)
The Hunger (1983)	*Thirst* (1989)
Fright Night (1985)	*Nightlife* (1989 TVM)
Lifeforce (1985)	*Beverly Hills Vamp* (1989)

Vance, Philo

S.S. Van Dine's dapper, erudite sleuth never made much of a hit on the screen. William Powell first played the part, enjoying modest success in four mysteries. Ironically, although Powell looked the part, he lacked the briskness of manner that made Vance such a memorable literary character and his portrayal is somewhat overrated. In his pre–Holmes days, Basil Rathbone made a more effective Vance in the slowly-paced, but cleverly-plotted *Bishop Murder Case* (the murderer wrote nursery rhymes containing clues about the identity of his next victim). Perhaps, the best Vance was Warren William, whose white gloves-and-cane portrayal sparkled in 1934's *The Dragon Murder Case*. Based on a Van Dine novel, this underrated puzzler found Vance investigating a young man's apparent drowning in a mysterious pool (haunted by a sea serpent?). William reprised the role in 1939's *The Gracie Allen Murder Case,* a comedy-mystery written for Allen by Van Dine. Other actors played the part, but none could make it their own. Later Vance films like *Philo Vance's Secret Mission* and *Philo Vance's Gamble* were Vance films in name only — their detectives were clearly closer to Philip Marlowe.

> *The Canary Murder Case* (1929) (William Powell)
> *The Greene Murder Case* (1929) (Powell)
> *The Benson Murder Case* (1930) (Powell)
> *The Bishop Murder Case* (1930) (Basil Rathbone)
> *The Kennel Murder Case* (1933) (Powell)
> *The Dragon Murder Case* (1934) (Warren William)
> *The Casino Murder Case* (1935) (Paul Lukas)
> *The Scarab Murder Case* (1936) (Wilfred Hyde-White)
> *The Garden Murder Case* (1936) (Edmund Lowe)
> *Night of Mystery* (1937) (Grant Richards)
> *The Gracie Allen Murder Case* (1939) (William)
> *Calling Philo Vance* (1940) (James Stephenson)
> *Philo Vance Returns* (1947) (William Wright)
> *Philo Vance's Gamble* (1947) (Alan Curtis)
> *Philo Vance's Secret Mission* (1947) (Curtis)

Ventriloquists

The difficulties inherent in injecting a distinct personality into a wooden dummy have caused identity problems for a number of movie ventriloquists. In the most chilling story in the classic anthology *Dead of Night* (1945), ventriloquist Michael Redgrave went insane after becoming convinced that his obnoxious dummy Hugo was looking for a new partner. Anthony Hopkins gave a tour-de-force performance in 1978's *Magic* as another mentally-unstable ventriloquist taking murderous advice from a dummy with an apparent mind of its own. Another dummy named Hugo (an obvious reference to *Dead of Night*) really did have a soul in the underrated 1964 fantasy *Devil Doll*. Bryant Halliday starred as Hugo's "partner," a ventriloquist who has transferred the soul of his assistant into his dummy. Aside from horror films, the most famous film ventriloquist remains Edgar Bergen. He enjoyed a prosperous career during the late 1930s accompanied by dummies Charlie McCarthy or Mortimer Snerd in comedies like *A Letter of Introduction* (1938), *Charlie McCarthy, Detective* (1939), and the W.C. Fields vehicle *You Can't Cheat an Honest Man* (1939). He earned a special Academy Award in 1937 for his creation of Charlie McCarthy. Major stars who have played ventriloquists include Erich von Stroheim in *The Great Gabbo* (1929), Danny Kaye in *Knock on Wood* (1954), and Lon Chaney in both the silent and talkie versions of *The Unholy Three* (1925 and 1930). In 1984's *Broadway Danny Rose,* theater agent Woody Allen had a hard time finding employment for a stuttering ventriloquist.

The Unholy Three (1925)
The Great Gabbo (1929)
The Unholy Three (1930)
A Letter of Introduction (1938)
You Can't Cheat an Honest Man (1939)
Charlie McCarthy, Detective (1939)

Dead of Night (1945)
Knock on Wood (1954)
Hypnosis (aka *Dummy of Death*) (1963)
Devil Doll (1964)
Magic (1978)
Broadway Danny Rose (1984)

Videotaped Films

American television movie producers, unlike their British counterparts, have long maintained that film's sharp, vibrant image compensates for its added expense when compared to videotape. As a result, very few U.S. made-for-TV movies have been shot on tape. The romantic ghost story *Sandcastles* (1972) was the first to employ a single videotape camera system, but even it was later transferred to film. The 1983 *Special Bulletin* was shot on videotape to simulate the "look" of a television newscast. Oddly, there have also been a handful of theatrical features shot originally on videotape and then transferred to film. The 1965 videotaped drama *Harlow,* starring Carol Lynley, was converted to film to compete theatrically with a rival biography of the blonde comedienne (confusingly, this second film was also called *Harlow* and starred Carroll Baker). Industrious producers dubbed this tape-to-film process "electronovision." The advent of high-definition videotape in the 1980s renewed interest in "filming" with videotape. However, *Julia and Julia* (1988), the first movie shot on high-definition tape, turned into a boxoffice disaster. Shortly after its U.S. theatrical release, it showed up—ironically—on videotape.

Harlow (1965)	*Hollywood Bowl* (1982)
Two Hundred Motels (1971)	*Special Bulletin* (1983 TVM)
The Catcher (1971 TVM)	*Desperate Intruder* (1983 TVM)
Sandcastles (1972 TVM)	*Emergency Room* (1983 TVM)
Numero Deux (1975)	*The Invisible Woman* (1983
Give 'Em Hell, Harry! (1975)	TVM)
Norman...Is That You? (1976)	*Julia and Julia* (1988)
Monty Python Live at the	

Vietnam

The "Forgotten War" was ignored in movies for most of its duration. The 1964 *A Yank in Vietnam,* a low-budget action picture, was the first to deal with U.S. involvement. The 1968 propaganda adventure *The Green Berets* glorified the fighting, while the searing 1974 documentary *Hearts and Minds* criticized it. Surprisingly, TV-movies dealt effectively with returning vets long before their theatrical counterparts. In 1967's *The Ballad of Andy Crocker,* Lee Majors returned home to find himself a stranger to those he loved. It seemed upbeat compared to the brutal frankness of Joseph Papp's production of the TV special *Sticks and Bones,* which several CBS affiliates refused to air. In the late 1970s, mainstream Hollywood finally addressed Vietnam in a roundabout fashion—*Coming Home* dealt with returning veterans, while Francis Coppola's *Apocalypse Now* portrayed the violence of war in a poetic manner. It was not until 1986's Academy Award winner *Platoon* and Stanley Kubrick's *Full Metal Jacket* that the major studios backed brutal, realistic portrayal of the Vietnam War. Those successes have been followed by low-budget clones (e.g. *Hamburger Hill* and *Platoon Leader*), big-budget clones *(Casualties of War)*, and one or two films of genuine originality *(84 Charlie Mopic)*.

A Yank in Vietnam (aka *Year of the Tiger*) (1964)	*The Dear Hunter* (1978)
	Go Tell the Spartans (1978)
The Anderson Platoon (1967)	*Apocalypse Now* (1979)
The Green Berets (1968)	*A Rumor of War* (1980 TVM)
The Ballad of Andy Crocker (1969 TVM)	*The Children of An Lac* (1980 TVM)
Hearts and Minds (1974)	*Uncommon Valor* (1983)
The Boys in Company C (1978)	*Missing in Action* (1984)
Coming Home (1978)	*Platoon* (1986)
Rolling Thunder (1978)	*P.O.W. The Escape* (1986)

Full Metal Jacket (1987)
Gardens of Stone (1987)
Good Morning, Vietnam (1987)
Hamburger Hill (1987)
The Hanoi Hilton (1987)
Dear America (1987 TVM)
Bat 21 (1988)

84 Charlie Mopic (1989)
Platoon Leader (1989)
Casualties of War (1989)
The Iron Triangle (1988)
Born on the Fourth of July
   (1989)

Vigilantes

Although contemporary vigilante films appeared prior to 1974, the genre began officially with 1974's *Death Wish* (q.v.), a highly manipulative revenge tale in which an average guy turns cold vigilante after punks kill his wife and rape his daughter. Charles Bronson clicked in the lead role and the film scored big at the boxoffice. In its wake, exploitative producers rushed out cheap imitations, like *Vigilante* and *Vigilante Force*. The most financially successful of these rip-offs was 1980's *The Exterminator*, which starred Robert Ginty as a Vietnam vet who used a flame-thrower to avenge a buddy's mugging. Abel Ferrera's feminist variation, 1981's *Ms. 45* (aka *Angel of Vengeance*), garnered some good reviews and has since earned minor cult status. *The Star Chamber*, *The Death Squad*, and the Dirty Harry picture *Magnum Force* showed vigilantism used by law enforcers to "correct" loopholes in our legal system, a plotline derived loosely from 1942's *The Strange Case of Dr. Rx.* See also **Death Wish.**

The Mad Executioners (1963)
Magnum Force (1973)
Outrage! (1973 TVM)
Death Wish (1974)
The Death Squad (1974 TVM)
Law and Disorder (1974)
Vigilante (aka Street Gang)
   (1976)
Vigilante Force (1976)
Dirty Knight's Work (aka Trial
   by Combat; Choice of
   Weapons) (1976)
Seige (1978 TVM)
The Exterminator (1980)
Ms. 45 (aka Angel of Ven-

geance) (1981)
Death Wish II (1982)
Fighting Back (1982)
The Star Chamber (1983)
Exterminator II (1984)
The Executioner, Part II (1984;
   there was no part I)
Death Wish III (1985)
Young Warriors (1985)
Streets of Justice (1985 TVM)
Brotherhood of Justice (1986
   TVM)
Shadows Run Black (1986)
Death Wish IV: The Crack-
   down (1987)

Violinists

Violinists (and other string musicians) have been faced with a variety of hard decisions. Young William Holden had to choose between a distinguished career as a violinist and a lucrative one as a prizefighter in *Golden Boy* (1939). That same year, Swedish violinist Leslie Howard had to decide whether to stay with his loyal wife (Edna Best) or run off with beautiful protegée Ingrid Bergman in *Intermezzo*. And in 1946's *Humoresque*, John Garfield played a moody musician torn briefly between wealthy patron Joan Crawford and his love of music. Real-life violin virtuoso Paganini was the subject of 1946's *The Magic Bow*. See also **Pianists; Trumpet Players.**

Golden Boy (1939)
Intermezzo (aka *Escape to Happiness; Intermezzo, A Love Story*) (1939)
My Love Came Back (1940)
The Phantom of the Opera (1944)
The Magic Bow (1946)
Humoresque (1947)

Rhapsody (1954)
All These Women (aka *Now About All These Women*) (1964)
Shame (1968)
Jeremy (1973)
The Man with One Red Shoe (1985)
The Living Daylights (1987)

Viral Epidemics

The threat of viral annihilation has been the subject of several movies. Quarantined scientists raced against the clock to combat an inexplicable, self-reproducing virus in *The Andromeda Strain* (1971). George Maharis tracked down a lunatic who stole a deadly experimental virus in 1965's *The Satan Bug*, a plot more or less borrowed by *Panic in the Streets* (1950) and *No Place to Hide* (1956). And Count Dracula revealed his plan to initiate viral warfare in the decidedly offbeat horror tale *The Satanic Rites of Dracula* (1973). In other horror films, Vincent Price met disease incarnate in 1964's *The Masque of the Red Death* and then battled a plague of vampirism in the underrated low-budget gem *The Last Man on Earth* (1964). A 1924 silent film also called *The Last Man on Earth* portrayed a world where a plague had wiped out most of the male population. A parasite, not a disease, was the culprit in David Cronenberg's 1975 cult thriller *They Came from Within*. In Lloyd C. Douglas's *Green Light* (1937), Errol Flynn discovered a cure for a more typical disease, Rocky Mountain spotted fever.

The Last Man on Earth (1924)
Yellow Jack (1938)
Isle of the Dead (1945)
Panic in the Streets (1950)
The Killer That Stalked New York (aka *Frightened City*) (1950)
No Place to Hide (1956)
The Last Man on Earth (1964)
The Masque of the Red Death (1964)
Spies a Go Go (aka *The Nasty Rabbit*) (1964)

The Satan Bug (1965)
What's So Bad About Feeling Good? (1968)
Shadow of Evil (1966)
Project X (1968)
On Her Majesty's Secret Service (1969)
Quarantined (1970 TVM)
No Blade of Grass (1970)
The Andromeda Strain (1971)
Killer by Night (1971 TVM)
The Satanic Rites of Dracula (aka *Count Dracula and His*

*Vampire Bride; Dracula Is
Alive and Well and Living in
London)* (1973)
The Crazies (aka *Code Name:
Trixie)* (1973)
*Where Have All the People
Gone?* (1974 TVM)
The Missing Are Deadly (1975
TVM)

The Cassandra Crossing (1977)
Panic in Echo Park (1977 TVM)
Killer on Board (1977 TVM)
Plague (aka *M3: The Gemini
Strain)* (1978)
Virus (1980)
The Plague Dogs (1982)
City Limits (1985)

Volcanoes

Mountainous rumbles and spurting lava have brought an end to numerous
South Seas sagas, displaying a particular affection for Dorothy Lamour
vehicles like *The Jungle Princess* (1936) and *Aloma of the South Seas*
(1941). Historical pictures, such as *Krakatoa, East of Java* (1969) and *St.
Helens* (1981), have tended to build plodding stories around their spectacular volcanic eruptions. *The Last Days of Pompeii* (1935) was an exception, thanks mostly to a fine performance by Basil Rathbone as Pontius
Pilate. Yet, despite Rathbone and the thrilling Mount Vesuvius finale, the
film lost almost $250,000 at the boxoffice. James Mason and crew entered
an extinct volcano at the beginning of their *Journey to the Center of the
Earth* (1959) and then were blown out the top of Mount Etna at the film's
climax (they managed to survive unharmed, though). The worldly Baron
Munchausen and his followers duplicated the same feat in 1989's *The
Adventures of Baron Munchausen*. Actually, the Baron and friends had
been enjoying the hospitality of Vulcan inside his volcano home until
Venus (aka Mrs. Vulcan) began displaying affection for the distinguished
Baron. Movie villains Fantomas and Ernst Blofeld have used extinct
volcanoes for elaborate hideouts in *Fantomas Strikes Back* (1965) and the
James Bond picture *You Only Live Twice* (1967), respectively.

East of Borneo (1931)
The Last Days of Pompeii
(1935)
The Jungle Princess (1936)
One Million B.C. (aka *Man and
His Mate; The Cave
Dwellers)* (1940)
Aloma of the South Seas (1941)
The Lost Volcano (1950)
Stromboli (1950)
Fair Wind to Java (1953)
*Journey to the Center of the
Earth* (1959)
The Last Days of Pompeii
(1960)

Atlantis, the Lost Continent
(1961)
The Devil at Four O'Clock
(1961)
Mysterious Island (1961)
Fantomas Strikes Back (1965)
One Million Years B.C. (1967)
You Only Live Twice (1967)
Krakatoa, East of Java (aka
Volcano) (1969)
Up Pompeii (1971)
Island at the Top of the World
(1974)
The Land That Time Forgot
(1974)

When Time Ran Out (1980)   *The Adventures of Baron*
St. Helens (1981)   *Munchausen* (1989)

Walking Tall

The real-life story of modern-day Tennessee sheriff Buford Pusser unexpectedly snowballed into a major hit in 1973. The film drew its biggest
audiences in the Southeastern U.S., the region where *Billy Jack* (q.v.), a
similar man-against-corruption tale, encountered sleeper success in 1971.
Screen heavy Joe Don Baker brought conviction—and a huge baseball
bat—to the role of Pusser. Elizabeth Hartman played his quiet, supportive
wife. When Baker showed no interest in a sequel, Bing Crosby Productions signed imposing Bo Svenson for the lead role. He played Pusser in
two sequels and a very brief 1981 TV series. Brian Dennehy also played
Pusser in the 1978 TV-movie *A Real American Hero.* The real Sheriff
Pusser was supposed to have played himself in another theatrical sequel
before he died in an automobile crash—under mysterious circumstances,
according to some sources.

Walking Tall (1973)   *Walking Tall: The Final*
Part 2: Walking Tall (aka   *Chapter* (1977)
    Legend of the Lawman)   *A Real American Hero* (1978
    (1976)   TVM)

Warsaw Trilogy

Andrzej Wajda's powerful trilogy of life in Poland during World War II
made him a major force in Eastern European cinema. *A Generation*
(1954), the first important post–World War II film to emerge from
Poland, dealt with the "lost generation" of Warsaw youth who became involved with the Resistance. *Kanal* (1956) followed a group of resisters
ordered to escape crumbling Warsaw through the city's intricate network
of sewers. Quickly lost in the darkness, they become stalked by the Nazis
above them. The 1958 *Ashes and Diamonds* shifted to the end of the war
and focused on a youth forced to choose between love and carrying out an
assassination. The title was derived from a grave stone inscription which
appears in the film and summarizes Wajda's themes: "Here nothing but
ashes will remain, the story in an instant to oblivion will sweep them;
from the ashes perhaps a diamond will emerge, shining victoriously for
centuries, it will have blossomed for you."

A Generation (aka *Pokolenie; Generation*) (1954)
Kanal (aka *They Loved Life; Sewer*) (1956)
Ashes and Diamonds (aka *Popiol i diament*) (1958)

Wax Museums

There are two basic types of wax museums movies. First, there's the one
about the resident insane sculptor who molds figures by pouring hot wax

over his murder victims. Lionel Atwill made this practice popular in 1933's *Mystery of the Wax Museum,* one of the first color horror films. Twenty years later, Vincent Price recreated the role in another technically historic horror film, the 3-D classic *House of Wax.* As the demented sculptors, Atwill and Price were splendid—no one has approached their level of depravity. Bad movie favorite Cameron Mitchell gave it a half-hearted shot in 1967's *Nightmare in Wax,* in which he injected folks with a drug that made them look (and act) like wax figures. The second type of wax museum film is the one where figures come to life. Although a popular television plot, it has been used sparingly on the big screen. In 1924's *Waxworks,* there was a nightmare sequence in which the wax figure of Jack the Ripper comes to life. Several decades later, another story called "Waxworks" was included in the anthology film *The House That Dripped Blood.* It starred Peter Cushing as a gentleman who becomes obsessed with an attractive, very life-like figure.

Waxworks (1924)
Mystery of the Wax Museum
   (1933)
Charlie Chan at the Wax
   Museum (1940)
The Frozen Ghost (1945)
House of Wax (1953)
Samson in the Wax Museum
   (aka *Santo in the Wax*
   Museum) (1963)

Chamber of Horrors (1966)
Nightmare in Wax (aka *Crimes*
   in the Wax Museum) (1969)
The House That Dripped Blood
   (1970)
Terror in the Wax Museum
   (1973)
Lisa and the Devil (aka *The*
   House of Exorcism) (1975)
Waxwork (1988)

Werewolves

The subject of silent films like *The Werewolf* (1913) and *The White Wolf* (1914), the werewolf made little impact until Universal Studios introduced it at the end of its first horror movie cycle with 1935's *Werewolf of London.* Featuring not one—but two—lycanthropes, it abandoned familiar werewolf lore in favor of a more novel approach (dealing with a rare flower that cures lycanthropy). For Universal's next furry film, *The Wolf Man* (q.v.), it returned to the basics, integrating a gypsy fortuneteller and a silver-handled cane into a contemporary terror tale. The film made Lon Chaney, Jr., a horror star and he repeated the role in four more movies. Hoping to capitalize on Universal's success, other studios also tried their hands at werewolf pictures. But sometimes, things were not always what they seemed to be. A plotting housekeeper convinced James Mason he was a werewolf in *The Night Has Eyes*—but he wasn't. June Lockhart suffered from the same delusion in *She-Wolf of London.* As the 1940s ended and science fiction films gained momentum, the popularity of the werewolf declined sharply. Fresh ideas were needed and they came unexpectedly in the late 1950s in the form of two low-budget drive-in features. *The*

Werewolf (1957) presented a creature created by a scientist, a theme aimed to please both science and horror fans. Far more successful was the following year's *I Was a Teenage Werewolf*, a trend-setting mixture of teen problems, rock'n'roll, and an adolescent werewolf (Michael Landon). In 1960, Britain's Hammer Studios tried to revive the European legends with *Curse of the Werewolf*, a brooding, literary picture which was a box-office flop. Except for a brief appearance in the anthology *Dr. Terror's House of Horrors*, the werewolf was silent through most of the 1960s. However, he rebounded strongly at the end of the decade in the guise of Spanish horror star Paul Naschy. His 1968 film *Mark of the Werewolf* (aka *Frankenstein's Bloody Terror*) was a European sensation and spawned eight sequels with colorful translated titles like *The Werewolf vs. the Vampire Woman* and *The Werewolf and the Yeti*. Still, the werewolf did not regain his popularity in the U.S. until the 1980s, when *The Howling* (q.v.) and *An American Werewolf in London* combined humor and horror for big boxoffice bucks. The most original werewolf movie of recent years remains the spellbinding 1984 British fantasy *The Company of Wolves*, a fanciful adult reworking of Little Red Riding Hood. In addition to the werewolf, there have been a handful of "were-cat" movies, such as *The Cat People*, its 1982 remake, *Cat-Man of Paris*, and *The Cat Girl*. And in 1933's *Island of Lost Souls*, a panther is surgically transformed into a beautiful girl. But that's not really lycanthropy. See also **Daninsky, Waldemar; The Howling; Humanimals; The Wolf-Man.**

The Werewolf (1913)
The White Wolf (1914)
Werewolf of London (1935)
The Wolf Man (1941)
The Undying Monster (1942)
The Night Has Eyes (aka *Terror House*) (1942)
Return of the Vampire (1943)
Cry of the Werewolf (1944)
She-Wolf of London (1946)
The Werewolf (1956)
I Was a Teenage Werewolf (1957)
Daughter of Dr. Jekyll (a mixed-up movie claiming Jekyll was a werewolf) (1957)
How to Make a Monster (an actor in makeup is the killer) (1958)
Curse of the Werewolf (1961)
Werewolf in a Girls' Dormitory (1961)
Dr. Terror's House of Horrors (1965)
The Maltese Bippy (1969)
Werewolves on Wheels (1971)
Moon of the Wolf (1972 TVM)
Blood (1973)
The Boy Who Cried Werewolf (1973)
The Werewolf of Washington (1973)
The Beast Must Die (1974)
Legend of the Werewolf (1975)
Wolfman! (1979)
An American Werewolf in London (1981)
Full Moon High (1981)
The Howling (1981)
The Company of Wolves (1984)
Silver Bullet (1985)
Teen Wolf (1985)
The Monster Squad (1987)
Teen Wolf Too (1987)
My Mom's a Werewolf (1989)

Whales

Whales on film have been portrayed as sympathetic creatures—with the notable exceptions of Herman Melville's immortal white whale *Moby Dick* and the people-eating Monstro in *Pinocchio*. Although Monstro was a true terror, it's hard to classify Moby as a villain, for Captain Ahab's crew perished solely because of its captain's obsession to kill the symbolic whale. The single-minded Ahab has been played by John Barrymore twice, in *The Sea Beast* (1926) and *Moby Dick* (1930), and by Gregory Peck in John Huston's 1956 adaptation. The killer whale *Orca* (1977) devoured quite a few humans, including Bo Derek, but his actions were in retaliation for the murder of his spouse (killer whales mate for life, we are told). Humans were also portrayed as thoughtless whale killers in *The White Dawn* (1974) and *A Whale for the Killing* (1981). Whales were glimpsed from a distance in the opening of *The Whales of August* (1987), but, again, they played a symbolic part in the tender story of two elderly sisters. The crew of the Enterprise went back in time to save some important humpback whales in *Star Trek IV: The Voyage Home* (1986). The cartoon compilation *Make Mine Music* (1946) featured a segment on Willie, the Singing Whale. See also **Dolphins; Fish; Sharks.**

The Sea Beast (1926)	*The White Dawn* (1974)
Moby Dick (1930)	*Orca* (aka *Orca, the Killer*
Pinocchio (1940)	*Whale*) (1977)
Make Mine Music (1946)	*A Whale for the Killing* (1981)
Moby Dick (1956)	*Star Trek IV: The Voyage*
Namu, the Killer Whale (1966)	*Home* (1986)
Island at the Top of the World (1974)	*The Whales of August* (1987)

The Whistler

In the mid-forties, when most detective series were coming to an end, Columbia launched this offbeat mystery anthology series. The films were inspired by a popular radio program, in which a mysterious narrator introduced each story with the ominous opening: "I am the Whistler—and I know many things." Only one film, 1948's *Return of the Whistler,* followed the radio format. The others were linked solely by their twisty plots and the presence of star Richard Dix. A former Oscar-nominated actor (for 1931's *Cimarron*) Dix was in the twilight of his career. The Whistler films allowed him to show his versatility, playing the hero in some pictures, the villain in others. In 1944's *The Whistler,* he played a husband so depressed over his wife's death that he hires a killer to murder him—only to discover his wife is alive. In 1945's *The Power of the Whistler,* Dix was a murderer suffering from amnesia. William Castle, best known for his gimmicky 1950s thrillers (e.g. *The Tingler*), produced and directed some of the entries. Following Dix's death in 1947, one more picture was made and then the series ended. Columbia revived it for television in 1954, producing 39 half-hour episodes.

The Whistler (1944)	(1946)
The Mark of the Whistler (1944)	*Mysterious Intruder* (1947)
The Power of the Whistler (1945)	*The Secret of the Whistler* (1947)
The Voice of the Whistler	*The 13th Hour* (1947)
	Return of the Whistler (1948)

Whistling in the Dark

Edward Childs Carpenter and Laurence Cross' hit Broadway comedy *Whistling in the Dark* was about a mystery writer forced to devise the perfect murder. MGM first filmed it in 1932 with Ernest Truex as the hero and Edward Arnold the villain. That version made a nifty profit, but was eclipsed by the 1941 remake starring Red Skelton as a radio sleuth called "The Fox," Ann Rutherford as his girlfriend, and Conrad Veidt as the heavy. The film's surprise success resulted in MGM's reuniting Skelton and Rutherford for two sequels. Their Southern honeymoon plans go astray when murder gets in the way in *Whistling in Dixie* (1942). Baseball and mystery provided the mixture for the last film *Whistling in Brooklyn* (1943). George Haight produced and S. Sylvan Simon directed all three films.

Whistling in the Dark (1932)	*Whistling in Dixie* (1942)
Whistling in the Dark (1941)	*Whistling in Brooklyn* (1943)

Windmills

No movie has been able to top the splendid climax of 1960's *Brides of Dracula* for imaginative use of a windmill. In Terence Fisher's lively vampire yarn, an athletic Van Helsing (Peter Cushing) dives onto a revolving windmill, his weight pulling the arms into the shape of a cross. The light of a full moon behind him casts the shadow of the cross onto the ground—thus destroying a hissing vampire caught in its path. The Frankenstein Monster was burned in a windmill at the end of 1931's *Frankenstein*, only to escape from the flames in the beginning of 1935's *Bride of Frankenstein*. Windmills were used to signal enemy planes in Hitchcock's *Foreign Correspondent* (1940). In the underrated 1986 fantasy *Highlander*, Christopher Lambert and Clancy Brown staged an elaborate swordfight throughout Lambert's windmill home. Michael Caine played a spy whose kidnapped son was being held hostage in *The Black Windmill* (1974). No discussion of windmills would be complete without mentioning *Don Quixote*, the gallant Spanish gentleman who imagined them to be dragons. Of related interest, Joanne Woodward's river mill home provided an atmospheric setting for the 1964 mystery-thriller *Signpost to Murder*.

Frankenstein (1931)
Bride of Frankenstein (1935)
Foreign Correspondent (1940)
Brides of Dracula (1960)

Don Quixote (1972)
The Black Windmill (1974)
Highlander (1986)

Witches

Not surprisingly, witches show up in all kinds of movies: children's fantasies, comedies, horror flicks, and literary adaptations. Margaret Hamilton played the most famous of them all—the Wicked Witch of the West in *The Wizard of Oz* (which also boasts Billie Burke as Glinda the Good Witch). Other children's films featuring notable witches include *Snow White and the Seven Dwarfs, Sleeping Beauty,* and *Bedknobs and Broomsticks.* Bewitching comedies have garnered laughs by casting against stereotype. Hence, instead of featuring witches with green skin and warts, both *I Married a Witch* and *Bell, Book, and Candle* offer curvaceous, blonde-haired witches (Veronica Lake and Kim Novak, respectively). The best horror film about witches is probably *Burn, Witch, Burn* (aka *Night of the Eagle*), in which Janet Blair resorts to witchcraft, first to further her husband's career and then to save his life. Barbara Steele was a revenge-minded witch in Mario Bava's eerie *Black Sunday* and Hope Lange discovers her neighbors belong to a witches' coven in *Crowhaven Farm.* On the literary side, prophesizing witches open up all film versions of *Macbeth* and Arthur Miller's *The Crucible* remains a potent condemnation of the infamous Salem witch trials.

Witchcraft Through the Ages
(aka *Haxan*) (1922)
Maid of Salem (1937)
Snow White and the Seven
Dwarfs (1938)
I Married a Witch (1942)
Day of Wrath (1943)
Weird Woman (1944)
The Woman Who Came Back
(1945)
Macbeth (1948)
The Undead (1956)
The Crucible (aka *Witches of Salem*) (1957)
Bell, Book, and Candle (1958)
The Day the Earth Froze (1959)
Sleeping Beauty (1959)
Black Sunday (1960)
Horror Hotel (aka *City of the Dead*) (1960)
The Witches' Curse (1960)
The Witches' Mirror (1960)

Burn, Witch, Burn (aka *Night of the Eagle*) (1962)
Snow White and the Three
Stooges (1961)
The Magic Sword (1962)
Terror in the Crypt (aka *Crypt of Horror*) (1963)
Witchcraft (1964)
The Devil's Own (aka *The Witches*) (1966)
The She-Beast (1966)
The Witch (1966)
A Witch Without a Broom
(1966)
The Conqueror Worm (aka
Witchfinder General) (1968)
Crowhaven Farm (1970 TVM)
Cry of the Banshee (1970)
Night of the Witches (1970)
Pufnstuf (1970)
The Witches' Mountain (1970)
Bedknobs and Broomsticks (1971)

The Blood on Satan's Claw (aka
   Satan's Skin; Satan's Claw)
   (1971)
Macbeth (1971)
Night of Dark Shadows (1971)
Simon, King of Witches (1971)
Touch of Melissa (aka *Touch of
   Satan; Night of the Demon*)
   (1971)
Necromancy (aka *The Witch-
   ing*) (1972)

Race with the Devil (1975)
Deathmoon (1978 TVM)
A Stranger in the House (1978
   TVM)
Witches' Brew (1980)
Midnight Offerings (1981 TVM)
Bay Coven (1987 TVM)
The Witches of Eastwick (1987)
Teen Witch (1989)
Witchery (aka *Witchcraft*)
   (1989)

(Despite their titles, the Disney kiddie adventures *Escape to Witch Mountain* and *Return to Witch Mountain* have nothing to do with witches—only alien children.)

Withers, Hildegarde

Edna May Oliver first brought Stuart Palmer's umbrella-toting school-teacher sleuth to the screen in 1932's *The Penguin Pool Murder*. It was a lively yarn, with a dramatic courtroom climax, but the film's highlight was the rapport between Oliver and co-star James Gleason as Inspector Oscar Piper. The gruff, wisecracking Piper masked his respect for Hildegarde, calling her a "nosy old dame" but later conceding: "That old battleaxe is the best friend I have in the world." The pair teamed for two more RKO series entries, then Oliver bowed out due to poor health. Helen Broderick replaced her for one film and then a miscast Zasu Pitts made the last two RKO Hildegarde Withers mysteries. James Gleason remained as Inspector Piper for all five films. In 1971, Eve Arden revived Hildegarde Withers for a TV pilot movie called *A Very Missing Person*, but a regular series never materialized.

> *The Penguin Pool Murder* (aka *The Penguin Pool Mystery*) (1932)
>   (Edna May Oliver)
> *Murder on the Blackboard* (1934) (Oliver)
> *Murder on a Honeymoon* (1935) (Oliver)
> *Murder on a Bridle Path* (1936) (Helen Broderick)
> *The Plot Thickens* (aka *The Swinging Pearl Mystery*) (1936) (Zasu
>   Pitts)
> *Forty Naughty Girls* (1937) (Pitts)
> *A Very Missing Person* (1971 TVM) (Eve Arden)

The Wizard of Oz

Published in 1900, L. Frank Baum's immortal children's novel was filmed twice in the silent era, first as a 1910 two-reeler starring Bebe Daniels (later a femme fatale) and then in 1925, with Dorothy Dwan as Dorothy and Oliver Hardy as the Tin Woodman. The screenplay for the latter version was written by L. Frank Baum, Jr. Of course, the most famous adaptation is MGM's classic 1939 musical *The Wizard of Oz*, which annually ranks among the most-watched films on television. Amazingly, it was not a commercial success when originally released. Budgeted at a hefty $2.8 million, it took *The Wizard of Oz* 20 years to recoup its cost. The cast, one of the finest ever assembled, was formed almost by accident. Shirley Temple, a huge boxoffice star in 1938, was the first choice to play Dorothy. However, 20th Century–Fox, which owned her contract, refused to cooperate with MGM. (To atone for its poor decision, Fox cast Shirley in 1940's *The Blue Bird,* a similar fantasy—and a financial flop.) The rest of the original cast included Ray Bolger as the Tin Man, Buddy Ebsen (later Jed on "The Beverly Hillbillies") as the Scarecrow, and Bert Lahr as the Cowardly Lion. However, Bolger, a Broadway dancer, lobbied for the role of the Scarecrow and he and Ebsen switched parts. Then, Ebsen developed an allergic reaction to the metallic paint used on his face and was replaced by Jack Haley, who gave his most memorable performance as the Tin Man. More liberal adaptations of Baum's book include the 1976 Australian rock musical *Oz* (aka *Twentieth Century Oz*), and *The Wiz* (1978), a film version of the hit Broadway play starring Diana Ross as an older Dorothy, Michael Jackson as the Scarecrow, and Richard Pryor as the Wiz. Although Baum wrote 13 additional Oz books (and many others have added to that total), few of those have made it to the screen. In 1914, he adapted his own novel *The Patchwork Girl of Oz* and then wrote and directed *His Majesty, the Scarecrow of Oz* (aka *The New Wizard of Oz*). An obscure musical version of *The Wonderful Land of Oz* appeared in 1969 and in 1971, Liza Minnelli (Judy Garland's daughter) and Margaret Hamilton provided voices for the animated *Journey Back to Oz.* In 1985, the Disney Studios released a costly, non-musical called *Return to Oz,* which was based on Baum's novels *The Land of Oz* and *Ozma of Oz.* Despite impressive technical wizardry, it received scathing reviews and died quickly at the boxoffice. Finally, Baum's original book played a major role in John Boorman's futuristic fantasy *Zardoz* (1974), which derived its title from The WiZARD of OZ.

The Wizard of Oz (1910)	*The Wonderful Land of Oz*
The Patchwork Girl of Oz	(1969)
(1914)	*Journey Back to Oz* (1971)
His Majesty, the Scarecrow of	*Oz* (aka *Twentieth Century of*
Oz (aka *The New Wizard of*	*Oz*) (1976)
Oz) (1914)	*The Wiz* (1978)
The Wizard of Oz (1925)	*Under the Rainbow* (1981)
The Wizard of Oz (1939)	*Return to Oz* (1985)

The Wolf Man

The Wolf Man appeared in five Universal films in the 1940s and yet it's difficult to classify these movies as a series. That's because he was the featured monster only once—in his 1941 debut *The Wolf Man.* This simply-plotted picture reaped benefits from a splendidly foggy atmosphere and a fine cast of Claude Rains, Ralph Bellamy, Warren William, Bela Lugosi, Maria Ouspenskaya, and Lon Chaney, Jr., as the sympathetic werewolf Larry Talbot. Despite a warm boxoffice reception, Universal decided that Chaney needed some horrorific support, so he was paired with the Frankenstein Monster (Lugosi) in 1943's *Frankenstein Meets the Wolf Man*. The two monsters' climactic confrontation lacked excitement and was cut short by a torrent of water released by the local villagers. But the film inspired Universal to package the Wolf Man, Dracula, the Frankenstein Monster, and a couple of mad scientists in *House of Frankenstein* (1944) and *House of Dracula* (1945). Thankfully, Chaney/Talbot/Wolf Man was cured in this last entry. He did, however, turn up in fur again in 1948's *Abbott and Costello Meet Frankenstein*. Lon Chaney, Jr., was the only actor to play Larry Talbot/the Wolf Man. North Carolina filmmaker Earl Owensby's *Wolfman!* had nothing to do with Talbot. See also **Werewolves**.

The Wolf Man (1941)	*House of Dracula* (1945)
Frankenstein Meets the Wolf Man (1943)	*Abbott and Costello Meet Frankenstein* (1948)
House of Frankenstein (1944)	

Wolfe, Nero

Rex Stout's heavyweight detective genius has been restricted to a handful of screen appearances. Edward Arnold made a delightfully self-indulgent Wolfe in 1936's *Meet Nero Wolfe,* an adaptation of Stout's classic mystery *Fer-de-Lance*. Arnold seemed well-cast and the critics were kind, but a series failed to materialize. The following year, Walter Connolly took over the role in *League of Frightened Men* (aka *League of Missing Men*). Lionel Stander played Wolfe's legman Archie Goodwin in both films. Over 40 years later, Stander was still playing in mysteries, as the Harts' chauffeur Max in the 1979–84 TV series "Hart to Hart." Nero made his own television debut in the 1977 TV-movie *Nero Wolfe,* starring Thayer David and Tom Mason as Archie. The movie was a pilot for a series that was postponed when Thayer died unexpectedly. However, the hour-long TV series "Nero Wolfe" finally aired in 1981 with William Conrad in the lead and Lee ("Matt Houston") Horsley as faithful Archie.

Meet Nero Wolfe (1936)	(1937)
League of Frightened Men (aka *League of Missing Men*)	*Nero Wolfe* (1977 TVM)

Wong, Mr. James Lee

Monogram initiated this low-budget film series in 1938, hoping to duplicate the success of the Charlie Chan and Mr. Moto mysteries. Hugh Wiley's Chinatown detective proved nowhere nearly as popular as either of his contemporaries and the films are pretty obscure today. Boris Karloff, who was eager to break from horror movie typecasting, played Mr. Wong in all but the last entry. In 1940's *Phantom of Chinatown*, Keye Luke, Charlie Chan's former #1 son, played Wong, but he didn't prove to be right for the part. The Wong series includes:

Mr. Wong, Detective (1938)	*Doomed to Die* (1940)
Mr. Wong in Chinatown (1939)	*The Fatal Hour* (1940)
Mystery of Mr. Wong (1939)	*Phantom of Chinatown* (1940)

Wrestling

Championship wrestling broadened its appeal — and its outrageousness — in the late 1970s and suddenly became a hot movie property. Subsequently, recent films have tended to focus on the sport's sillier side. In contrast, John Ford's *Flesh* (1932) was a gloomy tale about a German immigrant wrestler (Wallace Beery) involved with shady characters. Richard Widmark was a loser trying to break into the London wrestling racket — and running afoul of kingpin Herbert Lom — in Jules Dassin's moody *Night and the City* (1950). Early wrestling comedies include *Swing Your Lady* (1937), with Humphrey Bogart as a promoter who sets up a male/female wrestling match and 1945's *Here Come the Coeds,* which sent Lou Costello into the ring for one of his better vignettes. In Mexico in the 1960s, movie wrestlers turned into superheroes in highly-popular series such as Santo, Blue Demon, and Neutron (q.v.). These films typically pitted the masked wrestlers against armies of vampires, werewolves, and mummies. Probably, the most interesting films for American audiences were those starring the Wrestling Women. These rough-and-tumble señoritas never achieved the popularity of Santo, but they more than held their own against the baddies in wonderfully-titled pictures like *The Wrestling Women vs. the Aztec Mummy* (1964). In the dubbed English version, the Wrestling Women were known as Loretta and Ruby. In the early 1980s, stateside lady wrestlers were the subjects of *Below the Belt* (1980), *All the Marbles* (1981), and *Mugsy's Girls* (1985). Henry Winkler donned a blonde wig in the ring as a flamboyant wrestler trying to attract attention in 1978's *The One and Only.* Two 1985 movies, *Vision Quest* and *Hadley's Rebellion,* explored the world of high school wrestling. Sylvester Stallone took leave from the *Rocky* series (q.v.) long enough to make *Paradise Alley,* a nostalgic wrestling picture about three ambitious brothers. The 1985 *Grunt! The Wrestling Movie* was a documentary-style satire (e.g. *This Is Spinal Tap*) about an outrageous wrestler called Mad Dog Joe De Curso. Some real-life wrestlers made cameo appearances in the 1986 comedy *Bad Guys,* while wrestling superstar Hulk Hogan starred in his own feature, 1989's *No Holds Barred.* Paul Le Mat and Sylvester Stallone played arm wrestlers in, respectively, *P.K. and the Kid* (1982) and *Over the Top* (1987). See also **Blue Demon; Neutron; Santo.**

Flesh (1932)
Swing Your Lady (1937)
Here Come the Co-eds (1945)
Bodyhold (1949)
Night and the City (1950)
Mr. Universe (1951)
Doctor of Doom (1962)
The Wrestling Women vs. the
    Aztec Mummy (1965)
Mad Bull (1977 TVM)
The One and Only (1978)
Take Down (1978)
Blood and Guts (1978)

Paradise Alley (1978)
Below the Belt (1980)
All the Marbles (1981)
Tough Enough (1983)
Hadley's Rebellion (1985)
Mugsy's Girls (aka Delta Pi)
    (1985)
Vision Quest (1985)
Bad Guys (1986)
Grunt! The Wrestling Movie
    (1986)
No Holds Barred (1989)

Year in Title

Sweeping sagas with year-oriented titles include Bernardo Bertolucci's six-hour Italian epic *1900*, Horton Foote's nostalgic family drama *1918*, and Stanley Kubrick's science fiction classic *2001: A Space Odyssey*. George Orwell's bleak view of the future, *1984*, has been filmed twice, in 1956 and (appropriately enough) 1984.

One Million B.C. (1940)
Terror from the Year 5000
    (1958)
Panic in the Year Zero (1962)
Daleks—Invasion Earth 2150
    A.D. (aka Invasion Earth—
    2150 A.D.) (1966)
One Million Years B.C. (1966)
2001: A Space Odyssey (1968)
Summer of '42 (1971)
Dracula A.D. 1972 (aka Dracula
    Today) (1972)
Class of '44 (1973)

Class of '63 (1973 TVM)
1900 (1977)
September 30, 1955 (aka
    9/30/55; 24 Hours of the
    Rebel) (1978)
1941 (1979)
Class of 1984 (1982)
1990: The Bronx Warriors
    (1983)
1918 (1984)
2010 (1984)
1969 (1988)

Zombies

Commonly confused with ghouls, zombies are dead people brought back to life, usually by means of voodoo. Ghouls (q.v.) are dead, too, but—unlike zombies—they must feed upon the flesh of the living for their sustenance. With their slow movements and blank stares (apparently indicating a lack of wit), zombies rank among the screen's duller, less menacing monsters. Still, there is something bothersome about being chased by a dead person. And zombies often display great strength, which comes in handy for murder. There have been only two zombie classics: The Halperin Brothers' *White Zombie* (1932) and Val Lewton's *I Walked with a Zombie* (1943). In the primitive, but eerily effective *White Zom-*

bie, Bela Lugosi plays a zombie master named Murder Legendre. The film's most famous sequence shows a zombie falling silently to his "death" in a sugar mill, while his zombie coworkers continue to grind sugar emotionlessly. *I Walked with a Zombie* is a more literate movie, sort of *Jane Eyre* set in the West Indies. Darby Jones' brief, powerful appearance during a climactic walk through the sugar fields is startling — one of the cinema's finest moments of quiet terror. In addition to *White Zombie,* Lugosi appeared in two other zombie movies: *Voodoo Man* (1944), a Monogram programmer co-starring George Zucco and John Carradine, and the classically inept *Zombies on Broadway* (1945). In the latter film, gangsters import some real zombies (including Darby Jones again) as a novelty act for their night club. It was the only zombie foray into show business. A more common use of the undead was for soldiers, as in *Revolt of the Zombies* (1936), *King of the Zombies* (1941), and *Revenge of the Zombies* (1943). Cesare the somnambulist from the German classic *The Cabinet of Dr. Caligari* (1919) exhibited many zombie traits, although he was merely asleep, not dead. See also **Ghouls.**

White Zombie (1932)
Revolt of the Zombies (1936)
The Ghost Breakers (1940)
King of the Zombies (1941)
I Walked with a Zombie (1943)
Revenge of the Zombies (1943)
Voodoo Man (1944)
Zombies on Broadway (1945)
Scared Stiff (1953)
Creature with the Atom Brain (1955)
Voodoo Island (1957)
Zombies of Mora Tau (1957)
The Dead One (1961)
Plague of the Zombies (1964)
Zombies (aka *Zombie; I Eat Your Skin; Voodoo Blood*) (1964)
War of the Zombies (aka *Night Star — Goddess of Electra*) (1965)
Terror Creatures from the Grave (1965)
Sugar Hill (aka *The Zombies of Sugar Hill*) (1974)
The Dead Don't Die (1975 TVM)
Revenge of the Zombies (aka *Black Magic II*) (1981)
Zombie Island Massacre (1984)
I Was a Teenage Zombie (1987)
Zombie High (1987)
Dead Heat (1988)
Zombie Brigade (1988)
Hardrock Zombies (1988)
The Serpent and the Rainbow (1988)